COMMUNICATION MATTERS

Kory Floyd

ARIZONA STATE UNIVERSITY

 Connect
Learn
Succeed™

The McGraw-Hill Companies

Connect
Learn
Succeed™

Published by McGraw-Hill, an imprint of The McGraw-Hill Companies, Inc., 1221 Avenue of the Americas, New York, NY 10020. Copyright © 2011. All rights reserved. No part of this publication may be reproduced or distributed in any form or by any means, or stored in a database or retrieval system, without the prior written consent of The McGraw-Hill Companies, Inc., including, but not limited to, in any network or other electronic storage or transmission, or broadcast for distance learning.

3 4 5 6 7 8 9 0 DOW/DOW 9 8 7 6 5 4 3 2 1

ISBN: 978-0-07-338511-2
MHID: 0-07-338511-5

Vice President, Editorial: *Michael Ryan*
Publisher: *David S. Patterson*
Executive Editor: *Susan Gouijnstook*
Director of Development: *Rhona Robbin*
Senior Development Editors: *Jennie Katsaros and Sylvia Mallory*
Executive Marketing Manager: *Leslie Oberhuber*
Editing, Design, and Production Editor: *Melissa Williams*
Cover Designer: *Andrei Pasternak*
Interior Designer: *Elise Lansdon*
Manager, Photo Research: *Brian Pecko*
Media Project Manager: *Jennifer Barrick*
Illustrations: *Thompson Type*
Manufacturing Supervisor: *Louis Swaim*
Composition: *10/12 Times New Roman by Thompson Type*
Printing: *45# New Era Thin by R.R. Donnelley & Sons*

Cover image: *Superstock*

Credits: *The credits section for this book begins on page 435 and is considered an extension of the copyright page.*

Library of Congress Cataloging-in-Publication Data

Floyd, Kory.
  Communication matters / Kory Floyd. — 1st ed.
    p. cm.
  Includes bibliographical references and index.
  ISBN-13: 978-0-07-338511-2 (alk. paper)
  ISBN-10: 0-07-338511-5 (alk. paper)
  1. Human communication. I. Title.
BF637.C45F56 2010
153.6—dc22

2010008431038146

The Internet addresses listed in the text were accurate at the time of publication. The inclusion of a Web site does not indicate an endorsement by the authors or McGraw-Hill, and McGraw-Hill does not guarantee the accuracy of the information presented at these sites.

www.mhhe.com

Dear Readers:

I can still recall how my family reacted when I told them I wanted to study communication. *"You already know how to communicate,"* I remember one relative saying. Communication seemed like common sense to my family members, so they weren't entirely sure why I needed a PhD just to understand it.

As it turns out, my relatives are like a lot of other people in this regard. Because each of us experiences communication in some form nearly every day, it's hard not to think of communication as completely intuitive. What can we possibly learn from research and formal study that we don't know from our lived experience? Aren't we all experts in communication already?

For the sake of argument, let's say we are. Why, then, do we so often misunderstand one another? Why is the national divorce rate so high? How come it seems at times as if women and men are speaking different languages? What explains the popularity of self-help books, relationship counselors, and afternoon talk shows? If we're all experts at communicating, why do we often find it so challenging? Maybe communication isn't as intuitive as we might think.

My goal for *Communication Matters* is to help readers see how communication not only affects their social relationships but also influences their happiness, career objectives, and quality of life. *Communication Matters* guides readers through their **personal** experience of communication and illuminates the value of engaging in a **critical** investigation of communication processes and behaviors. *Communication Matters* targets those goals while encouraging readers to **actively** use both the program's content and its pedagogical tools to relate the course material to their own life experiences.

In short, *Communication Matters* makes the study of communication a meaningful endeavor that readers can positively extend to daily living. I hope you will find *Communication Matters* to comprise a fresh, contemporary, well-integrated program of materials for the introductory course.

Name: Kory Floyd

Education: I got my undergraduate degree from Western Washington University, my Masters degree from the University of Washington, and my PhD from the University of Arizona.

Current jobs: Professor, book writer

Favorite job growing up: Singing busboy

Worst childhood memory: Getting sent to the principal's office in third grade. (It's possible I haven't told my parents about that.)

Best childhood memory: The birth of my sister and brother

Hobbies: Playing piano, singing, reading, traveling, playing Wii tennis

Pets: I have a kitty, whose name is Kitty. I also have a family of goldfish in the pond in my back yard.

Favorite recent book: Outliers, by Malcolm Gladwell

Favorite TV show: NCIS (the original one)

Places I love: New Zealand, Starbucks, my parents' house

BRIEF CONTENTS

CONTENTS

CHAPTER 5 Communicating Nonverbally 101

CHAPTER 4 How We Use Language 75

PART THREE
Communication in the Public Sphere 259

BOXES

THE COMPETENT COMMUNICATOR

PUTTING COMMUNICATION TO WORK

Communication Matters
personally. critically. actively.

With Communication Matters, *students move beyond their intuitive appreciation of communication to examine the discipline's core principles.* By helping students to take **personal** responsibility for their communication, by encouraging **critical** reflection about communication behavior, and by **actively** applying the key concepts to the challenges of contemporary living, *Communication Matters* builds understanding of the many important ways that communication principles matter in personal relationships, classrooms, careers, and communities both real and virtual.

PERSONALLY.

Communication Matters invites students to explore the ways in which their personal background and circumstances influence communication behavior, and the processes by which they make sense of that behavior.

Personal Diversity

Communication Matters probes the ways that students' personal roots and contexts, and those of their communication partners, affect their communication. To set the foundation for this central theme, Chapter 2, "Communication and Culture," introduces the topics of culture and co-culture and surveys the crucial role of culture in communication. That chapter also illuminates how differences in individuals' mental and physical abilities can be the basis of a co-culture—examining, for example, the values and customs of the deaf community and the impact of those factors on members' communication. Other chapters consider the communicative diversity of socially marginalized groups such as the elderly, the homeless, and sexual minorities.

The Dark Side of Communication

The "dark side" of human communication, as it is called in the research literature, is a significant area of interest for both scholars and the public at large. The dark side encompasses the array of negative emotions and behaviors that can play a role in individuals' relational experiences. In each chapter, a Dark Side of Communication feature takes a close-up look at a specific dark side topic and promotes discussion of mature, effective ways of dealing with the challenges the issue presents to the lives (and communicative experiences) of individuals. For example, in Chapter 7, this feature investigates the serious problem of cyberbullying, and in Chapter 10 the selection looks at how the use of coercive power in communication can sometimes constitute emotional abuse.

THE DARK SIDE of Communication

Tell Me Lies: Misrepresentation in Online Dating Profiles

Online dating services—such as Match.com and Chemistry.com—have become enormously popular in recent years as a venue for meeting people and starting new relationships. On many such sites, participants create individual profiles for others to view. Profiles commonly include one or more photographs of the participant as well as information about the person's age, height and weight, profession, and interests.

Browsing the profiles of other participants can help us determine whom we might contact and communicate with, but how do we know whether the information in a profile is true? Research has shown—perhaps no surprisingly—that a large proportion of online date-seekers put false information in their profiles, usually to make themselves appear more attractive to potential partners. In fact, women and men tend to lie about different things. In a study involving over 5,000 online dating participants, communication researcher Jeff Hall and his colleagues found that women are more likely than men to lie about their weight. The researchers also found that men are more likely than women to lie about their income, interests, personality and age. The results from such studies encourage us to exercise caution when evaluating the profile of a potential dating partner.

Source: Hall, J. A., Park, N., Song, H., & Cody, M. J. (2010). Strategic misrepresentation in online dating: The effects of gender, self-monitoring, and personality traits. Journal of Social and Personal Relationships, 27, 117-135.

CRITICALLY.

Communication Matters encourages students to think analytically, to question their assumptions, and to use their insights to communicate successfully with others.

Fact or Fiction?

When it comes to forming perceptions, is more information always better? Is it always possible to resolve a conflict? The Fact or Fiction? selections in Chapter 3 and Chapter 10 challenge students to consider those intriguing questions. Showcased in every chapter, Fact or Fiction? fosters reflective analysis about applied research and issues related to communication. Ask Yourself questions are included for class discussion or homework.

Fact or Fiction?

Small Groups Can Aid Weight Loss

People who want to lose weight often choose to undertake that task in a small group. With others in the group to encourage them and share their struggle, many people believe the support and accountability they will receive from the group will help them lose more weight than they could on their own. Is that belief an illusion, or will people in a weight-loss group actually lose more weight than those working individually?

According to research, taking part in a weight-loss group is more effective than trying to lose weight individually. In one study, overweight adults worked with a weight-loss counselor for 26 weeks either on their own or in groups of 8 to 12. During each group session, participants reported on their progress and the counselor led a group discussion focused on rewarding progress and overcoming obstacles. Participants were also weighed and instructed in proper diet and exercise strategies. Those who worked with a counselor individually received all the same information and encouragement, just not in a group setting. By the end of the study, the participants who worked in groups had reduced their weight and body mass significantly more than had the participants who worked individually. Studies have similarly found that people more successfully quit using nicotine and cocaine when they take part in small groups designed to help them achieve those goals than when they try to quit alone.

ASK YOURSELF

- Why do you suppose working in small groups helps people improve their health more than working alone?
- What health problems, if any, do you think most people would solve more effectively alone than in groups?

Computer-Mediated Communication

In integrated examples in every chapter, as well as in various sidebar features and illustrations, *Communication Matters* analyzes how ever-evolving communication technologies are impacting individuals' sense of identity, expanding their communication choices and audiences, reshaping interactions in the workplace, and raising provocative new issues. The text critically investigates—and gives students invaluable insight into—the safe and responsible use of electronic media and resources, along with the ethical dimensions of using the new technologies.

Critical Assessment

Communication Matters can assess students' command of the material—online and at any time—so that they don't have to wait for a midterm for an update on their progress. Additionally, with consistent use of the adaptive diagnostic program throughout the course to identify areas where they can use more help, students can go into any test confident in their knowledge of the subject.

ACTIVELY.

Communication Matters makes students active participants in their learning. The fifteen chapters, including five chapters dedicated to public speaking skills and strategies, provide students with hands-on experience in applying communication principles to everyday communicative tasks—from personal conversation to public speaking, from the classroom to the community to cyberspace, and more.

THE COMPETENT COMMUNICATOR

Being a Mentor

One of the most important skills for socializing new members to groups is mentoring. How good a mentor are you already? For each of the following statements, indicate how well it describes you by assigning a number between 1 ("not at all") and 7 ("very well").

_____ I enjoy helping people.

_____ People frequently turn to me for advice.

_____ I like to take someone "under my wing" and help him or her succeed.

_____ I feel bad if a new person in my group seems uncomfortable.

_____ I am a good listener.

_____ Supporting people intellectually and emotionally makes me feel good.

_____ People tell me I am good at giving guidance.

_____ I like to "show people the ropes" when they are new to a group or situation.

_____ I try to be the kind of person that others can trust.

_____ I take my responsibilities toward other people seriously.

When you're finished, add up your scores. Your total score should fall between 10 and 70. A score of 10–25 suggests that mentoring is a skill you can build, and learning about small group communication is one way to do so. If you scored between 25 and 55, you are fairly good at mentoring, and as you have more opportunity to be a mentor, you can improve this skill even more. If you scored above 55, you are probably an experienced mentor already. As a result, you are well poised to help socialize new members into the small groups to which you belong.

The Competent Communicator

One way for students to improve their communication skills and ability is to think about how they communicate *now*. Featured in every chapter of *Communication Matters*, The Competent Communicator presents students with a self-assessment of a particular communication skill or tendency. For example, the selection in Chapter 4 invites students to explore how well they can distinguish opinions from factual claims; Chapter 10's example quizzes them on whether they are a high or low self-monitor.

Putting Communication to Work

Name Erika Lake

College(s) BA, SUNY Purchase College, May 2003; S, The College of New Rochelle, 2005

Major(s) Journalism (undergraduate); communication (graduate)

want to say with this feature? How will this text be perceived externally?" We are sending messages to our customers in everything we do—I got a better understanding of that concept from taking classes in communication studies. It makes you more in tune with what those around you are saying (verbally, non-verbally, visually) and what your own responses are.

Why Communication? I was a journalism major in college and went into communication studies for graduate school because I was unsure if I wanted to go to graduate school specifically for

Putting Communication to Work

Communication is an exciting major and a versatile field that is a springboard to a wide range of careers. *Communication Matters* explores career options for communication students through Putting Communication to Work selections that profile the diverse careers of former communication students—such as Chapter 4's interview with a managing editor at a multimedia publishing company and Chapter 15's conversation with a director of films, music videos, and commercials. The interviewees offer invaluable advice and insight on their career choices, as well as tips on how students can actively pave the way to their own career success.

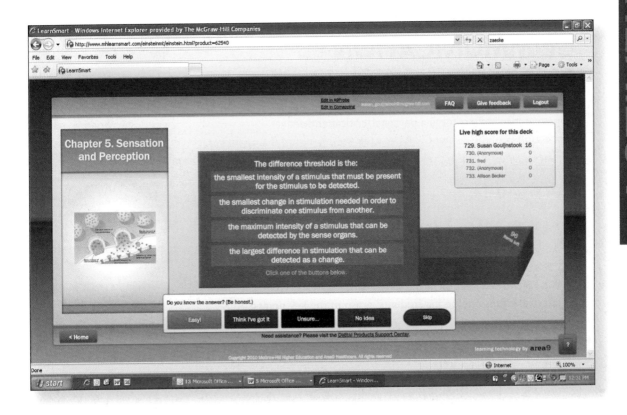

Active Assessment

Communication Matters puts students in charge of their learning with an adaptive diagnostic tool that generates a study plan specifically designed to address each student's strengths and weaknesses. Interwoven with the text content, the online assessment directs students to the exact section or paragraph where they need to clarify and reinforce their understanding. Once students demonstrate mastery of the topic at hand, they move on to the other concepts in their personal learning plan.

LEARNING WITH COMMUNICATION MATTERS

The practical, outcomes-oriented pedagogical elements of *Communication Matters* forge a personal, critical, and active connection with the content.

Personally.

- **AS YOU READ ... FOR REVIEW**

  A set of three As You Read questions following the chapter-opening vignette points students to the essential ideas of each chapter.

  The For Review section at the end of the chapter answers the three chapter-opening As You Read questions, thus reinforcing students' grasp of the key points.

- **TEST YOURSELF**

  A set of Test Yourself review questions at the end of each main text section allows students to pause and check their understanding of important take-away ideas. This recurrent feature serves as a handy tool for review, retention, and test preparation.

- **POP QUIZ**

  The chapter-ending Pop Quiz allows students to assess their understanding of the chapter as a whole and to prepare for tests.

Critically.

- **THOUGHT BUBBLES**

  These recurring questions, suitable for class discussion and journaling assignments, call on students to reflect analytically on the book's central concepts and ideas and to apply their learning to their own experiences.

- **BY THE NUMBERS**

  Interspersed throughout the chapters, By the Numbers presents statistically-based fun facts related to the topic at hand. This thought-provoking feature is suitable for generating class discussions and launching lectures.

Actively.

- **SHARPEN YOUR SKILLS**

  These regularly occurring, stand-alone skill-builders comprise active-learning exercises that may be carried out in a group or individually.

SHARPEN Your Skills

With a few students from your class, role-play a conversation in which you must decide on a policy for a controversial issue, such as stem-cell research or the use of prisoner torture during interrogations. Encourage your fellow students to voice their opinions even if others disagree. If conflict arises during the discussion, take note of when it arises and how the group deals with it. After the conversation, allow time for each student to assess how the group handled conflict during the role-play.

LEARNING

TEACHING WITH
COMMUNICATION MATTERS

The complete content of *Communication Matters* is available to instructors and students in traditional print format, as well as online with integrated and time-saving tools that involve students personally, critically, and actively.

The online tools, collectively called Connect Communication, make managing assignments easier for instructors—and make learning and studying more motivating and efficient for students.

- **Adaptive Diagnostic** This tool helps students "know what they know"—while guiding them to experience and learn what they don't know through interactive exercises and readings. Instructors using Connect report that their students' performance has jumped by a letter grade or more.

- **Speech Videos** More than two hours of student speech videos and video excerpts with assessment are featured, along with links to YouTube videos that illustrate communication concepts in action (with accompanying questions). In addition, Reel Interpersonal videos dramatize key concepts in interpersonal relationships.

- **Connect Speech Tools** Web-based speech preparation tools help students to select an appropriate speech topic, to outline effectively, and to conduct research geared toward analyzing their audience. Speech Capture allows students to upload their speech online for instructor review, grading, and feedback. Instructors have the option to assign peer review for the rest of the class.

- **Real-time Reports** These printable, exportable reports show how well each student (or section) is performing on each course segment. Instructors can use this feature to spot problem areas before they crop up on an exam.

- **Learning Objectives** Every assignment and every course resource can be sorted by learning objective, with point-and-click flexibility. Instructors can use this feature to customize the content and course materials to meet the particular needs of their syllabus.

- **Instructor's Manual** Written by Meredith K. Ginn of Georgia Highlands College, this rich resource provides learning objectives, ideas for lectures and discussions, key terms, additional readings, and websites. The Instructor's Manual incorporates tips for both new and experienced instructors.

- **PowerPoint Slides** Developed by *Communication Matters* author Kory Floyd, the PowerPoint slides present the key points of each chapter and include charts and graphs from the text. A time-saving organizational and navigational tool, the slides are integrated with examples and activities from an expert teacher. The selections can be used as is or modified to meet the needs of individual instructors.

- **Application & Assessment Source** Written by Marcie Pachter of Palm Beach State College–Lake Worth, this resource offers 70 multiple-choice and 20 scenario-based application questions for each chapter. Sample midterm and final exams are also included, and all test items are tied to Bloom's taxonomy. McGraw-Hill's computerized EZ Test allows the instructor to create customized exams using the publisher's supplied test items or the instructor's own questions. A version of the test bank is also provided in Microsoft Word files for instructors who prefer that format. Additional questions are available for use with in-class clicker systems through the Classroom Performance System (CPS), a wireless polling system that provides immediate feedback from every student in the class. A CPS tutorial is available at **www.einstruction.com.**

I was fortunate to have an exceptional group of reviewers, whose suggestions and insights have improved this book immeasurably.

Manuscript Reviewers

Patricia Amason, *University of Arkansas-Fayetteville*
Sandra Arumugam-Osburn, *Saint Louis Community College-Forest Park*
Jackie Barker, *Saint Louis Community College-Meramec*
Diane Bifano, *Palm Beach State College-Lake Worth*
Brett Billman, *Bowling Green State University*
Tonya Blivens, *Tarrant County College-SE*
Carol Bolton, *Phoenix College*
Lisa Heller Boragine, *Cape Cod Community College*
Thomas Bovino, *Suffolk County Community College-Selden*
Martin Brodey, *Montgomery College-Rockville*
Nader Chaaban, *Montgomery College-Rockville*
Tracie Clark, *Central Piedmont Community College*
Teri Colaianni, *University of Central Arkansas*
Julie Copp, *Saint Louis Community College-Florissant Valley*
Lori Crane, *Palm Beach State College-Lake Worth*
Jethro De Lisle, *Tacoma Community College*
Lynne Derbyshire, *University of Rhode Island-Kingston*
Ron Ellsworth, *Boise State University.*
Amber Finn, *Texas Christian University*
Fred Fitch, *Kean University*
Laura Fox, *Joliet Jr. College*
Brian Furio, *York College of PA*
Jodi Gaete, *Suffolk County Community College-Selden*
Rosemary Gallick, *North Virginia Community College-Woodbridge*
John Galyean, *Abraham Baldwin Agricultural College*
Meredith Ginn, *Georgia Highlands College*
Matthew Goken, *Illinois Central College*
Neil Goldstein, *Montgomery County Community College*
Angela Grupas, *Saint Louis Community College-Meramec*
Clint Haynes, *Western Kentucky University-South Campus*
Douglas Hoehn, *Bergen Community College*
Chris Holfester, *Suffolk County Community College-Brentwood*
Mary Hurley, *Saint Louis Community College-Forest Park*
Betty Jane Lawrence, *Bradley University*
Amy Lenoce, *Naugatuck Valley Community College*
Nancy R. Levin, *Palm Beach State College-Eissey*
Louie Lucca, *LaGuardia Community College*
Tobi Mackler, *Montgomery County Community College*
Sharon Lizabeth Martin, *Palm Beach State College-South*
Anne McIntosh, *Central Piedmont Community College*
Melanie McNaughton, *Bridgewater State College*
Lynn Meade, *University of Arkansas-Fayetteville*
Eric Morgan, *New Mexico State University-Las Cruces*
Thomas Morra, *Northern Virginia Community College*
Robert Mott, *York College of PA*

Travice Obas, *Georgia Highlands College*
Susan Olson, *Mesa Community College*
Marcie Pachter, *Palm Beach State College-Lake Worth*
Nan Peck, *Northern Virginia CC-Annandale*
Barbara Penington, *University of Wisconsin-Whitewater*
Sandy Pensoneau-Conway, *Wayne State University*
Keith Perry, *Abraham Baldwin Agricultural College*
Marlene Preston, *Virginia Polytechnic Institute*
Deborah Prickett, *Jacksonville State University*
Rody Randon, *Phoenix College*
Sherry Rhodes, *Collin County Community College-Plano*
Rhonda Richardson, *Phoenix College*
Adam Roth, *University of Rhode Island-Kingston*
Theresa Russo, *Central Piedmont Community College*
Elin Schikler, *Bergen Community College*
Susan Sellers, *Jacksonville State University*
Christopher Smejkal, *Saint Louis Community College-Meramec*
Blair Thompson, *Western Kentucky University*
Richard Underwood, *Kirkwood Community College*
Vivian Van Donk, *Joliet Jr. College*
Jennifer Willis-Rivera, *University of Wisconsin-River Falls*
Yin Zhang, *Suffolk Community College*

Connect Contributors

Diane Bifano, *Palm Beach State College*
Brett Billman, *Bowling Green State University*
Tonya Blivens, *Tarrant County Community College-SE*
Lisa Heller Boragine, *Cape Cod Community College*
Martin Brodey, *Montgomery College-Rockville*
Susan Caldwell, *Palm Beach State College-Lake Worth*
Irene Petersen Canal, *Miami Dade College*
Josie DeGroot, *Ohio University*
Jethro De Lisle, *Tacoma Community College*
Larry Edmonds, *Arizona State University*
Patricia S. Hill, *University of Akron*
Toz Jewell, *Bergen Community College*
Amy King, *Central Piedmont Community College*
Amy Lenoce, *Naugatuck Valley Community College*
Nancy R. Levin, *Palm Beach State College-Eissey*
Yvette Lujan, *Miami Dade College*
Tobi Mackler, *Montgomery County Community College*
Jennifer Pitts, *Volunteer State Community College*
Adam Roth, *University of Rhode Island-Kingston*
Denise Sperruzza, *St. Louis Community College-Meramec*
Jessica Swigger, *Western Carolina University*
Charlene Widener, *Hutchinson Community College*

ACKNOWLEDGMENTS

Few endeavors of any significance are achieved in isolation. There are always others who help us rise to—and exceed—our potential in nearly everything we do. I am delighted to acknowledge and thank those whose contributions and support are responsible for the book you are now reading.

This is my second book with McGraw-Hill, and I could not ask for a better team of editors, managers, and publishers to work with. Rhona Robbin, Jennie Katsaros, Katie Stevens, Leslie Oberhuber, David Patterson, Erika Lake, and Elena Mackawgy have truly become part of my extended family, and I am indebted to each of them for the opportunity to write this book and the consistent, professional support I received. I continue also to be grateful for the guidance of Nanette Giles, whose many lessons remain with me in everything I write.

I owe a very special word of thanks to my freelance development editor, Sylvia Mallory. She has dedicated countless hours to the task of making this book as fresh, contemporary, and student-friendly as possible. More important, she has done so with an extraordinary measure of patience, humor, and grace. The benefit of her input is evident throughout these pages, and I am most grateful to have been able to work with her so closely on this project.

My students, colleagues, and administrators at Arizona State University have, as always, been a joy to work with and a tremendous source of encouragement. Undertaking a project of this size can be daunting, and it is so valuable to have a strong network of professional support on which to draw.

I am eternally grateful for the love and support of my family and my lifelong friends. One needn't be an expert on communication to understand how important close personal relationships are—but the more I learn about communication, the more appreciative I become of the people who play those roles in my life. You know who you are, and I thank you from the bottom of my heart.

To Christina, Alan, Melissa, Colin, Perry, Alice, Jen, Adam, Lisa, and Doug

Thank you for everything you have taught me.

1

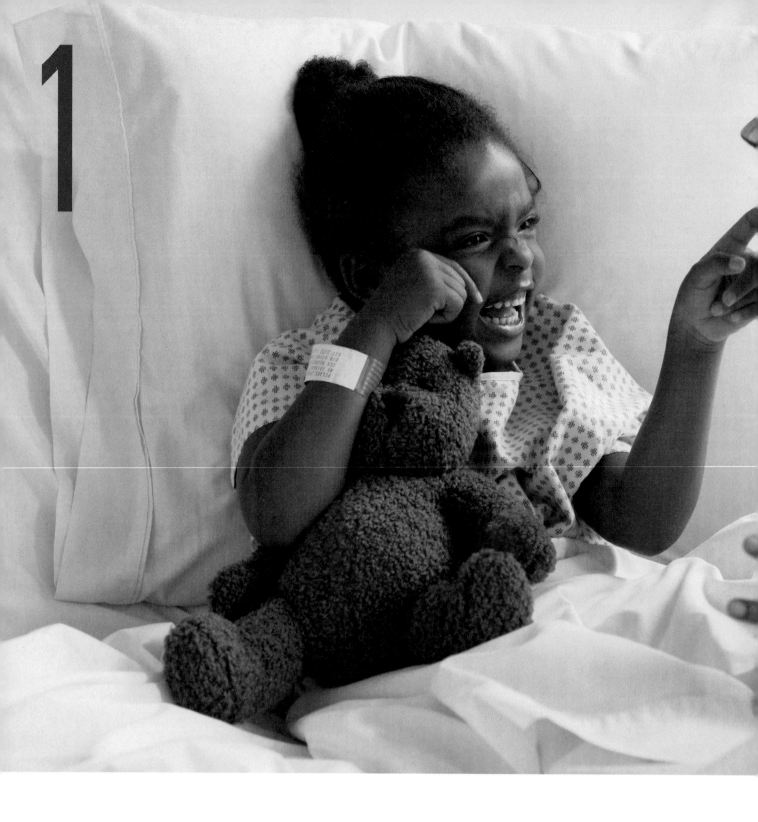

COMMUNIC

HUMOR:
NO LAUGHING MATTER

For Dr. Michael Titze, joking is serious business. As a clinical psychologist, Titze has long recognized that sharing a laugh with a loved one can alleviate stress, promote creativity, and even increase resistance to pain. Inspired by decades of research on the benefits of laughter, Titze founded HumorCare, an organization that promotes humor as a form of therapy. His patients learn to share jokes and express laughter with the people around them. The patients soon discover that communicating and behaving in humorous ways doesn't just put others at ease. It also reduces their own anxiety, makes them feel better physically, and gives them a more positive outlook on life. Titze is hardly alone in promoting humor therapy. In fact, hospitals, clinics, and nursing homes around the United States now use humor to enhance their patients' well-being and accelerate recovery from illness. Whether one is dealing with depression, chronic stress, or everyday aches and pains, it seems that humor and laughter may really be the best medicine.

ATION: A FIRST LOOK

1

As You READ

>>

- What needs does communication help us meet?
- How does communication work, and what misconceptions do we have about it?
- What particular skills characterize competent communicators?

Just as Michael Titze helps people battle depression and recover from illness by communicating humor, we communicate with others to affect several dimensions of our lives. For example, we communicate to form personal relationships, to maintain them, and even to end them. We communicate to order dinner at a restaurant, negotiate a car loan, and buy music online. Through communication interactions, teachers instruct us, advertisers persuade us, and actors entertain us. Very little about our lives isn't influenced by the way we communicate.

Because communication affects so many aspects of our existence, learning how to communicate effectively helps improve our lives in multiple ways. This course will give you the tools you will need to understand the communication process and improve your skills as a communicator.

communication The process by which people use signs, symbols, and behaviors to exchange information and create meaning.

>> Why We Communicate

Barely six minutes after leaving New York's La Guardia airport on January 15, 2009, US Airways Flight 1549 collided with a flock of Canada geese and made an emergency landing in the Hudson River that many have called miraculous. On a ferryboat 200 yards away from where the plane stopped, Janis Krums broadcast one of the first reports of the crash to the outside world. However, he wasn't a journalist delivering an on-air news report. Krums, a Florida businessman, sent word of the accident through Twitter. Twitter allows users to post messages, no longer than 140 characters in length, informing people in their networks about what they're doing. Posting a message—a *tweet*—allowed Krums to transmit information about the crash to family and friends, who then relayed the details to broader circles of people. Social networking services such as Twitter enable rapid and nearly continuous communication among their users. Over 54 million people around the world use Twitter each month to stay in contact with their social networks.[1]

Technologies such as Twitter give us communication abilities that are unprecedented in human history. **Communication** is the process by which we use signs, symbols, and behaviors to exchange information and create meaning.[2] Never before has it been as easy to communicate with others, given the profusion of digital communication media and devices—but what draws us to do so? *Why* do we communicate? As we'll see in this section, communication is vital to many different aspects of life, from our physical and everyday needs to our experiences with relationships, spirituality, and identity.

COMMUNICATION ADDRESSES PHYSICAL NEEDS

You might be surprised to hear it, but good communication keeps us healthy. We humans are such social beings that when we are denied the opportunity for interaction, our mental and physical health can suffer. That is a major reason why solitary confinement is considered to be such a harsh punishment. Several studies have shown that when people are prevented from having contact, and thus from communicating with others for an extended period, their health can quickly deteriorate.[3] Similarly, individuals who feel socially isolated because of poverty, homelessness, mental illness, or other stigmatizing situations can also suffer from the lack of quality interaction with others.[4]

It may sound like an exaggeration to say that we cannot survive without human contact, but that statement isn't far from the truth, as a bizarre experiment in the thirteenth century helped to show. Frederick II, emperor of Germany, wanted to know what language humans would speak naturally if they weren't taught any particular language. To find out, he placed 50 newborns in the care of nurses who were instructed only to feed and bathe them but not to speak to the babies or hold them. The emperor never discovered the answer to his question because all the infants died.[5] Clearly, Frederick's experiment was unethical by modern standards—that is, it did not follow established principles that guide people in judging whether something is morally right or wrong. Such an experiment wouldn't be repeated today. However, more recent studies in orphanages and adoption centers, conducted according to ethical guidelines, have convincingly shown that human interaction—especially touch—is critical for infants' survival and healthy development.[6]

Positive social interaction keeps adults healthy, too. Research shows that people without strong social ties such as close friendships and family relationships are more likely to suffer from major ailments (for example, heart disease and high blood pressure) and to die prematurely than are people who have close, satisfying relationships.[7] They are also more likely to suffer basic ailments, such as a cold, and they often take longer to recover from illnesses or injuries.[8] Certainly, not everyone needs the same amount of interaction to stay healthy. Nevertheless, communication plays an important role in maintaining health and well-being.

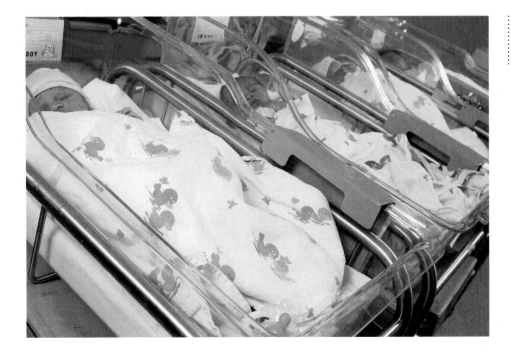

Human interaction, especially touch, is critical for infants' survival and healthy development.

COMMUNICATION MEETS RELATIONAL NEEDS

Besides our physical needs, each of us also has **relational needs**—the essential elements we look for in our relationships with other people. Relational needs include companionship and affection, relaxation, and escape.[9] We don't necessarily have the same needs in all our relationships—you probably value your friends for somewhat different reasons than you value your relatives, for instance. The bottom line, though, is that we need relationships in our lives, and communication is a large part of how we establish and maintain them.[10]

Many features of our day-to-day lives are designed to promote the development of human relationships. Neighborhoods, schools, workplaces, malls, theaters, and restaurants, for example, are all social settings in which we almost always interact with people in some way. Technology is also an avenue for promoting our relationships. Cell phones allow us to call or exchange text messages with virtually anyone at the touch of a button; the Internet offers multiple ways of connecting with others, and many people have met new friends or romantic partners online.[12] Just imagine how challenging it would be to form and maintain strong social relationships if you did not have the ability to communicate with others. The lack of communication channels is a common experience for many immigrants, who often struggle to adapt to their new culture and to learn its language—and who may feel lonely or ignored in the process.[13]

Some scholars believe that our need for relationships is so fundamental that we can hardly get by without them.[14] For example, research has shown that having a rich social life is one of the most powerful predictors of a person's overall happiness.[15] The single most important predictor of happiness in life—by far—is the degree to which an individual has a happy marriage.[16] Marital happiness is more important than income, job status, education, leisure time, or anything else in accounting for how happy people are with their lives. On the negative side, people in distressed marriages are much more likely to suffer from major depression, and they even report being in worse physical health than their happily married counterparts.[17]

The cause-and-effect relationship between marriage and happiness isn't a simple one. It may be that strong marriages promote happiness and well-being, or it may be that happy, healthy people are more likely than others to be married. Whatever the reason, personal relationships clearly play an important role in our lives, and communication helps us form and maintain them.

In what ways does your own communication behavior meet your relational needs?

Research indicates that the strongest predictor of happiness in life is the degree to which an individual has a happy marriage.

relational needs The essential elements people seek in their relationships with others.

COMMUNICATION FILLS IDENTITY NEEDS

Are you curious? Passive? Caring? Temperamental? Each of us can probably come up with a long list of adjectives to describe ourselves, but here's the critical question: How do you *know* you are these things? In other words, how do you form an identity?

The ways we communicate with others—and the ways that others communicate with us—play a major role in shaping the way we see ourselves.[18] As we'll consider in Chapter 3, people form their identities partly by comparing themselves to others. If you consider yourself intelligent, for instance, what that really means is that you see yourself as more intelligent than most other people. If you think you're shy, you see most other people as more outgoing than you are.

One way we learn how we compare to others is through our communication with those around us. If people treat you as intelligent, shy, or attractive, you'll probably begin to believe that you have those characteristics. In other words, those qualities will become part of your self-image. As we'll find in Chapter 3, identity develops over the course of life, and communication plays a critical role in driving that process. Good communicators also have the ability to emphasize different aspects of their identities in different situations. For example, during a job interview it might be important for you to portray your organized, efficient side, whereas on a date you might choose to project your fun-loving nature and sense of humor.

SHARPEN Your Skills

Recall a recent conversation you had, and identify how your communication behavior contributed to your physical, relational, identity, spiritual, and instrumental needs, if at all. Which need or needs took precedence? Why?

COMMUNICATION MEETS SPIRITUAL NEEDS

An important aspect of identity for many people is their spirituality. Spirituality includes the principles one values in life ("I value loyalty" or "I value equal treatment for all people"). It also encompasses one's *morals,* or notions about right and wrong ("It's never okay to steal, no matter what the circumstances" or "I would lie to save a life, because life is more important than honesty"). Finally, spirituality involves beliefs about the meaning of life, which often include personal philosophies, awe of nature, belief in a higher purpose, and religious faith and practices ("I trust in God" or "I believe I will reap what I sow in life").

A 2005 survey of more than 112,000 U.S. American college students found that many students consider some form of spirituality—however they choose to define it—to be an important part of their identity.[19] About 75 percent of those surveyed said they search for meaning and purpose in life and have discussions about those topics with their friends. In addition, more than 60 percent claimed that their spirituality was a source of joy in their lives, and almost 50 percent affirmed that they seek out opportunities to grow spiritually. For people who include spirituality as a part of their identity, communication provides a means of expressing and sharing spiritual ideas and practices with one another.

COMMUNICATION SERVES INSTRUMENTAL NEEDS

Finally, people communicate to meet their practical, everyday needs, which researchers refer to as **instrumental needs.** Some instrumental needs involve short-term objectives, such as ordering a drink in a bar, scheduling a haircut on the telephone, filling out a rebate card, and raising your hand when you want to speak in class. Others encompass longer-term goals, such as getting a job and earning a promotion. The communicative behaviors entailed in serving instrumental needs may not always contribute directly to our health, relationships, identity, or spirituality. Each behavior is valuable, however, because it serves a need that helps us get through daily life.

Meeting instrumental needs probably doesn't seem as interesting as forging new relationships or as meaningful as expressing spiritual beliefs. But it is important for two reasons. The first reason is simply that we have many instrumental needs. In fact, most of the communication we engage in on a day-to-day basis is probably mundane and routine—not heavy, emotionally charged conversations but instrumental interactions such as talking to

instrumental needs Practical, everyday needs.

Communication serves our instrumental needs, such as our need to be acknowledged when we wish to speak.

professors about assignments and taking orders from customers at work. The second reason that instrumental needs are important is that many of them—such as buying food at the store and ordering clothes online—have to be met before other needs—for example, maintaining quality relationships and finding career fulfillment—can be satisfied.[20]

- How is communication related to our physical well-being?
- What relational needs does communication help us fill?
- In what ways do communication behaviors meet our identity needs?
- How does communication help us express spirituality?
- What are some of the instrumental needs served by communication?

Test Yourself

>> The Nature and Types of Communication

When 14-year-old Santiago Ventura left his home in the Mexican state of Oaxaca for farm work in Oregon, he had no way of foreseeing the tragedy that would befall him. After the fatal stabbing of a fellow farm worker at a party, Ventura was questioned by a Spanish-speaking police officer. Ventura spoke neither Spanish nor English, however, but only the native language of Mixtec Indians. While being questioned, Ventura never made eye contact with the officer, because Mixtec Indians believe that it is rude to look people directly in the eye. Due to his poor grasp of Spanish, Ventura simply answered "yes" to all of the officer's questions, leading the officer to presume his guilt. After a trial in which his lawyer forbade him to testify because of his poor language abilities, Ventura was convicted of murder and sentenced to between 10 years and life in prison. Only after five years of protests by immigration advocates and jurors who were unconvinced of Ventura's guilt did another judge set aside the verdict, freeing Ventura from his wrongful imprisonment.

Had we been involved in Ventura's case, many of us would have interpreted his words and behaviors the same way the arresting officer did. If they asked Ventura whether he had committed a crime and he replied "yes" while also avoiding eye contact, most reasonable people would conclude that he was guilty. As his story illustrates, however, even seemingly straightforward communication behaviors can easily be misinterpreted, sometimes with tragic consequences. Ventura's problems began when the officer attributed the wrong meaning to his words and behaviors. So how do people express and interpret meaning accurately? What accounts for our ability to communicate in the first place?

We begin this section by examining different ways to understand the communication process. Next, we look at some important characteristics of communication and consider various approaches to thinking about communication in social interaction. Finally, we explore five types of communication in which humans engage. Even though you communicate all the time, you'll probably find that there are still many interesting things to learn about communication's central role in life.

VARIOUS MODELS EXPLAIN THE COMMUNICATION PROCESS

How would you describe the process of communicating? It's not as easy as it might seem, and even researchers have answered that question in different ways over the years. A formal description of a process such as communication is called a **model.** In this section we'll look at three different models that communication scholars have developed: the action, interaction, and transaction models. The action model was developed first, then the interaction model, and finally the transaction model. In that sense, those models represent the evolution of how communication researchers have defined and described communication over the years.

Communication as Action In the **action model,** we think of communication as a one-way process.[21] To illustrate, let's say that you need to leave work early next Tuesday to attend parent–teacher conferences at your children's school, and you're getting ready to ask your supervisor for permission. The action model starts with the **source**—the individual who has a thought that he or she wishes to communicate. In our example, the source is *you.* To convey the idea that you'd like to leave early, you must **encode** it, which means to put

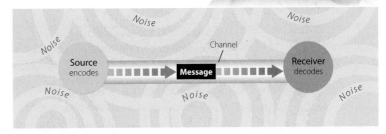

FIGURE 1.1 Action Model of Communication In the action model of communication, a sender encodes a message and conveys it through a communication channel for a receiver to decode.

your idea in the form of language or a gesture that your supervisor can understand. Through that process, you create a **message,** which consists of the verbal and/or nonverbal elements of communication to which people give meaning.[22] In this example, your message might be the question "Would it be all right if I left work a couple of hours early next Tuesday?"

According to the action model, you would then send your message through a communication **channel,** which is a type of pathway for conveying messages. For example, you can pose your question to your supervisor face-to-face, or you can send it by e-mail, through a text message, or by means of a phone call. Your supervisor acts as the **receiver** of the message, the person who will **decode** or interpret it.

The communication process also includes **noise,** which is anything that interferes with a receiver's ability to attend to your message. The major types of noise are *physical noise* (such as background conversation in the office or static on the telephone line), *psychological noise* (such as other concerns your supervisor is dealing with that day), and *physiological noise* (such as fatigue or hunger). Experiencing any of those forms of noise could prevent your supervisor from paying full attention to your question.

You can see that the action model is linear: A source sends a message through some channel to a receiver, and noise interferes with the message somehow (Figure 1.1). Many of us talk and think about the communication process in that linear manner. For example, when you ask someone "Did you get my message?" you are implying that communication is a one-way process. However, human communication is rarely that simple. In fact, it is usually more of a back-and-forth exchange than a one-way process—more similar to tennis than to bowling. Over time, researchers responded to that observation by creating an updated model of communication known as the interaction model.

model A formal description of a process.

action model A model describing communication as a one-way process.

source The originator of a thought or an idea.

encode To put an idea into language or gesture.

message Verbal and nonverbal elements of communication to which people give meaning.

channel A pathway through which messages are conveyed.

receiver The party who interprets a message.

decode To interpret or give meaning to a message.

noise Anything that interferes with the encoding or decoding of a message.

Communication as Interaction The **interaction model** takes up where the action model leaves off. It includes all of the same elements: source, message, channel, receiver, noise, encoding, and decoding, but it differs from the action model in two basic ways. First, the interaction model recognizes that communication is a two-way process. Second, it adds two elements to the mix: feedback and context.[23]

If you've taken physics, you learned that every action has a reaction. A similar rule applies to communication. Let's say that you're telling your office mate, Simone, about a long-lost friend with whom you recently made contact on Facebook. As you relate your story, Simone perhaps nods along and says "uh-huh" to show you that she's listening—or maybe she yawns because she was out late the night before. She might also ask you questions about when you originally met this person or how you got back in touch. In other words, Simone *reacts* to your story by giving you **feedback,** or various verbal and nonverbal responses to your message. Thus, Simone is not just a passive receiver of your message—instead, she is an active shaper of your conversation.

Now let's imagine that you're sharing your story with Simone while you're having coffee in a crowded employee cafe. Would you tell your story any differently than you would if the two of you were alone? What if you were in a classroom on campus? What if your parents were in the same room? All of those situations are part of the **context,** or the environment that you're in. Your environment includes both the physical and the psychological context. The *physical context* reflects where you are physically interacting with each other. In contrast, the *psychological context* involves factors that influence people's states of mind, such as the formality of the situation, the level of privacy, and the degree to which the situation is emotionally charged. According to the interaction model, we take context into account when we engage in conversation. That is, we realize that what is appropriate in certain contexts may be inappropriate in others, and we adapt our behaviors accordingly.

By taking account of feedback and context, the interaction model presents the communication process more realistically than the action model does. In the case of your telling Simone about your long-lost friend, for instance, your story and Simone's feedback would probably be affected by where you were speaking, how many other people could overhear you (if any), and whether those people were co-workers, classmates, family members, or strangers. The interaction model is illustrated in Figure 1.2.

Although the interaction model is more realistic than the action model, it still has limitations. One drawback is that it doesn't represent how complex communication can be. During conversations, it often seems as though both people are sending and receiving information simultaneously rather than simply communicating back and forth, one message at a time. The interaction model doesn't account for that overlapping two-way process, however. To understand that aspect of communication, we turn to the transaction model, currently the most complete and widely used of the three models on which we're focusing.

Communication as Transaction Unlike the action and interaction models, the **transaction model** of communication doesn't distinguish between the roles of source and receiver. Nor does it represent communica-

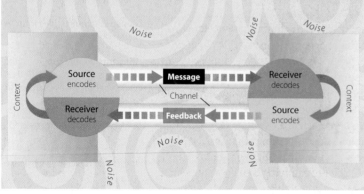

FIGURE 1.2 Interaction Model of Communication
The interaction model of communication explains that our messages are shaped by the feedback we receive from others and by the context in which we interact.

tion as a series of messages going back and forth. Rather, it maintains that both people in a conversation are simultaneously sources *and* receivers. In addition, it illustrates that the conversation flows in both directions at the same time.[24]

To understand the transaction model, imagine that you've taken your car in for service and you're describing the noise your engine has been making to the mechanic. As you attempt to communicate the noise, a confused look falls across the mechanic's face. According to the interaction model, that facial expression would constitute feedback to your message. In contrast, the transaction model recognizes that you will interpret that expression as a message in and of itself, making the mechanic a source and you a receiver. Note that this process occurs while you're describing your car problems to the mechanic. In other words, you are both sending messages to and receiving messages from the other at the same time. Figure 1.3 depicts the transaction model.

Not only does the transaction model reflect the complex nature of communication, but it also leads us to think about context more broadly. It suggests that our communication is affected not just by the physical or psychological environment, but also by our experience, gender, social class, and even the history of our relationship with the person or persons to whom we're talking. As we'll see throughout this book, communication is also influenced by our culture—the collection of shared values, beliefs, and behaviors of a group of people.

Let's go back to our previous example. If you have a history with the mechanic, you might help him understand your problem by referring to car trouble you've had in the past. If he isn't a native speaker of your language, you might have to speak more slowly and clearly than you otherwise would. Sometimes it's hard to consider how those cultural aspects of context might affect the way you communicate. According to the transaction model, however, they are always with you.

Applying the Models Clearly, then, researchers have different ways of understanding the communication process. Instead of debating which model is right, it's more helpful to look at the useful ideas each model offers. When we do so, we find that each model fits certain situations better than others.

For instance, sending a text message to your professor is a good example of the action model. You're the source, and you convey your message through a written channel to a receiver (your professor). Noise includes any difficulty your professor experiences in opening up the message or understanding the intent of your message because of the language you have used.

An apt example of the interaction model is the communication that occurs when you submit a report for your job, and a team of co-workers comments on it in writing. You (the source) have conveyed your message through your report, and your co-workers (the receivers) provide written feedback. Noise includes any difficulties either you or your co-workers experience in understanding what each other has said.

Most conversations are good examples of the transaction model, because both parties are sending and receiving messages simultaneously. That process occurs, for instance, when you strike up a conversation with someone sitting next to you on an airplane. You

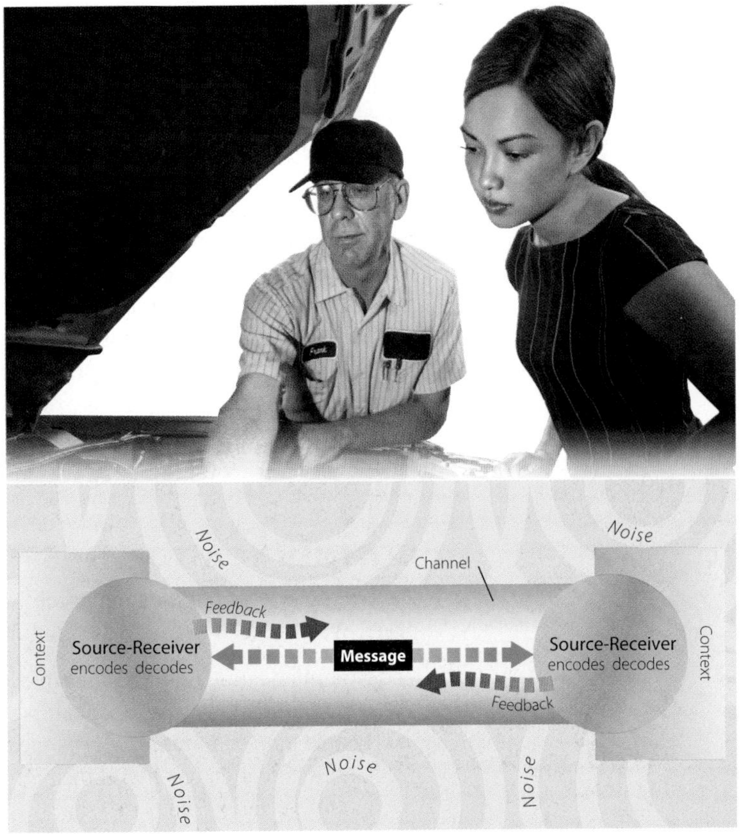

FIGURE 1.3 Transaction Model of Communication
The transaction model recognizes that both people in a conversation are simultaneously senders and receivers.

interaction model A model describing communication as a process shaped by feedback and context.

feedback Verbal and nonverbal responses to a message.

context The physical or psychological environment in which communication occurs.

transaction model A model describing communication as a process in which everyone is simultaneously a sender and a receiver.

might make small talk about where each of you is traveling that day or how the weather has been. As you do so, each of you is sending verbal and nonverbal messages to the other and is simultaneously receiving and interpreting such messages from the other. Your conversation is affected by the context, in that you may be communicating only to pass the time until you land. It is also affected by noise, including turbulence during the flight and the sound of the flight attendants' announcements.

Each model, then, is more useful in some situations than in others. The action model and interaction model are too simplistic to describe most face-to-face conversations, but when you're just leaving a note for someone or submitting a report for feedback, those models can describe the situation quite well. The transaction model, which many experts consider the most comprehensive of the three models, better describes complex face-to-face communications. As you come across examples of different communication situations in this book, you might ask yourself how well each model fits them.

Now that we've looked at different models of communication, let's consider some of communication's most important characteristics.

COMMUNICATION HAS MANY CHARACTERISTICS

Describing the communication process requires more than just mapping out how it takes place. We also need to catalog its important features. In this section, we'll discover that

- Communication relies on multiple channels.
- Communication passes through perceptual filters.
- People give communication its meaning.
- Communication has literal meanings and relational implications.
- Communication sends messages, whether intentional or unintentional.
- Communication is governed by rules.

Communication Relies on Multiple Channels How many different ways do people communicate with one another? Facial expressions telegraph how a person is feeling. Gestures and tone of voice help others interpret his or her messages. Touch can signal feelings such as affection and aggression. Even a person's clothing and physical appearance communicate messages about that individual to others.

Some situations are **channel-rich contexts**—environments that incorporate multiple communication channels at once. In face-to-face conversations, for instance, you can pay attention to people's words, see their expressions and gestures, hear their tone of voice, and feel their touch at the same time. You can evaluate the information from all those channels simultaneously. Other situations are **channel-lean contexts**—environments that use relatively fewer channels.[25] An example is tweeting, which relies on text alone; you don't experience a person's voice or gestures when he or she communicates with you on Twitter. As a consequence, you pay more attention to the person's words, because that's all you have to go on.

Communication Passes Through Perceptual Filters Anything you put through a filter—such as air, water, or light—comes out a little bit differently than it went in. The same happens when we communicate: What one person says is not always exactly what the other person hears. The reason is that we all "filter" incoming communication through our perceptions, experiences, biases, and beliefs.

Let's say you're listening to a senator speak on television. The way you process and make sense of the speech probably depends on how much you agree with the senator's ideas or whether you belong to the same political party. Two people with different political viewpoints may listen to the same speech yet hear something very different. One may hear a set of logical, well thought-out ideas, while the other may hear nothing but lies and empty promises.

Perceptual filters can also influence how two people understand their own words. In an episode of *Friends,* Rachel (played by Jennifer Aniston) and her boyfriend Ross (played by David Schwimmer) have a big fight and decide to go "on a break" from their relationship. They quickly learn, however, that they perceive the meaning of being "on a break" quite

channel-rich contexts Communication environments involving many channels at once.

channel-lean contexts Communication environments involving few channels at once.

Ross and Rachel both agreed that they were "on a break," but they had very different ideas of what that meant.

differently. To Rachel, it simply means not seeing each other for a while but keeping their relationship intact in the meantime. To Ross, being on a break means that his relationship with Rachel is effectively over. Thus, when Ross has sex with someone else during the "break," Rachel feels completely betrayed, and she and Ross end their relationship officially. Importantly, both Ross and Rachel agreed that they were "on a break" when Ross slept with someone else. They strongly differed, however, in their perceptions of what "on a break" meant.

Many aspects of our lives can influence our perception of communication. Whether we're aware of it or not, our ethnic and cultural background, gender, religious beliefs, socioeconomic status, intelligence, education, level of physical attractiveness, and experiences with illness, disease, and death can all act as filters, coloring the way we see the world and the way we make sense of communication. The officer who questioned Santiago Ventura filtered Ventura's behaviors through his own cultural expectations by assuming, incorrectly, that anyone from Mexico speaks Spanish and that a lack of eye contact is a sign of dishonesty.

People Give Communication Its Meaning When we write or speak, we choose our words deliberately so that we can say what we *mean*. What is the source of that meaning? Words have no meaning by themselves; they're just sounds or marks on a piece of paper or a monitor. A word is a **symbol,** or a representation of an idea, but the word itself isn't the idea or the meaning. The meaning of words—and many other forms of communication—comes from the people and groups who use them.

Almost all language is arbitrary in the sense that words mean whatever groups of people decide they mean. As a result, we can't assume that other people understand the meanings we intend to communicate just because we ourselves understand what we mean. For instance, what is a mouse? If you asked that question 40 years ago, the answer would have been along the lines of "a small rodent that likes cheese and gets chased by cats." Today, however, many people know a mouse as a pointing device for navigating within a computer screen. As another example, what is a robot? In the United States, it's a humanlike machine that performs mechanical tasks, but in South Africa, it's a traffic light.

symbol A representation of an idea.

Communication Has Literal Meanings and Relational Implications
Nearly every verbal statement has a **content dimension,** or the literal information that the

content dimension Literal information that is communicated by a message.

communicator is communicating.[26] When you say to your friend, "I'm kind of unhappy today," the content dimension of your message is that you're feeling sad, depressed, or angry. When your housemate says, "We're out of cereal again," the content dimension of the message is that you have no cereal left.

There's often more to messages than their literal content, though. Many messages also carry signals about the nature of the relationship in which they're shared. Those signals make up the **relational dimension** of the message. For example, by telling your friend that you're feeling unhappy, you may also be sending the message "I feel comfortable enough with you to share my feelings" or you may be signaling "I want you to help me feel better."

Likewise, you might interpret your housemate's statement that you're out of cereal as also saying "I'm sure you're aware of this, but I'm just reminding you," or you might take it as meaning "I'm irritated that you never replace the food you use up." Even though those messages were never spoken, we often infer meanings about our relationships from the tone and manner in which the statements are made.

What are some ways in which you metacommunicate?

One way that people distinguish between content and relational dimensions is through **metacommunication,** which is communication about communication. Let's say that Jude asks her husband, Han, to read over the speech she is preparing to give at a conference for small-business owners. Han reads the speech and marks it up with critical comments such as "this argument isn't convincing," "awkward wording," and "I can't tell what you're trying to say." After reading Han's comments, Jude is disheartened, and Han is confused by her reaction.

<u>Han:</u> *I thought you wanted my feedback. I was just trying to help you make your speech better; that's what you asked for. Why are you taking my comments so personally?*

<u>Jude:</u> *It's not so much what you said; it's how you said it.*

By focusing his attention on Jude's request for feedback, Han is attending to the content dimension of their conversation. He can't understand why Jude is so upset, because Jude had asked him for his feedback. To Jude, however, Han's comments are overly harsh and insensitive, and they imply that Han doesn't care about her feelings. Therefore, Jude's focus is on the relational dimension of their conversation. To highlight that distinction, Jude metacommunicates with Han by explaining that her hurt feelings were not caused by what Han said but by *the way he said it.* That phrase conveys Jude's thoughts about her communication with Han; thus, it is metacommunicative.

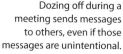

Dozing off during a meeting sends messages to others, even if those messages are unintentional.

Communication Sends Messages, Whether Intentional or Unintentional Much of what we communicate to others is deliberate. When you set up a job interview, for instance, you do so intentionally, having thought about why you want the job and how you will respond to the interviewer's questions. Very rarely do you schedule an interview by accident.

You may communicate a number of other messages, however, without intending to. For example, have you ever tried hard to stay awake in an important meeting? Despite your efforts to look engaged and interested, you might not have been aware that your slouching posture and droopy eyelids were signaling the fatigue you were feeling, perhaps after a long day of working at a part-time job and attending classes. In that instance, your behavior was sending unintentional messages.

Whether unintentional messages should qualify as communication has been a focal point of debate among communication scholars for many years. Some researchers believe that only deliberate, intentional messages are a part of communication, and that if you don't intend to communicate, then you aren't communicating.[27] Others subscribe to the belief that "you cannot *not* communicate," meaning that absolutely everything you do has communicative value.[28] The validity of that idea is the subject of the Fact or Fiction? box.

Communication Is Governed by Rules Rules tell us what behaviors are required, preferred, or prohibited in various social contexts.[29] Some rules

You Cannot *Not* Communicate

Some of the research findings you'll encounter in this course will make intuitive sense to you, and others will be more difficult to believe. Although our intuition is right much of the time, it can also fail us, and that potential for failure is one reason why the systematic study of communication is so useful. In the "Fact or Fiction?" boxes throughout this book, we'll examine some of the more intuitively appealing ideas about communication to see how valid they are.

For instance, Paul Watzlawick, an Austrian-born communication theorist, proposed that "one cannot *not* communicate." He believed that every behavior sends some message, whether intentional or not, so all behavior has communicative value. Because people are engaged in some type of behavior—watching television, crying, sleeping, dancing—at every moment, they cannot help but continuously communicate, according to Watzlawick. Other researchers have pointed out, however, that Watzlawick's idea treats all behavior as communication, and they have argued instead that unintentional behaviors are not necessarily communicative. They would propose, therefore, that if you don't *intend* for your behavior to convey a message, you aren't engaging in communication.

My own position lies somewhere in between. Although I don't believe that every possible behavior is a form of communication, neither do I think behaviors must be intentional to have communicative value. I would suggest that even unintended messages—such as the ones you might have expressed while trying to stay awake during a meeting—are forms of communication because they still convey meaning. Many aspects of appearance illustrate that idea. For instance, seeing someone in a wheelchair probably leads you to different conclusions than seeing someone in a white lab coat or an orange prison jumpsuit, yet those messages might be unintentional on that person's part.

ASK YOURSELF

- What do you think about Watzlawick's idea? Did it seem reasonable or unreasonable to you at first? Why?
- When and how do you communicate messages unintentionally?

Sources: Motley, M. T. (1990). On whether one can(not) not communicate: An examination via traditional communication postulates. *Western Journal of Communication,* *54,* 1–20; Watzlawick, T., Beavin, J., & Jackson, D. (1967). *The pragmatics of human communication.* New York: Norton.

---

for communication are **explicit rules,** meaning that someone has clearly articulated them. Perhaps your parents used to say "Don't talk with your mouth full." Many universities have explicit rules banning hate speech, such as statements that degrade ethnic or sexual minorities, at campus events and in school publications. Social networking websites such as MySpace and LinkedIn enforce specific guidelines regarding the content of text and photos. Those examples are all explicit communication rules because they directly express expectations for communicative behavior.

In contrast, many communication rules are **implicit rules**—rules that almost everyone in a certain social group knows and follows, even though no one has formally articulated them. People in North American cultures, for instance, follow implicit rules when riding in an elevator, such as "Don't get on if it's already full" and "Don't make eye contact with others while you're riding." Implicit rules also govern taking turns when you are waiting for some type of service, such as at a bank or grocery store; those rules include "Get into an orderly line" and "Don't cut ahead of someone else."

relational dimension Signals about the relationship in which a message is being communicated.

metacommunication Communication about communication.

explicit rules Rules that have been clearly articulated.

implicit rules Rules that have not been clearly articulated but are nonetheless understood.

Most people seem to know and accept implicit rules, even though they usually aren't posted anywhere. They're just a part of everyone's cultural knowledge. Because those rules are implicit, however, their interpretations are likely to vary more from person to person than do understandings of explicit rules. For example, some people believe that it is an implicit rule that one shouldn't talk on a cell phone while in a crowded environment such as a subway train during rush hour, whereas other people don't see that behavior as inappropriate.

FIVE TYPES OF COMMUNICATION

Communication comprises five basic types: intrapersonal, interpersonal, small group, public, and mass. These types differ primarily with respect to the size of the audience, but they also call for different communication skills.

Intrapersonal Communication The form of communication that includes the smallest audience is **intrapersonal communication,** the communication you have with yourself. When you mentally remind yourself to do something, or rehearse an upcoming conversation in your mind, you are engaging in intrapersonal communication.

Although it may be tempting to equate intrapersonal communication with *cognition*—the act of thinking—your thoughts and memories become communicative only when you put them into words in your mind. Perhaps you have the thought, "Don't forget to e-mail Mom about my holiday travel plans." In that instance, you have expressed your thought in words directed at yourself; that is, you have communicated intrapersonally.

Interpersonal Communication When you exchange instant messages with a friend, talk on the phone with a relative, or visit face-to-face with your supervisor, you are engaging in interpersonal communication. **Interpersonal communication** is communication that occurs between two people in the context of their ongoing relationship, and research indicates that it is the most common form of communication we enact.[30] Even in larger social groups, such as families and organizations, much of our communication is typically interpersonal in nature. We will delve more deeply into interpersonal communication in Chapters 7 and 8.

Interpersonal communication occurs between people in the context of their relationships.

Small Group Communication Almost all of us interact in small groups of people, such as sports teams, Bible study groups, organizational departments, and teams of students working on a class project. When we communicate with groups of about 3 to 20 people, we are engaging in **small group communication.** As we'll discover in Chapters 9 and 10, groups have specific ways of making decisions, negotiating power, and working together in the service of their common goals.

Public Communication **Public communication** occurs when we speak or write to an audience that is larger than a small group. If you give the wel-

intrapersonal communication Communication with oneself.

interpersonal communication Communication that occurs between two people in the context of their relationship.

small group communication Communication occurring within small groups of three or more people.

public communication Communication directed at an audience that is larger than a small group.

mass communication Communication to a large audience that is transmitted by media.

come speech at a convention for your fraternity or sorority or write a column for the convention's newsletter, you are engaging in public communication. Because your communication targets a larger audience, you might spend more time preparing and practicing your remarks than if you were talking only to a friend or a small group. In Chapters 11 through 15, we'll examine skills that are helpful for successful public communication.

Mass Communication Communication delivered to a large audience is considered public communication unless it is being transmitted via electronic or print media, such as magazines, television, newspapers, blogs, radio, and websites. Communication that is transmitted by such media is considered **mass communication.** Newspaper journalists, television personalities, bloggers, and radio announcers are among those whose words are disseminated to vast audiences of people with whom they have little or no personal connection. Because its audience is so large, mass communication works well for distributing news, commentary, and entertainment. It also is effective for marketing products and services through advertisements, but its breadth makes mass communication unsuited for developing relationships or making collective decisions.

Now that we've surveyed the nature and basic types of communication, we'll shift gears and look at some common beliefs about communication that are not as valid as they might seem.

Test Yourself

- What are the primary differences among the action, interaction, and transaction models of communication?
- What does it mean to say that communication has content and relational implications?
- How do the five types of communication differ from one another?

>> Dispelling Some Communication Myths

In one way or another, you've communicated practically every day of your life. At this point, then, you might feel that you already know what there is to know about communication. As you'll see, however, people have many different ideas about communication, some of which are not very accurate. In this section we'll examine five common communication myths so that you'll be better able to separate fact from fiction. Those myths are

- Everyone is a communication expert.
- Communication will solve any problem.
- Communication can break down.
- Communication is inherently good.
- More communication is always better.

MYTH: EVERYONE IS A COMMUNICATION EXPERT

Because people communicate constantly, it's easy to believe that just about everyone is an expert in communication. Indeed, in a nationwide survey of U.S. American adults conducted by the National Communication Association, fully 91 percent of participants rated their communication skills as above average.[31] It's important to remember, though, that having *experience* with something is not the same as having *expertise.* Many people drive, but that doesn't make them expert drivers. Many people have children, but that doesn't make them parenting experts. Experience can be invaluable, but expertise requires knowledge and ability

SHARPEN Your Skills

Using the Internet to help you, identify three communication experts outside of your college or university. Read about each person's background, and list the training, education, and/or work experiences that make that person an expert in communication. Share your findings with your instructor to ensure that you have identified appropriate markers of expertise for each person.

that go beyond personal experience. Thus, experts in driving, parenting, or communication have training in their fields and a level of understanding that most people who drive, parent, or communicate don't have.

MYTH: COMMUNICATION WILL SOLVE ANY PROBLEM

The classic Paul Newman movie *Cool Hand Luke* (1967) featured a prison warden who had his own special way of dealing with inmates. Whenever things went wrong, he would say, "What we've got here is a failure to communicate," after which he would beat the inmate unconscious and send him to solitary confinement. Sometimes it seems as though we could solve almost any problem—especially in our relationships—if only we could communicate better. It's easy to blame a lack of communication when things go wrong. Yet the fact is that poor communication isn't the cause of every problem.[32]

On his television talk show *Dr. Phil,* psychologist Phil McGraw often counsels couples encountering difficulties in their relationships. Suppose that Connie and Andy appear on *Dr. Phil* complaining that they have been drifting apart for some time. When they discuss their problems on the show, Connie says that she feels they need to communicate better to save their relationship. In the course of their conversation, however, Andy states very clearly that his feelings have changed and that he is no longer attracted to Connie.

Will communication ultimately solve this couple's marital problems? No—in fact, it will probably cause Connie to realize that their relationship is already over. Going their separate ways might be better for both of them in the long run, so we could say that communication will help them come to that realization. Nevertheless, it won't solve the problem of their drifting apart in the first place. Therefore, we must be careful not to assume that better communication can resolve any problem we might face in our relationships.

MYTH: COMMUNICATION CAN BREAK DOWN

Just as we sometimes blame our problems on a lack of communication, many of us also point to a "breakdown" in communication as the root of problems. When marriages fail, the spouses may say it was a breakdown in communication that led to their relational difficulties. When government agencies are slow to respond to a natural disaster, people frequently blame their sluggish response on communication breakdowns within those agencies.

The metaphor of the communication breakdown makes intuitive sense to many of us. After all, our progress on a journey is halted if our car breaks down, so it's easy to think that our progress in other endeavors is halted because our communication has broken down. The fact is that communication isn't a mechanical object like a car, a computer, or an iPod. Instead, it's a process that unfolds between and among people over time. It may be easy to blame a breakdown in communication for problems we face in personal relationships or during crisis situations. What is actually happening in those contexts, however, is that we are no longer communicating effectively. In other words, the problem lies not with communication itself but with the way we're using it. That is one reason why learning about communication—as you are doing in this class—can be so beneficial.

MYTH: COMMUNICATION IS INHERENTLY GOOD

Listen to people who are having relationship problems and you'll hear them say they no longer communicate with their romantic partners, parents, or friends. "Sure, we talk all the time," someone might say, "but we don't really *communicate* anymore." Reflected in that statement is the idea that *talking* means just producing words, but *communicating*

By the Numbers

53

Percentage of U.S. American adults who believe a "lack of effective communication" is the Number One reason why marriages fail.[33]

When have you felt that communication "broke down" in one of your relationships? What caused that feeling?

THE DARK SIDE of Communication

Tell Me Lies: Misrepresentations in Online Dating Profiles

Online dating services—such as Match.com and Chemistry.com—have become enormously popular in recent years as a venue for meeting people and starting new relationships. On many such sites, participants create individual profiles for others to view. Profiles commonly include one or more photographs of the participant as well as information about the person's age, height and weight, profession, and interests.

Browsing the profiles of others can help us determine whom we might want to contact and communicate with, but how do we know whether the information is true? Research has shown—perhaps not surprisingly—that a large proportion of online daters put false information in their profiles, usually to make themselves appear more attractive to potential partners. Interestingly, women and men tend to lie about different things. In a study involving over 5,000 online dating participants, communication researcher Jeff Hall and his colleagues found that women are more likely than men to lie about their weight. The researchers also found that men are more likely to lie about their income, interests, personality, and age. The results from such studies encourage us to exercise caution when evaluating the profile of a potential dating partner.

Source: Hall, J. A., Park, N., Song, H., & Cody, M. J. (2010). Strategic misrepresentation in online dating: The effects of gender, self-monitoring, and personality traits. *Journal of Social and Personal Relationships, 27*, 117–135.

means sharing meaning with another person in an open, supportive, and inherently positive manner.[34]

Thinking that communication is inherently good is similar to thinking that money is inherently good. Sometimes money is put to positive uses, such as providing a home for your family and donating to a worthy charity. At other times it is put to negative uses, such as providing funding for a terrorist group and gambling away hard-earned income. In either case, it isn't the money itself that is good or bad—rather, it's how it is used.

We can make the same observation regarding communication. We can use communication for positive purposes, such as expressing love for our parents and comforting a grieving friend. We can also use it for negative purposes, such as intimidating and deceiving people. In fact, deception has become common in certain communication venues, such as in online personal ads, as The Dark Side of Communication explains.

Regarding the "dark side" terminology: In recent years, several scholars in the area of interpersonal communication have been studying what they call the "dark side" of communication. This research focuses on how people sometimes use communication to hurt or manipulate others. As you encounter The Dark Side of Communication box in each chapter of this book, remember that communication itself is not positive or negative—it's what individuals do with communication that makes it good or bad.

> In many instances, people feel they are *talking* but not really *communicating*.

MYTH: MORE COMMUNICATION IS ALWAYS BETTER

Antonio thinks that if others don't agree with him, the reason is that they just don't understand him. In those situations, he talks on and on, figuring that others will eventually see things his way if he gives them enough information. Perhaps you know someone like Antonio. Is it really the case that more communication always produces a better outcome?

When people have genuine disagreements, more talk doesn't always help. In some cases, increasing communication can just lead to frustration and anger. A 2007 study of consultations between doctors and patients found that the more doctors talked, the more likely they were to get off-track and forget about the patients' problems, a pattern that can translate into worse care for the patient.[35] Another study found that the more people communicated with one another on cell phones, the less happy they were, the less satisfied they were with their families, and the more likely they were to say that their work lives "spilled over" into their family lives.[36]

We've already considered that communication cannot solve every problem, so it shouldn't surprise you to learn that more communication isn't always preferable. Indeed, sometimes it seems as though the less said, the better. As you'll learn in this book, the *effectiveness* of our communication—rather than the *amount* of communication—is often what matters. That fact explains why learning to be a competent communicator is so advantageous.

- **What is the difference between having experience and having expertise?**
- **Why do you think some people believe communication can solve any problem?**
- **If communication doesn't break down, what leads to communication problems?**
- **What are some positive and negative reasons for communicating?**
- **When is it better to communicate less rather than more?**

Test Yourself

>> Building Your Communication Competence

In February 2009, the National Association of Colleges and Employers asked over a thousand employers around the United States what skills and personal qualities they most look for in new college graduates whom they are considering hiring. As you can see in Table 1.1, verbal and written communication skills topped the list.[37] That survey—along with several others like it that have been conducted over the past decade—indicates that being an effective communicator gives someone a sizable advantage when he or she is looking for work.[38]

None of us is born a competent communicator. Rather, as with driving a car, playing a sport, or designing a web page, communicating competently requires skills that we must learn and practice. That doesn't mean that nature doesn't give some people a head start. Indeed, research shows that genes partly determine some of our communication traits—for example, how sociable, aggressive, or shy we are.[39] No matter which traits we are born with, though, we can still learn how to communicate competently. In this section, we probe what it means to be a competent communicator, which skills are necessary for competent communication, and how we learn those skills.

COMPETENT COMMUNICATION IS EFFECTIVE AND APPROPRIATE

communication competence Communication that is effective and appropriate for a given situation.

Think about five people whom you consider to be really good communicators. Who's on your list? Any of your friends or relatives? Teachers? Co-workers? Politicians or celebrities? Yourself? You probably recognize that identifying good communicators means first asking yourself what a good communicator is. Even communication scholars find that a tricky question. Nevertheless, most researchers seem to agree that **communication competence** means communicating in ways that are *effective* and *appropriate* in a given situation.[40] Let's take a closer look at what it means to communicate effectively and appropriately.

Communicating Effectively Effectiveness describes how well your communication achieves its goals.[41] Suppose that you want to persuade your neighbor to donate money to a shelter for abused animals. There are many ways to achieve that goal. You could explain how much the shelter needs the money and identify how many services it provides to animals in need. You could offer to do yard work in exchange for your neighbor's donation. You could even recite the times when you have donated to causes that were important to your neighbor.

Your choice of strategy may partly depend on what other goals you are trying to achieve at the same time. If maintaining a good relationship with your neighbor is also important to you, then asking politely may be the most effective course of action. If all you want is the money, however, and your neighbor's feelings are less important to you, then making your neighbor feel obligated to donate may help you achieve your goal, even though it might not be as ethical.

The point is that no single communication strategy will be effective in all situations. Because we often pursue more than one goal at a time, being an effective communicator means using behaviors that meet all of the goals we have in the specific context in which we have them.

Communicating Appropriately for the Social and Cultural Context Besides being effective, competent communication should also be appropriate. That means attending to the rules and expectations that apply in a social situation. As we considered earlier in this chapter, communication is governed by rules. A competent communicator takes those rules into account when deciding how to act. For instance, when a co-worker asks, "How are you?" you know that it's appropriate to say, "Fine, how are you?" in return. The co-worker probably isn't expecting a long, detailed description of how your day is going, so if you launch into one, your colleague may find that response inappropriate. Similarly, it's appropriate in most classrooms to raise your hand and wait to be called on before speaking, so it would be inappropriate in those cases to blurt out your comments.

Communicating appropriately can be especially challenging when you're interacting with people from other cultures. The reason is that many communication rules are culture-specific, so what might be perfectly appropriate in one culture may be inappropriate or even offensive in another.[42] As one example, if you're visiting a Canadian household and your hosts offer you food, it's appropriate to accept the food if you're hungry. In many Japanese households, however, it is inappropriate to accept the food, even if you're hungry, until you decline it twice and your hosts offer it a third time.

Even within a specific culture, expectations for appropriate communication can vary according to the social situation. Communication that's appropriate at home might be inappropriate at work and vice versa. Moreover, communication that's appropriate for a socially powerful individual is not necessarily appropriate for less powerful people. For that reason, it might not be out of line for your manager to demand better cooperation among the staff during a meeting, although expressing the same demand yourself would be inappropriate.

People who know how to communicate effectively can use their skills to succeed in a wide range of fields. Throughout this book, you'll meet individuals who majored in communication in college and are now using their communication training in a variety of careers. In the Putting Communication to Work box, you'll

Table 1.1	Personal Qualities Most Sought by Employers Among New College Graduates

1. Communication skills (verbal and written)
2. Strong work ethic
3. Teamwork skills (works well with others)
4. Initiative
5. Analytic skills

Source: National Association of Colleges and Employers. (2009). *Job Outlook 2009: Spring update.* Bethlehem, PA: Author.

Companies seek to hire employees with excellent communication skills.

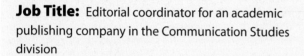

Name: Erika Lake

College(s): BA, SUNY Purchase College, May 2003; MS, The College of New Rochelle, 2005

Major(s): Journalism (undergraduate); communication (graduate)

Job Title: Editorial coordinator for an academic publishing company in the Communication Studies division

Salary: $34,000–$45,000

Time in Job: 4 years

Work Responsibilities: I am responsible for coordinating review projects and managing the work on various textbook revisions, doing marketing-related projects (to help ensure that new and revised texts will succeed), and acting as a liaison between the editorial team and our authors. I work on the Communication Studies and Criminal Justice lists. My background in communication allows me to look at the texts I help create and ask,

"What do we want to say with this feature? How will this text be perceived externally?" We are sending messages to our customers in everything we do— I got a better understanding of that concept from taking classes in communication studies. It makes you more in tune with what those around you are saying (verbally, nonverbally, visually) and what your own responses are.

Why Communication? I was a journalism major in college and went into communication studies for graduate school because I was unsure if I wanted to go to graduate school specifically for journalism. Communication offered a much broader scope and wider range of topics. I got to indulge my love of pop culture and its impact on our lives (you can study this in a mass communication class), and I got to understand how much my classroom topics and real life intersect. You are living the principles of communication all the time—you just don't know it sometimes.

My Advice to Students: They should appreciate that communication is something they already experience. You are being communicated with almost every single second of every day. Why not learn how to digest the information in an intelligent way and how to interpret the information for yourself?

see how one person applies her communication skills on a daily basis as an editorial coordinator for an academic publishing company.

Communication competence, then, implies both effectiveness and appropriateness. Note that those are characteristics of *communication,* not characteristics of people. Thus, the logical followup question is whether competent *communicators* share any traits. The answer is that competent communicators have many common characteristics, as we'll see next.

How would you describe your own level of self-monitoring— high or low—and why?

COMPETENT COMMUNICATORS SHARE MANY CHARACTERISTICS AND SKILLS

Look again at your list of five people who are good communicators. What do they have in common? Competence itself is situation-specific, so what works in one context may not work in another. Good communicators, however, tend to have certain characteristics that help them behave competently in most situations: They are self-aware, adaptable, empathic, cognitively complex, and ethical.

Competent Communicators Are Self-Aware

Good communicators are aware of their own behavior and its effects on others.[43] Researchers call that awareness **self-monitoring.** People who are "high self-monitors" pay close attention to the way they look, sound, and act in social situations. In contrast, people who are "low self-monitors" often seem oblivious to both their own behaviors and other people's reactions to them. For instance, you may know someone who never seems to notice that he dominates the conversation or who seems unaware that she speaks louder than anyone around her.

Self-monitoring usually makes people more competent communicators because it enables them to see how their behavior fits or doesn't fit in a given social setting. In addition, high self-monitors often have the ability to understand people's emotions and social behaviors accurately.[44]

Competent Communicators Are Adaptable

It's one thing to be aware of your own behavior; it's quite another to able to adapt it to different situations. Competent communicators are able to assess what is going to be appropriate and effective in a given context and then modify their behaviors accordingly.[45] That skill is important because what works in one situation might be ineffective in another. As we'll discover in Chapter 11, part of delivering a good speech is being aware of the audience and adapting one's behavior accordingly. A competent communicator would speak differently to a group of senior executives than to a group of new hires, for example, because what works with one audience may not work with the other.

High self-monitors pay close attention to the way they look, sound, and act.

Competent Communicators Are Empathic

Good communicators practice **empathy,** or the ability to be "other-oriented" and to understand other people's thoughts and feelings.[46] When people say "Put yourself in my shoes," they are asking you to consider a situation from *their* perspective rather than your own. Empathy is an important skill because people often think and feel differently than you do about the same situation.

Suppose that you want to ask your instructor for a one-week extension on an assignment. You might think, "What's the big deal? It's only a week." To your instructor, on the other hand, the extension might mean that she will be unable to complete her grading in time for her planned vacation. If the situation were reversed, how would you feel? An empathic approach would be to consider the situation from the instructor's perspective and tailor your behaviors accordingly.

People who don't practice empathy tend to assume that everyone thinks and feels the same way they do, and they risk creating problems when that assumption isn't accurate. How empathic are you? Take the quiz in The Competent Communicator box on page 23 to find out.

Empathy is a particular challenge for individuals with conditions such as autism and Asperger's disorder, both of which impair a person's ability to interpret other people's nonverbal behaviors. You may have little difficulty judging when a friend is being sarcastic, for instance, because you infer that from his facial expressions and tone of voice. For people with autism or Asperger's disorder, however, those nonverbal signals may not be as evident, making it more challenging to understand and adopt another person's perspective.

Competent Communicators Are Cognitively Complex

Let's say that you see your friend Annika coming toward you in the hallway at school. You smile and get ready to say hi, but she walks right by as if you're not there. How would you interpret her behavior? Maybe she's mad at you. Maybe she was concentrating on something when she passed and didn't notice anyone around her. Maybe she actually did smile at you and you just didn't see it.

self-monitoring Awareness of one's behavior and how it affects others.

empathy The ability to think and feel as others do.

cognitive complexity The ability to understand a given situation in multiple ways.

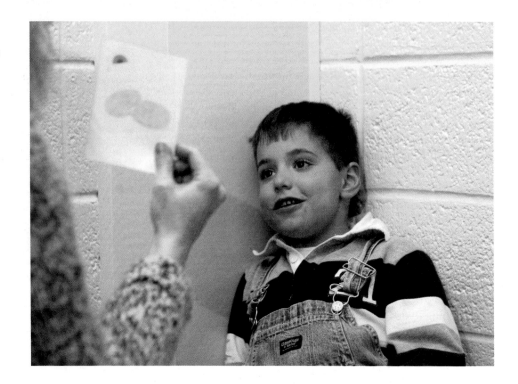

Children with autism often have difficulty interpreting other people's nonverbal behaviors.

SHARPEN Your Skills

Choose a reality TV show, and think about the characters and their communication behaviors. Based on what you've learned in this section, how would you rate each character in terms of communication competence? What makes some characters more communicatively competent than others? Try to identify specific skills, such as empathy and cognitive complexity, that differentiate the characters from one another. Consider how each person might improve his or her communication competencies.

ethics Principles that guide judgments about whether something is morally right or wrong.

The ability to consider a variety of explanations and to understand a given situation in multiple ways is called **cognitive complexity.** Cognitive complexity is a valuable skill because it keeps you from jumping to the wrong conclusion and responding inappropriately.[47] Someone with little cognitive complexity might feel slighted by Annika's behavior and might therefore ignore her the next time they meet. In contrast, someone with more cognitive complexity would remember that behaviors do not always mean what we think they mean. That person would be more open-minded, considering several possible interpretations of Annika's behavior.

Competent Communicators Are Ethical Finally, competent communicators are ethical communicators. **Ethics** are principles that guide us in judging whether something is morally right or wrong. Ethical communication generally dictates that we treat people fairly, communicate honestly, and avoid immoral or unethical behavior. Communicating ethically can be easier said than done, however, because people often have very different ideas about right and wrong. What may be morally justified to one person or one culture may be considered completely unethical to another.

Ethical considerations are often particularly important when we're engaged in compliance-gaining strategies, trying to change the way another person thinks or behaves. Referring back to a previous example, is it ethical to make your neighbor feel obligated to contribute money to your cause? To some people, that compliance-gaining strategy would seem unfair because it may lead your neighbor to donate even if he or she doesn't want to. Depending on why you need the money, however, or what you have done for your neighbor in the past, you might not consider that strategy to be unethical, even if others do. Competent communicators are aware that people's ideas about ethics vary. They are also aware of their own ethical beliefs, and they communicate in ways that are consistent with these beliefs.

Take one last look at your list of five good communicators. Are they generally aware of their own behaviors and able to adapt these behaviors to different contexts? Can they adopt

Stepping into Others' Shoes: How Empathic Are You?

One of the ways to improve your communication ability is to think about how you communicate now. Each "The Competent Communicator" box will help you do so by presenting one self-assessment of a communication skill or tendency. For instance, how empathic are you? For each of the following statements, indicate how well it describes you by assigning a number between 1 ("not at all") and 7 ("very well").

_____ It makes me sad to see a lonely stranger in a group.

_____ I become nervous if others around me seem nervous.

_____ I tend to get emotionally involved with a friend's problems.

_____ Sometimes the words of a love song can move me deeply.

_____ The people around me have a great influence on my moods.

_____ Seeing people cry upsets me.

_____ I get very angry when I see someone being ill-treated.

_____ I cannot continue to feel okay if people around me are depressed.

_____ I am very upset when I see an animal in pain.

_____ It upsets me to see helpless elderly people.

When you're finished, add up your scores. Your total score should fall between 10 and 70. A score of 10–25 suggests that empathy is a skill you can work on. Learning more about empathy, as you are doing in this class, might help you become more empathic. If you scored between 25 and 55, you are already moderately empathic, and you have a good ability to understand other people's emotions. Continued practice can improve this skill even more. If you scored above 55, you are a highly empathic person. Chances are that this ability helps you to communicate effectively in interpersonal situations.

  Remember that your score on this quiz—and on every "The Competent Communicator" quiz in this book—reflects only how you see yourself at this time. If your score surprised you, take the quiz again later in the course to see how studying communication might have changed the way you assess your communication abilities.

Source: Items adapted from Mehrabian, A., & Epstein, N. (1972). A measure of emotional empathy. *Journal of Personality, 40,* 525–543.

other people's perspectives and consider various ways of explaining situations? Do they behave ethically? Those aren't the only characteristics that make someone a competent communicator, but they are among the most important. To the extent that we can develop and practice those skills, we can all become better at the process of communication.

Test Yourself

• **What is the difference between communication effectiveness and communication appropriateness?**

• **How does cognitive complexity affect behavior?**

For REVIEW >>

- **What needs does communication help us meet?**

  We use communication to help us stay physically healthy, form and maintain important relationships, understand and express our identities, convey our spiritual beliefs, and accomplish mundane, instrumental tasks.

- **How does communication work, and what misconceptions do we have about it?**

  Communication can be described as action, interaction, or transaction, depending on the situation. Many people mistakenly believe that everyone is a communication expert, communication will solve any problem, communication can break down, communication is inherently good, and more communication is always better.

- **What particular skills characterize competent communicators?**

  Competent communicators express themselves effectively and appropriately in whatever situation they're in. They are self-aware, adaptable, empathic, cognitively complex, and ethical.

Pop Quiz

Multiple Choice

1. Garry is having difficulty paying attention to what his sister is saying because he is feeling tired and ill. The type of noise that is interfering with his ability to understand his sister is

   a. physical noise
   b. psychological noise
   c. cultural noise
   d. physiological noise

2. A sign that reads "Please turn off all cell phones" exemplifies an

   a. explicit communication rule
   b. implicit communication rule
   c. empathic communication rule
   d. ethical communication rule

3. Empathy is best defined as

   a. feeling sorry for someone else
   b. identifying, feeling, and relating to what others are feeling
   c. keeping other people's feelings separate from your own
   d. paying attention to how others are evaluating your social skills

4. All of the following are examples of a psychological context *except*

   a. the formality of the situation
   b. the level of privacy
   c. the degree to which the situation is emotionally charged
   d. the temperature of the room

5. Research has found that having a strong, positive social network can
   a. increase a person's susceptibility to depression
   b. decrease a person's susceptibility to colds
   c. decrease a person's life expectancy
   d. increase a person's cognitive complexity

Fill in the Blank

6. The tendency to behave in morally correct ways is a characteristic of someone who is _____.

7. Most U.S. American adults believe that a lack of _____ is the Number One cause of divorce.

8. The _____ model is the most contemporary model of human communication.

9. The ability to modify your behavior according to the demands of the situation is known as _____.

10. Communication is _____ if it attends to the rules and expectations that apply in a given social situation.

Answers: 1. d; 2. a; 3. b; 4. d; 5. b; 6. ethical; 7. effective communication; 8. transaction; 9. adaptability; 10. appropriate

KEY TERMS

communication 2
relational needs 4
instrumental needs 5
model 7
action model 7
source 7
encode 7
message 7
channel 7
receiver 7
decode 7
noise 7
interaction model 8
feedback 8
context 8
transaction model 8
channel-rich contexts 10
channel-lean contexts 10
symbol 11
content dimension 11
relational dimension 12
metacommunication 12
explicit rules 13
implicit rules 13
intrapersonal communication 14
interpersonal communication 14
small group communication 14
public communication 14
mass communication 15
communication competence 19
self-monitoring 21
empathy 21
cognitive complexity 22
ethics 22

COMMUN
AND CULTURE

A TRIUMPH OF CULTURAL UNITY

For athletes such as Danny Silva, competing in the Olympics isn't about winning gold. In the 2010 Winter Games in Vancouver, the 37-year-old cross country skier from Portugal finished dead last in his only event—the men's 15-kilometer race. Yet Silva and competitors like him have the rare privilege of taking part in what is perhaps the grandest celebration of cultural unity in human history. Every two years, during the Olympic opening ceremonies, athletes and coaches from each country parade into the host stadium in separate groups but quickly form one large mass of people, divided by languages and cultures but united around a common love of sports. Although the competitions pit each nation's best athletes against one another, the Olympics have come to symbolize the ability of humans from vastly different cultures and walks of life to interact in peaceful, respectful, and joyous ways. In so doing, they reinforce both the rich differences and the enduring similarities among human societies.

ICATION

- What is culture?
- How does culture influence communication behavior?
- In what ways can we improve our cultural communication skills?

Although few of us will ever take part in an Olympic opening ceremony, nearly all of us will communicate with people from different cultures at some point in our lives. Culture is a powerful influence on communication behavior. It can affect not only how we express ourselves but also how we interpret and react to others. In this chapter, we'll examine many ways that culture influences us as communicators. We begin by defining culture and considering the sources of our cultural ideas. We then look at some key ways in which cultures differ, focusing in particular on how communication behavior varies from society to society. Finally, we explore strategies for improving our communications with people of other cultures.

>> Understanding Cultures and Co-Cultures

Even if we don't realize it, our cultural traditions and beliefs influence how we make sense of communication behavior. Each of us is affected by the culture in which we grew up, and we tend to notice other cultures only when they differ from ours. To many people, culture—like an accent—is something that only *other* people have. Let's begin by understanding in what sense we *all* have cultural traits and biases.

SHARPEN Your Skills

Describe an interaction you have had with someone whose language, values, or traditions differed markedly from your own. What communication challenges did each of you face? How did you manage those challenges? How might you have managed them more effectively?

WHAT IS CULTURE?

We use the term *culture* to mean all sorts of things. Sometimes we connect it to a place, as in "Norwegian culture" and "New England culture." Other times we use it to refer to an ethnic or a religious group, as in "Asian American culture" and "Jewish culture." We also speak of "deaf culture" and "the culture of the rich." What makes a culture?

Although the word *culture* can have different meanings, we will define **culture** as the totality of learned, shared symbols, language, values, and norms that distinguish one group of people from another. That definition tells us that culture isn't a property of countries or ethnicities or economic classes. Rather, it's a property of *people*. We'll refer to the groups of people who share common symbols, language, values, and norms as **societies.**

Naturalized citizens bring many different cultural beliefs and practices to the United States.

Each of us identifies with one or more societies. Many of us are keenly aware of which societies we do and do not identify with. A fundamental aspect of our human nature, in fact, is to notice people's similarities and differences with respect to ourselves, so that we know which groups of people we belong to and which ones we are separate from. That distinction comprises the difference between in-groups and out-groups.

DISTINGUISHING BETWEEN IN-GROUPS AND OUT-GROUPS

Researchers use the term **in-groups** to refer to groups we identify with and **out-groups** to describe groups we see as different from ourselves.[1] If you grew up in the American South, for example, you probably see other Southerners as part of your in-group, whereas if you were raised in the Northwest, you do not. Similarly, when you are traveling in foreign countries, the residents may perceive you as an out-group member if you look or sound different from them or if you behave differently.

In-Groups and Out-Groups, Facebook-Style If you're an active social networker on Facebook, you already have an understanding of the difference between in-groups and out-groups. On Facebook, your in-group comprises those people on your friend list. By comparison, your out-group includes people who are not your Facebook friends—among them, those you have "unfriended," or deleted from your friend list.

Should Facebook qualify as its own culture? Check out Table 2.1 and see what you think.

The Challenges of Out-Group Status For some people, being perceived as different can be an exciting or intriguing experience, particularly if they do not typically stand out in their regular environments. For others, however, their differences can be stressful. For instance, research shows that many immigrants experience abnormally high levels of stress during their first year in their new homeland.[2] That stress can contribute to disorders such as depression, high blood pressure, and heart disease.[3]

Some researchers point out that our ability to distinguish between people who are similar to and different from ourselves probably helped our ancestors survive by encouraging them to associate with people whose goals and priorities were similar to their own.[4] That tendency to seek out familiar others endures today, as research shows that many people

culture The totality of learned, shared symbols, language, values, and norms that distinguish one group of people from another.

societies Groups of people who share common symbols, language, values, and norms.

in-groups Groups of people with which a person identifies.

out-groups Groups of people with which a person does not identify.

Table 2.1   The United States of Facebook?

Has the social-networking site Facebook become so large that it should qualify as its own culture? Consider the following:

- Facebook has over 350 million registered users. If Facebook were its own country, it would be the third most populous country in the world, after China and India.
- Although Facebook began in the United States, 7 out of 10 users today are from other countries.
- Facebook is available in 70 different languages.
- More than 3.5 billion pieces of content are shared on Facebook each week.*

What symbols, language, values, and norms would you identify as being unique to the Facebook culture?

*Figures are according to *The Economist*, January 30, 2010, pp. 3–5.

strongly prefer individuals and groups whom they perceive to be similar to themselves. By the same token, many people are more suspicious and less trusting of individuals whose ethnic, national, or cultural background is different from their own.[5] The reality of such feelings can make it uncomfortable for an individual to live or work someplace where he or she is considered a minority, especially if the person feels discriminated against on the basis of cultural or ethnic background. For example, read about the experiences of some Muslim students attending U.S. American colleges in The Dark Side of Communication.

The in-group/out-group distinction is a major reason why so many countries struggle with the issue of immigration. How open should a country be to letting people from other cultures—whom the nation's citizens consider to be out-groups—become part of the country's culture and in-group? Some countries, including Sweden and the United States, have relatively lenient policies that allow many applicants for immigration to move to those countries and eventually to become citizens. Other countries have much stricter policies concerning whom they will accept as immigrants or eventually as permanent residents. Denmark, for instance, has drawn criticism in the last decade for significantly toughening its immigration policies and thus making it harder for foreign-born people to immigrate and to become citizens.[6]

Should U.S. immigration policies be more lenient or more restrictive? Defend your answer.

How best to manage immigration—and the population of immigrants living in the country illegally—is currently a highly controversial issue in the United States. The experiences of Sweden, the United States, and Denmark all illustrate the complex and sometimes contentious relationship between in-groups, such as current citizens or residents of a country, and out-groups, such as those who wish to move to that country.

ACQUIRING A CULTURE

How does each of us acquire a culture? Because cultures and societies vary so broadly around the world, it might seem as though we simply inherit our culture genetically, the same way we inherit our eye color and other physical characteristics, but that isn't the case. Culture is not necessarily related to or based on our **ethnicity,** which is our perception of our ancestry or heritage. Neither is culture necessarily related to our **nationality,** which is our status as a citizen of a particular country. Rather, culture is learned. It is determined by who raised you and what their symbols, language, values, and norms were. Researchers use the term **enculturation** to describe the process of acquiring a culture.

For instance, a Cambodian-born citizen raised in the United States will likely adopt the language and practices common to where she is brought up. Her ethnicity and citizenship are Cambodian, but her culture is the U.S. American culture. Likewise, someone

ethnicity People's perceptions of ancestry or heritage.

nationality One's status as a citizen of a particular country.

enculturation The process of acquiring a culture.

THE DARK SIDE of Communication

Cultural Intolerance: Discrimination Against Muslim Students on U.S. College Campuses

During the years of the U.S. wars in Iraq and Afghanistan, many Muslim students have felt like outsiders at the U.S. colleges and universities they attend. Some receive hostile looks or threatening e-mail messages. Others feel excluded from social events where they once would have felt welcome. Some have been the target of verbal abuse blaming all Muslims for the terrorist actions of a few.

Distinguishing between in-groups and out-groups may be a natural tendency among human beings and other species, but it can lead to erroneous judgments about others. After 19 Islamic extremists carried out deadly attacks on the United States on September 11, 2001, many U.S. Muslims felt as though they were being treated as terrorists themselves simply because they shared a cultural and religious background with the hijackers. Although the attacks were genuine atrocities, in truth the vast majority of Muslims had nothing to do with them. In fact, many major Islamic organizations explicitly condemned the terrorist strikes. Such discrimination against Muslims provides evidence of how, during times of stress or uncertainty, it may be especially easy to make broad generalizations about groups of people. For competent communicators, however, it is vitally important to remember not to condemn an entire group based on the actions of a few individuals.

Source: Kerr, M. (2009, May 17). Muslims face discrimination and intolerance. *The Statesman*. Retrieved February 17, 2010, from http://www.sbstatesman. com/2.892/muslims-face-discrimination-and-intolerance-1.38633

born in New Zealand but raised in Nigeria may adopt the Nigerian culture as his own, even if he is Caucasian. The point is that we acquire our culture by learning the traditions, values, and language of the people by whom we are raised.

WHAT IS A CO-CULTURE?

When you think about culture as shared language, beliefs, and customs, it may seem as though you belong to many different cultures at once. If you grew up in the United States, you likely feel a part of the U.S. American culture. At the same time, if you enjoy comic books, vintage cars, or skateboarding, you may notice that the people who share your interests appear to have their own customs and vocabularies. Or perhaps you observe that people in your generation have different values and customs than people who are older than you—or that different ethnic or

Culture is learned. Regardless of our citizenship, most of us learn the language and cultural practices common to the place where we grow up.

religious groups at your school seem to have their own traditions and beliefs. Does each of those groups have a culture of its own? In a manner of speaking, the answer is yes.

Defining Co-Cultures Within many "large" cultures—such as the Italian, Thai, and U.S. American cultures—is a host of "smaller" cultural groups that researchers call co-cultures. **Co-cultures** are groups of people who share values, customs, and norms related to mutual interests or characteristics besides their national citizenship. Your co-culture isn't based on the country in which you were born or the national society in which you were raised. Instead, it is composed of smaller groups of people with whom you identify.

The Bases of Co-Cultures Some co-cultures form around shared activities or beliefs. If you're into fly fishing, organic gardening, or political activism, there are co-cultures for those interests. Similarly, Buddhists have beliefs and traditions that distinguish them from Baptists, regardless of where they grew up.

Some co-cultures develop around differences in mental or physical abilities. For instance, many deaf populations have values and customs that differ from those of hearing populations, including social customs.[7] Consider that whereas many people are uncomfortable having constant eye contact with another person while talking, deaf people frequently maintain a steady mutual gaze while communicating through sign language. In addition, they often make a point of notifying others in the group if they are leaving the room, even if just for a few moments. Because deaf individuals cannot hear one another call out from another room, that practice makes frantic searches for the departed person unnecessary. In contrast, among hearing people, it would be considered annoying at the very least to announce every departure from a room. Sharing those and other customs, then, helps deaf people interact with one another as members of a shared co-culture.[8]

The deaf co-culture also places a strong emphasis on the distinctions between in-group and out-group members. Many individuals who are deaf point out that a person cannot genuinely understand the physical experience of deafness—or the social experience of being treated as deaf—unless he or she is deaf. Consequently, people who are deaf often express a strong preference for interacting with other deaf individuals. They may treat sign language interpreters and the hearing parents of deaf children as "honorary deaf people,"

The deaf co-culture often places a strong emphasis on the distinctions between in-group and out-group members.

co-cultures Groups of people who share values, customs, and norms related to mutual interests or characteristics besides their national citizenship.

but they are frequently hesitant to accept hearing people as part of the deaf co-culture.[9] Such reluctance was in evidence when, in 1988, students at Gallaudet University in Washington, DC, whose undergraduate student body consists entirely of deaf people, staged an eight-day protest demanding the appointment of a deaf president for the university. The board of trustees responded by appointing the first deaf president in the school's 130-year history.

Identifying with Multiple Co-Cultures Many people identify with several co-cultures at once. You might relate to a co-culture for your age group, ethnicity, religion, sexual orientation, musical tastes, athletic interests, and even your college major. Each may have its own values, beliefs, traditions, customs, and ways of using language that distinguish it from other groups. Some co-cultures even contain smaller co-cultures within them. For example, the deaf co-culture includes people who advocate using only sign language and others who advocate the use of cochlear implants, devices surgically inserted in the ear to help a person hear.

Co-Cultures Online The Internet offers multiple opportunities for people to develop and participate in co-cultures that are specific to the online world. For instance, those who are interested in online games or science fiction, or in the development of free software, can find extensive communities of people with similar interests on the web. Each such community may develop its own terminology, values, and communication practices and interact as a co-culture even though its members may be geographically disbursed.

The Internet also provides opportunity for people to find others who share co-cultural interests that are not unique to the cyberworld. Search engines such as Google and Yahoo host thousands of Usenet groups where people can communicate with others who share their passion for bird watching, silent movies, Eastern philosophy, or African art.[10] Although such co-cultures are not specific to the Internet environment—in the way that, say, online gaming is—they often thrive on the web, where people separated by thousands of miles can communicate whenever they wish.

Test Yourself

- How are cultures and societies different?
- What are in-groups and out-groups?
- How do we acquire a culture?
- What is a co-culture?

>> Components of Cultures and Co-Cultures

Cultures and societies vary enormously. Imagine a group composed of people raised in Saudi Arabia, Vietnam, Iceland, Botswana, Paraguay, Israel, and the U.S. Southwest. The members would differ not only in their native languages but also, most likely, in their religious beliefs, political viewpoints, sports interests, food preferences, clothing, and ideas about education, marriage, money, and sexuality. Indeed, we might have a harder time identifying the members' similarities than their differences. That's how powerful an influence culture can be.

As we'll see later, values, beliefs, and preferences often vary even among different groups of people within the same country. For example, native Hawaiians, native Texans, and native New Yorkers might vary considerably in their customs and values, even though they were all raised in the United States. Similarly, opera buffs, country music lovers, and acid rock fans might seem to have more differences than similarities, even in cases where these followers of various music styles all grew up in the same neighborhood. In short, culture can distinguish not only people with different nationalities but also those with different interests and social characteristics.

Culture distinguishes people with different interests. Opera lovers and country music fans—even if they live in the same community—often seem more different than similar.

The United States has often been called a melting pot to acknowledge that it comprises multiple cultural groups. In fact, students are frequently encouraged to learn more about intercultural communication precisely because of the notion that the country's cultural diversity continues to increase. Is that assumption true, though? Check out the Fact or Fiction? box to find out.

No matter what their differences, cultures have some common components, as our definition of culture made clear. Those components are symbols, language, values, and norms. Let's take a close look at each one.

CULTURES VARY IN THEIR SYMBOLS

As we saw in Chapter 1, a symbol is something that represents an idea. Words are symbols, for example. In addition, every culture has its own symbols that stand for ideas that are vital to that culture.

With what cultural symbols do you most strongly identify?

When we hear that something is "as American as baseball and apple pie," the speaker is using baseball and apple pie as symbols of U.S. American life. The U.S. flag, the bald eagle, and "The Star-Spangled Banner" are also common symbols of the United States.

Each society uses symbols that carry particular meanings for its members. For instance, the Chinese national anthem, "Yiyongjun Jinxingqu" ("March of the Volunteers"), serves as a symbol of Chinese culture. Similarly, "Die Stem van Suid-Afrika" ("The Call of South Africa"), the national anthem of South Africa, symbolizes that country's culture.

CULTURES VARY IN THEIR LANGUAGES

Researchers believe there are approximately 6,800 languages used in the world today.[11] Furthermore, according to the New York State Comptroller's Office, more languages are spoken in Queens, New York, than in any other city on earth: 138 at last count.[12] Language allows for written and spoken communication, and it also ensures that cultures and cultural ideas are passed from one generation to the next.

Today, Chinese, English, and Spanish—in that order—are the three most commonly spoken languages in the world. Unfortunately, many other languages are in danger of extinction. In fact, researchers believe that at least 10 percent of the world's languages are currently spoken by fewer than 100 people each.[13] We will examine language use further in Chapter 4.

By the Numbers

2,159,000,000

Number of people in the world who speak Chinese, English, and/ or Spanish.

Change Is Inevitable: The United States Is Becoming More Culturally Diverse

Communication professors often encourage students to learn more about intercultural communication on the argument that the United States is becoming more diverse over time. Is that notion fact or fiction?

Projections from the U.S. Census suggest that it's a fact. Using data compiled from previous census counts, the U.S. Census Bureau predicts that the United States will have greater diversity with respect to both ethnicity and age over the next half century. The table below presents the percentages of the U.S. population that fit each ethnic and age category in 2000 and are projected to fit each category in 2025 and 2050.

Year	Ethnic Category				Age Category		
	African American	White/Caucasian	Asian American	Other Ethnicities	0–19	20–64	65+
2000	12.7	81.0	3.8	2.5	28.5	59.0	12.4
2025	13.7	76.7	5.8	3.8	26.3	55.5	18.2
2050	14.6	72.1	8.0	5.3	26.0	53.4	20.6

2025 percentages for ethnicity represent aggregates of 2020 and 2030 projections. Some percentages do not sum to 100 due to rounding.

As the table illustrates, the U.S. Census Bureau forecasts greater ethnic and age diversity over the next 40 years. For instance, whereas Asian Americans composed 3.8 percent of the population in 2000, they are expected to rise to 8 percent of the population in 2050. Similarly, senior citizens 65 years of age and older were only 12.4 percent of the U.S. population in 2000 but are expected to make up 20.6 percent—more than one-fifth—of the population in just four more decades. Given this growth, the ability to communicate effectively with people from other demographic groups will be increasingly advantageous in the years to come.

ASK YOURSELF

- What communication challenges will Americans face as ethnic and age diversity increases?
- What particular communication skills do you think might help society meet those challenges?

Source: Shrestha, L. B. (2006). *The changing demographic profile of the United States.* Congressional Research Service report for Congress. Retrieved February 5, 2010, from www.fas.org/sgp/crs/misc/RL32701.pdf

CULTURES VARY IN THEIR VALUES

A culture's *values* are the standards it uses to judge how good, desirable, or beautiful something is. In other words, values are cultural ideas about *what ought to be*. Sociological research indicates that U.S. American culture values ideas such as equal opportunity, material comfort, practicality, efficiency, achievement, democracy, free enterprise, and individual choice.[14] In other countries, citizens might have cultural values that are dramatically different from U.S. values.

CULTURES VARY IN THEIR NORMS

Finally, *norms* are rules or expectations that guide people's behavior in a culture. As an example, consider the norms for greeting people when you first meet them. In North

Whether a kiss is an intimate act between lovers or a routine social greeting may depend on the culture in which it occurs.

American countries, people typically shake hands and make a courteous statement such as "Nice to meet you." In another culture it may be normal to hug, kiss on both cheeks, or, in some cases, even to kiss on the lips.

Cultures also vary in their norms for politeness. A behavior that is considered very polite in one culture may be frowned upon in another. When receiving a compliment, for instance, U.S. Americans consider it polite to say "Thank you." By comparison, a Chinese person would consider that reply boastful and would instead respond by suggesting that he or she was not worthy of the compliment in the first place.[15]

DISTINCTIVE FEATURES OF CO-CULTURES

Like cultures, co-cultures often adopt distinctive symbols, language, values, and norms that distinguish their members from outsiders. A co-cultural symbol might be a logo, such as the pink triangle used by the GLBT (gay, lesbian, bisexual, and transgender) community, or it might be an action, such as a secret handshake, that allows members of a fraternal organization to identify one another. Although co-cultures may not adopt entirely distinctive languages, they frequently use terminology—called *jargon*—that is understood only by others in the same co-culture. Surfers, for instance, might say "getting tubed" to describe being completely covered by the top of a wave, and firefighters call someone who always has trouble gearing up for a fire a "door dancer." Such terms are understood within the co-cultural community but are frequently incomprehensible to outsiders. We will delve further into the topic of jargon later in this chapter.

Co-cultural groups often arise precisely because their members share specific values. The co-culture of veganism—which promotes diets free of animal products—largely shares values related to the preservation of animal life, whereas the co-culture of Civil War re-enactors—who stage dramatizations of famous Civil War battles—shares values related to the recognition of that major event in U.S. history. Finally, co-cultures adopt their own norms, such as the norm of silent worship among Quakers and the norm of dressing alike among the community of twins.

SHARPEN Your Skills

Select a culture that seems substantially different from your native culture. Using the Internet, research the values and norms that are common in that other culture. In a short essay, describe the values and norms of that culture and discuss how you would use that knowledge to communicate effectively with people of that cultural background.

Test Yourself

- What are cultural symbols?
- What various functions does language serve?
- Which values characterize your culture?
- In what ways do cultures differ with respect to their norms?
- In what ways do co-cultures vary in their use of symbols, language, values, and norms?

>> How Culture Affects Communication

If you've ever had difficulty communicating with someone from a different cultural background, you've experienced the challenge of overcoming cultural differences in communication. Dutch social psychologist Geert Hofstede and American anthropologist Edward T. Hall have pioneered the study of cultures and cultural differences in behavior. Their work and that of others points in particular to six cultural differences that influence how people communicate with one another. Those variations—our focus in this section—are related to (1) the emphasis placed on individuals versus groups, (2) the communicative context, (3) power distance, (4) views about masculinity and femininity and about men's and women's roles, (5) orientation toward time, and (6) uncertainty avoidance.

The phenomenal popularity of *American Idol* reflects the highly individualistic nature of U.S. American culture.

INDIVIDUALISTIC VERSUS COLLECTIVISTIC CULTURES

Cultures differ as to how much they emphasize individuals rather than groups. In an **individualistic culture,** people believe that their primary responsibility is to themselves. Children in individualistic cultures are raised hearing messages such as "Be yourself," "You're special," and "There's no one else in the world who's just like you." Those messages emphasize the importance of knowing oneself, being self-sufficient, and being true to what one wants in life.[16] Indeed, the motto in an individualistic culture might be "I gotta be me!" People in individualistic societies also value self-reliance and the idea that people should "pull themselves up by their own bootstraps"—that is, help themselves when they need help instead of waiting for others to come to their aid. Research shows that the United States, Canada, Great Britain, and Australia are among the most individualistic societies in the world.[17] The United States is so individualistic that *American Idol*—the talent show in which undiscovered singers compete to land lucrative recording contracts and achieve superstar status—is one of television's top-rated programs.

In contrast, people in a **collectivistic culture** are taught that their primary responsibility is to their families, their communities, and their employers. In other words, collectivistic cultures focus on the importance of taking care of the needs of the group rather than the individual. People in collectivistic cultures place a high value on duty and loyalty and see themselves not as unique or special but as a part of the groups to which they belong. Among the Kabre of Togo, for instance, individuals try to give away many of their material possessions in order to build relationships and benefit their social groups.[18] The motto in a collectivistic culture might be "I am my family and my family is me." Collectivistic cultures include Korea, Japan, and many countries in Africa and Latin America.[19]

individualistic culture A culture in which people believe that their primary responsibility is to themselves.

collectivistic culture A culture in which people believe that their primary responsibility is to their families, their communities, and their employers.

How individualistic or collectivistic a culture is can affect communication behavior in several ways. When people in an individualistic culture experience conflict with one another, for instance, they are expected to express it and work toward resolving it. In comparison, people in a collectivistic culture are taught to be much more indirect in the way they handle disagreements, to preserve social harmony.[20]

Another difference between the two types of culture centers on people's comfort level with public speaking. Many people feel anxious when they have to give a speech, but that experience of nervousness is especially common in collectivistic societies, where people are taught to blend in rather than to stand out. Asserting oneself and standing up for oneself are valued in individualistic cultures, but they can cause embarrassment and shame for people in a collectivistic culture.

Some researchers have gone so far as to suggest that the individualistic–collectivistic distinction is the most fundamental way that cultures differ from one another. Other researchers disagree, maintaining that this distinction by itself cannot adequately characterize cultures.[21]

LOW- VERSUS HIGH-CONTEXT CULTURES

If you have traveled much, you perhaps have noticed that people in various parts of the world differ in how direct and explicit their language is. On your trips, you may have spent time in both low- and high-context cultures, with *context* here referring to the broad range of factors surrounding every act of communication.

In a **low-context culture,** people are expected to be direct, to say what they mean, and not to "beat around the bush." Individuals in low-context cultures value expressing themselves, sharing opinions, and trying to persuade others to see things their way.[22] The United States is an example of a low-context society, as are Canada, Israel, and most northern European countries.

In contrast, people in a **high-context culture** are taught to speak in a much less direct way than individuals in a low-context culture. In high-context societies—examples of which are Korea, the Maori of New Zealand, and Native Americans—maintaining harmony and avoiding offense are more important than expressing one's true feelings.[23] Consequently, people speak in a more ambiguous manner and convey much more of their meaning through subtle behaviors and contextual cues, such as facial expressions and tone of voice.

The impact of the communicative context is evident in the ways in which people handle criticism and disagreement in different societies. In a low-context culture, a supervisor might reprimand an irresponsible employee openly, to make an example of the individual. The supervisor would probably be direct and explicit about the employee's shortcomings, the company's expectations for improvement, and the consequences of the employee's failing to meet those expectations.

In contrast, in a high-context culture, the supervisor probably wouldn't reprimand the employee publicly for fear that it would put the employee to shame and cause the worker to "lose face." Criticism in high-context cultures is more likely to take place in private. The supervisor would also likely use more ambiguous language to convey what the employee was doing wrong, "talking around" the issue instead of confronting it directly. To reprimand an employee for repeated absences, for example, a supervisor might point out that responsibility to one's co-workers is important and that letting down the team would be cause for shame. The supervisor may never actually say that the employee needs to improve his or her attendance record. Instead, the employee would be expected to understand that message by listening to what the supervisor says and paying attention to the supervisor's body language, tone of voice, and facial expressions.

When people from low- and high-context cultures communicate with one another, the potential for misunderstanding is great. To appreciate that point, imagine that you have asked two of your friends if they'd like to meet you tomorrow evening for a coffee tasting at a popular bookstore cafe. Your friend Tina, who's from a low-context culture, says, "No, I've got a lot of studying to do, but thanks anyway." Lee, who grew up in a high-context culture, nods his head and says, "That sounds like fun." Thus, you're surprised later when Lee doesn't show up.

low-context culture A culture in which people are expected to be direct and to say what they mean.

high-context culture A culture in which people are taught to speak in an indirect, inexplicit way.

low-power-distance culture A culture in which people believe that no one person or group should have excessive power.

high-power-distance culture A culture in which certain groups, such as the royal family or the members of the ruling political party, have much greater power than the average citizen.

masculine culture A culture in which people cherish traditionally masculine values and prefer sex-specific roles for women and men.

How can you account for those different behaviors? The answer is that people raised in a high-context culture are often reluctant to say no—even when they mean no—for fear of causing offense. Another person from Lee's culture might have understood from Lee's facial expression or tone of voice that he didn't intend to go to the coffee tasting. Because you grew up in a low-context society, however, you interpreted his answer and his nods to mean he was accepting your invitation.

LOW- VERSUS HIGH-POWER-DISTANCE CULTURES

Cultures also differ from one another in the degree to which power is evenly distributed within the society. Several types of assets can give someone power, including money or other valuable resources, education or expertise, age, popularity, talent, intelligence, and experience. In democratic societies such as the United States and western European nations, people believe in the value of equality across the sexes and groups.

The belief that all men and women are created equal and that no one person or group should have excessive power is characteristic of a **low-power-distance culture.** The United States and Canada fall in that category, as do Israel, New Zealand, Denmark, and Austria.[24] People in lower-power-distance societies are raised to believe that although some individuals are born with more advantages (such as wealth or fame), no one is inherently better than anyone else. That doesn't necessarily mean that people in those societies *are* treated equally, only that they value the idea that they should be.

In a **high-power-distance culture,** power is distributed less evenly; certain groups, such as the royal family or the members of the ruling political party, have great power, and the average citizen has much less. People in high-power-distance societies are taught that certain people or groups deserve more power than others and that respecting power is more important than respecting equality. Mexico, Brazil, India, Singapore, and the Philippines are all examples of high-power-distance societies.[25]

Power distance affects many aspects of communication. For example, people in low-power-distance cultures usually expect friendships and romantic relationships to be based on love rather than social status. In contrast, people in high-power-distance cultures often feel pressure to choose friends and mates from within their social class.[26]

Another difference involves the way people think about authority. Individuals in a low-power-distance society are often taught that it is their right—even their responsibility—to question authority. In such a society it's not unexpected for people to ask "Why?" when a parent or teacher tells them to do something. In contrast, individuals in a high-power-distance society learn to obey and respect those in power, such as parents and teachers, without question.[27]

That difference is also evident in individuals' relationships and communication patterns with their employers. Workers in a low-power-distance culture value *autonomy*—freedom of choice about the way they do their jobs—as well as opportunities to influence decisions that affect them. Such workers might provide their input, for example, through unions or employee satisfaction surveys. In contrast, employees in a high-power-distance culture are used to having little or no say about how to do their jobs. Instead, they expect their employers to make the decisions and are more likely to follow those decisions without question.

MASCULINE VERSUS FEMININE CULTURES

We usually use the terms *masculine* and *feminine* when we're referring to people. Hofstede has suggested that we can also apply those terms to cultures.[28] In a highly **masculine culture,** people tend to cherish traditionally masculine values, such as ambition, achievement, and the acquisition of material goods. They also value sex-specific roles for women and men, preferring that men hold the wage-earning and decision-making positions (such

Saudi Arabia has a high-power-distance culture. Members of the royal family have considerably more power than the average citizen.

Do you agree with researchers who characterize the United States as having a low-power-distance culture? Does that assessment match your own experiences? Why or why not?

By the Numbers

450

Days of paid maternity leave guaranteed by law in Sweden, one of the world's most feminine cultures.

as corporate executive) while women occupy the nurturing positions (such as homemaker). Examples of masculine cultures are Austria, Japan, and Mexico.

By comparison, in a highly **feminine culture,** people tend to value nurturance, quality of life, and service to others, all of which are stereotypically feminine qualities. They also tend *not* to believe that men and women's roles should be strongly differentiated. Therefore, in a feminine culture, it is not unusual for a man to care for children or for a woman to be her family's primary wage earner. Furthermore, most feminine cultures provide new mothers with more paid maternity leave than do masculine cultures, so that those mothers can focus their attention on their new infants. Examples of feminine cultures are Sweden, Chile, and the Netherlands.

According to Hofstede's research, the United States has a moderately masculine culture. U.S. Americans tend to value sex-differentiated roles—although not as strongly as Austrians, Japanese, and Mexicans do—and they place a fairly high value on stereotypically masculine qualities such as achievement and the acquisition of resources.[29]

MONOCHRONIC VERSUS POLYCHRONIC CULTURES

Cultures also vary with respect to their norms and expectations concerning the use of time. Societies that have a **monochronic** concept of time—such as Swiss, Germans, and most U.S. Americans—view time as a commodity. Americans save time, spend time, fill time, invest time, and waste time as though time were tangible. They treat time as valuable, believe that "time is money," and talk about making time and losing time.[30]

A monochronic orientation toward time influences several social behaviors. Because people in monochronic cultures think of time as valuable, they hate to waste it. Therefore, they expect meetings and classes to start on time (within a minute or so), and when that doesn't happen, they are willing to wait only so long before leaving. They also expect others to show up when they say they will.

In comparison, societies with a **polychronic** orientation—which include Latin America, the Arab part of the Middle East, and much of sub-Saharan Africa—conceive of time as more holistic and fluid and less structured. Instead of treating time as a finite commodity that must be managed properly to avoid being wasted, people in a polychronic culture perceive it more like a never-ending river, flowing infinitely into the future.[31]

In societies with a polychronic time orientation, schedules are more fluid and flexible than they are in monochronic societies. In Pakistan, for instance, if you're invited to a wedding that begins at 4:30 in the afternoon and you arrive at 4:25, you will most likely be the first one there. A bank or restaurant may not open at a specified time—as it would be expected to do in a monochronic society—but whenever the owner or manager decides to open. Students in a polychronic society would not expect a professor to begin class at an appointed hour; instead, students would arrive over a period of time, and the class would begin whenever the professor was ready. Further, people in a polychronic culture don't prioritize efficiency and punctuality but instead attach greater value to the quality of life and to their relationships with others.

Check out "Putting Communication to Work" to see how one former communication major has used her skills and training to interact effectively with people from a wide variety of cultures.

UNCERTAINTY AVOIDANCE

Humans have a natural tendency to avoid unfamiliar and uncomfortable situations. In other words, we dislike uncertainty—and in fact, uncertainty causes many of us a good deal of stress.[32] Not all cultures find uncertainty to be equally problematic, however. Rather, cultures vary in what Hofstede called **uncertainty avoidance,** or the extent to which people try to avoid situations that are unstructured, unclear, or unpredictable.[33]

Individuals from cultures that are highly uncertainty avoidant are drawn to people and situations that are familiar, and they are relatively unlikely to take risks, for fear of failure. They are also uncomfortable with differences of opinion, and they tend to favor rules and

feminine culture A culture in which people cherish traditionally feminine qualities and prefer little differentiation in the roles of women and men.

monochronic culture A culture that views time as a finite and tangible commodity.

polychronic culture A culture that views time as holistic, fluid, and infinite.

uncertainty avoidance The extent to which people try to avoid situations that are unstructured, unclear, or unpredictable.

Putting Communication to Work

Name: Deborah Therrien

College(s): Associate degree, College of Southern Maryland, 2007; BA, University of Maryland University College, 2009

Major(s): Communication

Job Title: Logistics Management Specialist, Department of the Navy

Salary: 3-year career development intern positions start at $35,000+/year; most positions pay $65,000+ after successful completion of the program

Time in Job: 8 months

Work Responsibilities: Life Cycle Logistics Specialists plan and coordinate integrated logistics support activities to provide the manpower, training, facilities, equipment, computer resources, transportation, and technical data needed to support U.S. Navy and Marine Corps ships, aircraft, and weapons systems. My job is managing and supporting technical data as a technical data rights expert. I am learning about policies and laws relevant to intellectual property and technical data rights as they relate to the acquisition and support of defense weapons and equipment.

Why Communication?: I am 51 years old, and my background was working in advertising for the *Los Angeles Times* and in volunteer promotions. I pursued a communication degree because I was somewhat familiar with the work required in public relations—my intended career path.

In my intercultural communication class, I gained insight into successful communication in a diverse workforce. I remember being surprised to learn that an individual's behavior and actions can be influenced by his or her culture's perception of time, space, and power distance. My intercultural communication class served to increase my understanding of the actions and reactions of others so that I can manage my responses and effectively communicate with anyone.

My Advice to Students: Consider that a working knowledge of communication elements is vital to success in any field, not just those typically associated with communication, such as public relations, journalism, and broadcasting. Explore other career choices. I would never have dreamed that I would end up in a technical position such as logistics. Yet my interviewers recognized that my communication expertise would be a positive contribution to the organization because it would help me to understand and convey instructions and ideas, learn unfamiliar tasks and responsibilities, and interact effectively with diverse team members, clients, and management.

---

laws and maximize security and reduce ambiguity. Argentina, Portugal, and Uruguay are among the countries whose cultures are the most uncertainty avoidant.

In contrast, people in uncertainty-accepting cultures are more open to new situations and more accepting of people and ideas that are different from their own. They take a "live and let live" approach, preferring as few rules as possible that would restrict their behaviors. Societies with cultures that are highly accepting of uncertainty include Hong Kong, Jamaica, and New Zealand. Hofstede has determined that the U.S. culture is more accepting than avoidant of uncertainty, but it is closer to the midpoint of the scale than many countries are. Co-cultures within the United States, however, vary in how tolerant they are of uncertainty. For instance, Amish communities—which adhere to strict guidelines

SHARPEN Your Skills

Write a short paragraph identifying and explaining three ways in which your cultural orientation toward time—whether monochronic or polychronic—influences your communication behaviors.

Although the United States is relatively accepting of uncertainty, particular groups—such as the Amish—are highly uncertainty avoidant.

regarding dress, behavior, and the use of modern technology—are often highly uncertainty avoidant. In comparison, actors, sculptors, and other artists may have a high tolerance for uncertainty if it facilitates their creativity.

Test Yourself

- What messages do individualistic and collectivistic cultures teach their children?
- How direct is verbal communication in a high-context culture?
- What do people in low-power-distance cultures think of social equality?
- In what ways can a culture be characterized as masculine or feminine?
- What approach to time do people take in a monochronic culture?
- How does a culture's uncertainty avoidance affect people's behaviors?

>> Communicating with Cultural Awareness

The opportunity to know and communicate with people from other cultures is greater now than at any time in history. Many U.S. colleges and universities enroll large populations of international students, and social networking on the Internet makes it as easy to communicate with someone in New Guinea as with someone in New Jersey. Consequently, the ability to communicate effectively with people from different cultural backgrounds has never been more advantageous. In this section, we'll explore some essential qualities for communicating with cultural awareness: being open-minded about cultural differences, knowledgeable about cultural communication codes, and flexible and respectful when interacting with others.

BE OPEN-MINDED ABOUT CULTURAL DIFFERENCES

People with different cultural backgrounds don't just communicate differently—in many cases, they also truly *think* differently. Those differences in communicating and thinking can present real challenges when people from different cultures interact. As we'll see in this section, one way to combat those challenges is to be open-minded about similarities and differences. Open-mindedness requires first being mindful of potential differences and then avoiding the tendency to judge all differences negatively.

Be Mindful People from different cultures are often unaware of *how* they differ. A U.S. American college professor might think a Japanese student is being dishonest because the student doesn't look him in the eye when she speaks to him. In the United States, that behavior can suggest dishonesty. In Japan, however, it signals respect. If neither the professor nor the student is aware of how the other is likely to interpret the behavior, it's easy to see how a misunderstanding might arise.

Communicating effectively with people from other cultures requires us to be **mindful,** or aware of how their behaviors and ways of thinking are likely to differ from our own. Unfortunately, being mindful is easier said than done. Many of us operate on what researchers call a *similarity assumption*—that is, we presume that most people think the same way we do, without asking ourselves whether that's true. In the preceding example, the professor thought the student was being dishonest because he assumed her lack of eye contact had the same meaning for her that it did for him. The student likewise assumed the professor would interpret her lack of eye contact as a sign of respect, because that's how she understood and intended it.

Questioning our cultural assumptions can be a real challenge because we're often unaware that we hold them in the first place. At the same time, however, it is one of the basic ways in which studying communication and learning about the influences of culture can make us more mindful and competent communicators.

Avoid Ethnocentrism It's one thing to be *aware* of how patterns of thought and behavior differ among cultures. It's another thing to avoid judging all other cultural practices as inferior to one's own.

Do you react ethnocentrically when you encounter cultural practices that are different from your own?

mindful Aware—as in being aware of how other cultures' behaviors and ways of thinking are likely to differ from one's own.

ethnocentrism The tendency to judge other cultures' practices as inferior to one's own.

The first time she traveled through the south of Africa, for instance, Gretchen was put off by certain of the cultural practices she encountered. People would kiss her on the lips when they met her for the first time. Strangers sat uncomfortably near her on public buses, and their closeness bothered her even more because few of them used deodorant. Most of the men had multiple wives and sent their children to witch doctors when they got sick.

Instead of accepting those characteristics as normal parts of the societies she visited, Gretchen found them backward and wrong. "What messed-up cultures!" she said upon returning to the United States. In making that assessment, Gretchen was displaying **ethnocentrism,** the tendency to judge other cultures' practices as inferior to one's own. Had she been more open-minded, Gretchen might have learned why people behaved differently than she expected with regard to their greeting behavior, respect of personal space, and beliefs about marriage and medicine. She may have even come to appreciate that her own cultural practices aren't the only valid ways of interacting with others.

Think of a time when you have acted in an ethnocentric manner. How could you have handled the situation with greater cultural awareness?

Particularly if you haven't had exposure to a broad range of cultures, it can be easy to believe that your values and traditions are the *right* values and traditions for everyone. If you think that way, consider how much your concept of culture reflects nothing more than where you were raised. Had you been raised in the south of Africa, for instance, you would likely find it normal and right for a man to have several wives and for people to kiss on the lips when they meet, and you would think cultural values and traditions such as Gretchen's were abnormal and wrong. In other words, every cultural group—not just one's own—considers its ways of living to be right. When you communicate with people from other cultures, it is therefore valuable to resist ethnocentrism by remembering that being *different* does not necessarily mean being *wrong.* Perhaps you put a lot of stock in the use of deodorant and view consultations with witch doctors as primitive, but bear in mind that those are simply your cultural values. Although they may seem right to you, they aren't right to everyone.

Overcoming ethnocentrism takes practice. A first step is to recognize any tendencies you might have to judge other cultures' practices as inferior to your own. Check out The Competent Communicator to assess where you stand.

BE KNOWLEDGEABLE ABOUT DIFFERENT COMMUNICATION CODES

Another requirement for communicating with cultural awareness is to remember that cultures differ from one another in their use of **communication codes,** verbal and nonverbal behaviors whose meanings are often understood only by people from the same culture. Three kinds of communication codes—idioms, jargon, and gestures—differ significantly from society to society, and the variations can make communicating across cultures and co-cultures challenging. Being knowledgeable about those differences can boost the effectiveness of one's intercultural communication.

Cultures Use Different Idioms An *idiom* is a phrase whose meaning is purely figurative; that is, we can't understand its meaning by interpreting the words literally. For example, most U.S. American adults know that the phrase "kicking the bucket" has nothing to do with kicking a bucket. In U.S. American culture, that idiom means to die. If you grew up in the United States, you can probably think of several other common idioms, including "a dime a dozen" to mean very common or nothing special, having "two left feet" to mean being a poor dancer, "shaking a leg" to mean hurrying, and "pulling my leg" to mean joking with you.

Every society has its own idioms whose meanings are not necessarily obvious to people from other cultures. In Portugal, for instance, a person who "doesn't give one for the box" is someone who can't say or do anything right. In Finland, if something "becomes gingerbread," that means it goes completely wrong. If someone in Brazil says, "Fish don't pull wagons," she is encouraging you to eat red meat. Likewise, if someone in Australia is "as flash as a rat with a gold tooth," he's very pleased with himself. When you interact with people from other cultures, it's very helpful to be aware that they may use phrases that are not familiar to you, and you may be using idioms that are unfamiliar to them.[34]

Who, Me? Being Aware of Ethnocentrism

What do you think about other cultures' values and traditions as compared to your own? On a scale of 1 to 7, indicate your level of agreement with each statement shown below. A score of 7 means you strongly agree; a score of 1 means you strongly disagree.

1. _____ Most other cultures are backward compared with my culture.

2. _____ I see people who are similar to me as virtuous.

3. _____ The values and customs of other cultures have nothing to do with me.

4. _____ People in other cultures just don't know what's good for them.

5. _____ Most people would be happier if they lived like the people in my culture.

6. _____ Lifestyles in other cultures are not as valid as those in my culture.

7. _____ I do not trust people who are different.

8. _____ It is hard for me to respect the customs and traditions of other cultures.

9. _____ Other cultures should try to be more like my culture.

10. _____ People from other cultures act in strange and unusual ways when they come into my culture.

When you're finished, add up your score, which should range from 10 to 70. That is your general ethnocentrism score. If your score is 40 or below, you are relatively low on ethnocentrism. A score above 40 indicates relatively high ethnocentrism.

ASK YOURSELF

- Were you surprised by your score? Why or why not? What factors do you think your score reflects?
- How can learning about cultural influences on communication affect a tendency toward ethnocentrism?

Source: Items adapted from Neuliep, J. W. (2002). Assessing the reliability and validity of the generalized ethnocentrism scale. *Journal of Intercultural Communication Research, 31*, 201–215.

Cultural differences in language use can also make it difficult to translate phrases and slogans from one culture to the next. As Table 2.2 illustrates, some humorous mistranslations can result.

Table 2.2 Lost in Translation: Some Mistranslated Slogans	
Sign in a Bangkok dry cleaner:	*Drop your trousers here for best results!*
Sign in a Copenhagen airline ticket office:	*We take your bags and send them in all directions.*
Sign in a Hong Kong tailor shop:	*Ladies may have a fit upstairs.*
Sign in an Acapulco restaurant:	*The manager has personally passed all the water served here.*
Sign in a Moscow hotel room:	*If this is your first visit to the USSR, you are welcome to it.*

communication codes Verbal and nonverbal behaviors whose meanings are often understood only by people from the same culture.

Cultures Use Different Jargon A specific form of idiomatic communication—and one that often separates co-cultures in particular—is jargon. *Jargon* is language whose technical meaning is understood by people within a given co-culture but not necessarily by those outside it. Physicians, for instance, use precise medical terminology to communicate among themselves about medical conditions and treatments. In most cases, such jargon is used only with people in the same co-culture. Therefore, although your doctor might inform her nurse that you have "ecchymosis on a distal phalange," the physician would probably tell you that you have a bruise on your fingertip. Similarly, if your dentist orders a "periapical radiograph," he wants an X-ray of the roots of one of your teeth.

Not understanding jargon such as that can make you feel like an outsider. In addition, you might get the impression that doctors and dentists talk that way just to reinforce their in-group status. Jargon can serve an important function, however, by allowing people who use it to communicate with one another in ways that are very specific, efficient, and accurate. Just bear in mind that when you use jargon with people who don't belong to your in-group, they might have difficulty understanding your meaning. Culturally aware communicators know when they need to *code-switch,* or shift between using jargon and plain language, in order to be understood by others.

Cultures Use Different Gestures Cultures also differ a great deal in their use of *gestures,* which are movements, usually of the hand or the arm, that express ideas. The same gesture can have different meanings from society to society. For instance, U.S. American parents sometimes play the game "I've got your nose!" with infants by putting a thumb between the index and middle finger. That gesture means good luck in Brazil, but it is an obscene expression in Russia and Indonesia. Similarly, holding up an index and pinky finger while holding down the middle and ring finger is a common gesture for University of Texas Longhorns fans. In Italy, however, people use that gesture to suggest that a man's wife has been unfaithful.[35] Being aware of cultural differences in the meaning of such gestures can steer you away from unintentionally embarrassing yourself or insulting others.

BE FLEXIBLE AND RESPECTFUL WHEN INTERACTING WITH OTHERS

Finally, remember that cultures sometimes vary a good deal in how they communicate. When you interact with people from other cultures, it is therefore helpful to expect some level of ambiguity, to be aware of potential differences in access to communication technology, and to adapt to the behavior patterns you observe.

Expect Ambiguity Communication experts have long recognized that we value certainty in our interactions with others.[36] Most of us can recall being in social situations in which we were unsure of what to do or how to act. Such occasions present us with *ambiguity,* or a lack of certainty. Because cultures can differ so substantially in their communication patterns, such ambiguity is common when we interact cross-culturally.

It's easy to feel uncomfortable and discouraged when we experience ambiguity and to long for the certainty of our own cultural practices. Good communicators remember, however, that ambiguity is normal when they interact with people from another culture. Instead of fearing the ambiguity, they use it as an opportunity to learn more about the other culture.

Paul and Ethan discovered the value of expecting ambiguity when they traveled to Indonesia one summer. On the bus from the airport on the day they arrived, they were constantly pushed and shoved by other passengers. At their hotel, the guest checking in before them appeared to be haggling with the manager over the cost of the room, and the bargaining delayed Paul and Ethan's check-in. Once they finally reached the check-in desk, the manager refused to take Ethan's credit card when he offered it in his left hand. After completing their transaction, Paul and Ethan were told their luggage would be delivered to their room shortly, yet they waited nearly two hours before it arrived.

As experienced travelers, Paul and Ethan knew, however, to take the ambiguity of those interactions in stride. They soon discovered that Indonesians often push and shove while in crowds but consider that jostling to be normal, not an expression of anger or malice. They learned that bargaining over prices is expected in many business transactions and that it is polite to give or receive items only with the right hand, never the left. And because Indonesia is a highly polychronic society, people are far less concerned with punctuality than Paul and Ethan are used to—hence the delayed delivery of the luggage. Even though this was their first trip to Indonesia, Paul and Ethan knew that ambiguity comes with the territory in intercultural communication and that it offers a chance to learn about the values and traditions of culturally different people.

Appreciate Differences in Access to Communication Technology An erroneous assumption many people make when interacting cross-culturally is that everyone has the same access to communication technology, such as the Internet. In fact, access to technology varies greatly around the world, particularly between countries that are economically *developed* (such as the United States, Australia, France, and Japan) and those that are economically *developing* (such as Bolivia, Angola, Pakistan, and Laos). Social scientists use the term *digital divide* to acknowledge the cultural gap between societies that do and do not have regular Internet access.[37]

Figure 2.1 charts the number of people, per 100 inhabitants, with reliable Internet access in the developed and developing world. Notice how the gap has widened—not shrunk—over the years.

Erroneously assuming that everyone has the same access to communication technology can create frustration. For instance, whereas electronically scanning a proposal and sending it as an e-mail attachment may be a simple task for you, a potential business client in a developing country may not have easy access to the equipment or the Internet service to be able to retrieve it. If you know that ahead of time, however, you can make alternative arrangements to send your proposal, saving your client frustration—and potentially saving the business transaction.

Adapt to Others As you interact with people of other cultures and learn about their customs—particularly those related to communication behavior—it's advantageous to adapt to those customs. To **adapt** means to change your behavior to accommodate what others are doing. If you find that people in a particular social setting are all speaking very quietly, for instance, then lowering your own speaking volume demonstrates adaptation. If others are bowing when they greet a leader or a learned person, you can adapt by doing the same. Good intercultural communicators adapt to the communicative behaviors of their conversational partners to emphasize similarity, convey respect, and promote unity.[38]

One of the most significant barriers to adaptation is ethnocentrism, which we examined earlier. To the extent that we judge other cultures' practices as inferior to our own, we find it difficult to understand why we *should* adapt to those customs—and even more difficult to do so. Ethnocentrism takes concerted effort to overcome, but if we can remember that "different" doesn't mean "wrong," we are often more comfortable adapting to the cultural practices of others.

Adaptation can help your intercultural communication flow smoothly, but only if others perceive the adaptation as respectful. If they perceive that you are copying their behavior to mock them, you can cause offense. Whenever Margene speaks to someone with an accent, she inadvertently adopts the same accent in her own speech. If the other speaker

Internet users per 100 inhabitants 1997–2007 (Source ITU)

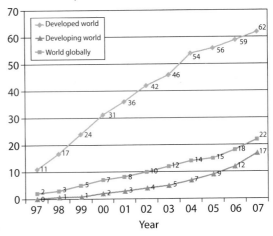

FIGURE 2.1 The Global Digital Divide
Note the widening gap in recent years between people with and without reliable Internet service.

Source: International Telecommunication Union: http://www.itu.int/ITU-D/ict/statistics/ict/graphs/internet.jpg

adapt To change one's behavior to accommodate what others are doing.

doesn't consciously notice, then Margene's adaptation likely helps to make the interaction positive. Researchers know that we like people who adapt to our vocal behavior because we subconsciously think of them as similar to ourselves.[39] If the other speaker does notice that Margene has adopted his accent, however, he may feel she is making fun of his speech, even if Margene is unaware that she has adapted to his accent in the first place.

When you adapt your behavior to others, do so in a way that conveys your interest in following their example and accommodating their traditions rather than in a way that mocks or disrespects them. The distinction can be a fine line, but being aware of the potential for conveying disrespect is a crucial first step.

Test Yourself

- What does it mean to be mindful of cultural differences?
- How are idioms an example of a cultural communication code?
- Why is it advantageous to expect ambiguity when communicating interculturally?

For REVIEW >>

- What is culture?

  Culture is the totality of learned, shared symbols, language, values, and norms that distinguish one group of people from another.

- How does culture influence communication behavior?

  Culture influences communication behavior through variations in (1) the emphasis placed on individuals versus groups, (2) the communicative context, (3) power distance, (4) views about masculinity and femininity and about men's and women's roles, (5) orientation toward time, and (6) uncertainty avoidance.

- In what ways can we improve our cultural communication skills?

  We can be open-minded about cultural differences, knowledgeable about cultural communication codes, and flexible and respectful when communicating with people from other cultures.

Pop Quiz

Multiple Choice

1. Garrett's culture has specific rules and expectations that guide people's behavior. We would call those rules and expectations his culture's

   a. symbols
   b. language
   c. values
   d. norms

2. When Trudy communicates with others, she generally expects them to be direct and to say what they mean. Trudy is probably from a culture that is

   a. high-context
   b. low-context
   c. high-power-distance
   d. low-power-distance

3. Pieta thinks of time as holistic, fluid, and loosely structured. She does not expect her classes to start on time but to begin whenever the instructor is ready. She is likely from a culture that is

   a. monochronic
   b. feminine
   c. masculine
   d. polychronic

4. The type of culture in which children are taught to put the needs of their families, villages, and employers ahead of their personal desires or ambitions is called

    a. individualistic
    b. uncertainty avoidant
    c. collectivistic
    d. low-context

5. The phrase "kick the bucket" is, for speakers of English, an example of a cultural

    a. idiom
    b. custom
    c. symbol
    d. gesture

Fill in the Blank

6. Groups of people who share a common culture are called a _____.

7. The process by which we acquire a culture is called _____.

8. A _____ is a group of people who share values, customs, and norms related to mutual interests or characteristics besides their national citizenship.

9. People who are _____ judge other cultural practices as inferior to their own.

10. Good intercultural communicators _____, meaning that they change their behavior to accommodate what others are doing.

Answers: 1. d; 2. b; 3. d; 4. c; 5. a; 6. society; 7. enculturation; 8. co-culture; 9. ethnocentric; 10. adapt

KEY TERMS

culture 28	low-power-distance culture 39
societies 28	high-power-distance culture 39
in-groups 29	masculine culture 39
out-groups 29	feminine culture 40
ethnicity 30	monochronic culture 40
nationality 30	polychronic culture 40
enculturation 30	uncertainty avoidance 40
co-cultures 32	mindful 43
individualistic culture 37	ethnocentrism 44
collectivistic culture 37	communication codes 44
low-context culture 38	adapt 47
high-context culture 38	

3

PERCEIVING

FIRST IMPRESSIONS CAN MISS THE MARK

Susan Boyle didn't exactly project the image of a celebrity. When the plain-looking 47-year-old Scottish woman took the stage on *Britain's Got Talent* in April 2009, many in the audience were skeptical of her quest to become a professional entertainer. Some laughed at her; others booed and hissed—until she began to sing. Her performance was remarkable. After belting out the first line of the song "I Dreamed a Dream" from the musical *Les Misérables,* Boyle received a standing ovation from the audience and two of the three judges on the televised talent show. When she finished, judge Piers Morgan said, "Without a doubt, that was *the* biggest surprise I have had in three years on this show." Boyle instantly became a media sensation: In the two months following the broadcast, the video of her strikingly impressive performance was viewed over 100 million times on YouTube. Recognizing that Boyle's talent far surpassed the audience's first impressions of her, Morgan remarked, "Everyone was laughing at you. No one is laughing now. That was stunning."

THE SELF AND OTHERS

PERCEPTION IS A PROCESS

Our minds usually select, organize, and interpret information so quickly and so subconsciously that we think our perceptions are objective, factual reflections of the world. Suppose you had a conflict with your roommate before leaving for school or work this morning, and throughout the day he failed to respond to your text messages reminding him that it's his turn to pick up groceries. You might perceive that your roommate is ignoring you because he is not replying to you. In fact, however, you have created the perception that he's ignoring you based on the information you *selected* for attention (he doesn't respond to your text messages), the way you *organized* that information (he is deliberately being inconsiderate because he is angry about your conflict), and the way you *interpreted* it (he's ignoring me).[3]

Selection, organization, and interpretation are the three basic stages of perception. Let's examine each in turn.

A loud conversation in a library would grab your attention because it would be unusual in that environment.

What sensory information do you pay the most attention to when your communication instructor teaches your class?

Selection Perception begins when one or more of your senses are stimulated. You pass a construction site and hear two workers talking about the foundation they're pouring. You see one of your classmates smile at you. You feel a co-worker bump you on the shoulder as he walks past. Those sensory experiences of hearing, seeing, and being bumped can initiate your formation of perceptions.

In truth, your senses are constantly stimulated by events in your environment. It's impossible, though, to pay attention to everything you're seeing, hearing, smelling, tasting, and feeling at any given moment.[4] When you're walking past that construction site, you're probably no longer hearing the sounds of traffic going by. Rather than paying attention to all the stimuli in your environment, you engage in **selection,** the process by which your mind and body help you isolate certain stimuli to pay attention to. For example, you notice that your spouse failed to take out the trash but overlook that he got the car washed. Clearly, the information we attend to influences the perceptions we form.

A key point is that we don't necessarily make conscious decisions about which stimuli to notice and which to ignore. How, then, does selection occur? Research indicates that three characteristics in particular make a given stimulus more likely to be selected for attention.

First, being unusual or unexpected makes a stimulus stand out.[5] You might not pay attention to people talking loudly while walking across campus, but if the same loud conversation were to take place in the library, it would grab your attention because it would be unusual in that environment. Second, repetition, or how frequently you're exposed to a stimulus, makes it stand out.[6] For example, you're more likely to remember radio ads you've heard repeatedly than ones you've heard only once. Similarly, you tend to notice more characteristics about the people you see frequently than about individuals you don't see often, such as their physical appearance and behavior patterns. Third, the intensity of a stimulus affects how much you take notice of it. You are more aware of strong odors than weak scents, and of bright and flashy colors than dull and muted hues.[7]

With so much sensory information available to you, how do you avoid becoming overwhelmed? A part of your brain called the *reticular formation* serves the important function of helping you focus on certain stimuli while ignoring others.[8] It is the primary reason why, when you're having a conversation with a friend in a crowded, noisy restaurant, you can focus on what your friend is saying and tune out the many other sights and sounds that are bombarding your senses at the time.

selection The process of paying attention to a certain stimulus.

organization The process of categorizing information that has been selected for attention.

perceptual schema A mental framework for organizing information.

Organization Once you've noticed a particular stimulus, the next step in the perception process is **organization,** the classification of information in some way. Organization helps you make sense of the information by allowing you to see its similarities to and differences from other things you know about. To classify a stimulus, your mind applies a **perceptual schema** to it, which is a mental framework for organizing information into categories we call *constructs*.

According to communication researcher Peter Andersen, we use four types of schema to classify information we notice about other people:[9]

- *Physical constructs* emphasize people's appearance, causing us to notice objective characteristics such as height, age, ethnicity, and body shape, as well as subjective characteristics such as physical attractiveness.
- *Role constructs* emphasize people's social or professional position, so we notice that a person is a teacher, an accountant, a father, and so on.[10]
- *Interaction constructs* emphasize people's behavior, so we notice that a person is outgoing, aggressive, shy, or considerate.
- *Psychological constructs* emphasize people's thoughts and feelings, causing us to notice that a person is angry, self-assured, insecure, or carefree.

Whichever constructs we notice about people—and we may notice more than one at a time—the process of organization helps us determine the ways in which various pieces of information that we select for attention are related to one another.[11] If you notice that your neighbor is a Little League softball coach and the father of three children, for example, then those two pieces of information go together because they both relate to the roles he plays. Likewise, if you notice that he seems irritated or angry, those pieces of information go together as examples of his psychological state.

Which constructs would you use to describe these people?

Interpretation After noticing and classifying a stimulus, you have to assign it an **interpretation** to figure out its meaning for you. Let's say one of your co-workers has been especially friendly toward you since last week. She finds numerous occasions to run into you, brings you coffee, and offers to run errands for you over her lunch break. Her behavior is definitely noticeable, and you've probably classified it as a psychological construct because it relates to her thoughts and feelings about you.

What is her behavior communicating, though? How should you interpret it? Is she being nice because she's getting ready to ask you for a big favor? Does she want to look good in front of her boss? Or does she like you? If she does like you, does she like you as a friend, or is she making a romantic gesture?

To address those questions, you likely will pay attention to three factors: your *personal experience*, your *knowledge* of this co-worker, and the *closeness of your relationship* with

Our interpretations of another person's behaviors rely on personal experience, knowledge, and the closeness of our relationship with that individual.

interpretation The process of assigning meaning to information that has been selected for attention and organized.

her. First, your personal experience helps you assign meaning to behavior. If some co-workers have been nice to you in the past just to get favors from you later, then you might be suspicious of this co-worker's behavior.[12] Second, your knowledge of the person helps you interpret her actions. If you know she's friendly and nice to everyone, you might interpret her behavior differently than you would if you notice that she's being nice only to you.[13] Finally, the closeness of your relationship influences how you interpret a person's behavior. When your best friend does you an unexpected favor, you probably interpret it as a sincere sign of friendship. In contrast, when a co-worker does you a favor, you may be more likely to wonder whether the person has an ulterior motive.[14]

The Nonlinear Nature of Perception Although perception occurs in stages, the process is far from linear. Instead, the three stages of perception—selecting, organizing, and interpreting information—all overlap.[15] How we interpret a communication behavior depends on what we notice about it, for example, but what we notice can also depend on the way we interpret it.

Let's assume, for example, that you're listening to a speech by a political candidate. If you find her ideas and proposals favorable, you might interpret her demeanor and speaking style as examples of her intelligence and confidence. In contrast, if you oppose her ideas, you might interpret her demeanor and speaking style as reflecting arrogance or incompetence. Either interpretation, in turn, might lead you to select for attention only those behaviors or characteristics that support your interpretation and to ignore those that don't. So, even though perception happens in stages, the stages don't always take place in the same order. We're constantly noticing, organizing, and interpreting things around us, including other people's behaviors.

As we consider next, perception, like other skills, takes practice. In addition, our perceptions are more accurate on some occasions than others.

WE COMMONLY MISPERCEIVE OTHERS' COMMUNICATION BEHAVIORS

Although we constantly form perceptions of others and of their communication behaviors, we are hardly experts at it. In fact, perceptual mistakes are easy to make. Let's say, for example, that on your overseas trip, you perceive that two adults you see in a restaurant are having a heated argument. As it turns out, you discover that they are not arguing but

Our feelings about a politician's ideas often influence our interpretation of his or her behaviors.

engaging in behaviors that, in their culture, communicate interest and involvement.

Why do we commit such a perceptual error despite our accumulated experience? The reason is that each of us has multiple lenses through which we perceive the world. Those lenses include our cultural and co-cultural backgrounds, stereotypes, primacy and recency effects, and our perceptual sets. In each case, those lenses have the potential to influence not only our own communication behaviors but also our perceptions of the communication of others.

Cultures and Co-Cultures Influence Perceptions One powerful influence on the accuracy of our perceptions is the culture and co-cultures with which we identify. Recall from Chapter 2 that culture comprises the learned, shared symbols, language, values, and norms that distinguish one group of people—such as Russians, South Africans, or Thais—from another. Co-cultures are smaller groups of people—such as single parents, liberals, and history enthusiasts—who share values, customs, and norms related to mutual interests or characteristics besides their national citizenship.

Many characteristics of cultures can influence our perceptions and interpretations of other people's behaviors.[16] For instance, people from individualistic cultures frequently engage in more direct, overt forms of conflict communication than people from collectivistic cultures. In a conflict, then, an individualist might perceive a collectivist's communication behaviors as conveying weakness, passivity, or a lack of interest. Likewise, the collectivist may perceive the individualist's communication patterns as overly aggressive or self-centered. Those perceptions can arise even though each person is enacting his or her culturally normative communication behaviors.

Co-cultural differences can also influence perceptions of communication. Teenagers might perceive their parents' advice as outdated or irrelevant, for instance, whereas parents may perceive their teenagers' indifference to their advice as naïve.[17] Liberals and conservatives may each perceive the others' communication messages as rooted in ignorance.[18]

Stereotypes Influence Perceptions A **stereotype** is a generalization about a group or category of people that can have a powerful influence on how we perceive other people and their communication behavior.[19] Stereotyping is a three-part process:

- First, we identify a group to which we believe another person belongs ("you are a man").
- Second, we recall a generalization others often make about the people in that group ("men don't know how to express their emotions").
- Finally, we apply that generalization to the person ("therefore, you must not know how to express your emotions").

You can probably think of stereotypes for many groups.[20] What stereotypes come to mind for elderly people? How about people with physical or mental disabilities? Wealthy people? Homeless people? Gays and lesbians? Science fiction fans? Immigrants? Athletes? What stereotypes come to mind when you think about yourself?

Many people find stereotyping distasteful or unethical, particularly when stereotypes have to do with characteristics such as sex, race, and sexual orientation.[21] Unquestionably, stereotyping can lead to inaccurate, even offensive, perceptions of other people. The reason is that stereotypes underestimate the differences among individuals in a group. It may be true, for instance, that adolescents communicate in a more self-centered way than individuals in other age groups, but not *every* adolescent communicates in a self-absorbed way. Similarly, people of Asian descent may often be more studious than those from other ethnic groups, but not every Asian is a good student, and not all Asians do equally well in school.[22]

The culture and co-cultures with which we identify often influence the accuracy of our perceptions.

stereotype A generalization about a group or category of people that is applied to individual members of that group.

What stereotypes come to mind when you think of people such as these?

There is variation in almost every group, but stereotypes focus our attention only on the generalizations. In fact, we have a tendency to engage in *selective memory bias*—to remember information that supports our stereotypes while forgetting information that doesn't.[23] During conflict communication, for instance, both women and men tend to remember only their partners' stereotypical behaviors.[24] Men may recall that women nagged and criticized them but might forget that they also listened carefully. Likewise, women may recall that men tuned them out but might overlook their apologies and signs of remorse.

Although perceptions about an individual made on the basis of a stereotype are often inaccurate, they aren't necessarily so.[25] For example, consider the stereotype that women love being around children. If you met a woman and assumed (on the basis of that stereotype) that she enjoyed being around children, you might be wrong—however, you also might be right. Not every woman enjoys spending time with children, but some do. By the same token, not every adolescent is self-centered, but some are. The point is that just because your perception of someone is consistent with a stereotype, that perception isn't necessarily inaccurate. Just as we shouldn't assume that a stereotypical judgment is accurate, we should not assume that it's inaccurate.

Before assuming that your perceptions of others are correct, genuinely get to know those people, and let your perceptions be guided by what you learn about them as individuals. By communicating with them, you can begin to discover how well other people fit or don't fit the stereotypical perceptions you formed of them.

Primacy and Recency Effects Influence Perceptions As the saying goes, you get only one chance to make a good first impression. There's no shortage of advice on how to accomplish that, from picking the right clothes to polishing your conversational skills. Have you ever noticed that no one talks about the importance of making a good *second* impression?

According to a principle called the **primacy effect,** first impressions are critical because they set the tone for all future interactions.[26] Our first impressions of someone's communication behaviors seem to stick in our mind more than our second, third, or fourth impressions do. In an early study of the primacy effect, psychologist Solomon Asch found that a person described as "intelligent, industrious, impulsive, critical, stubborn, and envious"

SHARPEN
Your Skills

Watch the movie *Crash* (2005), which highlights numerous cultural stereotypes. Identify as many stereotyped beliefs as you can from the movie, and take note of the ways in which each character's beliefs influenced his or her behaviors toward other characters.

By the Numbers

0.05

Number of seconds it takes the average person to form an impression of a website.[27]

was evaluated more favorably than one described as "envious, stubborn, critical, impulsive, industrious, and intelligent."[28] Notice that most of those adjectives are negative, but when the description begins with a positive adjective *(intelligent),* the effects of the more negative ones that follow it are diminished.

Asch's study illustrates that the first information we learn about someone tends to have a stronger effect on how we perceive that person than information we receive later.[29] That finding explains why we work so hard to communicate competently during a job interview, on a date, or in other important situations. When people evaluate us favorably at first, they're more likely to perceive us in a positive light from then on.[30]

As most entertainers know, it's equally important to make a good *final* impression, because that's what the audience will remember after leaving. Standup comedians will tell you that the two most important jokes in a show are the first and the last. That advice follows a principle known as the **recency effect,** which says that the most recent impression we have of a person's communication is more powerful than our earlier impressions.[31]

Which is most important, the first or the most recent impression? The answer is that *both* appear to be more important than any impressions that we form in between.[32] To grasp this key point, consider the last significant conversation you had with someone. You probably have a better recollection of how the conversation started and ended than you do of what was communicated in between. Figure 3.1 illustrates the relationship between the primacy effect and the recency effect by showing how our first and most recent impressions of people overshadow our other perceptions of them.

Perceptual Sets Influence Perceptions "I'll believe it when I see it," people often say. However, an individual's perception of reality is influenced by more than what the person sees. Perception is also affected by one's biases, expectations, and desires. Those elements can create what psychologists call a **perceptual set,** or a person's predisposition to perceive only what he or she wants or expects to perceive.[33] An equally valid motto might therefore be "I'll see it when I believe it."

For example, our perceptual set regarding gender guides the ways we perceive and interact with newborns. Without the help of a contextual cue such as blue or pink baby clothes, we sometimes have a hard time telling whether an infant is male or female. However, research shows that if we're told, say, that an infant's name is David, we perceive that child to be stronger and bigger than if the same infant is called, say, Diana.[34] Our perceptual set tells us that male infants are usually bigger and stronger than female ones, so we "see" a bigger, stronger baby when we learn that it's a boy. Our perceptions can then affect our communication behavior: We may also hold and talk to the "female" baby in softer, quieter ways than the "male" baby.

Our perceptual set also influences how we make sense of people, circumstances, and events. Deeply religious individuals may talk about healings as miracles or answers to prayer, whereas others may describe them as natural responses to medication.[35] Highly homophobic people are more likely than others to perceive affectionate communication between men as sexual in nature.[36]

In summary, perception is a complex process, susceptible to many different biases and patterns. As we'll discover in the next section, we are vulnerable to mistakes not only when we form perceptions but also when we try to explain what we perceive.

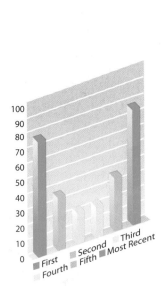

Many successful comedians understand that the final impression they make on an audience is just as important as the first impression.

FIGURE 3.1
Primacy Effect and Recency Effect
Our first impressions and our most recent impressions are more important than those that come in between.

primacy effect The tendency to emphasize the first impression over later impressions when forming a perception.

recency effect The tendency to emphasize the most recent impression over earlier impressions when forming a perception.

perceptual set A person's predisposition to perceive only what he or she wants or expects to perceive.

>> How We Explain Our Perceptions

Moments into her speech accepting the 2009 MTV Video Music Award for Best Female Video, country singer Taylor Swift—along with her audience—was stunned when rapper Kanye West suddenly appeared onstage, grabbed the microphone from her hands, and declared that a video from pop singer Beyoncé should have won the award instead. "Taylor, I'm really happy for you," West said. "I'll let you finish, but Beyoncé had one of the best videos of all time. One of the best videos of all time!" Visibly shaken, Swift walked offstage moments after West's outburst, leaving viewers to wonder why he had so rudely interrupted Swift's acceptance speech.

When we perceive social behavior, especially behavior we find surprising, our nearly automatic reaction is to try to make sense of it.[37] We need to understand what is happening to know how to react to it. Think about it: If you perceive that someone is communicating out of anger or jealousy, you'll likely react to that behavior differently than if you perceive it is motivated by humor or sarcasm. The ability to explain social behavior—including our own behavior—is therefore an important aspect of how we perceive our social world. In this section, we'll see that we explain behaviors by forming attributions for them, and we'll discover how to avoid two of the most common errors people make when formulating attributions for communication behavior.

WE EXPLAIN BEHAVIOR THROUGH ATTRIBUTIONS

An **attribution** is an explanation, the answer to a "why" question.[38] You notice your brother ignoring his girlfriend, for instance, and you wonder what to attribute his behavior to. Although we can generate countless attributions for a given behavior, our attributions vary along three important dimensions: locus, stability, and controllability.[39]

How would you explain Kanye West's behavior at the Video Music Awards presentation? How confident are you that your explanation is accurate?

Locus Locus refers to where the cause of a behavior is "located," whether within ourselves or outside ourselves.[40] Some of our behaviors have *internal* causes in the sense that they're caused by a particular characteristic of ourselves. Other behaviors have *external* causes, meaning they're caused by something outside ourselves. If your boss is late for your 9 A.M. performance review, an internal attribution you might make about her is that she has lost track of time or she's making you wait on purpose. An external attribution you might form about her is that the traffic is heavy that morning or that an even earlier meeting she is attending has run long.

Stability A second dimension of attributions is whether the cause of a behavior is stable or unstable.[41] A *stable* cause is one that is permanent, semipermanent, or at least not easily changed. Why was your boss late? Rush hour traffic would be a stable cause for lateness, because it's a permanent feature of almost everyone's morning commute. The attribution that she is rarely punctual would likewise be stable, because it identifies an enduring aspect of her behavior. In contrast, a traffic accident or an overly long morning meeting would be an *unstable* cause for your boss's lateness, because those events occur only from time to time and are largely unpredictable.

Controllability Finally, causes for behavior vary in how controllable they are.[42] You make a *controllable* attribution for someone's behavior when you believe the cause of

attribution An explanation for an observed behavior.

the behavior was under that person's control. In contrast, an *uncontrollable* attribution identifies a cause that was beyond the person's control. If you perceive that your boss is late for your appointment because she has spent too much time socializing with other co-workers beforehand, that is a controllable attribution because socializing is under her control. Alternatively, if you perceive she's late due to a car accident on the way to work, that is an uncontrollable attribution because she couldn't help but be late if she wrecked her car.

AVOIDING TWO COMMON ATTRIBUTION ERRORS

Although most of us probably try to generate accurate attributions for other people's behaviors, we are still vulnerable to making attribution mistakes.[43] Those errors can create communication problems because, as noted above, our responses to other people's behaviors are often based on the attributions we make for those behaviors.

Let's say that Adina and her 14-year-old son Craig argue one night about whether Craig can go on a school-sponsored overseas trip. After their argument, they both go to bed angry. When Adina gets up the following morning, she finds that Craig hasn't done the dishes or taken out the trash, two chores he is responsible for doing every night before bed. It turns out that Craig was so upset by the argument that his chores slipped his mind. Adina makes a different attribution, however: She perceives that Craig didn't do the chores because he was deliberately disobeying her. On the basis of her attribution, she tells Craig he's grounded for a week and is definitely not going on the trip. Her actions only prolong and intensify the conflict between them. Had Adina correctly attributed Craig's behavior to an honest oversight, she might have been able to overlook it instead of making it the basis for additional conflict. In other words, recognizing a common attribution error might have equipped Adina to avoid a mistake that made a bad situation worse.

We might think we always explain behavior objectively and rationally, but the truth is that we're all prone to taking mental shortcuts when generating attributions. As a result, our attributions are often less accurate than they ideally should be. Two of the most common attribution errors—which we can better prepare ourselves to avoid by understanding them—are the self-serving bias and the fundamental attribution error.

Self-Serving Bias   The **self-serving bias,** which relates primarily to how we explain our own behaviors, refers to our tendency to attribute our successes to stable, internal causes while attributing our failures to unstable, external causes.[44] For instance, if you gave a great informative speech in your class, you say that it's because you were well prepared, but if your speech went poorly, you say that the assignment was unfair or that other students were distracting you. Such attributions are self-serving because they suggest that our successes are deserved but our failures are not our fault.

Although the self-serving bias deals primarily with attributions we make for our own behaviors, research shows that we often extend this tendency to important people in our lives.[45] In a happy marriage, for instance, people tend to attribute their spouse's positive behaviors to internal causes ("She remembered my birthday because she's thoughtful") and negative behaviors to external causes ("He forgot my birthday because he's been very preoccupied by his job"). In a distressed relationship, the reverse is often true: People attribute negative behaviors to internal causes ("She forgot my birthday because she's completely self-absorbed") and positive behaviors to external causes ("He remembered my birthday only because I reminded him five times").

Fundamental Attribution Error   Think about how you reacted the last time someone cut you off in traffic. What attribution did you make for the driver's behavior? You might have reasoned, "She must be late for something important" or "He must have a car full of noisy children," but you probably didn't. "What a jerk!" may be closer to your reaction.

We can attribute a person's lateness to either internal or external causes. Was your boss late because she lost track of time—or because she got caught in heavy traffic?

Many people have a self-serving bias when it comes to explaining their own behaviors.

self-serving bias   The tendency to attribute one's successes to stable internal causes and one's failures to unstable external causes.

The reason for that response is the human tendency to commit what scientists call the **fundamental attribution error,** in which we attribute other people's behaviors to internal rather than external causes.[46] The high school student ran the pledge drive because he's a caring, giving person, not because he earned extra credit for doing so. The cashier gave you the wrong change because she doesn't know how to count, not because she was distracted by an announcement over the store's audio system.

As a student of communication, you should bear in mind that people's behaviors—including your own—are often responses to external forces. For instance, when the new doctor you're seeing spends only three minutes diagnosing your condition and prescribing a treatment before moving on to the next patient, you might perceive that she's not very caring. That would be an internal attribution for her communication behavior, which the fundamental attribution error makes more likely. To judge the merits of that attribution, however, ask yourself what external forces might have motivated the doctor's behavior. For example, might she have rushed through your consultation because another doctor's absence that day left her with twice as many patients as usual? Good communicators recognize the tendency to form internal attributions for people's behaviors, and they force themselves to consider external causes that might also be influential.

As with other forms of perception, attributions are important but prone to error. That observation doesn't imply that we *never* make accurate attributions for people's behaviors (including our own). It simply acknowledges that the self-serving bias and the fundamental attribution error are easy mistakes to commit. The more we know about those processes, therefore, the better we can base our communication behaviors on accurate perceptions of ourselves and others.

SHARPEN Your Skills

For a few days, keep a list of all the attributions you give to others about your own behaviors. At the end of that time, go back through your list and evaluate each attribution for accuracy. How many attributions fit the self-serving bias? How many were genuine? Were any of your attributions overly negative?

- **What does it mean to say that attributions vary according to locus, stability, and controllability?**
- **How are the self-serving bias and the fundamental attribution error examples of attribution mistakes?**

Test Yourself

>> How We Perceive Ourselves

As much as your communication depends on your ability to perceive others, it also depends on your ability to perceive yourself. Ask yourself: Who am I? How do I relate to others? What is the *self* in *myself*? Grappling with those challenging questions will allow you to communicate and to form relationships with a sure understanding of who you are and what you have to offer.

In this section, we'll discover that each of us perceives ourself through our self-concept, and we'll examine the characteristics of a self-concept. We'll also learn how self-concept influences communication behavior and relates to self-esteem.

SELF-CONCEPT DEFINED

Let's say you are asked to come up with 10 ways to answer the question "Who am I?" What words will you pick? Which answers are most important? Each of us has a set of ideas about who we are that isn't influenced by moment-to-moment events (such as "I'm happy right now") but is fairly stable over the course of our lives (such as "I'm a happy person"). Your **self-concept** is composed of those stable ideas about who you are. It is your **identity,** your understanding of who you are. As we'll see in this section, self-concepts are multifaceted and partly subjective.

fundamental attribution error The tendency to attribute others' behaviors to internal rather than external causes.

self-concept The set of perceptions a person has about who he or she is; also known as *identity*.

identity The set of perceptions a person has about who he or she is; also known as *self-concept*.

Johari window A visual representation of components of the self that are known or unknown to the self and to others.

Self-Concept Is Multifaceted We define ourselves in many different ways. Some of these ways rely on our name: "I'm Sunita" or "I'm Deepak." Some rely on physical or social categories: "I am a woman" or "I am Australian." Others make use of our skills or interests: "I'm artistic" or "I'm a good cook." Still others are based on our relationships to other people: "I am an uncle" or "I do volunteer work with homeless children." Finally, some rely on our evaluations of ourselves: "I am honest" or "I am impatient." You can probably think of several other ways to describe who you are. Which of those descriptions is the *real* you?

The answer is that your self-concept has several different parts, and each of your descriptions taps into one or more of those parts. What we call *the self* is a collection of smaller *selves*. If you're female, that's a part of who you are, but it isn't everything you are. Asian, athletic, agnostic, or asthmatic may all be parts of your self-concept, but none of those terms defines you completely. All the different ways you would describe yourself are pieces of your overall self-concept.

One way to think about your self-concept is to distinguish between aspects of yourself that are known to others and aspects that are known only to you. In 1955, U.S. psychologists Joseph Luft and Harry Ingham created the **Johari window,** a visual representation of the self as composed of four separate parts.[47] According to this model, which is illustrated in Figure 3.2, the *open area* consists of characteristics that are known both to the self and to others. Those probably include your name, sex, hobbies, academic major, and other aspects of your self-concept that you are aware of and freely share with others. In contrast, the *hidden area* consists of characteristics that you know about yourself but choose not to reveal to others, such as emotional insecurities or traumas from your past that you elect to keep hidden.

An innovative aspect of the Johari window is that it recognizes dimensions of our self-concept of which we may be unaware. For instance, others might see us as impatient or moody even if we don't recognize these traits in ourselves. Those characteristics make up the third part of the model, the *blind area*. Finally, the *unknown area* comprises aspects of our self-concept that are not known either to ourselves or to others. For example, no one—including you—knows what kind of parent you will be until you actually become a parent.

Self-Concept Is Partly Subjective Some of what we know about ourselves is based on objective facts. For instance, I'm 5'8" tall and have brown hair, I was born in Seattle but now live in Phoenix, and I teach college for a living. Those aspects of my self-concept are objective—they're based on fact and not on someone's opinion. That doesn't mean I have no choice about them. I chose to move to Arizona and to take a teaching job, and although I was born with brown hair, I could change my hair color if I wanted to. Referring to those personal characteristics as "objective" simply means that they are factually true. Many aspects of our self-concept are subjective rather than objective, however. "Subjective" means that they're based on the impressions we have of ourselves rather than on objective facts.

It is often difficult for people to judge themselves accurately or objectively. Sometimes our self-assessments are unreasonably positive. For instance, you might know individuals who have unrealistic ideas about their intelligence, talents, or understanding of the world or other people. In one study, the College Board (the company that administers the SAT college entrance examination) asked almost a million U.S. American high school seniors to rate their ability to get along with others. *Every single*

	Known to Self	Unknown to Self
Known to Others	OPEN	BLIND
Unknown to Others	HIDDEN	UNKNOWN

FIGURE 3.2 Johari Window In the Johari window, the open area represents what you know and choose to reveal to others, and the hidden area depicts what you know but choose not to reveal. The blind area reflects what others know about you but you don't recognize in yourself, and the unknown area comprises the dimensions of yourself that no one knows.

SHARPEN Your Skills

Select three people who are important to you. Considering your relationship with each person separately, draw a Johari window that reflects your self-concept with that person. Make the *open, hidden, blind,* and *unknown* portions of the window larger or smaller depending on how you see yourself. Then write a short paragraph explaining why the panes of your Johari window differ in size for each relationship and how they reflect your communication behaviors with each of those people.

student in the study responded that he or she was "above average"—a result that is mathematically impossible! Moreover, 60 percent claimed their ability to get along with others was in the top 10 percent, and a whopping 25 percent rated themselves in the top 1 percent, both of which are highly improbable.[48]

In contrast, sometimes our judgments of ourselves are unreasonably negative, as is especially true for people with low self-esteem. Several studies have shown that such individuals tend to magnify the importance of their failures.[49] They often underestimate their abilities, and when they get negative feedback, such as a bad evaluation at work or a disrespectful remark from someone they know, they are likely to believe that it accurately reflects their self-worth.

Several studies have also suggested that people with low self-esteem have a higher-than-average risk of clinical depression, a condition that impairs not only mental and emotional well-being but also physical health and the ways people communicate in their social relationships.[50] We will return to self-esteem a little later in this chapter.

AWARENESS AND MANAGEMENT OF THE SELF-CONCEPT

Part of being a competent, skilled communicator is being aware of your self-concept and managing its influences on your communication with others. Two pathways by which self-concept can shape communicative behavior are self-monitoring and the self-fulfilling prophecy.

Self-Monitoring Recall from Chapter 1 that *self-monitoring* is an awareness of how you look and sound and how your behavior is affecting those around you. The tendency toward self-monitoring ranges along a continuum from high to low. People on the high end of the scale pay attention to how others are reacting to their own behaviors, and they have the ability to adjust their communication as needed. People on the low end express whatever they are thinking or feeling without paying attention to the impression they're creating.

To understand how self-monitoring operates, imagine that you've fixed up your friends Caleb and Keith to go on a blind date. As a high self-monitor, Caleb pays a great deal of attention to his clothes and grooming to make sure he looks and smells good. In contrast, as a low self-monitor, Keith doesn't spend much time thinking about those things. During their date, Caleb is aware of what he's saying, so he comes across as nice, easygoing, and funny. Keith, however, says whatever is on his mind, without considering what Caleb might think. Caleb notices if his behavior seems to make Keith uncomfortable, and he adjusts his actions accordingly. In contrast, Keith doesn't tune in to what he's doing and how he's affecting Caleb.

From that example, you might get the impression that it's best to be a high self-monitor. Self-monitoring certainly has its advantages. High self-monitors tend to be better at making whatever kind of impression they want to make, because they are aware of their communication behaviors and others' responses to them. They often find it easier than low self-monitors to put other people at ease in social situations. High self-monitors also tend to be good at figuring out what others are thinking and feeling, and that skill gives them a clear advantage in many social settings.

Being a low self-monitor also has advantages, however. Low self-monitors spend less time and energy thinking about their appearance and behavior, so they are probably more relaxed than high self-monitors in many situations. In addition, because they are less aware of, or concerned with, the impressions they make, they are often more straightforward communicators. They may even be seen as more genuine and trustworthy than high self-monitors.

Self-Fulfilling Prophecy You've probably had the experience of waking up in a bad mood and saying to yourself it was going to be an awful day. After that, everything seems to go wrong. Because you're in a bad mood, you're cranky and you speak impatiently with people, and they treat you poorly in return. You think to yourself, "See? I *knew* everyone would be awful to me today." When you have to give a speech in class that afternoon, you figure it's not worth putting much effort into it because you're going to get a mediocre grade anyway. When you get a C–, you think, "See? I *knew* this speech would go badly." You feel as though you shouldn't have gotten out of bed that morning.

Why did your predictions about a lousy day come true? Most likely, the cause is a phenomenon called a **self-fulfilling prophecy**—a situation in which an expectation prompts you to act and communicate in ways that make that expectation come true.

What do self-fulfilling prophecies have to do with our communication? Consider that sometimes our expectations influence our communication behavior, as in the example above where we think it's going to be a bad day and we then have a bad day. Similarly, when we expect our relationships to succeed, we behave in ways that strengthen them, and when we expect to be socially rejected, we perceive and react to rejection even when it isn't really there.[51]

There is one very important clarification about self-fulfilling prophecies. For a prophecy to be self-fulfilling, it's not enough that you expect something to happen and then it does. Rather, it has to be the case that your expectation *causes* it to happen. To illustrate that point, let's say that yesterday morning you expected it to rain, and later it did rain. That isn't a self-fulfilling prophecy, because your expectation didn't cause the rain: It would have rained regardless of whether you thought it would. In other words, your expectation was fulfilled, but it was not *self*-fulfilled. A self-fulfilling prophecy is one in which the expectation itself causes the behaviors that make it come true.

VALUING THE SELF: SELF-ESTEEM

Knowing your self-concept and *being happy with* your self-concept are two different things. How do you feel about yourself? Are you satisfied with your looks? Your accomplishments? Your personality? Your relationships? Do you feel confident about and proud of who you are? Such questions concern your **self-esteem,** your subjective evaluation of your value and worth as a person.

As with self-monitoring, your level of self-esteem ranges along a continuum from high to low. If you evaluate yourself positively and feel happy about who you are, you probably have high self-esteem. In contrast, if you are pessimistic about your abilities and dissatisfied with your self-concept, you probably have low self-esteem. Take a minute to respond to the questions in The Competent Communicator to evaluate your level of self-esteem.

Maintaining a positive image of ourselves does appear to have its advantages when it comes to communication behavior. Compared to people with lower self-esteem, individuals with higher self-esteem are generally more outgoing and more willing to communicate and build relationships with others.[53] They are more comfortable initiating relationships, and they're more likely to believe that their partners' expressions of love and support are genuine.[54]

By the Numbers

17

Percentage increase in self-esteem experienced by college students after taking part in a five-session Internet conversational task.[52]

self-fulfilling prophecy An expectation that gives rise to behaviors that cause the expectation to come true.

self-esteem One's subjective evaluation of one's value and worth as a person.

Are You Happy with You? Measure Your Self-Esteem

How much do you agree with each of the following statements? On the line before each statement, record your level of agreement on a 1 to 7 scale. A higher number means you agree more; a lower number means you agree less.

_____ On the whole, I am satisfied with myself.

_____ Most of the time, I think I'm a good person.

_____ I feel I have a number of good qualities.

_____ I am able to do things as well as most other people.

_____ I feel I have much to be proud of.

_____ I rarely, if ever, feel useless.

_____ I feel that I'm a person of worth, at least on an equal plane with others.

_____ I have a good deal of respect for myself.

_____ All in all, I am inclined to feel I am a success.

_____ I take a positive attitude toward myself.

When you're finished, add up your scores. Your total score should fall between 10 and 70. A score of 10 to 25 suggests that your self-esteem is relatively low right now. If you scored between 25 and 55, you have a moderate level of self-esteem. A score above 55 suggests that your self-esteem is relatively high.

Source: Rosenberg, M. (1965). *Society and the adolescent self-image.* Princeton, NJ: Princeton University Press.

Despite its advantages, high self-esteem also has some drawbacks, particularly for adolescents and young adults. Although several researchers have speculated that having low self-esteem promotes aggressive and antisocial behavior, the reverse is true. Research confirms that aggressive people tend to have higher self-esteem, not lower.[55] Adolescents with higher self-esteem are also more prone to be sexually active and to engage in risky sexual behaviors than teens with lower self-esteem.[56] Finally, when their relationships run into problems, people with high self-esteem are more likely than their low self-esteem counterparts to end those relationships and seek out new ones.[57]

In this section, we've considered that we perceive ourselves through our self-concepts, which are multifaceted and partly subjective. We've seen how we exercise awareness of our self-concepts through self-monitoring and self-fulfilling prophecies, and we've examined self-esteem and learned about its benefits and drawbacks. All of those concepts help people to form and modify their perceptions of themselves. As we'll discover in the next section, people use a variety of communication behaviors to express their desired self-perceptions to others.

- What does it mean to say that self-concepts are partly subjective?
- How do high self-monitors communicate differently than low self-monitors?
- In what circumstances is having high self-esteem problematic, according to research?

Test Yourself

>> Managing Our Image

As discussed in the preceding section, our self-concept is related to *the way we see ourselves*. When we communicate with other people, we are also interested in *the way we want them to see us*. In some situations, we might want others to regard us as friendly, outgoing, and fun. In other situations, we might want people to view us as reliable, competent, and serious.

When we consider how we want others to perceive us, our concern is the kind of **image** we want to project—that is, the personal "face" we want others to see. In this section, we'll examine what scholars call image management, and we'll look into research that has shed light on that process.

COMMUNICATION AND IMAGE MANAGEMENT

In the film *Meet the Parents* (2000), Greg Focker (played by Ben Stiller) plans to propose to his girlfriend during a weekend trip to her parents' house and finds himself working hard to make a good impression on her distrusting father (played by Robert De Niro). When the goal, like Greg Focker's, is to make a positive first impression on others, you've probably heard that it's best just to "be yourself." Indeed, many of us try to project an image that accurately reflects our self-concept.

At times, though, we adjust our behavior to reflect a specific image we wish to project. It might be an image that suits the particular occasion or an outcome we desire. That process of behavioral adjustment to project a desired image is known as **image management.** In the following discussion, we'll consider that image management is collaborative, that we manage multiple identities, and that managing an image is complex.

Image Management Is Collaborative To some extent, managing your image is an individual process. After all, your image is yours. Yet you also get a lot of help managing your image from the people around you. As psychologist Dan McAdams has suggested, each of us develops a **life story,** a way of presenting ourselves to others that is based on our self-concept but is also influenced by other people.[58]

In many situations, we carefully consider how we want others to perceive us. That is the process of image management.

image The way one wishes to be seen or perceived by others.

image management The process of projecting one's desired public image.

life story A way of presenting oneself to others that is based on one's self-concept but is also influenced by other people.

If others accept the image you portray, they'll tend to behave in ways that encourage that image. Let's say you see yourself as a confident person, and you project that image when you interact with others. If other people see you as confident, they'll treat you as though you are—and their behavior will strengthen that part of your identity in your own mind. If others don't accept the image of yourself that you portray, however, they may treat you as less credible or as untrustworthy.

Perhaps you have encountered people who seem as though they are trying to be someone they aren't or who are portraying an image that you don't accept as genuine. Many of us find it hard to take such people seriously, and we react to them accordingly. In October 2009, millions watched television coverage of a runaway homemade helium balloon floating in the sky over Colorado. A seemingly distraught man, Richard Heene, reported that his 6-year-old son Falcon was trapped onboard. After the balloon landed and the boy was nowhere to be found in it, authorities discovered that Falcon had been at home all along. Widespread suspicions were raised that the father had staged the event to attract media attention. Although he initially denied doing so, the elder Heene pleaded guilty the following month, revealing himself to lack credibility and trustworthiness.

We Manage Multiple Identities If you think of all the people who know you, you'll probably realize that most of them know you only in certain contexts. You have your circle of friends, who know you as a friend. You have your family members, who might know you as a mother, a son, an aunt, a brother, a cousin, or a grandchild. Your boss and co-workers know you as an employee.

Each of those contexts carries its own distinctive role expectations, so you probably enact a somewhat different identity in each one. You likely communicate differently at work than at home, and your friends probably know you differently than your instructors do. In fact, we all manage multiple identities. That is, we show different parts of ourselves to different people in our lives.

Managing Multiple Identities in Instances of Invisible Medical Conditions

The challenge of managing multiple identities is especially pronounced for individuals with "invisible" medical conditions—illnesses or disorders that are not necessarily apparent to others. Conditions such as Down syndrome, stuttering, developmental disabilities, and confinement to a wheelchair are relatively visible in the sense that many people will notice those conditions after seeing or listening to someone who has them. However, individuals can, to varying degrees, hide the fact that they have other kinds of conditions, such as cancer, diabetes, asthma, and depression, if they don't want others to know. Most people can't identify someone with diabetes or asthma, for example, simply by observing the person.

People with invisible conditions have both the responsibility and the ability to determine how to incorporate their conditions into the image they project. Many individuals with such conditions must continually decide whom to tell about their conditions, when to make those disclosures, and how to do so. That decision can be particularly agonizing for individuals suffering from invisible conditions that are also socially stigmatized, such as mental health disorders and HIV-positive status, because of the fear of how others will react to their disclosures. The Dark Side of Communication addresses this issue as it pertains to individuals who are HIV positive.

Managing Multiple Identities Online
In the virtual world of the Internet, a person can create and maintain as many different identities as he or she chooses, simply by generating multiple e-mail addresses or web pages or participating in various virtual communities.[59] For instance, you might have one e-mail address associated with your college or university that indicates both your name and the school (mine is kory.floyd@asu.edu). You might have another address from a free e-mail server, such as Yahoo or Gmail, containing no identifying information about yourself (for example, mybro4816@gmail.com). Perhaps you use such an anonymous address when you want to communicate online without revealing your identity. In virtual communities, such as chat rooms and Second Life, you can even manipulate your identity to appear as though you are of a different gender, different ethnicity, or even a different species.[60] Some people may create multiple online identities to protect themselves when

Under what conditions, if any, is it unethical to misrepresent your identity online?

THE DARK SIDE of Communication

Risks of Disclosing HIV-Positive Status

Discovering they are infected with HIV is a traumatic experience for many people. Being HIV positive puts individuals at risk for developing AIDS, a terminal disease with no known cure. It also requires them to choose with whom they're going to share the news of their infection.

Many people with HIV have difficulty deciding whether to disclose their condition to others. On the one hand, disclosing the illness may help individuals acquire both medical and emotional support, and it may encourage others to adopt safer sexual or drug-use behaviors themselves. However, disclosure can be risky. Psychologists Valerian Derlega and Barbara Winstead explain that individuals who are HIV positive may have several reasons for choosing not to disclose their condition:

- *Privacy:* It's no one else's business but their own.
- *Self-blame:* They feel guilty for being HIV positive.
- *Communication difficulties:* They don't know how to tell others about their condition.
- *Fear of rejection:* They worry about others rejecting or even hurting them.
- *Fear of discrimination:* They fear that employers, landlords, or others will discriminate against them.
- *Protection of others:* They don't want others to worry about them.
- *Superficial relationships:* They don't feel close enough to others to trust them with this information.

Despite these risks, Derlega and Winstead emphasize that disclosing HIV status can be useful in many ways. Beyond helping individuals to secure needed medical attention and emotional support, disclosure can also help to strengthen relationships, particularly with others who are also HIV positive.

Disclosure is also critical for the health and safety of a romantic or sexual partner. To protect potential partners, in fact, several U.S. states have enacted laws making it a felony to expose someone else knowingly to HIV without that person's consent.

Source: Derlega, V. J., & Winstead, B. A. (2001). HIV-infected persons' attributions for the disclosure and nondisclosure of the seropositive diagnosis to significant others. In V. Manusov & J. H. Harvey (Eds.), *Attribution, communication behavior, and close relationships* (pp. 266–284). New York: Cambridge University Press.

interacting with strangers; others may do so for amusement or to explore various aspects of their personalities.

One online venue in which portraying multiple identities is surprisingly *un*common is the blog, a website that features running commentary, news, and/or personal thoughts about one or more topics. Although some blogs belong to companies or organizations, many are created and maintained by individuals—most frequently adolescents—who often use them as a type of online diary. A 2004 study of communication on personal blogs found that 67 percent of bloggers provided their real names on their blogs, whether their full names (31 percent) or just their first names (36 percent). In contrast, only 29 percent used a fake name, with the remainder providing no name whatsoever. Further, more than half of the bloggers in the study provided explicit demographic information about themselves, such as their age, occupation, or geographic location.[61]

More recent research has found that male and female bloggers differ somewhat with respect to the identifying information they post. Specifically, male bloggers are more likely than their female counterparts to provide information about their location, to use emoticons that indicate sadness or flirtatiousness, and to reveal their sexual identity as homosexual. In comparison, female bloggers are more likely to include links to their personal web pages.[62]

Image Management Is Complex Image management is often complicated and may involve competing goals for our interactions with others. Let's say you've been offered a prestigious internship at a startup company in California's Silicon Valley and you ask your older sister and her romantic partner, who live close to that area, if you can move in with them for the semester. You want your sister to think of you as a mature, responsible adult rather than as the naïve teenager you were when she moved out of your parents' house. You therefore have to present your request in a way that projects your image as a grown, responsible person. At the same time, though, you want to persuade your sister and her partner that you really need a place to stay, and you can't afford to rent one because your internship pays poorly and rents are expensive. That goal may prompt you to project the image that you need help. Thus, you may find your image needs in conflict: You want to appear responsible but also in need of assistance. Managing those competing image needs—while still persuading your sister to let you move in—can be complex.

Communication researcher Myra Goldschmidt found that when people ask others for favors, they often create narratives—ways of telling their stories—that help them to maintain their image while still being persuasive.[63] To your sister, you might make statements such as "I need a place to stay only for a couple of months while I do this internship" and "I promise to help around the house." Such strategies can help preserve your image as a responsible individual even in a situation where that image might be threatened.

We've seen that managing your image is a collaborative process that often requires you to negotiate several identities in a complex way. How do we determine what our image needs are in the first place?

COMMUNICATION AND FACE NEEDS

Helping someone "save face" means helping that person to avoid embarrassment and preserve dignity in a situation where that dignity is threatened. The very reason we hate getting embarrassed is that it threatens the image of ourselves we're trying to project, and that threat is a function of our need to save face. Sometimes we associate the concept of saving face with collectivistic cultures such as Korea and Japan. In reality, saving face is important in many cultures.[64] Let's consider what happens when our desired public image is threatened.

face A person's desired public image.

facework The behaviors people use to establish and maintain their desired public image with others.

face needs Important components of one's desired public image.

fellowship face The need to be liked and accepted by others.

autonomy face The need to avoid being imposed upon by others.

competence face The need to be respected and viewed as competent and intelligent.

face-threatening act Any behavior that threatens one or more face needs.

Face and Face Needs Each of us has a desired public image—a certain way that we want others to see and think of us—and we work to maintain that image through the ways we communicate. For instance, if you want others to see you as intelligent and competent, you will likely communicate in ways that nurture that impression and will try to avoid situations that would make you look uninformed or incompetent. Sociologist Erving Goffman coined the term **face** to describe our desired public image and the term **facework** to describe the behaviors we use to project that image to others.[65]

Researchers believe that our face is made up of three different **face needs,** or important components of our desired public image.[66] You might find it easy to remember those face needs by noting that the first letters of their names—fellowship, autonomy, and competence—are also the first three letters in the word *face*.

Fellowship face refers to the need to have others like and accept us. That is the part of our identity that motivates us to make friends, join clubs and social groups, and communicate pleasantly with others. **Autonomy face** refers to our need to avoid being imposed upon by others. It's our autonomy face that motivates us to be in control of our time and resources and to avoid having other people make decisions for us. Finally, **competence face** is our need to be respected—to have others acknowledge our abilities and intelligence. That need drives us to seek careers and hobbies in which we can excel and to avoid situations that will embarrass us.

In relationships, people try to project a desired public image, known as *face*.

Face Threats Each of us has a different desired public image, and so our face needs vary. Some people have a very strong fellowship face need, meaning it is extremely important that others like them. Other people much prefer to be respected than liked. Similarly, one person may have a very high need for autonomy, whereas another person doesn't mind having decisions made for himself or herself. Those differences are part of what makes everyone's identity unique.

We often become consciously aware of our face needs only when they're threatened. Let's say you apply to join an honor society but are not accepted. That decision not to include you could threaten your fellowship face. It could also threaten your competence face by making you feel you aren't smart enough to get into the group. The rejection of your application, therefore, is a **face-threatening act** because it hinders the fulfillment of one or more of your face needs.

Face-threatening acts often lead people to behave in ways that help them restore their face. In the case of the honor society, you might say to others, "I didn't really want to be in that group anyway."[67] In truth, you probably *did* want to be in the honor society, or you wouldn't have applied. So, you would likely make such a statement as a way of managing your image with others—that is, you would want it to *appear* that your face needs have not been threatened. That statement is thus a type of *defense mechanism*—a response that minimizes the effects of a face-threatening act on you.

SHARPEN Your Skills

With others in your class, role-play a conversation in which you have to criticize someone else's work. Practice delivering your critiques to each other in ways that will minimize face threats for the recipients.

Face Threats in Socially Marginalized Groups Face threats are common in many socially marginalized populations. For example, many elderly people experience threats to their autonomy face as a result of various physical and cognitive limitations associated with aging.[68] Similarly, people with certain disabilities may perceive threats to their autonomy face if they are unable to do activities that others can do, such as driving a car. Still other groups may feel their autonomy is jeopardized when they don't have the legal authority to make certain decisions for themselves, as in the case of lesbian and gay adults who (in most states) cannot choose to marry their romantic partners.

Being marginalized also leads many people to feel disrespected and shamed. Such feelings can threaten both their fellowship face and their competence face. In U.S. American society, for example, there are stigmas associated with being homeless, poor, old, disabled, lesbian, gay, mentally ill, and (in some circles) divorced, even though a person may have no choice about belonging to any of these groups.[69] Stigmatized people might feel that they don't fit in with those around them, and those perceptions threaten their fellowship face by making them feel unaccepted. Those individuals may also perceive that others judge them not on the basis of their intelligence or abilities but because of their stigmatized condition. Such perceptions threaten their competence face by causing them to feel disrespected.

Whether we're aware of it or not, each of us is constantly managing our public image, hoping that others will perceive us the way we want them to. Through communication behavior, we manage multiple identities in multiple ways, and we protect our face needs and respond to situations that threaten them.

- **What does it mean to say that image management is collaborative?**
- **When are a person's fellowship, autonomy, and competence face threatened?**

Test Yourself

For REVIEW >>

- How do we form perceptions of others?

  Perceiving others is a process whereby we select information for attention, organize that information according to a perceptual schema, and then interpret it to give it meaning.

- What influences our perceptions?

  Our cultural background, stereotypes, primacy and recency effects, and perceptual sets are among the most potent influences on our perceptions. Our attributions for behavior are also influenced by the self-serving bias and the fundamental attribution error.

- How do we manage our image?

  Over the course of life, we create and refine a self-concept. Our communication behavior reflects our self-concept through the way we manage our image, both in person and online.

Pop Quiz

Multiple Choice

1. Noticing that someone is a communication major is an example of the schema for classifying information about people known as
   a. physical
   b. interaction
   c. psychological
   d. role

2. When Jacob makes attributions about his roommate's communication behaviors, his attributions might include all of the following dimensions *except*
   a. locus
   b. stability
   c. controllability
   d. self-serving bias

3. The predisposition to perceive only what we want or expect to perceive is known as

   a. interpretation
   b. perceptual set
   c. attribution
   d. perceptual schema

4. The Johari window is a representation of self that consists of all of the following parts *except*

   a. open
   b. hidden
   c. visual
   d. unknown

5. The need to avoid being imposed upon by others is known as

   a. fellowship face
   b. competence face
   c. saving face
   d. autonomy face

Fill in the Blank

6. The first of the three stages of perception is the _____ stage.

7. According to the _____, first impressions are crucial because they set the tone for future interactions.

8. The _____ causes us to attribute others' communication behaviors more to internal causes than external causes.

9. The subjective evaluation of one's value and worth as a person is known as one's _____.

10. A _____ is a behavior that threatens one's face needs.

Answers: 1. d; 2. d; 3. b; 4. c; 5. d; 6. selection; 7. primacy effect; 8. fundamental attribution error; 9. self-esteem; 10. face-threatening act

KEY TERMS

perception 52	Johari window 63
selection 54	self-fulfilling
organization 54	prophecy 65
perceptual schema 54	self-esteem 65
interpretation 55	image 67
stereotype 57	image management 67
primacy effect 58	life story 67
recency effect 59	face 71
perceptual set 59	facework 71
attribution 60	face needs 71
self-serving bias 61	fellowship face 71
fundamental attribution error 62	autonomy face 71
	competence face 71
self-concept 62	face-threatening
identity 62	act 71

4

HOW
WE USE LANG

WHAT'S IN A WORD?

Like holidays themselves, debates over whether to wish people "Merry Christmas" or "Season's Greetings" have become annual traditions. In the past several years, retail giants such as Wal-Mart and Target have generated public controversy by adopting the phrase "Happy Holidays" in their advertisements and store displays. Some people point out that nonspecific language such as "Happy Holidays" and "Season's Greetings" respects diversity by acknowledging all holidays equally, regardless of their religious origin. Others argue that such phrases disrespect Christians by failing to recognize one of their most important religious holidays by name.

Why does it matter which greeting a store uses? It matters because the holiday shopping period can account for as much as half of a retailer's annual sales. As a result, few companies can afford to alienate customers by offending them through a particular choice of words.

If you were in charge of a store's marketing campaign, and you knew millions of dollars in sales were potentially at stake, how would you decide which holiday greeting to use?

UAGE

- What are the defining characteristics of language?
- For what reasons do people use language?
- How can you use language more effectively?

Words can shape our lives in extraordinary ways. By announcing in 1776 that "all men are created equal," Thomas Jefferson and the Second Continental Congress declared to the world the emergence of a new sovereign nation founded on the principle of individual liberty. Nearly two centuries later, Martin Luther King Jr. described his vision for civil rights and racial equality by proclaiming "I have a dream." In those and many other cases throughout history, powerful words have inspired women and men to enact dramatic social change.

Because language can be so consequential, we have to choose our words carefully in many situations. Using the right words in a job interview, a political campaign, a marriage proposal, and a retail chain's holiday advertisements may make the difference between failure and success. Being a competent communicator therefore requires us to use language in a deliberate and informed way.

>> The Nature of Language

Abraham Lincoln was purportedly fond of asking people, "How many legs does a dog have if you call its tail a leg?" Think about how you would respond to that question. Many replied to Lincoln by saying that if you call the dog's tail a leg, then a dog has five legs. When he encountered that reply, Lincoln responded by saying that no, dogs have only four legs, because calling a tail a leg doesn't make it one.

Some would say the former U.S. president was correct. They would claim that simply changing the way we talk about an object doesn't change the nature of the object itself. We may call a studio apartment a mansion, such people might say, but it's still a studio apartment. Others, however, would observe that Lincoln's assessment was incorrect, claiming that words have only the meanings we choose to assign them. Those individuals would point out that the term *leg* only means what it does because English language speakers allocate that meaning to it—so, if we call a tail a leg, it is therefore a leg. Lincoln's riddle illustrates one reason why it's so important for us to understand language: We use words to refer to objects, events, ideas, and other entities in the real world, but most words have only the meanings that we, as the users of a language, give them.

What is language in the first place? According to researchers, **language** is a structured system of symbols used for communicating meaning. You can probably think of many behaviors and items that represent or symbolize some type of meaning. A smile often

SHARPEN Your Skills

Invent a new word or expression. Write out a definition for it, and begin using it in everyday conversation with your friends. Take note of how well your word or expression catches on and whether your friends begin using it in their own conversations. This is an example of how words gain meaning.

language A structured system of symbols used for communicating meaning.

symbolizes happiness, for instance; a red traffic light symbolizes the need to stop. Many gestures also have symbolic meaning, in that they represent a particular concept or idea. For example, you probably wave to say "hello" and shrug your shoulders to indicate "I don't know." Although facial expressions, traffic lights, and gestures all symbolize meaning, however, none qualifies as language. Why? The answer is that language is characterized by the use of a specific type of symbol: words.[1]

Words are the building blocks of language and verbal communication. As we'll see in this chapter, we use words to represent ideas, observations, feelings, and thoughts. Words—whether we speak or write them—can have a profound influence on how we relate to others. In this section, we'll see that language is symbolic, is usually arbitrary, is governed by rules, has layers of meaning, varies in clarity, and is bound by context and culture.

LANGUAGE IS SYMBOLIC

When we say that language is symbolic, we mean that each word represents a particular object or idea, but it does not constitute the object or idea itself. For example, the word *textbook* represents a bound collection of printed material to be read as a supplement for lectures and in-class activities in a course. The word itself is not the object, though; it merely symbolizes it. Similarly, the word *five* represents a specific quantity of something (one more than four, and one fewer than six), yet the word itself is not the quantity; it simply represents it.

One way to understand the symbolic nature of language is to remember that different languages often have different words for the same object. The English word *textbook,* for instance, is *läromedel* in Swedish, 教科書 in Japanese, учебник in Bulgarian, and كتاب in Arabic. Those are completely different symbols, but they all represent the same entity, a textbook. If you were to invent your own language, you could create any term you wanted to represent the concept of a textbook.

We often acquire new words, and new meanings for older words, as technology advances. The widespread use of computer-mediated communication, for instance, has added new terms to our everyday conversations, such as *blog, e-mail,* and *instant messaging.* In addition, it has generated new meanings for existing words, such as *web, crash, tweet,* and *net.* As computer technology continues to develop, new words will likely be added to our vocabulary to help us communicate about it.

The word *tweet* is used to refer to the sound a bird makes. Today, we use the same word to describe a message sent on Twitter.

LANGUAGE IS USUALLY ARBITRARY

Why do words symbolize the particular things they do? For the most part, words have only an arbitrary connection to their meanings. Think of the word *car.* That word doesn't look or sound like a car, so why does it make us think of one? The only reason is that speakers of English have agreed to give the word *car* that particular meaning. They could just as easily have called cars "whickles" or "geps" or "mumqualls." These words don't mean anything to speakers of English, but they would if we were to assign them a meaning. The point is that the meaning of almost all words is arbitrary: Words literally mean whatever we, as users of a language, choose for them to mean.

Language can be arbitrary precisely *because* it is symbolic. As we saw above, words only symbolize their meanings; they don't constitute their meanings themselves. For that reason we can select almost any word to symbolize a particular meaning, and so the connection between language and meaning is arbitrary. In that sense, then, Abraham Lincoln was wrong when he said that calling a tail a leg doesn't make it one. It's true that calling a tail a leg doesn't change any of its physical properties, but because of the arbitrary nature of language, we can choose to make *leg* the appropriate term to describe a tail . . . or a rainbow, a fishing boat, a salt shaker, or any other object or idea we wish to describe.

Why do we call a car a car?

LANGUAGE IS GOVERNED BY RULES

Where did you learn all of the rules associated with your native language?

We have said that language is symbolic and that the meaning of most words is arbitrary. If those statements are both true, then how do we all understand one another? The answer is that every language is governed by rules.

You already know many of the rules that frame your native language. Even if you can't articulate them, you usually take notice when they're violated. To a native speaker of English, for instance, the statement "I filled the bottle with water" sounds correct, but "I filled water into the bottle" does not. Even if you aren't quite sure *why* the second sentence sounds wrong, you probably still recognize that it does. Along these same lines, when you learn a new language, you don't learn just the words; you also learn the rules for how the words work together to convey meaning.

Researchers distinguish among four different types of language rules:

- *Phonological rules* deal with the correct pronunciation of a word, and they vary from language to language. If you speak French, for example, you know that the proper way to pronounce *travail* is "trah-VYE." According to English phonological rules, however, the word looks as though it should be pronounced "trah-VALE."
- *Syntactic rules* govern the order of words within phrases and clauses. The question "What is your name?" makes sense to an English speaker because the words are in the proper order. To ask the same question in American Sign Language, a system of visual signs used by hearing-impaired people to communicate, we would sign "your – name – what?" Signing "what – your – name?" is incorrect because it violates the syntactic rules of American Sign Language.
- *Semantic rules* have to do with the meaning of individual words. Those meanings may be arbitrary, as we saw above, but they are agreed upon by speakers of a language. When you hear the word *lawyer,* for instance, you think of an attorney, not a paper mill or a cell phone or a Caribbean vacation. It is a semantic rule that connects *lawyer* with *attorney* and not with one of those other meanings.
- *Pragmatic rules* deal with the implications or interpretations of statements. Think of hearing the phrase "Nice to meet you," a common greeting among speakers of English. Depending on the context and the speaker's tone of voice, you might think the speaker really *is* happy to meet you, or you might infer that he or she is just saying so to be polite. If there's a sarcastic tone in the speaker's voice, you might even infer that he or she is *unhappy* to meet you. In each instance, pragmatic rules lead you to your conclusion.

No matter how we communicate verbally, we observe phonological, syntactic, semantic, and pragmatic rules for language.

As children acquire a language, they gain an almost intuitive sense of its phonological, syntactic, semantic, and pragmatic rules. That knowledge allows native speakers of a language to speak and write fluently. In contrast, people who are less familiar with the language are more likely to violate those rules.[2] You'll read about how one individual applies her mastery of the rules of the English language in the Putting Communication to Work box.

LANGUAGE HAS LAYERS OF MEANING

Many words imply certain ideas that are separate from their literal meanings. The literal meaning of a word—the way a dictionary defines it—is its **denotative meaning.** Think of the word *home,* for instance. Its denotative meaning is "a shelter used as a residence." When you hear the word *home,* however, you may also think along the lines of "a place where I feel safe, accepted, and loved" or "a space where I am free to do whatever I want." Those are examples of the word's **connotative meaning,** the ideas or concepts that the word suggests in addition to its literal definition.

denotative meaning The literal meaning of a word.

connotative meaning The ideas or concepts a word suggests in addition to its literal definition.

The Semantic Triangle To illustrate the relationship between words and their denotative and connotative meanings, psychologist Charles Ogden and English professor Ivor

Putting Communication to Work

Name: Jennifer Hesse

College(s): BA, Whitworth University, 2002

Major(s): Journalism (within Communication program)

Job Title: Assistant Managing Editor

Salary: $30,000–$45,000

Time in Job: 5 years

Work Responsibilities: I work as an editor at OpenSystems Media, a multimedia publishing company. I coordinate editorial production for print and online media formats, a process that entails helping authors formulate article content; fact-checking; and editing for grammar, spelling, and style. I work with graphic designers as they lay out the print magazines, and collaborate with web designers as they develop content for the websites and electronic newsletters. My knowledge and understanding of communication principles and strategies, particularly those associated with conflict resolution and interpersonal relationship building, come into play as I deal with tardy contributors and sales personnel who do not always share the same goals as the editorial staff.

Why Communication? Our communication program offered either a journalism track or a general communications studies track. I opted for the journalism track because I wanted to pursue a career as a newspaper or magazine editor and writer. That track involved writing-intensive classes that especially appealed to me. I also took general communication studies classes such as media history, interpersonal communication, and communication ethics. Aside from my journalistic training, my background in communication has helped me interact more effectively with co-workers and clients by implementing basic interpersonal and organizational communication skills such as active listening, affirmative nonverbal cues, and awareness of cultural rules and values.

My Advice to Students: No matter what your ultimate vocational goal is, the path to achieve it can be circuitous, and whatever industry you choose, the expectations will be continually evolving. So, take advantage of the opportunity to learn and explore diverse topics that might not only further your career but also expand your overall knowledge base.

Richards developed the *semantic triangle* (Figure 4.1).[3] In its three corners, the semantic triangle portrays three necessary elements for identifying the meaning in language. The first element is the *symbol*, which is the word being communicated. In the second corner is the *referent*, which is the word's denotative meaning. Finally, there's the *reference*, which is the connotative meaning.

If several listeners hear the same word, they might attribute the same denotative meaning to it but different connotative meanings. For instance, if I say the word *euthanasia*, the word itself is the symbol, and its referent is a medically assisted death. To one listener, the word represents a merciful way to end a person's pain and suffering. To another person, it represents

FIGURE 4.1 The Semantic Triangle
The semantic triangle portrays three necessary elements for identifying meaning in language: the symbol, the referent, and the reference.

HOME

a form of homicide. To still other listeners, it represents an unfortunate but sometimes justified component of the death experience. Those are all differences in the word's reference, or connotative meaning, rather than in its denotative meaning.

Loaded Language In October 2008, the U.S. Congress passed the Economic Stimulus Act, which allowed the federal government to purchase up to $700 billion in troubled assets as a way to rouse the faltering economy. The law was highly controversial among members of Congress and other U.S. citizens, and the controversy was reflected in the language people used to describe it. For those who favored it, the Economic Stimulus Act was a "rescue plan," but for many who opposed it, it was a "bailout." Both of those terms are examples of **loaded language,** words with strongly positive or negative connotations. Notice that the term *rescue plan* sounds positive because it conjures images of a hero saving the innocent victims of a crisis. The term *bailout,* however, sounds negative because it connotes begrudgingly helping people deal with problems they themselves have created.

Loaded language reflects the observation that denotations and connotations represent different layers of meaning. At a denotative level, for instance, the word *cancer* simply refers to a malignant growth or tumor in the body. For many people, however, the term connotes any evil condition that spreads destructively. For instance, you might hear someone describe conditions such as poverty and bigotry as "cancers on society." That example illustrates that people can use the word *cancer* as a loaded term when they wish to evoke feelings of fear, disgust, or anger on the part of listeners. People can also use loaded words to evoke positive emotions. Terms such as *peace, family,* and *freedom* have emotionally positive connotations even if their denotative meanings are emotionally neutral.[4]

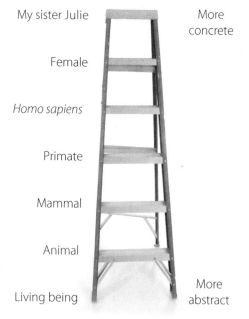

My sister Julie

Female

Homo sapiens

Primate

Mammal

Animal

Living being

More concrete

More abstract

FIGURE 4.2 Hayawaka's Ladder of Abstraction Note how the example begins at the bottom with a broad, abstract category and how, as we move up the ladder, the concepts become more and more concrete and specific.

LANGUAGE VARIES IN CLARITY

Josh is driving his brother Jeremy to a doctor's appointment, and Jeremy has the directions. As they approach an intersection, they have the following conversation:

> Josh: *I need to turn left at this next light, don't I?*
>
> Jeremy: *Right.*

Which way should Josh turn? When Jeremy responded to Josh's question by answering "right," was he saying that Josh was accurate in thinking that he should turn left, or was he correcting Josh by instructing him to turn right? We don't really know, because Jeremy has used **ambiguous language** by making a statement that we can interpret to have more than one meaning. Jeremy's reply was ambiguous because the word *right* could mean either "you are correct" or "turn right" in that situation.

A certain amount of ambiguity is inherent in our language. In fact, according to the *Oxford English Dictionary,* the 500 most frequently used words in the English language have an average of 23 different meanings each. The word *set* has so many different meanings—nearly 200, more than any other English word—that it takes the *Oxford English Dictionary* 60,000 words to define it![5] One reason that language varies in clarity is that some words are more *concrete* than others. A word that is concrete refers to a specific object in the physical world, such as a particular laptop computer, a specific restaurant, or an individual person. In contrast, a word that is *abstract* refers to a broader category or organizing concept of objects. According to English professor Samuel Hayakawa, words can be arrayed along a "ladder of abstraction" that shows their progression from more abstract to more concrete.[6]

Figure 4.2 gives an example of Hayakawa's ladder of abstraction. At the bottom of the ladder is a reference to all living beings, which is a broad, abstract category. As we move upward in the diagram, the concepts become more and more concrete, referencing all animals and then all mammals, all primates, all *Homo sapiens,* and all females before reaching the most concrete reference—to a specific individual, Julie.

loaded language Words with strongly positive or negative connotations.

ambiguous language Words that can have more than one meaning.

LANGUAGE IS BOUND BY CONTEXT AND CULTURE

Finally, meaning in language is affected by the social and cultural context in which people use it. Societies and cultures differ in their degree of individualism and their use of communication codes. Many of those differences are evident in people's verbal messages. For instance, "I'm looking out for Number One" is a very individualistic message that would be relatively uncommon in a collectivistic society. In fact, a common adage in Japan, and one that reflects that nation's collectivistic culture, states, "It is the nail that sticks out that gets hammered down."[7]

In what became known as the **Sapir-Whorf hypothesis,** anthropologist Edward Sapir and linguist Benjamin Whorf proposed that language shapes our views of reality. Their notion was that language influences the ways that members of a culture see the world—and that a people's attitudes and behaviors are reflected in its language.[8] The Sapir-Whorf hypothesis embodies two specific principles. The first, *linguistic determinism,* suggests that the structure of language determines how we think. In other words, we can conceive of something only if we have a term for it in our vocabulary.[9] Imagine a language that includes no term describing the emotion of envy. According to the principle of linguistic determinism, people who speak that language would not experience envy because they could experience something only if they had words to describe it.

The second principle, *linguistic relativity,* suggests that because language determines our perceptions of reality, people see the world differently depending on which language they speak. Whorf discovered, for instance, that the language of the Hopi Indians of the American Southwest makes no distinction between nouns and verbs. Whereas English uses nouns to refer to *things* and verbs to refer to *actions,* the Hopi language describes just about everything as an action or a process. Compared to English speakers, then, the Hopi tend to see the world as being constantly in motion.[10]

The Sapir-Whorf hypothesis is provocative, but is it true? Check out the Fact or Fiction? box for insight into this question.

By the Numbers

Number of new words added to the *Oxford English Dictionary* in 2007 alone.

Test Yourself

- What does it mean to say that language is symbolic?
- Why is the meaning of almost every word arbitrary?
- How do syntactic rules differ from semantic rules?
- What is the difference between a word's denotative meaning and its connotative meaning?
- When is a word or phrase ambiguous?
- What is the Sapir-Whorf hypothesis?

>> Appreciating the Power of Words

English writer Rudyard Kipling, author of *The Jungle Book,* once called words "the most powerful drug used by mankind." To understand his point, think about how you feel when someone you love expresses affection to you, or when you listen to a speech by a politician you can't stand, or when you comfort a friend who is grieving the loss of a family member. Words can literally change a person's day—or a person's life—in positive or negative ways.

Entire books have been written about the power of language. Here we focus on four important functions that language serves in our daily lives. Specifically, we'll discover that language expresses who we are, connects us to others, separates us from others, and motivates action.

LANGUAGE EXPRESSES WHO WE ARE

Think about playing a game in which you have to select one word to represent your identity. Should you pick an adjective, such as *adventurous, conservative,* or *shy?* Maybe you

Sapir-Whorf hypothesis
A theory that language shapes a person's views of reality.

I Speak, Therefore I Think: Language Determines Thought

Sapir and Whorf proposed that our thoughts are rooted in language, so we can think about something only if we have a word or words for it. This idea implies that if we don't have a word for a particular concept, then we can't experience that concept. It also implies that people will see the world differently *because of the differences in their languages.* Are those ideas fact or fiction?

It's hard to tell for certain, but the Sapir-Whorf hypothesis has been widely criticized by researchers. Three criticisms are common:

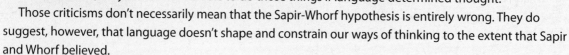

- First, although the Sapir-Whorf hypothesis proposes that language shapes our thoughts, it is equally possible that our thoughts shape our language. For instance, an experienced fashion designer might look at four different jackets and label their colors "scarlet," "ruby," "crimson," and "vermilion." You might look at the same jackets and call them all "red." Does the designer think of the four colors as different because she has more terms for them than you do? Or does she have more terms because she has more experience thinking about differences among colors? It's difficult to know for sure, but either idea is possible.

- Second, not having a word for a particular experience doesn't necessarily mean that people don't have that experience. People in a society may feel jealous, for instance, even if they don't have a word to describe that feeling.

- Third, as linguist Steven Pinker has pointed out, even people who don't acquire language, perhaps because of mental deficiencies, are able to think, count, and interact with others; they would not be able to do those things if language determined thought.

Those criticisms don't necessarily mean that the Sapir-Whorf hypothesis is entirely wrong. They do suggest, however, that language doesn't shape and constrain our ways of thinking to the extent that Sapir and Whorf believed.

ASK YOURSELF

- What did you think of the Sapir-Whorf hypothesis when you first read about it? Did it seem reasonable or unreasonable to you at first? Why?
- Do you think only in words? Do you ever think in numbers or colors or sounds?

Source: Pinker, S. (1994). *The language instinct.* New York: HarperCollins.

should choose a verb instead, such as *think, sing,* or *run.* That game is challenging because any word we choose might represent a part of who we are but may not represent us fully. As humans, we express our identities in many ways—by our clothes, jobs, preferred leisure activities, and the language we use to communicate with others.

Language expresses who we are in at least two ways: by naming and identifying us and by enhancing our credibility. Let's take a look at each.

Names Define and Differentiate Us What's something that belongs to you yet is constantly used by others? The answer is *your name*. By itself, a name is simply a linguistic device that identifies something or someone. Your name does more, however, than differentiate you from others—it's also an important component of your sense of self. Naming is therefore one way you gain information about other people and represent yourself to the world.

A person's first name, for instance, can suggest information about the person's characteristics. One such characteristic is the person's sex. For example, in Western societies, we usually assign names such as Jacob, Michael, and Caleb only to males and names such as Emma, Savannah, and Nicole only to females. Names can also provide clues about a person's ethnicity. You might infer that LaKeisha is African American, Huong is Asian, and Santiago is Latino. Some names even suggest a person's age group, so you might assume that Jennifer, Emily, and Hannah are younger than Edna, Mildred, and Bertha.

In addition to demographic information, names can suggest information about our disposition and sense of self. For instance, we might perceive an adult man who goes by the name Richard differently from one who goes by Ricky, even though those are two forms of the same name. Indeed, research shows that we do make assumptions about people— whether accurately or not—on the basis of their names.[11] In one study, people made more positive evaluations of men named David, Jon, Joshua, and Gregory than they did of men named Oswald, Myron, Reginald, and Edmund, even though they were given no information about the men other than their names.[12] Other studies have shown that people whose names strongly suggest a non-white ethnicity sometimes experience discrimination based only on their names.[13]

Language Enhances or Diminishes Credibility A second way in which words express who we are is by reflecting our credibility. **Credibility** is the extent to which others perceive us to be competent and trustworthy. Some speakers have credibility on certain topics because of their training and expertise. You'll probably have more confidence in medical advice if you hear it from a doctor, for instance, than from the barista at your local coffee shop. If the advice is about making a great latte, however, you'll probably trust your barista more than your doctor. In either case, you are assigning credibility on the basis of the speaker's specific expertise.

Language is intimately tied to issues of credibility. Irrespective of our training or credentials, our words can portray us as confident, trustworthy communicators, or they can make us appear unsure of ourselves. In either situation, our ability to get what we want is affected by the credibility that our language use gives us. As we'll see next, several specific forms of language have the potential either to enhance or to diminish our credibility.

A barista has credibility when it comes to making great coffee but not when it comes to giving medical advice.

Clichés *Clichés* are words or phrases that were novel at one time but have lost their effect due to overuse. When politicians talk about "the promise of change," business leaders refer to "thinking outside the box," and community activists talk about "making a difference," they may lose credibility with their audiences; those phrases are clichés that can make speakers sound uninformed or out-of-touch. Even if a cliché expresses the point you want to make, you will usually be more persuasive if you use different words. Encouraging someone to "evaluate your situation from a different perspective" can be more powerful than telling the person to "think outside the box" because the latter phrase is so overused.

Dialects People can also enhance or diminish their credibility by using *dialects,* language variations shared by people of a certain region or social class. Many U.S. Americans, for example, can tell the difference between a speaker from the South and one from New England on the basis of some of the words and expressions they use. The Southern speaker might employ words characteristic of that region's dialect, such as "y'all" to mean

credibility The extent to which others perceive us to be competent and trustworthy.

"you"; the New Englander's speech might reflect that area's dialect, such as using "wicked good" instead of "very good." According to *communication accommodation theory,* developed by communication scholars Howard Giles and John Wiemann, we may be able to enhance our credibility by speaking in a dialect that is familiar to our audience.[14] In contrast, when we use a dialect that is different from that of our listeners, we can cause them to see us as an outsider, and such a perception might lead them to question our credibility.

Equivocation Another form of language that sometimes influences a speaker's credibility is *equivocation,* language that disguises the speaker's true intentions through strategic ambiguity. We often choose to use equivocal language when we're in a dilemma, a situation when none of our options is a good one. Suppose, for example, that you're asked to provide a reference for your friend Dylan, who is applying for a job on your town's police force. One of the questions you're asked is how well Dylan handles pressure. Even though Dylan is your friend, you can immediately think of several occasions when he hasn't dealt well with pressure. Now you're in a bind. On one hand, you want Dylan to get the job because he's your friend. On the other hand, you don't want to lie to the police lieutenant who's phoning you for the reference.

Several studies have shown that—to get out of such situations, when we're faced with two unappealing choices—we often use equivocal language.[15] In response to the lieutenant's question about how well Dylan handles pressure, you might say, "Well, that depends; there are different kinds of pressure." As you can probably tell, that statement doesn't give the lieutenant much information at all. Instead, it might imply that you don't know how well Dylan deals with pressure, but you don't want to admit that you don't know. It might also imply that you do know how well Dylan handles pressure but don't want to say. In either case, you are likely to come across as less credible than if you had answered the question directly.[16] Researchers John Daly, Carol Diesel, and David Weber have suggested that those sorts of conversational dilemmas are common and that we frequently use equivocal language in such situations.[17]

Weasel Words A form of language related to equivocation is *weasel words,* terms or phrases intended to mislead listeners by implying something that they don't actually say. Advertisers often use weasel words when making claims about their products. When you hear that "four out of five dentists prefer" a certain brand of toothpaste, the implication is that 80 percent of *all* dentists prefer that brand. That level of preference would be really impressive—but the statement does not actually make that specific claim. For all we know, only five dentists were surveyed. If that were the case, the support of "four out of five" would appear much less impressive.

Allness Statements One specific form of weasel words is an *allness statement,* a statement implying that a claim is true without exception. For instance, when you hear someone claim that "experts agree that corporal punishment is emotionally damaging to children," the implication is that *all* experts agree. Note, however, that the speaker provides no evidence to back up that implication. Likewise, when someone says, "There's no known cure for depression," the implication is that no cure exists. All the statement *actually* means, however, is that no cure is known to the speaker.

Naming and enhancing our credibility aren't the only ways language reflects who we are, but they are among the most noticeable. We also use language to form positive connections with others, as we'll consider next.

What makes one speaker more credible than another to you? What qualities reinforce credibility?

LANGUAGE CONNECTS US TO OTHERS

For many years, the telecommunications company AT&T ran an advertising campaign whose slogan was "Reach out and touch someone." The phrase was meant to suggest that by calling someone on the telephone, we could establish or reinforce a personal bond with that person. Today, many of us use social networking websites such as Facebook and MySpace for the same purposes: to meet new people and to stay connected with those we already know. Even texting and tweeting help us reinforce relational bonds with others, as some of the abbreviations in Table 4.1 illustrate.

Language can help us connect with others; it allows us to express affection, provide comfort and support, and share social information. Let's look at each of those primary social functions of language.

Language Expresses Affection Think about the people in your life to whom you feel the closest. How do you convey your feelings of love and appreciation to them? Although you probably use some nonverbal behaviors—such as smiling, hugging, and kissing—chances are you also express your feelings verbally.

Language has a profound ability to communicate affection. Some statements express our fondness for another person, such as "I like you." Others reinforce the importance of our relationship with the person, such as "You're my best friend." Still others convey hopes or dreams for the future of the relationship, including "I can't wait until we get married." Finally, some statements express the value of the relationship by noting how we would feel without it, such as "My life would be empty without you." Statements such as those are characteristic of our closest personal relationships.

Research indicates that communicating affection is good both for relationships and for the people in them. For example, family studies researcher Ted Huston and his colleagues found that the more affection spouses communicated to each other during their first 2 years of marriage, the more likely they were to remain married 13 years later.[18] Other studies have found that expressing and receiving affection can produce several health benefits, including lower stress hormones,[19] better cardiovascular health,[20] lower cholesterol,[21] an improved ability to recover from stress,[22] lower average blood sugar (a risk factor for diabetes),[23] better mental health,[24] and lesser risk of developing clinical depression and anxiety.[25]

Language Provides Comfort From time to time, you probably need to comfort someone in distress. Your spoken exchanges with the individual can be mundane, as when you soothe a child with a stubbed toe, or they can occur in extraordinary circumstances, as when you offer support to someone grieving the loss of her romantic partner to a fatal

Table 4.1 Connecting by Text and Tweet

When communicating by text or tweet, many people use abbreviations for common phrases to connect to others efficiently. Here are some popular abbreviations and their meanings.

WRUD	What are you doing?
FYEO	For your eyes only
UG2BK	You've got to be kidding
TTYL	Talk to you later
HAND	Have a nice day
LOL	Laugh out loud
PCM	Please call me
KUTGW	Keep up the good work
LMIRL	Let's meet in real life
^5	High five

Research shows that communicating affection with our loved ones helps to keep us happy and healthy.

war injury. Perhaps you can recall situations when you have been in distress yourself and another's comforting words calmed you.

We also use written messages to convey support to others. Consider that the U.S. greeting card industry is a $10 billion-a-year business. Although people send cards to acknowledge birthdays and to communicate good wishes for holidays, they also use greeting cards, such as get-well and sympathy cards, to extend verbal messages of comfort.[26] In addition, there are cards that express gratitude and ones that convey hope. Bluemountain.com, a website from which people can send free electronic greeting cards, offers e-cards in several special categories related to comfort and healing, including cards for the families of deployed military personnel and for the remembrance of victims of the September 11 attacks.[27]

Language Conveys Social Information A third way in which language connects people is by allowing us to share social information, which includes facts and opinions we have of others. We often do so by engaging in **gossip,** which is informal—and frequently judgmental—talk about people who are not present during the conversation. Gossip is a common communicative behavior in all sorts of social group settings, from neighborhoods to offices to churches and synagogues.[28]

Many people frown on gossip—even those who engage in it themselves—because it frequently involves spreading negative information about others. Although we sometimes gossip about people's positive qualities, such as talking about a coworker's new promotion, research shows that we are far more likely to gossip about a person's negative features or behaviors.[29] Moreover, studies indicate that most people enjoy hearing negative gossip more than positive gossip.[30] How, then, does engaging in gossip help us connect with others?

According to researchers, gossip serves to strengthen the social bonds between those who exchange it.[31] Like sharing secrets, sharing gossip with someone requires us to trust that person to handle the information sensitively. Thus, we don't typically share gossip with strangers or people we don't like; rather, it's usually with people we trust and feel close to. Sharing gossip with someone therefore implies a level of trust in, and closeness to, that person. In that way, engaging in gossip can reinforce personal relationships among

gossip Informal, and frequently judgmental, talk about people who are not present.

the people in the conversation, even if it involves sharing negative information about someone who is not present.

The utility of gossip has spurred a proliferation of gossip websites on the Internet. Most of those provide gossip about celebrities and their lives. Many gossip sites are extraordinarily popular. One such site—omg.yahoo.com—boasts over 14 million visitors per month, a testament to how much people enjoy engaging in gossip about others.[32]

As we've seen, we can use language to express feelings of love and affection, provide comfort and support, and reinforce our social bonds through gossip. In these ways, language can serve to connect us to others. Language can also separate us from others by causing hurt, as the following discussion reveals.

LANGUAGE SEPARATES US FROM OTHERS

During election years, it is common for political candidates to run negative campaign advertisements that focus on the shortcomings of a candidate's opponent. Such ads make misleading claims about an opponent's position on issues, or derogatory statements about his or her character and values. Although viewers often perceive negative campaign ads as distasteful, research demonstrates that these appeals can strongly influence voters by mobilizing them around their candidate of choice[33] and encouraging them to vote accordingly.[34] In those ways, the negative language in such advertisements is effective not by bringing people together but by separating them—ideologically, at least—from one another.

Although gossip is frequently judgmental, sharing gossip can reinforce our social bonds to others.

You may have grown up hearing that "sticks and stones might break my bones, but words can never hurt me." According to this common American idiom, language has no power to cause people pain. Your own experiences, however, have probably taught you that the opposite is true: Words can hurt us in profound and enduring ways. Two forms of language that can be especially harmful are criticisms and threats.

Criticisms **Criticism** is the act of passing judgment on someone or something. When you say what you like or dislike about an organization's public relations campaign, a coworker's new reading glasses, or your grandmother's cooking, you're expressing criticism.

Criticism is often difficult to hear. Especially when it comes from people whom we respect or love, criticism can make us feel hurt, unappreciated, and incompetent. These reactions are magnified when we receive *destructive criticism,* which occurs when we feel that someone is criticizing us to put us down or destroy our self-confidence. As The Dark Side box describes, destructive criticism that is too frequent or harsh can constitute verbal abuse. Most of us would likely prefer to receive *constructive criticism,* as we do when we feel that someone is criticizing us to help us improve.

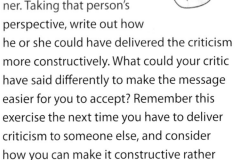

SHARPEN
Your Skills

Recall the last time someone criticized you in a harsh manner. Taking that person's perspective, write out how he or she could have delivered the criticism more constructively. What could your critic have said differently to make the message easier for you to accept? Remember this exercise the next time you have to deliver criticism to someone else, and consider how you can make it constructive rather than destructive.

Threats A second form of language that can cause hurt is a **threat,** a declaration of the intention to harm someone. Some threats promise harm only if the receiver does or doesn't do something specific ("If you touch my car, I'll break your neck"). Statements such as those are intended to motivate or to prevent particular actions. Instead of using persuasion to accomplish those goals (a topic we'll take up later in this chapter), threats telegraph the promise of harm. As a result, they often evoke fear on the part of the receiver, who may feel coerced into doing as the speaker says to avoid being hurt. Threats of physical harm to another person, a person's family, or a person's property violate the law in most jurisdictions in the United States, even if the threatened harm is never enacted.

Criticisms and threats can separate us from others by causing emotional pain and fear. Those negative feelings are probably magnified when the person criticizing or threatening us is someone with whom we have close emotional ties, such as a family member, a good friend, or a romantic partner.

criticism The act of passing judgment on someone or something.

threat A declaration of the intention to harm someone.

Crossing the Line:
When Criticism Becomes Abuse

In personal relationships, when one person continually criticizes another in destructive rather than constructive ways, that behavior can qualify as *verbal abuse*. Verbal abuse can produce long-term psychological and emotional damage and can also be accompanied by physical aggression or violence.

Verbal abuse is especially damaging to children, who depend on their parents and loved ones for protection and who lack the ability to process criticism cognitively rather than emotionally. According to the organization Prevent Child Abuse America, verbally abused children are likely to become depressed and socially withdrawn and to have difficulty making and keeping friends. That organization strongly encourages parents to seek help if they have difficulty managing stress so that they won't take their stress out on their children in the form of critical language.

Thus far, we've seen how language can express who we are, connect us to others, and separate us from others. Words can also motivate us to behave in certain ways, a topic we'll explore next.

LANGUAGE MOTIVATES ACTION

One of an advertiser's most powerful tools for selling a product or a service is the *slogan,* a short and memorable phrase that will motivate people to become customers. Effective slogans become ingrained in our subconscious, causing us to recall them with minimal effort. How many times have you heard "Visa—it's everywhere you want to be," "Nike—just do it," and "What happens in Vegas, stays in Vegas"? The purpose of an advertising slogan isn't just to be memorable, however: It's also to motivate you to buy the advertised product or service.

Just as advertisers use language, in the form of slogans, to motivate buying behavior, we can use various forms of language to motivate others to think or act in particular ways. Words can be powerfully persuasive if we choose them correctly. **Persuasion** is the process of convincing people that they should think or act in a certain way. Every time we watch a TV commercial, read a pop-up ad on the Internet, or listen to a political speech, someone is trying to influence what we believe or how we will behave.

Let's say that you've decided to run in a 10-kilometer race to benefit the local children's hospital, and you're trying to persuade your relatives, friends, and co-workers to make pledges to sponsor you. What are some ways of asking for their sponsorship that would encourage them to agree?

persuasion The process of convincing people to think or act in a certain way.

anchor-and-contrast approach A persuasion technique by which one precedes a desired request with a request that is outrageously large.

Anchor and Contrast One strategy is to use what researchers call an **anchor-and-contrast approach.** With that technique, you first craft a request that is so large that few people will agree to do it. That sweeping request is the anchor. After people reject the anchor, you ask for what you actually want, which, by comparison to the anchor, will seem reasonable to most people and thus will encourage them to comply. To solicit sponsors for your 10K run, for instance, you could write a letter giving people the following sponsorship options:

- $40 per kilometer, or $400 in total
- $20 per kilometer, or $200 in total
- $10 per kilometer, or $100 in total
- $5 per kilometer, or $50 in total

If you simply asked people to pledge $50 or even $100, many probably would decline on the grounds that those amounts are too costly. But $50 doesn't seem so unreasonable when it is contrasted with anchors of larger amounts, such as $200 and $400. In fact, it appears quite reasonable by comparison, and the fact that your potential sponsors will see it as such will likely increase the persuasive success of your appeal.[35]

Norm of Reciprocity You may have heard the old saying, "One good turn deserves another." This idea suggests that when someone gives you some type of gift or resource, you are expected to return the favor. Sociologist Alvin Gouldner called that expectation the **norm of reciprocity.**[36] Because of the norm of reciprocity, we should feel a sense of duty to help people who have helped us in the past.[37] Businesses and organizations appeal to reciprocity any time they offer you free samples of their products. You might employ that persuasive technique when soliciting sponsorships for your 10K race by reminding people of ways in which you have helped them in the past.

Social Validation A third persuasive strategy is to invoke the **social validation principle,** which maintains that people will comply with requests if they believe that others are also complying.[38] Whenever advertisers say that "four out of five people preferred" a certain brand of car, refrigerator, or toilet bowl cleaner, they are hoping you will want to buy the same brand that most people are buying. The idea is that you gain social approval by acting the way others act. So, to the extent that social approval is important to you, the quest for approval can influence the decisions you make. When soliciting sponsors for your 10K race, you could invoke the social validation principle by pointing out how many others have already sponsored you.

Expressing our identities, connecting us to others, separating us from others, and motivating action aren't the only functions that language serves. However, they are among the most relevant to our day-to-day lives as communicators.

Test Yourself

- **What forms of language are related to credibility?**
- **In what ways do we express affection to others verbally?**
- **What is the difference between a criticism and a threat?**
- **How can you use the social validation principle to persuade someone?**

>> Ways We Use and Abuse Language

We've seen that language serves a wide variety of functions. Now let's survey the ways in which language also varies in its form. Some forms, including humor, are generally positive and can produce good outcomes, such as entertaining others, strengthening relationships, and even contributing to healing. Other forms, such as hate speech, can cause devastating hurt. In this section, we explore several different forms of language—humor, euphemism, slang, defamation, profanity, and hate speech—and discover that many of these forms are neither entirely good nor entirely bad.

HUMOR: WHAT'S SO FUNNY?

A few years ago, psychologist Richard Wiseman designed a study on the Internet with an ambitious goal: to discover the world's funniest joke. More than 2 million people from

norm of reciprocity The expectation that favors are reciprocated.

social validation principle The idea that people will comply with requests if they believe that others are also complying.

around the world visited his website and rated some 40,000 jokes for their level of humor. Here was the winning entry—the funniest joke in the world:

> *Two hunters are out in the woods when one of them collapses. He doesn't seem to be breathing, and his eyes are glazed. The other guy takes out his phone and calls the emergency services. He gasps: "My friend is dead! What can I do?" The operator says: "Calm down, I can help. First, let's make sure he's dead." There is a silence, then a gunshot is heard. Back on the phone, the guy says: "Okay, now what?"* [39]

Humor can enhance the closeness of our social and personal relationships. It can also demean or offend others if used inappropriately.

Not everyone finds that joke funny, and some may even find it offensive. Regardless, you can probably recognize the humor in it. The joke contains what researchers believe to be the most important aspect of humor: a violation of our expectations. [40] Most of us would interpret the operator's statement ("Let's make sure he's dead") as a suggestion to check the hunter's vital signs, not as a recommendation to shoot him. It's this twist on our expectations that makes the joke funny. In fact, researchers have discovered that specific parts of the brain process humor and that without the violation of expectations—without the punch line—those neurological structures don't "light up" or provide the mental reward we associate with a good joke. [41]

Humor can enhance our communication and associations with others in many ways. It can bring us closer to people and make social interaction more pleasant and enjoyable. [42] It can defuse stress, such as the tension that occurs when people are in conflict with one another. [43] Within relationships, "inside jokes" can reinforce people's feelings of intimacy. Humor can provide so many personal and social benefits, in fact, that a good sense of humor is a strongly desired characteristic that both women and men seek in a romantic partner. [44]

Not all effects of humor are positive, however. Humor can also demean individuals and social or cultural groups, as in the case of racial jokes and gags about elderly people or persons with disabilities. Moreover, even when they are made without the intention to offend, jokes told at another's expense can cause embarrassment or distress and might even qualify as harassment. [45] When using humor, it's therefore essential to take stock of your audience to make certain that your jokes will amuse rather than offend.

EUPHEMISMS: SUGAR COATING

Some topics are difficult or impolite to talk about directly. In those cases, we might use a **euphemism,** a vague, mild expression that symbolizes and substitutes for something that is blunter or harsher. Instead of saying that someone has died, for instance, we might say that he has "passed away," and rather than mentioning that she is pregnant, a woman might say that she's "expecting." You can probably think of many different euphemisms, including to "let go" (instead of to "fire") and to "sleep together" (instead of to "have sex"). In February 2004, when Janet Jackson's top came undone on live television during the half-time show of the Super Bowl, network executives infamously downplayed the incident by referring to it euphemistically as a "wardrobe malfunction."

Typically, the euphemistic term sounds less harsh or less explicit than the term it stands for, and that's the point. We use euphemisms when we want to talk about sensitive topics without making others feel embarrassed or offended. [46] Yet euphemisms require more than just a technical understanding of the language (English, French, Japanese, and so on) in which they are made; they also require an understanding of cultural idioms. That understanding is necessary because euphemisms often have a literal meaning that differs from their euphemistic meaning. For example, at a literal level, the phrase "sleep together" simply means to engage in sleep while together. If you didn't realize that is a cultural euphemism for "have sex," then you wouldn't understand the meaning when it is used in that way.

euphemism A vague, mild expression that symbolizes and substitutes for something blunter or harsher.

slang Informal and unconventional words often understood only within a particular group.

SLANG: THE LANGUAGE OF CO-CULTURES

Closely related to euphemism is **slang,** the use of informal and unconventional words that often are understood only by others in a particular group. If you grew up in Boston, for instance, you probably know that "Rhodie" is a slang term for people from nearby Rhode Island. In Australia, "snag" is slang for "sausage." On the Internet, a "blog" is a web page featuring ongoing news or commentary, and a "hacker" is someone who creates or modifies computer software.

Slang can serve an important social function by helping people distinguish between those who do and don't belong to their particular social networks. Many social, cultural, and religious groups have their own terminology for certain ideas, and a person's ability to use a group's slang appropriately can "mark" him or her as belonging to that group. For instance, if you don't know that "bubbly-jock" means "turkey," you're probably not from Scotland, and if you don't know whether you're in "T Town" (Texarkana) or "Big T" (Tucson), chances are you're not a trucker.

A form of informal speech closely related to slang is **jargon,** the technical vocabulary of a certain occupation or profession. Jargon allows members of that occupation or profession to communicate with one another precisely and efficiently. For example, many law enforcement officers in North America talk to one another using *ten-codes,* or number combinations that represent common phrases. In that jargon, "10-4" means that you've received another person's message. Health care providers also use jargon specific to their profession—for instance, referring to a heart attack as a "myocardial infarction." Other occupations and professions that have their own jargon include attorneys, engineers, dancers, airplane pilots, television producers, and military personnel.

Like humor and euphemisms, slang and jargon are neither inherently good nor inherently bad. As we've considered, those forms of language serve many positive purposes, among them reaffirming our membership in a particular social community. Whether you're into surfing or wine tasting, doing calligraphy or restoring vintage cars, learning and using the slang appropriate to those interests serves as a type of membership badge that connects you with others like yourself.

By the same token, however, using slang and jargon can also make people feel like outsiders. If you're a police officer, for instance, saying that you're "10-7" instead of "done for the day" might make people around you who are not in law enforcement feel excluded from the conversation. For that reason you should consider how your use of slang and jargon might come across to others around you.

SHARPEN
Your Skills

Many groups of people have their own slang. Pair up with a classmate whose hobbies and interests are very different from yours, and learn some of the slang common to groups that pursue such interests.

DEFAMATION: HARMFUL WORDS

In January 2008, baseball pitcher Roger Clemens filed a lawsuit against former New York Yankees trainer Brain McNamee. In a report released a month earlier, McNamee had informed investigators that while working as Clemens's strength trainer, he had repeatedly injected the pitching ace with Winstrol, a performance-enhancing steroid, in violation of

In 2008, Roger Clemens sued his former trainer, Brian McNamee, for defamation.

jargon Technical vocabulary of a certain occupation or profession.

91

the law. In his lawsuit, Clemens claimed that McNamee's statements not only were untrue but had damaged Clemens's professional reputation.

Clemens's claim was that McNamee had engaged in **defamation,** language that harms a person's reputation or gives that person a negative image. Defamation comes in two forms. The first, *libel,* refers to defamatory statements made in print or some other fixed medium, such as a photograph or a motion picture. The second, *slander,* is a defamatory statement that is made aloud, within earshot of others.

For instance, let's say that Aliyah wants to open a day care center in a town where Toni also operates one. To discourage parents from using Aliyah's center, Toni circulates rumors that Aliyah has been charged with child molestation. That statement is defamatory because it harms Aliyah's reputation and could cause her financial damage in the form of lost business.

Should making negative statements about a person qualify as slander if those statements are true? Why or why not?

Does it matter whether Toni's accusation is true? Usually the answer is yes: Under most legal systems, a statement must be false to be considered libel or slander. There are situations, however, when even a true accusation can qualify. Those cases often involve public figures, such as politicians and celebrities, and they hinge on the importance of the information for the public. Disclosing in print that a senator has tested positive for HIV, for example, might qualify as libel even when it is true, *if* disclosing the information serves no prevailing public interest.

PROFANITY: OFFENSIVE LANGUAGE

Profanity is language that is considered vulgar, rude, or obscene in the context in which it is used. We sometimes call profane terms *swear words* or *curse words,* and they come in many forms. Some profane terms are meant to put down certain groups of people, as in calling a person a "bitch" or a "fag." (Many of those also qualify as instances of hate speech, our next topic.) Other terms attack religious beliefs or figures considered sacred by followers of a particular religion. Still others describe sexual acts or refer to people's sexual organs or bodily functions. Finally, some are general expressions of anger or disappointment, such as "Damn!"

Like other forms of language, profanity is context-specific: What makes a word profane is that it is considered rude or obscene in the language and context in which it is used. For instance, calling a woman a "bitch" might be profane, but using the same term to describe a female dog is not. In the United States, "fag" is derogatory expression for gay men, but to the British, it refers to a cigarette. Some swear words translate across languages; for example, the expression "Damn" in English is "Zut" in French and "Verflucht" in German and can be profane in all of them. Other words appear to be unique to certain languages; for instance, a Dutch speaker might say "Krijg de pest!" which translates to "Go get infected with the plague!"

Profanity has many different effects on social interaction. Often, it makes people feel uncomfortable or insulted. In recent years, some social groups have recognized that they can negate the effect of certain profane terms themselves by making the terms more commonplace, in this way reducing or eliminating their shock value. That practice is called *reclaiming* the term. For instance, when homosexuals call one another "queers," their intent is not to offend but rather to remove the power to insult from the word.

Not all effects of profanity are negative. In certain contexts, the use of profanity can act as a social lubricant by maintaining an informal social atmosphere. Profanity is a common element in comedy, for instance, partly because it creates an expectation that nothing is taboo in that context and that ideas can flow freely. In addition, using profanity within one's own social network can reinforce interpersonal bonds by sending the metamessage that "I feel comfortable enough with you to use profanity in your presence."

defamation Language that harms a person's reputation or image.

profanity Language considered to be vulgar, rude, or obscene.

hate speech Language used to degrade, intimidate, or dehumanize specific groups of people.

HATE SPEECH: PROFANITY WITH A HURTFUL PURPOSE

Hate speech is a specific form of profanity meant to degrade, intimidate, or dehumanize people based on their sex, national origin, sexual orientation, religion, race, disability status, or political or moral views.[47] Calling people derogatory names, intimidating them, and advocating violence against groups of individuals might all qualify as hate speech. For instance, the terms *bitch* and *fag* can be used not only as profanity but also as hate speech if they're directed at women or homosexuals with the intent to degrade or intimidate them.

Two notorious incidents have brought widespread public attention to the issue of hate speech. After being pulled over and detained in July 2006 on suspicion of driving while intoxicated, film actor Mel Gibson reportedly made several derogatory comments to deputies about Jewish people. Four months later, during a standup routine at a comedy club, television actor Michael Richards made inflammatory remarks about African Americans, reportedly using the "n-word" more than half a dozen times. Although authorities did not formally charge either star with having committed a hate crime, those incidents have fueled public debate over whether hate speech should be illegal.

Many instances of hate speech have incited violence, particularly when they have touched on sensitive issues such as race.

As communication professor Michael Waltman and his colleagues have noted, the use of hate speech is increasingly common online.[48] In 2006, the Federal Bureau of Investigation (FBI) arrested Randall Ashby in Delaware for allegedly sending hate speech by e-mail to the National Association for the Advancement of Colored People (NAACP).[49] In his e-mail message, Ashby had told NAACP members that "you are no match for our numbers and our power" and suggested that they would be victimized in their sleep. The FBI determined that the e-mail message violated a federal law prohibiting the interstate communication of a threat. Several laws and regulations in North America restrict hate speech and other acts of intimidation against minority groups and punish people who engage in them.

In summary, language comes in many forms, including humor, euphemism, slang, libel and slander, profanity, and hate speech. Some of those forms, such as humor, generally have positive effects but can also produce unwanted negative outcomes. Other forms, such as profanity, are generally negative even though they can have positive effects on the people using them. Understanding the positive and negative aspects of these diverse forms of language helps us to appreciate the power and complexity of verbal communication.

By the Numbers

5

Number of U.S. states that do not have hate crime laws punishing behavior such as hate speech. Those states are Wyoming, Arkansas, Indiana, South Carolina, and Georgia.

Test Yourself

- **What makes a joke funny?**
- **What are the purposes of using euphemisms?**
- **In what ways does the use of slang reflect a person's co-cultures?**
- **How does libel differ from slander?**
- **What makes a word or phrase profane?**
- **What is hate speech?**

>> Improving Your Use of Language

This section presents three pieces of advice for improving verbal communication. Some of those tips may be more relevant to one situation than another, but collectively they can serve as a useful road map for fine-tuning your language use. Specifically, we will explore how to separate opinions from factual claims, speak at an appropriate level, and own your thoughts and feelings.

SEPARATE OPINIONS FROM FACTUAL CLAIMS

Many communicators have a tendency to conflate factual claims with personal opinions. A factual claim makes an assertion that we can verify with evidence and show to be true or false ("I've taken piano lessons for 10 years"). An opinion expresses a personal judgment or preference that we could agree or disagree with but that is not true or false in an absolute sense ("I'm a terrific piano player"). Competent communicators know how to keep opinions and factual claims separate in verbal communication. Unfortunately, distinguishing factual claims from opinions is easier said than done, especially when we're dealing with strong opinions on emotionally heated issues.

Let's say that you and several friends are discussing an upcoming election in which you're choosing between two candidates. Half of you prefer Candidate C, the conservative, and the other half prefer Candidate L, the liberal. Imagine that one of your friends makes the following statements:

- "Candidate C has more experience in government." That is a factual claim because we can show it to be true or false by looking at the candidates' records.
- "Candidate L is the better choice for our future." That is an opinion because it expresses a value judgment (this candidate is *better*) that we cannot objectively validate.
- "Candidate C is immoral." That is an opinion because the truth of the claim depends on the speaker's (in this case, your friend's) morals. Morals are subjective; therefore, the statement can't be proved true or false in an absolute sense.
- "Candidate L accepted illegal bribes." That is a factual claim because it is possible to examine the evidence to discover whether it's true.

Opinions and factual claims require different types of responses. Suppose that you tell me "Candidate C has never held an elective office," and I reply by saying "I disagree." That isn't a competent response. You have made a factual claim, which by definition is either true or false. Therefore, whether I agree with it is irrelevant. I can agree or disagree

Which pianist is expressing an opinion, and which is making a factual claim?

How Well Can You Distinguish Opinions from Factual Claims?

The ability to separate opinions from factual claims is an essential skill for effective verbal communication. How well can you spot the difference? Read each of the following statements. Assuming nothing more than what the statement tells you, indicate whether you think the statement is an opinion or a factual claim by placing a checkmark in the appropriate column.

		Opinion	Factual Claim
1.	Britney Spears is the best singer in the world.	_____	_____
2.	Television was invented in the 1920s.	_____	_____
3.	Religious people are happier than nonreligious people.	_____	_____
4.	The United States is better off with a Democrat as president.	_____	_____
5.	Men talk as much as women do.	_____	_____
6.	Same-sex couples should not be allowed to marry.	_____	_____
7.	Children should be required to learn a foreign language.	_____	_____
8.	Neil Armstrong was the first person to walk on the moon.	_____	_____
9.	Dogs have a keener sense of smell than people do.	_____	_____
10.	Abortion should be legal in the United States.	_____	_____

Statements 1, 4, 6, 7, and 10 are all opinions. Statements 2, 3, 5, 8, and 9 are all factual claims. How well did you do? If you missed some of the answers, don't worry—distinguishing opinions from factual claims can be harder than it seems.

---

with an opinion, but a factual claim is either true or false no matter how I feel about it. Instead, if I had responded to your statement by saying "I think you're incorrect," that would be a competent reply because we would now be discussing the *truth* of your statement rather than my agreement with it.

How good are you at distinguishing opinions from factual claims? Check out The Competent Communicator box to find out.

As you develop that skill, keep two principles in mind. First, *opinions are opinions whether you agree with them or not*. If you believe that abortion should be legal in the United States, for instance, you might be inclined to call that statement a fact. It isn't, though. It is still a statement of opinion because it expresses an evaluation about what "should be." Second, *factual claims are factual claims whether they are true or not*. If you think it's untrue that religious people are happier than nonreligious people, for instance, you might be inclined to call that statement an opinion. It isn't, though. Even if the statement isn't true, it is still a factual claim because it expresses something that can be verified by evidence.

Although it's probably more difficult to separate opinions from facts when you feel strongly about an issue, that's often when it is most important to do so. Instead of telling others that their positions on sensitive issues are right or wrong, state that you agree or disagree with their

SHARPEN
Your Skills

Separating facts and opinions can be tricky, not only when you're speaking but also when you're listening to others. Practice that skill by watching a television newscast or reading an Internet blog. For each statement you hear or read, ask yourself if it is a fact, an opinion, or some other type of statement (such as an instruction). Remember that facts make claims that can be verified with evidence, whereas opinions express a person's judgments or evaluations about something. With practice, you'll sharpen your ability to distinguish opinions from facts.

positions. That language expresses your own position and acknowledges that different—even contradictory—opinions may also exist.

SPEAK AT AN APPROPRIATE LEVEL

Efficacious linguistic devices must demonstrate isomorphism with the cerebral aptitude of the assemblage. If the meaning of that statement isn't exactly clear, the reason is that the language is inappropriately complex. What the statement means is that good messages must be understandable to listeners.

Part of being an effective verbal communicator is knowing how simple or how complex your language should be for your audience. A competent instructor, for instance, knows to use simpler language when teaching an introductory course than when teaching an advanced course because students in each class will have different levels of understanding. When you use language that is too complex for your listeners, you are *talking over their heads.* If you have been in a situation where someone has talked over your head, you know how hard it can be to understand what the speaker is trying to say.

The opposite problem is *talking down* to people, or using language that is inappropriately simple. Talking down often happens by mistake. You might provide unnecessary detail when giving someone driving directions, for example, because you don't realize that he or she is familiar with the area. At other times, overly simple language is used on purpose. That behavior can make listeners feel patronized, disrespected, or even insulted.

OWN YOUR THOUGHTS AND FEELINGS

People often use language that shifts responsibility for their thoughts and feelings onto others. Perhaps, for example, when your academic adviser doesn't understand you, she typically says "You're not being clear," but when you don't understand her, she says "You're not paying attention." By using that language pattern, your adviser blames you for misunderstandings but takes no responsibility for her own role in the communication process. In reality, the problem may be that your adviser herself might not be paying attention or that she might not be using clearly understandable language.

I-statement A statement that claims ownership of the communicator's feelings or thoughts.

you-statement A statement that shifts responsibility for the communicator's feelings or thoughts to the other party in the communication.

Good communicators take responsibility for their thoughts and feelings by using I-statements rather than you-statements. An **I-statement** claims ownership of what a communicator is feeling or thinking, whereas a **you-statement** shifts that responsibility to the other person. Instead of saying, "You're not being clear," your adviser might say, "I'm hav-

Table 4.2 Examples of You-Statements and I-Statements

You-Statement	I-Statement
You're making me mad.	I'm mad right now.
You're not listening to me.	I'm feeling ignored.
You don't know what you're doing.	I don't think this task is getting done right.
You hurt my feelings.	My feelings are hurt.
You're not making any sense.	I'm having trouble understanding you.

ing a hard time understanding you." Rather than saying "You make me mad," you might say "I'm angry right now." Table 4.2 provides examples of you-statements and I-statements.

I-statements don't ignore the problem; instead, they allow the communicator to claim ownership of his or her feelings. That ownership is important because it acknowledges that the individual controls how he or she thinks and feels. Constructive I-statements include four parts that clearly express that ownership:

- "I feel _____" *This expresses responsibility for your own feelings.*
- "when you _____" *This identifies the behavior that is prompting your feelings.*
- "because _____" *This points to the characteristic of the behavior that is prompting your feelings.*
- "and I would appreciate it if you would _____" *This offers an alternative to the behavior.*

When do you tend to use you-statements? When are you more likely to use I-statements?

Remember that other people can't control our thoughts and feelings unless we let them. Effective communicators therefore speak in ways that acknowledge responsibility for and ownership of the ways they feel and think.

You were not born using language. Rather, you had to *learn* how to use it. You can also learn to use it better. By distinguishing opinions from statements of fact, speaking at a level that is appropriate for your audience, and taking ownership of your thoughts and feelings, you will be empowered to express yourself effectively in a broad range of social and professional situations.

Learning how to communicate better is an ongoing process.

- How do we distinguish opinions from facts?
- Why is it important to speak at an appropriate level?
- What are the four components of a constructive I-statement?

For REVIEW >>

- **What are the defining characteristics of language?**

  Language is a structured system of symbols used for communicating meaning. Language is symbolic, usually arbitrary, and rule-governed; it has layers of meaning and varies in clarity; and it is bound by context and culture.

- **For what reasons do people use language?**

  People use language to express who they are, to connect to others, to separate themselves from others, and to motivate action. Common uses and abuses of language include humor, euphemism, slang, defamation, profanity, and hate speech.

- **How can you use language more effectively?**

  You can improve your language skills by separating opinions from factual claims, speaking at an appropriate level for your audience, and owning your thoughts and feelings.

Pop Quiz

Multiple Choice

1. The dictionary definition of a word is its _____ meaning, whereas the implication of that word is its _____ meaning.
   a. denotative; connotative
   b. connotative; denotative
   c. denotative; relational
   d. connotative; relational

2. The term for the type of rule that governs the order of words within phrases is
   a. phonological
   b. syntactic
   c. semantic
   d. pragmatic

3. The idea that language shapes our views of reality by influencing how various cultures see the world is reflected in
   a. the semantic triangle
   b. the ladder of abstraction
   c. the Sapir-Whorf hypothesis
   d. communication accommodation theory

4. A vague, mild expression that symbolizes something that is blunter or harsher is
   a. a euphemism
   b. an equivocation
   c. euthanasia
   d. an ambiguity

5. Reminding others of favors you have done for them in the past can constitute the persuasive tactic known as
   a. anchor and contrast
   b. norm of reciprocity
   c. social validation
   d. pragmatic rules

Fill in the Blank

6. Because language is _____, each word represents a particular object or idea, but it does not constitute the object or idea itself.

7. A statement that we can interpret to have more than one meaning is an example of _____.

8. _____ rules allow an individual to connect the word *lawyer* with the meaning "attorney."

9. The idea that we can conceive of something only if we have a word for it is known as _____.

10. Terms or phrases that are intended to mislead listeners by implying something that they don't actually say are known as _____.

KEY TERMS

language 76

denotative meaning 78

connotative meaning 78

loaded language 80

ambiguous language 80

Sapir-Whorf hypothesis 81

credibility 83

gossip 86

criticism 87

threat 87

persuasion 88

anchor-and-contrast approach 88

norm of reciprocity 89

social validation principle 89

euphemism 90

slang 90

jargon 91

defamation 92

profanity 92

hate speech 92

I-statement 96

you-statement 96

5

COMMUN

A TOUCHING MOMENT FOR THE FIRST LADY

In April 2009, during her first visit to England as First Lady of the United States, Michelle Obama created a public stir when she put her arm around Queen Elizabeth II as a gesture of friendship. Although such friendly physical contact is natural in U.S. culture, it was a breach of protocol in Great Britain, where visitors to the royal palace are sternly warned never to touch the queen unless reciprocating a handshake. The no-touch rule reflects a long historical tradition of considering kings and queens to possess divine powers, including the power to cure disease through touch. If a monarch's touch could heal, people believed, the ruler should conserve that power by not allowing others to touch him or her.

Even though such beliefs are no longer widely held, official protocol still prohibits touching a king or queen in most instances. Many people in England were therefore shocked to see Michelle Obama with her arm around the queen. The queen's spokespeople insisted afterward, however, that she took no offense at the First Lady's affectionate gesture.

ICATING
NONVERBALLY

- How do people communicate nonverbally?
- How do culture and sex influence nonverbal behavior?
- In what ways can you improve your nonverbal communication skills?

Nonverbal communication is powerful stuff. Sometimes the smallest gesture—a glance; a warm vocal tone; a brief, affectionate touch with a foreign head of state—can send unmistakable messages about ourselves to others. Moreover, so much of what we learn about other people's thoughts and feelings comes not through listening to their words but through observing their body language—watching their facial expressions, seeing how they move and gesture, and taking note of their eye contact. Those and other behaviors can "speak" volumes about people in efficient and sometimes subtle ways.

>> The Nature and Functions of Nonverbal Communication

On the animated TV show *The Simpsons,* Marge Simpson is seldom shy about expressing disapproval when her husband Homer or her son Bart misbehaves. She frequently communicates her feelings through her facial expressions, posture, and stressful grunts when she's annoyed. Those and other nonverbal communication behaviors clearly convey Marge's state of mind to everyone around her. What makes nonverbal behavior such an effective form of communication? We'll find out in this section, first by differentiating nonverbal from verbal communication and then by examining five of its most important characteristics.

WHAT IS NONVERBAL COMMUNICATION?

Nonverbal means just what it sounds like—not verbal. Nonverbal communication requires neither words nor language. How else do we communicate with others, if not with words and language?

The answer is, in many ways. We can tell a great deal about people by watching their facial expressions, for instance, or by listening to the tone of their voice. Think about it: When you listen to your doctor tell you the results of your recent blood tests, you might hear tension in her voice and determine that something is wrong, or you might see a pleasant look on her face and conclude that everything is fine. We also interpret people's gestures and the way they carry themselves: You see two teenage boys punching each other and determine from their behaviors that they are playing rather than genuinely fighting. Sometimes we even perceive others based on the way they use their time and the space around them: Perhaps you try talking with your boss about your

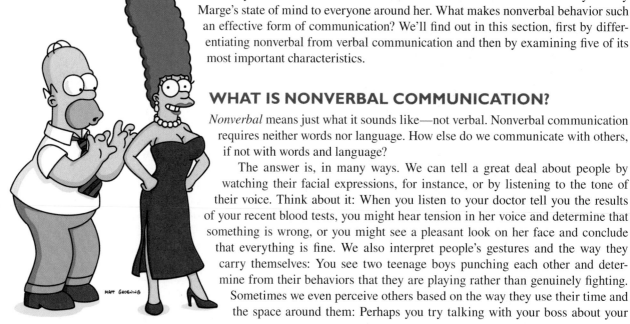

MATT GROENING

recent evaluation and you feel ignored because he keeps looking at his iPhone. People routinely communicate more information through their nonverbal behaviors than they do through spoken language. So when it comes to communication, actions often do speak louder than words.

We can define **nonverbal communication** as those behaviors and characteristics that convey meaning without the use of words. Importantly, nonverbal communication behaviors sometimes *accompany* verbal messages, to clarify or reinforce them. For instance, if someone asks you which direction to go to find the bookstore, and you point and say, "It's that way," your nonverbal behavior (pointing) clarifies the meaning of your verbal message. If you just say, "It's that way" without pointing, your verbal message is ambiguous—and not especially helpful. At other times, however, nonverbal communication behaviors convey meaning on their own. If you ask me where the bookstore is and I shrug my shoulders, you will probably infer from my behavior that I don't know, even though I never actually said so.

Nonverbal behavior is a powerful way of communicating, and it comes naturally to many of us. In fact, we often engage in nonverbal behavior so effortlessly that you might wonder why you need to study it. The truth is, even though we frequently enact nonverbal behaviors and encounter them in others, there's a lot more to interpreting them than you might think. In an episode of the TV sitcom *Seinfeld,* for instance, Jerry, Elaine, and George visit with Jerry's accountant, Barry, who seems to be sniffing frequently. After Barry leaves, Jerry and his friends try to figure out how to interpret Barry's sniffing behavior. Unable to settle on the cause, Jerry becomes increasingly concerned that Barry might be sniffing because of a drug addiction. Only at the end of the episode does Jerry discover that Barry was sniffing because he was allergic to the material in Jerry's sweater.

On the basis of nonverbal behaviors, we interpret the behavior of others as playful rather than aggressive.

SIX CHARACTERISTICS OF NONVERBAL COMMUNICATION

It's difficult to imagine life without nonverbal communication. The capacity to communicate without words is critical for those lacking in language ability. Such individuals include infants, who haven't learned yet how to speak, and people with certain neurological problems, like the effects of a stroke, that might limit their language use. But even people with language ability depend immensely on nonverbal communication. Because she had only a limited knowledge of Spanish, for instance, Bergitta relied heavily on nonverbal behaviors while traveling through Bolivia, Uruguay, and Argentina after graduation. She was frequently amazed at how well she could understand others simply by observing their gestures and facial expressions. Her communication was more challenging than it would have been if she had known the language, but she was still able to understand—and to be understood by others—through nonverbal behaviors.

Let's take a look at some of the most compelling reasons why nonverbal communication plays such an important role in human interaction.

Nonverbal Communication Is Present in Most Communication Contexts Whether you talk with people one-on-one or in a group, you have access not only to their spoken words but also to several dimensions of nonverbal communication. In many situations, you can watch people's facial expressions for signs of how they're feeling. For instance, you might tell from his facial expression that your supervisor is bored at a business lunch and eager to go home. Voice also conveys data about a person's state of mind. At a party, you can judge from the tone of her voice when your host is being serious and when she's kidding. Even the way people dress and smell can send you information. Glancing around the auditorium at a large business event, you might be able to guess which people are managers and which are staff members by the formality of their clothing. We are flooded with nonverbal signals in many kinds of social situations.

nonverbal communication Behaviors and characteristics that convey meaning without the use of words.

Communication in computer-mediated formats, such as e-mail, instant messaging, and text messaging, relies heavily on language. Even in these environments, however, people can still introduce nonverbal facial expressions through the use of emoticons (a word that means *emotional icons*). Here are some of the most common emoticons:

Smiles	:)	😊
Laughs	:D	😄
Frowns	:(	🙁
Winks	;)	😉
Kisses	:X	😚
Confusion	:/	😕
Sticking out tongue	:P	😛

FIGURE 5.1   Emoticons

In other communication contexts, such as talking on the telephone and sending e-mail messages, we don't have access to as many nonverbal cues as we do in face-to-face conversation. We still make use of what's available, however. Even if we haven't met those to whom we're speaking on the telephone, we can make judgments about them from certain qualities of their voices—noticing, for example, how fast they're talking, how loudly, with what tone, and with what type of accent. In electronically mediated communication—such as e-mail, instant messaging, and text messaging—we can introduce nonverbal cues through the use of **emoticons,** the familiar textual representations of facial expressions (Figure 5.1). There are also other cues to help us make judgments in electronic media, such as pauses and the use of all capital letters.

Most human communication includes at least some form of nonverbal behavior, and when we only have a few nonverbal signals to go on, we pay extra attention to those cues. For example, vocal characteristics, such as the tone and sound of one's voice, are important nonverbal cues in face-to-face conversation, but they are even more important on the telephone, where so many other nonverbal signals are unavailable. By the same token, when we lose the ability to use one of our senses in our communications, we typically compensate by relying more heavily on the remaining senses. People who are deaf pay extra attention to visual cues when communicating with others because they are unable to interpret vocal characteristics. Similarly, individuals with impaired vision often rely more heavily on hearing and touch to help them communicate, because they are unable to see gestures and facial expressions.

Nonverbal Communication Often Conveys More Information Than Verbal Communication Go to the self-help section of almost any bookstore, and open up titles such as *How to Read a Person Like a Book* and *The Power of Non-Verbal Communication: What You Do Is More Important Than What You Say.*[1] You'll probably get the impression that nearly all the information we get by communicating with others comes through nonverbal behavior. In fact, some unreliable but frequently cited studies have estimated that as much as 93 percent of meaning is transmitted nonverbally, leaving only 7 percent to be accounted for by the words we use.[2] Nonverbal communication isn't quite that powerful, however. More realistic estimates from nonverbal communication scholar Judee Burgoon suggest that 65 to 70 percent of meaning comes from nonverbal clues, whereas 30 to 35 percent comes from language.[3] In many situations, therefore, we do communicate more information through nonverbal behavior than we do through our words.

The most likely reason why nonverbal communication adds up to such a significant percentage is that it makes use of many **nonverbal channels,** which are the various behavioral forms that nonverbal communication takes. Some of those channels, including facial expressions, gestures, and personal appearance, rely on our sense of vision. Vocal characteristics—such as loudness, pitch, and tone of voice—engage our sense of hearing. We also use our senses of touch and smell to communicate. We often express different messages with a handshake and a hug, and we convey subtle messages about attraction to others through our use of smell.

We sometimes rely on clues from nonverbal channels to make sense of a situation when talking to others isn't a good option. Rick has learned that his alcoholic mother, Claudia,

emoticons Textual representations of facial expressions.

nonverbal channels The various behavioral forms that nonverbal communication takes.

has very unpredictable mood swings. When he gets home from school each day, he's never sure how she'll be feeling. Some days she's happy and outgoing; other days she's sullen and withdrawn. Occasionally, she'll start yelling at the slightest provocation. Over time, Rick has noticed that he can determine Claudia's mood without even talking to her: He needs only to look at her posture and facial expression to tell whether she's cheerful, depressed, or angry.

Why do you suppose that some people are better at "reading" nonverbal behaviors than others?

Nonverbal Communication Is Usually Believed over Verbal Communication It's not uncommon to get conflicting messages between what a person says and does. Most of the time, we believe the nonverbal clues.[4] Let's say you're waiting for your friend Joel at your favorite coffee shop. When he walks in, Joel slumps into the seat next to you, rolls his eyes, and sighs heavily. You ask him how he's doing, and he says, "It's been a *great* day." Joel's verbal behavior is sending you one message ("I'm having a great day"), but his nonverbal behavior is suggesting something quite different ("I'm having a lousy day"). Which of these contradictory messages do you believe? Most of us would put more stock in what Joel is *doing* than in what he is *saying*. In other words, as multiple studies have shown, we would believe his nonverbal message.

Why do we put our trust in nonverbal communication? Experts think we do so because most of us believe people have a harder time controlling nonverbal signals than verbal ones, so we think nonverbal behaviors more accurately reflect what a person is really thinking or feeling. It's easy for Joel to *say* he's having a great day, but if he feels frustrated or depressed, it's probably tougher for him to *act* as if his day is going well. When he slumps, rolls his eyes, and sighs, you probably conclude that his day is going poorly, despite what he says.

The human preference for believing nonverbal signals even when they conflict with words is especially critical for detecting **deception**—the act of leading someone to believe something one knows to be untrue—because people often have inconsistent verbal and nonverbal behaviors when they're lying. Imagine that Tawny misses her group study session for the third time because she overslept, yet she tells her study group that she was in the emergency room with a severe migraine. Tawny might feel nervous telling such a lie, especially because she knows she could be kicked out of the group if she were to get caught. Chances are that her nervousness will affect her nonverbal behavior. She might perspire, get dry in the mouth, sound unusually tense, and appear especially rigid in her posture. If Tawny really had been in the hospital as she said, there's probably no reason she would be nervous telling her study group about it. She would be able to explain her

We can often interpret a person's emotional state from his or her nonverbal signals.

deception The act of leading others to believe something the speaker knows to be untrue.

55

Percentage of time
when most people
can accurately detect
deception.[5]

medical emergency calmly and apologize for her absence. So, if she looks or sounds nervous, those nonverbal messages will contradict her verbal message and may give her group reason to think she's not telling the truth.

Nonverbal Communication Is the Primary Means of Expressing Emotion We have a large verbal vocabulary for describing our emotions, but our nonverbal behaviors do it much more efficiently. How many times have you been able to tell how someone is feeling just by looking at him or her? We might not always be right about the emotions we sense—and some of us are better than others at interpreting people's emotions—but research shows that humans are acutely sensitive to nonverbal emotion cues.[6] As we saw in the example above about Rick and his mother Claudia, Rick has developed the ability to interpret Claudia's emotional state accurately with just a glance, by paying attention to her facial expressions and posture.

Emotion is a powerful influence on our behavior, and our primary way of communicating how we feel is through our nonverbal behaviors. Two channels of nonverbal behavior that are particularly important in the communication of emotion are facial expressions and vocal behaviors.

Humans are highly visual beings, meaning that we tend to pay a lot of attention to people's facial expressions when we want to figure out their emotional state. We take close note of these expressions whether we're talking with them face-to-face, listening to them speak to a group, or even watching them on television. On reality TV shows such as *The Bachelor, Project Runway,* and *Extreme Makeover: Home Edition,* producers often shoot close-ups of people's faces during critical moments, to capture their facial expressions of emotion. Most of us can easily think of the type of facial expression that connotes happiness: The eyes tend to be wide and bright, and the person tends to be smiling. That look of happiness differs notably from the facial expressions we associate with anger, sadness, surprise, and disappointment. The distinctive patterns we perceive for each are keys to helping us interpret other people's emotions.

In fact, several studies suggest that facial expressions of these basic emotions are interpreted similarly across cultures.[7] For instance, psychologist Paul Ekman took photographs of people communicating six basic emotions through their facial expressions, including happiness, fear, disgust, anger, sadness, and surprise. He then showed the photos to participants in five different countries, including Chile, Brazil, Argentina, Japan, and the United States. He asked the participants to match each photograph with what they believed was the emotion being displayed. Ekman then compared the participants from different coun-

Reality television shows often capture images of intense emotional expressions.

tries and found that they were equally accurate at describing which emotion was displayed in each photograph.[8]

Similar studies have repeated those results using groups from a range of cultures, including Greek, Chinese, Turkish, Malaysian, Ethiopian, Swedish, Italian, Sumatran, Estonian, and Scottish.[9] The degree of similarity in interpretations of emotion displays does differ from culture to culture. It also differs from emotion to emotion, with certain facial displays of some emotions, such as happiness, being interpreted more consistently than others, such as fear.[10] Overall, however, it appears that facial expressions of our most basic emotions are interpreted similarly around the world.

We also pay attention to vocal cues to understand a person's emotional state. When someone is yelling and using harsh vocal tones, we usually infer that the person is angry, whereas laughter and lots of pitch variation suggest happiness or excitement. It turns out that we may be even more accurate at interpreting emotions through vocal cues than through facial expressions.[11] That appears to be particularly true when the vocal channel is the only accessible channel, such as when we're speaking with someone on the telephone. We don't necessarily get *more* information about individuals' emotional state from their voice than we do from their facial expressions, but we may get *more accurate* information.

SHARPEN
Your Skills

Consider how tone of voice can influence meaning. Take a simple phrase such as "She made me do that." Say it as though you're angry, then surprised, and finally sarcastic. How does your voice change each time, even though the words are the same?

Nonverbal Communication Metacommunicates As discussed in Chapter 1, metacommunication is communication *about* communication, and we often metacommunicate verbally. When we use statements such as "Let me tell you what I think," "Don't take this the wrong way," and "I'm just kidding," we are sending messages related to our other messages—that is, we're communicating about our communication. Usually, we do so to avoid misunderstandings and to provide listeners with greater clarity about the meaning of our statements. Communicating clearly is a very important feature of social interaction, and several nonverbal behaviors also help us to achieve this goal.

Suppose, for example, that you're sitting at the dinner table with your brother and he leans over to you, lowers his voice to a whisper, and cups his mouth with his hand as though he's about to tell you a secret. That combination of nonverbal behaviors sends you the message, "What I'm about to say is meant for only you to hear." In other words, your brother's nonverbal behavior metacommunicates his intentions to you.

We often use nonverbal behaviors such as facial expressions and gestures to indicate how someone else should interpret our messages. For instance, we might smile and wink to indicate that we're being sarcastic, or raise our eyebrows to signal that what we're saying is very serious. All those are examples of how we can use nonverbal cues to metacommunicate with others.

Nonverbal behavior can metacommunicate. For instance, we can use nonverbal signals to indicate the meta-message that "this is a secret."

Nonverbal Communication Serves Multiple Functions Beyond its role in emotional expression, nonverbal communication serves several additional functions that help us interact effectively with others. Let's take a quick look at some of those key functions.

- *Nonverbal communication helps us manage conversations.* We can use nonverbal signals—such as raising a hand in class—to indicate that we wish to speak. We can also use eye contact to convey that we understand what a speaker is saying.[12]
- *Nonverbal communication helps us maintain relationships.* We reinforce many of our important relationships through the use of **immediacy behaviors,** nonverbal signals of affection and affiliation. In many relationships, such behaviors include smiling, engaging in affectionate touch, using warm vocal tones, and standing or sitting close to each other.[13]
- *Nonverbal communication helps us form impressions.* By observing how another person looks, sounds, dresses, and carries himself or herself, we can form impressions

immediacy behaviors Nonverbal signals of affection and affiliation.

about that individual's personality, education level, cultural and ethnic background, economic status, political affiliation, and sexual orientation.[14] Our impressions may not always be accurate, but we rely heavily on nonverbal cues when we form them.

- *Nonverbal communication helps us influence other people.* When we attempt to cause others to think or act in a certain way, we can manipulate some visual cues, such as our clothing, to appear more authoritative.[15] We can also use nonverbal immediacy behaviors to enhance our affiliation with others; in this way, we might lead them to be more open to our suggestions than they otherwise might be.[16]
- *Nonverbal communication helps us conceal information.* Several nonverbal behaviors coincide with our attempts to deceive other people. When we try to conceal the truth, we often speak in a higher voice than normal,[17] and our smile looks more fake or forced.[18] We also use fewer gestures and adopt a more rigid posture, probably because we're trying to control signs of nervousness.[19]

- **What determines whether a form of communication is verbal or nonverbal?**
- **Why are we more likely to believe nonverbal behaviors than words when the two conflict?**
- **What multiple functions does nonverbal communication serve?**

Test Yourself

>> Ten Channels of Nonverbal Communication

Nonverbal communication engages nearly all of our senses, so it's probably no surprise that we experience it in so many different forms, or channels. Those channels include facial displays, eye behaviors, movement and gestures, touch behaviors, vocal behaviors, the use of smell, the use of space, physical appearance, the use of time, and the use of artifacts.

FACIAL DISPLAYS

It's difficult to overstate the importance of **facial displays,** or facial expressions, in nonverbal communication. Indeed, according to the *principle of facial primacy,* the face communicates more information than any other channel of nonverbal behavior.[20] That communication power is especially evident in three important functions of facial displays: revealing identity, signaling attractiveness, and expressing emotion.

- *Identity.* First, the face is the most important visual clue that humans use to identify one another.[21] After all, most of us don't display photos of our family's and friends' hands, legs, or feet—we display pictures of their faces, because the appearance of the face is our most reliable clue to identity.
- *Attractiveness.* Second, the face plays a large role in attractiveness. Two properties that appear to be especially important are symmetry and proportionality. **Symmetry** is the similarity between the left and right sides of your face (Figure 5.2). **Proportionality** refers to the relative size of your facial features. It may seem odd to identify symmetry and proportionality as primary contributors to facial attractiveness, because we so often think of attractiveness as a highly individual assessment. However, as you'll learn in the Fact or Fiction? box on page 110 we're much more similar than dissimilar when it comes to judging a person's attractiveness.
- *Emotion.* Finally, as noted above, facial behavior is our primary means of communicating emotion. Our facial muscles give us the ability to make hundreds of different expressions. We use those expressions to convey a host of emotions—from happiness, surprise, and determination to anger, fear, sadness, and contempt.

Facial expressions are also extremely useful for those who communicate through sign language. In sign language, facial expressions are sometimes called *non-manual signals*

facial displays Facial expressions that are an important source of information in nonverbal communication.

symmetry The similarity between the left and right sides of a face or body.

proportionality The relative sizes of facial or body features.

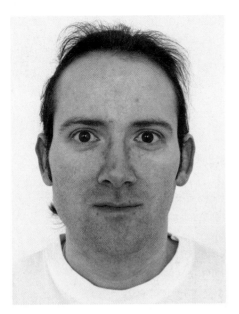
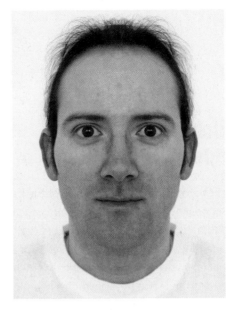

FIGURE 5.2 Asymmetrical and Symmetrical Faces All else being equal, symmetrical faces are more attractive than asymmetrical faces. When researchers study facial symmetry, they often do so by taking a photograph of a face and modifying it with computer software to make it appear more symmetrical. For instance, the image on the left is an original, un-retouched photo of an adult man's face, and the image on the right is a modified version of the same face that increases its symmetry. Research indicates that most people would find the face on the right to be more attractive.

because they work alongside hand signs to help express a particular meaning. For instance, when someone asks a yes or no question using sign language, the eyes are wide open, the eyebrows are raised, and the head and shoulders are pushed forward. Sometimes a person can change the entire meaning of a sign just by changing the facial expression that goes with it (Figure 5.3).[22]

FIGURE 5.3 Facial Expression in American Sign Language Facial expression plays a vital role in communicating ideas in American Sign Language (ASL). In some instances, the same hand sign is associated with different meanings if it is accompanied by different facial expressions. Both photographs in the figure feature the hand sign for "you," but they involve different facial displays. The photo on the left would be interpreted as a question, such as "Are you?" or "Did you?" The photo on the right, however, would be interpreted as an exclamation, such as "It's you!" Although the hand signal is the same in both photographs, the meaning differs because of the accompanying facial expression.

Fact or Fiction?

In the Eye of Which Beholder?
Cultures Vary Widely in Perceptions of Beauty

Most of us have heard the cliché that "beauty is in the eye of the beholder," meaning that what one group finds attractive may not be appealing to another. Surprisingly, this idea dates back at least to the third century B.C., indicating that humans have long considered beauty to be subjective, a matter of individual taste. If that were the case, then we would expect to find little agreement from person to person, and from culture to culture, about what is physically attractive. Exactly how true is that idea, though?

Not very, according to research. In fact, a host of studies has shown just the opposite: People are remarkably consistent when it comes to judging attractiveness. In 2000, researcher Judith Langlois and her colleagues reviewed 130 of those studies and found that within cultures, people showed 90 percent agreement with one another when judging someone's attractiveness. Moreover, people from different cultures agreed in their judgments of attractiveness 94 percent of the time. Thus, although we sometimes think of beauty as being culturally specific, Langlois and her team found that there was substantial agreement both *within* cultures and *across* cultures in assessing attractiveness.

Those findings indicate that people are much more similar than different when it comes to judging looks. Therefore, people who are considered attractive by one social group are also likely to be considered attractive by other groups.

ASK YOURSELF

- Why does the idea that "beauty is in the eye of the beholder" persist?
- What do you find most physically attractive in members of the other sex? How about in members of your own sex?

Source: Langlois, J. H., Kalakanis, L. E., Rubenstein, A. J., Larson, A. D., Hallam, M. J., & Smoot, M. T. (2000). Maxims or myths of beauty: A meta-analytic and theoretical review. *Psychological Bulletin, 126,* 380–423.

EYE BEHAVIORS

Because the eyes are part of the face, it may strike you as odd that researchers study eye behavior separately from facial behavior. Just as facial behavior communicates more than any other nonverbal channel, however, the eyes communicate more than any other part of the face—thus, we treat **oculesics,** the study of eye behavior, as a separate nonverbal channel.

When many people think about eye behavior, eye contact first comes to mind, for good reason. Eye contact plays a role in several important types of relational interaction. We use eye contact to signal attraction to someone and to infer that someone is attracted to us. We use it to gain credibility and to come across as sincere or trustworthy. We use it to persuade others, as well as to signal that we are paying attention and understanding what others are saying. We can even use eye contact when we want to intimidate someone or take a dominant or an authoritative position in a conversation or a group discussion. Indeed, there are few times when we feel as connected to another person—in either positive or negative ways—as when we are looking each other in the eye. As we'll see later in the chapter, however, those functions of eye contact often vary by culture.

Another eye behavior with communicative value is pupil size. The pupil is the dark spot right in the center of each eye, which you can see in a mirror. Your pupils control how

oculesics The study of eye behavior.

much light enters your eyes; as a result, they continually change in size. In darker environments, they dilate, or open wider, in order to take in all available light. In brighter environments, they contract, or become smaller, to avoid taking in too much light at once. What communication researchers find interesting, however, is that your pupils also dilate when you look at someone you find physically attractive and when you feel arousal, whether it is a positive response, such as excitement or sexual arousal, or a negative response, such as anxiety or fear. Watching how a person's pupils react to different social situations or conversational partners can therefore tell us something about the individual's interest and arousal.

MOVEMENT AND GESTURES

Think about the different ways you walk. When you're feeling confident, you hold your head high and walk with smooth, consistent strides. When you're nervous, you probably walk more timidly, stealing frequent glances at the people around you. Your *gait,* or the way you walk, is one example of how your body movement can communicate various messages about you to others, such as "I feel proud" or "I feel scared." The study of movement, including the movement of walking, is called **kinesics.**

Now consider how you use your arms and hands to communicate. Perhaps it's to wave at your neighbor when you see her at the grocery store. Maybe it's to hold up two fingers to signal that you want two hot dogs at the football game concession stand. The use of arm and hand movements to communicate is called **gesticulation.** Research indicates that most people—even those who are born blind—use gestures even before they begin speaking.[23]

Communication scholars divide gestures into several forms, including emblems, illustrators, affect displays, regulators, and adaptors.

- **Emblems** are any gestures that have a direct verbal translation. Whenever you see an emblematic gesture, you should be able to translate it into words. Examples include the wave for "hello" or "goodbye" and the upright extended palm for "stop."
- **Illustrators** are gestures that go along with a verbal message to clarify it. If you hold up your hands a certain distance apart when you say the fish you caught was "this big," your gesture serves as an illustrator to clarify what you mean by "this big."
- **Affect displays** are gestures that communicate emotion *(affect).* You probably know people who wring their hands when they're nervous or cover their mouth with their hands when they're surprised. Those are both affect displays because they coincide with particular emotions.

We often infer people's emotional state from the way they walk.

kinesics The study of movement.

gesticulation The use of arm and hand movements to communicate.

emblems Gestures that have a direct verbal translation.

illustrators Gestures that go along with a verbal message to clarify it.

affect displays Gestures that communicate emotion.

- **Regulators** are gestures that control the flow of conversation. One regulator with which you're probably very familiar is raising your hand when you're in a group and wish to speak. Gestures such as that help regulate who is speaking, and when, so that communication can flow smoothly.
- **Adaptors** are gestures you use to satisfy some personal need, such as scratching an itch or picking lint off your shirt. When we do those behaviors to ourselves, we call them *self-adaptors*. When adaptors are directed at others (say, picking lint off of someone else's shirt), they're called *other-adaptors*.

Research indicates that physical affection—including affectionate touch—is essential for our physical and mental health.

TOUCH BEHAVIORS

Touch is the first of our five senses to develop. Even before an infant can see, hear, taste, or smell, his or her skin can respond to stimuli in the environment. Touch is also the only sense without which we cannot survive. Consider that no matter how much we may cherish our other senses, it's entirely possible to survive without being able to see, hear, taste, or smell. Without touch, however, we would constantly be susceptible to burn, frostbite, and other potentially life-threatening forms of injury.

Haptics is the study of how we use touch to communicate. In terms of human communication, there are five major areas in which touch plays a critical role in conveying meaning: affection, caregiving, power and control, aggression, and ritual.

- *Affectionate touch.* Behaviors such as hugging, kissing, and handholding communicate love, intimacy, commitment, and safety and are commonplace in many romantic relationships, parent–child relationships, and friendships.[24] One reason affectionate touch is so important is that it contributes to our physical and mental well-being. Infants who are regularly cuddled, for instance, experience faster physical development than those who are not.[25]

Caregiving touch helps people to accomplish instrumental needs.

- *Caregiving touch.* We often receive touch from others while receiving some form of care or service. When you get your hair cut, have your teeth cleaned, or work with a personal trainer, for instance, you're touched in ways that correspond to those activities. Caregiving touch is distinguished from affectionate touch because although it *can* reflect positive emotion for the person being touched, it does not necessarily do so.

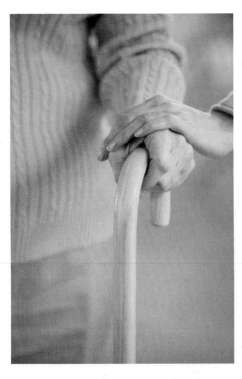

- *Power and control touch.* Still other touches are used to exert power over people's behavior. We sometimes touch people merely to suggest a certain course of behavior, as when the host of a party puts his hand on a guest's back to guide her in a certain direction. In other cases, we touch people to control their behavior against their wishes, such as when police officers hold a suspect on the ground while applying handcuffs.
- *Aggressive touch.* Behaviors done to inflict physical harm—such as punching, pushing, kicking, slapping, and stabbing—are all forms of aggressive touch. Using touch behaviors to inflict physical harm on others almost always constitutes a criminal act. Despite the legal constraints on such behaviors, incidents of violence and abuse using aggressive touch are unfortunately still common in North America and many societies around the world.
- *Ritualistic touch.* Some touches are ritualistic, meaning that we do them as part of a custom or tradition. In North America, shaking hands is one such example; when we shake hands with people as part of a greeting ritual, we understand that the handshake does not convey any particular meaning about the relationship (the way that, say, holding hands would).

VOCAL BEHAVIORS

Perhaps you have a high, breathy voice or a deep, booming voice. Maybe you usually talk very fast or quite loudly. Perhaps you have an accent that indicates to others where you grew up. And there are times when you speak with a particular tone in your voice, to suggest that you are irritated, amused, or bored. Those and other characteristics of the voice are referred to, collectively, as **vocalics.** We also refer to them as **paralanguage** (meaning "beside language") to indicate that they go along with the words we speak to convey meaning.

Some people are surprised to learn that the voice is a channel of nonverbal communication. After all, we speak with our voices, and spoken communication is verbal, right? That statement is true, but the only verbal aspect of spoken communication is *what we say*—the words themselves. Everything else about our voices, including the following characteristics, is nonverbal.

- *Pitch.* The pitch of your voice is an index of how high or deep your voice sounds. On average, women's voices have a higher pitch than men's voices, and adults have deeper voices than children.
- *Inflection.* When we talk about the inflection in your voice, we're referring to your variation in pitch. Voices that have a lot of inflection are usually described as very expressive; those with little inflection are said to be monotone.[26]
- *Volume.* Volume is an index of how loud or quiet your voice is. Most of us alter our vocal volume as the social context demands, such as by speaking quietly in a library and more loudly at a crowded reception.
- *Rate.* Vocal rate refers to how fast or slowly you speak. The average adult speaks at a rate of approximately 150 words per minute,[27] but we might speak faster when we're excited or slower when we're unsure of ourselves.
- *Filler words.* Filler words are non-word sounds such as "umm" and "er" that people often use to fill the silence during pauses. If we have to pause while speaking—say, to remember the word we want to use—we can use filler words to indicate that we intend to continue speaking.
- *Pronunciation.* Pronunciation reflects how correctly you combine vowel and consonant sounds to say a word. For example, how would you pronounce the word *victuals*? Although it looks as though it should be pronounced "VIK-tules," its correct pronunciation is "VIT-tles."
- *Articulation.* Articulation, also known as enunciation, is how clearly you speak. People who mumble their words or speak with their mouth full demonstrate poor articulation. In contrast, individuals whose words are clear and easily understandable are good articulators.
- *Accent.* An accent is a pattern of pronouncing vowel and consonant sounds that is representative of a particular language or geographic area. Everyone speaks with an accent—even you—although we typically only notice accents that are different from ours.
- *Silence.* Silence is the absence of sound. We frequently use silence to convey meaning in conversations.[28] For instance, we often become silent when we are unsure how to respond to a question or when we have said as much as we wish to about a topic.

THE USE OF SMELL

Of all the channels of nonverbal behavior, you might have the hardest time figuring out what smell has to do with human communication. It turns out that your sense of smell, which we call **olfactics,** operates subtly but powerfully to influence your reactions to other people. In fact, two phenomena that are central to the human experience and to communication—memory and sexual attraction—are profoundly affected and regulated by smell.

Memory Smells can affect our communication behavior by influencing our memories and moods. Have you ever smelled a particular scent—maybe a certain food or cologne—and instantly remembered a particular person, event, or place? Maybe the aroma of banana bread makes you think of your grandmother's kitchen, or the smell of newspaper

regulators Gestures that control the flow of conversation.

adaptors Gestures used to satisfy a personal need.

haptics The study of the sense of touch.

vocalics Characteristics of the voice that communicate meaning.

paralanguage Vocalic behaviors that communicate meaning along with verbal behavior.

olfactics The study of the sense of smell.

ink makes you recall the paper route you had as a kid. Those connections are examples of *olfactic association,* the tendency of odors to bring up specific memories. Why do olfactic associations matter for communication? It happens that memories often come with specific emotions, so when a smell reminds us of a particular person or place, it has the potential to affect our mood and behavior.

Sexual Attraction Smell also affects our communication by playing a role in determining to whom we are sexually attracted. That connection between smell and attraction may surprise you, because chances are you think of sexual attraction as being driven mostly by visual cues—whether you think an individual *looks* attractive. In fact, your judgments about a person's sexual attractiveness are strongly affected by the way he or she smells to you. More specifically, research tells us that when we are looking for opposite-sex romantic partners, we are drawn to people whose natural body scent is the most different from our own. Why?

If two people have very similar scents, scientists have determined that their genes are also very similar, and this similarity can increase their probability of producing genetically abnormal children. People produce much healthier children when they mate with partners who are genetically dissimilar to them. It happens that a person's natural body scent sends a signal to your brain that tells you how similar his or her genes are to yours. The more dissimilar a person's body odor is to yours, therefore, the more sexually attractive you will instinctively judge that individual to be.

Of course, not all instances of sexual attraction coincide with the desire to reproduce. Nonetheless, nature has connected smell to sexual attraction to help motivate healthy mate choices when procreation is our goal. We don't sniff out a person's scent profile consciously, however; rather, our brain is adapted to pick up on those olfactic signals subconsciously.

Many smells invoke specific memories. The smell of banana bread might make you think of your grandmother's kitchen

What olfactic associations do you have? How might they influence your communication behavior?

THE USE OF SPACE

When we interact socially, we constantly negotiate our use of space. That negotiating process becomes particularly apparent when our personal space is limited; think of being in a crowded elevator or on a full airplane. Many of us find such situations uncomfortable, but why? The scientific study of spatial use, known as **proxemics,** tells us that we each have a preferred amount of personal space that we carry like an invisible bubble around us. How much personal space we prefer depends on our temperament, the situation we're in, and our level of familiarity with those around us.

We each prefer a certain amount of personal space. As a result, we often feel uncomfortable in crowded conditions.

Anthropologist Edward T. Hall discovered that in Western cultures, people use four different spatial zones, or levels of personal distance, when interacting with one another.[29] **Intimate distance,** which ranges from 0 to approximately 1½ feet, is the zone we willingly occupy with only our closest and most intimate friends, family members, and romantic partners. With other friends and relatives, we typically maintain a **personal distance,** which Hall defined as extending from 1½ to about 4 feet. With customers, casual acquaintances, or others whom we don't know very well, we occupy a **social distance.** That ranges from about 4 to 12 feet and conveys more formal, impersonal interaction. Finally, **public distance** typically applies when someone is giving a speech or performing in front of a large audience. The purpose is to keep the presenter far enough away from the group that he or she is safe and visible to everyone. Public distances are usually 12 to 25 feet or greater, depending on the circumstance.

PHYSICAL APPEARANCE

We place extraordinary importance on physical appearance. Whether we intend to or not, we make all sorts of judgments about people based on their looks. In particular, we have a strong predisposition to attribute positive qualities to physically attractive people, a tendency that researchers refer to as the **halo effect.** In other words, when a person *looks* good, most of us subconsciously assume that he or she *is* good. Indeed, research has shown that we think attractive people are friendlier, more competent, and more socially skilled than less attractive people.[30]

Those perceptions translate into some real advantages for attractiveness. For instance, attractive people have higher self-esteem and more dating experience than less attractive people.[31] We are also nicer and more cooperative toward attractive people and more lenient toward attractive criminal defendants.[32] So if it seems at times that good-looking people get all the breaks, research tells us that is often the case. Much as we may like to claim otherwise, most of us are strongly influenced by physical appearance when making assessments about other people.

That preference for beauty has a dark side, however. Because physical attractiveness is so highly valued, some people go to dangerous extremes to achieve it. As you'll see in "The Dark Side of Communication," one of the unfortunate effects of the quest for beauty is the prevalence of eating disorders.

THE USE OF TIME

Chronemics is to the way we use time. You might not immediately think of time usage as nonverbal behavior, but the way we give (or refuse to give) our time to others can send them important messages about how we feel about them. Because most of us spend our time on the people and activities that matter to us, for instance, the way we use time communicates messages about what we value. When we give our time to others, we imply that we value those people.

Our use of time also sends messages about power. When you go to see someone who is in a position of power over you, such as your supervisor, it is not uncommon to be kept waiting. However, you would probably consider it bad form to make a more powerful person wait for you. Indeed, the rule seems to be that the time of powerful people is more valuable than the time of less powerful people.

The way we use time can send important messages to others.

THE USE OF ARTIFACTS

Each of us has certain physical environments that we inhabit and control, such as a house or apartment, a dorm room, and an office. **Artifacts** are the objects and visual features within an environment that reflect who we are and what we like. One office you routinely visit, for instance, may be plush and opulent, with an oak desk, leather furniture, soft lighting, and expensive paintings on the walls. Another office may be plain and basic, featuring a metal desk and chairs, fluorescent lighting, and bare walls. What messages might those different artifacts send you about the occupants of those two offices?

The way artifacts such as furniture are placed within an environment can facilitate or inhibit communication. For example, teachers at Phillips Exeter Academy, a private preparatory school in New Hampshire, practice the Harkness method of teaching, which involves arranging up to 12 students and a teacher around an oval table. That arrangement is meant to diminish the separation between students and teachers and to encourage everyone to interact in an open, engaging way. In contrast, people who wish to discourage conversation in their office or work environment might place their desk so that their back is to others.

The ten different channels by which we communicate with others nonverbally encompass almost all our senses, making nonverbal communication a truly engaging experience. Not everyone enacts nonverbal behavior in the same ways, however. As we'll see in the next section, culture and sex are both powerful influences on our styles of communicating nonverbally.

proxemics The study of the use of space.

intimate distance The zone of space willingly occupied only with intimate friends, family members, and romantic partners.

personal distance The zone of space occupied with close friends and relatives.

social distance The zone of space occupied with casual acquaintances.

public distance The zone of space maintained during a public presentation.

halo effect A predisposition to attribute positive qualities to physically attractive people.

chronemics The use of time.

artifacts Objects and visual features that reflect a person's identity and preferences.

THE DARK SIDE of Communication

Eating Disorders and the Pressure to Be Attractive

There's little question that being physically attractive is an advantage in everyday life. Because of the halo effect, we think attractive people are nicer, smarter, friendlier, more honest, and more competent than unattractive people, and we treat them accordingly. Most of us grow up learning that physical attractiveness is prized. That lesson can create enormous social and psychological pressure on people to look as attractive as possible.

Particularly in Western societies, people see thin, slim bodies as attractive and overweight bodies as unattractive. Because of the pressure to be attractive and because being attractive means being thin, an alarming number of people suffer from eating disorders. According to the U.S. National Institute of Mental Health, eating disorders are of two major types. *Anorexia nervosa* derives from the desire to be as thin as possible. Individuals with anorexia pursue thinness relentlessly through excessive dieting and exercise, self-induced vomiting, and the abuse of laxatives or diuretics. *Bulimia nervosa* is a disorder characterized by binging on large quantities of food and then compensating for overeating by vomiting, abusing laxatives or diuretics, or fasting. Whereas people with anorexia are often excessively thin, those with bulimia are often of normal weight for their age and height. Like those with anorexia, though, individuals with bulimia fear gaining weight and are intensely unhappy with their body. Both anorexia and bulimia elevate the risk of several health problems, including low blood pressure, cardiac arrest, clinical depression, gastrointestinal disorders, and suicide.

ASK YOURSELF

- Why do you suppose thinness is considered attractive in so many cultures, particularly for women?
- Besides developing eating disorders, what are some other examples of the dangerous extremes to which people will go in their quest for attractiveness?

Sources: National Institute of Mental Health: http://www.nimh.nih.gov/health/publications/eating-disorders/what-are-eating-disorders.shtml; National Eating Disorders Association: www.nationaleatingdisorders.org.

- What are three primary communicative functions of the face?
- How is pupil dilation affected by attractiveness?
- When is a gesture an emblem?
- Why is touch the most important sense for survival?
- Which aspects of the voice are verbal and which are nonverbal?
- How does smell affect memory and sexual attraction?
- What are Hall's four spatial zones?
- What is the halo effect?
- How does the use of time communicate messages about power?
- What is an artifact?

Test Yourself

>> Culture, Sex, and Nonverbal Communication

Suppose you've won an Olympic gold medal. As you stand atop the podium listening to your national anthem, with your friends and family beaming with pride from the stands, imagine the immense joy you would feel. In that scenario, what nonverbal behaviors would you likely be engaged in? How would you stand? What expression would be on your face? What gestures might you make?

If you can picture yourself in that situation, it's easy to imagine that everyone would behave the same way you would. Research tells us, however, that our ways of communicating nonverbally are affected not only by our individual emotions and the demands of the situation, but also by two major influences on nonverbal communication: culture and sex. We'll take a look at each in this section.

CULTURE INFLUENCES NONVERBAL COMMUNICATION

When they watch the Olympic Games on television, many U.S. Americans are surprised by some of the nonverbal behaviors of athletes from different cultures. For instance, athletes from around the world have different ways of greeting one another than are common in the United States. They may stand closer to—or farther from—each other than is typical in U.S. culture. The reason is that those and many other nonverbal behaviors are shaped by the cultural practices with which people are raised. As an example of how one former communication student applies his knowledge of cultural variation in nonverbal behavior, see "Putting Communication to Work."

Consider these many ways in which culture influences nonverbal communication:

- *Emblems:* The specific messages that an emblem symbolizes often vary by culture. The "come here" gesture commonly used in the United States means "goodbye" in China, Italy, and Columbia.[33] Gestures such as A-OK, thumbs up, and crossed fingers have sexual or obscene meanings in many parts of the world.[34]

Differences in greeting behaviors are one way in which athletes in international competitions display cultural differences.

Putting Communication to Work

Name: Robert Schlehuber

College(s): Undergraduate degree, University of Illinois, May 2008

Major(s): Double major: communication and political science

Job Title: Peace Corps Volunteer, Youth Development Group

Salary: Volunteer position; small stipend to pay for food, accommodations, and travel

Time in Job: 6 months so far; I will be in Ukraine for 27 months total

Work Responsibilities: I work with kids between age 12 and 21 at a school in the easternmost part of Ukraine. I run all of the afterschool programs—chess/checkers, English, and sports clubs. I also am developing a school newspaper with the help of a USAID Small Projects Assistance Grant. In addition, I am designing a volunteer exchange program in partnership with local organizations in Rockford, Illinois, that would develop pen pal relationships between students and would potentially allow three American students to travel to Ukraine and three Ukrainian students to travel to the United States to help run two-week volunteer projects.

Why Communication? I majored in communication because of its broad appeal. Every industry, every relationship, every job you will ever have will involve what you can learn as a communication major. Knowing that I wanted to work in international relations and international development, I found that the Communication College offered classes on communication not only within organizations but also with other cultures. I have gained a mindset that allows me to work with large groups of people and to design projects quickly. My perspective allows me to get the best out of all participating members.

What I learned from my classes about nonverbal communication, including body language, has significantly helped with my job, because in Ukrainian culture people communicate much more through nonverbal behavior than with words. In addition, my communication courses taught me about the small differences in communication between different cultures at home and abroad. Little cultural differences come to light a lot more quickly now, tremendously helping my communication with other cultures.

My Advice to Students Look at the wide range of topics that communication classes offer—these can help you pursue different career paths. I took classes that covered communication in politics, psychology, philosophy, business, management, and public relations, all of which have been helpful in my post-college life.

- *Affect displays:* Some displays of affect (emotion) are specific to certain cultures. In China, for example, women express emotional satisfaction by holding their fingertips over their closed mouths. Similarly, a man in Uruguay will hold his fists together and turn them in opposite directions, as if wringing out a wet cloth, to express anger.
- *Personal distance:* People from Arab countries generally converse with each other at closer distances than do U.S. Americans.[35] One study found that because of differences in their preferred conversational distance, Arab college students regarded those from the United States as aloof, whereas the U.S. American students regarded the Arab students as overbearing.[36]
- *Eye contact:* In many Western cultures, direct eye contact signifies that someone is sincere, trustworthy, and authoritative, whereas the lack of eye contact elicits negative evaluations from others.[37] In comparison, some Asian, Latin American, and Middle

Eastern cultures emphasize the lack of eye contact as a sign of deference or respect for authority.[38]

- *Facial displays of emotion:* As noted above, decades of research indicate that people around the world express emotions—particularly primary emotions such as happiness, sadness, fear, anger, surprise, and disgust—in highly similar ways.[39] What tends to differ across cultures is how expressive people are of emotion, with those in individualistic cultures routinely being more emotionally expressive than those in collectivistic cultures.[40]

- *Greeting behavior:* People in Western countries typically greet social acquaintances with a handshake, whereas people in Mediterranean countries usually kiss each other on both cheeks. In Asian countries, it is common to greet others by bowing, with the longest and lowest bows reserved for the most respected individuals.[41]

- *Time orientations:* Recall from Chapter 2 that some cultures—including the United States, Canada, Finland, Great Britain, and Germany—are *monochronic,* meaning that they see time as a tangible commodity, expect events to begin "on time," and dislike having their time wasted.[42] Other cultures—including France, Brazil, Mexico, and Saudi Arabia—are *polychronic,* meaning they see time as flexible and diffused and don't necessarily expect punctuality.[43]

- *Touch:* People in *high-contact cultures,* which include France, Mexico, and Greece, touch each other significantly more often than do people in *low-contact cultures,* such as Japan, Sweden, and Finland.[44] Research indicates that the United States is most accurately classified as a *medium-contact culture.*[45]

- *Vocalics:* Besides their readily noticeable differences in accents, cultures also differ in their use of filler words.[46] Although "umm" and "er" are common filler words for English speakers, Chinese speakers often say "zhege zhege zhege"—which translates to "this this this"—as filler words.

Greeting behaviors vary significantly from culture to culture. Some people shake hands, some kiss each other on the cheek, and others bow when meeting someone new.

Before we proceed, it's important to acknowledge that not *every* nonverbal behavior differs by culture. People around the world interpret a smile as an expression of joy.[47] Parents in every known culture speak *babytalk*—soft, high-pitched vocal tones and highly simplified language—to their infants.[48] The fact that two people come from different cultures doesn't mean they can't communicate with each other nonverbally. It simply means they should be aware of the many ways in which each of their cultural backgrounds is influencing how they do so.

SEX INFLUENCES NONVERBAL COMMUNICATION

A second major influence on our nonverbal communication is our sex. Perhaps you've noticed that women and men sometimes react with different nonverbal behaviors—or to different degrees—to the same situation. The question of *why* sex influences nonverbal communication has intrigued researchers for decades.

One explanation is that beginning in early childhood, boys and girls are socialized to communicate in gender-specific ways (masculine for boys, feminine for girls).[49] Another explanation is that anatomical and physiological differences between the sexes cause them to behave in different ways.[50] Both possibilities have received extensive support from research, but not always for the same behaviors. In other words, sex differences in some nonverbal behaviors appear to be more influenced by socialization than biology, whereas others are more affected by biology than socialization.

No matter what the reason, sex influences several forms of nonverbal communication, including

- *Emotional expressiveness:* Several studies document that women are more expressive than men with respect to a variety of emotional states, including joy,[51] affection,[52] sadness,[53] and depression.[54] Some research indicates that men are more expressive

By the Numbers

108

Number of times per hour French adolescents touch one another, compared to 36 for U.S. American adolescents, according to one study.[55]

than women of anger,[56] although other studies have found no sex difference in anger expression.[57]

- *Eye contact:* When communicating with others of their same sex, women engage in more eye contact than do men,[58] a difference that has been demonstrated in both the United States and Japan.[59] In fact, female pairs use higher amounts of gaze than do male pairs when speaking, while listening, and even during silence.[60] Research indicates that male–female pairs are similar to female–female pairs in terms of eye contact.[61]
- *Personal space:* In comparison to men, women are approached more closely, give way more readily to others, stand and sit closer to each other, and tolerate more violations of their personal space than do men.[62] In opposite-sex interactions, men are also more like to violate women's personal space than women are to violate men's.[63]
- *Vocalics:* On average, men's voices have a lower average pitch than do women's. The primary reason why is that men have a larger voice box and longer vocal cords—which produce the sound of the voice—than women do, as a result of physiological changes that occur during puberty.[64] Research indicates that men also use more filler words and pauses while speaking than do women.[65]
- *Touch:* Among adults, men are more likely to touch women than women are to touch men, unless the touch is occurring as part of a greeting (such as a handshake).[66] In same-sex pairs, however, women touch each other more than men do, although that sex difference is smaller in close friendships than among acquaintances.[67]
- *Appearance:* Sex differences in appearance are also influenced by culture. Moreover, women and men typically adorn themselves in notably different ways. In Western cultures, for example, cosmetic use is significantly more common for women than for men.[68] Also, women and men usually wear different styles of clothing and jewelry and adopt different hairstyles, and those conventions further accentuate the differences in their appearance.

As with culture, it's important to note that not every nonverbal behavior differs by sex. Perhaps more important is to acknowledge that sex differences, even when they're present, aren't always substantial. Popular author John Gray, who wrote the highly successful book *Men Are from Mars, Women Are from Venus,*[69] has suggested that women and men communicate so differently that they might as well be from different planets. Although many communication behaviors do differ by sex, research tells us that those sex differences are often relatively small, not nearly as significant as Gray proposed. Indeed, communication scientist Kathryn Dindia has suggested a more modest metaphor for sex differences: "Men are from North Dakota, women are from South Dakota."[70]

Culture and sex aren't the only important influences on nonverbal communication. Another significant influence—and one in which our ability to communicate nonverbally is continually evolving—is computer-mediated communication. Table 5.1 highlights some of the ways in which changes in technology—and in our use of it—have impacted our nonverbal behavior.

Table 5.1	Get Connected: Computer-Mediated Nonverbal Communication

Although early computer-mediated communication relied exclusively on text, people eventually developed ways of expressing themselves nonverbally online. These include:

- **Emoticons:** As we noted earlier in this chapter, textual representations of a facial expression can help to convey a person's emotional state :)
- **Capitalization:** When you type something in all capital letters, IT IS OFTEN INTERPRETED AS YELLING.
- **Random symbols:** Instead of using obscenities in an e-mail message, a series of random keyboard symbols will often do the %#@&* trick.
- **Images:** You can incorporate both still pictures and video clips in computer-mediated communication to add a visual dimension to your message.

- How do people from different cultures vary in their facial displays of emotion?
- Why are men's voices deeper, on average, than women's?

>> Improving Your Nonverbal Communication Skills

In the NBC TV comedy series *The Office,* the character Michael Scott is the regional manager of a paper distribution company. Scott is socially awkward. In conversations with employees and customers, he often has difficulty expressing his emotions and uses inappropriate humor to mask feelings of insecurity or inadequacy. At the same time, he frequently fails to notice when others react negatively to his communication style. Although he tries to get people to like him—and even comes across as likeable—Scott is not a particularly skilled nonverbal communicator.

Michael Scott would be well advised to read this section, in which we'll explore some ways of improving two particular types of nonverbal communication skills: interpreting nonverbal communication and expressing messages nonverbally.

INTERPRETING NONVERBAL COMMUNICATION

As we've seen in this chapter, people use nonverbal communication to express many types of messages, including those related to emotions and attitudes, power and dominance, persuasion, and deception. An important skill for communicators, therefore, is the ability to decode, or interpret, the nonverbal behaviors of others. That ability requires two separate but interrelated skills, as we'll now consider.

Be Sensitive to Nonverbal Messages One skill involved in interpreting nonverbal communication is being sensitive to others' nonverbal messages. When your daughter grimaces after learning you're serving broccoli for dinner, or your son has an excited tone in his voice when talking about his last fencing match, do you notice those nonverbal emotion cues? When a competitor at work intentionally keeps you waiting for an appointment or seems unusually tense during your conversation, do you pick up on those potential signs of dominance or deception?

Sensitivity to nonverbal behaviors is essential because we can't interpret messages unless we first take note of them. Although research indicates that some of us are naturally more nonverbally sensitive than others, it is possible to increase our nonverbal sensitivity through mindful awareness—that is, by tuning in closely to what's happening around us.[71] When you're interacting with someone, try these approaches:

- Pay particular attention to facial expressions for signs of what the person is feeling. Remember that the face communicates more emotion than all other nonverbal channels.
- Take note of his or her tone of voice and body movements, as those are particularly relevant for signaling dominance and deception.

Decipher the Meaning of Nonverbal Messages Nonverbal messages sometimes carry multiple meanings. If you notice a young man smiling as he interacts with another person, it might mean he's happy. Alternatively, it might mean that he's persuading a customer to make a purchase, comforting a relative who has just shared bad news, or

flirting.[72] If you hear him speaking loudly, it might mean he's excited, or it may mean he's angry, surprised, or talking with someone who's hard of hearing.

An essential part of interpretation, therefore, is deciphering the meaning of nonverbal behaviors that others enact. Accurately deciphering a nonverbal behavior means taking it to mean what the sender intended.[73] Suppose that while describing your grandmother's failing health to your friend Vanessa, she squeezes your hand to convey her support. If you take her behavior as a gesture of support, then you have accurately deciphered her nonverbal message. If you take it to mean she's trying to persuade you or is interested in you romantically, however, then you have deciphered her message inaccurately.

To improve your skill at deciphering nonverbal messages, try the following strategies:

- Consider both the social situation a person is in and the other nonverbal behaviors he or she is enacting. If you notice a man crying, your first instinct might be to conclude that he's sad. Perhaps you also notice, however, that he is surrounded by smiling people who are hugging him and patting him on the back. You even hear him laugh, although tears are running down his face. Armed with these additional pieces of information, you might take his crying to mean that he is happy or relieved rather than sad.
- Keep in mind that cultural differences sometimes influence the meaning of a nonverbal message—particularly for gestures and eye behaviors. Using the thumbs-up gesture or failing to make eye contact while taking with someone can have different meanings in different cultures. The more you learn about cultural variation in nonverbal behavior, the more accurately you'll be able to decipher it.
- When you're unsure of how accurately you've deciphered someone's nonverbal message, ask the person. Let's say you're relating the details of a new product to a client and her facial expression suggests confusion. Instead of assuming you've deciphered her expression accurately, you might ask her directly, "Did my description make sense?" If she replies that she found it confusing, you can explain the product again, using simpler language. If she instead replies that she is developing a headache, you will learn that the expression you deciphered as confusion was actually one of discomfort. Asking is a way to check your interpretation of someone's nonverbal message and to make sure you have deciphered it correctly.

As you practice your sensitivity and deciphering skills, you should be able to improve your ability to interpret the meaning of nonverbal behaviors.[74]

EXPRESSING NONVERBAL MESSAGES

Some of us are good at interpreting the nonverbal behaviors of others but not particularly skilled in expressing ourselves nonverbally. Skill in communicating nonverbal messages is valuable for the same reason that interpretation skill is important: People communicate more information nonverbally than verbally. If you're skilled at expressing nonverbal messages, you'll therefore be able to communicate with others more effectively and more efficiently than someone who is less skilled.

Just as with interpretation skills, some people are naturally more expressive, charismatic, and outgoing than others.[75] To improve your own skill at expressing nonverbal messages, try the following ideas:

SHARPEN
Your Skills

Record an episode of one of your favorite TV shows and then watch a few minutes of it with the sound turned of. Pay attention to the characters' nonverbal behaviors and try to figure out what emotions they are experiencing at the time. Once you have an idea of a character's emotion, ask yourself what other conclusions you might have drawn with the information available to you. Then watch the same few minutes again with the sound turned on to determine how accurate you were.

Nonverbal Know-How: Rate Your Interpretation and Expression Skills

How much do you agree with each of the following statements? On the line before each statement, record your level of agreement on a 1 to 7 scale. A higher number means you agree more; a lower number means you agree less.

1. _____ When I feel depressed, I tend to bring down those around me.

2. _____ It is nearly impossible for people to hide their true feelings from me.

3. _____ I have been told that I have expressive eyes.

4. _____ In social settings I can instantly tell when someone is interested in me.

5. _____ Quite often I tend to be the life of the party.

6. _____ People often tell me that I am a sensitive and understanding person.

When you're finished, add up your scores from items 1, 3, and 5. That is your score for expressiveness. Next add up your scores for items 2, 4, and 6. That is your score for interpretation. Both scores should range from 3 to 21.

    If your scores on both scales are between 16 and 21, then you are already quite good at nonverbal interpretation and expressiveness. If your scores are between 9 and 15, you have a moderate ability to interpret and express nonverbal behavior, and the suggestions offered in this chapter may help you sharpen those abilities. If your scores are between 3 and 8, then you especially can benefit from the guidance provided in this chapter for improving your skills. You may also find that one of your scores is considerably higher than the other. If that's the case, then you know which skill you're already good at and which skill could benefit from more practice.

Source: Riggio, R. E. (1986). Assessment of basic social skills. *Journal of Personality and Social Psychology, 51*, 649–660.

- Spend time with highly expressive people. Some researchers have suggested that we can learn how to become more nonverbally expressive by being around extroverted and charismatic people.[76] Research also suggests that highly expressive people are attracted to certain professions, which include teachers and lecturers, actors and singers, politicians, salespeople, diplomats, customer service representatives, counselors and therapists, and members of the clergy.[77] Each of those professions requires an ability to communicate clearly and competently with others, which is served by being nonverbally expressive.

- Take part in games and activities that exercise your nonverbal expression skills. A good example is playing charades, which involves acting out a word or phrase without speaking, while members of your team try to guess the answer based on your depiction. Because success in charades depends on your ability to depict your word or phrase nonverbally, it can be a good exercise of your expression skill. Another example is role playing, which involves acting out the roles of characters in a specific situation the way you would if you were actually in that situation.

Why is your ability to express yourself nonverbally important?

Being skilled at expressing nonverbal messages requires more than simply being expressive; you also must be able to express yourself using nonverbal behaviors that others will accurately interpret. Spending time around people who are skilled at nonverbal expression may help you learn or improve this ability, and taking part in activities such as charades and role playing can give you the chance to exercise your skills.

    You can take a first step toward improving your skills at nonverbal interpretation and expression by assessing how skilled you are now. Complete the exercise in The Competent Communicator to evaluate your current interpretation and expression abilities.

- What is the difference between being sensitive to a nonverbal message and deciphering its meaning?
- What are some professions in which you would commonly find highly expressive people?

For
REVIEW >>

- How do people communicate nonverbally?

  Nonverbal communication comprises those behaviors and characteristics that convey meaning without the use of words. People communicate nonverbally via several channels, including facial displays, eye behaviors, movement and gestures, touch, vocal behaviors, smell, use of space, physical appearance, use of time, and use of artifacts.

- How do culture and sex influence nonverbal behavior?

  Culture and sex affect multiple nonverbal communication behaviors, including gestures, personal distance and touch, eye contact, time orientation, vocalics, and emotional expression.

- In what ways can you improve your nonverbal communication skills?

  You can improve your nonverbal communication skills by being sensitive to the nonverbal messages you encounter, learning to decipher their meanings accurately, and practicing your nonverbal expressiveness.

Pop Quiz

Multiple Choice

1. The two characteristics that contribute most to facial attractiveness are

   a. symmetry and proportionality
   b. symmetry and expressiveness
   c. proportionality and diameter
   d. proportionality and expressiveness

2. Diane announces that she is doing a study of oculesics. The form of nonverbal communication that she is studying is

   a. the use of smell
   b. the influence of attractiveness
   c. emotional expressiveness
   d. eye behaviors

3. A manicurist touches Suzi's hands while giving her a manicure. The type of touch Suzi is receiving is

   a. affectionate
   b. caregiving
   c. ritualistic
   d. power and control

4. How high or low a voice sounds is an index of the vocal characteristic known as

   a. inflection
   b. volume
   c. rate
   d. pitch

5. Because she's from this type of culture, Laila sees time as flexible and diffused and doesn't necessarily expect punctuality.

   a. monochronic culture
   b. high-contact culture
   c. polychronic culture
   d. low-contact culture

Fill in the Blank

6. _____ is the first of the five senses to develop in humans.

7. The study of smell is called _____.

8. Non-word sounds such as "umm" and "uh" are called _____.

9. People in _____ cultures touch each other significantly more than do people in other cultures.

10. The _____ is the idea that the face communicates more information than any other nonverbal behavior channel.

KEY TERMS

6

LISTEN

LISTENING SO THAT OTHERS CAN LISTEN

It's no exaggeration to say that Diana Tuan-Li Liao spent most of her career listening. Born to British-educated parents in Hong Kong, Liao was raised speaking English and three separate dialects of Chinese. After majoring in comparative literature at the University of Hong Kong and working as a reporter in Paris, she put her communication skills to work by becoming an interpreter at the United Nations headquarters in New York City. Liao's primary responsibility on the job was to listen carefully to what various speakers said and to repeat their words immediately in a different language. For instance, she might listen to a speech being given in French and interpret the speech into Chinese, English, Spanish, or Russian, depending on her audience. As Liao quickly learned, effective interpreting required that she not only hear and understand a speaker's words but also make sense of the message the speaker was attempting to communicate. Liao was so proficient at her job that she became the chief interpreter at the United Nations headquarters before retiring in 2004 after 32 years of helping people listen effectively to one another.

ING
EFFECTIVELY

As You READ

>>

- What does it mean to listen effectively?
- Why is listening effectively so challenging?
- How can you improve your listening skills?

You've probably had the frustrating experience of feeling as though someone was *hearing* you but not really *listening*. If so, you know that effective communication involves more than understanding the words that another person is speaking. You must also make sense of the speaker's intended message.

As you might imagine, problems with listening are fairly common in many types of relationships, from marital and family relationships to the relationships among delegates of different countries.[1] In addition, students often struggle to listen effectively to lectures and class presentations. Why? The reason is that proficient listening is a tough challenge. As Liao's career reflects, listening is a skill you have to learn and practice. When you do it properly, listening adds much to the quality of your relationships and your learning; when you don't listen effectively, your communication, relationships, and learning suffer.

>> What It Means to Listen

You probably don't give much thought to how well you listen. You can take classes to become a better speaker or a better writer, but few schools offer courses on improving listening skills. Yet if you're like most people, you spend much more time listening than you do speaking, writing, or engaging in other communicative behaviors. That's one reason why listening effectively is such a valuable skill.

WHAT IS LISTENING?

Listening is one of the most important concepts in human communication, yet many people find effective listening hard to define. When someone says, "You're not listening to me!" what exactly does that statement mean?

We can think of **listening** as the active process of making meaning out of another person's spoken message.[2] Several details about that definition are important to note. First, listening is an active process. That means it isn't automatic; you have to *make* yourself listen to someone. Second, listening isn't just about **hearing,** which is the sensory process of receiving and perceiving sounds—listening is about creating meaning from what you hear. It is about **attending** to someone's words, or paying attention well enough to understand what that person is trying to communicate.

Even if people are hearing the same message, they may construct different meanings for it, an indicator that they are listening differently. For instance, you might listen to your brother's description of his new officemate and conclude that he finds her competent and likable. After listening to the same description, however, your mother might conclude that

listening The active process of making meaning out of another person's spoken message.

hearing The sensory process of receiving and perceiving sounds.

attending Paying attention to someone's words well enough to understand what that person is trying to communicate.

your brother feels threatened by his officemate's intelligence and self-confidence. You and your mother both heard the same description, but you listened to it differently.

Finally, listening deals with spoken messages. We certainly pay attention to written messages, as well as to nonverbal messages, which influence our interpretation of people's behaviors. But we can engage in listening only when someone is speaking.

Listening to someone doesn't necessarily mean listening *effectively*. Effective listening requires listening with the conscious and explicit goal of understanding what the speaker intends to communicate. You might never know for certain whether you have understood a speaker's meaning *exactly* as he or she intended. If you're listening with the goal of understanding the speaker's meaning as best you can, however, you're listening effectively.

As we'll consider in this chapter, several barriers exist that make effective listening difficult, and different situations call for different types of listening. Understanding those dimensions of listening can help each of us improve our ability to listen effectively. That's a worthwhile goal, as we'll now see.

THE IMPORTANCE OF LISTENING EFFECTIVELY

One reason it's vital to understand listening is that we listen so much of the time. How much of your day do you think you spend listening? In one study, researchers Kathryn Dindia and Bonnie Kennedy found that college students spend more time listening than doing any other communication activity. As depicted in Figure 6.1, participants spent 50 percent of their waking hours listening.[3] In contrast, they spent only 20 percent of their time speaking, 13 percent reading, and 12 percent writing. Other studies have found similar results, at least with college students, suggesting that most of us spend a similar percentage of our communication time listening.[4]

The ability to listen effectively is important to our success in a variety of contexts. Good listening skills are essential in the workplace. Suppose, for instance, that your employees don't listen when you tell them the alarm they will soon be hearing will signal a fire drill, not a real fire. Some might panic at the sound of the alarm, and some might injure themselves as they rush frantically from their workspaces. Now suppose that your manager at work doesn't listen to the staff's warnings about problems with the company's equipment. As a result, a critical production line breaks down, stalling operations for a week.

Those examples illustrate how consequential effective listening can be in the workplace. In one survey, a thousand human resource professionals ranked listening as the single most important quality of effective managers.[5] In other research, listening also topped the list of the most important communication skills in families and personal relationships.[6] Being a good listener is vital to just about every social and personal bond we have.[7]

FIGURE 6.1 Percentages of Various Communication Activities Among College Students College students spend more time listening than communicating in other ways.

Despite the importance of listening skills, many of us nevertheless overestimate our listening abilities. In one study, 94 percent of corporate managers rated themselves as "good" or "very good" at listening, whereas not a single one rated himself or herself as "poor" or "very poor." Their employees told quite a different story, however; several rated their managers' listening skills as weak.[8] There appears to be very little association, in other words, between how good *we* think we are at listening and how good *others* think we are.[9]

As we'll see below, many obstacles can get in the way of our ability to listen well. The good news, though, is that listening is a skill we can improve, and in this chapter we'll look at some ways to do just that.[10]

MISCONCEPTIONS ABOUT LISTENING

Are you surprised to learn that people often overestimate their listening abilities? Here are some other misunderstandings about the listening process.

Should people in certain professions, such as medicine and counseling, be required to pass a proficiency test proving they are effective listeners before being licensed?

Effective listening is an essential skill for health workers. Many medical schools now teach new physicians how to listen effectively to patients.

Myth: Hearing Is the Same as Listening Some people use the terms *hearing* and *listening* interchangeably, but they aren't the same activity. Hearing is merely the perception of sound. Most people hear sounds almost continuously—you hear your roommate's music, the neighbor's dogs barking, the car alarm that wakes you in the middle of the night. Hearing is a passive process that occurs when sound waves cause the bones in your inner ear to vibrate and send signals to your brain.

As we've seen, *hearing* something doesn't mean we're *listening* to it. Unlike hearing, listening is an active process of paying attention to a sound, assigning meaning to it, and responding to it. Hearing is a part of that process, but listening requires much more than just perceiving the sounds around you.

By the same token, we sometimes listen without hearing, and our understanding can be impaired as a result. A series of television ads aired by the Cingular/AT&T telephone company illustrated this point humorously. Each ad depicts a call between two people in which they unknowingly lose their cellular connection halfway through the conversation. In every case, one speaker interprets the other's silence as meaningful when in fact it is simply the result of the dropped call. For instance, just after telling her husband that she is expecting a baby, one woman's call is dropped without her knowledge. Although her husband is exclaiming his excitement about the pregnancy, all she hears is silence, which she incorrectly interprets as indifference or fear on his part. Even though she was *listening,* that is, she wasn't *hearing.* As those ads illustrate, listening and hearing are related but separate processes.

Myth: Listening Is Natural and Effortless It's easy to think of listening as a completely natural, mindless process, much like breathing. In reality, listening is a *learned skill,* not an innate ability. We have to acquire our listening abilities. Just as we are taught to speak, we have to be taught to listen—and to listen effectively.

We learn from our experiences. Perhaps, for example, you can recall instances when you didn't listen effectively to a supervisor's instructions about how to accomplish a work project and you made poor decisions as a result. Maybe you have been in a situation with a romantic partner when you didn't listen as effectively as you could have, and the consequence was an unnecessary argument. Those types of unhappy experiences have probably taught you about the importance of effective listening, because good communicators learn from their mistakes. We also learn through instruction, such as the instruction you are receiving in your introductory communication course. The more you learn about what makes listening effective and what barriers to watch out for, the better equipped you'll be to listen effectively to others.

The fact that listening is a skill also means that people vary in their listening abilities. Just as some people are better than others at drawing or singing or writing, some are better listeners than others. Finally, like most other skills, your listening ability can improve with education and training.[11] Counselors and social workers, for instance, are trained to listen effectively to clients, a skill that improves the quality of their work. In recent years, medical schools around the United States have added coursework on effective listening and other interpersonal skills to their curricula for training new physicians. People in many professions, from education and ministry to customer service and politics, can benefit from training in effective listening.

People in monochronic cultures may quickly become impatient when listening, because those cultures emphasize efficiency. In contrast, people in polychronic cultures may be more patient when listening, because their cultural context emphasizes social harmony.

HOW CULTURE AFFECTS LISTENING BEHAVIOR

Cultural messages shape many communication behaviors, and listening is no exception. Research indicates that culture affects listening behavior in at least three ways: expectations for directness, nonverbal listening responses, and understanding of language.

Culture Affects Listeners' Expectations for Directness Listening behavior is influenced by how people in a given culture think about the importance of time. Reflecting their monochronic culture, U.S. Americans commonly say that "time is money" and conceive of time as something that can be saved, spent, and wasted. Listeners in a monochronic culture value direct, straightforward communication and become impatient with speakers who don't get to the point.[12] In contrast, people in polychronic cultures such as China and Korea emphasize social harmony over efficiency. As part of their listening behavior, they often pay close attention to nonverbal behaviors and contextual cues to determine the meaning of a speaker's message.[13]

Culture Affects Nonverbal Listening Responses Cultural expectations can also influence what individuals consider to be appropriate listening responses, particularly with respect to nonverbal behavior. For instance, people in U.S. American culture typically expect listeners to maintain eye contact with them while they're speaking. Listeners who look down or away usually seem as though they aren't listening. Within Native American culture, however, looking down or away while listening is a sign of respect rather than a signal that one is not listening.[14]

Culture Affects Understanding of Language When people speak a language in which listeners aren't fluent, listeners can have a difficult time understanding what is being said. That difficulty arises for at least two reasons. One reason, which we examined in Chapter 4, is that many languages include idioms—phrases often understandable only to native speakers of that language—that are incomprehensible to non-native listeners. For instance, you might tell an overseas visitor that you're "on Cloud 9" with respect to your upcoming graduation, but if English isn't her first language, she may not understand that you mean you're very happy. Consequently, she would have difficulty listening effectively to you.

The second reason why language differences can lead to listening challenges is that listeners may not comprehend the words being spoken, due to their insufficient grasp of the language a speaker is using. When I have foreign exchange students in my classes, I try to be aware of terms and phrases that they may be unable to interpret because of their limited knowledge of English, and I provide an explanation for those words. That approach is especially helpful when I'm using highly technical terms with which non-native listeners may be unfamiliar.

Listeners for whom English is a non-native language can improve their listening abilities online by visiting http://wiki.vec.hku.hk/index.php/listening. That virtual English Wiki site offers links to a wide variety of other websites providing listening materials, songs, television links, and exercises for those whose native language is other than English.

Test Yourself

- How is listening different from merely hearing?
- Approximately how much of a person's communication time is spent listening?
- Why isn't listening a natural, effortless process?
- What are three ways that culture affects listening behavior?

>> Ways of Listening

Until now, we've been talking about listening as though it were a single activity. In truth, listening *effectively* has *several* stages, all of which are equally important.

STAGES OF EFFECTIVE LISTENING

Judi Brownell, an expert on listening, developed the **HURIER model** to describe the stages of effective listening.[15] The six stages, from whose first letters the model is named, are *h*earing, *u*nderstanding, *r*emembering, *i*nterpreting, *e*valuating, and *r*esponding. We don't necessarily have to enact those stages in order; sometimes listening effectively requires us to go back and forth among them. Nonetheless, when we listen effectively, those are the behaviors we adopt.

Hearing Hearing, the physical process of perceiving sound, is where listening begins. Yet we can certainly hear someone without listening to that person. Hearing without listening is common when we're tired or uninterested in what a person is saying or when we're hearing multiple voices at once, as in a crowded restaurant. However, we can't really listen effectively to someone unless we can first hear the person.

The sensory task of hearing may be difficult for individuals with hearing impairments. Some read lips, and others use sign language to communicate. For individuals without hearing problems, though, hearing is the first step in effective listening.

On what occasions and under what circumstances do you have a hard time understanding a speaker?

Understanding It's not enough simply to hear what someone is saying—you also have to understand it. That means comprehending the meanings of the words and phrases you're hearing.[16] If someone is speaking in a language you don't comprehend, you might be able to hear but you won't be able to listen effectively. That is why foreign language interpreters such as Diana Tuan-Li Liao, whom you met at the beginning of this chapter, are so useful in helping people to listen to one another. The same is true when you hear technical language or jargon with which you're unfamiliar: Even if the speaker is speaking your language, you can't effectively listen if you do not understand the words. If you're uncertain whether you understand what a speaker is saying, the most effective course of action is usually to ask the person questions so that you can check your understanding.

HURIER model A model describing the stages of effective listening as hearing, understanding, remembering, interpreting, evaluating, and responding.

Remembering The third stage of the HURIER model of effective listening is remembering, or being able to store something in your memory and retrieve it when needed.[17]

Remembering what you hear is often important for interpersonal communication, because it can help you to avoid awkward situations with others. For instance, you might have had the embarrassing experience of running into someone whose name you can't remember, even though you have met the person on several prior occasions. In such an encounter, the ability to remember what you heard previously—the person's name in this instance—can help you communicate more effectively.

As a student, you probably have your memory skills tested on an ongoing basis. If you're particularly good at remembering the details of a conversation, you're in the minority. Research shows that most people can recall a mere 25 percent of what they hear—and even then, they remember only about 20 percent of it accurately.[18] The average person is therefore not especially good at remembering. Fortunately, short-term memory is a skill you can practice and improve.

Mnemonics are tricks that can aid our short- and long-term memory. Such devices come in several forms. If you've ever studied music, for instance, perhaps you learned to recall the lines of the treble staff—  EGBDF—by treating the letters as an acronym for a phrase such as "Every good boy does fine." You might also develop rhymes to help you remember certain rules, such as the spelling convention "*I before E, except after C.*" In another mnemonic device, you might treat an acronym as if it were a word. For instance, if you remember the elements of Brownell's effective listening model by learning the word HURIER, you are employing that type of mnemonic device. Research suggests that using mnemonic devices can significantly enhance our memory of what we hear.[19]

Interpreting Besides hearing, understanding, and remembering, an effective listener must interpret the information he or she receives. Interpreting has two parts. The first part of interpreting is paying attention to all the speaker's verbal and nonverbal behaviors so that you can assign meaning to the person's message. Suppose your friend Maya says, "It's a beautiful day outside!" Based on her facial expressions and tone of voice, you might interpret her message as sincere—meaning that Maya thinks today's weather *is* beautiful—or sarcastic—meaning that she thinks the weather is lousy. Those are very different interpretations of Maya's message, even though her words are the same.

The second part of interpreting is signaling your interpretation of the message to the speaker. If you interpret Maya's statement as sincere, you might smile and say you're looking forward to getting outside to enjoy the great weather. If you interpret her statement as sarcastic, however, you might laugh or respond with a cynical remark of your own. Signaling, in other words, not only lets the speaker know we're following along with the message but also allows us to check our interpretations. Suppose, for instance, that Maya intended her comment about the weather to be sarcastic but you interpreted it as sincere. If you smiled and said you were looking forward to getting outside, you would probably be signaling to Maya that you have misinterpreted the intent of her statement. She might then say "I was just kidding" to correct your interpretation by indicating that she meant her comment to be sarcastic.

Evaluating Several things happen at the evaluation stage, another crucial step for effective listening. For one thing, you're judging whether the speaker's statements are accurate and true. You're also separating facts from opinions and trying to determine the reason for the speaker's particular message. Finally, you're considering the speaker's words in the context of other information you have from that speaker or others. All those processes help you to be an active, engaged listener rather than a passive recipient of information.

Responding The last stage of effective listening is responding, or indicating to a speaker that we are listening. We sometimes refer to that process as "giving feedback." We respond both verbally and nonverbally using a variety of strategies.[21]

SHARPEN Your Skills

Electronically record someone in your family telling you a story about his or her childhood. As you listen to your relative speak, visualize as much of the story as you can, using all of your senses. Create a mental representation of the sights, sounds, tastes, smells, and feelings the speaker describes. A week later, retell the story to yourself, and then play your recording of the original story to see how many details you correctly recalled.

By the Numbers

51

Percentage increase in memory accuracy among the elderly when using a mnemonic device.[20]

mnemonics Devices that can aid short- and long-term memory.

Below are seven types of listening responses you might use, arranged in order from the most passive to the most active strategies:

- *Stonewalling:* Responding with silence and a lack of expression on your face. Stonewalling often signals a lack of interest in what the speaker is saying.
- *Backchanneling:* Using facial expressions, nods, vocalizations such as "uh-huh," and verbal statements such as "I understand" and "That's very interesting" to let the speaker know you're paying attention.
- *Paraphrasing:* Restating in your own words what the speaker has said, to show that you understand.
- *Empathizing:* Conveying to the speaker that you understand and share his or her feelings on the topic being discussed.
- *Supporting:* Expressing your agreement for the speaker's opinion or point of view.
- *Analyzing:* Providing your own perspective on what the speaker has said.
- *Advising:* Communicating advice to the speaker about what he or she should think, feel, or do.

Table 6.1   HURIER Model of Effective Listening

Brownell's model suggests that effective listening has six elements, represented by the acronym HURIER.

Hearing	Physically perceiving sound
Understanding	Comprehending the words we have heard
Remembering	Storing ideas in memory
Interpreting	Assigning meaning to what we've heard
Evaluating	Judging the speaker's credibility and intention
Responding	Indicating that we are listening

Depending on the situation, some of those responses may be more useful or appropriate than others. For instance, if you are listening to a friend who has just lost her favorite uncle to cancer, empathizing and supporting responses are probably the most fitting. Stonewalling, backchanneling, or paraphrasing might make it seem as though you don't care about your friend, whereas analyzing or advising might seem insensitive. In contrast, if you're listening to a client who is wondering how she can make the most of her stock portfolio, then analyzing and advising are probably called for.

To summarize, the stages of effective listening are hearing, understanding, remembering, interpreting, evaluating, and responding. (Keep in mind that mnemonic word *HURIER.*) A brief recap appears in Table 6.1. According to Brownell's model, those stages characterize effective listening no matter why we happen to be listening in the first place. As you probably know, we listen to others for several different reasons. We'll take a close look at three of the most common types of listening next.

TYPES OF LISTENING

When we talk about different *types* of listening, we're referring to the different *goals* we have when we listen to other people. Sometimes we listen to learn, sometimes to evaluate, and sometimes to empathize. Those goals aren't necessarily exclusive; sometimes we listen with more than one goal in mind. When we distinguish among types of listening, we are therefore considering what our *primary* listening goal is at a given time.

Informational Listening Much of the listening you do in class or at work is **informational listening,** or listening to learn. Whenever you watch the news or listen to driving directions or pay attention to a professor's lecture, you're engaged in informational listening.

Informational listening is one of the most important ways we learn. It is also a relatively passive process. When we engage in informational listening, we're simply taking in information. That is, although we may be listening effectively and even taking notes, we are listening primarily to learn something new rather than to critique what we're hearing or to support the person saying it.

informational listening
Listening to learn.

Critical Listening When our goal is to evaluate or analyze what we're hearing, we are engaged in **critical listening.** You listen carefully to a television commercial to see whether you want to buy the product being advertised. You listen to a sales presentation or a political speech and evaluate the merits of what you're hearing. You listen critically to your mother's description of her recent medical appointment to determine how worried she is about the results of her blood test.

Critical listening doesn't necessarily mean criticizing what you're hearing. Instead, it means analyzing and evaluating the merits of a speaker's words. Compared to informational listening, critical listening is therefore a more active, engaging process. It requires not only taking in information but also evaluating and judging it. As you will see at the end of this chapter, practicing critical listening skills is one of the best ways of becoming a better listener.

Empathic Listening The most challenging form of listening is often **empathic listening,** which occurs when you are trying to identify with the speaker by understanding and experiencing what he or she is thinking or feeling.[22] When talking to a friend who has just lost a beloved pet, or when listening to a family member describing the stress of her divorce, you can use empathic listening to give comfort and support.

When you listen to an instructor for the purpose of learning something, you are engaged in informational listening.

Effective empathic listening requires two separate skills. The first, *perspective taking,* is the ability to understand a situation from another's point of view.[23] The second skill, *empathic concern,* is the ability to identify how someone else is feeling and to experience those feelings yourself.[24] When listening to a co-worker describing his recent diabetes diagnosis, for instance, you can practice perspective taking by trying to think about the situation as he would think about it. You can practice empathic concern by imagining how he must feel and by sharing in those emotions.

Empathic listening is different from *sympathetic listening,* which involves feeling sorry for another person. If your neighbors lost their young grandson to leukemia, for instance, you might be able to sympathize with them even if you can't truly understand their grief. With empathic listening, however, the goal is to understand a situation from the speaker's perspective and to feel what he or she is feeling. You might be listening to a friend who didn't get into her first-choice graduate school, and trying to convey that you feel and share her disappointment. Listening empathically can be a challenge, because our own perceptions can cause us to focus on how *we* would be feeling in the same situation, when our goal is to understand the *speaker's* feelings.

Empathic listening occurs when we try to feel what the speaker is feeling.

critical listening Listening to evaluate or analyze.

empathic listening Listening to experience what the speaker thinks or feels.

People, Action, Content, Time: What's *Your* Listening Style?

We have seen that people listen for different reasons—sometimes to learn, sometimes to evaluate, and sometimes to provide empathy to others. Did you know that each of us also has a primary listening style? A *listening style* is a set of attitudes and beliefs about listening, and researchers have identified four distinct styles. We can adopt any of these styles as the situation dictates, but research suggests that most of us have one style that we use most often. Which one best describes you?

- **People-oriented style:** This style emphasizes concern for other people's emotions and interests. Someone with this style tries to find common interests with others. For example, when listening to his middle-school students, Lorenzo tries to understand what they think and feel so that he can relate to them effectively.
- **Action-oriented style:** This style emphasizes organization and precision. Someone with this style likes neat, concise, error-free presentations. For instance, Monica loves it when her interns fill her in on the week's activities in a clear, straightforward way, and she gets frustrated when she can't understand them.
- **Content-oriented style:** This style emphasizes intellectual challenges. Someone with this style likes to attend to details and think things through. Emma really enjoys listening to political commentators, for example, because they make her think about her own social and political views.
- **Time-oriented style:** This style emphasizes efficiency. Someone with this style prefers conversations that are quick and to-the-point. As an emergency room physician, for instance, Ben relies on short and fast reports on a patient's condition from paramedics and nurses, and he gets impatient when they give him irrelevant information

Each listening style has its strengths and weaknesses, and none is inherently better than the others. If you're primarily a people-oriented listener, you're likely to get to know others well, but you may not be able to work as efficiently as a time-oriented listener. If you're an action-oriented listener, you might do best in a major that emphasizes clarity and precision, such as engineering or computer science, whereas a content-oriented listener might prefer a major that involves greater ambiguity and room for debate, such as fine arts or political science.

Source: Watson, K. W., Barker, L. L., & Weaver, J. B. (2005). The listening styles profile (LSP-16): Development and validation of an instrument to assess four listening styles. *International Journal of Listening, 9,* 1–13.

Other Types of Listening Informational, critical, and empathic listening aren't the only types of listening. For example, sometimes we engage in *inspirational listening,* which is listening to be inspired by what someone is saying. That type of listening is common when we're taking in a sermon or a motivational speech. Other times, we engage in *appreciative listening,* which is listening for pure enjoyment. We adopt that style when listening to someone telling a funny story or singing one of our favorite songs. When it comes to interacting with others, however, informational, critical, and empathic listening are among the most common and most important types.

In addition to engaging in different *types* of listening, many of us also differ in our *styles* of listening. Check out "The Competent Communicator" to see what listening style best describes you.

- What are the differences between interpreting a message and responding to it?
- How do the goals of informational, critical, and empathic listening differ?

>> Common Barriers to Effective Listening

In the 2006 movie *The Break Up*, Brooke Meyers (played by Jennifer Aniston) asks her boyfriend Gary Grobowski (played by Vince Vaughn) to bring home a dozen lemons for a dinner party she is throwing for their families. Gary doesn't listen and ends up bringing home only three lemons. Brooke finds Gary's goof distressing because their company is arriving shortly, so she expresses her concern to Gary—who watches television while talking to her:

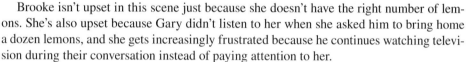

Brooke: *You got three lemons.*

Gary: *What my baby wants, my baby gets; you know that.*

Brooke: *I know, but I wanted 12, baby wanted 12.*

Gary: *Why would you want 12 lemons?*

Brooke: *Because I'm making a 12-lemon centerpiece.*

Gary: *So no one's actually even eating them, they're just show lemons?*

Brooke: *Yeah, they're just show lemons. To go in the center of the table. I'm glad you find that amusing, but I cannot fill a vase with only three lemons.*

Brooke isn't upset in this scene just because she doesn't have the right number of lemons. She's also upset because Gary didn't listen to her when she asked him to bring home a dozen lemons, and she gets increasingly frustrated because he continues watching television during their conversation instead of paying attention to her.

Why are so few of us good listeners? The answer is that various factors can get in our way, acting as barriers to our ability to listen well. We will take a look at several of those obstacles next, beginning with noise.

NOISE

How many different stimuli are competing for your attention right now—or perhaps at work, where your boss, customers, and co-workers may all be trying to talk to you at once? In the context of listening, **noise** is anything that distracts you from listening to what you wish to listen to. That distraction could be *physical noise,* which consists of actual sound, or *psychological noise,* which comprises anything else we find distracting.

Most of us find it tougher to listen to a conversational partner when there are other sounds in the environment, such as a TV or loud music.[25] TV and music are examples of physical noise. However, it isn't just sound that can distract us. If we're hungry or tired, or if we're in an especially hot or cold environment, those influences qualify as psychological noise because they distract us and thus reduce our ability to listen effectively.[26]

When faced with such distractions, focus your attention on your conversational partner and listen intently to what he or she is saying. That strategy requires being conscientious of noise in your environment and identifying the factors that are drawing your attention away from your conversation. If you can eliminate or ignore sources of noise, such as by turning off your car radio or disregarding your ringing cell phone, you will better focus attention on your partner. If you're being distracted by noise that you can't ignore or reduce, it may be best to reschedule your conversation for a time when fewer stimuli are competing for your attention.

PSEUDOLISTENING AND SELECTIVE ATTENTION

At one time or another, you've probably pretended to pay attention to someone when you weren't really listening, a behavior called **pseudolistening.** When you are pseudolistening, you use feedback behaviors that make it *seem* as though you're paying attention, even

noise Anything that distracts people from listening to what they wish to listen to.

pseudolistening Pretending to listen.

though your mind is elsewhere. A variation of pseudolistening is **selective attention,** which means listening only to what you want to hear and ignoring the rest.[27] With selective attention, you are actually listening to some parts of a person's message but pseudolistening to other parts. In her job as an insurance adjustor, for instance, Sue-Ann receives an evaluation from her supervisor every January. Most of her supervisor's comments are usually positive, but some suggest ways in which Sue-Ann could improve. The problem is, Sue-Ann doesn't listen to those suggestions. Instead, she listens selectively, paying close attention to her supervisor's praise but only pretending to listen to his critiques.

People engage in pseudolistening and selective attention for many different reasons. Think about your own experiences. Maybe you're bored with what a speaker is saying, but you don't want to seem rude. Maybe you don't understand what you're hearing, but you're embarrassed to say so. Maybe you're paying attention to something else while someone is talking to you, or maybe you simply don't like what is being said. Whatever the reason, pseudolistening and selective attention are not only barriers to effective listening; they also can be a source of frustration for those you're pretending to listen to, because (as you probably know from your own experience) people are often aware of when others aren't listening to what they're saying.

INFORMATION OVERLOAD

A third barrier to effective listening is **information overload,** which refers to the state of being overwhelmed by the huge amount of information that each of us takes in every day. We talk to people, watch television, listen to the radio, surf the Internet, thumb through magazines, and read newspapers and college textbooks. At times, the sheer volume of information we have to attend to can seem overwhelming. When it is, we find it hard to listen effectively to new information.

Sources and Effects of Information Overload Consider how many advertising messages you see or hear on a daily basis. We view ads on television, in magazines and newspapers, on billboards, on people's clothing, in junk mail, and in movie previews. We receive ads by fax, hear them on the radio, and find them in product inserts. We see them at gas pumps, at automated teller machines, on banners flying behind airplanes, and on the stickers we peel off apples and bananas. We also receive them in the form of e-mail spam and pop-up announcements on the Internet.

It might seem as though information overload is a product of the digital age, as massive amounts of information have become so easily and immediately available at the stroke of a key. In fact, the term *information overload* was coined in 1970 by sociologist Alvin Toffler in a book discussing the downsides of rapid technological change.[28] Thus, people were experiencing the distracting effects of information overload long before computer-mediated communication was widely used.

One of the biggest problems with information overload is that it can interrupt our attention. If you're e-mailing with an important client, for instance, your ability to pay attention to her messages can be compromised repeatedly by each new radio advertisement you hear, each new faxed announcement you receive, and each new pop-up ad you see. Those interruptions might seem small and inconsequential when considered individually, but when you think about their effects on the entire population over time, they become a significant distraction. In fact, a 2007 analysis by a New York–based management research firm estimated the annual cost to U.S. companies of unnecessary interruptions from information overload to be a staggering $650 billion.[29]

Information overload can be particularly troubling for people with *attention-deficit hyperactivity disorder (ADHD),* a developmental disorder. Individuals with ADHD are often easily distracted and have trouble focusing their attention for very long at a time. They are often also overly active and restless.[31] Although ADHD symptoms usually appear during

Children diagnosed with attention-deficit hyperactivity disorder find information overload significantly problematic.

childhood, a majority of children diagnosed with ADHD will continue to suffer from it as adults.[32] Because of their impaired ability to focus and susceptibility to distraction, individuals with ADHD may have an especially difficult time coping with the volume of information most of us encounter every day.

Avoiding Information Overload from Computer-Mediated Sources You can employ several strategies to reduce the distracting effects of information overload. For example,

- During meetings and important conversations, turn off the ringer on your cell phone or PDA (personal digital assistant) so that you won't be distracted by incoming calls, text messages, and e-mails.
- Set the filters on your e-mail system to reduce spam, and use a pop-up blocker to eliminate ads when you're online.
- Contact the Direct Marketing Association to have your address removed from junk mail lists.
- Use your DVR (digital video recorder) to record your favorite TV shows so that you can watch them at your convenience and skip the commercials.

Employing such strategies will help you to focus more of your attention on others and less on the blitz of information emanating from computer-mediated and other communication sources.

GLAZING OVER

A fourth reason why effective listening is challenging is that the mind thinks much faster than most people talk. Most of us are capable of understanding up to 600 words per minute, but the average person speaks fewer than 150 words per minute.[33] That gap leaves a lot of spare time for the mind to wander, during which we can engage in what researchers call **glazing over,** or daydreaming.

For instance, Rochelle picks up her 6-year-old daughter and 9-year-old son every afternoon, and during the drive home the children describe what they did in school that day. Although she listens to what they say, Rochelle allows her mind to wander as they talk. She thinks about the novel she's reading and ponders her grocery list. Because her children speak more slowly than she can listen, and because the reports of their school activities are similar every day, Rochelle often glazes over when listening to them.

Glazing over is different from pseudolistening, which, as you'll recall, means only pretending to listen. When you're glazing over, you actually *are* listening to the speaker. It's just that you're allowing your mind to drift while doing so.

Glazing over can lead to at least three different problems. First, it can cause you to miss important details in what you're hearing. If you're glazing over while listening to a lecture in your communication course, for instance, you might fail to hear a critical piece of information about the term paper assignment. Second, glazing over might lead you to listen less

selective attention Listening only to what one wants to hear and ignoring the rest.

information overload The state of being overwhelmed by the enormous amount of information encountered each day.

glazing over Daydreaming or allowing the mind to wander while another person is speaking.

critically than you normally would. For example, if your mind is wandering while you're listening to a salesperson describe the terms of a car loan, you might not realize that the deal isn't as good as it seems. Finally, glazing over can make it appear to a speaker that you aren't listening to what he or she is saying, even though you are. In those instances, you can come across as inattentive or dismissive. An effective listener will work to keep his or her focus on what the speaker is saying, instead of daydreaming or thinking about other topics.

REBUTTAL TENDENCY

Regan has recently started work as a customer service representative for an electronics retailer, but his first two weeks on the job have not gone well. He knows he should listen nonjudgmentally to customers as they describe their frustrations with the products they bought, and then offer them his assistance and advice. Instead, Regan begins arguing with customers in his mind, even while they're still speaking. Rather than listening carefully to their concerns, he jumps to conclusions about what the customers have done wrong, and he formulates his response even before the customers have stopped talking.

Regan is enacting a **rebuttal tendency,** the propensity to debate a speaker's point and formulate a reply while that person is still speaking.[34] According to research by business professor Steven Golen, the tendency to think of how you're going to respond to a speaker, arguing with the speaker in your mind, and jumping to conclusions before the speaker has finished talking are all barriers to effective listening.[35] There are two reasons why.

First, the rebuttal tendency requires mental energy that should be spent paying attention to the speaker. That is, it's difficult to listen effectively when all you're thinking about is how to respond. Second, because you're not paying close attention to the speaker, you can easily miss some of the details that might change your response in the first place. Regan had that very experience when a woman returned a wireless Internet router she was having trouble installing. Regan concluded too quickly that she hadn't followed the instructions, and he got sidetracked thinking about what he was going to say in response. Consequently, he didn't hear the customer say that she'd already had a technician guide her through the installation procedure and advise her that the router was defective. If Regan had heard that important detail, he could have exchanged the product efficiently and sent the customer on her way. Instead, he spent 10 minutes telling the customer to do what she had already done, leaving her feeling frustrated and dissatisfied.

We're closed-minded when we refuse to listen to anything with which we disagree.

CLOSED-MINDEDNESS

Another barrier to effective listening is **closed-mindedness,** the tendency not to listen to anything with which one disagrees.[36] Perhaps you know people whom you would describe as closed-minded: They typically refuse to consider the merits of a speaker's point if it conflicts with their own views. They also tend to overreact to certain forms of language, such as slang and profanity, and stop listening to speakers who use them.[37]

Many people who are closed-minded are that way only about particular issues, not about everything. For example, as an educator, Bella prides herself in being open to diverse opinions on a range of topics. When it comes to her own religious beliefs, however, she is so thoroughly convinced of their merits that she refuses to listen to religious ideas that she doesn't already accept. It's as if Bella is shutting her mind to the possibility that any religious ideas besides her own can have value. Many of her teaching colleagues find this reaction off-putting. It prevents Bella not only from learning more about their religious traditions, but also from teaching others about her beliefs, because she refuses to talk about religion with anyone who doesn't already share her views.

Bella should remember that we can listen effectively to people even if we disagree with them. As the Greek philosopher Aristotle (384–322 B.C.) wrote, "It is the mark of an educated mind to be able to entertain a thought without accepting it." When we refuse even to listen to ideas with which we disagree, we limit our ability to learn from other people and their experiences. If you find yourself feeling closed-minded toward particular ideas, remind yourself that listening to an idea doesn't necessarily mean accepting it.

What topics or issues do you tend to be closed-minded about? Why do you think you react that way?

COMPETITIVE INTERRUPTING

Normal conversation is a series of speaking "turns." You speak for a while, and then you allow another person to have a turn, and the conversation goes back and forth. Occasionally, though, people talk when it isn't their turn. We call that behavior *interrupting,* and there are many reasons why people do it. Sometimes they interrupt to express support or enthusiasm for what the other person is saying ("Yeah, I agree!"); sometimes they do so to stop the speaker and ask for clarification ("Wait, I'm not sure what you mean"); and sometimes they talk out of turn to warn the speaker of an impending danger ("Stop! You're spilling your coffee!").

For some people, however, interrupting can be a way to dominate a conversation. Researchers use the term **competitive interrupting** to describe the practice of using interruptions to take control of the conversation. The goal in competitive interrupting is to make sure that you get to speak more than the other person does and that your ideas and perspectives take priority. You can probably think of people who engage in that behavior—individuals with whom you feel you "can't get a word in edgewise."

Although research shows that most interruptions *aren't* competitive, talking with a competitive interrupter can be frustrating.[38] Some people respond by becoming competitive themselves, turning the conversation into a battle of wits; others simply withdraw from the interaction. Studies suggest that on average, men interrupt more often than women.[39] How else do women and men differ in their listening behaviors? Check out the Fact or Fiction? box to find out.

Table 6.2 summarizes the barriers to effective listening. Bear in mind that each of them can be overcome. Specifically, with training and practice, most of us can improve our abilities to listen well, as we'll now consider.

Test Yourself

- What constitutes noise (in the context of listening)?
- What do people do when they pseudolisten?
- How does information overload affect listening ability?
- What does it mean to glaze over?
- When people have a rebuttal tendency, what do they tend to do while listening?
- What does it mean to be closed-minded?
- When are interruptions competitive?

Table 6.2   Barriers to Effective Listening

Noise	Anything that distracts you from listening to what you wish to listen to
Pseudolistening	Using feedback behaviors to give the false impression that you are listening
Selective attention	Listening only to points you want to hear, while ignoring all other points
Information overload	Being overwhelmed with the large amount of information you must take in every day
Glazing over	Daydreaming when you aren't speaking or listening during a conversation
Rebuttal tendency	Propensity to argue inwardly with a speaker and formulate your conclusions and responses prematurely
Closed-mindedness	Refusal even to listen to ideas or positions with which you disagree
Competitive interrupting	Interrupting others to gain control of a conversation

rebuttal tendency The propensity to debate a speaker's point and formulate a reply while that person is still speaking.

closed-mindedness The tendency not to listen to anything with which one disagrees.

competitive interrupting The practice of using interruptions to take control of the conversation.

Sex Matters: Men and Women Listen Differently

In this book we examine several stereotypes about how women and men communicate. Some are outright false; others are true; and some are true but highly exaggerated. One idea that relates to listening is that women and men have different listening styles: Women are more interested in people, whereas men are more interested in facts. Are these distinctions fact or fiction?

Recent research suggests that these assumed differences are true. In a study of adults' listening styles, researchers Stephanie Sargent and James Weaver found that women scored themselves higher on people-oriented listening than men did, a result suggesting that women use their listening skills to learn about people and to make connections with others. In contrast, men scored themselves higher on content-oriented listening than women did, an outcome suggesting that men use their listening skills to take in content and solve intellectual challenges. Those findings do not mean women don't engage in content-oriented listening and that men don't engage in people-oriented listening—they certainly do in both cases. Rather, the study results show that women and men—overall—have different approaches to listening, just as the stereotype suggests.

You might recall reading earlier in this chapter that people often overestimate their listening abilities, so you may wonder how you can have confidence in the result of a study that relies on self-reports. Because virtually every study of listening styles uses a self-report method for collecting data, that's a critical question. The answer is that reporting on *how* you listen is different from reporting on *how well* you listen. Many of us do have a tendency to exaggerate how well we listen, but research suggests that we are much more accurate at reporting the style of listening we use.

How can we apply the information about sex differences in listening styles to improve our communication abilities? When communicating with members of the other sex, we can consider their listening tendencies and formulate our messages accordingly. Let's say you're describing a recent conflict you had with your romantic partner to different friends. Because you know that men tend to focus on the content of what they're hearing, you might tailor your description to male friends to highlight what the conflict was about and what each person's position was. Because you know that women tend to focus on the interpersonal aspects of what they're hearing, you might adapt your description to female friends to focus on what the conflict taught you about your relational partner and yourself. Importantly, although the sex differences in listening preferences are just tendencies, they can still give you clues for communicating optimally with members of each sex.

ASK YOURSELF

- How do those general sex differences compare to the listening behavior of women and men you know?
- Is one style of listening better than another, in your opinion? How might men's and women's styles of listening be appropriate in different situations?

Source: Sargent, S. L., & Weaver, J. B. (2003). Listening styles: Sex differences in perceptions of self and others. *International Journal of Listening*, 17, 5–18.

>> Honing Your Listening Skills

In this chapter we've explored several examples of ineffective listening. We've seen that in the movie *The Break Up,* Gary doesn't listen to Brooke when she says she needs a dozen lemons. We've witnessed that Regan doesn't listen effectively to his customers' complaints and that Rochelle glazes over when listening to her children describe their day at school.

Listening effectively to others can be challenging. Fortunately, effective listening is a skill rather than an innate ability, so it is possible to become a better listener through education and practice. In this section, we'll look at various strategies you can use to improve your skills for informational, critical, and empathic listening.

BECOME A BETTER INFORMATIONAL LISTENER

When you engage in informational listening, your goal is to understand and learn from the speaker's message. For instance, you might be attending a presentation about saving for retirement or listening to your CEO talk about a merger your firm has just completed. How can you make the most of those opportunities?

Separate What Is and Isn't Said One important strategy for improving your informational listening skills is to beware of the tendency to "hear" words or statements that aren't actually said. Think about the last time you saw a TV commercial for a pain reliever, for instance. A common tactic for advertisers is to claim that "nothing is more effective" than their product. What do you learn from hearing that statement? In other words, how would you restate the message in your own words?

The advertisers are hoping you learn that their particular pain reliever is the strongest one available—but that's not really what they said, is it? All they said is that nothing is more effective, a statement that could mean that there may be several other products *just as effective* as theirs. It may also mean that all of the products are equally ineffective! If you listened to that type of ad and concluded that the product was the most effective one available, you arrived at that conclusion on your own. When you are engaged in informational listening, practice being aware of what is actually being said versus what you are simply inferring.

Perhaps the most effective way to determine whether you have understood a speaker's message is to paraphrase it. As we saw earlier in the chapter, paraphrasing means restating a speaker's message in your own words in order to clarify its meaning. If you paraphrase a statement in a way that accurately reflects its meaning, many speakers will reply by confirming your understanding.

Let's suppose that while leaving a theater after a movie, your roommate Dean and you have the following exchange:

> Dean: *I think we should swing by that new barbecue place on the way home.*
>
> You: *You want to pick up some dinner?*
>
> Dean: *Yeah, I'm starving.*

You conclude that Dean is implying that he's hungry and wants to get some food, but that isn't actually what he said. To check your understanding, you therefore paraphrase his statement by putting it into your own words. Because you understood his statement correctly, he replies by confirming your interpretation.

If you paraphrase a statement in a way that changes its meaning, many speakers will reply by correcting your understanding. Let's say the exchange with Dean goes like this:

> Dean: *I think we should swing by that new barbecue place on the way home.*
>
> You: *You want to pick up some dinner?*
>
> Dean: *No, I want to see if my friend Blake is working tonight.*

In that instance, your interpretation of Dean's statement was inaccurate. By paraphrasing his statement, you invited him to correct your understanding, and he did. Paraphrasing is a simple but very efficient way to determine whether you have correctly separated what a speaker has and has not said.

Avoid the Confirmation Bias The **confirmation bias** is the tendency to pay attention only to information that supports our values and beliefs, while discounting or ignoring information that doesn't.[40] This tendency becomes a problem for listening when it causes us to make up our minds about an issue without paying attention to all sides.

Let's say that your close friend Tim is having a conflict with his partner, Eric. Tim confides in you about the negative things Eric has been saying and doing, and because Tim is your friend, you're biased toward believing him. When Eric comes to talk to you about the situation, you tune him out because you've already made up your mind that he's at fault. In this scenario, you're falling victim to the confirmation bias. Because you've already concluded that Tim is behaving fairly, you pay attention only to information that confirms your belief, while tuning out information that does not.

Good informational listeners are aware, however, that their beliefs are not necessarily accurate. Thus, another strategy for improving your informational listening skills is to ask yourself whether you have listened to all sides of an issue before you form a conclusion—or whether, instead, you are simply avoiding information that would lead you to question your beliefs.

Listen for Substance More Than Style The psychological principle called the **vividness effect** is the tendency of dramatic, shocking events to distort our perceptions of reality.[41] We watch news coverage of a deadly plane crash, for instance, and we worry about flying even though we have heard from reliable sources that the probability of dying in a plane crash is only about 1 in 8 million.[42] The vividness effect was also in evidence when, two days after the 1999 massacre at Columbine High School, 63 percent of U.S. Americans indicated in a survey that they thought a shooting at their own child's school was likely, even though only 10 percent of all public schools report just one episode of violent crime in an entire year.[43] The same effect can occur in relationships. For example, if your parents went through a traumatic divorce when you were a child, that experience might make you think that marriage is more likely to fail than it actually is. The reason for all of these mistaken conclusions is that dramatic events are more vivid and memorable than everyday events, so we pay more attention to them.

We can experience much the same problem during informational listening if we focus only on what's most vivid. Let's say that in your history class yesterday, the lecture included dramatic stories and flashy PowerPoint slides that you found highly entertaining, but in today's class the lecture was comparatively dry and lacked those bells and whistles. You shouldn't conclude that the flashy presentation contained better information than the dry one did, or that you necessarily learned more from it. Similarly, you might love being in classes with engaging, humorous teachers, but that doesn't necessarily mean you'll learn more from them than from more serious teachers.

Being a good informational listener means being able to look past what is dramatic and vivid to focus on the *substance* of what you're hearing. That skill starts with being aware of the vividness effect and remembering that vivid experiences can distort your perceptions. The next time you go through a dramatic event or listen to a particularly engaging speaker, ask yourself whether you are listening and paying attention to accurate information instead of being swayed by the event's drama or the speaker's charisma.

BECOME A BETTER CRITICAL LISTENER

Many interpersonal situations require you to assess the reliability and trustworthiness of what you're hearing. Here are three ways to hone that ability.

Be a Skeptic Being a good critical listener starts with being skeptical of what you hear. **Skepticism**—an attitude that involves raising questions or having doubts—isn't about being cynical or finding fault; it's about evaluating the evidence for a claim. As we noted above with respect to the confirmation bias, some people pay attention only to evidence that supports what they already believe. Being skeptical means setting aside your biases

confirmation bias The tendency to pay attention only to information that supports one's values and beliefs, while discounting or ignoring information that does not.

vividness effect The tendency of dramatic, shocking events to distort one's perceptions of reality.

skepticism An attitude that involves raising questions or having doubts.

Good critical listeners set aside their feelings and biases and focus on the merits of the idea.

and being willing to be persuaded by the merits of the argument and the quality of the evidence. A good critical listener doesn't accept claims blindly but questions them to see whether they're valid.[44]

Suppose your co-worker Fahid has come up with a business opportunity, tells you about his plan, and asks you to consider investing in it. Poor critical listeners might make their decision based on how they feel about Fahid or how excited they are at the prospect of making money. If you're a good critical listener, though, you'll set aside your feelings and focus on the merits of Fahid's idea. Does he have a sound business plan? Is there a genuine market for his product? Has he budgeted for advertising? Did he explain how he would use your investment? Being a critical listener doesn't mean criticizing his plans—it means evaluating them to see whether they make sense.

Evaluate a Speaker's Credibility Besides analyzing the merits of an argument, a good critical listener pays attention to the credibility of the speaker. As we've seen, *credibility* refers to the reliability and trustworthiness of someone or something. All other things being equal, you can generally presume that information you hear from a credible source is more believable than information you get from a non-credible source.

Several qualities make a speaker more or less credible. One is expertise. It makes more sense for us to trust medical advice we receive from a physician than from a professional athlete, for instance, because the doctor is a medical expert and the athlete is not. At the same time, it doesn't make sense to trust a physician for legal or financial advice, because he or she isn't an expert in those realms.

It's sometimes easy to confuse *expertise* with *experience*. Having experience with something may give a person credibility in that area, but that experience doesn't necessarily make the individual an expert. Consider Hannah, the mother of six children. In the course of raising her kids, Hannah has become a very experienced parent, and so she has sufficient credibility to give advice to other moms insofar as she can draw on her many experiences. Yet Hannah isn't an expert on parenting, because her only source of credibility is her individual experience. For example, she isn't a recognized authority on parenting issues, nor, as it happens, does she even have a degree in child development.

Conversely, people can be experts on topics and areas with which they have no direct personal experience. As a board-certified obstetrician and gynecologist, Tyrell is an expert on pregnancy and women's health, even though, as a man, he has not personally experienced a pregnancy or a disease to which women are subject. Similarly, Young Li is an outstanding marital therapist who has helped countless couples even though she has never married. How can a man be a good obstetrician and a single person be a good marital

Some researchers think it's even more important to be skeptical of claims that you tend to believe than claims that you don't. Why might that be the case?

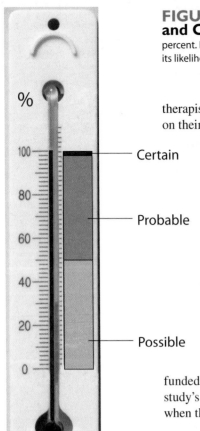

FIGURE 6.2 The Relationship Among Possibility, Probability, and Certainty A statement is *possible* if its likelihood of being true is between 1 percent and 50 percent. It is *probable* if its likelihood of being true is between 51 percent and 99 percent. It is *certain* only if its likelihood of being true is 100 percent.

%

100 — Certain

80 —
— Probable
60 —

40 —

20 —
— Possible
0 —

Truth

therapist? The answer is that they draw on their training and expertise to help others, not on their individual experiences.

Another characteristic that affects a speaker's credibility is bias. If a speaker has a special interest in making you believe some idea or claim, that bias tends to reduce his or her credibility. For instance, if a tobacco company executive claimed publicly that smoking has health benefits, a good critical listener would be highly skeptical because the executive is a biased source. That bias might seem obvious because it is so public, but sometimes you have to dig below the surface to investigate the source behind a particular idea in order to evaluate its credibility. For example, you might be intrigued to hear about a research report claiming that using your cell phone while driving does not increase your risk of being in a collision. You might assume that the study was conducted by a reputable source, such as a research team at a major university, and that assumption would enhance the report's credibility. You decide to investigate further, however, and you discover that the study was funded by a group that lobbies on behalf of the telecommunications industry. Given its purpose, such a group would have had a vested interest in research results that are favorable to cell phone use. The fact that the study was funded by a group with a vested interest in its results doesn't necessarily mean that the study's conclusions are wrong. It does mean, though, that you should be more skeptical when thinking about the results.

Understand Probability Evaluating the merits of a claim means speculating about the likelihood that the claim is true. Such speculation can be tricky, however, because we sometimes confuse what's possible with what's probable, and we sometimes confuse what's probable with what's certain. An event or fact is *possible* if there's even the slightest chance, however small, that it might be true. In contrast, to be *probable,* a statement has to have greater than a 50 percent chance of being true. Finally, a statement is *certain* only if its likelihood of being true is 100 percent and nothing less. Figure 6.2 illustrates the relationship among possibility, probability, and certainty.

Consider a claim such as "I can survive without water for a month." There's a possibility that assertion could be true, but the likelihood is pretty small. The claim certainly isn't probable, and a good critical listener wouldn't treat it as though it were. The statement "I will get married someday" is not only possible, it's also probable, because a very large majority of people marry at least once in their lives. Is that claim therefore certain? No, because there's a chance, however small, that it might not happen. For a claim to be certain, there can be *absolutely no chance* that it isn't true. A claim such as "I will die someday" is certain, because every living being eventually dies. Good critical listeners understand the differences among possibility, probability, and certainty. They bear in mind that a claim that is possible isn't necessarily one that is worth believing.

BECOME A BETTER EMPATHIC LISTENER

Within our relationships, a common goal for listening is to provide empathy and support. Being a good empathic listener can be challenging at times, but it's not impossible.

Listen Nonjudgmentally When we listen to learn, and especially when we listen to evaluate, we often make judgments about the information we're taking in. But good empathic listening is about being open-minded and nonjudgmental.

SHARPEN Your Skills

Television commercials offer ample opportunity to sharpen your critical listening skills. During the next TV show you watch, choose three of the commercials and think about the claims they are making. For each, write a paragraph addressing these questions: How credible are the sources? How probable are the claims? What inferences, unsupported by evidence, do the commercials encourage you to make?

Two strategies are particularly helpful here. First, listen without interrupting. Being supportive and empathic means letting the other person say what he or she needs to say without jumping into the middle of the message. Fight the urge to interrupt, and simply listen to the other person. Second, don't offer advice unless asked. When we're hearing other people tell us their problems, our tendency is often to respond with advice on solving those problems.[45] A good empathic listener remembers that people aren't always looking for advice—they often just want someone to listen to them.

Acknowledge Feelings Empathizing is about understanding how someone else is feeling and trying to relate to those feelings. It's *not* the same as sympathizing, which is feeling sorry for the other person. An important strategy for good empathic listening, therefore, is to acknowledge a speaker's feelings and allow him or her to continue expressing them.

We do so by responding to speakers with *continuer statements,* phrases that identify the emotions a person is experiencing and allow him or her to communicate them further. In contrast, it is important to avoid *terminator statements,* phrases that fail to acknowledge a speaker's emotions, shutting down his or her opportunity to express them. After listening to a patient describe her concerns about the progress of her illness, for instance, empathic physicians can use continuer statements such as "That must make you feel very uncertain" and "I can imagine how scary this must be" to convey to the patient that they understand and appreciate her feelings. Physicians with less empathic ability will be more likely to use terminator statements such as "We're doing everything we can" and "You just need to give this some time." Those types of responses imply to the patient that her feelings are unimportant.

In a 2007 study, researchers examined conversations between advanced cancer patients and their oncologists.[46] With permission, the researchers recorded nearly 400 conversations between patients and oncologists and listened for times when patients expressed negative emotions such as sadness, fear, and anxiety. When those moments arose, the researchers found that oncologists replied with continuer statements only 22 percent of the time. Younger physicians were more likely than older ones to use continuers, and female physicians were more likely than male doctors to do so. Importantly, that finding doesn't mean that oncologists lack empathy. Rather, it illustrates that they may have trouble communicating their empathy through emotionally supportive listening responses, which are particularly important for individuals struggling with a terminal illness such as cancer.

There are times when it may be difficult to empathize with others. For example, if you haven't experienced a great deal of grief in your life, it can be hard to understand the power of that emotion. The Dark Side of Communication box suggests some ways of practicing effective empathic listening during times of grief.

Communicate Support Nonverbally One of the most important aspects of being a good empathic listener is communicating your support nonverbally. When you're listening rather than speaking, your nonverbal behaviors convey your interest, understanding, and empathy to the speaker.

Perhaps the most important nonverbal behavior in this situation is eye contact. Others often watch your eye behaviors to see whether you're paying attention to what they're saying. If you allow yourself to be distracted by your environment, you can convey the message that you aren't really listening. Other important empathic behaviors are your use of facial expressions and touch. A reassuring smile and a warm touch can make people feel as though you understand, support, and empathize with them.[47]

Test Yourself

- What is the vividness effect?
- When should you question another person's credibility?
- Why is it important to listen nonjudgmentally?

THE DARK SIDE of Communication

Times of Grief: Providing Effective Empathic Listening

Dealing with grief—as we do, for instance, when we lose a loved one—is among life's most traumatic experiences. When someone you care about is grieving, one of the ways you can be most supportive is to be a good listener. Listening during times of grief often reflects the dark side of communication because it involves actively attending to something that is difficult to hear. Here are some tips for listening empathically during times of grief:

- Appreciate that everyone grieves differently and that there is no right or wrong way to go through a loss.
- Avoid telling the grieving individual "I know exactly how you feel" unless you have been through the same type of loss yourself.
- Encourage the person to take care of his or her needs, especially physical needs. If you're close to the person and feel it's appropriate, suggest that major personal, financial, and professional decisions be put off until the person is in a better frame of mind.
- Don't try to diminish the person's grief by using a statement such as "you have to be strong" or "look how much you still have." Such imperatives can unfairly make people feel ashamed of their grief.
- Remind the person that you are willing to listen and to help however you can.

Source: Adapted from St. Mary's College Counseling Center Grief and Loss Guidelines: http://www.stmarysca.edu/prospective/undergraduate_admissions/student_life_and_services/student_support/counseling_center/grief.html

For REVIEW >>

- **What does it mean to listen effectively?**

  We listen effectively when we hear, understand, remember, interpret, evaluate, and respond to what someone has said. Cultural messages shape listening, just as they influence many communication behaviors.

- **Why is listening effectively so challenging?**

  Many barriers exist to effective listening, including noise, pseudolistening, selective attention, information overload, glazing over, rebuttal tendency, closed-mindedness, and competitive interrupting.

- **How can you improve your listening skills?**

  You can be a better informational listener by separating what is and isn't said, avoiding the confirmation bias, and listening for substance. You can improve your critical listening skills by being skeptical, evaluating credibility, and understanding probability. You can become better at empathic listening by listening nonjudgmentally, acknowledging a speaker's feelings, and communicating support nonverbally.

Pop Quiz

Multiple Choice

1. Which of the following the statements most accurately reflects how culture affects listening behavior?

   a. In individualistic cultures, people tend to think of time as something that can be saved or spent, and listeners tend to be impatient when speakers do not get to the point.

   b. In collectivistic cultures, people tend to think of time as something that can be saved or spent, and listeners tend to be impatient when speakers do not get to the point.

   c. When listening, people in individualistic cultures pay close attention to nonverbal behaviors to determine the meaning of a speaker's message.

   d. When listening, people in collectivistic cultures pay close attention to nonverbal behaviors to determine the meaning of a speaker's message.

2. The type of listening that involves trying to understand a situation from a speaker's perspective is

   a. informational listening
   b. appreciative listening
   c. critical listening
   d. empathic listening

3. Marilyn's listening style, which emphasizes organization and precision, is best described as

   a. people-oriented
   b. action-oriented
   c. time-oriented
   d. content-oriented

4. In class, Charyn cannot keep her mind off her problems at work. Instead of skipping class, she attends and pretends to listen to the professor's lecture. This behavior (and barrier to effective listening) is known as

   a. information overload
   b. closed-mindedness
   c. pseudolistening
   d. competitive interrupting

5. Understanding probability is crucial for being a good critical listener. Evaluate the following messages and identify which one is true.

   a. For a message to be probable, it has to have at least a 1 percent chance of being true.

   b. For a message to be certain, it must be true 99 percent of the time.

   c. For a message to be possible, it need have only the slightest chance of being true.

   d. For a message to be certain, it has to have a 51 percent chance of being true.

Fill in the Blank

6. Using facial expressions and verbal statements such as "I understand" to let the speaker know you are paying attention is called _____.

7. Jack's tendency to daydream when he isn't listening increases his chances of _____.

8. The _____ style of listening emphasizes efficiency.

9. The tendency to pay attention only to information that supports our values and beliefs, while discounting or ignoring information that does not, is called the _____.

10. _____ is anything that distracts you from listening to what you wish to listen to.

Answers: 1. a; 2. d; 3. b; 4. c; 5. c; 6. backchanneling; 7. glazing over; 8. time-oriented; 9. confirmation bias; 10. noise

KEY TERMS

listening 128	selective attention 138
hearing 128	information overload 138
attending 128	
HURIER model 132	glazing over 139
mnemonics 133	rebuttal tendency 140
informational listening 134	closed-mindedness 140
critical listening 135	competitive interrupting 141
empathic listening 135	confirmation bias 144
noise 137	vividness effect 144
pseudolistening 137	skepticism 144

7

COMMUNIC
AND PROFESSIONAL

FRIENDS IN NEED ARE FRIENDS INDEED

Although he was among the most successful professional basketball players in U.S. history, Steve Kerr has experienced great sorrow in his personal life. While Kerr was an undergraduate student and basketball player, his father—who was then serving as president of the American University of Beirut—was shot and killed by suspected militant nationalists. Understandably devastated by his father's murder, Kerr drew needed emotional support from his coach, his teammates, and the community. During one especially difficult game shortly after his father's death, fans of the opposing team heartlessly taunted Kerr in order to throw off his playing ability. Determined not to let him falter, his teammates and close friends communicated their love and support for Kerr. With that encouragement, he played an outstanding game, leading his team to victory despite the taunting. To this day, Kerr remains appreciative of the crucial role his social and personal relationships played during that dark period in his life.

ATING IN SOCIAL RELATIONSHIPS

- Why do social relationships matter so much to us?
- Which characteristics of friendships make them vital to our social experience and well-being?
- How do we manage social relationships in the workplace?

Imagine what life would be like without friends. Families and romantic relationships are important to us, but our friends and acquaintances contribute significantly to our well-being. Sometimes we look to friends for social and emotional support. Sometimes we seek out our friends when we just want to hang out and relax, and sometimes we do so when we need help making a decision or talking through a problem. Just as his teammates did for Steve Kerr, friends lift our spirits and remind us we're not alone in the world.

This chapter probes the importance of social and professional relationships, such as those between friends and co-workers, and focuses on how we use interpersonal communication to manage them. All relationships are social to some extent. Because romantic and familial relationships often meet different social needs than friendships and workplace relationships, we will examine them in the next chapter.

>> Why Social Relationships Matter

Strong social relationships improve the quality of our life in many ways.

Ann Atwater and C. P. Ellis were never destined to become friends. In the 1970s, Atwater, a poor African American welfare mother, was a civil rights activist in Durham, North Carolina, where Ellis was a leader in the Ku Klux Klan, a violent white supremacist organization. During 10 days of community talks about school desegregation, Ellis came to believe that both whites and minorities would benefit from desegregation, and he and Atwater became partners in the civil rights movement. They also became close personal friends. Together, they struggled against oppression and social stereotypes, and they leaned on each other heavily for support. When Ellis died of Alzheimer's disease in 2005, Atwater, having lost a dear—and most unlikely—friend, gave the eulogy at his funeral.

Each of us can probably think of many friends who support us through life's ups and downs. Having strong social ties with friends,

need to belong theory A psychological theory proposing a fundamental human inclination to bond with others.

People don't just *enjoy* social interaction— they truly *need* it.

By the Numbers

91

Percentage of inmates who experience severe psychological trauma as a result of solitary confinement, according to one study.[1]

neighbors, co-workers, and others improves the quality of our life in multiple ways. In this opening section, we'll see that we form social relationships because we have a strong need to belong. We'll also examine some benefits of our social relationships, as well as certain costs we incur by maintaining them.

WE FORM RELATIONSHIPS BECAUSE WE NEED TO BELONG

In his book *Personal Relationships and Personal Networks* (2007), communication scholar Mac Parks wrote: "We humans are social animals down to our very cells. Nature did not make us noble loners."[2] He's right. One reason social relationships matter is that it's in our nature to form them. In fact, evolutionary psychologists argue that our motivation toward social relationships is innate rather than learned.[3]

That fundamental human inclination to bond with others is the idea behind psychologist Roy Baumeister's **need to belong theory.**[4] His theory says that each of us is born with a drive to seek, form, maintain, and protect strong social relationships. To fulfill that drive, we use communication to form social bonds with others at work, at school, in our neighborhoods, in community and religious organizations, on sports teams, in online communities, and in other social contexts. According to the theory, each of those relationships helps us feel as though we aren't alone because we belong to a social community.

What We Need from Social Relationships The need to belong theory suggests that for us to satisfy our drive for relationships, we need social bonds that are both interactive and emotionally close. For example, most of us wouldn't be satisfied if we had emotionally close relationships with people with whom we never got to communicate. Being cut off from social interaction can be physically and psychologically devastating. That's one of the reasons why solitary confinement is considered such a harsh punishment for prisoners.[5] Women and men who are deployed for military service,[6] and many elderly individuals who live alone,[7] also experience loneliness when they don't see their families or friends for extended periods.

By the same token, interacting only with people for whom we have no real feelings would be unrewarding as well. Imagine, for instance, that you move to a large city where you don't know anyone. Even though you'd have plenty of interactions with people—taxi drivers, grocery store clerks, an eye doctor, the neighborhood dry cleaner—you might not initially encounter anyone to whom you feel close. Although task-oriented relationships help you to accomplish various needs, such as getting from one place to another and having your vision checked, they don't fulfill your need to belong because they usually aren't emotionally close.

Why do you feel the need to belong?

Meeting Our Social Needs Online We develop many of our important relationships in face-to-face contexts. However, we form others online—and research shows that those relationships are often just as emotionally close and involve just as frequent interaction as do our face-to-face relationships.[8] Many of us therefore meet our need to belong partially via electronically mediated communication channels such as e-mail, Facebook, text messaging, and Twitter.

For instance, in a study of adolescents' use of text messaging and instant messaging (IM), communication researchers J. Alison Bryant, Ashley Sanders-Jackson, and Amber Smallwood found that participants used IM as a primary means of communicating with their social networks. In fact, seven of the top eight reasons why adolescents report using IM involved interacting with people they knew, which helped them to maintain (or in some cases to end) their social relationships.[9] Table 7.1 lists the top eight reasons for using IM.

Who forms social relationships online? Only a decade or so ago, people who developed relationships online were somewhat stigmatized as lacking the self-confidence and social skills to form face-to-face bonds.[10] Today, online relationships are so common that it is difficult to distinguish those who form them from those who don't. A study of college students, for example, found no differences in self-esteem, social skills, loneliness, anxiety, or number of face-to-face relationships between individuals who had and had not formed social relationships online.[11]

Just as the Internet provides multiple opportunities for forming positive social relationships, it unfortunately also allows people to offer their friendship in a deceptive, self-serving way. As "The Dark Side of Communication" explains, such behavior can have devastating effects on its victims.

Whether formed online or in person, many social relationships fulfill our needs for interaction and emotional closeness. Each of those social relationships can help us feel connected to others in meaningful and significant ways. The natural "need to belong" is not the only reason social relationships matter to human beings, but Baumeister's need to belong theory suggests that it's one of the biggest reasons.

Table 7.1 Meet Me in Cyberspace: Relating by Instant Message	
Top Eight Reasons for Using Instant Messaging	**Percentage of Respondents**
1. Keep in touch with friends	92%
2. Make plans with friends	88%
3. Play games with IM software	62%
4. Play a trick on someone	60%
5. Ask someone out on a date	44%
6. Write something you wouldn't say in person	42%
7. Send non-text information	39%
8. Break up with someone	24%

THE DARK SIDE of Communication

Cyberbullying

Cyberbullying means using the Internet to inflict emotional or psychological harm on someone, and it often has devastating consequences. In October 2006, for example, teenager Megan Meier from Missouri committed suicide after being lulled into a fake online friendship by the mother of a former friend who was posing on MySpace as a 16-year-old boy named Josh Evans. After weeks of being friendly with Megan, "Josh" suddenly began insulting her and spreading rumors about her to her real-life friends. Two days later, Megan took her own life.

Cyberbullying reflects the dark side of forming and maintaining friendships online. According to research:

Megan Meier, 1992–2006

- Among adolescents, 43 percent have experienced some form of online harassment.
- The most common cyberbullying acts are posting messages on semipublic spaces (such as social networking pages) that make fun of another person, distributing gossip to an individual's social network via e-mail or text message, and posting or distributing embarrassing photos of someone without his or her permission.
- Girls are twice as likely as boys to be the victims of cyberbullying. They are also twice as likely as boys to be the perpetrators of cyberbullying.
- Cyberbullying affects all age groups that interact online, but it is most prevalent among individuals 15 to 16 years old.
- The most common reason people give for perpetrating cyberbullying is to get revenge on the victim.
- Online victims of cyberbullying are 8 times as likely to have carried a weapon to school in the previous 30 days than non-victims.

Source: Hinduja, S., & Patchin, W. J. (2009). *Bullying beyond the schoolyard: Preventing and responding to cyberbullying*. Thousand Oaks, CA: Sage.

SOCIAL RELATIONSHIPS BRING REWARDS

Besides fulfilling our need to belong, social relationships matter also because they bring us rewards. We'll now look at three types of rewards—emotional, material, and health—and find that they are often intertwined in our social relationships.

Social Relationships Bring Emotional Rewards Friends provide at least two types of emotional rewards. One is emotional support, or encouragement during times of emotional turmoil. Whether you're going through a serious crisis or just having a bad day, friends can provide comfort and empathy to help you make it through.[12] When Steve Kerr was dealing with the emotional trauma of losing his father, for instance, his close friends and teammates made sure he knew they were there to listen to and support him. Although the experience was difficult for Kerr, his friends' emotional support helped him to cope.

The second emotional reward of having friends is happiness. We enjoy interacting with friends because it's fun and relaxing and because our friends entertain us. One of

cyberbullying Using the Internet to inflict emotional or psychological harm.

Erin's favorite ways to spend a Friday night, for example, is by inviting her good friends over to cook dinner, watch DVDs, and talk about what's going on in their lives. Hanging out with her close friends always makes Erin feel good. Indeed, many of our happiest times are spent with our close friends around us.[13]

Social Relationships Bring Material Rewards A second way social relationships benefit us is by helping to meet our material needs, such as our needs for money, food, shelter, and transportation. People tend to share those types of resources with others to whom they feel close. When you need help moving, or a place to stay for the weekend, or a few extra dollars to tide you over until payday, you're more likely to have those material needs met if you have strong social relationships to draw on than if you don't. You're also more likely to offer those material rewards to your close friends than to strangers or people you don't know well.

Social Relationships Bring Health Rewards Positive social relationships also promote good health. A study by psychologist Sheldon Cohen and his colleagues found, for instance, that the more social relationships people had, the better able they were to fight off the common cold.[14] Another study reported that people with a strong social network were twice as likely as those without strong relationships to survive after a heart attack.[15] In fact, after reviewing over 60 published studies on the topic, sociologist James House and his colleagues determined that the lack of strong, positive social relationships is as big a risk to premature mortality as cigarette smoking, obesity, and elevated blood pressure.[16] Research suggests that close relationships help people manage the negative effects of stress[17] and maintain a healthy lifestyle.[18]

SOCIAL RELATIONSHIPS CARRY COSTS AS WELL AS BENEFITS

It's relatively easy to think of the benefits of social relationships—they bring us emotional support, help during times of need, and even make us healthier. However, friendships and other social relationships carry costs as well as rewards. Think about what it "costs" you to be friends with someone. A friendship takes time that you might spend doing something rewarding by yourself. It requires an emotional investment, particularly when your friend is in need of your support. There can be material costs associated with doing things together, such as the expenses involved in taking road trips and going out to dinner. Friendships often require physical investments as well—you may not *want* to help your friend move into her new apartment, but you do it anyway because she's your friend.

Much of the time, we decide that the benefits of friendship are well worth the costs. We invest our energies and resources in our friends because they reward us. We spend our time and money with our friends because we feel happy and entertained by their friendship. Some social relationships, however, eventually reach the point where the costs of staying in the relationship outweigh the benefits. As we'll see in the next section, a social exchange orientation suggests that being in that kind of "under-benefited" state can motivate people to end relationships—or at least make them feel unsatisfied in those relationships.

SHARPEN
Your Skills

For a week, record the time, energy, and other resources (money, help, and so on) your friends give you, as well as those you give your friends. How equitable are your friendships in terms of the exchange of resources?

- What is the theory of the need to belong?
- In what ways do social relationships benefit us?
- What sorts of costs are associated with maintaining a friendship?

>> Forming and Maintaining Social Bonds

We've examined why social relationships matter and how we are rewarded by them. In this section, we'll look at several theories that explain the various interpersonal forces that are at work in the formation and development of social relationships. Some of those theories help us to understand with whom we choose to form social relationships, including

- Attraction theory, which describes why we are drawn to others
- Uncertainty reduction theory, which indicates why we initially interact with others

Other theories explain why and how we maintain social relationships once we form them, including

- Social exchange theories, which indicate how we compare our current relationships with our alternatives and how we count our costs and benefits
- Relational maintenance behaviors theory, which concerns the communication behaviors we use to sustain our relationships

ATTRACTION THEORY

Attraction theory explains why individuals are drawn to others. The process of forming most relationships begins with **interpersonal attraction,** the force that draws people together.

You're probably already familiar with the concept of **physical attraction,** or being drawn to someone because of his or her looks, but there are at least two other ways to be attracted to another person. A second type of interpersonal attraction is **social attraction,** which means being attracted to someone's personality. For example, you might like your new officemate at work because of her positive attitude or a great sense of humor. A third kind of interpersonal attraction is **task attraction,** or being attracted to someone's abilities and dependability.[19] You might feel positive toward your new carpool partner because he shows up on time every day, rain or shine, or toward your suitemate because of her excellent karaoke technique. Any or all of those types of attraction can draw you to others and make you want to get to know them.

To consider how physical, social, and task attraction play a role in your own social relationships, think of your closest friend and then respond to the items in The Competent Communicator.

A variety of qualities in a new acquaintance can spark interpersonal attraction, but research suggests that four factors are especially powerful: personal appearance, proximity, similarity, and complementarity. Let's look at each and then also consider the role that culture plays in what we find attractive about others.

We Are Attracted by Appearance When we say that a person is attractive, we often mean that he or she *looks* attractive. Humans are very visually oriented, so finding someone physically attractive often motivates us to get to know that person better. There are at least two reasons for this attraction. One is that we value and appreciate physical attractiveness, so we want to be around people we think are attractive.[20] Another reason is that throughout history, humans have sought others who are physically attractive as mates.[21] Because attractive people often have very healthy genes, their children are likely to have especially good health because they will inherit those genes.[22]

We Are Attracted by Proximity Another important predictor of attraction is **proximity,** or closeness, including how closely together people live or work and thus how often they interact. We're more likely to form attraction—particularly social and task attraction—with people we see often than with those we see rarely.[23] For example, we tend

attraction theory A theory that explains why individuals are drawn to others.

interpersonal attraction The force that draws people together.

physical attraction Attraction to someone's appearance.

social attraction Attraction to someone's personality.

task attraction Attraction to someone's abilities or dependability.

proximity Closeness, as in how closely together people live or work.

What Draws You? Attraction in Your Closest Friendship

Close friendships always include one or more forms of interpersonal attraction. We might be attracted to someone's personality. We might find the person physically attractive. We might also be drawn to someone as a work partner. Think about your current closest friendship. On a scale of 1 (strongly disagree) to 7 (strongly agree), how much would you say you agree or disagree with each of the following statements?

Social Attraction

_____ I find this person easy to be around.

_____ I really enjoy his or her personality.

_____ We get along really well with each other.

_____ He or she is the kind of person I like to spend time with.

Physical Attraction

_____ I think this person is good looking.

_____ He or she has a nice appearance.

_____ Most people would find this person physically attractive.

_____ This person has a nice look.

Task Attraction

_____ This person would be fun to work with.

_____ I can always count on this person.

_____ I would enjoy studying with this person.

_____ This person is very dependable.

Add up your scores for each scale. Each score will range from 4 to 28. For each type of attraction, a score of 4–12 indicates that you don't perceive that type of attraction very strongly for your friend. A score of 13–20 suggests you have a moderate level of that form of attraction. A score of 21–28 indicates that you perceive a good deal of that form of attraction for your friend.

You may find that your scores for each scale differ quite a bit from one another. If so, that simply means your friendship is based more heavily on some forms of attraction than others. In any event, this exercise will give you a chance to reflect on what you find most attractive about your closest friendship.

Source: Items adapted from McCroskey, J. C., & McCain, T. A. (1974). The measurement of interpersonal attraction. *Speech Monographs, 41*, 261–266.

to know our next-door neighbors better than the neighbors down the road, and we're more likely to become friends and maintain friendships with classmates and co-workers than with people we seldom see, such as other students at school or other employees at work.

We Are Attracted by Similarity We've all had the experience of getting to know someone and marveling at how much we have in common with that person. When we meet people with backgrounds, experiences, beliefs, and interests that are similar to our own, we find them to be comfortable and familiar. Sometimes it's almost as if we already know them.

We find similarity to be very attractive, particularly with respect to social attraction. Research shows we're more likely to form social relationships with people who are similar

Magnetic Force? When It Comes to Forming Friendships, Opposites Attract

You've probably heard the expression that "opposites attract." That notion suggests that we find differences attractive and will be drawn most strongly to people who are different from us. Is that fact or fiction?

When we're forming friendships, difference *can* be attractive to us, but only if we see the difference as complementary—that is, if it benefits us in some way, such as by reflecting a positive personality trait that we lack. Study after study has shown, however, that we find similarity to be much more attractive.

In one study, researchers paired up college students at the beginning of a semester with strangers of their same sex and ethnicity. Both people in each pair reported on their individual attitudes, personalities, and ways of seeing the world. Over the next eight weeks, they also reported how much they liked each other. The researchers found that having similar attitudes was the strongest predictor of initial attraction. If their attitudes were highly dissimilar, the students tended not to like each other. The study also found that having similar personalities and ways of seeing the world was the strongest predictor of whether students remained friends after being initially drawn to each other. The results of this and dozens of other studies suggest that when it comes to forming friendships, the more accurate statement would be that "similars attract."

ASK YOURSELF

- Why do you suppose so many people believe that opposites attract?
- Why do we find similarity to be rewarding in a friend?

Source: Neimeyer, R. A., & Mitchell, K. A. (1988). Similarity and attraction: A longitudinal study. *Journal of Social and Personal Relationships, 5,* 131–148.

to us.[24] We often find social validation in those who are familiar to us. In other words, being attracted to people who are similar to us is, in a way, like being attracted to ourselves. We might be especially drawn to individuals who share our hobbies, sense of humor, or worldview, because those people make us feel good about who we are.[25] We don't necessarily think about that effect at a conscious level, but it may nonetheless be one of the reasons we find similarity to be attractive.

We Are Attracted by Complementarity As the Fact or Fiction? box confirms, similarity is often more attractive than difference. Still, opposites can sometimes attract. Specifically, we can be attracted to those who are unlike us if we see their differences as providing **complementarity**—a beneficial supplement by another person of something we lack in ourselves. A shy teenage boy might be drawn to an outgoing female friend because she can help him become more sociable, and a retiree who prefers to plan activities ahead of time might be attracted to a more spontaneous individual.

Culture Sometimes Influences Our Perceptions of Attractiveness Culture influences so many of the ways we interact with others that it shouldn't be a surprise to learn it influences our perceptions of attractiveness as well. According to research, we see the effects of culture most directly on perceptions of physical attractiveness. Some notions of beauty vary widely from culture to culture. Consider weight, for example. In North America and western Europe, a thin, physically fit body type is generally considered most

complementarity The beneficial provision by another person of a quality that one lacks.

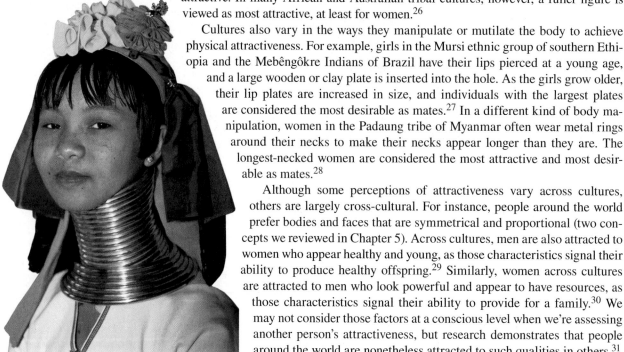

attractive. In many African and Australian tribal cultures, however, a fuller figure is viewed as most attractive, at least for women.[26]

Cultures also vary in the ways they manipulate or mutilate the body to achieve physical attractiveness. For example, girls in the Mursi ethnic group of southern Ethiopia and the Mebêngôkre Indians of Brazil have their lips pierced at a young age, and a large wooden or clay plate is inserted into the hole. As the girls grow older, their lip plates are increased in size, and individuals with the largest plates are considered the most desirable as mates.[27] In a different kind of body manipulation, women in the Padaung tribe of Myanmar often wear metal rings around their necks to make their necks appear longer than they are. The longest-necked women are considered the most attractive and most desirable as mates.[28]

Although some perceptions of attractiveness vary across cultures, others are largely cross-cultural. For instance, people around the world prefer bodies and faces that are symmetrical and proportional (two concepts we reviewed in Chapter 5). Across cultures, men are also attracted to women who appear healthy and young, as those characteristics signal their ability to produce healthy offspring.[29] Similarly, women across cultures are attracted to men who look powerful and appear to have resources, as those characteristics signal their ability to provide for a family.[30] We may not consider those factors at a conscious level when we're assessing another person's attractiveness, but research demonstrates that people around the world are nonetheless attracted to such qualities in others.[31]

Cultures vary significantly in how they manipulate or mutilate the body to make it physically attractive.

UNCERTAINTY REDUCTION THEORY

A second major theory of why we form relationships focuses not on attraction but on the uncertainty we feel when we don't know others very well. Let's say you meet someone and want to get to know the person better. What does it *mean* to get to know that individual? According to communication scholars Charles Berger and Richard Calabrese, it means you're reducing your level of uncertainty about the person.[32]

When you first meet a new co-worker, for instance, you don't know much about her, so your uncertainty about her is high. Berger and Calabrese's **uncertainty reduction theory** suggests that you will find uncertainty to be unpleasant, so you'll be motivated to reduce your uncertainty by using communication behaviors to get to know your new co-worker. At first, you probably talk about basic information, such as where she lives and what she does outside of work. As you get to know her better, she will probably disclose more personal information about herself. You might also learn about her by paying attention to nonverbal cues, such as her personal appearance, the sound of her voice, and her use of gestures. According to uncertainty reduction theory, each new piece of information you gain further reduces your uncertainty.

Importantly, uncertainty reduction theory also proposes that the less uncertain we are, the more we will like a new acquaintance. Because we dislike having uncertainty about people, according to the theory, we will like people more as our uncertainty about them decreases. The relationship between liking and uncertainty, as reflected in uncertainty reduction theory, is shown in Figure 7.1.

What happens if you don't *like* the information you learn about your co-worker? Although your uncertainty has been reduced, does that change guarantee you'll want to get to know her better? Theories developed since uncertainty reduction theory say no. In his *predicted outcome value theory,* communication professor Michael Sunnafrank explained that we consider the merits of what we learn about other people when

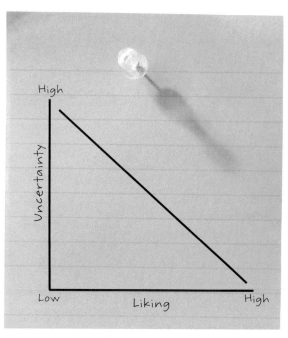

FIGURE 7.1 The Relationship Between Liking and Uncertainty According to Uncertainty Reduction Theory This theory says that as uncertainty about a person goes down, liking for that person goes up.

forming opinions of them.[33] In contrast to uncertainty reduction theory, Sunnafrank's theory suggests that when we dislike the information we learn about others, that information can cause us to like them less, not more.[34]

Research has also shown that cultural background influences how people deal with uncertainty. Recall from Chapter 2 that some cultures accept uncertainty as a normal part of life, whereas others tend to avoid it whenever possible. Some studies have compared participants from Japan—an uncertainty-avoiding society—and the United States—an uncertainty-accepting society. That research has shown that compared to U.S. American adults, Japanese adults are less engaged and less likely to reveal information about themselves when they know little about the person with whom they're interacting. Importantly, that cultural difference emerges whether people are communicating online[35] or in simulated face-to-face conversations.[36]

Even if we do form a social relationship with someone, that doesn't guarantee that we'll want to maintain it. For instance, some friendships start strong but fade over time. Others, though, do continue to grow and flourish. We'll look next at two theoretic traditions that in particular help us to understand why and how we maintain the social relationships we have formed: theories of cost/benefit calculations and theories of relational maintenance behaviors.

SOCIAL EXCHANGE AND EQUITY THEORIES: WEIGHING COSTS AND BENEFITS

Suppose you're drawn to someone, you get to know that person, and now the two of you are friends. You've formed a social relationship—but how will you decide whether you want to stay in it? One way to understand why we maintain certain friendships while letting others fizzle out is by examining the give-and-take of relational costs and benefits.

Earlier in this chapter, we saw that relationships carry costs as well as rewards. We give certain things to a friendship, such as our time, attention, and money, and we get certain benefits out of it, such as emotional support, entertainment, and help. Two specific theories help us understand how those costs and benefits influence which relationships we are most likely to maintain: social exchange theory and equity theory.

Social Exchange Theory The guiding principle of **social exchange theory** is that people seek to maintain relationships in which their benefits outweigh their costs.[37] Think of your relationship with a neighbor. There are costs involved in being neighborly: You have to be willing to help when needed, and there might be a loss of privacy if your

Relationships entail both costs and benefits. According to social exchange theory, we prefer relationships in which the benefits outweigh the costs.

uncertainty reduction theory Theory suggesting that people find uncertainty to be unpleasant, so they are motivated to reduce their uncertainty by getting to know others.

social exchange theory Theory suggesting that people seek to maintain relationships in which their benefits outweigh their costs.

neighbor is aware of your comings and goings. There are also benefits to a neighborly relationship, including knowing your neighbor is there to watch your place when you're away and having someone close by whom you enjoy being around. The question, according to social exchange theory, is whether you think the benefits outweigh the costs. If you do, then you're likely to stay in that relationship; if not, then you're less inclined to maintain it.

An important concept in social exchange theory is **comparison level,** our realistic expectation of what we want and think we deserve from a relationship. That expectation comes both from experience with social relationships and from cultural norms for such relationships. For example, perhaps you think neighbors should be friendly and should offer help when you need it but should otherwise mind their own business. Those ideas would form part of your comparison level for your own neighborly relationships. Perhaps you believe that friends should care about your well-being, always keep your secrets, and support you even when they disagree with your decisions. Those desires and expectations would therefore be part of your comparison level for your own friendships.

Equally important is our **comparison level for alternatives,** which measures how much better or worse our current relationship is than other options. Are you satisfied with your neighborly relationships, or do you think you could find better neighbors if you moved? Likewise, are you happy with your current friendships, or do you think you'd be better off ending those relationships? Social exchange theory suggests that we maintain relationships when we think that maintaining them is better than our alternatives, such as ending those relationships and developing new ones. The theory also indicates that we are most likely to end relationships if we believe staying in them is worse than our alternatives.

Research suggests that in some relationships, our comparison level for a particular relationship will strongly influence *how satisfied we are in that relationship*.[38] Significantly, though, our comparison level for alternatives will more strongly influence *whether that relationship will last*. Even satisfying friendships can end if the alternatives are more appealing. On the other hand, sometimes unsatisfying friendships endure. The association between the comparison level and the comparison level for alternatives is depicted in Figure 7.2.

Social exchange theory therefore provides a rationale for why people maintain relationships that appear to be costly. For example, it helps explain why anyone would stay in an abusive friendship. Any type of abuse—whether physical, psychological, or emotional—represents a cost, rather than a benefit, of being in a relationship. For the person being abused, however, the choice between maintaining and ending the abusive relationship is rarely as simple as it seems to outsiders. Some victims of abuse perceive that an abusive friend's positive qualities make up for his or her negative characteristics; thus, they have a favorable comparison level. Others believe the costs of ending the relationship—which might include loneliness, loss of other friends, or even the threat of violence—exceed the costs of staying in the relationship. In that case, their comparison level exceeds their comparison level for alternatives because they believe that even if the relationship is bad, ending it would be worse.

Equity Theory If we think of social relationships as having costs and rewards, then it's easy to see that both people in a given relationship might not benefit equally. Imagine that your friend Chandra is always texting you about her problems but never seems to have time to listen to you communicate about yours. She's getting the benefit of your time and attention without the cost of giving her own time and attention to you. You, on the other hand, are putting more into the friendship than you're getting from it.

FIGURE 7.2 Comparison Level and Comparison Level for Alternatives in Social Exchange Theory Social exchange theory says that four outcomes are possible when we cross our comparison level with our comparison level for alternatives.

comparison level A realistic expectation of what one wants and thinks one deserves from a relationship.

comparison level for alternatives An assessment of how much better or worse one's current relationship is than one's other options.

over-benefited A state in which one's relational benefits outweigh one's costs.

under-benefited A state in which one's relational costs outweigh one's benefits.

equity theory Theory that a good relationship is one in which a person's ratio of costs and benefits is equal to his or her partner's.

relational maintenance behaviors theory Theory specifying the primary behaviors people use to maintain their relationships.

In that situation, Chandra is **over-benefited** and you are **under-benefited.** According to equity theory, such inequality will lead to trouble.[39] **Equity theory** borrows the concepts of cost and benefit from social exchange theory and extends them, stating that a good relationship is one in which our ratio of costs and benefits is equal to our partner's. It's fine if you're working harder on your relationship than your friend is, as long as you're getting more out of it than she does. For example, if you're doing all the cooking every night but Chandra is letting you share her apartment for free, you're probably getting more out of the friendship than Chandra is, even though you might also be putting more effort into it.

However, if both partners get the same level of benefit but one partner's costs are greater than the other's, equity theory predicts that the partner with the greater costs won't want to maintain that relationship. That doesn't mean relationships have to be equitable every moment or in every instance—just in the long run. In many long-term friendships each friend may be over-benefited at some points and under-benefited at others, but as long as they experience equal costs and rewards in the long run, equity theory predicts that their friendship will be stable.

Our costs and benefits in friendships aren't just a matter of money or other tangible goods. We also invest time, attention, and care in our friends; in an equitable relationship, we reap those rewards back from them. In some situations, however, we may go through prolonged periods when our investments far outweigh our returns, such as when we provide substantial care for someone suffering a significant health problem.

In which relationships, if any, do you feel over-benefited? Why?

RELATIONAL MAINTENANCE BEHAVIORS THEORY

Social exchange theory and equity theory both explain *why* we choose to maintain relationships. In contrast, **relational maintenance behaviors theory** explains *how* we maintain them—specifically, it focuses on the primary behaviors we use to do so.

Let's imagine now that you've made friends with someone, and you're both satisfied with the costs and benefits of your friendship. You'll therefore want to maintain your relationship so that it grows and thrives. How do you do so? Communication researchers Laura Stafford and Dan Canary have found that people use five primary relational maintenance behaviors:[40]

- *Positivity* includes behaviors such as acting friendly and cheerful, being courteous to others, and refraining from criticism. Individuals who engage in positivity behaviors smile a lot, express affection and appreciation for others, and don't complain—in other words, they're pleasant and fun to be around. Those types of behaviors tend to make people well liked.[41]
- *Openness* describes a person's willingness to discuss his or her relationship with a friend or other relational partner. People who use this relational maintenance strategy are likely to disclose their thoughts and feelings, to ask how their friend feels about the relationship, and to confide in their friend. Although it's certainly possible to have too much openness in a relationship, an optimal amount will help maintain the relationship and keep it strong.[42]
- *Assurances* are verbal and nonverbal behaviors that people use to stress their faithfulness and commitment to others. A statement such as "Of course I'll help you; you're my best friend" sends the message that one is committed to the relationship, and it reassures the friend or partner that the relationship has a future.[43]
- *Social networks* include all the friendships and family relationships you have. An important relational maintenance behavior is to share

SHARPEN
Your Skills

Choose one of your friendships and make a point of practicing the five relational maintenance behaviors—positivity, openness, assurances, social networks, and sharing tasks—with that friend over the next few weeks. What changes in your friendship do you notice in that time?

your social networks with another. You and a close friend, for instance, are likely to know each other's family, co-workers, and other friends. When you do, we say that your and your friend's social networks have *converged*. Research shows that convergence is an important way to keep relationships stable and strong.[44]

- *Sharing tasks* means performing one's fair share of the work in a friendship. If your friend gives you a ride to the airport whenever you need it, for example, then it's only fair that you help her paint her apartment when she asks. As we've seen, being in a social relationship requires investments of energy and effort—so, one way of maintaining a relationship is to make sure you're both contributing equally.[45]

You may have additional ways of maintaining your social relationships, such as doing favors for a friend and always asking about his or her day. Many friends also maintain their relationships by participating together in their shared interests, such as watching sporting events, going to movies, and trying out new recipes.[46] In various ways, each of those behaviors conveys the message that you appreciate and value your friend and enjoy his or her company. Because friendships are largely voluntary, feeling appreciated and valued can motivate you to stay in them.

Test Yourself

- What are the differences among physical, social, and task attraction?
- According to uncertainty reduction theory, how is uncertainty related to liking?
- What is a comparison level for alternatives?
- In what ways do people maintain their social relationships?

>> Revealing Ourselves in Relationships

Now that we've explored why and how we form social relationships, let's examine how we communicate about ourselves in those relationships. **Self-disclosure** is the act of intentionally giving others information about ourselves that we believe is true but that we think they don't already have. From intimate conversations about our hopes and dreams to mundane chats about our favorite restaurants, self-disclosure involves revealing a part of ourselves to someone else through communication. In this section, we'll first look at several characteristics of self-disclosure and review some of the benefits that self-disclosure can bring to us and to our relationships. We'll then survey some risks of self-disclosure— and thereby gain insight into avoiding those dangers.

CHARACTERISTICS OF SELF-DISCLOSURE

Most of us engage in some form of self-disclosure on an ongoing basis. Self-disclosure has several important attributes.

self-disclosure Act of intentionally giving others information about oneself that one believes is true but thinks others don't already have.

social penetration theory Theory indicating that the depth and breadth of self-disclosure help us learn about a person we're getting to know.

breadth The range of topics one discusses with various people.

Self-Disclosure Is Intentional and Truthful For an act of communication to qualify as self-disclosure, it must meet two conditions. First, we must deliberately share the information about ourselves. Second, we must believe that the information is true.

Let's say that through a momentary lapse in attention, your friend Dean accidentally mentions his financial problems to you. That incident would not constitute an act of self-disclosure according to the definition provided above, because Dean did not share the information deliberately. Perhaps you can think of instances in which you've unintentionally told another person something about yourself. Those situations are examples of verbal "leakage"—information unintentionally shared with others.

Now let's say that you tell a co-worker that you've never traveled outside your home country. That statement qualifies as self-disclosure if you believe it to be true. Importantly, it's your belief in the truth of the information that matters, not the absolute truth of the statement. Perhaps you traveled outside the country when you were too young to remember. If you believe the information you're providing is true, however, then it qualifies as self-disclosure.

Self-Disclosure Varies in Breadth and Depth **Social penetration theory,** developed by researchers Irwin Altman and Dalmas Taylor and depicted in Figure 7.3, illustrates how self-disclosure over time is like peeling away the layers of an onion: Each self-disclosure helps us learn more and more about a person we're getting to know.[47]

According to social penetration theory, peeling away the layers to get to know someone requires sharing disclosures that vary along two dimensions: breadth and depth. **Breadth** describes the range of topics one discusses with various people. With some people, we might disclose about only certain aspects of our life. In those relationships, our self-disclosure has little breadth, because we disclose about a limited range of topics. With

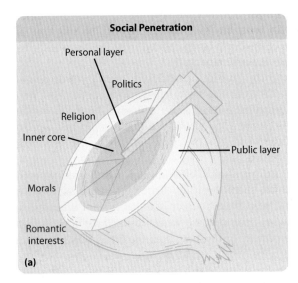

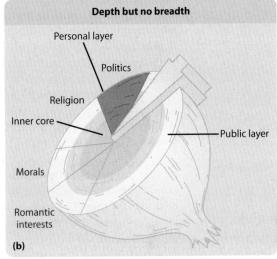

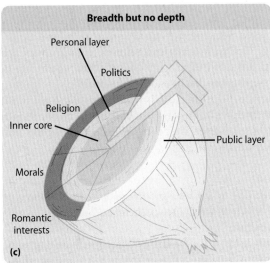

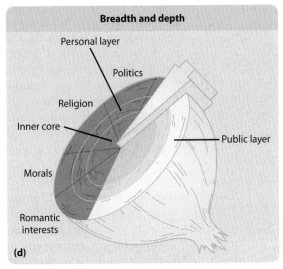

FIGURE 7.3 Social Penetration Theory Researchers use the image of a multilayered onion to represent the process of social penetration in a relationship. The outer layer represents breadth of self-disclosure, and the inner layers reflect depth of self-disclosure. Our close relationships are usually characterized by both breadth and depth.

close friends and co-workers, however, we probably talk about several different aspects of our life, such as our work and school experiences, financial concerns, professional ambitions, health, spiritual or religious beliefs, political opinions, and desires for the future. Our disclosure in those relationships is characterized by greater breadth because we disclose about a wider range of topics.

The second dimension, **depth,** measures how personal or intimate one's disclosures are. The depth of our self-disclosures largely reflects how carefully we feel we must guard the information we might give out. Let's say that Ramona and her romantic partner are having problems. Ramona might describe her difficulties in detail with her mother, not only because she values her opinion but also because she trusts her mother to keep the information private. Because she doesn't feel the need to guard the information from her mother, Ramona can engage in disclosure that has great depth. With her assistant, however, Ramona discloses that she is having difficulty, but she doesn't go into detail because she doesn't feel comfortable entrusting her assistant with the specifics. In that instance, Ramona engages in self-disclosure of lesser depth.

Self-Disclosure Varies Among Relationships
Not every relationship is characterized by the same breadth and depth of self-disclosure. Some relationships involve depth of disclosure but very little breadth. With your accountant, for instance, you might disclose in depth about financial matters but not about anything else. In Figure 7.3b, that type of relationship is depicted by one wedge of the circle being colored from the outermost ring to the innermost, while the other circles remain untouched.

Other relationships are characterized by breadth of disclosure but very little depth. With casual friends at school or work, for example, you might disclose a little about several areas of your life—family, hobbies, political ideas, career ambitions—but not provide intimate details about any of them. As Figure 7.3c reflects, you would depict that type of relationship by coloring in several of the wedges on the circle but only on the outermost ring, leaving the smaller internal rings untouched.

Still other relationships, such as close friendships, often involve high degrees of both breadth and depth. In those relationships, people typically share both public and private information about multiple aspects of their lives. You can see that type of relationship depicted in Figure 7.3d by the coloring of several of the wedges around the circle—with the color extended all the way to the center—to illustrate both the breadth and depth of self-disclosure.

Self-Disclosure Is Usually Reciprocal
You may have heard the adage "One good turn deserves another." That saying suggests that when someone gives you a gift or shares a resource, you should return the favor. Sociologist Alvin Gouldner called that expectation the **norm of reciprocity.**[48] In North American cultures, among others, the norm of reciprocity usually extends to self-disclosure; that is, when we disclose to other people, we typically expect them to disclose to us in return.[49]

There are exceptions to that rule. For example, when we disclose to a physician or counselor, we don't expect that individual to disclose back to us. In our friendships and other personal relationships, however, we generally expect that others will share information with us as we share it with them.

Self-Disclosure Is Influenced by Cultural and Gender Roles
Many factors affect how much information we are willing to disclose to other people, such as the type of relationship we have with them and how long we've known them. Self-disclosure is also affected by the norms for our sex and culture.[50]

Regarding sex, many people probably believe that women self-disclose more than men, because disclosure and emotional expressiveness are a bigger part of the feminine gender role than the masculine gender role, especially in North America.[51] Is that generalization true? The evidence does suggest that women, on average, self-disclose more than men, although the difference is smaller than many people believe.[52]

Self-disclosure is also affected by the norms for the culture in which one grows up. In some cultures, such as those in North America and northern Europe, people are often

When do you choose not to reciprocate another person's self-disclosures?

depth The intimacy of one's self-disclosures.

norm of reciprocity The social expectation that favors should be reciprocated.

encouraged to express themselves and to self-disclose to their friends and family. Other cultures, such as most Asian and Middle Eastern cultures, value discretion and encourage people to disclose only under more limited circumstances. For instance, people in those cultures may be inclined to disclose personal information only within their families or romantic relationships rather than with social or professional acquaintances.[53]

Whereas people in North America and northern Europe are often encouraged to express themselves, people in Asian and Middle Eastern cultures are frequently taught to value discretion.

BENEFITS OF SELF-DISCLOSURE

Self-disclosure can be good for us and for our relationships. Here we take a brief look at four key benefits of self-disclosure: enhancement of relationships and trust; reciprocity; emotional release; and assistance to others.

- *Enhancement of relationships and trust.* One benefit of self-disclosure is that it often helps us maintain high-quality relationships. We tend to disclose the most to people we like—and we also tend to like people who disclose to us.[54] Sharing appropriate self-disclosure in close relationships helps us to maintain those relationships and to reinforce the trust we share with those individuals.[55]

- *Reciprocity.* As noted above, many of us follow a norm of reciprocity when it comes to self-disclosure: When we disclose to others, they tend to disclose back to us.[56] Thus, one way to get to know other people is to tell them about ourselves. When we share personal information with others, they may feel more comfortable doing the same in return.

- *Emotional release.* Sometimes the best part of self-disclosing is just the feeling of getting something "off your chest." Perhaps you've had the experience of holding on to a secret that you felt you just had to talk to someone about. Appropriate self-disclosures can often bring emotional release.[57] Also, as several studies have shown, self-disclosures can reduce the stress of holding on to a secret. That stress reduction is an important benefit because it can improve our mental and physical health.[58]

- *Assistance to others.* We can also self-disclose in ways that help other people, particularly when we are consoling individuals who are going through hard times. If your friend is having difficulty handling his father's death, you might disclose how you managed traumatic situations in your own life. That disclosure can provide comfort and

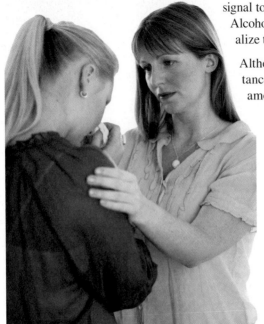

signal to your friend that he's not alone. Many self-help programs, among them Alcoholics Anonymous, encourage such disclosures to help their members realize they are all going through a similar struggle.[59]

Although enhanced relationships, reciprocity, emotional release, and assistance to others are not the only benefits provided by self-disclosure, they're among the most important for social relationships.

RISKS OF SELF-DISCLOSURE

Like many communication behaviors, self-disclosure isn't always a positive action; it has both good and bad aspects. Here we'll look at four potential risks of self-disclosure: rejection; chance of obligating others; hurting others; and violating privacy.

- *Rejection.* When we self-disclose, we allow others to know information about us that they didn't know before. What if the people to whom we're disclosing don't like what we tell them? Let's say your co-worker decides to confide to you that he's gay. His disclosure might bring you closer together. If his sexuality is a problem for you, however, his disclosure could lead you to reject him. Often, the way a person reacts to a disclosure will determine whether its outcome is positive or negative.
- *Chance of obligating others.* The reciprocity of self-disclosure can be a very good thing if we are trying to get to know someone better. On the other hand, it can make the other person feel put on the spot and uncomfortable about disclosing something back. That discomfort may cause awkward silences and uneasiness. Even worse, it could encourage the person to avoid us in the future.
- *Hurt to others.* Beyond making someone uncomfortable, it's possible to hurt others with disclosures that are too critical or too personal. Despite the idea that honesty is the best policy, uncensored candor can lead to wounded feelings and resentment. Indeed, we have all heard that if we can't say something nice, we shouldn't say anything at all. That rule for politeness is meant to reduce the chances that someone may be hurt by a self-disclosure that is too critical.
- *Violation of other people's privacy.* Inappropriate disclosures can even hurt people who aren't participating in the conversation. People in many relationships—including families, friendships, and workplace relationships—share private information with one another that is not meant to be shared with others. When we disclose that information to third parties without permission, we risk hurting our loved ones and damaging their trust in us.

Referring to those outcomes of self-disclosure as risks implies that although they *can* occur when we self-disclose, they aren't guaranteed. When managed with care and sensitivity, self-disclosure can reinforce the most positive aspects of our social and professional relationships.

Self-disclosure can help us console others during difficult times.

- **What are the characteristics of self-disclosure?**
- **How can an individual's self-disclosure benefit other people?**
- **Why is self-disclosure sometimes harmful?**

Test Yourself

>> Characteristics of Friendships

Our friendships with others are likely as different and individual as the friends themselves. Some are probably long-term friendships that seem almost like family ties. Other relationships might be specific to a certain context, such as our job, school, the gym where we

peer A person similar to oneself in status or power.

work out, or the place where we volunteer. Yet nearly all friendships have certain qualities in common. As we'll see in this section, a typical friendship is a voluntary relationship between peers that is governed by rules and differs by sex. Although a particular friendship might be an exception to any of those characteristics, most friendships reflect them all.

FRIENDSHIPS ARE VOLUNTARY

One of the defining characteristics of friendship is that it is *voluntary*.[60] We choose our friends and they choose us; we don't *have to* be friends with anyone. Part of what makes a friendship so special is that both friends are in the relationship by choice.

What friendships do you have, if any, that you feel are involuntary?

When we meet someone we want to be friends with, initiating a friendship requires communication behaviors. Not only do we need to interact with that person to form the friendship in the first place, we also must use relationship maintenance behaviors such as positivity, openness, assurances, network convergence, and sharing tasks to maintain our friendship.

FRIENDSHIPS ARE USUALLY AMONG PEERS

A second important characteristic of friendship is that it is usually a relationship between equals. A **peer** is someone who is similar to us in power or status. We aren't a peer of our professors, boss, or parents, because they all exercise some measure of control over us, at least temporarily. Most of us conceive of friendship as a relationship between peers—people who are our equals, no more or less powerful than we are.

We *can* have satisfying friendships with others who have some type of power over us. Those relationships can be complicated, however, because people in power sometimes have to make decisions that conflict with the friendship. A supervisor might want to share news about an upcoming layoff with a friend who works for her, for instance, but may feel she cannot because of her supervisory position. In such friendships, it is often best to discuss these competing expectations directly and agree on ground rules for addressing them.

FRIENDSHIPS ARE GOVERNED BY RULES

In some ways, a friendship is like a social contract to which both parties agree. By being someone's friend, we acknowledge—at least implicitly—that we expect certain things from that person and that he or she can expect certain things from us. Those expectations are possible because friendships have rules. Even if the rules aren't explicitly stated, most people within a given society usually know and understand them.[61]

As Table 7.2 shows, researchers have studied many of the rules of friendship. Some relate to a specific behavior, such as standing up for our friends or not criticizing them. Others relate to the way we should think or feel about our friends, such as trusting them and not being jealous of their other friendships. Perhaps you've been in a friendship in which one or more of those implicit rules were broken. For example, maybe you found out a friend was criticizing you behind your back, or maybe he consistently failed to show up when you made plans together. Just as with communication rules in general, friendship rules often become explicit only when someone violates them. As research tells us, most people agree there simply are right and wrong ways to treat our friends.[62]

Table 7.2 Friendship Rules

One way to understand a relationship is to think about the rules or expectations that govern it. Researchers Michael Argyle and Monika Henderson have discovered that people have certain rules for friendships. When the parties to the relationship observe these rules, their friendships tend to be stronger. Here are some of the most important friendship rules the researchers found. What rules would *you* add to this list?

- Stand up for your friend in his or her absence.
- Trust each other.
- Offer help when your friend needs it.
- Don't criticize your friend in public.
- Keep your friend's secrets.
- Provide emotional support when needed.
- Respect your friend's privacy.
- Don't be jealous of his or her other friends.

Source: Argyle, M., & Henderson, M. (1984). The rules of friendship. *Journal of Social and Personal Relationships, 1,* 211–237.

FRIENDSHIPS DIFFER BY SEX

You have probably noticed differences between your friendships with women and those with men. Researchers have written volumes about sex differences and similarities in friendships and friendship behaviors. Let's examine those separately for same- and opposite-sex friendships.

Same-Sex Friends For same-sex friends, one of the most consistent findings in research is that women and men value different aspects of their friendships. Friendships between women often emphasize conversational and emotional expressiveness more than do friendships between men.[63] Best friends Juanita and Linsay, for instance, frequently get together just to talk and catch up. Their visits often include sharing their feelings about what's going on in their lives. They would say their ability to share, disclose, and express feelings with each other is what makes their friendship so close.

Compared to women's friendships, men's friendships tend to place a heavier emphasis on shared activities and common interests.[64] For instance, the time Alex spends with his best friend Jake almost always revolves around some activity. It might be playing a round of golf and then having nachos and beer at a sports bar, or working together on Jake's vintage car. For Alex and Jake, it's the *doing,* not the *talking,* that makes their friendship close.

Two aspects of those sex differences are important to note. First, as with nearly all sex differences in behavior, differences in same-sex friendships are just averages. They don't characterize all friendships. Some women's friendships focus more on shared activities than conversation, and some men routinely share personal conversations with their male friends even if they aren't engaged in an activity together. Second, those differences don't mean friendships are any more important to one sex than the other. Some people believe women's friendships are closer and more satisfying than men's because women self-disclose more to each other than men do. Research has instead shown that women and men report equal levels of closeness in their same-sex friendships.[65] What differs between the sexes is simply the characteristics that make those friendships close. For women, it's often shared conversation; for men, it's frequently shared activity.

Opposite-Sex Friends What about opposite-sex friendships, then? Research suggests that both men and women value them as a chance to see things from each other's perspective.[66] Opposite-sex friendships can provide opportunities for men to be emotionally expressive and for women to enjoy shared activities that their same-sex friendships do not.[67] In addition, many opposite-sex friends feel some degree of physical or romantic attraction toward each other,[68] and they often communicate in ways that resemble romantic relationships, such as flirting with each other[69] and sharing sexual humor.[70]

In a study of 324 U.S. American college students, in fact, communication scientists Walid Afifi and Sandra Faulkner found that half of the students reported having engaged in sexual activity in a non-romantic opposite-sex friendship.[71] Some researchers have suggested that sexual activity changes the fundamental nature of an opposite-sex friendship from a platonic to a romantic relationship.[72] Yet more than half of the students in Afifi and Faulkner's study who had engaged in sexual activity with an opposite-sex friend reported no such change in the nature of their relationship. Research by communication scholars Mikayla Hughes, Kelly Morrison, and Kelli Jean Asada suggests that such relationships are more positive if the friends observe certain rules, such as not getting emotionally attached and always practicing safe sex.[73]

Whether they are attracted to each other or not, many opposite-sex friends have specific reasons for not wanting their friendship to evolve into a romantic relationship. In surveys of more than 600 U.S. American college students, communication scholars Susan Messman, Dan Canary, and Kimberly Hause discovered that people avoid romance in their opposite-sex friendships for six primary reasons:[74]

Many opposite-sex friends communicate in ways that resemble romantic relationships, such as by flirting with each other and sharing sexual humor.

- They aren't physically attracted to their friend.
- Their relatives and other friends wouldn't approve of a romantic relationship with the friend.
- They aren't ready to be in a romantic relationship.
- They want to protect their existing friendship.
- They fear being disappointed or hurt.
- They are concerned about a third party, such as a sibling who is romantically interested in the friend.

Studies show that same- and opposite-sex friendships each offer unique rewards. Both women and men report that their same-sex friends are more loyal and helpful than their opposite-sex counterparts.[75] Opposite-sex friendships, however, allow women and men to enjoy those aspects of friendship most valued by the other sex.

Test Yourself

- What does it mean to say that friendship is voluntary?
- What is a peer?
- Which rules are common for friendships?
- Do people report feeling greater loyalty to their same- or opposite-sex friends? Explain.

>> Social Relationships in the Workplace

Nearly all of us will be employed at some point in life, and many of our jobs will require us to interact with other people. It's therefore realistic to assume that most of us will have to relate to and communicate with people we know from work, whether they're co-workers, superiors, subordinates, or customers. Further, many public agencies and private corporations expect specific behaviors from their employees, which might include communicating honestly, treating people with dignity, listening attentively, and being open to others' opinions. All of those communication behaviors contribute to a civil and respectful work environment, and they can also facilitate the formation of workplace friendships.[76]

Friendships at work can be a dual-edged sword. On the one hand, having friends at work can make the workday fun and pleasant and provide us with help and support when we need it. On the other hand, friendship roles and work roles sometimes conflict. For instance, your friends may want to visit with you at work, but if you have tasks to complete by a deadline, you may not have the time to socialize.

Workplace friendships may also be more challenging to control than regular friendships. If you have an argument with a regular friend, you can choose to avoid him or her until you both cool down. Because of your work obligations, however, you may not have that option with workplace friends.

For all of the foregoing reasons, it is particularly useful to understand the dynamics of workplace friendships, so that we can deal with the challenges they present. Let's examine those dynamics in three specific workplace relationships: between co-workers, between superiors and subordinates, and with clients.

SOCIAL RELATIONSHIPS WITH CO-WORKERS

Perhaps the most likely opportunity for forming friendships at work arises with respect to our immediate co-workers. One reason is that co-workers are usually peers rather than superiors or subordinates, so they tend to have levels of power and responsibility similar to ours.[77] Another reason is that by virtue of being co-workers, they share some common experiences with us, such as working for the same company and perhaps the same department and supervisor. On top of that, we typically spend a great deal of time with our co-workers, perhaps even more time than we spend with friends outside work. Thus, there is a ready-made basis for friendship with co-workers.[78]

Research has shown that the quality of people's friendships with their co-workers affects their job satisfaction.[79] That is, the closer we are to our co-workers, the happier we are at work.

As beneficial as they are, friendships with co-workers can be challenging. The reason is that the workplace relationship has both a *social dimension* and a *task dimension,* and those different aspects of the friendship can come into conflict. The social dimension is our personal relationship with a co-worker; the task dimension is our professional relationship.

Let's say you're friends with your co-worker Tonya, who's up for a promotion. *As her friend,* you want her to have the promotion. *As her co-worker,* however, you don't think she deserves it, because in your opinion she hasn't earned it. It's easy to see how your opinion

By the Numbers

9.5

Percentage more likely women are than men to report having friendships with co-workers.[80]

Putting Communication to Work

Name: Mary Dawson

College(s): BA, Boise State University, 2005; MA, Boise State, 2007

Major(s): Undergraduate, mass communication journalism; graduate, organizational communication

Job Title: Grant Administrator and Membership Development Consultant

Salary: Starting between $60,000 and $72,000 annually

Time in Job: 2 years

Work Responsibilities: I am currently employed with a private company that provides firefighter, EMS (emergency medical services), and law enforcement associations with organizational support. In my position I fill several roles, including grant acquisition and management, membership growth campaigns, legislative lobbying, strategic marketing, public and media relations, and web and technology management. In a typical workweek, one day I may be writing and submitting a federal grant and the next day producing commercials for an integrated media campaign. This is the beauty of the position—it allows me to utilize a variety of communication skills learned during the pursuit of my degree.

Why Communication? I took an entry-level communication course and realized it was exactly what I was seeking. I enjoyed the versatility of the degree and the opportunities it provided. The skills I learned as a communication major allow me to interact successfully with people in a variety of careers.

My Advice to Students Become active in your local community. The relationships you develop just might lead to a future job placement, whether you become involved on campus, volunteer in the nearby community, or intern with a local business. In the current economic climate, companies often hire someone they know or someone recommended by a current employee rather than trying to sift through thousands of resumes. The most important thing you can do for your future is to begin building authentic relationships now. Don't forget: Your friend majoring in engineering now may, down the road, be your point of access to a position that otherwise might not have been available to you. Look not only at where your peers are now but where they will be in the future.

might be troublesome for your friendship, but being friends with your co-workers means having to balance the personal and professional sides of the relationship at all times.

In that situation, you might decide it's important to tell Tonya you support her, to voice enthusiasm if she receives the promotion, and to express disappointment if she doesn't, because she's your friend. Even though you don't feel she's earned the promotion, your friendship with Tonya may motivate you to be supportive of her anyway. On the other hand, you might remind Tonya that the promotion is very competitive, that employees with more experience and seniority than she has are competing for the promotion, and that she shouldn't be surprised if she doesn't get it. You might even say "I'm telling you this as your co-worker" to make it clear that you are speaking from the perspective of your professional rather than personal relationship. Which approach you choose will probably depend on the closeness of your friendship and on similar situations you have experienced.

One person who understands the importance of social relationships in the workplace is Mary Dawson, whose story is profiled in Putting Communication to Work.

Have you experienced tensions in your work friendships before? How were they resolved, and with what effects?

SOCIAL RELATIONSHIPS BETWEEN SUPERIORS AND SUBORDINATES

Even though they can be tricky, friendships among co-workers are fairly common. Friendships between superiors and subordinates are considerably more complicated because they include a power differential that co-worker friendships generally do not entail.[81] As we saw earlier in this chapter, one of the defining characteristics of a typical friendship is that it's a relationship between equals. When two friends are a supervisor and an employee, the power difference between them introduces a task dimension that friendships between co-workers usually don't have.

Genuine friendships between superiors and subordinates certainly aren't impossible to form or maintain. Indeed, research shows that being friends with the boss usually adds to a person's job satisfaction.[82] That effect makes sense: If we like our supervisor, we'll probably enjoy working for him or her. The challenge is that what's best for the superior–subordinate relationship isn't always what's best for the friendship. If you're the employee, for instance, you may find yourself disliking decisions your boss makes about the company's policies or future direction, particularly when those decisions might significantly affect you. If you're the supervisor, you may agonize about such decisions, realizing that what's best for the organization is not always what's best for each individual employee.

To save money, for instance, your supervisor may announce that the company will reduce the office support staff on whom you depend to get your work done. How would that decision make you feel as an employee? Or, to accommodate a new business strategy, your boss may decide to cancel a promotional campaign you've been developing. In those cases, it may be hard not to take your boss's actions personally, and they can strain your friendship.[83] In a study of superior–subordinate friendships, communication scholar Theodore Zorn found that superiors commonly experienced those types of tensions between their work responsibilities and their friendships with subordinates.[84] Still, friendships between superiors and subordinates aren't necessarily doomed.

Often, it's best if both parties in a power-imbalanced friendship acknowledge that their friendship and their work relationship might conflict and if they agree to keep those relationships separate. It's helpful, too, if the two can discuss the potential for conflicts directly, particularly if they started their relationship as peers and one of them was later promoted. By acknowledging the possibility of conflicts and establishing their expectations for how to address clashes of interests *before they occur*, a supervisor and an employee can lay the groundwork for a successful friendship. Although doing so doesn't mean they'll avoid the tensions that often accompany that type of relationship, they will be better able to handle those tensions when they arise.

SOCIAL RELATIONSHIPS WITH CLIENTS

In most professions, you'll also interact with customers. For instance, you might work for a financial or technology firm that offers ongoing consulting services to a number of long-term business clients. Depend-

SHARPEN
Your Skills

Suppose you're good friends with your supervisor, Kyle, whose quarterly sales figures have been dismal. Kyle asks you to let him take credit for some of your sales so that he has a chance of getting a satisfactory performance review from his superiors. On the one hand, you recognize the value of making your supervisor look good, and you know Kyle will repay your generosity. On the other hand, you are uncomfortable lying, and you resent the idea of Kyle's taking credit for your hard work. With a friend or classmate, role-play a conversation in which you discuss this situation with Kyle and try to reach agreement on how to resolve it.

ing on the nature of your job, you may have clients you see or talk to on a regular basis, and so it's reasonable to expect that you may form social relationships with some of them.[85] Those relationships can be highly rewarding personally, and they can also benefit your organization because they may be a large part of the reason why your customers continue to buy from you or your company.[86] After all, most of us prefer dealing with a service provider or a salesperson with whom we can develop a comfortable and trusting relationship.

Friendships with customers can run into some of the same task-versus-social tensions that occur with friendships between co-workers and with friendships between superiors and subordinates. Our customers may be our friends, but they still expect us to furnish a high-quality product or service, and we still expect them to provide full and prompt payment. If either party doesn't uphold its end of the bargain, the customer–provider relationship can be disrupted and the friendship can suffer.

Perhaps to avoid those tensions, some companies discourage their employees from developing personal friendships with customers. Although friendliness is critical in customer relations, many businesses recognize that the feelings of loyalty and favor we often have for friends can interfere with the professional relationship. When he took a position as a sales representative for a cable television company, for instance, Deion became close friends with several clients. Because he liked them, he began giving them discounts on their cable service that other customers didn't receive. Because his client-friends liked Deion, they consistently gave him the highest possible scores on customer satisfaction surveys. Those special deals and preferential treatments continued for almost a year before Deion's regional manager realized what was happening. She reprimanded Deion for allowing his friendships with clients to compromise his professional relationships with them.

The separation of personal and professional relationships is particularly important in the health care setting. In the United States, ethical guidelines of the American College of Physicians discourage doctors from treating friends, relatives, intimate partners, or others with whom they have close personal relationships.[87] A doctor's professional judgment and objectivity could be compromised by his or her personal feelings for the patient. If objectivity is lost, then the doctor might not make proper decisions about the patient's condition or treatment and might put the patient's health at risk.

If you do become friends with customers, be especially clear with them about the boundaries between your personal and professional relationships. While conducting business, treat them as you would treat any other customer, and ask them to treat you as they would any other provider. A personal friendship with customers can be successful if the friends agree that their professional relationship is separate and should be treated professionally.

In both our professional and our personal lives, having friends and other social relationships enriches us. English poet Samuel Taylor Coleridge once called friendship a "sheltering tree" to point out that friends can shield and protect us from many of the stresses of life. Friends make our life safer, happier, and more meaningful than it otherwise would be.

Test Yourself

- What do we mean by the terms *social dimension* and *task dimension* in work relationships?
- How are superior–subordinate relationships different from co-worker relationships?
- Why are health care providers discouraged from treating friends?

For REVIEW >>

- Why do social relationships matter so much to us?

  We have a natural need to belong that motivates us to seek, form, and maintain social relationships. Those relationships in turn provide us with emotional, material, and health rewards.

- Which characteristics of friendships make them vital to our social experience and well-being?

  Friendships are voluntary relationships, usually among peers, that are governed by rules and differ by sex.

- How do we manage social relationships in the workplace?

  In relationships with co-workers, superiors, subordinates, and clients, it is important to separate the social dimension of the relationship from its task dimension and to be aware of power differences.

Pop Quiz

Multiple Choice

1. When she meets her neighbor Carma for the first time, Patrice is immediately attracted to her personality. Patrice is experiencing
   a. task attraction
   b. physical attraction
   c. role-limited attraction
   d. social attraction

2. Uncertainty reduction theory states that
   a. uncertainty about someone creates mystery and facilitates attraction toward him or her
   b. we like uncertainty because what we do not know cannot hurt us
   c. uncertainty is unpleasant, and through communication we seek to reduce it
   d. we dislike uncertainty but there is not much we can do about it

3. Jake and Peter are best friends who both invest heavily in their friendship. According to equity theory, the best scenario for Jake is that
   a. his rewards outweigh his costs
   b. his costs outweigh his rewards
   c. his ratio of costs to rewards is the same as Peter's
   d. none of the above

4. The theory illustrating how self-disclosure over time is like peeling away the layers of an onion is
   a. attraction theory
   b. social penetration theory
   c. predicted outcome value theory
   d. social exchange theory

5. Workplace relationships can be challenging because they contain both a social dimension and a
   a. task dimension
   b. complementarity dimension
   c. role-limited dimension
   d. network convergence dimension

Fill in the Blank

6. The theory that says that each of us is born with a desire to seek, form, and maintain social relationships is _____.

7. We can be attracted to others who are different from ourselves if we perceive their differences as _____, or beneficial to ourselves.

8. _____ describes the range of topics we discuss with other people.

9. Because friendships are _____, we choose our friends and they choose us.

10. Relationships between subordinates and superiors can be complicated because they include a _____ difference that co-worker relationships generally do not include.

Answers: 1. d; 2. c; 3. c; 4. b; 5. a; 6. need to belong theory; 7. complementary; 8. Breadth; 9. voluntary; 10. power

KEY TERMS

need to belong theory 153

cyberbullying 155

attraction theory 157

interpersonal attraction 157

physical attraction 157

social attraction 157

task attraction 157

proximity 157

complementarity 159

uncertainty reduction theory 160

social exchange theory 161

comparison level 162

comparison level for alternatives 162

over-benefited 163

under-benefited 163

equity theory 163

relational maintenance behaviors theory 163

self-disclosure 164

social penetration theory 165

breadth 165

depth 166

norm of reciprocity 166

peer 169

8

COMMUNICA

A ROMANTIC LOOK AT ROMANCE

For many people who are raised in Western cultures such as North America and western Europe, a first understanding of intimate relationships comes from fairy tales such as *Cinderella, Sleeping Beauty,* and *Snow White and the Seven Dwarfs.* Those classic stories all offer a similar portrayal of love: A handsome prince rescues a beautiful young woman in distress, and the couple lives happily ever after. Fairy tales provide a romantic—if not realistic—depiction of intimate relationships. Cinderella and her prince never end up in marital therapy. Snow White doesn't argue with her husband about who's taking the kids to school. In real life, however, as individuals grow older, many come to realize that their intimate relationships—such as those with their romantic partners and relatives—entail multiple challenges. The difficulties of intimate relationships may be especially poignant because they conflict so directly with the idealized relationships of childhood stories.

TING IN INTIMATE RELATIONSHIPS

- What makes some relationships intimate?
- How do we form, maintain, and dissolve romantic relationships?
- What makes a family, and how do we communicate in families?

It's difficult to overstate the importance of our intimate relationships. We may have many close friends, co-workers, and other acquaintances, but our relationships with romantic partners and family members are special. Those are the people whose lives affect us the most and with whom we share our deepest sorrows and greatest joys. Most of us invest more in, and feel more committed to, those relationships than any others. The intimate relationships we develop with our families and romantic partners truly shape our lives in unique and important ways.

Family life and romantic relationships also influence each other. Growing up in a family gives most of us our first exposure to the concept of personal relationships and our first examples of romantic unions. Moreover, when we form romantic relationships in adulthood, those often provide the basis for starting new families. Thus, although romantic and familial relationships are different in some notable respects, there is often an intimate connection between the two.

Actor Patrick Swayze was deeply dependent on the commitment of his wife, Lisa Niemi, during his year and a half of treatment for pancreatic cancer, which claimed his life in 2009.

>> The Nature of Intimate Relationships

Many people think specifically of romantic relationships when they hear the word *intimate,* but intimacy is about more than just romance. **Intimacy** means significant emotional closeness that we experience in a relationship, whether romantic or not. Several characteristics are common to intimate relationships. As we'll see in this section, intimate relationships require deep commitment, foster interdependence, require continuous investment, and spark dialectical tensions.

INTIMATE RELATIONSHIPS REQUIRE DEEP COMMITMENT

After being diagnosed with advanced pancreatic cancer in January 2008 that would eventually claim his life, actor Patrick Swayze relied heavily on the commitment of his wife of 34 years, Lisa Niemi. During the 20 months of his illness and treatment, Niemi helped her husband deal with physical and emotional turmoil, and she was at his side when he died in September 2009.

Like Niemi, most of us are more committed to our intimate relationships than we are to other relationships in our lives. For instance, we may be more willing to put aside minor differences and make compromises to preserve our intimate relationships. **Commitment** is our desire to stay in a relationship no matter what happens. When people are committed to each other, they assume they have a future together. That assumption is important because most intimate relationships—such as families and romantic relationships—experience conflict and distress from time to time. What allows us to deal with those difficult times is the belief that our relationship will survive them.

How do we commit ourselves to others? Intimate relationships usually include some level of *emotional commitment,* or a sense of responsibility for each other's feelings and emotional well-being. For example, it's your emotional commitment to your sibling that leads you to listen to his or her problems, even if they seem trivial to you. Our intimate relationships also involve a level of *social commitment,* which motivates us to spend time together, to compromise, to be generous with praise, and to avoid petty conflict. In some romantic relationships, social commitment takes the form of spending time with a partner's friends or family members even if one doesn't enjoy their company. Finally, some intimate relationships are bound by *legal* and *financial commitments,* which are more formal expressions of people's obligations to each other. Parents have a legal responsibility to provide housing, food, clothing, health care, and education for their children who are minors, and family members often take on financial obligations to care for relatives who are aging or who have specific physical or mental needs. No matter what form it takes, commitment is one of the foundations of intimate relationships.

Although deep commitment is important for many relationships, people can take commitment too far. At an extreme level, commitment can turn into obsession, a topic explored in The Dark Side of Communication.

SHARPEN Your Skills

Write a letter to your romantic partner, one of your parents, or another person with whom you have a close relationship and express why you feel so committed to that relationship. Even if you never give the letter to that individual, putting your reasons for your commitment into words can help clarify the importance of that relationship for you.

INTIMATE RELATIONSHIPS FOSTER INTERDEPENDENCE

Another hallmark of intimate relationships is that they include high degrees of **interdependence,** meaning that what happens to one person affects everyone else in the relationship. Because people in families and romantic relationships depend on one another, one person's actions influence others. For instance, how parents use their time and money depends not only on themselves but also on their children's needs. Likewise, how children perform in school and how they treat their siblings also affect their parents. Parents and children are therefore interdependent. So are romantic partners: If a woman is offered a

intimacy Significant emotional closeness experienced in a relationship, whether romantic or not.

commitment The desire to stay in a relationship no matter what happens.

interdependence The state in which what happens to one person affects everyone else in the relationship.

THE DARK SIDE of Communication

When Commitment Becomes Obsession

Although deep commitment is necessary in intimate relationships, an excessive level of commitment can turn into an unhealthy obsession with another person. According to communication scholars William Cupach and Brian Spitzberg, intimate relationships are healthy and satisfying only if both partners desire approximately the same level of connection and interaction with each other. When one partner expresses a substantially higher level of interest in the relationship than the other, the result can be what Cupach and Spitzberg call *obsessive relational intrusion,* or ORI. ORI sometimes occurs between strangers but can also arise in the context of an established relationship in which one partner feels significantly more invested than the other.

ORI can prompt an individual to enact several specific behaviors aimed at increasing intimacy with the target of his or her affections. Those include spying on the target or invading his or her privacy, sending the person unwelcome expressions of attraction or love, and engaging in sexually harassing behaviors. They can also include demanding that the target curtail communication with others and commit to an exclusive relationship with the person.

Although relational intrusion can occur in face-to-face contexts, it is also becoming increasingly common online. Using the Internet, e-mail, or other electronic means to intrude on another person's life is called *cyberstalking.* Intrusive behaviors can have various negative effects on the recipients, including physical and psychological stress, disruptions in everyday routines, loss of sleep or appetite, and diminished trust in others.

Sources: Cupach, W. R., & Spitzberg, B. H. (2004). *The dark side of relationship pursuit: From attraction to obsession and stalking.* Mahwah, NJ: Lawrence Erlbaum Associates; Spitzberg, B. H., & Hoobler, G. (2002). Cyberstalking and the technologies of interpersonal terrorism. *New Media & Society, 4,* 71–92.

Interdependence means that an event or a decision that impacts one person in a relationship—such as taking a job or moving—affects everyone else in the relationship.

job promotion that requires her to relocate, for example, her decision will affect her romantic partner as much as it will affect her. The essence of interdependence is the idea that our actions influence other people's lives as much as they influence our own.

Almost all relationships have some measure of interdependence; what distinguishes intimate relationships is their *degree* of interdependence. You might feel very close to your best friend, but you probably wouldn't sell your house and move if his job were relocated. If your supervisor at work broke her leg, you might send flowers or visit her in the hospital, but you probably wouldn't offer her round-the-clock care.

Like most social relationships, friendships and professional relationships are interdependent to a degree. What typically sets our romantic and familial relationships apart, however, is their *higher* level of interdependence. That higher degree of interdependence often motivates us to engage in greater relational maintenance behaviors than we do with friends or co-workers.

INTIMATE RELATIONSHIPS REQUIRE CONTINUOUS INVESTMENT

Compared to other relationships, intimate relationships usually also involve a higher degree of **investment**—that is, the commitment of our energies and our other resources to those relationships, particularly resources such as time, energy, and attention. We also expect to benefit from that investment—think of our expectations from financial investments, for instance—but we know we cannot retrieve the resources we've dedicated to the relationship if it comes to an end. For example, if we drift apart from our siblings during adulthood, we may retain memories of our relationships, but we cannot retrieve the time, attention, and material resources we invested in them.

People in romantic relationships are often especially aware of how much—and how equitably—they are each investing in the relationship. Research shows that romantic partners are happiest when they feel they are both investing in their relationship to the same degree.[1] If you think you are putting more into your relationship than your partner is, it's easy to feel resentful. The most satisfying intimate relationships appear to be those in which both parties are investing equally.

INTIMATE RELATIONSHIPS SPARK DIALECTICAL TENSIONS

What investments do you make in your most important relationships?

Have you ever felt as though you wanted to be closer to someone but you also wanted to maintain your individuality? In your relationships, have you wished to have more self-disclosure but still wanted to keep some thoughts private? Maybe you enjoy novelty and surprise in your relationships but you also desire them to be stable and predictable. If you can relate to any of those feelings, you have experienced what relationship researchers call **dialectical tensions**—conflicts between two important but opposing needs or desires. Dialectical tensions are common in intimate relationships.[2] Within families, romantic relationships, and even friendships, three dialectical tensions in particular often arise.

Autonomy Versus Connection A common tension in intimate relations is between *autonomy*—the feeling of wanting to be one's own person—and *connection*—the desire to be close to others. People often observe that tension in their children. Especially as children enter adolescence, it's natural for them to desire greater autonomy. After all, adolescence is a period of life when teenagers begin to develop independent identities and make decisions for themselves.[3] Many adolescents, however, still want to be emotionally close to their parents. Even as they are learning to behave like adults, they still need and crave the security of family closeness. In fact, it's not uncommon for parents and children to experience that dialectical tension for some time, even as the children grow into adulthood.

Openness Versus Closedness A second often-experienced dialectical tension in intimate relationships is the conflict between *openness*—the desire for disclosure and honesty—and *closedness*—the desire to keep certain facts, thoughts, or ideas to oneself. Suppose your mother asks you how your new relationship is going. On one hand, you might want to confide in her as a way of reinforcing your closeness to her. On the other hand, you may feel it's best to keep some of the details to yourself, out of respect for your partner's privacy. In other words, part of you desires openness, and another part desires closedness.

Predictability Versus Novelty Finally, many intimate relationships experience conflict between *predictability*—the desire for consistency and stability—and *novelty*—the desire for fresh, new experiences. After nearly 20 years of marriage, for instance, Pauline and Victor were so settled into their routines that their relationship had become highly predictable. Such predictability can be comforting, but at times it made their marriage feel stale and left them longing for something new. They found that trying new activities—such

investment The commitment of one's energies and resources to a relationship.

dialectical tensions Conflicts between two important but opposing relational needs or desires.

as taking a foreign language class together and volunteering at a soup kitchen—provided a refreshing change from the predictability of their life together. By the same token, however, they recognized that predictability gave their relationship an orderliness and certainty they both appreciated.

Researchers believe that dialectical tensions are a normal part of any close, interdependent relationship and that they become problematic only when people fail to manage them constructively. We'll look at several strategies relational partners use to manage dialectical tensions at the end of this chapter.

Test Yourself

- What is commitment?
- What does it mean to be interdependent?
- How do relational partners invest in each other?
- What is a dialectical tension?

>> Characteristics of Romantic Relationships

The most intimate of intimate relationships is often with a romantic partner. Forming romantic relationships is a nearly universal human experience. Some 95 percent of us will get married at least once in our lifetime, and many of those who don't marry will have at least one significant, marriage-like romantic relationship.[4]

Marriages and long-term relationships are very important to our health and well-being. Multiple studies have shown, for instance, that married people live longer[5] and healthier[6] lives than those who never marry. One reason for those findings is that being married reduces a person's likelihood of engaging in risky health behaviors. In line with that idea, research demonstrates that married people, compared to unmarried people, drink less[7] and are less likely to use an illicit drug such as marijuana.[8] They are also less likely to suffer from a psychological disorder such as depression.[9] Several studies have shown that the health benefits of marriage are greater for men than for women.[11] However, women are also healthier if married than if single, particularly if they are unemployed and lack the social support and financial resources employment provides.[12]

By the Numbers

250

Percentage decrease in premature mortality for married men, as compared to single men, other things being equal.[10]

People in every known society form romantic unions, and although many romantic relationships share certain characteristics, there is also diversity among them. Let's look at variations in the extent to which romantic relationships are exclusive, voluntary, based on love, and composed of opposite-sex partners.

If a person in an exclusive relationship interacts sexually with someone else online, does that behavior constitute infidelity—or is the behavior permissible because the sexual interaction didn't occur in "real life"?

ROMANTIC RELATIONSHIPS AND EXCLUSIVITY

One common expectation for romantic relationships is that they are exclusive. Usually, exclusivity takes the form of **monogamy,** which means being in only one romantic relationship at a time and avoiding romantic or sexual involvement with others outside that relationship. Exclusivity is an expression of commitment and faithfulness that romantic partners share and trust each other to uphold. As a result, relational **infidelity,** which means having romantic or sexual interaction with someone outside of one's romantic relationship, is often an emotionally traumatic experience for the partner who is wronged.

However, not all romantic partners expect their relationship to be exclusive. Instead, some choose to have "open" relationships in which romantic and/or sexual involvement with people outside the relationship is accepted.[13] Although it's difficult to know exactly how common this type of relationship is, research indicates that open relationships are observed between heterosexuals,[14] bisexuals,[15] gay men,[16] and lesbians alike.[17]

ROMANTIC RELATIONSHIPS AND VOLUNTARINESS

Another common expectation for romantic relationships is that they are voluntary, meaning that people choose for themselves whether to be romantically involved—and if they decide to, they get to select their romantic partner. That expectation presumes that a relationship is strong and satisfying only if both partners have freely chosen to participate in it. One indicator of that expectation in the United States is the abundance of online and in-person dating services, which allow customers to browse the profiles of prospective partners and choose the ones with whom they want to make contact. One such service—Match.com—boasts over 15 million registered clients.[18]

Even if people enter into romantic relationships voluntarily, they do not always stay in them voluntarily. Indeed, research shows that many people are unhappy in their relationships but stay in them anyway.[19] According to relationship scholars Denise Previti and Paul Amato, the most common reasons people stay in relationships involuntarily are

- They want to provide stability for their children.
- Their religious beliefs disallow separation or divorce.
- They are concerned about the financial implications of separating.
- They see no positive alternatives to their current relationship.[20]

ROMANTIC RELATIONSHIPS AND LOVE

In much of the Western world, people think of marriage and other romantic relationships as being based on love. In individualist societies such as the United States and Canada, that is, people tend to believe not only that they should get to choose their romantic partner but that their choice should be based on love and attraction.[21] Indeed, the typical American wedding ceremony (whether religious or civil) emphasizes the importance of love in the marital relationship, whereas a lack of love is frequently cited as a reason why relationships fail.[22]

Whether or not they love each other, however, some people enter into romantic relationships for other reasons. Some form relationships for financial stability.[23] Others form relationships to gain, consolidate, or protect power,[24] such as when members of royal or politically powerful families intermarry.

Same-sex marriage is a controversial issue in the U.S. and abroad.

ROMANTIC RELATIONSHIPS AND SEXUALITY

People form romantic relationships with others whether they are heterosexual or homosexual. In many ways, people communicate similarly in same- and opposite-sex romantic relationships.[25] Both kinds of relationships value intimacy and equality between relational partners.[26] They both experience conflict[27] and do so over similar topics.[28] They both seek emotional support from family members and friends.[29] Further, they both negotiate how to accomplish mundane (or "instrumental," in researchers' terms) needs such as everyday household chores.[30] Research indicates, in fact, that people in same-sex romantic relationships report levels of relationship satisfaction equal to those of opposite-sex dating, engaged, and married couples.[31]

Despite those similarities, same- and opposite-sex romantic relationships in most parts of the world differ with respect to the legal recognition of their relationships. In the United States and abroad, the question of whether same-sex romantic partners should be allowed to marry has been socially and politically controversial for decades. People in many same-sex relationships live as *domestic partners,* often jointly owning property and raising children together, so many have demanded that they be allowed to legally marry. Supporters of same-sex marriage argue that people should be permitted to marry whomever they love

monogamy The state of being in only one romantic relationship at a time and avoiding romantic or sexual involvement with others outside that relationship.

infidelity Romantic or sexual interaction with someone outside one's romantic relationship.

Some cultures endorse the practice of arranged marriage, in which individuals are expected to marry the partner their parents select for them.

and that it is discriminatory to deny marriage rights to people based on their sex. Opponents say that marriage is inherently a reproductive relationship and that allowing same-sex couples to marry threatens the sanctity of marriage and the family. The issue is likely to remain controversial for some time.

ROMANTIC RELATIONSHIPS AROUND THE WORLD

As we've seen, every common expectation for romantic relationships has exceptions. Each expectation also varies by culture, as we'll discover next.

Culture Affects Expectations for Exclusivity Although exclusivity is often expected for romantic relationships in the Western world, people in many other cultures don't share that expectation. In fact, many countries—primarily in Africa and southern Asia—allow the practice of **polygamy,** in which one person has two or more romantic partners at once. Some people in a polygamous relationship report that they appreciate the closeness and intimacy they share with multiple partners. Others indicate that feelings of jealousy and resentment can lead to increased conflict in such relationships.[32]

Culture Affects Expectations for Voluntariness People in Western cultures usually expect to be able to choose their own romantic partners. In much of the world, however, it is common for other people—usually one's parents—to choose an individual's romantic partner. In fact, according to the practice of *arranged marriage* (which is most common in the Middle East, Asia, and Africa), many people are expected to marry the partner their parents select for them. Sometimes children can reject their parents' selection of a spouse, in which case the parents look for someone else. In other cases, children may be pressured to marry the person their parents have chosen. In either situation, an arranged marriage is not entirely voluntary.

Culture Affects Expectations for Love Would you marry someone you didn't love? Although many people in individualistic Western cultures would say no, many people in collectivistic societies would say yes. For example, in China and India, the choice of

polygamy The state of having two or more romantic partners at once.

So, What Do You Expect?
Your Expectations for Romantic Relationships

People come into romantic relationships with a variety of expectations. What are yours? Read the statements below and circle the numbers for each statement with which you agree. You can take this quiz whether you are currently in a romantic relationship or not.

1. I expect my romantic partner to be my best friend.
2. I expect my romantic relationship to be only one of several important relationships in my life.
3. I expect my romantic relationship to be problem-free.
4. I expect any romantic relationship to have its share of problems.
5. I think the most important aspects of a good romantic relationship are love and attraction.
6. I think a romantic relationship can be successful and satisfying even without high degrees of love and attraction.
7. I expect that once I get married or enter into a significant relationship, I will remain in that relationship until one of us dies.
8. I don't necessarily expect to spend the rest of my life with the same romantic partner.
9. I think living together before marriage sets up the marriage to fail.
10. I think living together before marriage is realistic and wise.

When you're finished, count how many odd-numbered statements you circled. Then count how many even-numbered statements you circled. Which number is greater? If you circled more odd-numbered statements, your expectations for romantic relationships are mostly *idealistic*. You believe in the ideal version of romantic relationships and want that for yourself. If you circled more even-numbered statements, your expectations are mostly *pragmatic*. You may want a good romantic relationship for yourself, but you don't necessarily expect it to be perfect or permanent.

a spouse often has more to do with the wishes and preferences of family and social groups than it does with love, even if the marriage isn't arranged. One study found that only half of the participants in India and Pakistan felt that love was necessary for marriage, whereas 96 percent of the U.S. American participants did.[33] Sociologist Frances Hsu explained that when considering marriage, "an American asks, 'How does my heart feel?' A Chinese [person] asks, 'What will other people say?'"[34]

Culture Affects Expectations for Sexuality Social and legal acceptance of same-sex romantic relationships varies dramatically among different cultures. Currently, same-sex partners can marry with full legal recognition in eight countries: Argentina, Belgium, Canada, the Netherlands, Norway, South Africa, Spain, and Sweden. Several other countries—including Colombia, Denmark, Iceland, Slovenia, and Switzerland—recognize civil unions or domestic partnerships. In sharp contrast, many other countries prohibit people of the same sex from being romantically or sexually involved at all. In some countries—such as Guyana, Uganda, Pakistan, and Tanzania—people convicted of engaging in same-sex relations face a sentence of life in prison. Other countries—including Mauritania, Somalia, Yemen, and Saudi Arabia—impose the death penalty on those who violate laws banning same-sex relations.

Whatever their form, romantic relationships are clearly among the most significant of all human relationships. To examine your own expectations for romantic relationships, see The Competent Communicator.

- What is relational infidelity?
- Why do individuals sometimes stay in relationships involuntarily?
- Other than love, what are some primary reasons that people enter into romantic relationships?
- In what ways is communication in same- and opposite-sex romantic relationships similar?
- What is an arranged marriage, and in what parts of the world is this practice common?

Test Yourself

>> Forming and Communicating in Romantic Relationships

Romantic relationships don't form overnight. Instead, like many important relationships, they evolve. In this section, we'll see that people follow some fairly consistent steps when they develop a romantic relationship. They also vary in how they handle several common communication tasks, and they tend to end their relationships in stages.

GETTING IN: STAGES OF RELATIONSHIP DEVELOPMENT

Communication scholar Mark Knapp has suggested that relationship formation involves five separate stages: initiating, experimenting, intensifying, integrating, and bonding.[35] Let's first take a brief look at each stage:

- *Initiating.* The **initiating stage** occurs when people meet and interact for the first time. For instance, you might make eye contact with someone on the first day of class and decide to introduce yourself, or you might find yourself sitting next to someone on an airplane and strike up a conversation. "What's your name?" and "Where are you from?" are common questions people ask at this initial stage.
- *Experimenting.* When you meet someone in whom you're initially interested, you might move to the **experimenting stage,** during which you have conversations to learn more about that person. Individuals in the experimenting stage might ask questions such as "What movies do you like?" and "What do you do for fun?" to gain basic information about a potential partner. This stage helps individuals decide if they have enough in common to move the relationship forward.
- *Intensifying.* During the **intensifying stage,** people move from being acquaintances to being close friends. They spend more time together and might begin to meet each other's friends. They start to share more intimate information with each other, such as their fears, future goals, and secrets about the past. They also increase their commitment to the relationship and may express that commitment verbally through statements such as "You're really important to me."
- *Integrating.* The **integrating stage** occurs when a deep commitment has formed, and the partners share a strong sense that the relationship has its own identity. At that stage, the partners' lives become integrated with each other, and they also begin to think of themselves as a pair—not just "you" and "I" but "we." Others start expecting to see the two individuals together and begin referring to the pair as a couple.
- *Bonding.* The final stage in Knapp's model of relationship development is the **bonding stage,** in which the partners make a public announcement of their commitment to

initiating stage The stage of relationship development at which people meet and interact for the first time.

experimenting stage The stage of relationship development at which people converse to learn more about each other.

intensifying stage The stage of relationship development at which people move from being acquaintances to being close friends.

integrating stage The stage of relationship development at which a deep commitment has formed, and the partners share a strong sense that the relationship has its own identity.

bonding stage The stage of relationship development at which partners make a public announcement of their commitment to each other.

each other. That might involve moving in together, getting engaged, or having a commitment ceremony. Beyond serving as a public expression of a couple's commitment, bonding also allows individuals to gain the support and approval of people in their social networks.

Individual and Cultural Variations in Relationship Formation Not every couple goes through the stages of relationship development in the same way. Some may stay at the experimenting stage for a long time before moving into the intensifying stage. Others may progress through the stages very quickly. Still others may go as far as the integrating stage but put off the bonding stage. Furthermore, the stages of relational development are not exclusive to opposite-sex romantic couples. Researchers have found that same-sex romantic relationships develop according to the same kinds of steps.[36]

Relationship formation is not necessarily the same in all cultures. In countries that practice arranged marriage, for instance, the process of forming a marital relationship would look much different. It would include negotiation and decision making by the parents and less input (if any) from the children. In countries where polygamy is common, the integration and bonding stages would also look different, because one person may be joining multiple spouses at once. As noted earlier in this chapter, cultures vary in their expectations about romantic relationships—and as their expectations differ, so do their ways of forming relationships.

Forming Relationships Online The Internet provides a wide range of options for meeting people and developing relationships, including social networking sites, chat rooms, bulletin boards, and multi-user dungeons (MUDs). Because the communication capabilities of these various options differ from one another—and from face-to-face interaction—we might expect that relationships would develop quite differently online than in real life. Yet several studies indicate that individuals follow largely the same steps whether forming relationships online or in face-to-face contexts.[37] Even though certain forms of computer-mediated communication impose limits on the ways people can communicate with others, most individuals appear to overcome those limitations and to follow similar trajectories for relationships formed online and offline.[38]

Romantic relationships are as individual as the people in them. Several of the ways people differ are related to their communication behaviors within the relationship, as we consider next.

"Hey...here's a hot prospect...likes catching frisbees, chasing squirrels, hanging head out of car windows..."

COMMUNICATING IN ROMANTIC RELATIONSHIPS

We can learn a lot about the quality of romantic relationships by looking at how the partners communicate with each other. Although couples engage in many forms of communication, four communication behaviors have particular influence on romantic partners' satisfaction with their relationship: conflict, privacy, emotional communication, and instrumental communication.

Romantic Relationships Vary in How They Handle Conflict Conflict is a common characteristic of many romantic relationships. Communication scholars William Wilmot and Joyce Hocker define **conflict** as "an expressed struggle between at least two interdependent parties who perceive incompatible goals, scarce resources, and interference from the other party in achieving their goals."[39] Partners in a romantic relationship can have conflicts about many issues, including how they spend their time and money, raise their children, manage their personal and professional obligations, and enact their sex life. Although conflict isn't fun, it isn't necessarily bad for a relationship. The way

conflict An expressed struggle between at least two interdependent parties who perceive incompatible goals, scarce resources, and interference from the other party in achieving their goals.

couples handle conflict—rather than the amount of conflict they have—is what influences the success of their relationship.

Much of what we know about how romantic partners handle conflict comes from research on marriage. For instance, social psychologist and marital therapist John Gottman has spent many years studying how spouses communicate during conflict episodes.[40] His work suggests marital couples can be classified into four groups, depending on how they handle conflict:[41]

- *Validating couples* talk about their disagreements openly and cooperatively. In such couples, spouses communicate respect for each other's opinions even when they disagree with them. They stay calm when discussing hotly contested topics. They also use humor and expressions of positive emotion to defuse the tension that conflict can create.
- *Volatile couples* also talk about their disagreements openly, but in a way that is competitive rather than cooperative. In volatile couples, each spouse tries to persuade the other to adopt his or her point of view. Conflicts in such couples tend to be marked with expressions of negative rather than positive emotion. Those conflicts, however, are often followed by intense periods of affection and "making up."
- *Conflict-avoiding couples* talk about their disagreements covertly rather than openly. To avoid the discomfort of engaging in conflict directly, spouses in such couples try to defuse negative emotion and focus on their similarities. They feel there is little to be gained by engaging in conflict directly, believing that most problems will resolve themselves. They often "agree to disagree," a position that can side-step conflict but can also leave their points of disagreement unresolved.
- *Hostile couples* have frequent and intense conflict. During conflict episodes, spouses in such couples use negative emotion displays, such as harsh tones of voice and facial expressions of anger or frustration. They also engage in personal attacks, insults, sarcasm, name calling, blaming, and other forms of criticism with each other.

Although Gottman developed his categories with reference to married couples, more recent work by researchers Thomas Holman and Mark Jarvis has indicated that the same categories also apply to unmarried heterosexual couples.[42] Less research has examined the conflict communication of lesbian and gay couples, but Gottman's studies have identified some differences in the conflict styles of homosexual and heterosexual couples. Specifically, his research has found that compared to heterosexual couples, gay and lesbian couples

- Use more humor and positive emotion during conflict conversations
- Are less likely to become hostile after a conflict
- Use fewer displays of dominance and power during a conflict episode
- Are less likely to take conflict personally
- Stay calmer emotionally and physiologically during conflict

For many romantic relationships, conflict is an unpleasant but unavoidable fact of life. We will learn more about successful strategies for managing conflict later in this chapter.

Romantic Relationships Vary in How They Handle Privacy In every romantic relationship, the partners must choose for themselves how to manage information they consider to be private. When Kali and Neal were having difficulty conceiving a child, for instance, they carefully considered whom they were going to tell. Neal felt the information was no one's business but theirs and preferred to keep it private. Kali wanted to tell her family and close friends because she needed their emotional support. Their problems conceiving were causing enough stress in their relationship already; disagreeing on whether to keep the problems private was only making matters more stressful.

Communication scientist Sandra Petronio believes that we all experience tensions between disclosing certain information and keeping it private. She developed **communication privacy management (CPM) theory** to explain how individuals and couples manage those tensions.[43] CPM theory would say that Kali and Neal *jointly own* the information about their problems. The information belongs to them, and so they must decide whether to keep it to themselves or share it with others.

communication privacy management (CPM) theory A theory explaining how people in relationships negotiate the tension between disclosing information and keeping it private.

Individuals and couples vary in their approach to privacy. Some of us are "open books"—that is, uninhibited about disclosing private information to others. Others are discreet, sharing private information only with a select few. Research indicates that some of us are simply more inclined than others to disclose private information. In most cases, however, our decisions about sharing information are influenced by the people to whom we are disclosing it, by how much we trust them, and by how much they have disclosed to us.[44] No matter what our reasons for disclosing to others, we should always be cognizant of information that a romantic partner expects us to keep private.

Romantic Relationships Vary in How They Handle Emotional Communication Emotional communication is an important part of most romantic relationships. Research tells us that how romantic partners express emotion to each other can say a lot about the quality of their relationship.[45] Specifically, it reflects how satisfied the partners are with each other.[46]

Suppose for example that Anita and her husband Jonah have been together for eight years. They co-own a home where they run a small pottery studio and raise Jonah's twin girls from a previous marriage. They have their challenges just like any couple, but they are both highly satisfied with their relationship. Now suppose that Brad and Lynne live across the street from Anita and Jonah. They have been together for almost 10 years but have separated twice in that time. Their most recent separation lasted seven months and would have ended their relationship permanently were it not for pressure from Lynne's family for the couple to work out their difficulties. Both Brad and Lynne would describe their relationship as very unsatisfying.

According to research, one of the most noticeable differences in the communication patterns of those two couples will be in their expression of emotion. Over the course of several studies, social psychologists John Gottman and Robert Levenson have identified two patterns of emotional communication that differentiate happy from unhappy couples.

First, happy partners such as Anita and Jonah communicate more positive emotion and less negative emotion with each other than do unhappy partners such as Brad and Lynne.[47] In particular, people in satisfying relationships express more affection, use more humor, and communicate more assurances (that is, verbal expressions of their commitment to the relationship). In comparison, people in unsatisfying relationships express more negative emotion in the form of anger, contempt, sadness, and hostility.[48] Gottman's work has found, specifically, that people in satisfying couples maintain a ratio of approximately five positive behaviors for every one negative behavior.[49]

Romantic partners must communicate about several instrumental tasks, such as making dinner and taking children to soccer practice.

The second pattern of emotional communication Gottman and Levenson identified is that unhappy couples are more likely than happy couples to reciprocate expressions of negative emotion.[50] When Lynne criticizes or expresses anger toward Brad, for example, he often reciprocates her behavior by expressing criticism or anger back at her. That type of response escalates the negativity in their conversation. As a result, they often find it difficult to address the issues underlying their conflict because they are so focused on the negative emotion they're each communicating. In comparison, people in happy couples are more likely to respond to negative expressions with positive or neutral ones.

Romantic Relationships Vary in How They Handle Instrumental Communication People in most romantic relationships communicate with each other about instrumental (day-to-day) topics such as who's making dinner and who's taking the children to soccer practice.[51] The fact that instrumental communication addresses the necessary daily tasks couples face

Romantic partners don't always divide instrumental tasks along traditional gender lines. Thus, a woman may elect to take responsibility for both child care and home maintenance.

explains why it is one of the most common forms of communication among romantic partners.[52] It can also be one of the most contentious issues couples face, as romantic partners often disagree over the division of responsibilities for instrumental tasks.[53]

How partners negotiate the division of everyday tasks matters for their relationship for at least two reasons. First, day-to-day tasks such as cleaning, cooking, and childcare *need* to be completed, so most couples cannot leave decisions about who will do them to chance. Second, the way in which partners divide mundane, everyday tasks often reflects the balance of power in their relationship.[54] If one partner assumes greater power and control than the other, that partner is in a greater position to dictate how tasks will be divided. If instead both partners see themselves as equally powerful, the division of instrumental tasks can be more equitable.[55]

Romantic relationships vary greatly in how the partners communicate about the division of day-to-day tasks. In opposite-sex relationships, partners who believe in traditional gender role behaviors will often divide instrumental tasks along stereotypical gender lines.[56] Thus, men perform tasks such as yard maintenance and auto repair, whereas women take responsibility for meal preparation and childcare. In contrast, partners who do not necessarily adopt traditional gender role behaviors frequently have a conflict over how instrumental tasks should be divided.[57] Specifically, women often wish their partners would take greater responsibility for household tasks and childcare than they actually do.[58] Compared to men, women are more likely to feel that the division of instrumental tasks is unfair, and those feelings reduce their relational satisfaction.[59]

With regard to same-sex relationships, recent research has speculated that homosexual partners may divide instrumental tasks more equally than opposite-sex partners, with each same-sex partner sharing in both stereotypically masculine and stereotypically feminine responsibilities. In a survey of 113 same-sex romantic couples from around the United States, communication researcher Justin Boren discovered that such a pattern was common, particularly among couples who were highly satisfied with their relationships.[60]

SHARPEN Your Skills

Identify a couple in which the partners have been together for at least 10 years, and ask the partners (together or separately) how their communication patterns have changed in the time they've been together. Also, ask them what advice they would give to others about communicating successfully in relationships. Document your findings.

GETTING OUT: ENDING ROMANTIC RELATIONSHIPS

Just as romantic relationships develop over time, they also come apart over time. Communication researcher Mark Knapp has described five stages that relationships go through when they end: differentiating, circumscribing, stagnating, avoiding, and terminating.[61]

differentiating stage The stage of relationship dissolution at which partners begin to view their differences as undesirable or annoying.

circumscribing stage The stage of relationship dissolution at which partners begin to decrease the quality and quantity of their communication with each other.

stagnating stage The stage of relationship dissolution at which the relationship stops growing and the partners feel as if they are just "going through the motions."

- *Differentiating.* Partners in any romantic relationship are similar to each other in some ways and different in other ways. In happy, stable relationships, partners see their differences as complementary. At the **differentiating stage,** however, partners begin to view their differences as undesirable or annoying.
- *Circumscribing.* When romantic partners enter the **circumscribing stage,** they begin to decrease the quality and quantity of their communication with each other. Their purpose in doing so is to avoid

dealing with conflicts.[62] At the circumscribing stage, partners start spending more time apart.[63] When they're together, they usually don't talk about problems, disagreements, or sensitive issues in their relationship and instead focus on "safe" topics and issues about which they agree.

- *Stagnating.* If circumscribing progresses to the point where the partners are barely speaking to each other, the relationship enters the **stagnating stage,** at which time the relationship stops growing, and the partners feel as if they are just "going through the motions." Partners avoid communicating about anything important because they fear it will only lead to conflict. Many relationships stay stagnant for long periods of time.

- *Avoiding.* When partners decide they are no longer willing to live in a stagnant relationship, they enter the **avoiding stage,** during which they create physical and emotional distance from each other. Some partners take a direct route to creating distance, such as by moving out of the house or saying "I can't be around you right now." Others create distance indirectly, for example by making up excuses for being apart ("I have company in town all next week, so I won't be able to see you") and curtailing availability to the other person by screening phone calls or not responding to instant messages.

- *Terminating.* The last stage in Knapp's model of relationship dissolution is the **terminating stage,** at which point the relationship is officially judged to be over. In nonmarital relationships, that usually involves one or both partners' moving out if the partners shared a residence. It also includes dividing property, announcing to friends and family that the relationship has ended, and negotiating the rules of any future contact between the partners. For legally married partners, relational termination means getting a **divorce,** which is the legal discontinuation of the marriage. In the United States today, approximately 40 percent of all marriages end in divorce.[64]

The decision to terminate a romantic relationship is a significant one. It often requires a substantial reorganization of the family, and it can take an enormous mental and emotional toll, particularly on children. Research shows that children can be negatively affected by divorce or relationship dissolution well into their own adulthood.[65] That isn't always the case, though. When the romantic relationship is highly conflicted, neglectful, or abusive, for instance, children and their parents are often better off after the relationship ends.[66]

Test Yourself

- What are the stages of relationship development?
- How are validating, volatile, and conflict-avoiding couples different?
- What are the stages of relationship dissolution?

>> Communicating in Families

It's hard to overestimate the importance of family to one's life. For most of us, our first relationships are with our family members. Familial relationships can provide us with a feeling of belonging, a sense of our own history, and a measure of unconditional love and support we cannot find anywhere else. Growing up in a family also introduces us to the concept of relationships and can help us form mental models for how to engage in friendships and romantic relationships in adolescence and adulthood. Families can moreover be a source of great frustration and heartache—and many family relationships experience both peace and conflict. The depth of our engagement with families, and the fact that they can be both so positive *and* so negative, make families one of our most important intimate relationships.

avoiding stage The stage of relationship dissolution at which partners create physical and emotional distance from each other.

terminating stage The stage of relationship dissolution at which the relationship is officially deemed to be over.

divorce The legal discontinuation of a marriage.

In this section, we'll examine what makes a family a family and what characteristics familial relationships often share. We'll also survey types of family structures and discover what communication issues are common in family relationships.

WHAT MAKES A FAMILY?

If you were asked to draw a picture of your family, whom would you choose to include? Some people might be obvious options, such as your parents, spouse, siblings, and children. How about your grandparents? Nieces and nephews? In-laws? What about your stepsiblings? Maybe there are close friends or longtime neighbors whom you think of as family—would you include them?

Even researchers have difficulty defining exactly what makes a family a family, yet many scholars agree that most family relationships have one or more of three important characteristics: genetic ties, legal obligations, and role behaviors. Let's briefly examine each.

If you had to come up with a definition of family, what would it be?

Genetic Ties Many family members are related "by blood," meaning they share a specified proportion of their genetic material. For instance, you share about 50 percent of your genes with your biological mother, biological father, and each full biological sibling (or 100 percent if you're an identical twin or triplet). With your grandparents, aunts and uncles, and any half-siblings, you share about 25 percent of your genes, and with cousins, it's about 12.5 percent.

However, a genetic link isn't the only characteristic that defines family relationships. Consider that we typically share zero percent of our genes with our spouses, steprelatives, and adopted relatives, yet we generally consider them to be family. Moreover, although sharing a genetic tie makes two people biological relatives, it does not necessarily mean they share a social or an emotional relationship.

Legal Obligations Another aspect of many family relationships is that they involve legal bonds. For example, parents have many legal obligations toward their minor children, and neglecting their responsibilities to house, feed, educate, and care for their children is a crime.[67] Furthermore, marriage is the most heavily regulated family relationship from a legal perspective—in the United States, well over a thousand different federal laws govern some aspect of marriage.[68]

The law also regulates adoptive relationships and domestic partnerships, and even stepfamily relationships are affected by the laws regulating the stepparents' marriages. The existence of a legal familial bond is therefore another characteristic of many family relationships. Family members may feel they have responsibilities to one another even without the law's saying so, but laws formalize those responsibilities and help to ensure that they are met.

Identical twins are called "identical" because they share 100 percent of their genetic material with each other. Fraternal twins share only 50 percent of their genes—the same as other biological siblings.

Role Behaviors Regardless of whether a relationship is bound by genetic or legal ties, many people believe that the most important characteristic that defines a family is that the people in it *act* like family. According to that idea, there are certain behaviors or roles that family members are expected to enact. Those may include living together, taking care of and loving one another, and representing themselves as a family to outsiders. People who enact such behaviors and who think of themselves as family are therefore family, according to that definition.

These elements—genetic, legal, and role—are not mutually exclusive, and some relationships, such as parental relationships, include all three. Rather, they are characteristics that often help to define a relationship as familial. How researchers define family is important because that determines, in part, which relationships family scholars study and which they do not. How *you* define family is also important because that can influence whom you invite to significant occasions in your life, with whom you share resources, and to whom you entrust secrets or sensitive information.

TYPES OF FAMILIES

One of the reasons it can be tricky to talk about families is that they come in so many forms. We'll examine some of the diversity of family types in this section.

Let's begin by distinguishing between what researchers call family of origin and family of procreation. **Family of origin** is the family we grew up in, so it typically consists of our parents or stepparents and any siblings we have. **Family of procreation** is the family we start as an adult, and it consists of our spouse or romantic partner and/or any children we raise as our own. Most adults would say they belong to both a family of origin and a family of procreation; others, however, may identify with only one type of family or with neither type.

Families of origin and families of procreation develop in many forms. Perhaps the most traditional profile consists of a married woman and man and their biological children. Researchers often call that configuration a *nuclear family,* and it is the traditional family form in the United States. Is the nuclear family still the most common type today? See the Fact or Fiction? box to find out.[69] One family type that is becoming increasingly common is the *blended family,* with two adult partners (who may be married or cohabiting and of

Families come in many forms.

family of origin The family in which one grows up, usually consisting of parents and siblings.

family of procreation The family one starts as an adult, usually consisting of a spouse or romantic partner and children.

Still Going Nuclear:
The Average U.S. Family Remains a Nuclear Family

In the 1950s TV show *Leave It to Beaver,* the Cleaver family was like most U.S. American families at the time: a legally married husband and wife and their biological children living together in the same household. For decades, people have referred to that arrangement as the "average American family," and in the 1950s, almost two-thirds of families in the United States fit that description. The Simpsons, from the animated series of the same name, represent the same family configuration. Is the average American family of today still nuclear in form?

The answer is no. According to the U.S. Census Bureau, fewer than 50 percent of families in the United States are now headed by a married couple. That statistic doesn't mean fewer people are marrying—rather, it means more U.S. American families are now headed by single adults, cohabiting opposite-sex couples, and cohabiting same-sex couples than at any point in U.S. history.

Furthermore, typical family arrangements vary around the country. According to the Census Bureau's American Community Survey, the highest percentage of families headed by a married couple is in Utah County, Utah, at nearly 70 percent. The lowest, at just 26 percent, is in Manhattan, New York.

ASK YOURSELF

- Do you consider your family of origin to be average or typical? If so, in what ways?
- How do you think changes in the family structure affect the ways family members communicate?

Source: U.S. Census Bureau. (2006). American community survey. Available online at: http://www.census.gov/acs/www/

the same or opposite sex) raising children who are not the biological offspring of both partners. The children might be adopted, or they might be the biological offspring of one of the parents and the stepchildren of the other.

A third family form is the *single-parent family,* in which one adult raises one or more children. As in blended families, the children may be the parent's biological offspring or they may be adopted or stepchildren. There are more than 12 million single-parent families in the United States, and 10 million of those are headed by a single mother.[70]

COMMUNICATION ISSUES IN FAMILIES

As in all significant relationships, communication plays a big part in making or breaking family relationships. We'll examine four communication issues that families commonly encounter: roles, rituals, stories, and secrets.

Family Roles Family roles embody the functions people serve in the family system. One person might be the problem solver; another might act as the family jokester or the family peacemaker. One sibling may be the troublemaker, whereas another is the caregiver or the helpless victim. Notice that roles are different from family positions, so we wouldn't talk about the "role of the father," for instance, or the "role of the daughter." *Positions* such as father and daughter are based on the structure of our relationships with others, but *roles* are based on the social and emotional functions our behavior serves within the family.

family rituals Repetitive activities that have special meaning for a family.

Family roles often become particularly relevant when the family is in conflict. Expert family therapist Virginia Satir has suggested that four roles are especially common during conflict episodes.[71] The first role is the *blamer,* who holds others responsible for whatever goes wrong but accepts no responsibility for his or her own behaviors. A second role is the *placater,* the peacemaker who will go to any lengths to reduce conflict. That person may simply agree with whatever anyone says to keep others from getting angry. A third role is the *computer,* who attempts to use logic and reason—rather then emotion—to defuse the situation. Finally, there's the *distracter,* who makes random, irrelevant comments so that the rest of the family will forget about the conflict. Each role leads people to communicate in different ways. Some role behaviors, such as computing and placating, can be useful for resolving conflict or at least preventing it from escalating. The behavior of blamers and distracters, on the other hand, might make conflict worse by taking attention away from the topic of the conflict.

Family Rituals Many families have their own important traditions. One family's tradition might be to spend every Thanksgiving serving turkey dinners at a shelter for homeless veterans. Another's might be to attend drag races together every summer. We call those behaviors **family rituals,** or repetitive activities that have special meaning for a family. Rituals serve a variety of functions in family interactions, among them reinforcing a family's values and providing a sense of belonging. A family ritual such as an annual road trip isn't just about the trip; it's also about spending time together, creating memories, and emphasizing the importance of family relationships.

According to communication scholars Dawn Braithwaite, Leslie Baxter, and Anneliese Harper, rituals can be especially important in blended families of stepparents and stepchildren. Their research found that people often "import" rituals from their original family into their blended family.[72] Sometimes those rituals are retained or adapted in the blended family; other times, they are not. For instance, Braithwaite and her colleagues described one family in which a widowed mother and her children would have a pizza "picnic" in the living room on a regular basis. The children would cuddle with the mother on the couch, eat pizza, and talk, and all considered it to be a special time. When the mother remarried and acquired stepchildren, however, the ritual stopped, perhaps because the stepchildren would have been uncomfortable taking part.

Braithwaite and colleagues also found that it's important for blended families to develop their own rituals. In one such family, a young man described how his new stepfather began a ritual of watching the Super Bowl with his brother and him. According to this young man, that ritual served as a means of promoting communication with his stepfather.[73]

Family Stories Many of us can think of particular stories we've heard over and over again from members of our family. Maybe your grandparents were fond of describing how they overcame hardships when they were first married, and your parents have a favorite story about your childhood antics. Even events that were stressful or unpleasant at the time but turned out well, such as fixing a flat tire while on vacation, can serve a reassuring or cautionary function when they become part of the family lore. Stories are common in families, and communication scholar Elizabeth Stone suggests that they do more than provide entertainment. Family stories, she says, give families a sense of their

SHARPEN
Your Skills

Take a minute to recall a family ritual that you remember from when you were growing up. Consider what that ritual reflected about your family's rules, values, and beliefs. How did it reinforce the strength of your family relationships? Document your recalled experience.

Creating a family web page is easy, thanks to several Internet resources. Here are a few sites designed to help families generate their own web pages:

- www.yourfamily.com
- www.myfamily.com
- www.familylobby.com
- www.familydetails.com
- www.familywebsite.com
- www.mygreatbigfamily.com

history, express what family members expect of one another, and reinforce connections across different generations.[74]

Family stories are as varied as families are, but they all tend to have at least two characteristics in common. First, they're told and retold, often over long periods of time. In that way, they become part of a family's collective knowledge: After a while, most everyone in the family has heard each story over and over. Second, family stories convey an underlying message about the family, such as "We are proud," "We overcome adversity," or "We stick together no matter what."

These days, many families choose to tell parts of their family stories on family web pages. As Table 8.1 notes, the Internet provides several resources for families who wish to create and maintain a family web page.

Family Secrets Many families have secrets they intentionally keep hidden from others. Those secrets often contain information the family considers private and inappropriate for sharing with outsiders, such as details of religious practices, health or legal issues, family conflicts, or financial information. When you were growing up, you may remember your parents telling you not to talk about such issues with people outside your family. Keeping family secrets doesn't just protect private family information, though; it also reinforces the family's identity and exclusivity, because only family members are allowed to know the secrets.[75]

Secrets can also be kept *within* families. For instance, Marco may not want his parents to know that he has moved in with his girlfriend, so he swears his sister to secrecy. Erin and Tammy may not want their kids to know that Tammy has breast cancer, so they agree to keep it secret. People might choose to keep secrets from other family members for many reasons, such as avoiding embarrassment or conflict, protecting another's feelings, and maintaining a sense of autonomy and privacy.

- How do genetic ties, legal obligations, and role behaviors matter to the definition of families?
- What is the difference between a family of origin and a family of procreation?
- What are family roles, and how might they affect communication within families?

Test Yourself

>> Improving Communication in Intimate Relationships

Because romantic and familial relationships are so important to us, it's in our best interests to communicate as competently as we can within them. In this section, we'll look at four strategies for improving communication within your intimate relationships: emphasizing excitement and positivity, handling conflict constructively, having realistic expectations, and managing dialectical tensions.

GO FOR FUN: EMPHASIZE EXCITEMENT AND POSITIVITY

You might have heard the saying, "The family that plays together, stays together." That bit of folk wisdom has some truth to it. Research by relationships scholar Art Aron and his colleagues has shown that partners who engage together in exciting or exhilarating forms of play—such as rollerblading, riding a roller coaster, and going to a suspenseful movie—increase their level of relationship satisfaction.[76] Less exhilarating activities such as playing cards and going out to dinner, even if they are pleasant, don't have the same effect. Why is that the case? Aron suggests that when partners engage in activities that elevate their physical arousal—the way riding a roller coaster or watching a thriller movie can—they may attribute their elevated arousal to each other instead of to the activity. Subconsciously, that is, people may notice their physical arousal and conclude that their partner, rather than the activity, is causing it. Sharing exhilarating play activities together can therefore help partners keep a level of positivity and freshness in their relationship that might otherwise fade with time.

You can use the knowledge gained from the Aron research to improve your own relationships. With your romantic partner, family members, and even your friends, make opportunities to share exciting and novel experiences. You may well find that your relationships become closer as a result.

There are other ways to emphasize positivity in family relationships. An important technique is the use of **confirming messages,** behaviors that indicate how much we value another person.[78] Those are the opposite of **disconfirming messages,** behaviors that imply a lack of respect or value for others. Several decades ago, researcher Jack Gibb observed that people can communicate confirming and disconfirming messages in several ways.[79] Table 8.2 identifies and explains six types of supportive, confirming messages people use in their close relationships. Table 8.3 summarizes six types of disconfirming messages that Gibb believed created a defensive, unsupportive climate in relationships.

By the Numbers

0.8

Number of positive behaviors enacted for every negative behavior in marriages with a high risk of divorce.[77]

What role do excitement and positivity play in your intimate relationships?

Table 8.2	Six Types of Confirming Messages
Descriptive	Messages that communicate support clearly and specifically, without judgmental words
Inquiry Orientation	Messages that invite others to work cooperatively to solve problems or understand issues
Spontaneity	Messages that are unplanned and free of hidden motives
Empathy	Messages that express understanding of, and interest in, another's thoughts and feelings
Equality	Messages that seek others' viewpoints and express value for others' ideas
Provisional	Messages that convey points of view but invite alternative views

Table 8.3	Six Types of Disconfirming Messages
Evaluative	Messages that convey judgments of what's right and wrong, good and bad
Control	Messages that attempt to impose one's ideas on others and coerce others to agree
Strategy	Messages that suggest the speaker is trying to direct others' behaviors
Neutrality	Messages that imply indifference or a lack of interest in others
Superiority	Messages that imply that the speaker is superior to his or her listeners
Certainty	Messages that convey that the speaker's ideas are absolutely true and that no other viewpoints are valid

confirming messages Behaviors that convey how much another person is valued.

disconfirming messages Behaviors that imply a lack of respect or value for others.

Research shows that confirming messages are particularly important in marital relationships. Psychologist John Gottman has spent much of his career looking at why marriages succeed or fail. As we considered earlier in this chapter, he has found that stable, satisfied couples have a 5 to 1 ratio of positive to negative communication. In other words, spouses who are happy with their marriages enact at least five positive behaviors (such as confirming messages) for every one negative behavior. Gottman has found that couples with lower positive-to-negative ratios have an elevated risk of divorce.[80]

DEAL WITH THE DARK SIDE: HANDLE CONFLICT CONSTRUCTIVELY

Even the happiest, most stable relationships experience conflict from time to time. Conflict comes about when people in an interdependent relationship have competing goals. How can we manage conflict in a constructive way?

It turns out that handling conflict constructively is more about what we *don't do* than what we *do*. That is, couples who manage conflict in a positive manner do so by avoiding certain problematic behaviors. To identify the behaviors to avoid, Gottman has spent years studying how romantic partners interact with each other during conflict episodes. We might expect that couples who fight frequently are most likely to split up. In fact, Gottman's research has found otherwise. According to Gottman, *how* couples argue, and not how frequently they argue, predicts their chances for staying together.[81] His work has identified four specific behaviors that are warning signs for separation or relational dissolution: criticism, contempt, defensiveness, and stonewalling. Gottman refers to those behaviors as the "Four Horsemen of the Apocalypse" to indicate that they signal distress.[82] Let's take a close look at each.

Criticism According to Gottman, the first warning sign occurs when partners engage in **criticism** or complaints about each other. Criticism isn't always bad, but it becomes counterproductive when it focuses on people's personality or character rather than on their behavior. Statements such as "You always have to be right" and "You never care about my feelings" focus on attacking the person and assigning blame.

Criticisms also tend to be global statements about a person's value or virtue instead of specific critiques about the topic of the conflict. For example, a distressed partner might say "You never think of anyone but yourself" rather than "You should be more attentive when I describe my feelings to you." Because criticisms often come across as personal attacks instead of as accurate descriptions of the sources of conflict, they tend to inflame conflict situations. At that point, criticism becomes a sign of a distressed relationship.

Contempt A second warning sign occurs when partners show **contempt** for each other—hostile behavior in which they insult each other and attack the other's self-worth. That behavior can include name calling ("You stupid idiot!"), using sarcasm or mockery to make fun of the other person, and engaging in nonverbal behaviors that suggest a low opinion of the partner, such as sneering and eye rolling. It can also include ridiculing the person in front of others and encouraging others to do the same.

Contempt functions to put down and degrade the other person. Research indicates that responding to conflict with contempt often increases the partners' stress. Elevated stress in turn can impair their physical health as well as their relational satisfaction.[83]

criticism Complaints about another person or the person's behaviors.

contempt Hostile behavior in which people insult each other and attack the other's self-worth.

Defensiveness A third danger sign is that partners become defensive during their conflict. **Defensiveness** means seeing oneself as a victim and denying responsibility for one's behaviors. Instead of listening to their partners' concerns and acknowledging that they need to change certain behaviors, defensive people whine ("It's not fair"), make excuses ("It's not my fault"), and respond to complaints with additional complaints ("Maybe I spend too much money, but you never make time for the kids and me"). People are particularly prone to defensiveness when they recognize that the criticisms have merit but they don't want to accept the responsibility of changing their behavior.

Stonewalling The last of Gottman's "Four Horsemen" is **stonewalling,** or withdrawing from the conversation. People who engage in stonewalling often act as though they are "shutting down." They stop looking at their partners, stop speaking, and stop responding to what their partners are saying. In some cases, they physically leave the room to end the conversation. The reason for their departure isn't to calm down, which might be an effective strategy. Rather, it is to shut down the conversation entirely.

Gottman's research has suggested that people stonewall when they feel emotionally and psychologically "flooded," or incapable of engaging in the conversation any longer. Unfortunately, when one partner stonewalls, it becomes almost impossible for the couple to resolve their disagreements. Research has also shown that when men stonewall during a conflict, women often experience significant increases in stress hormones.[84]

Gottman's research therefore tells us that *constructive* conflicts are characterized not by the behaviors that are present but by those that are absent. When we are able to engage in conflict without criticizing, showing contempt, becoming defensive, and stonewalling, we stand a much better chance of preserving the quality of our relationship even as we work with our partner to resolve our differences.

GET REAL: HAVE REALISTIC EXPECTATIONS

Another way to improve communication in intimate relationships is to make sure that *everyone* in those relationships has realistic expectations for them. When expectations are unrealistic, relationships are likely to fail, causing the individuals involved to feel disappointed, hurt, or betrayed. Only through open communication can everyone's expectations come to light and can they reach agreement on how realistic they are.

Six months after marrying Carla, for instance, Gregory stopped spending time with his parents, brother, and even his close friends. He wanted to spend all of his time with Carla and began feeling anxious when they were apart. Carla started to feel smothered, and she explained to Gregory that they both needed other people in their lives besides each other. She encouraged him to reconnect with his family and friends. Gregory in turn explained that spending time with Carla helped him feel secure about their relationship. Eventually, they agreed on a new expectation for spending time together that seemed more reasonable to both of them. By communicating about their different expectations for their marriage and coming to an agreement on what they both considered realistic, Carla and Gregory were able to strengthen their feelings of satisfaction with each other.

As in Gregory's case, it's common to want to spend a lot of time with a romantic partner. However, it is important to be realistic about what we expect from our relationships. No one person—not even a spouse—can meet *all* of our social and emotional needs. Expecting someone to do so places an unfair burden on that person and may lead to disappointment.

A better approach is to appreciate each relationship individually and to remember that the important people in our life are important for different reasons. For example, you might talk to your romantic partner about most issues, but maybe you feel more comfortable discussing your worries about your dad's health or your daughter's financial difficulties with your brother or sister. Further, just as no single person can meet all of *your* needs, you cannot meet someone else's every need. Being realistic about your expectations helps you appreciate the most positive aspects of each of your relationships.

defensiveness Seeing oneself as a victim and denying responsibility for one's behaviors.

stonewalling Withdrawing from a conversation.

Table 8.4   Strategies for Managing Dialectical Tensions

Denial

Denial entails responding to only one side of the tension and ignoring the other. Were Moira to adopt this strategy, she might deny her desire for autonomy and focus all her attention on being connected with Albee.

Disorientation

Disorientation involves ending the relationship in which the tension exists. Moira may feel so disoriented by the tension between her desires for autonomy and connection that she calls off her engagement to avoid it.

Alternation

Alternation means going back and forth between the two sides of a tension. On some days, Moira might act in ways that enhance her autonomy and individuality. On other days, she might act in ways that strengthen her connection to Albee.

Segmentation

Segmentation involves dealing with one side of a tension in some aspects of a relationship and with the other side of the tension in other aspects of that relationship. Moira might emphasize her connection to Albee by sharing intimate disclosures, but she might stress her autonomy by keeping her finances separate from his. Rather than going back and forth between the two sides of the tension, as in alternation, she addresses one side of the tension in some segments of her relationship and the other side in other segments.

Balance

Balance involves trying to compromise, or find a middle ground, between the two opposing forces of a tension. For instance, Moira may disclose most but not all of her feelings to Albee. She may not feel as autonomous as she wants *or* as connected as she wants, but she may feel she is satisfying each desire to some degree.

Integration

Integration entails developing behaviors that will satisfy both sides of a tension simultaneously. Moira feels connected to Albee when they spend their evenings together, but she also likes to choose how she spends her time. To integrate those needs, she reads or does crossword puzzles while Albee watches television in the same room, an option that allows her to feel autonomous and connected at the same time. Unlike the balance strategy, which focuses on compromising each desire, integration involves finding ways to satisfy both desires without compromising either.

Recalibration

Recalibration means reframing a tension so that the contradiction between opposing needs disappears. By communicating about their needs and expectations for their relationship, Moira and Albee might realize that autonomy and connection are both desirable. As a result, they may come to see autonomy and connection as complementary rather than opposing needs.

Reaffirmation

Reaffirmation means simply embracing dialectical tensions as a normal part of life. Moira may come to realize that she will always feel torn between being autonomous and being connected. Instead of fighting the tension or struggling to resolve it, she accepts the tension as a normal feature of her relationship. Whereas reframing means eliminating the tension by seeing the opposing needs as complementary, reaffirmation means accepting the tension as normal.

PUSH AND PULL:
MANAGE DIALECTICAL TENSIONS

As we saw earlier in this chapter, people in romantic and familial relationships often experience dialectical tensions—conflicts between two opposing needs. Managing dialectical tensions can help improve communication in intimate relationships. Researchers have identified eight different strategies to manage dialectical tensions.[85] None of these is inherently positive or negative. Whether they work depends on our goals for the relationship and the context in which we are using them.

Let's suppose Moira is engaged to Albee and has been spending a lot of time with him. She is experiencing the tension between autonomy and connection. She strongly desires to retain her own individuality and autonomy but also passionately wants to be connected to Albee. Different strategies she might use to manage that tension include denial, disorientation, alternation, segmentation, balance, integration, recalibration, and reaffirmation. Table 8.4 explains each strategy and shows how it could be applied to Moira and Albee's situation.

Individuals in families and romantic relationships commonly try several of those strategies, and they may find some more effective than others. Improving your communication in intimate relationships doesn't require you to adopt specific strategies and ignore others. Rather, if you're aware of the options for managing dialectical tensions, you can use the ones that work best for you.

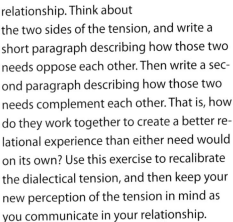

SHARPEN
Your Skills

Identify a dialectical tension you are currently experiencing in a romantic or familial relationship. Think about the two sides of the tension, and write a short paragraph describing how those two needs oppose each other. Then write a second paragraph describing how those two needs complement each other. That is, how do they work together to create a better relational experience than either need would on its own? Use this exercise to recalibrate the dialectical tension, and then keep your new perception of the tension in mind as you communicate in your relationship.

Test Yourself

- What is an example of a confirming message?
- When is compromising a useful strategy for managing conflict?
- Why are unrealistic expectations problematic for a relationship?
- How is alternation different from segmentation as a strategy for managing dialectical tensions?

For
REVIEW >>

- **What makes some relationships intimate?**
  Intimate relationships require deep commitment, foster interdependence, require continuous investment, and spark dialectical tensions.

- **How do we form, maintain, and dissolve romantic relationships?**
  Forming romantic relationships involves initiating, experimenting, intensifying, integrating, and bonding. We maintain our relationships by the way we handle conflict, privacy, emotional communication, and instrumental communication. Ending romantic relationships involves differentiating, circumscribing, stagnating, avoiding, and terminating.

- **What makes a family, and how do we communicate in families?**
  Family relationships typically involve some combination of genetic ties, legal obligations, and role behaviors. We use family roles, rituals, stories, and secrets to maintain communication in our familial relationships.

Pop Quiz

Multiple Choice

1. Johann and his partner Cris go out to dinner and see a movie every Friday night. That routine bores Johann but provides stability that Cris values. The dialectical tension Johan and Cris are experiencing is

   a. openness versus closedness
   b. autonomy versus connectedness
   c. presence versus absence
   d. predictability versus novelty

2. The idea that romantic relationships occur between individuals who choose to be together reflects the characteristic that romantic relationships are

   a. exclusive
   b. voluntary
   c. composed of opposite-sex partners
   d. based on love

3. The stage of Knapp's relational model that helps individuals decide whether they have enough in common to move the relationship forward is

   a. initiating
   b. intensifying
   c. differentiating
   d. experimenting

4. The practice in which one person has two or more romantic partners at a time is called

    a. monogamy
    b. infidelity
    c. polygamy
    d. annulment

5. Doug's family has a tradition of calling his grandmother every Sunday morning. That practice exemplifies a family

    a. ritual
    b. role
    c. secret
    d. story

Fill in the Blank

6. Connectedness is in dialectical tension with _____.

7. Discussions about topics such as who's doing the laundry and who's taking out the paper and glass for recycling are examples of _____ communication.

8. According to Gottman, couples who talk openly about disagreements and stay calm throughout conflict episodes are called _____ couples.

9. According to _____ theory, partners in a romantic relationship jointly own information about their problems.

10. A romantic relationship is _____ when the partners are going through the motions of a relationship that is no longer satisfying.

KEY TERMS

intimacy   180
commitment   181
interdependence   181
investment   183
dialectical
     tensions   183
monogamy   184
infidelity   184
polygamy   186
initiating stage   188
experimenting
     stage   188
intensifying stage   188
integrating stage   188
bonding stage   188
conflict   189
communication privacy
     management (CPM)
     theory   190
differentiating
     stage   192

circumscribing
     stage   192
stagnating stage   193
avoiding stage   193
terminating stage   193
divorce   193
family of origin   195
family of
     procreation   195
family rituals   197
confirming
     messages   199
disconfirming
     messages   199
criticism   200
contempt   200
defensiveness   201
stonewalling   201

COMMUN
IN SMALL GROUPS

SMALL IN SIZE, LARGE IN STATURE

The U.S. Supreme Court is a small group with extraordinary responsibilities. Composed of nine justices who are appointed for life, the Supreme Court serves as the highest judicial body in the nation. Its principal duty is to make the final decisions on highly controversial cases, many of which require rendering interpretations of the U.S. Constitution. Throughout its history, the Court has issued landmark rulings on slavery, civil liberties, presidential power, due process, abortion, and other topics that define and redefine what it means to be an American.

Because many of their cases are so controversial and have such far-reaching effects on the country, Supreme Court justices must learn to work together productively, despite their frequent differences of opinion. They do so by communicating with one another regularly, both in writing and in face-to-face conferences. When they meet to discuss the merits of a case, they follow rules and traditions that ensure everyone's right to be heard. They listen to one another's arguments and try to persuade others of their own positions. Although the justices are often sharply divided in their opinions, the small group communication patterns they follow have helped the Court to function in its critical role since 1789.

ICATING

As You READ >>

- What are small groups, and what do they do?
- Why and how do people join small groups?
- How can you communicate better in a small group?

We humans have lived, worked, and communicated in small groups for thousands of years. Archeologists tell us our prehistoric ancestors lived in small groups of hunters and gatherers and may have interacted with only a couple dozen people over their entire lives.[1] Although the world is considerably different today, our tendency to interact in small groups endures.

Communicating in small groups can be difficult, however. People often have strikingly different ideas about what decisions a group should make and how those decisions should be implemented. Coming together on ideas can therefore be a challenging process. For that reason, it's beneficial to know how small group communication operates and how we can excel at it. We can apply that knowledge to almost any small group to which we belong. Even Supreme Court justices employ many of the same principles of small group communication that we will review in this chapter.

Habitat for Humanity, which has built more than 300,000 homes, began as a small group.

small group A collection of people working interdependently to accomplish a task; small groups typically include 3 to 20 members.

>> What Is a Small Group?

In 1942, a small group of farmers near Americus, Georgia, began communicating with one another about a concept they called "partnership housing." Their idea was that people in need of safe, adequate shelter would work alongside volunteers to build simple, affordable houses. The homes would be sold—at no interest and for no profit—to those who needed them. As the group communicated its ideas with others, it received the help and capital it required to launch its mission. What began nearly seven decades ago as a small group of farmers grew into today's Habitat for Humanity, an international charitable organization that has built more than 300,000 homes, providing affordable shelter for more than 1.5 million people in over 3,000 communities around the world.[2]

In this and countless other instances, people communicating in a small group have had a positive influence on the lives of others. That success doesn't mean small group communication is without its problems. Indeed, working in small groups can be stressful and even frustrating. Further, as we'll see, small groups don't always make the smartest, most informed decisions, despite their best efforts. If we know how to conduct small group communication effectively, however, and we learn the problems to avoid, we stand a better chance of making our small group experiences positive and productive.

We can define a **small group** as a collection of three or more people working cooperatively interdependently to accomplish a task.[3] Small groups address a broad range of tasks, whether it's creating a dramatic presentation, organizing a fundraiser, making a policy recommendation, interpreting the Constitution, or providing affordable housing. Although small groups have diverse missions, they share important similarities that distinguish them from other social units. In this section, we'll see that

- Small groups are distinguished by their size.
- Small groups are interdependent.
- Small groups are cohesive.
- Small groups enforce rules and norms.
- Small groups include individual roles.
- Small groups have their own identities.
- Small groups have distinctive communication practices.
- Small groups often interact online.

SMALL GROUPS ARE DISTINGUISHED BY THEIR SIZE

An important part of what distinguishes a small group is its size. A 1,500-person church, a 90-piece orchestra, and the 435-member U.S. House of Representatives are all groups, but most researchers wouldn't classify any of them as a small group. Rather, communication scholars consider small groups to comprise at least 3 members (as noted in the formal definition above) and no more than about 15 or 20.[4]

The size of a small group matters because most of us communicate differently in larger and smaller collections of people. When we interact with only one other person, we are engaged in interpersonal communication rather than small group communication. Interpersonal communication usually focuses on the development and maintenance of a personal relationship, whereas small group communication is concerned with the performance of tasks. When we interact with *larger* groups of people, our communication can become impersonal because we may not know the others very well. Indeed, if the group is too large, we might feel as though our input won't be heard. However, interpersonal communication and large group communication both have their functions.

Many of us form and maintain interpersonal relationships *within* groups. We use our understanding of interpersonal communication in those relationships. Yet communicating effectively with a small group utilizes a distinct set of skills.[5]

A small group's size depends on its purposes. If the small group is a barbershop quartet, it needs exactly four people. If it's a jury, it will usually have 12 members plus a couple of alternates. Focus groups, committees, support groups, sports teams, and other small groups vary in size according to the tasks they have to accomplish. If there are too few members, the group may not have sufficient help to complete its goals. Likewise, if there are too many members, scheduling and coordinating the group's activities can be cumbersome. For those reasons, each small group must evaluate for itself what its optimal number of members will be.[6]

SMALL GROUPS ARE INTERDEPENDENT

When professional chefs create new recipes, they keep in mind that each ingredient will affect, and will be affected by, each of the others. Too little salt will make a soup taste bland; too much salt will overpower the individual flavors of the chicken and the vegetables. The appropriate amount of water—essential for a good broth—depends on the volume of the soup ingredients. Because each ingredient in a recipe influences, and is influenced by, every other ingredient to compose the tasty finished product, we would say that the ingredients are **interdependent.**

According to *systems theory,* members of a small group are also interdependent in the sense that each member affects and is affected by every other member in some way.[7] Whenever the National Aeronautics and Space Administration (NASA) launches the space shuttle, for instance, a group of 16 flight controllers monitors every aspect of the mission. Each individual controller oversees specific dimensions of the flight, such as communication with the crew, deployment and retrieval of the spacecraft's payload, flight navigation, electrical generation, and the execution of spacewalks. To ensure the success of the mission and the safety of the shuttle and its crew, the flight controllers must work interdependently. Although each person's responsibilities are different, everyone's actions influence, and are influenced by, everyone else's. For instance, communication with the crew is impaired if electrical generation malfunctions. Spacewalks are safe only if the flight navigation is accurate. In this interdependent group of flight controllers, the members must communicate to understand how their behaviors and decisions affect the others.

In small groups, interdependence doesn't necessarily mean that each member's influence on all other members is always positive. Perhaps you can recall attending small group gatherings in which two or three people expressed a disagreement that soon escalated into a full-scale argument within the group. In that instance, group members were influencing one another in a *negative* way by letting a conflict get out of hand. They were still demonstrating interdependence, however, because the moods and behaviors of some members affected, and were affected by, the moods and behaviors of others.

SMALL GROUPS ARE COHESIVE

If you've ever studied music, you know that a song's melody is its primary tune and that other pitches are added to the melody to create harmonies. Most melodies aren't quite as beautiful without harmonies, and most harmonies are incomplete without the melodies. When melodies and harmonies work together, though, they can produce something truly

special. The same principle applies in small groups. To be effective, small groups must have **cohesion,** which means that the members work together—as melodies and harmonies do—in the service of a common goal.[8] Cohesion takes interdependence a step further: Groups are interdependent if the members all influence one another, but they are cohesive only if the members work together toward the same goal.[9]

Two types of cohesion are particularly important for small groups. The first is what researchers call *task cohesion,* which is the extent to which everyone in the group is working together toward the same objectives.[10] Task cohesion is high when all the group members know their specific tasks and follow through on them. If only some members follow through on their assignments while others neglect their

THE DARK SIDE of Communication

Working at Odds: Dysfunctional Groups

A cohesive group is effective because everyone is contributing to the group's collective goals. When cohesion breaks down, and some members behave in ways that inhibit the group's goals, the group becomes *dysfunctional* because it is no longer operating to pursue a collective purpose. According to researchers who study small groups, four behaviors in particular can cause a group to become dysfunctional.

The first dysfunctional behavior, *parasitism,* occurs when some group members persuade or coerce others to do their work for them. The second behavior, *interpersonal aggression,* refers to actions that undermine the physical or psychological well-being of others, such as bullying and intimidation. Third, *boastfulness* means exaggerating the value of one's own contributions in relation to those of other group members. Finally, *misuse of resources* occurs when group members waste important materials or misuse equipment, reducing their availability for the rest of the group.

Dysfunction does not just cause groups to become unproductive. Research finds that it also increases stress and impairs the psychological well-being of the individuals in the group. As you communicate within small groups, it is therefore helpful to watch out for parasitism, interpersonal aggression, boastfulness, and misuse of resources. If everyone is aware that those behaviors are problematic, then your group stands a better chance of avoiding dysfunction.

Source: Aubé, C., Rousseau, V., Mama, C., & Morin, E. M. (2009). Counterproductive behaviors and psychological well-being: The moderating effect of task interdependence. *Journal of Business and Psychology, 24,* 351–361.

---

responsibilities, then task cohesion is low. Perhaps you've taken part in small groups in which only a few members did the majority of the work. If so, then you know that being in such groups is often unsatisfying.

The second important type of cohesion is *social cohesion,* which refers to the level of positive regard group members have for one another.[11] In groups with high social cohesion, the members generally get along well and maintain positive relationships among themselves. They trust and listen to one another, and they respect one another's opinions, even in cases in which they disagree. In contrast, members of groups with low social cohesion are often distrustful of the other members. They disregard one another's opinions and don't seem to care much about each other. In some groups, low social cohesion causes members to argue frequently; in others, it causes members to ignore one another. Not surprisingly, most people are more satisfied participating in groups with high social cohesion than in those with low social cohesion.[12]

When members act contrarily to a group's goals, the group can become dysfunctional and counterproductive. Let's take a closer look at group dysfunction in The Dark Side of Communication.

SMALL GROUPS ENFORCE RULES AND NORMS

In the 2004 movie *Mean Girls,* Cady Heron (played by Lindsay Lohan) enrolls in a public high school for the first time. There, she meets and befriends a small group known as the

interdependence With respect to groups, a state in which each member of a group affects, and is affected by, every other member.

cohesion The force by which the members of a group work together in the service of a common goal.

Plastics, composed of the school's most popular girls. She soon realizes that like all small groups, the Plastics have both rules and norms. A group's *rules* are its explicitly stated principles for governing what its members can and cannot do. Shortly after she joins the Plastics, for instance, Cady receives instruction in some of its rules by fellow member Gretchen Wieners (played by Lacey Chabert):

Gretchen: *You can't wear a tank top two days in a row, and you can only wear your hair in a ponytail once a week, so I guess you picked today. Oh, and we only wear jeans or track pants on Fridays. If you break any of these rules, you can't sit with us at lunch. I mean, not just you . . . any of us. Okay look, if I was wearing jeans today, I'd be sitting over there with the art freaks. Oh, we always vote before we ask someone to eat lunch with us, because you have to be considerate of the rest of the group. I mean, you wouldn't buy a skirt without asking your friends first if it looked good on you.*

Cady: *I wouldn't?*

Gretchen: *Right. Oh, and it's the same with guys. I mean, you may think you like someone, but you could be wrong.*

In this scene, Gretchen explains some of the guidelines about how to dress and how to interact with others in the group that all members of the Plastics are expected to observe. Those guidelines constitute rules because they are explicitly communicated.

Other principles for how group members should behave are never officially stated, however, but seem to be understood implicitly within the group. Those are called the group's *norms,* and even though they aren't expressly communicated, they nonetheless affect behavior. While in the Plastics, for instance, Cady realizes she is expected to talk only to certain people, attend specific parties, keep other group members' secrets, and gossip about other students. Although these expectations are never communicated to her explicitly, she infers them from observing how others in the group behave.

Nearly every small group has both rules and norms that its members are expected to follow. Some rules and norms govern how group members should interact with one another, such as "we stick together no matter what." Other rules and norms dictate how the group should function, such as "we always vote before asking someone to have lunch with us." Still other rules and norms focus on the nature of the group's mission, such as "everything we do must be done with the utmost professionalism." Table 9.1 gives additional examples of small group rules and norms. As we'll see later in this section, introducing members to the group's rules and norms is an important part of socializing new members into the group.

Small groups, such as the Plastics in the movie *Mean Girls,* enforce rules and norms that their members are expected to observe.

What rules and norms are enforced in small groups to which you belong?

Table 9.1 Examples of Rules and Norms in a Small Group

Behavior in most small groups is influenced by explicit rules and implicit norms. Here are some examples of rules and norms that a college study group might use.

Rules

Study sessions always start at 8 P.M.
Members always share study materials.
Everyone produces a weekly reading outline.
One person brings snacks each week.
No music is to be played during meetings.

Norms

Send a text message if you're going to be late.
Don't discuss the group with others.
Come to each meeting prepared.
Always cooperate with one another.
If one person falls behind, help that person to catch up.

SMALL GROUPS INCLUDE INDIVIDUAL ROLES

Most small groups have one or more collective goals or purposes. Tennis teams exist to compete with other teams in tennis matches. Jazz bands exist to create and perform music. In each case, everyone is expected to work together toward the group's collective mission, but that doesn't mean everyone contributes in the same ways. Rather, individual members of the group often take on specific **roles,** patterns of behavior that define a person's function within a group or a larger organization.[13]

Some roles in small groups are *formal roles,* meaning they are specifically assigned to people to help the group fulfill its mission. On a tennis team, for instance, one person usually plays the role of captain, the individual who is in charge of organizing team meetings and boosting players' morale. Because they are specifically assigned, formal roles usually receive official recognition both inside and outside the group. For example, all the players on a team know who the captain is because someone selected him or her and officially bestowed that title.

Other roles are better described as *informal roles,* meaning that they are not formally assigned and that anyone in the group can choose to take them on.[14] Unlike formal roles, which often ensure that important group assignments get fulfilled, informal roles more frequently relate to how well or poorly the group functions while carrying out its mission. In a jazz band, for instance, one member might play the role of humorist, always making funny observations to lighten the mood. Another might enact the role of mediator, helping members to find common ground when conflicts arise. A third member might play the nurturer, always attending to everyone else's emotional and physical needs. Whereas each formal role is generally assigned to a specific person, informal roles are usually filled by members taking on whatever work fits their personality. Consequently, an individual member might have more than one informal role, and a given informal role might be fulfilled by more than one member at a time.

Because formal roles are assigned and officially recognized, it's tempting to conclude that they're more important to a group's success than informal roles. That's not always the case, however. Although a team captain can keep a group organized and on task, members who enact helpful informal roles might make equally important contributions to a satisfying and productive group atmosphere.[15] Formal and informal roles can therefore complement each other, creating a positive small group experience.

As captain of the Mexican women's soccer team, Monica Gonzales fulfills a formal role.

SMALL GROUPS HAVE THEIR OWN IDENTITIES

When two people get married, it's often as if their relationship takes on a life of its own. They may say to each other, "There used to be you and me, but now there's you, me, and *us.*" That sentiment reflects the idea that the relationship has become an entity unto itself, one with its own identity. Many small groups have the same experience: Once people come together to form a small group, the group takes on its own identity. When that happens, people begin referring to "the group" as well as to individual members, and they start to think about the group's needs and desires, reflecting the idea that the group has become an entity unto itself.

One reason group identities are important is that they set boundaries around a group's membership by defining who belongs to the group and who does not. Some groups establish and maintain their boundaries in elaborate ways. For instance, members of the Freemasons, an international fraternal organization, are thought to use secret knocks, hand signals, passwords, and other covert signs to differentiate true members from individuals posing as members.[16] Likewise, fraternities and sororities often put new pledges through highly involved initiation rituals, during which they may teach them secret handshakes or code words by which they can signify their membership.[17] Similarly, many gangs require new members to get specific tattoos to signify their affiliation and allegiance with the gang.[18]

Other groups establish and maintain their boundaries in less dramatic ways. For example, the Red Hat Society is a social organization for women over 50 whose members wear red hats and purple clothing whenever they meet in groups.[19] Their attire therefore serves as a marker of membership, distinguishing those who belong to the group from those who do not. In the same vein, Alcoholics Anonymous members attending small group meetings recite the "serenity prayer," which symbolizes their inclusion in the group. Membership cards, lapel pins, member jackets, and similar tokens also signify who belongs to a group and who does not. In each of those ways, groups express and reinforce their identity both to those in the group and to outsiders.

role A pattern of behavior that defines a person's function within a group or larger organization.

SMALL GROUPS HAVE DISTINCTIVE COMMUNICATION PRACTICES

Central to accomplishing any group's mission is the practice of communication.[20] Can you imagine any small group that could meet its goals if its members couldn't communicate with one another? Without communicating, members wouldn't be able to share ideas, encourage one another, make collective decisions, assign individual tasks, or stay informed on what other members are doing.

Although members of many small groups communicate on an ongoing basis, they don't always communicate in the same ways. In fact, researchers have discovered four specific types of communication that characterize small groups.[21] The first type, *problem-solving communication,* focuses on the details of how a small group can accomplish its tasks. *Role communication,* the second type, relates to the formal and informal roles that each member plays within the group. *Consciousness-raising communication,* the third type, involves the group's identity and the morale of its members. Finally, *encounter communication* comprises the interpersonal interactions that occur among group members.

To illustrate each type of communication, let's say you're on an advisory board charged with reviewing the policies of the student health center on your campus. At your first meeting, you and the other board members will probably identify each of your specific tasks, discuss how often you need to meet, and determine how you'll communicate with one another about your progress in between meetings. Those are all examples of problem-solving communication because they relate to your goals and your strategies for meeting them. You might also talk about who's going to be in charge of your board, who's going to keep the records of your meetings, and who will be responsible for communicating with the health center administrators. That conversation is an example of role communication because it concerns the individual roles that board members will play.

Suppose the advisory board experiences several challenges while attempting to complete its mission, and you and the other board members are feeling overwhelmed and discouraged. Perhaps the leader of your group gives everyone a pep talk about the importance of your task, stressing that you'll be successful if you all stick together and work as a team. That is an example of consciousness-raising communication because it is meant to raise morale and reinforce your identity as a group. Let's say that you've been particularly discouraged lately because of the stresses of school and your part-time job, and you confide in another group member about your feelings. That is an example of encounter communication because it reflects an interpersonal conversation that occurs within the group.

SHARPEN Your Skills

Select two small groups to which you belong. For each one, list the ways in which the group is distinguished by its size, is interdependent, experiences cohesion, enforces rules and norms, includes individual roles, has its own identity, and follows distinctive communication practices. Identify the characteristics the two groups have in common and those in which they differ.

SMALL GROUPS OFTEN INTERACT ONLINE

An increasing number of small groups interact either primarily or exclusively online.[22] Some small groups communicate online because their members are located in different cities or countries, and so face-to-face communication is impractical.[23] Other groups interact online because computer-mediated communication can be more efficient than face-to-face conversation. Technologies such as e-mail, instant messaging, message boards, texting, and videoconferencing allow group members to interact whenever—and wherever—they choose.

Nonetheless, online groups pose challenges. Research shows that compared to people in face-to-face groups, individuals who interact with other group members online report being less committed to the group and less happy while working with it. Small group researchers Stefanie Johnson, Kenneth Bettenhausen, and Ellie Gibbons found that those negative outcomes are particularly likely in groups that interact via computer-mediated communication more than 90 percent of the time.[24] Other research has found that regardless of their culture, people feel less confident in their ability to be productive in virtual groups as compared to face-to-face groups.[25]

What makes an online small group successful? Researchers Ann Majchrzak, Arvind Malhotra, Jeffrey Stamps, and Jessica Lipnack offer the following suggestions:[26]

- *Take advantage of diversity.* In communicating electronically, groups can find it difficult to ensure that everyone's input is heard when a decision must be made. By actively seeking and considering divergent opinions, online groups can make decisions that better reflect their members' needs.
- *Simulate reality.* One of the downsides of technologies such as e-mail is that it doesn't allow group members to interact with one another in *real time,* as they would in a face-to-face conversation. Consequently, members can feel disengaged or left out of the dialogue. Successful groups use computer-mediated technologies that simulate real-life interactions, such as videoconferencing and virtual workspaces (websites where people can talk and share documents or graphics in real time).
- *Keep the team together.* The lessened commitment often felt by members of virtual groups (relative to face-to-face groups) increases the chance that the members of online groups will become bored with the group and decide to leave. Communicating on a daily basis with group members may help to reduce that possibility by keeping members involved in the group's business.

Communicating online—as in a videoconference—is often more efficient than interacting in person, particularly for groups whose members are geographically dispersed.

As we've seen in this section, several characteristics define the small group experience: group size, interdependence, cohesion, rules and norms, individual roles, unique identities, and communication practices. In addition, people in many small groups interact—either primarily or exclusively—online. Why might someone choose to take part in the small group experience at all? We'll probe some of the most important reasons in the next section.

Test Yourself

- How many people are usually in a small group?
- In what ways are group members interdependent?
- Why is cohesion important within a group?
- How do members learn about a group's rules and norms?
- What is the difference between formal and informal roles?
- Why do groups identify group boundaries?
- In what ways do groups enact distinctive communication practices?
- What are the advantages and challenges of virtual groups?

>> Functions of Small Groups

Once a month, community members in towns and cities across the United States come together for a dinner in which they eat locally grown foods and discuss ways to make food production more sustainable. They are members of the Slow Food movement, an organization that began in Italy in 1986 to promote long, leisurely dining experiences that encourage conversation and an appreciation of the food being eaten. The movement, which opposes the quick consumption of mass-produced food, now has over 80,000 worldwide members. Yet despite the organization's size, Slow Food members meet in small groups to enjoy and celebrate their good meals. Whether we're talking about a Slow Food group, service organization, committee, or sports team, we'll discover in this section that small groups can have several different functions.

Members of the Slow Food movement meet in small groups to enjoy leisurely dining experiences.

SMALL GROUPS HAVE MANY FUNCTIONS

Groups don't come together by accident. Rather, we form small groups when we believe they'll help us in some way. In this section, we'll see that small groups

- Focus on discrete tasks
- Evaluate and advise
- Create art and ideas
- Provide service and support
- Promote social networking
- Compete
- Help us learn

Figure 9.1 illustrates the functions that small groups can serve. As you read and examine these functions, bear in mind that they aren't mutually exclusive. Any given group can serve multiple functions at once.

Some Small Groups Focus on Discrete Tasks

One function of some groups is to accomplish specific assigned tasks. In 2002, for example, a small group was appointed in Washington, DC, to "prepare a full and complete account of the circumstances surrounding the September 11, 2001 terrorist attacks, including preparedness for and the immediate response to the attacks."[27] The group, which came to be known as the 9/11 Commission, was composed of ten individuals, most of whom were attorneys and former politicians. The 9/11 Commission investigated the September 11 attacks for more than a year and a half, interviewing over 1,200 people and reviewing some 2.5 million pages of documents.[28] In 2004, the 9/11 Commission completed its assigned task by releasing a 604-page report detailing its findings.

Similarly, whenever a jury is assembled for a criminal or civil trial, it hears evidence, takes part in deliberation, and then fulfills its mission by communicating a verdict. Like a jury or the 9/11 Commission, most small groups that focus on discrete tasks usually disband after their tasks are complete.

Some Small Groups Evaluate and Advise
The purpose of some small groups is to discuss and evaluate particular issues and give advice on how those issues should be addressed. The president of the United States, for instance, appoints a cabinet of 15 individuals who head major governmental agencies, such as the departments of State, Justice, Defense, Homeland Security, Education, and Commerce. The cabinet meets regularly to advise the president on issues related to domestic and foreign policy.[29] Although its individual members change, the cabinet has been a permanent group since the presidency of George Washington in the late eighteenth century.

Other small groups evaluate and advise on an as-needed basis. To evaluate the merits of a new product, for instance, many companies turn to *focus groups*.[30] Focus groups are usually composed of 6 to 10 people who may use and provide their feedback on a new product before it is available to the public. They may also give input on the new product's name or packaging. In those ways, focus groups evaluate a company's new product ideas and advise the company on how best to market the products to consumers. Other small groups that evaluate and advise are an award selection committee, an advisory board, and an employee performance evaluation committee.

Some Small Groups Create Art and Ideas
The Dave Matthews Band is a small group whose purpose is to create, perform, and record rock music. Composed of five musicians, the Grammy Award–winning band has sold over 30 million albums in the United States alone and is one of the most successful creative small groups in history.[31]

Like the Dave Matthews Band, many small groups exist primarily to create forms of art. A string quartet, a sculpting class, and the cast of *Saturday Night Live* are all examples of small groups that produce artistic expressions. Other groups are charged with creating

Focus on discrete tasks

Evaluate and advise

Provide service and support

Compete

Small Groups

Help us learn

Promote social networking

Create art and ideas

FIGURE 9.1 Some Functions of Small Groups

ideas instead of art. Many companies and organizations, for instance, use *brainstorming groups,* which are small groups of people who are assembled to generate innovative ways of thinking. When a county hospital needed a more efficient way of processing patients in the emergency room, for instance, it brought together a small group of nurses, medical technicians, paramedics, and volunteers to compile a list of suggestions. After listening to one another's experiences and concerns, the members of the brainstorming group were able to generate ideas for improving efficiency that hospital administrators had not previously considered.

Some Small Groups Provide Service and Support Many small groups focus on providing community service to those who need it. For instance, local chapters of Kiwanis International serve their local communities through activities such as building playgrounds, running food drives, and raising money for pediatric medical research.[32] Similarly, local chapters of the Lions Club raise funds to aid victims of natural disasters and to support screening for blindness and hearing loss.[33] Although Kiwanis and the Lions Club are international organizations, their members frequently work in small groups to accomplish community service missions. Many colleges, universities, and religious organizations also sponsor groups whose purpose is to provide community services.

Other small groups provide social and emotional support for people dealing with difficult circumstances. Some *support groups* aid those battling health concerns, such as diabetes, alcoholism, depression, and acne. Other support groups help people cope with the prejudice and discrimination they experience because they are mentally or physically disabled or sexual minorities. People in support groups often benefit by communicating with others whose circumstances are similar to their own.[34] A woman with a gambling addiction, for instance, may feel the only people who understand her are others battling the same addiction. Listening to others' stories in a support group therefore may help the individual feel less alone and better able to control the problem behavior. Research has shown, in fact, that taking part in support groups for health conditions can improve physical and mental health.[35] Although some support groups meet in person, many now meet online, providing emotional encouragement and support to members worldwide.[36]

Some Small Groups Promote Social Networking

At one point or another, many of us have joined small groups simply to meet other people. Groups with this purpose, known as *social networking groups,* allow people to meet, communicate, and get to know each other.[38] On the day she moved into her new residence hall, for instance, Lindsay and her fellow residents were divided into groups of 10 and were given time to get to know one another. Taking part in that type of social networking group ensured that Lindsay knew at least nine other people when she began the year in her residence hall.

Although social networking groups sometimes meet in person, as in Lindsay's case, they are particularly common on the Internet. For instance, chat rooms allow people to communicate online in real time, via text or web cams. Chat rooms often focus on a particular shared interest (such as pop culture or video gaming) or appeal to a specific demographic (such as single fathers or women over 40). Their primary purpose, however, is typically to allow people to communicate and get to know one another.[39] Social networking websites, such as MySpace and Facebook, also allow users to interact with others in groups. Like chat rooms, many of the groups are organized to appeal to a specific population, such as fans of a certain celebrity or alumni of a particular high school. Although some groups and chat rooms can get quite large—growing to several hundred members— they often include only small numbers of people who are interacting and sharing their interests online at a given time.[40]

Some Small Groups Compete

Many small groups are organized to take part in team competitions. For instance, colleges and universities around the United States sponsor groups of 8 to 12 students who compete in Quiz Bowl.[41] Quiz Bowl is an academic competition in which students respond to questions posed by a moderator about a wide range of subjects. Whichever team correctly answers the most questions in the shortest time wins the match, so members of a Quiz Bowl team must work interdependently to accomplish their mission.

Similarly, the teams organized for many athletic competitions are small groups. Your school may have a wrestling, diving, or gymnastics team, for example, that has 20 or fewer members and therefore functions as a small group. The purpose of competitive groups is to train and practice a particular set of skills and then to compete with similar groups to win material prizes (such as trophies) or recognition.

Some Small Groups Help Us Learn

Finally, we join some small groups because they help us learn. For instance, you may have taken part in *study groups,* which usually comprise a small number of students who help one another understand the material and prepare for the exams in a specific course. Workshops and Bible studies are also examples of small groups that help us learn.

Research has shown that taking part in learning groups enhances critical thinking skills, such as the ability to analyze and evaluate ideas.[42] When we come together with others for the purpose of learning, we are able to contribute our own understanding of the material for the benefit of others and to take advantage of what others can teach us.

As we've seen, small groups can enact several different functions, including accomplishing discrete tasks, evaluating and advising, creating, providing service and support, promoting social networking, competing, and helping us learn. It's important to keep in mind that these functions are not mutually exclusive. That is, many groups focus on more than one of these functions at once. A nonprofit organization might form a committee to evaluate its public relations efforts, for instance, but the committee might also create new ideas, implement those ideas in the form of a new public relations campaign, and provide an opportunity for social networking among its members. A support group might provide encouragement for people suffering from arthritis, but in the process its members might learn more about their condition and the options available for treatment. As these examples illustrate, participating in small groups often helps people in many different ways.

Test Yourself

- **What are seven functions of small groups?**
- **What functions are served by a small group such as the 9/11 Commission and a local chapter of Alcoholics Anonymous?**

>> Joining Small Groups

The first group to which most of us belong is a family—and because we're either born or adopted into our family, we have little say over our membership. Over the course of our life, however, we may join and leave a wide variety of small groups. Although every group is different, we can understand the process of joining small groups by considering why and how we do so. We'll begin this section by exploring some of the major reasons people have for joining small groups. We'll then look at the process by which people become socialized into groups.

WE JOIN SMALL GROUPS FOR MANY REASONS

Thinking back on your own small group experiences, you'll likely realize that you joined different groups for different reasons. Perhaps you joined some groups enthusiastically, primarily for social reasons, whereas you might have joined others because you felt compelled to join. People take part in small groups for a variety of reasons: because they need to belong, because groups provide protection, because group membership can improve their performance, and because they feel pressure to join.

We Join Small Groups Because We Need to Belong In the 1999 comedy *Never Been Kissed*, Drew Barrymore plays Josie Geller, a 25-year-old newspaper copy editor assigned to pose as a high school student and write an undercover story about adolescent life. During her own high school years, Josie was an intelligent but socially awkward teenager who yearned for acceptance and popularity. As she begins her undercover assignment, she is inhibited by insecurity. On her first day of school, however, her classmate Aldys (played by Leelee Sobieski) invites her to join the Denominators, a small group of students who excel in math and compete in math competitions. The Denominators wear matching sweatshirts, sit together during lunch, and provide Josie with an immediate group of friends who give her a sense of belonging.

Humans are highly social beings. We don't just *want* to belong to social networks; we *need* to. Friendships and families can meet many of our social needs, but small groups can also give us a sense of social belonging. Especially in situations when we feel out of place or unsure of ourselves—as Josie did when she began her undercover assignment—having a group to belong to and identify with can be comforting.

We Join Small Groups for Protection The expression "There's safety in numbers" suggests we are better protected against threats or problems when we're part of a group than when we're alone. The reason is that group members can take care of one another, and those who are stronger can protect those who are weaker.

In some instances, the protection we gain from groups is physical. You and your immediate neighbors might form a neighborhood watch group, for example, in which you agree to look out for one another's safety and property. Belonging to the group provides you the assurance of knowing that if something goes wrong, neighbors will seek help on your behalf. Religious and community groups may also come together to provide aid when a member is sick and unable to care for himself or herself. In those cases, being in a small group gives some measure of protection for one's physical health and well-being.

We can also gain social or emotional protection from groups. Many people facing chronic or life-threatening illnesses find comfort by participating in support groups. The emotional support they receive from others who are experiencing the same illness can encourage them and remind them they aren't alone in their struggles. In support groups for addiction to alcohol, drugs, or gambling, members are routinely assigned a sponsor to whom they are accountable for their behavior. When they feel the urge to gamble or use alcohol or drugs, they can call on their sponsor for the support necessary to resist those behaviors.

We Join Small Groups to Improve Our Effectiveness A third reason people join small groups is to improve their skills or to become more effective at some task.[43] For instance, contestants on the NBC series *The Biggest Loser* form small groups led by personal trainers who help them lose weight. The members of each group work out together, offer mutual encouragement, and hold one another accountable for maintaining their diet and exercise regimens. Participating in their small groups often makes contestants much more effective at losing weight than they could be alone. In fact, many individuals who are trying to lose weight seek support and encouragement from small groups because they believe it will help them. Will it? Check out the Fact or Fiction? box to find out.

Membership in various other kinds of small groups can also help us improve particular skills. Joining an investment group may teach you things you didn't know about money and help you become a more effective investor. Joining a golf team may expose you to the skills of other players and give you opportunities to sharpen your own skills through competition. Joining a small standup comedy group might make you a better, more confident performer on stage.

We Join Small Groups Because We Feel Pressure to Join Although we often join small groups by choice, we sometimes join because we feel pressured into doing so. Perhaps you've been enrolled in college courses that required you to participate in a group project. In such cases, your group participation wasn't voluntary. Similarly, if many of your friends at work are joining a small group to support a certain political candidate, you might feel pressured to do the same, even if that wouldn't have been your choice.

Feeling pressure to join a small group doesn't necessarily mean that your experience in that group will be negative. After being assigned to a group for a class project, for example, you might develop a friendship with some of the other members. Whether you join a group by choice or for another reason, your experience in that group will be as positive or negative as you make it.

Now that we've identified some of the reasons why we join small groups, let's take a look at how we become socialized into them.

Small Groups Can Aid Weight Loss

Individuals who want to shed weight often join a small weight-loss group. Many people believe that the support and accountability they receive from the group will help them lose more weight than they could on their own. Is that belief fact or fiction?

According to research, taking part in a weight-loss group is more effective than trying to reduce weight individually. In one study, overweight adults worked with a weight-loss counselor for 26 weeks either on their own or in groups of 8 to 12. During each group session, participants reported on their progress, and the counselor led a group discussion focused on rewarding progress and overcoming obstacles. Participants were also weighed and instructed in proper diet and exercise strategies. Those who worked with a counselor individually received all the same information and encouragement, just not in a group setting. By the end of the study, the participants who worked in groups had reduced their weight and body mass significantly more than had the participants who worked individually.

Other studies have produced similar results. For instance, people are more successful at giving up nicotine and cocaine when they take part in small groups designed to help them than when they try to quit on their own.

ASK YOURSELF

- Why do you suppose working in small groups helps people improve their health more than working alone?
- What health problems, if any, do you think most people would resolve more effectively alone than in groups?

Sources: Renjilian, D. A., Perri, M. G., Nezu, A. M., McKelvey, W. F., Shermer, R. L., & Anton, S. D. (2001). Individual versus group therapy for obesity: Effects of matching participants to their treatment preferences. *Journal of Consulting and Clinical Psychology, 69,* 717–721; Schmitz, J. M., Oswald, L. M., Jacks, S. D., Rustin, T., Rhoades, H. M., & Grabowski, J. (1997). Relapse prevention treatment for cocaine dependence: Group vs. individual format. *Addictive Behaviors, 22,* 405–418; Stead, L. F., & Lancaster, T. (2005). Group behaviour therapy programmes for smoking cessation. *Cochrane Database of Systematic Reviews, 18,* CD001007.

WE ARE SOCIALIZED INTO SMALL GROUPS

Think back to your first day of college. You can likely remember the anticipation, some uncertainty about your courses, and the excitement about being part of a campus community. You probably found that these feelings faded as you learned what to expect and became accustomed to your college routine. The process by which you gained greater certainty about the college experience is called *socialization,* and the same process occurs when you join a small group.

Researchers believe we are socialized into small groups in five phases—the antecedent phase, the anticipatory phase, the encounter phase, the assimilation phase, and the exit phase (Figure 9.2). Let's review each.

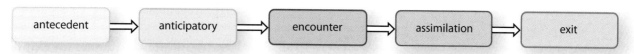

FIGURE 9.2 The Five Phases of Socialization into Small Groups

Antecedent Phase The first phase of socialization begins before we even enter a new group. We develop certain beliefs, attitudes, and expectations about small groups before joining the group. At the *antecedent phase* of socialization, we apply those beliefs, attitudes, and expectations to the group we're joining.

Let's say that in the last three classes in which you've worked on a group project, you ended up doing the bulk of the work while other members shirked their responsibilities. As a result, you've come to believe that group work is never fair. You've developed a negative attitude about small groups and the expectation that you will always have to do more than your share of the work. The next time you decide to join a small group, you therefore approach the group less optimistically than you might if your previous experiences had been more positive.[44]

Anticipatory Phase When we first decide to join a group, we make judgments about what we expect from that group and its other members. The process of forming those judgments is called the *anticipatory phase*. Some of our judgments might be based on the beliefs, attitudes, and expectations we formed from previous experiences with small groups. Others may be influenced by what we've heard about the group's objectives or traditions. Researchers point out that the anticipatory phase can be stressful if our expectations for a group are unrealistic.[45]

For instance, you might join a study group expecting it will help you understand the course material, only to discover that the group's primary purpose is social, not academic. In such a case, you may alter your expectations for the group or you may decide to join a different group instead.

Encounter Phase The *encounter phase* encompasses the first time we meet with others as a group. For some groups, that meeting will occur face-to-face. For others, it may occur in electronically mediated formats, such as teleconferencing, or in virtual reality, by which the group interacts online.

In general, do you prefer to interact in face-to-face or online groups? Why?

At least three important tasks are typically addressed during the encounter phase. First, groups often use their initial meeting to establish their mission and define their goals. A committee might identify its specific tasks, whereas a support group might discuss the needs of the people it is supporting. Second, groups often assign specific roles during the encounter phase. Individual group members might be allocated responsibility for specific projects; others might be given the roles of leader or record-keeper for the group. Finally, groups may use the encounter phase to remind members of expectations for their behavior. Those expectations compose part of the group's culture, and they often take the form of statements such as "Everyone in this group is expected to do his or her fair share of the work" and "In this group, no one is more important than anyone else."

In a small group such as a Little League team, new members are socialized into the group's norms and expectations.

Assimilation Phase Once the expectations for a group's culture are known, individual members must decide whether to accept those expectations. If they do, then they enter the *assimilation phase*. It's at this stage of socialization that the group acquires its own identity. Members begin to identify with the group and to think of themselves not as "you and me" but as "we."

During the assimilation phase, group members may begin enacting specific rituals or communication behaviors that signify their membership in the group. Those might include wearing specific signs of membership, such as matching sweatshirts or lapel pins, or conforming to the group's traditions by greeting other members with a secret handshake or reciting a specific pledge at every group meeting. Some members may accept a group's culture outright; others may accept it but attempt to change it over time.[46] Members who do not accept a group's culture or who find themselves at odds with a group's purpose often enter the final stage of group socialization—the exit phase.

Exit Phase Membership in most small groups has a life span. Individual members may leave a small group, either voluntarily or involuntarily. Leaving a group signifies the final stage of socialization, the *exit phase*. For instance, you might grow dissatisfied with the advisory board you're on at work after the board's new leader changes the group's mission significantly, and so you may choose to leave the group voluntarily. Instead, if you were to be laid off from your job, you would have to leave the advisory board whether you wanted to or not.

Members also exit groups when the groups themselves cease to exist.[47] Many small groups meet only long enough to accomplish a specific task, such as studying for exams in a college course, painting a mural in a neighborhood park, or drafting a policy on yard maintenance for a homeowners' association. Once the task is complete, such groups often disband. Other small groups stop meeting because of a lack of interest on members' part or because the resources they require are diminished. No matter what the reason, many small groups—if not most—will disband at some point, causing their members to exit the group.[48]

In this section, we've seen that people join small groups for various reasons and that becoming socialized into a small group has many phases. Next we'll explore some of the advantages and challenges of communicating in small-group settings.

Test Yourself

- In what ways can groups improve our effectiveness?
- What characterizes each phase of group socialization?

>> Advantages and Challenges of Small Group Communication

On the ABC drama *Grey's Anatomy,* the group of surgeons at Seattle Grace Hospital experiences many of the benefits and the trials of small group communication. Although the closeness of their group provides the doctors with emotional support and assistance with their jobs, it can also invite conflict and cause the doctors to wear on one another's nerves. Seattle Grace Hospital is fictitious, but the advantages and challenges of communicating in small groups are not. In this section, we'll explore some of the benefits we can accrue and some of the tribulations we can encounter when participating in a small group.

The surgeons depicted in *Grey's Anatomy* are subject to both the advantages and the challenges of small group communication.

COMMUNICATING IN SMALL GROUPS HAS ADVANTAGES

Participating in small groups confers some specific benefits. In this section, we'll examine three advantages of small groups: They provide resources, they experience synergy, and they expose us to diversity.

Small Groups Provide Resources Accomplishing almost any task requires the availability of **resources,** which are entities that enable us to be productive. Some resources are tangible, such as money, space, materials, and equipment. Others are intangible, such as time, information, talent, and expertise. Each of us has different resources at our disposal. When we come together with people in a small group, we gain access to the resources of others.[49]

resources Entities that enable a group to be productive.

Suppose you're on a committee to raise funds for a renovation of your local high school's computer facilities. As a busy college student, you don't have much free time to go door to door or make phone calls soliciting donations, but other committee members have the time to do so. Your training in communication allows you to craft good persuasive messages for the committee to use, however. Other committee members can provide materials for making signs, cars to use for canvassing neighborhoods, or money to cover expenses. In this small group, as in many small groups, each of you can take advantage of the resources of other group members.

Small Groups Experience Synergy In many small groups, members can accomplish more by working together than they could by working individually. When they do, researchers say they are experiencing **synergy,** a collaboration that produces more than the sum of its parts.

Let's say you and two friends are each running for separate seats on your county's board of supervisors. By campaigning as individuals, each of you might generate approximately 25,000 votes, for a total of 75,000 votes. Instead, however, you decide to campaign as a group by publicly endorsing one another, representing yourselves as three running mates and encouraging people to vote for all three of you. By adopting that strategy, you are able to pool your money to buy more advertising time and post more campaign signs around your county than your individual opponents can afford. As a result, each of you generates 40,000 votes. That's a total of 120,000 votes, or 45,000 more than you would have generated by working individually. Can you think of occasions when you have taken part in a small group that experienced synergy?

Small Groups Expose Us to Diversity The expression "Two heads are better than one" reflects the idea that getting input from others can help us make better, more informed decisions than we would make on our own. The reason is that each person brings a different set of ideas, experiences, insights, and values to bear on a decision. Listening to the perspectives of other people often makes us consider aspects of a decision that hadn't occurred to us before. Thus, one important advantage of participating in a small group is exposure to ways of thinking that are different from our own.[50]

Suppose two "juries" were to hear the same fictitious criminal case in a law school's mock trial exercise. Jury A is composed of 12 people with highly diverse work experience, cultural background, educational level, and socioeconomic status. Jury B consists of 12 people with highly similar characteristics. After hearing the case, Jury B arrives at a unanimous verdict quickly. Because the members of Jury B are so similar, they paid attention to the same pieces of evidence, were persuaded by the same arguments, and brought similar biases and prejudices to bear on their decision. In contrast, Jury A takes much longer to arrive at a unanimous verdict. Because of their diversity, the members of Jury A each paid attention to different aspects of the case. Whereas some found the physical evidence persuasive, others listened more carefully to the eyewitness accounts or watched the defendant's facial expressions while testimony was being presented.

When it came time for the juries to reach a verdict, the members of Jury A drew from a much more diverse set of ideas, arguments, and biases. Even though arriving at a unanimous decision was a long and difficult process for Jury A, the panel's verdict was better informed because it was fully considered from many different points of view. Although working in diverse groups can present challenges, it can also help us to think in more open-minded ways—and thereby to come to better decisions.

In what situations is diversity problematic rather than beneficial?

COMMUNICATING IN SMALL GROUPS POSES CHALLENGES

Taking part in small groups can be extremely rewarding, but it isn't always easy. At least three challenges are common to small groups: they require sacrifices, they can experience conflict, and they can be difficult to coordinate.

Small Groups Require Sacrifices Belonging to a small group sometimes requires making sacrifices for the benefit of the group. Let's say you're on a committee at work that

synergy A collaboration that produces more than the sum of its parts.

social loafing The tendency of some members of a group to contribute less to the group than the average member does, particularly as the group grows in size.

Table 9.2   Ways to Reduce Social Loafing

When group members engage in social loafing, the group's productivity suffers and other members can become resentful. Here are some strategies for reducing social loafing.

- *Name names.* Make every member's specific contributions to the group known to the rest of the group, so that if a specific person is being unproductive, others will know.
- *Be specific about goals.* Social loafing is easier when the group's goals are ambiguous; make sure each person knows exactly what he or she is meant to do.
- *Make the consequences clear.* People are less likely to engage in social loafing if they understand *how* their individual behaviors contribute to the group's goal.

is charged with selecting a new marketing slogan. Your deadline is fast approaching, so the group decides to hold a meeting on Sunday afternoon, a time you usually spend with your family. As a result, you may have to sacrifice your family time for the sake of the group's mission.

Besides sacrificing time, group members sometimes find they have to do more work than their fellow members to make sure tasks get completed. The reason is that some group members may engage in **social loafing,** meaning that they contribute less to the group than the average member, particularly as the group grows in size.[52] Perhaps you've been in small groups at school in which one or two people did the bulk of the work and others did hardly any. If so, you know that can be a frustrating experience for those who take responsibility for the group's productivity.[53] In effect, members who do more than their share of work are sacrificing their time and effort so that the group can accomplish its goals. Table 9.2 presents some strategies for reducing social loafing in small groups.

Small Groups Can Experience Conflict Whenever small groups have to make decisions, they are likely to experience some measure of conflict. As we considered in Chapter 8, conflict arises when two or more parties perceive that their goals are incompatible and their resources are limited. Such a situation is probable in many group decision-making contexts.

Suppose you and some close friends are trying to decide on a graduation gift for one of the friends in your group. You intend to pool your money to purchase one gift on behalf of the group, but you're undecided about what to buy and how much to spend. One person thinks you should get a new printer for your friend's computer. Another thinks a gift card for a trendy new restaurant would be a better idea. Two people

SHARPEN
Your Skills

With a few students from your class, role-play a conversation in which you must decide on a policy for a controversial issue, such as stem cell research or the use of prisoner torture during interrogations. Encourage your fellow students to voice their opinions even if others disagree. If conflict arises during the discussion, take note of when it occurs and how the group deals with it. After the conversation, allow time for each student to assess how the group handled conflict during the role-play.

Many small groups experience conflict. As a normal part of human communication, conflict isn't necessarily problematic. What matters is how groups handle conflict.

in the group think you should just give your friend money, and you think it would be best to buy your friend some work clothes for the job he is about to begin.

Because you have a finite amount of money to spend, your group has to choose just one gift, and because different people prefer different outcomes, members may experience conflict in the process of making a decision. As we saw in Chapter 8, conflict is a normal part of human communication, and it isn't necessarily problematic. What matters is how groups handle conflict when it arises. If it is managed inappropriately, conflict can be a destructive force in a group, leading to resentment and hurt feelings and a general lack of productivity for the group. If conflict is managed constructively, however, it can lead groups to make more informed and more creative decisions than they otherwise would. We'll examine strategies for managing group conflict appropriately in Chapter 10.

Small Groups Can Be Difficult to Coordinate If you've ever been in charge of coordinating a group's meetings or activities, then you know how challenging that task can be. Even in groups that have only three or four members, finding dates and times to meet that fit everyone's schedule can be difficult. That challenge is even more pronounced in groups with 15 or more members. Some groups may even find it necessary to divide their work, assigning specific tasks to pairs of people who can more easily coordinate their schedules rather than trying to get the entire group together.

Scheduling isn't the only challenge for small groups. Particularly as groups grow in size, members often find it increasingly difficult to communicate efficiently with one another. As a result, larger groups tend to communicate less about their tasks than do smaller groups.[54] People in larger groups also encounter more challenges when trying to maintain their relationships with one another than do their counterparts in smaller groups.[55]

Although small groups require sacrifice, can experience conflict, and can be tough to coordinate, those realities don't mean that participating in them isn't worth the effort. On the contrary, belonging to a small group can be a positive and rewarding experience. That outcome is all the more likely if we are aware of the challenges of small group communication and can manage those challenges productively.

- **When is synergy advantageous?**
- **In what ways do groups require sacrifices?**

Test
Yourself

>> Becoming a Better Small Group Communicator

If you've participated in many small groups, some of your experiences were probably more favorable than others. Although your experiences in groups will vary, you can use your knowledge of small group communication to make them positive. Two particularly important communication skills for small groups are socializing new members constructively and maintaining positive group relationships.

SOCIALIZE NEW MEMBERS CONSTRUCTIVELY

Becoming part of a small group requires more than signing one's name to a membership roster. New members must also be socialized into the group. They must be informed about the group's expectations, roles, ways of working, and culture. If new members are not properly socialized, they may feel unwelcome or unenthusiastic about having joined the group. They may also unintentionally disrupt activities because they aren't aware of the group's norms and expectations. Part of communicating competently in small groups therefore involves helping to socialize new members.

One on One: Mentoring a New Group Member

One of the most important skills for socializing new members to groups is mentoring. How good a mentor are you already? For each of the following statements, indicate how well it describes you by assigning a number between 1 ("not at all") and 7 ("very well").

_____ I enjoy helping people.

_____ People frequently turn to me for advice.

_____ I like to take someone "under my wing" and help him or her succeed.

_____ I feel bad if a new person in my group seems uncomfortable.

_____ I am a good listener.

_____ Supporting people intellectually and emotionally makes me feel good.

_____ People tell me I am good at giving guidance.

_____ I like to "show people the ropes" when they are new to a group or situation.

_____ I try to be the kind of person that others can trust.

_____ I take my responsibilities toward other people seriously.

When you're finished, add up your scores. Your total score should fall between 10 and 70. A score of 10–25 suggests that mentoring is a skill you can build, and learning about small group communication is one way to do so. If you scored between 25 and 55, you are fairly good at mentoring, and as you have more opportunity to be a mentor, you can improve that skill. If you scored above 55, you are probably an experienced mentor. You are well poised to help socialize new members into the small groups to which you belong.

Experts point out that two sets of skills are necessary for proper socialization.[56] As we'll now consider, the first set comprises skills required of the group the person is joining, and the second set encompasses skills required of the new member.

Socialize New Members to the Group When new members join a group, it is important to welcome them. Researchers have suggested four behaviors in particular by which to socialize new members positively and constructively:

What can you do to help new members feel welcome in a group to which you belong?

- *Recruit good members.* Seek out potential members who will contribute to the group's mission. Be on the lookout for individuals who fit the group's personality, and encourage them to consider joining.
- *Create a group orientation.* Spend time with new members and teach them about the group's history, norms, expectations, and procedures. Helping new members learn about these aspects of the group will aid them in being positive contributors.[57]
- *Include new members in activities.* Ensure that new members are included in group functions and activities. If, for example, the work team meets every Wednesday morning for breakfast, invite the new members. They will feel welcomed and encouraged to participate when they are included in the group's plans.
- *Be a mentor.* An experienced group member can be a mentor for a new member.[58] A *mentor* is someone who serves as a trusted friend, counselor, or teacher for another person. Even if new members are properly initiated when they first join a group, they may benefit from having a seasoned mentor. How good are you at mentoring? Take the quiz in The Competent Communicator to find out.

Those behaviors are useful ways of socializing new members into groups to which you already belong. What if *you* are the new member, however? Let's look at four ways you can help ensure successful socialization for yourself.

Join a Group When you join a new group, you can aid your own process of socialization by following four steps:

- *Embrace the group's culture.* If you've made the effort to join a small group, you probably already support that group's goals, norms, values, and behaviors. Thus, part of socializing yourself into a new group is communicating in ways that reflect the group's culture.
- *Acquire appropriate skills.* If you are to become an active member of a group, you'll need to develop the skills to carry out your role and responsibilities. If you've joined a community outreach group, for instance, you may need to brush up on your conversational skills so that you can interact with the public. Think about the skills you'll need to contribute to the group's mission, and look for ways to acquire or improve those skills.
- *Learn what matters.* Groups often have multiple goals that require members to juggle several demands on their time and attention. In most cases, however, some goals are more important to the group than others. A key aspect of socializing yourself into a new group is learning how the group prioritizes competing demands. If you understand what matters to the group, you are well positioned to work toward the group's most valued goals.
- *Contribute to the group.* When you're new to a group, if you're like most people, you probably require a period of adjustment during which you learn about the group's mission and culture. Once you are socialized into the group, take responsibility for contributing to that group and its members.[59]

Joining a group can be intimidating for anyone. Whether you're helping to socialize a new member into your group or attempting to join a new group yourself, you can contribute to a more positive socialization experience by following the steps we've examined.

MAINTAIN POSITIVE GROUP RELATIONSHIPS

Your experiences in almost any small group will be more productive and meaningful if you develop and maintain positive relationships within the group. That doesn't necessarily mean that you have to become a friend with every member. Indeed, you can establish positive relationships in two other specific ways: by contributing to the creation of a constructive group environment and by helping to build group cohesion.

Contribute to a Constructive Group Environment Maintaining positive relationships within a group is easiest if an optimistic, constructive attitude prevails. When group members believe they have the resources to achieve their tasks and deal successfully with challenges, they feel better about themselves and others. Here are a few tips to help you contribute to a constructive group environment:

- *Celebrate success.* When someone in the group receives good news or achieves success in a task, ask that person if you can share the news with the group. Many people are uncomfortable telling others of their own good fortune for fear they will be seen as bragging, but they appreciate when others relate their good news for them. That way, everyone can celebrate members' successes.
- *Defuse stress.* It's normal for groups to experience stress from time to time. When interactions among group members become tense, try to defuse the stress. Suggest a group outing, such as going on a hike or taking in a movie. Use humor to reduce tensions and help people relax. When group members feel less stressed, they will likely get along better and be more productive.

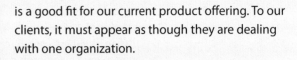

Name: Mary Peternel

College(s): BA, University of Illinois, 2003

Major(s): Communication

Job Title: Manager of Vendor Relations

Time in Job: 2 years

Work Responsibilities: For several of our products and services, my company must outsource certain components. Working as the intermediary between the company and the outside vendor, I maintain all aspects of the relationship—from creating shared marketing messages, to monitoring vendor compliance to contractual obligations, to presenting a joint sales presentation to prospects. It is my job to make sure that the outside company is a good fit for our current product offering. To our clients, it must appear as though they are dealing with one organization.

Why Communication? I realized that communication courses would serve a practical value in any career and throughout my whole life. When studying organizational communication, for example, I gained tremendous value from learning about the business side of communication, including leadership and working within groups and teams. I experienced a great deal of group work in my courses and tried to apply the lessons from those experiences to my jobs. I always try to balance both the task and the social dimensions of group work, as well as to understand the various roles individuals can play in groups.

My Advice to Students Take a variety of courses. Also, get to know faculty members, who can be a tremendous asset for advice in the field, as well as for writing letters of recommendation.

- *Respect others.* In almost any group, there are people whose perspectives are at odds. Creating a positive group environment doesn't mean that everyone has to agree or that individuals have to give up their own viewpoints. Rather, group members show respect for others by listening to different perspectives. Acknowledge the positive aspects of others' ideas and then present your own. When people treat one another respectfully, their diversity can benefit them by helping them to consider all of the possibilities in a given situation.

The ability to build and maintain positive relationships in groups is a particular asset in the workplace. To see how one former communication major has applied her learning about groups to her jobs, check out Putting Communication to Work.

Help to Build Group Cohesion Recall from earlier in this chapter that group cohesion is the extent to which everyone in the group works together toward a common goal. Research shows that cohesive groups are more productive and have happier, more satisfied members than groups lacking cohesion.[60] Contributing to group cohesion is therefore an important way to build positive group relationships. You can promote cohesion in the groups to which you belong in the following ways:

- *Emphasize collective goals.* Encourage the group to identify its shared goals clearly. Some goals will be broad, such as "Support economic development in the community." Others will be specific, such as "Plan a rally for next Thursday evening." Whatever the group's goals, cohesion suffers when members lose sight of their collective goals. Take opportunities to remind others in the group of the common goals. When members concentrate on their shared objectives, group cohesiveness often increases.
- *Keep track of progress.* When a goal takes longer to achieve than a group planned, or when members encounter unanticipated problems along the way, those who are working toward a common goal can get discouraged. You can help by acknowledging your group's progress so far. Stress what members have already accomplished, not what they haven't yet achieved. When they are raising funds, for instance, some groups create a large drawing of a thermometer, which they post in a visible place and fill in with color to indicate how much money they have collected. When group members pay attention to what they have achieved, they may focus more on their collective goals than on the challenges of meeting those goals.
- *Remind others of their value to the group.* Almost everyone has a need to belong and appreciates feeling valued. Therefore, another way you can contribute to group cohesion is to point out the reasons why you value others in the group. Some of those reasons might directly relate to the group's task; for instance, you might value one member because of her skill at generating publicity or her knack for organizing efficient workspaces. More generally, you might value a member's empathy or sense of humor. In either case, people are often more committed to groups or causes if they feel valued than if they don't, so reminding people of the ways in which you appreciate them can increase the cohesiveness of the group.

Test Yourself

- **What skills are necessary for the proper socialization of new members to a group?**
- **How can you contribute to a positive group environment?**

For REVIEW >>

- What are small groups, and what do they do?

  Small groups are collections of 3 to 20 people who focus on discrete tasks, evaluate and advise, create art and ideas, provide services and support, promote social networking, compete, and/or help their members learn.

- Why and how do people join small groups?

  People join small groups because they need to belong, they seek protection, they want to improve their effectiveness at a skill, and/or they are pressured into joining. Whatever the reason, people are socialized into small groups in several stages.

- How can you communicate better in a small group?

  You can contribute to a positive socialization experience for new members, and you can maintain good group relationships by contributing to a constructive environment and helping to build group cohesion.

Pop Quiz

Multiple Choice

1. The term for the ability of group members to work together in the service of a common goal, much as do melodies and harmonies in music, is
   - a. cohesion
   - b. independence
   - c. formal roles
   - d. introversion

2. The phase of group socialization that occurs when individual members decide to accept the expectations for the group's culture is the
   - a. anticipatory phase
   - b. assimilation phase
   - c. encounter phase
   - d. antecedent phase

3. While working in a group to complete a class project, Ron contributes far less than anyone else in the group. Ron is engaging in
   - a. synergy
   - b. role communication
   - c. social loafing
   - d. the need to belong

4. Greta has been elected president of her homeowners' association. Being president is an example of a(n)
   - a. group role
   - b. formal role
   - c. norm
   - d. informal role

5. On a NASA flight crew, each member affects, and is affected by, every other member. That is an example of the crew's
   - a. interdependence
   - b. social cohesion
   - c. task communication
   - d. resources

Fill in the Blank

6. A fan club on Facebook would be an example of a group that serves the function of _____ .

7. The entities that enable us to be productive—such as money, equipment, and expertise—are known as _____ .

8. Quiz Bowl teams exemplify groups that _____ .

9. A collaboration that produces more than the sum of its parts is known as _____ .

10. At the _____ phase of group socialization, you meet with a small group for the first time.

Answers: 1. a; 2. b; 3. c; 4. b; 5. a; 6. social networking; 7. resources; 8. compete; 9. synergy; 10. encounter

KEY TERMS

small group 209	resources 223
interdependence 210	synergy 224
cohesion 210	social loafing 225
role 212	

10

DECISION LEADERSHIP

ANCIENT PROCESS FOR A MODERN DECISION

For the group of cardinals serving as senior leaders in the Catholic Church, no decision is more important than the selection of a new pope. The pope serves not only as the head of state for the Vatican City but also as spiritual leader for more than a billion Catholics worldwide. When a pope dies in office, cardinals from around the globe convene in the Sistine Chapel, a church near the pope's official residence in the Vatican City. There the cardinals begin a *papal conclave,* a highly ritualized and closely guarded meeting in which they elect the next pope.

Adhering to a decision-making process that has been refined over nearly 2,000 years, the cardinals cast secret paper ballots to record their votes. Each vote is carefully counted under the leadership of a senior cardinal who is not eligible for election himself. Conclave rules require that the pope be elected by at least two-thirds of the votes unless multiple votes have failed to produce a winner; in that case, only a majority of votes is required. Because of the magnitude of the pope's influence and visibility, billions of people wait in anticipation of the cardinals' decision whenever a papal conclave is under way.

MAKING
AND
IN GROUPS

As You READ

>>

- How do groups generate ideas and make decisions?
- How do leaders enact leadership and exercise power?
- What communication skills improve group decision making?

No matter what its primary functions are, almost every group makes decisions. A criminal jury decides whether a defendant is guilty. A faculty committee may have decided to select this textbook for your class. From time to time, cardinals in the Catholic Church decide who will be the next pope. Those decisions are all very different, but as you'll discover in this chapter, they have more in common than you might think.

Whether groups make good or bad decisions often depends on how their members interact. As we'll see, the quality of a group's choices can be influenced by how those choices are made. It can also be influenced by who leads the group and how that leader exercises power. Because so many groups make decisions that affect the lives of others—often in significant ways—learning about leadership and decision making can help you contribute more productively in the groups to which you belong.

>> Generating Ideas and Making Decisions

In the wake of the economic recession plaguing much of the United States, small businesses are fighting to survive. Increased competition from large retail chains and decreased disposable income from consumers have forced many merchants to lay off employees or to shut their doors altogether. Rather than give up, however, several small retailers in the city of Hanford, California, came together to generate ideas for surviving the recession. So far, the group has devised several business-boosting plans, which include sponsoring community events and improving the landscaping downtown, where most of the retailers are clustered. The group hopes that these and other ideas will help the city's small businesses to weather the economic downturn.[1]

For many groups—such as the Hanford merchants—the ability to make good decisions is essential for their livelihood and quality of life. Fortunately, groups have several options for generating and choosing among ideas, as we'll see in this section. We'll also consider that several cultural and social characteristics can influence which decision-making options are best.

GROUPS GENERATE IDEAS THROUGH VARIOUS METHODS

brainstorming An idea-generating process in which group members offer whatever ideas they wish before any are debated.

A personnel committee may need to decide how to advertise the three new positions it must fill. A musical group may need to choose a repertoire of songs to perform for an up-

A musical group can use a variety of decision-making methods to choose its repertoire of songs for an upcoming performance.

coming concert series. In both cases, generating a list of possible options is an important first step in the decision-making process. Here we'll examine three of the most common methods groups use to generate ideas: brainstorming, the nominal group technique, and ideawriting.

Groups Can Brainstorm Brainstorming is a technique popularized in the 1950s to stimulate creative decision making.[2] **Brainstorming** means allowing group members to offer any ideas they wish and creating a list of all the proposed ideas before any are debated. The concept behind brainstorming is that if people feel free to think in unorthodox ways without the fear of being ridiculed, they may generate better and more creative ideas.[3]

Groups usually begin a brainstorming session by identifying the question to be answered or the problem to be solved. During the session, group members are encouraged to pose ideas they have, no matter how outlandish they might seem at first. All ideas are added to a master list, and the process continues until no one expresses any new ideas. At that point, the group considers the merits of each idea, with the goal of selecting the best one or more. During that process, the group discards some ideas in favor of others and may even combine two or more ideas. Finally, the group may decide which idea or ideas to adopt. We will consider various methods of group decision making later in this chapter.

Brainstorming can be a very effective method of generating ideas.

To brainstorm productively, groups should observe four general rules that are clearly communicated to group members before the brainstorming session begins. That way, everyone knows what to expect. Those rules are[4]

- *Focus on quantity:* Generate as many different ideas as possible in the allotted time.
- *Don't criticize:* While ideas are being generated, don't criticize them. Put all discussion about the merits of ideas on hold until later.
- *Encourage creativity:* Welcome unusual ideas, even those that may sound crazy or nonsensical at first.
- *Piggyback:* Allow members to build off of one another's ideas or to combine ideas.

SHARPEN Your Skills

With a small group of students from your class, spend 15 minutes brainstorming to generate a list of actions you could take to address a social problem in your community. First, identify the problem you want to address—such as homelessness, unequal access to health care, hunger, inadequate child care, or low adult literacy. Next, follow the principles of brainstorming to list various actions that your group could take to improve the lives of those affected. Afterward, spend a few minutes discussing what you found most enjoyable and most challenging about brainstorming. You might present your final list of ideas to the rest of the class as a way to encourage community involvement.

Researchers suggest that brainstorming sessions last no longer than about 30 minutes so that the group's energy and creativity don't wane.[5] When done properly, brainstorming can lead a group to generate useful and innovative ideas.

Groups Can Use the Nominal Group Technique

Brainstorming works well when all members of the group feel comfortable offering ideas and sharing opinions. Sometimes, though, people felt uncomfortable expressing their ideas in a group. Because brainstorming calls for group members to generate ideas collaboratively, members who are shy or who fear being ridiculed may be unlikely to participate. In that situation, a more productive option may be to use the **nominal group technique (NGT).**[6] NGT calls for group members to generate their initial ideas silently and independently and then to combine them and consider them as a group.

Like brainstorming, NGT begins with the identification of a question to be answered or a problem to be solved. Instead of having members contribute their initial ideas aloud in front of the group, however, NGT involves having each member make a list of ideas on his or her own, working silently. Afterward, a group facilitator asks each member to read his or her ideas aloud, one at a time, while the facilitator writes them onto a master list. Alternatively, the facilitator can collect the ideas and compile the master list on his or her own so that no one knows who came up with each idea.[7]

Once a master list is in place, NGT follows essentially the same process as brainstorming. The group considers the merits of each idea on the list, discarding some and debating or modifying others. Finally, the group selects whichever idea it believes to be the best. The major advantage of NGT over brainstorming is that it can encourage participation from members who might be uncomfortable contributing their ideas aloud.[8]

Groups Can Ideawrite

A third method groups can use to generate ideas is ideawriting.[9] **Ideawriting** encourages members to generate and evaluate ideas in writing while working independently.

Like brainstorming and NGT, ideawriting starts with the description of a specific question to be answered or problem to be solved. The ideawriting process then proceeds in four steps. In the first step, each member creates a list comprising three to four ideas and including the reasons why each idea has merit. Afterward, members put their individual lists in a pile. In the second step, each member chooses a list from the pile that is not his or hers. Working alone, members read all the ideas and reasons shown on the list they select, and they offer comments about the strengths and weaknesses of each idea. When they're done, they return the list to the pile, select another list, and do the same. The second step continues until every member has read and commented on every other member's ideas.

In the third step, members retrieve the list of ideas they originally created, which now contains written comments from everyone else in the group. Each member reads and responds in writing to the comments made about his or her ideas. That process allows group members to react to feedback and potential criticism of their ideas in a nonthreatening way. Finally, in the fourth step, group members come together to create a master list of ideas they think are worthy of additional discussion. They then work toward selecting the best idea, as they would in brainstorming and NGT.

Of the three idea-generation methods we've surveyed, ideawriting is the least collaborative, because group members accomplish most of the steps in ideawriting while working individually rather than as a group. The major advantage of ideawriting is that it allows each member to offer ideas, respond to others' ideas, and react to criticisms of his or her own ideas in a private manner.[10] Privacy can help shield group members from the feelings of resentment or defensiveness that might arise in a public process.

nominal group technique (NGT) An idea-generating process in which group members generate their initial ideas silently and independently and then combine them and consider them as a group.

ideawriting An idea-generating process in which each member adds three or four ideas to a pile and then offers comments on others' ideas. Afterward, members respond to comments made about their ideas and generate a master list of ideas worthy of consideration.

Having used a technique such as brainstorming, NGT, or ideawriting to generate ideas, groups usually must choose the best idea from among the various options. That process requires them to use a decision-making method, our next point of focus.

GROUPS MAKE DECISIONS IN MANY WAYS

To illustrate the various methods by which groups can make decisions, let's imagine that you're an employee of Star Bank. You are assigned to a team charged with choosing a marketing slogan for the bank's new account options, which were designed to meet the needs of senior citizens. Your team has generated several ideas for slogans and has narrowed the list down to three:

- *Star Bank: Where Seniors Reach for the Stars*
- *Star Bank: The Right Choice for Your Active Lifestyle*
- *Protect Your Golden Years with Star Bank*

Your team must select one slogan from this list. Let's examine five methods by which the team members might arrive at their decision: consensus, majority rule, minority rule, expert opinion, and authority rule.

Some Groups Decide by Unanimous Consensus One option for making a decision is to try to get everyone to agree about which slogan is best. Once you begin discussion, for instance, you might find that all the members of your team prefer the first marketing slogan to the other two. If everyone in the group prefers the same slogan, then the group has **unanimous consensus,** which is uncontested support for a decision. In some instances, unanimous consensus is the only option for group decision making. A jury hearing a criminal case, for example, must arrive at a unanimous verdict about the defendant's innocence or guilt. Verdicts on which not all jurors agree are considered invalid. Even if it isn't required, however, unanimous consensus can be advantageous because group members are likely to support more enthusiastically a decision on which they all agree.

Achieving unanimous consensus isn't always easy, though. Particularly if the decision to be made is controversial, group members may vary dramatically in the outcomes they prefer. In that case, arriving at a decision may require the group to engage in long, often frustrating discussions. Even so, such discussions may end in a **stalemate,** an outcome where members' opinions are so sharply divided that unanimity is impossible to achieve. In the event of a stalemate, a group may have to resort to one of the other forms of decision making *if* it has the option of doing so.

When trying to decide by unanimous consensus, groups must also be careful not to achieve **false consensus,** which occurs when some members of the group say they support the unanimous decision even though they do not. If most members appear to support the same outcome, then those who prefer a different outcome may feel pressure to support the majority's wishes so that unanimity can be reached. What is actually achieved in such a situation is false consensus, which reduces the chance that all members will be enthusiastic about the group's decision. Groups often discover false consensus after the fact, when members who felt pressured to vote with the majority begin voicing their concerns about the decision. The likelihood of achieving false consensus is diminished if group members feel safe expressing their opinions, even if those opinions contradict the views of their fellow members.

Some Groups Decide by Majority Rule Instead of choosing a marketing slogan by unanimous consensus, your team might reach its decision by **majority rule,** a decision-making process that follows the will of the majority. If someone says "Let's take a vote" when a group decision is looming, he or she is probably recommending majority rule. To select among your marketing slogans, therefore, each member of your team might cast a vote for one of the slogans. The slogan receiving the fewest votes would be discarded, and

unanimous consensus Uncontested support for a decision—sometimes the only option in a group's decision-making process.

stalemate An outcome where members' opinions are so sharply divided that consensus is impossible to achieve.

false consensus An outcome where some members of a group say they support the unanimous decision even though they do not.

majority rule A decision-making process that follows the will of the majority.

then each member would vote for one of the remaining two options. If more people vote for one slogan than the other, that slogan will have been chosen by majority rule.

Majority rule operates on the democratic principle that decisions should reflect what most people want, not what a smaller number of more powerful people prefers. The primary advantage of majority rule is that by definition, it ensures that most people in the group support the decision being made. People raised in democratic societies are used to majority rule as a form of decision making, and under most circumstances, they accept that the will of the majority should be followed even if they themselves voted with the minority.

When a vote is particularly close, however, the minority can feel that the decision was arbitrary. For instance, if one marketing slogan received eight votes from your team and the other slogan received seven votes, those who favored the second slogan might feel the decision was unfair because the margin of victory was so small. As a result, those in the minority may be less inclined to support the team's decision than if the winning slogan had won by more votes. When using majority rule to make decisions on controversial issues, it may thus be useful to remind everyone in the group of the importance of supporting the majority decision, whatever it is.

Majority rule can be problematic in groups that have an even number of members, because of the possibility of a tie vote. If each marketing slogan had won 50 percent of the vote, neither slogan would have received a majority of the votes. In cases in which an even number of votes will be cast, groups should determine ahead of time what procedures to follow in the event of a tie. For example, a group might determine that its leader will cast a vote only if a tie vote arises and the leader's vote is necessary to break the tie. To prevent the possibility of a tie vote, some groups decide ahead of time to have an odd number of members.

Some Groups Decide by Minority Rule A third form of decision making is **minority rule,** a process in which a small number of members makes a decision on behalf of the group. Decision makers often use minority rule for the sake of efficiency.

Let's say your Star Bank team wants to host a reception to unveil its new marketing slogan. Instead of having the entire team discuss where and when to hold the event, the leader might delegate that responsibility to two or three team members. Those members then have the ability to make decisions about the reception on the team's behalf. The minority rule strategy saves the team's time for discussing more important decisions, such as which marketing slogan to adopt.

By definition, minority rule excludes the input of most members of the group. For that reason, it is rarely a good option for making decisions that are controversial or consequential.

Some Groups Decide by Expert Opinion Some groups include people whose training or experience makes them experts on the type of decision the groups are making. Such groups may reach their decisions by deferring to **expert opinion,** or the recommendations of individuals with expertise in a particular area. Let's assume your Star Bank team includes someone with a master's degree in marketing. Because of that person's expertise, your team might ask his or her advice on which marketing slogan to adopt, instead of taking a vote or trying to achieve unanimous consensus.

Expert opinion works on the principle that certain people have better judgment or more informed opinions on specific topics and that consequently these experts often make better decisions than non-experts. It's important to bear in mind, however, that expertise is always specific to particular topics or matters. No one is an expert on everything. If the group is going to rely on expert opinion, members therefore should make certain they're listening to someone with appropriate expertise.

Some Groups Decide by Authority Rule Suppose that instead of building unanimous consensus, taking a vote, assigning the decision to a minority, or consulting an expert, your team at Star Bank leaves the choice of a slogan to the team leader. That approach is an example of **authority rule,** a process by which the leader of the group makes the decisions. Authority rule is a common method of decision making in some groups. In a class or workshop, for instance, a teacher usually makes decisions about the group's

minority rule A decision-making process in which a small number of members makes a decision on behalf of the group.

expert opinion Recommendations of individuals who have expertise in a particular area that are sometimes the basis of a group's decision-making process.

authority rule A decision-making process in which the leader of the group makes the decisions.

Authority rule is best if one person has the experience and responsibility to make decisions for everyone else in the group.

activities. In a group of firefighters responding to a blaze, the senior commander makes the decisions and issues the orders.

Authority rule is best in such situations—that is, when someone in the group has legitimate authority over other members. Teachers and fire commanders make decisions on behalf of their groups because it's their responsibility and their prerogative to do so. Authority rule is also very efficient. If firefighters had to meet to consider and vote on all possible approaches to dealing with an emergency, lives would be lost in the time their discussions would take. If the commander makes the decisions, however, the group can act on those decisions more quickly, and this consideration is critical when time is short.[11]

Authority rule can be problematic, however, when exercised in groups that have no legitimate authority figure. If someone on your work team were to say, "I've decided we should choose the second slogan," the other members would likely resent that person's attempt to exercise authority over the team. When no one in the group is a legitimate authority figure, other methods of decision making are likely to be more effective.

The Choice of Method Depends on Various Factors Which method of making decisions is best depends on several factors that vary from decision to decision. One factor is the importance of the decision itself. Relatively unimportant decisions may be best made by authority rule or minority rule because those methods are efficient. More important decisions—those that will affect many people or require a great deal of money—might be better made by unanimous consensus, majority rule, or expert opinion because those methods often entail a closer, more critical consideration of the options.

A second factor in determining the right decision-making method is whether the decision requires expert knowledge. Expert opinion is often the most effective method of making decisions that require specialized knowledge not shared by everyone in the group. Authority rule can also be effective in such situations if the leader has authority *because of his or her expertise,* as, for example, a fire commander usually does.

A third factor influencing the choice of decision-making method is how quickly the decision must be made. Authority rule is often the fastest way of making decisions, whereas building unanimous consensus is frequently the most time-intensive. When selecting its method of decision making, a group might consider the time constraints on the decision.

Which methods of decision making do you generally prefer? Why?

CULTURAL CONTEXT AFFECTS DECISION MAKING

Cultural and social characteristics of a group also can influence the decision-making method that the group prefers. They include individualism, power distance, and time orientation. We examined those characteristics in Chapter 2; now let's see how they can affect group decision making.

Individualism Affects Decision Making People in individualistic cultures are taught that their primary responsibility is to themselves. Competition, self-reliance, and individual achievement are valued in highly individualistic cultures. In contrast, people in collectivistic cultures believe their primary responsibility is to their families, their communities, and their employers. Collectivistic cultures value collaboration, harmony, and solidarity rather than competition and individual achievement.

Whether a group hails from an individualistic or a collectivistic culture can influence how that group makes decisions. Groups in collectivistic cultures, for instance, may place great emphasis on reaching group consensus. Because collectivistic cultures stress collaboration, group members value what's best for the group, even if that means having to compromise on their individual preferences. In contrast, groups in individualistic cultures are more likely to encourage members to voice their opinions on decisions, even if those opinions differ. Because individualistic cultures emphasize competition, group members may be less interested in reaching consensus than in persuading others to agree with their position.

Power Distance Affects Decision Making Recall that cultures vary in how they expect power to be distributed within a society. In high-power-distance cultures, certain groups of people have great power and the average citizen has much less. In low-power-distance cultures, people value equality and believe no one person or group should have excessive power over others.

A culture's power distance can influence how groups within that culture arrive at decisions. Groups in high-power-distance cultures may be particularly deferential to authority, for instance. Consequently, they may prefer to make decisions by authority rule or by following expert opinion. In contrast, groups in low-power-distance cultures are more likely to prefer majority rule as a decision-making method given that majority rule treats everyone's vote as equal to everyone else's.

Time Orientation Affects Decision Making Cultures differ with respect to their norms and expectations concerning the use of time. Monochronic cultures view time as a tangible commodity. As a result, people in monochronic cultures enjoy "saving" time and try to avoid "wasting" it. In contrast, polychronic cultures conceive of time as more fluid. People in polychronic cultures don't prioritize efficiency and punctuality to the same extent that people do in monochronic cultures. Instead, they attach greater value to the quality of their lives and to their relationships with others.

A group's preferred decision-making method may depend on whether its culture is monochronic or polychronic. Groups from monochronic cultures may opt for majority rule, minority rule, or authority rule because those methods often use time efficiently. However, groups from polychronic cultures, which have less incentive to make decisions quickly, may be more likely to try achieving unanimous consensus if they believe that method will produce a better decision.

In summary, groups have many options for making decisions. Individualism, power distance, and time orientation can each influence the decision-making methods a group *prefers*, but they do not necessarily *determine* which methods that group will use. As we've seen, a group's method of decision making is also affected by the nature of the decision to be made. Nonetheless, cultural influences can be powerful, shaping not only how groups make decisions but also how satisfied they are with those decisions.

- **What are the advantages of brainstorming, nominal group technique, and ideawriting?**
- **What are five decision-making methods for groups? Under what conditions is each method an appropriate choice?**
- **How do individualism, power distance, and time orientation influence the decision-making practices a group prefers?**

>> Being a Leader

Mary Ellen Diaz knows about effective leadership. A world-class chef who trained at the famed Le Cordon Bleu in Paris, Diaz has worked in exclusive restaurants, including at the Ritz-Carlton hotel in Chicago. Although she prepared gourmet meals for her restaurants' clients, she felt personally drawn to the cause of providing food for the hungry. Importantly, however, she didn't want to feed people leftover scraps or second-rate food but the same high-quality meals she prepared in Chicago's restaurants. With a small group of staff members, Diaz founded First Slice, an organization that distributes fresh, expertly prepared food to the needy. Because of her leadership and the decisions her group has made, First Slice delivers more than 1,400 meals each month to the hungry, homeless, and disenfranchised in Chicago.

With effective leadership and constructive decision-making techniques, groups of people can achieve great things. What does it mean to be a leader, however? In this section, we'll examine the characteristics and behaviors of effective leaders, and we'll discover that leaders enact distinct leadership styles.

LEADERS OFTEN SHARE SPECIFIC TRAITS

One way to understand leadership is to look at some common traits of leaders. **Traits** are distinguishing characteristics of a person that are often relatively enduring and not easily changeable. Each of us has certain physical traits, such as our eye color, sex, and height. We also have psychosocial traits, such as our self-esteem, temperament, and level of anxiety when faced with a communication task. Physical traits tend to be more enduring than psychosocial traits.

None of these traits, however, necessarily determines who's going to be a good leader and who isn't. Rather, most of us can learn to be an effective leader no matter what physical and psychosocial traits we possess. In fact, sometimes the responsibilities of leadership are assigned to us whether or not we want them. Still, researchers have discovered that leaders often share particular traits, as we'll now consider.

Physical Traits The body's attributes are referred to as its **physical traits.** Studies have found that three physical traits in particular can influence who is likely to become leaders and how effective leaders are perceived to be.

One such trait is the sex of the leader. Some studies have reported that people perceive women less favorably than men as potential leaders and that they evaluate the work of female leaders less positively than the work of male leaders.[12] Importantly, those findings don't mean that men actually *are* more effective leaders, only that they are sometimes perceived to be. Other research has found that people in groups have more negative nonverbal reactions, such as facial expressions and gestures, toward female leaders than male leaders,[13] particularly when female leaders enact stereotypically masculine behaviors, such as dominance and aggression,[14] but some studies have not found that sex difference.[15] Although people may respond to male and female leaders differently, they appear to judge female and male leaders as being equally competent.[16]

A second physical trait that can affect leadership is height.[17] In Western cultures, people often associate height with dominance, competence, and power.[18] It therefore may not surprise you to learn that taller people are more likely than shorter people to be nominated or elected to leadership positions.[19] For example, 29 of the 44 U.S. presidents have been taller than the average U.S. adult man, and since 1990, the taller candidate for president has won the popular vote 66 percent of the time.[20] Perhaps because the average adult man is taller than the average adult woman, however, height is a stronger predictor of leadership success for men than it is for women.[21]

Finally, physical appearance influences leadership. Studies have shown, for instance, that leaders with masculine-looking faces are judged as more competent than are leaders with feminine-looking faces.[22] Masculine faces typically feature a wide, square jaw and small eyes, whereas feminine faces feature large eyes and a small, rounded jaw. Research-

By the Numbers

66.5

Height, in inches, of the average U.S. American adult.[23]

traits Defining characteristics of a person that are often relatively enduring and not easily changeable.

physical traits The body's physical attributes.

Most U.S. presidents—including Bill Clinton and George W. Bush—have been taller than the average U.S. American man.

ers speculate that people associate masculine faces with competent leadership because they think of men as being more dominant and powerful than women.[24]

Regardless of whether they appear masculine or feminine, however, leaders are more likely to be physically attractive than unattractive.[25] As you might know from your own experience, people associate physical attractiveness with a range of positive qualities, including intelligence, honesty, and competence. It should therefore come as no surprise that physically attractive people are perceived to be better leaders than less attractive individuals.

It's worth repeating that although sex, height, and physical appearance are *related to* leadership, none of those traits determines who will be a good leader and who will not. Leadership is a skill you can develop and nurture over time, regardless of your physical traits.

Psychosocial Traits Many effective leaders share particular **psychosocial traits,** which are characteristics of their personality and ways of relating to others. Much of the research has focused on three particular traits: self-esteem, self-monitoring, and outgoingness.

Recall from Chapter 3 that self-esteem is a person's subjective evaluation of his or her value and worth. Because having self-esteem gives us confidence in ourselves, it seems likely that people are better leaders if their self-esteem is higher rather than lower. In line with that idea, research tells us that people with high self-esteem rate themselves as better leaders than do those with low self-esteem.[26] Surprisingly, though, a leader's self-esteem doesn't predict how *other people* rate his or her leadership abilities.[27] Although having high self-esteem improves how leaders perceive themselves, it doesn't improve how others perceive them.

A second psychosocial trait that has been studied with reference to leadership is self-monitoring. Recall that self-monitoring is our awareness of our own behavior and its effects on others. Some researchers have suggested that people who are high self-monitors are able to perceive the needs of others in a group and adapt their own behavior to meet those needs. In line with that idea, several studies have found that self-monitoring is strongly related to leadership emergence in groups.[28] Curiously, some research has shown that self-monitoring predicts leadership only for men,[29] but most research indicates that both female and male leaders are likely to be high self-monitors. How high a self-monitor are you? Take the quiz in The Competent Communicator to find out.

Finally, several studies have indicated that leaders are more likely to be outgoing and expressive rather than shy and withdrawn. One project examined the findings of 73 different studies and found that people are more apt to become leaders—and more apt to be *effective* leaders—to the extent that they are extroverted rather than introverted.[30] **Extroversion** is a personality trait shared by people who are friendly, assertive, and outgoing with others. Leadership is inherently social, so extroverts tend to excel at leadership because they are comfortable interacting socially with others. In contrast, **introversion** characterizes people who are shy, reserved, and aloof. Because of their more reserved nature, introverts often experience **communication apprehension,** anxiety or fear about communicating with others. Apprehensive communicators often have difficulty leading. One study found that people who scored high on a test of communication apprehension perceived themselves—and were perceived by others—as less likely to be good leaders than were people who scored low on communication apprehension.[31]

Just as not every effective leader is male, tall, and physically attractive, not every effective leader scores high on self-esteem, self-monitoring, and extroversion. Examining traits that many leaders share tells us only part of the story about effective leadership. To understand leadership more fully, we must look not only at *who leaders are* but also at *how leaders behave,* our next topic.

Think of the five leaders you most respect. What physical traits do they have in common?

psychosocial traits Characteristics of one's personality and ways of relating to others.

extroversion A personality trait shared by people who are friendly, assertive, and outgoing with others.

introversion A personality trait shared by people who are shy, reserved, and aloof.

communication apprehension Anxiety or fear about communicating with others.

Your Self-Monitoring—High, Low, or No?

Self-monitoring is an awareness of your behaviors and their effects on others. How high a self-monitor are you? Read each of the following statements and indicate whether you think it is true or false with respect to yourself. There are no right or wrong answers. Simply respond to each statement in whatever way seems to represent you.

	True	False
I find it easy to imitate the behavior of other people.	_____	_____
I can argue in favor of ideas even if I don't believe in them.	_____	_____
I guess I put on a show to impress or entertain people.	_____	_____
When I am uncertain how to act in a social situation, I look to the behavior of others for cues.	_____	_____
I would probably make a good actor.	_____	_____
I laugh more when I watch a comedy with others than by myself.	_____	_____
In groups of people, I am often the center of attention.	_____	_____
I often act differently in different situations or when I'm around different people.	_____	_____
I'm good at making other people like me.	_____	_____
I rarely feel awkward in social settings.	_____	_____

When you're finished, add up the number of statements you marked as true. The total should be between 0 and 10. If your total was 7 or above, you are a high self-monitor. You are highly aware of your own behavior and of how other people perceive you. If your total was between 4 and 6, you are a moderate self-monitor. You're aware of yourself and your effect on others, but not to a substantial degree. If your total was 3 or lower, you would be classified as a low self-monitor. You tend not to direct your attention to your own behavior or to your interactions with others.

Source: Items adapted from Snyder, M. (1974). Self-monitoring of expressive behavior. *Journal of Personality and Social Psychology, 30,* 526–537.

LEADERS ENACT DISTINCT STYLES

Think about the leaders of groups to which you've belonged. How would you describe their leadership styles? Regardless of his or her physical or psychosocial traits, chances are each leader had a specific way of enacting leadership responsibilities. Many years ago, a team of social psychologists determined that most leaders enact one of three distinct styles in the way they lead others—democratic, autocratic, and laissez-faire. Let's take a quick look at each.

Some Leaders Are Democratic One of the underlying principles of a democracy is that every citizen has the right to participate in decision making. Group leaders who enact a **democratic style** reflect that principle in their leadership.[32]

Let's say that Taylor chairs the committee overseeing the adult literacy outreach program at her community center. When the committee needs to generate ideas about how to raise community awareness, Taylor strives to get everyone's input. She cultivates a non-judgmental environment in which committee members can feel free to express their ideas. She makes sure that the committee considers every opinion, even ideas that may conflict

democratic style A leadership style in which every member of a group has the right to participate in decision making.

with her own views. When it's time for the committee to make a decision, she counts everyone's vote equally, and she supports the will of the majority even if it doesn't reflect her own preferences. As a leader with a democratic style, Taylor therefore sees herself as a facilitator for the group's mission.

Some Leaders Are Autocratic As the organizer of his calculus study group, Adya believes it's his responsibility to make decisions on behalf of his group. He sets the schedule for group meetings and decides where each one will be held. Whenever the group gets together, Adya takes charge and controls how the study session proceeds. Adya is enacting an **autocratic style** of leadership.[33] That is, he sees himself as having both the authority and the responsibility to take action on his group's behalf. When decisions need to be made, he makes them, usually without asking others in the group what they want. When tasks need to be done, he assigns them to individuals in the group instead of soliciting volunteers. Unlike Taylor, Adya considers himself to be the most important member of his group.

Some Leaders Are Laissez-Faire Meghan has just been promoted to the lieutenant in charge of eight patrol officers in her police precinct. Her philosophy is that patrol officers should work independently, with little direction or personal involvement from her. She rarely interacts with her officers, and she gives them little feedback on their job performance. When she is forced to oversee decisions or mediate conflicts, she involves herself only as long as is necessary. Afterward, she resumes her general lack of involvement in the operations of her division. All of those characteristics reflect Meghan's **laissez-faire style** of leadership.[34] It's not that she doesn't care about her patrol officers; she simply thinks they function at their best with minimal supervision. Thus, unlike Taylor and Adya, Meghan often sees herself as the person who is least important to the success of her group.

Each Leadership Style Has Its Strengths Which type of leader—democratic, autocratic, or laissez-faire—would you prefer? If you were raised in a country with a democratic style of government, such as the United States, you might be inclined to say democratic leaders are best because they value everyone's input equally. You might also like laissez-faire leaders because they allow you to work autonomously. If you value equality and autonomy, you might be inclined to say that autocratic leaders are least preferable because they would give you neither equality nor autonomy.

Preferences aside, each style of leadership is best under certain circumstances. When it's important that everyone in a group feels he or she has an equal voice in decision making, the democratic style of leadership is the most likely to accomplish that goal.[35] Even if not everyone agrees on the group's decision, the democratic style helps to ensure that no one feels neglected or unimportant.

If the group's priority is to accomplish its tasks quickly, however, the autocratic style is best because only one person needs to make the decisions. The autocratic style is also the most effective when the leader has knowledge or expertise that the group members at large lack. If a senior physician is leading a group of interns in a complicated surgery, for instance, it's best for everyone if the physician takes charge and gives orders rather than taking a vote about how to proceed with the surgery, because the surgeon's experience confers knowledge that the interns don't yet have.

In groups composed of people who are proficient at working on their own, the laissez-faire style can be best because it provides group members with the greatest autonomy to do their work. Although most leaders need to provide some level of oversight, a laissez-faire leader lets his or her group members work independently, giving direction only when absolutely necessary. That approach backfires when group members lack the skills or training to work autonomously, but it can be very effective when group members are proficient at working on their own.

SHARPEN
Your Skills

Make a short list of democratic, autocratic, and laissez-faire leaders. Next to each leader's name, explain why he or she exemplifies the leadership style you indicated.

autocratic style A leadership style in which leaders see themselves as having both the authority and the responsibility to take action on a group's behalf.

laissez-faire style A leadership style in which leaders offer minimal supervision.

power The ability to influence or control people or events.

reward power A form of power based on the leader's ability to reward another for doing what the leader says.

- Which physical and psychosocial traits are often associated with leaders?
- How are democratic, autocratic, and laissez-faire styles of leadership different?

>> Exercising Power

Regardless of which styles of leadership they enact, leaders rely on the exercise of power to achieve their goals. **Power** is the ability to influence or control people or events.[36] To be an effective leader requires having some form of power.

People exercise influence or control over others in many ways. In this section, we will explore the various forms of power that leaders can possess. We will observe that power does not reside in leaders themselves but in their relationships with the people they lead.

LEADERS EXERCISE MANY FORMS OF POWER

Exercising power over people may seem relatively straightforward: A leader tells people what to do and they do it. The important question, however, is *why* they do it. Some people might follow instructions because they are being paid to do so. Others might follow along because they want to please the leader or because they fear the consequences of disobeying.

In their now classic studies, social psychologists John French and Bertram Raven determined that the reason *why* a leader is followed constitutes the form of power that leader has. French and Raven proposed that power comes in six specific forms: reward, coercive, referent, legitimate, expert, and informational.[37] As we take a close look at these forms, keep in mind that they aren't mutually exclusive. Rather, one person may exercise multiple forms of power in different situations or even within the same situation.

Leaders Exercise Reward Power As its name implies, **reward power** operates when a leader has the ability to reward another for doing what the leader says. The supervisor of your work team has power over you, for instance, because she pays you and can promote you for following her instructions. In this case, your pay and the possibility of advancement are the rewards. If your supervisor loses the ability to pay or promote you (say, if your company goes bankrupt or she leaves her job), she also loses her power over you.

Leaders can exercise many different forms of power over others.

THE DARK SIDE of Communication

When Coercion Becomes Abuse

Any form of power can be put to positive or negative uses. Coercive power is a positive force if it encourages people to act in their best interests, as when a parent threatens to withhold cell phone privileges if her teenage son breaks curfew. However, those who are threatened with excessive consequences—especially when they are encouraged to act contrary to their best interests—are often the victims of emotional abuse. A corrupt sheriff threatens to have his dispatcher's mother deported unless she sleeps with him. A bank manager threatens to "out" her closeted gay teller unless he works weekends and holidays. In those and similar cases, someone in a leadership position induces extreme fear to elicit the behaviors he or she desires from a subordinate. That exercise of coercive power can intimidate or even terrorize the victim and thus constitutes emotional abuse.

Sustained emotional abuse often has many negative effects on its victims, including severe anxiety and depression, low self-esteem, diminished physical health, and even heightened risk of suicide. Like many other forms of abuse, emotional abuse is most commonly perpetrated on the most vulnerable people in a society, such as the poor, the disabled, the elderly, women, children, and minorities. To help someone you suspect of being victimized by excessive coercion, identify sources of aid, such as a company's human resources office and a county abuse hotline.

Source: National Clearinghouse on Family Violence Information

Having reward power requires the ability not just to provide a reward to those who follow one's instructions but to provide a *sufficient* reward. People who feel they are not rewarded adequately for following someone are likely to stop following that person eventually. When employees perceive that they are not receiving fair wages in exchange for their work, for instance, their willingness to follow the company leadership decreases.[38]

Leaders Exercise Coercive Power The opposite of reward power is **coercive power,** or power that comes from the ability to punish. When you go to court, for example, the judge has power over you because a judge can punish you with fines or imprisonment for not doing as he or she says. Throughout history, dictators have exercised coercive power over their populations by ordering imprisonment or even death for those who don't follow their orders.

Just as reward power requires the ability to provide a *sufficient* reward, coercive power requires the ability to issue a *sufficient* punishment. For instance, most of us would follow the directions of a university administrator who had the power to expel us. If the worst punishment that administrator could dole out were a memo of reprimand that would get buried in some file drawer, however, we might feel less obligated to follow his or her directions.

Although exercising coercive power can be an effective way of achieving one's goals, research shows that it entails certain disadvantages. One study, for example, found that the more often a manufacturing company exercised coercive power over its dealers, the less of the other forms of power it was perceived to have.[39] As The Dark Side of Communication explains, excessive use of coercive power can also constitute emotional abuse.

coercive power A form of power that comes from the ability to punish.

referent power A form of power that derives from attraction to the leader.

legitimate power A form of power in which leaders' status or position gives them the right to make requests with which others must comply.

expert power A form of power that stems from having expertise in a particular area.

Leaders Exercise Referent Power

French and Raven used the term **referent power** to refer to the power of attraction, the idea being that we tend to comply with requests made by people we like, admire, or find attractive in some way. In a study group, for instance, you might work harder for a group leader you like than for one you dislike. The reason you do so is that it's human nature to desire the approval of people we like and admire. By following their directions, we hope to gain that approval. In contrast, gaining the approval of people we don't like or admire is usually not a high priority.

In a similar vein, many of us are persuaded to buy products or services that are endorsed by celebrities we like or find attractive.[40] Because we usually don't know the celebrities personally, we aren't trying to gain their approval when we follow their recommendations. Instead, we are trying to *be* like them. Researchers have shown that we have a strong tendency to emulate—or act like—people we find attractive.[41] Therefore, when a handsome singer or a glamorous actress endorses a particular brand of car, protein bar, or cable TV service, we are often persuaded to buy those brands out of a desire to be like that individual.

We tend to comply with requests made by people we like, admire, or find attractive. That type of power is known as referent power.

Leaders Exercise Legitimate Power

People exercise **legitimate power** when their status or position gives them the right to make requests with which others must comply. When the president of the United States meets with the cabinet, for instance, members of that group follow the president's directives because the president is in a position of legitimate authority.

Because legitimate power is granted by people's status or position, it is no longer effective when people lose their status or leave their position. Suppose you have been promoted to the job of interim department head at your company to fill in for someone who is on maternity leave. During the time you fill that position, you have legitimate power to issue instructions, make purchasing decisions, conduct employee evaluations, and hire and fire at your discretion. Each of those abilities is a legitimate exercise of the position you hold. When the permanent department head returns from maternity leave, however, you will return to your previous position. At that point, you will no longer have the powers you exercised as the interim department head because you will no longer have legitimate claim to those powers.

SHARPEN Your Skills

Suppose you supervise a group of high school student volunteers at a local children's hospital. One of your responsibilities is to ensure that the volunteers clock in and out properly when they start and end their shifts. With another student, brainstorm ways that you could use referent power to influence the volunteers' behavior.

Leaders Exercise Expert Power

The fifth form of power on French and Raven's list is **expert power,** power that stems from having expertise in a particular area. In a chamber orchestra, for instance, the musicians follow the instructions of the conductor because he or she has the musical expertise to make the orchestra sound as good as possible. In many cases, we perceive that it is in our best interests to comply with the directions of experts, because their experience or training gives them specialized knowledge that we lack.

It can be tricky to identify exactly what constitutes expertise. For the most part, we recognize expertise through agreement: A person is an expert if the right people consider him or her to be so. For instance, a physician is considered a medical expert because he or she graduated from medical school, completed a residency, and was certified to practice medicine by other medical professionals. That individual's doctoral degree and medical license indicate that there is consensus about his or her qualifications as an expert. Other people may have the same level of

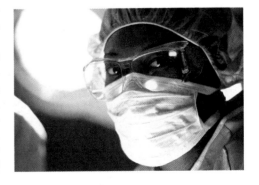

Table 10.1   Forms of Power

According to French and Raven, leaders exercise six forms of power in their relationships with others.

Reward	Power based on the ability to reward for compliance
Coercive	Power based on the ability to punish for noncompliance
Referent	Power based on liking, admiring, and being attracted to the leader
Legitimate	Power based on rightfully granted status or position
Expert	Power based on knowledge, training, experience, and/or expertise
Informational	Power based on access to valued information

medical knowledge as the doctor but may not exercise expert power because their expertise is not formally recognized. Later in this section, we will further discuss the importance of recognizing power.

Leaders Exercise Informational Power   A final form of power is **informational power,** power that stems from the ability to control access to information. Many socialist and communist governments exercise informational power over their populations, for example, by controlling all of the media in their countries. Citizens in those societies are exposed only to news that their governments want them to know, and thus they become dependent on their government leaders for information.

In what instances have you exercised power in your relationships with others? Which forms of power have you exercised?

A similar process can occur in smaller groups if one person has news or information that others want. In that case, the person holding the information has power over the others until he or she releases that information. A person's informational power is usually greatest when the information he or she has is valuable and cannot be obtained elsewhere.

Table 10.1 summarizes the six forms of power leaders can exercise.

POWER RESIDES IN RELATIONSHIPS, NOT IN PEOPLE

As we saw in the last section, people wield many forms of power in many different situations. Because some people seem to have more power than others, we might think of them as being *powerful people,* as though their power resides within them. In truth, however, power doesn't exist within people—it exists within relationships. As we'll see in this section, we have power only over particular people and only when our power is recognized. In other words, power is an inherently social experience.

Power Is Relative   One characteristic of power is that it is *relative,* meaning that people have power only *in relation to* other people. No person has absolute power. Regardless of what forms of power we possess, each of us exercises power only over particular people in particular situations. Your manager may have some power over you, but that doesn't mean she also has power over your friends and neighbors. She is powerful only relative to the people who work for her.

We often acknowledge the relative nature of power when people overstep their boundaries by attempting to exert power they don't have, as when a child rejects direction from an older sibling with the response "You're not the boss of me!" That statement reflects the opinion that the older sibling does not have power relative to the younger one. Similarly, adults may feel defensive when they receive direction from people who have no reward, coercive, referent, legitimate, expert, or informational power over them.[42] In such situations, individuals recognize that any person's power is limited to specific people in particular contexts, and they may resent or reject attempts to control their behavior by people without power over them.

informational power A form of power that stems from the ability to control access to information.

Power Requires Recognition In groups and organizations, powerful people have only the power that their followers recognize in them. For example, a charismatic religious leader may exercise referent power over her followers, but she does not have that power over others who don't share her followers' desire to please her and gain her approval.

Importantly, recognizing that someone has power does not necessarily mean we give our consent to be governed. If a police officer stops you while you're driving, for instance, you would likely recognize the power he has over you even if you don't want to be subject to that power. In other words, we don't always enjoy having others tell us what to do, even though we may still recognize their right to do so. We can therefore say that a person can have power over others only if others recognize that power.

We've seen in this section that leaders can exercise many different forms of power, that all power is relative, and that power requires recognition. To end this section, let's also acknowledge that power itself is neither positive nor negative. Rather, it's how we *use* power that makes it good or bad. When we abuse the power we have over others or exercise it unwisely, we can cause harm and heartache; in such instances, we may not hold on to that power for long. As former U.S. senator Elizabeth Dole observed, however, "Power is a positive force if it is used for positive purposes." Using power in a positive way can therefore improve the lives of those who follow us.

Many of us resent illegitimate attempts to exert power over us.

Test Yourself

- In what ways are reward power, coercive power, referent power, legitimate power, expert power, and informational power different?
- What does it mean to say that power resides in relationships?

>> Leadership and Decision-Making Skills

Effective leadership and decision making are not always easy to achieve or sustain. Many factors can inhibit the ability of leaders and groups to function at their best. The more we understand about leadership and decision-making skills, the better equipped we are to contribute positively to the groups to which we belong. As we'll see in this section, three particular skills that are useful for groups and their leaders are their ability to

- Manage conflict constructively
- Avoid groupthink
- Listen carefully

MANAGE CONFLICT CONSTRUCTIVELY

Because the members of a group are interdependent, they are bound to experience conflict from time to time. Recall that conflict occurs when two or more interdependent parties express a struggle over goals they perceive to be incompatible. Especially when groups are faced with making decisions, conflict can arise because of perceived differences in the goals of individual members. Conflict is not necessarily problematic. In fact, conflict can motivate groups to make more creative decisions than they otherwise might. What matters is how groups manage conflict when it arises.

According to researchers Robert Blake and Jane Mouton, our options for dealing with conflict are based on two underlying dimensions: our concern for our own needs and

Concern for Self

High   Low

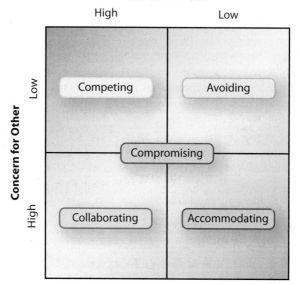

Competing	Avoiding
	Compromising
Collaborating	Accommodating

Concern for Other: Low / High

FIGURE 10.1 Five Styles of Conflict Our options for dealing with conflict rest on two underlying factors: concern for *our own* needs and desires, and concern for *the other party's* needs and desires. These factors give rise to five main strategies for engaging in conflict: competing, avoiding, accommodating, compromising, and collaborating.

Source: Adapted from Blake, R. R., & Mouton, J. S. (1984). *The managerial grid III* (3rd ed.). Houston: Gulf.

desires, and our concern for the other party's needs and desires.[43] When plotted on a graph (Figure 10.1), these dimensions give rise to five major strategies for engaging in conflict: competing, avoiding, accommodating, compromising, and collaborating. Some of those strategies may seem more appropriate or more desirable than others. As we examine them, however, consider that each strategy may be best under certain circumstances.

Competing The *competing* style represents a high concern for one's own needs and desires and a low concern for those of the other party. The goal is to win the conflict while the other party loses. Engaging in conflict in this style is much like playing football. There are no tie games—rather, one team's win is the other team's loss.

Competing might be appropriate in situations when there is a concrete outcome that cannot be shared, such as when two people are vying to become a committee chair. People may also see ongoing competition as a positive aspect of their relationship, insofar as it might motivate each person to perform at his or her best.[44] The competing style of managing conflict becomes problematic, however, when it leads to resentment or to a desire to get even with people to whom one has "lost" a competition.[45]

In what situations do you avoid conflict? Is avoidance the best option in those situations? Why?

Avoiding A very different approach to conflict is the *avoiding* style, which involves a low concern for both the self and the other party. Adopting this style means ignoring the conflict and hoping it will go away on its own. Some people choose avoidance because they are uncomfortable engaging in conflict. Others choose it because they don't care enough about the outcome of the conflict to bother.

Avoiding conflict isn't always the wrong choice; many people in groups opt to ignore or avoid certain points of contention among themselves to maintain harmony.[46] When avoidance becomes a group's primary way of managing conflict, however, it often leaves

In collectivistic societies, accommodating in response to conflict is often expected and is viewed as respectful or noble.

important matters unresolved. In this situation, the result can be dissatisfying relationships within the group.[47]

Accommodating *Accommodating* is the opposite of competing in that accommodating reflects a high concern for the other party but a low concern for the self. In the accommodating style, one's goal is to sacrifice so that the other party wins. People in a group sometimes accommodate to keep the peace. That strategy may work well in the short term. In the long run, however, continually accommodating the other party can lead to resentment.

Cultural ideas play an important role in the use of accommodation. In collectivistic societies, accommodating in response to conflict is often expected and is viewed as respectful or noble.[48] In contrast, in individualistic societies, people may be seen as weak or spineless if they consistently accommodate others.

Compromising *Compromising* reflects a moderate concern for everyone's needs and desires. In this strategy, both parties in the conflict give up something in order to gain something. No one gets exactly what he or she wants, but everyone leaves the conflict having gained something valuable.

Let's say you're negotiating a job offer with a new work group, and you want a higher salary than the group leader wants to pay. Through your negotiation, you agree to accept a lower salary than you originally wanted, and the group leader agrees to give you an extra week of vacation in return. Neither of you got exactly what you wanted, but you each got something you valued in return for giving up something else. Compromising takes time and patience, but it often leads to more satisfying outcomes than do competing, avoiding, or accommodating.

Collaborating The *collaborating* style represents a high concern for the needs of both sides in a conflict. The goal is to arrive at a win–win situation that maximizes both parties' gains.

After they unexpectedly had a third child, for example, Mick and Laura felt the strain of paying for day care while Mick worked and Laura went to school. Their other children, Tara and Tana, were excited about having a younger sibling but upset about the reduced attention they would get. Soon, the tensions gave rise to conflict within the family. After collaborating on a solution, the family decided that Mick would cut his work hours, and Laura would enroll in online courses so that at least one of them would be home every day. The money they saved in day care ex-

Work at It: Groups Can Resolve Any Conflict If They Try Hard Enough

There are multiple ways to manage conflict in groups. That observation may lead you to believe that if you have the right skills and try hard enough, your group can eventually resolve any conflict it might encounter. That outcome would be great, but the truth is that some conflicts are simply irresolvable.

Let's say you're part of a jury hearing a lawsuit brought against a pharmaceutical company. The plaintiff in the case has alleged the company was negligent when it failed to warn consumers that its prescription pain relievers should not be given to animals. During your deliberation, you discover that some jurors steadfastly believe the company is negligent. Other jurors believe just as strongly that reasonable people should know not to give animals medications that are prescribed for humans, so the company should not be required to make that warning explicitly. The longer your deliberation goes, the more entrenched jurors become in their opposing viewpoints. As a result, you report to the judge that the jury is hopelessly deadlocked, and the case is dismissed.

This courthouse scenario illustrates that when people's opinions are diametrically opposed, and when those people are unwilling or unable to change their positions, they are unlikely to resolve their conflicts, no matter how hard they try. In such cases, the only real options are to avoid the conflict, to agree to disagree, and to try to minimize the effects of the conflict on other aspects of the group's relationship.

ASK YOURSELF

- What conflicts have you experienced that seemed impossible to resolve?
- When should a group give up trying to resolve a conflict? When should a group continue trying to resolve a conflict, even if it seems irresolvable?

penses more than made up for Mick's reduced income. Moreover, both Laura and Mick felt better because they were able to care for their new child themselves, and Tara and Tana got to spend more time with their parents than they had before.

In many situations, collaborating is the best way for groups to handle conflict. Yet collaborating can require a great deal of energy, patience, and imagination. Even when it is the ideal approach to managing conflict, it can therefore also be the most time-consuming and laborious solution.

Managing conflict appropriately can be very beneficial for groups, but can *every* conflict be resolved? Take a look at the Fact or Fiction? box to find out.

SHARPEN
Your Skills

With two or three other people, generate a topic of conflict and then role-play resolving that conflict using each of Blake and Mouton's conflict styles. Afterward, discuss which style or styles seemed most appropriate for the conflict you were having, and consider how other styles might have been more appropriate for a different type of conflict.

AVOID GROUPTHINK

Let's suppose you're part of a group of engineers designing a new toy for children. The toy is colorful and fun to play with, and the manufacturer is pressuring your group to approve the toy's design so it can put the toy into production in time for the holiday shopping season.

Although you like the toy, you are concerned that the paint on its exterior could be unsafe for children. When the group meets to consider approving the design, however, you feel pressured to keep your concerns to yourself. You sense that some other engineers are also concerned about safety, but most don't speak up. When someone asks whether the paint is safe for children, the group leader says, "Yes, it's safe; now let's move on." Soon, you hear people say it's important that the group approve the toy's design unanimously so that consumers will have confidence in the product. Although you have serious doubts about the toy's safety, you feel pressured to ignore your misgivings—and, along with everyone else in the group, you vote to approve the design.

That example illustrates the problem of **groupthink,** which occurs when group members seek unanimous agreement despite their individual doubts.[49] According to psychologist Irving Janis, a pioneer of groupthink research, there are eight major warning signs that a group has fallen victim to groupthink:[50]

- *Illusion of invulnerability:* Group members are overly confident in their position, ignoring obvious problems.
- *Collective rationalization:* Members "explain away" any ideas that are contrary to the group's position.
- *Illusion of morality:* Members believe the decisions they make are morally correct, ignoring any arguments to the contrary.
- *Excessive stereotyping:* Members construct negative stereotypes of anyone who disagrees with them.
- *Pressure for conformity:* Members feel pressure to conform to the group's decision and are branded as disloyal if they do not.
- *Self-censorship:* Members don't speak up if they have dissenting viewpoints.
- *Illusion of unanimity:* Members falsely perceive that everyone agrees with the group's decision, because they don't hear anyone offering counterarguments.
- *Mindguards:* Some members actively prevent the group from hearing about arguments or evidence against the group's position.

According to researchers, groupthink is particularly likely to occur when a group has a strong, authoritarian leader; is composed of members with similar backgrounds; and is isolated from outside influence.[51] Under those conditions, groups can produce decisions that appear both unanimous and well informed but are actually neither. Indeed, decisions produced by groupthink tend to be problematic because they are not subjected to critical thought. Instead, groupthink discourages all attempts to consider a decision critically, because critical analysis might prevent members from reaching consensus.

As a result, decisions reached by groupthink can have disastrous effects, such as exposing thousands of children to potentially unsafe paint on a new toy. In fact, researchers have identified groupthink as a contributing factor for several national disasters, including the attack on Pearl Harbor, the Cuban Missile Crisis, the Watergate scandal, and the explosion of the space shuttle *Challenger.*[53] What is most troubling about those examples is that they might all have been avoided if the groups in charge had thought critically about their decisions instead of falling victim to groupthink.

Avoiding groupthink is therefore an important aspect of communicating competently in groups.[54] According to researchers, group members can take several specific steps to prevent groupthink from occurring:

- *Be aware of the potential for groupthink.* Teach others in the group about what groupthink is, why it is so problematic, and what its warning signs are. If you detect any of the warning signs, speak up and remind others how important it is to avoid groupthink.
- *Make sure the group has sufficient time to make decisions.* Groupthink can occur when members feel pressured to arrive at a decision quickly. If your group is making an important decision, remind members to allow sufficient time for discussion. If the decision-making process feels rushed, say "It might be better to put off making this decision until we have more time."

By the Numbers

191

Percentage that members are more likely to voice disagreement if groupthink is *not* occurring than if it is.[52]

Groupthink played a role in the explosion of the space shuttle Challenger.

groupthink A situation in which group members seek unanimous agreement despite their individual doubts.

- *Encourage dissenting viewpoints.* When it appears that most members have the same position on an issue, ask, "What are some alternative ideas?" Encourage members to play devil's advocate by questioning the merits of one another's positions. Remind the group not to accept any ideas at face value and to examine each idea critically.
- *Solicit input from outside the group.* Suggest that group members consult with people outside the group who might offer useful input on the group's decision. Look up relevant research and bring it to the group's attention.
- *Give important decisions a second chance.* Even after the group has made its decision, recommend that members meet once more to reconsider it. Encourage members to express any doubts or second thoughts they have about the decision. Listen to all arguments, whether they are for the decision or against it. Then ask the group to vote on its decision once again.

It might seem that these recommendations would discourage a group from reaching any decision at all. Their purpose, however, is to help the group make a *good* decision by avoiding the problems of groupthink.

LISTEN CAREFULLY

When we interact with others, our ability to communicate effectively relies heavily on how well we listen. That observation is especially true when we interact within groups, a setting where multiple ideas or positions are often discussed at the same time. One way to become a better group communicator is to build listening competence. Particularly useful strategies in this regard are knowing how to recognize barriers to effective listening and practicing listening skills.

Recognize Barriers to Effective Listening in Groups A starting point for honing your listening skills is to acknowledge factors that might be inhibiting your ability to listen attentively. Barriers to effective listening common in many groups include

- *Noise:* Noise is anything in the physical environment (such as sound) or in your individual experience (such as hunger) that distracts you from listening effectively. If noise interferes with your ability to listen in a group, try to identify what is causing the noise and do what you can to reduce its effect.
- *Boredom:* When you're bored, effective listening becomes difficult because your mind wanders. If you find that boredom is preventing you from listening effectively,

Boredom makes it difficult to listen effectively.

suggest to the group that members take a break and come back to the discussion later. If a break isn't possible, try to identify some aspect of what's being said that you find interesting, and focus on that aspect. Doing so may help you overcome your boredom and allow you to listen more actively.

- *Information overload:* Many of us have difficulty listening effectively when we feel we're being bombarded with information. If a member of your group is overloading you with information, politely suggest that he or she identify the most critical pieces of information and focus specifically on those.

- *Rebuttal tendency:* We saw in Chapter 6 that the rebuttal tendency is the propensity to debate a speaker's point and formulate your reply while the person is still speaking. The rebuttal impulse can be a particularly common barrier to effective listening in groups that evaluate or analyze—such as juries, focus groups, and advisory boards—because members of such groups may disagree on the merits of the various ideas they're discussing. If you notice the rebuttal tendency in yourself, remind yourself to listen to everything a speaker says *before* you formulate your response.

Practice Listening Listening is a skill, not an innate ability. As with most skills, you can hone your ability to listen through practice.

Perhaps you're unsure about how you can *practice* listening. If so, remember that people listen with various goals in mind. As we considered in Chapter 6, people sometimes engage in informational listening, which is listening to learn. At other times, they engage in critical listening, which is listening to evaluate and analyze what they hear. Individuals also engage in empathic listening, when the goal is to experience what another person is thinking or feeling. Those goals are quite different from one another. You can therefore practice your listening skills by paying attention to the specific listening goals that are most useful to you in a given situation.

Informational listening skills are particularly important when you need to understand and retain what you're hearing, such as when you take part in a study group. To ensure you have understood what you've heard, try paraphrasing the speaker's message. Paraphrasing is restating the speaker's message in your own words to clarify its meaning. If you paraphrase a statement in a way that accurately reflects its meaning, the speaker will usually reply by confirming your understanding. If you paraphrase in a way that changes the meaning of a statement, however, the speaker will generally correct your misunderstanding. Paraphrasing can therefore help you to understand a speaker's message more accurately.

Critical listening skills are especially important in groups that have to make important decisions, such as a state legislature and a corporate board of directors. To improve your critical listening skills, remind yourself not to accept what you hear at face value. Instead, question what you hear. Start by considering the credibility of the speakers. Are they experts on the topic about which they're speaking? Are they biased toward one point of view? If you find the speakers to be credible, ask yourself whether their statements have merit. Are their assertions logical and well thought out, or do they seem inconsistent? Do the speakers make claims that are improbable? Keep in mind, too, that it's relatively easy to listen critically when you are hearing ideas or claims you don't like, because you may already be inclined to discredit such information. It's when you *approve* of the speakers or their message that it is most important to listen critically. Doing so will help ensure you accept ideas on their merits rather than at face value.

Finally, empathic listening skills are most important in groups that provide comfort, such as support groups. In such groups, people often listen to understand how others are thinking or feeling. If that's your goal, practice listening without interrupting. As you probably know from your own experience, being interrupted while you're speaking is frustrating. Particularly when people are sharing personal or sensitive information—as they often do in a support group—they appreciate being able to speak without interruption. Also, practice listening without offering advice. Unless they specifically ask for your advice, many people would prefer that you simply listen to what they have to say.

The effectiveness of communication in many groups depends on the ability of members to listen to one another. By acknowledging the barriers to effective listening and practicing the listening skills appropriate to the situation, you can improve your own ability to communicate effectively in groups.

- How can people in groups manage conflict effectively?
- Why is it important to avoid groupthink?
- What tactics and skills can help group members become better listeners?

For REVIEW >>

- How do groups generate ideas and make decisions?

  Groups can use brainstorming, nominal group technique, and ideawriting to generate ideas, and they can make decisions by unanimous consensus, majority rule, minority rule, expert opinion, and authority rule. The preferred decision-making technique depends on the nature of the decision and on the cultural context of the group.

- How do leaders enact leadership and exercise power?

  Leaders can enact democratic, autocratic, or laissez-faire leadership styles, each of which has its strengths. Leaders exercise several forms of power—including reward, coercive, referent, legitimate, expert, and informational power—over the people they lead.

- What communication skills improve group decision making?

  Group members should learn to manage conflict appropriately, avoid groupthink, and listen carefully to contribute positively to group decision making.

Pop Quiz

Multiple Choice

1. To choose a theme for next year's conference, a student group votes on three possible themes and selects the one that receives the most votes. The group's decision-making process is

   a. unanimous consensus
   b. majority rule
   c. minority rule
   d. authority rule

2. The style of managing conflict that represents a high level of concern for the needs of the self and the needs of the other party is

   a. competing
   b. avoiding
   c. accommodating
   d. collaborating

3. The style of leadership that reflects the philosophy that group members should work independently, with minimal involvement from the leader, is

   a. democratic
   b. autocratic
   c. laissez-faire
   d. legitimate

4. Everyone in Arianne's group follows her suggestions because they all admire her and want to please her. Arianne's form of power is

   a. reward power
   b. referent power
   c. legitimate power
   d. informational power

5. The eight major warning signs that a group has fallen victim to groupthink include all of the following *except*

   a. illusion of anonymity
   b. illusion of morality
   c. illusion of invulnerability
   d. illusion of unanimity

Fill in the Blank

6. Leaders who score high on _____ are highly aware of their own behavior and how it affects others.

7. When using _____ to make a decision, group members generate their initial ideas silently and independently and then combine them and consider them as a group.

8. A(n) _____ leader believes it is his or her right and responsibility to make decisions on behalf of the group.

9. Leaders who exercise _____ power punish people for not doing what the leaders want them to do.

10. To avoid groupthink, groups should encourage members to play _____ by questioning the merits of one another's positions.

Answers: 1. b; 2. d; 3. c; 4. b; 5. a; 6. self-monitoring; 7. nominal group technique or NGT; 8. autocratic; 9. coercive; 10. devil's advocate

KEY TERMS

brainstorming 235
nominal group
    technique
    (NGT) 236
ideawriting 236
unanimous
    consensus 237
stalemate 237
false consensus 237
majority rule 237
minority rule 238
expert opinion 238
authority rule 238
traits 241
physical traits 241
psychosocial traits 242

extroversion 242
introversion 242
communication
    apprehension 242
democratic style 243
autocratic style 244
laissez-faire style 244
power 245
reward power 245
coercive power 246
referent power 247
legitimate power 247
expert power 247
informational
    power 248
groupthink 253

11

CHOOSING, RESEARCHING

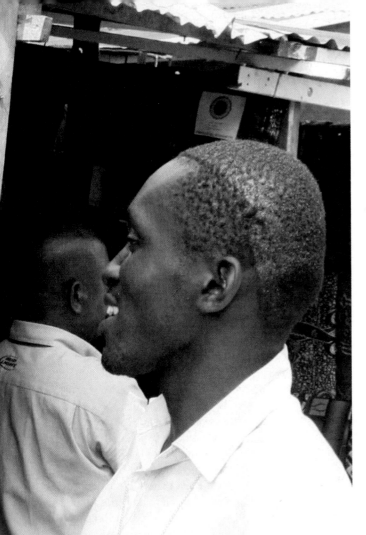

WORDS CAN CHANGE LIVES

When Matt and Jessica Flannery attended a lecture at Stanford Business School one day in 2003, they had no way of knowing how many people they would eventually help as a result. The speaker was Muhammad Yunus, a Bangladeshi economist who would later win the Nobel Peace Prize for combating poverty and advancing social and financial development in some of the world's neediest countries. Yunus spoke that day about lending small amounts of money to help struggling entrepreneurs set up businesses and become self-sufficient. His speech inspired the Flannerys to establish Kiva, a nonprofit organization allowing people to lend money online to help poor entrepreneurs around the world. Many recipients of Kiva's microloans require only a few hundred dollars to purchase supplies or equipment for family farms, bakeries, laundromats, clothing stores, and other small enterprises. As recipients pay back their loans over time, Kiva is able to fund other applicants. As of August 2010, Kiva had made over 395,000 loans, averaging only $400 each, to help people across the globe gain economic security. Yunus's speech had profoundly influenced the Flannerys. Indeed, his words motivated them to take actions that would change many people's lives for the better.

DEVELOPING, AND
A TOPIC

As You READ

>>

- For what reasons might you plan a speech?
- How can you select a topic that is right for you and your audience?
- Where can you find supporting information?

At the end of the Second World War, the nation of Germany was divided into two states: West Germany, which was democratically governed, and East Germany, which was under communist rule. In the German capital of Berlin, a concrete wall nearly a hundred miles long divided the city, preventing people from crossing from one side to the other. For over a quarter century, the Berlin Wall stood as a symbol of the ongoing tension between communism and democracy. In 1987, in what would be one of the most memorable speeches of his U.S. presidency, Ronald Reagan stood at the Berlin Wall and exhorted communist leader Mikhail Gorbachev, "Tear down this wall!" East and West Germany lifted their travel restrictions two years later, and by 1990, the wall was gone. Spurred by Reagan's persuasive and memorable speech, a nation torn apart by war eventually reunited.

Even if you find that story inspiring, you may think it has little to do with you. Perhaps you find public speaking to be a chore, one of those necessary evils of studying communication that won't matter to your life. The thought of speaking before a group may even bring on pangs of anxiety. If you feel that way, you're in good company. Research indicates that most of us would rather do almost anything other than getting up in front of others and giving a speech—particularly if we feel our words won't accomplish much.

Obviously, not every speech will reunite a country or inspire others to help the poor around the world. As you'll see in this chapter, however, you don't have to be a U.S. president or a Nobel Peace Prize recipient to give competent, effective public presentations that can help your listeners. Whether your purpose is to inform, to entertain, or to persuade, you can learn to develop speeches that will meet your goals and connect with your audience.

Although he appears regularly on television, Jon Stewart undertook extensive preparation before hosting the Academy Awards broadcasts in 2006 and 2008.

>> Know Why You're Speaking

Although some 1.5 million people watch him on *The Daily Show* each weekday,[1] Jon Stewart still reacted with awe at the responsibility of hosting the Academy Awards broadcast, as he did in 2006 and 2008. With a viewing audience of more than 30 million in the United States alone, the awards show is usually one of the highest-rated television events every year.[2] Hosting the broadcast required Stewart to prepare an entertaining opening monologue and introductions to all the guests who would appear throughout the evening. Even though he's a seasoned television entertainer, Stewart required weeks of preparation and practice to perform his role successfully.

Preparing to host the Academy Awards is much like preparing to give any type of public presentation, just on a larger scale. You can learn to create successful speeches by following many of the same steps performers such as Stewart follow when preparing for large broadcasts. As you'll see in this section, creating an effective presentation starts with identifying your goals.

Acting students are taught to ask themselves "What's my motivation?" when practicing for a performance. That question leads them to consider why their character should be saying or doing what's described in the scene. If the script calls for a character to appear aggressive toward others, for instance, a performer must know *why* the character is being aggressive to make his or her portrayal believable. Because characters can have several different motivations, it's useful for performers to consider which motivations are relevant to the scenes they are practicing.

Preparing a public presentation is no different. To be effective, you must begin by asking about your *own* motivation. Good public speakers carefully consider the goals of the speeches they prepare. As we'll see in this section, we can speak with many different goals in mind, such as to inform, to persuade, to entertain, to introduce, and to give honor. Those goals are not necessarily mutually exclusive; sometimes a speaker has more than one goal for the same speech. Just like actors who consider their characters' motivations, you can improve your performance as a speaker by identifying the goal or goals you want to accomplish in your speech.

WE SPEAK TO INFORM

Anthony Sullivan knows about informative speaking. Having appeared in television advertisements for nearly two dozen household products, Sullivan is an expert at teaching audiences how a product works in 20 seconds or less. In one commercial, for instance, he informs viewers about a cordless sweeping device called the Swivel Sweeper by explaining how it works and demonstrating its effectiveness on dirty floors. Regardless of whether they eventually buy the product, viewers learn what the Swivel Sweeper can do by watching and listening to Sullivan's informative speech.

Millions of Swivel Sweepers have been sold on television thanks to informative speaking by pitchmen such as Anthony Sullivan.

When we speak to inform, our goal is to teach listeners something they don't already know. Teaching a seminar for lifeguards, leading a workshop for senior citizens, and demonstrating a product at a trade fair are all examples of informative speaking. In each case, the speaker has knowledge on a particular topic that he or she wishes to impart to the audience. To do so successfully, the speaker must make the material interesting, clear, and easy for listeners to follow. We'll further examine informative speaking in Chapter 14.

WE SPEAK TO PERSUADE

On the reality TV series *Big Brother,* contestants live together for three months in a house isolated from the outside world but under constant video surveillance. Each week, two contestants are nominated for eviction, and the others vote to decide which one will stay. Immediately before the voting, the nominated contestants have a few minutes to appeal to their housemates not to evict them. In these short speeches, the nominees are speaking to persuade others to let them remain in the Big Brother house for another week.

As we saw in Chapter 4, persuasion is the process of guiding people to adopt a specific attitude or enact a particular behavior. When we speak to persuade, we are therefore appealing to our listeners to think or act in a certain way. During a motivational halftime speech in the locker room, a basketball coach can persuade her team to play more effectively in the game's second half. During an inspiring commencement address, a celebrity or political figure can persuade the new graduates to believe in themselves. For decades, social scientists have studied the most effective ways to persuade others. We'll explore the components of a good persuasive speech more fully in Chapter 15.

WE SPEAK TO ENTERTAIN

Whenever Chris Rock, Dane Cook, and Kathy Griffin take the stage to do standup comedy, they speak for the purpose of entertaining their listeners. Similarly, many motivational speakers seek to entertain their audiences with fun, inspirational stories. When we speak to entertain, our goal usually isn't to teach new information or to persuade our audience to adopt certain attitudes or behaviors. Rather, we seek to amuse our listeners and help them have an enjoyable time.

Although speaking to entertain may sound like more fun than speaking to inform or to persuade, it isn't necessarily easier. To be effective, speakers who entertain must be keenly aware of who their listeners are and what that audience is likely to find amusing. For example, in terms of what would inspire or entertain them, inner-city schoolchildren probably differ from retired nurses, and computer sales reps most likely differ from religious missionaries. Many a comedian has had the experience of bombing on stage by telling jokes the audience found inappropriate, incomprehensible, or simply not funny. Speaking to entertain therefore requires the ability to fit your material to the characteristics and interests of your listeners.

WE SPEAK TO INTRODUCE

In August 2008, Beau Biden, the attorney general of Delaware, introduced his father, Joseph Biden, now vice president of the United States, at the Democratic National Convention in Denver. During his speech, the younger Biden spoke of his father's struggles during childhood and young adulthood, as well as his dad's accomplishments during his 36 years in the U.S. Senate. At the conclusion of his remarks, Beau Biden asked his listeners to welcome his father to the stage.

Like Biden, many of us will give public presentations to introduce other people. When we do so, our aim is often to inform listeners of the person's background and notable characteristics. Suppose you were introducing a new colleague to your project team at work. In your presentation, you might say a few words about the person's hometown, education, prior work experience, and hobbies or interests. Good speeches of introduction are usually short and focused on information that the listeners will find interesting.

We also speak to introduce ourselves. Perhaps you've been called upon to introduce yourself to your classmates on the first day of the academic term. If so, you may have informed your audience of your major, career goals, and reasons for taking that particular course. Just as when we introduce others, we want to select a few pieces of information our listeners will find interesting when we introduce ourselves.

SHARPEN Your Skills

Identify an important political figure and search online for the text of one of his or her most notable speeches. Read the text and identify the speaking goal or goals you see reflected in the speech.

WE SPEAK TO GIVE HONOR

On many occasions, we speak to give honor. Speaking at the funeral of his sister Diana, Princess of Wales, Charles Spencer described Diana as "the very essence of compassion, of duty, of style, of beauty" and as a "symbol of selfless humanity" worldwide. His remarks were part of a *eulogy,* a speech made to honor the memory of people after their death. We use eulogies and many other types of presentations to give honor to people, places, or significant points in history.

At a social gathering such as a wedding reception or graduation party, it's common for particular guests to give a *toast,* a short speech of tribute to the person or people being celebrated. Most toasts offer comments on the honoree's positive qualities and congratulations on his or her accomplishments. Similarly, one might deliver a *speech of recogni-*

tion to honor someone who is receiving an award. Such presentations usually explain the criteria for the award and then identify the recipient by describing his or her achievements.

Speakers also give speeches to honor important places. In December 2008, for instance, Nancy Pelosi, the Speaker of the U.S. House of Representatives, delivered a *speech of dedication* to honor the completion of the new Capitol Visitor Center in Washington, DC. As is common during speeches of dedication, Pelosi spoke of how the site came to be and what important roles it will play. Perhaps the most famous speech of dedication in U.S. history was President Abraham Lincoln's Gettysburg Address, delivered in November 1863, during the Civil War, to dedicate a new national cemetery for soldiers. Finally, we can use speeches to honor significant points in history. On the fifth anniversary of the September 11 terrorist attacks on the United States, for example, President George Bush gave a *speech of commemoration*. Bush honored the memory of the victims and rescue workers who had lost their lives, and he re-emphasized the government's commitment to prosperity and peace.

In summary, informing, persuading, entertaining, introducing, and honoring are not the only reasons we give public presentations, but they are among the most common. Table 11.1 describes those reasons. In addition, many presentations have multiple goals. For instance, salespeople often attempt to persuade customers to buy a product by informing them of the item's positive features. The best man at a wedding might give a toast to honor the couple but also to entertain the guests with funny stories about the new spouses. Even if a speech has one primary goal, it can also have one or more secondary goals.

Once you have identified the goal or goals for your presentation, you should think about an appropriate topic on which to speak. We'll examine that key step next.

Which type of speaking (to inform, to persuade, to entertain, to introduce, to give honor) do you think you would find most challenging? Why?

Table 11.1   Five Reasons Why We Speak

To inform	Teaching listeners about something they don't already know
To persuade	Affecting listeners' attitudes or behaviors
To entertain	Causing listeners enjoyment
To introduce	Informing listeners of someone's background
To give honor	Giving recognition or commemoration to a person, place, or event

- When you give a speech to inform, what is your goal?
- What does it mean to persuade?
- Why must speakers who entertain be keenly aware of their audiences?
- What are the characteristics of good speeches of introduction?
- On what occasions might you give a speech of honor?

>> Choose an Appropriate Topic

When you are invited to give a speech, you may be assigned a topic that is based on your specific knowledge—whether it's your cultural experiences and adventures from your extensive travel or your expertise in retirement planning, Pilates, or deep-sea fishing. Other times, however, you may select the topic for your speech. When you're in that situation, you can identify appropriate topics by following four steps:

- Brainstorm to identify potential topics.
- Identify topics that are right for you.
- Identify topics that are right for your audience.
- Identify topics that are right for the occasion.

BRAINSTORM TO IDENTIFY POTENTIAL TOPICS

When no speech topic has been assigned, start by brainstorming to generate a list of potential topics. As you may recall from Chapter 10, brainstorming encourages you to identify as many ideas as possible without stopping to evaluate them. You can use two questions to guide your brainstorming: What topics do you care about, and what topics are in the news?

What Topics Do You Care About? One way to identify potential topics is to consider what interests you. What experiences, hobbies, beliefs, attitudes, values, and skills do you have? How do you enjoy spending your time? What issues do you care about? Jot down as many topics as you can think of. Some of your topics might be questions; others might be statements. Don't stop to evaluate your ideas just yet; for now, your goal is to generate as many ideas as possible. Your list might look something like this:

> History of hip-hop music
> Challenges of multiple births
> Five reasons to learn a foreign language
> Common financial mistakes
> How to make the perfect lasagna
> Who is Desmond Tutu?
> Caring for someone with dementia
> The right way to view an eclipse
> Latin American pottery
> Tips for taking digital photos
> What does the secretary of state do?
> Surviving a hurricane
> The Emancipation Proclamation
> Why be ethical?

Considering what you already care about is a good first step toward generating a list of potential speech topics. The Competent Communicator provides hints for creating an inventory of topics that interest you. As we'll consider next, you can also identify potential speech topics by looking at issues in the news.

What Moves You? Selecting Your Speech Topic

A good first step in selecting a speech topic is to create a list of issues that are important to you or about which you already have some knowledge. If you need inspiration in selecting your speech topic, try the following exercise. Read each question in the left column. Write down the first three answers that come to mind in the middle column. Afterward, consider two ways you might talk about each answer and write them in the third column. When you're done, you will have a list of potential topics.

Questions	Your Answers	Your Topics
What do you talk about the most with your friends and family?		
What do you find intriguing, confusing, or bewildering?		
What are your favorite websites?		
What is your fantasy career?		
What are your favorite ways to spend free time?		
With which people, living or dead, would you most like to have a conversation?		

One way to choose a speech topic is to consider issues that are currently in the local, national, or international news.

What Topics Are in the News? A second way to brainstorm potential topics is to consider issues in the local, national, or international news. Fortunately, most of us have multiple sources of news available at all hours of the day and night. We can watch news broadcasts on network and cable television. We can pick up any of the hundreds of newspapers or news magazines published every day. Perhaps most conveniently, we can log into websites that highlight contemporary news stories. Those sites include search engines, such as www.yahoo.com and news.google.com, as well as dedicated news sites, such as www.cnn.com and www.msnbc.msn.com. Updated multiple times per day, most search engines and news sites provide ongoing coverage of important and current issues. A list of contemporary topics might look like this:

> Pros and cons of stem cell research
> How secure is online voting?
> Three ways to conserve energy
> iPhone apps
> Effectiveness of airport security screening
> Reality television
> Guantánamo Bay detention camp (Gitmo)
> The search for extraterrestrial life
> Marriage versus civil union
> The future of Social Security
> What is intelligent design?
> School vouchers
> Efficiency of hybrid cars
> Copyright laws and the Internet

You can combine the list of topics you care about with the list of topics in the news to create a master list of potential topics. You'll then need to select one topic as the focus of your speech, being sure that is appropriate for you, for your audience, and for the occasion.

IDENTIFY TOPICS THAT ARE RIGHT FOR YOU

When homing in on your presentation topic, first consider whether the topic is right for you. Ask yourself

- *What do I already know about this topic?* If you choose to speak about an issue with which you're already familiar, you will speak with credibility and confidence.

By the Numbers

29,800,000

Number of hits on google.com in response to the term "speech topics."

- *What do I need to learn about this topic?* Even if you're already familiar with your topic, you should still be willing to invest some time to ensure that your knowledge is up to date.
- *How much do I care about this topic?* Choosing a topic you care about will make preparing your speech more enjoyable, and your presentation will be more engaging for your listeners.
- *How valuable is the topic?* If you're going to the trouble of researching and preparing a speech, don't waste your energy on a trivial topic. Select something that is meaningful and valuable to you.

Answering those four questions won't always lead you toward the same topic. For instance, you might know a great deal about impressionist paintings, cell mitosis, or the Electoral College, but you may care more about car repair, the greenhouse effect, or Barack Obama's path to the presidency. Some speakers may be drawn to topics such as Cuban agriculture, homeschooling, and online banking, whereas others might find the same topics trivial or boring.

Even if your answers to those questions don't lead you to a specific topic, they ought to narrow the field of potential topics. Once they do, there's a key question to consider: whether the topic is appropriate for your audience.

If you have ever had difficulty generating good topics for a speech, how did you overcome the problem?

IDENTIFY TOPICS THAT ARE RIGHT FOR YOUR AUDIENCE

To give an effective speech, you need to select a topic that is right not only for yourself but also for your listeners. Once you have a potential topic in mind, ask yourself

- *How appropriate is this topic for my audience?* Consider whether your topic will be suitable for your listeners. Topics that are appropriate for adults, for instance, may not be appropriate for children.
- *How much will my audience care about this topic?* Consider whether your listeners will likely care about your topic. If the answer is yes, they will be more attentive to your speech and more likely to remember what you say.

We will return to this discussion of ways to analyze your audience later in this chapter. For now, though, if you narrowed your list of potential topics by considering which are right for you, then you should have narrowed it even further by considering which are right

Before committing to a particular speech topic, be sure to ask yourself what kind of topics would be appropriate for the speaking occasion.

SHARPEN
Your Skills

SHARPEN
Your Skills

Suppose your community group is sponsoring a charity auction to benefit juvenile diabetes research, and you have been asked to speak at the event. You anticipate that your audience will comprise businesspeople and community leaders, parents of juvenile diabetics, and local media representatives. Go through the four steps described in this section to identify at least two possible topics for your speech. Create your own version of Figure 11.1 by brainstorming to generate a list of potential topics and then narrowing down that list by considering what's right for you, your audience, and the occasion.

for your audience. However, before settling on a specific topic, you will want to ask yourself what kind of topics would be appropriate for the speaking occasion.

IDENTIFY TOPICS THAT ARE RIGHT FOR THE OCCASION

To give an effective speech, you need a topic that is appropriate for the situation. With your potential topic in mind, ask yourself

- *Why am I speaking?* Is your goal to inform, or persuade, or entertain? Are you introducing or honoring someone? Select a topic that will fit the primary goal of your speech.
- *What is the emotional tone of the event?* Is the occasion joyous and celebratory, such as a wedding or commencement? Is it somber, such as a memorial service? Is it formal but emotionally neutral, such as a stockholders' meeting? You want to make sure your topic fits the tone of the occasion.

If you start with a broad list of potential topics, you can narrow it by considering first which topics are right for you, then which topics are right for your audience, and finally which topics are right for the occasion. That process should leave you with a "short list" of excellent options from which to make your final selection.

As an illustration, let's suppose that Jarnell has been asked to speak at the annual awards banquet for an organization of high school seniors who study literature. The ceremony's coordinator says that the choice of topic is up to Jarnell, who recently finished his degree in English and is now an associate editor for a literary magazine. Having never before given such a speech, Jarnell first brainstorms to identify potential topics. He then evaluates which topics are right for him, his audience, and the occasion. That process leads him to three excellent potential topics. Figure 11.1 illustrates Jarnell's steps to identify his speech topics.

Test Yourself

- In what ways can you brainstorm potential speech topics?
- How do you know whether a topic is right for you?
- Why should you consider the needs of your audience when choosing a speech topic?
- What aspects of the occasion should you evaluate?

>> Analyze Your Audience

Since capturing seven Olympic medals, swimmer Amanda Beard spends much of her time making public appearances. On one day, she may be speaking to a group of advertising executives. The next day, her audience might be a group of underprivileged children at an after-school swimming program or several dozen reporters at a press conference. Like other celebrities who give frequent public appearances, Beard knows she must tailor each presentation to the audience if she is to speak effectively. Doing so requires Amanda to know who her listeners are and to understand the situation they are in.

CONSIDER WHO YOUR LISTENERS ARE

Good public speakers engage in **audience analysis,** which means thinking carefully about the characteristics of their listeners so they can address their audience in the most effective way. An important part of audience analysis is taking account of listeners' *demographic characteristics,* which include their age and facility with computer-mediated communica-

audience analysis Carefully considering the characteristics of one's listeners when preparing a speech.

Step 1: Brainstorm. Jarnell begins by generating a list of potential topics. At this point, his priority is to generate ideas, not to evaluate them. Here's his first list:

Military history	Human cloning
Bird flu	Welfare reform
Nelson Mandela	Amnesty
Celebrating milestones	Air Force One
How to swing a golf club	Eyewitness testimony
French feminism	Clinical depression
National parks	Amelia Earhart
Condoms in schools	Personal responsibility
Samuel Beckett	The Latin language
Gone With the Wind	Aromatherapy

Step 2: What's Right for Him? Using his first list, Jarnell considers the topics he knows and cares about, and he eliminates the others. Here's his revised list:

Celebrating milestones	Amnesty
Nelson Mandela	Air Force One
How to swing a golf club	Clinical depression
Samuel Beckett	Personal responsibility
Gone With the Wind	The Latin language

Step 3: What's Right for His Audience? Jarnell knows his listeners are high school literature students, most of whom plan to go to college. Considering his listeners, he identifies what he thinks are appropriate topics and eliminates the others. Here's his revised list:

Celebrating milestones	Personal responsibility
Samuel Beckett	The Latin language

Step 4: What's Right for the Occasion? Because he's speaking at an awards ceremony, Jarnell knows the occasion will be celebratory. Thus, he considers which topics will fit the occasion, and he eliminates the others. Here's his final list:

Celebrating milestones	Personal responsibility

FIGURE 11.1 Selecting a Speech Topic

A frequent public speaker, Olympic medalist Amanda Beard understands the importance of adapting to her audience.

tion, sex and sexual orientation, culture, socioeconomic status, physical and mental characteristics, and political orientation. Knowledge about those features can help you craft your presentation for maximum effect.

Age and Facility with Computer-Mediated Communication

To know your listeners, consider their age. The age of your audience matters because it may influence the things with which your listeners are familiar. Suppose you're speaking on communicating with family and friends while traveling abroad. If your listeners are teens or young adults, they may follow along easily as you describe IMing friends and relatives through Facebook, talking online through Skype, and blogging about your travel experiences because people in those age groups have grown up communicating in those ways. If your audience is composed of senior citizens, however, many listeners will not understand your references, as computer-mediated communication has been in widespread use only since the early 1990s. Age matters as well when a talk includes references to popular culture: Consider that musical acts such as twentieth-century greats Count Basie, Glenn Miller, and Benny Goodman may not be familiar to young adults, just as Alicia Keys, Kanye West, and Coldplay may be unfamiliar to seniors.

Your listeners' age can also affect which forms of presentation will best grab and hold their attention. Children, adolescents, and young adults often appreciate presentations that use multiple, diverse forms of media. When speaking to such groups, you may thus choose to incorporate music, PowerPoint slides, and video clips into your speech. Some older adults or seniors, however, may find the use of multiple media distracting and might prefer a no-frills presentation style.

Listeners' sex and sexual orientation can both influence how they respond to a public presentation.

Sex and Sexual Orientation Effective speakers also consider the audience's sex composition, particularly if their topic will be of greater interest to one sex than another. On average, women and men differ from each other in their attitudes about particular topics. Studies show that although there are individual variations, men are often more interested in issues such as finance, national security, athletics, and career achievement. Women, on the other hand, are often more interested in issues such as health care, education, social justice, and personal relationships. If your audience is composed primarily of one sex or another, it's best to tailor your presentation to appeal to their interests.

Especially when speaking to large, diverse audiences, effective presenters also bear in mind that listeners may vary in their sexual orientation. That matters because some forms of language reflect only the experiences of heterosexual people. Suppose that a community business leader, while delivering the commencement address at a local college, encourages graduates to thank their "spouses and families" for their support. To heterosexual people, such a statement may sound like an important reminder to acknowledge the sacrifices their relatives have made while they went to school. To gay and lesbian listeners, however, the statement may sound dismissive because the word *spouses* implies legally recognized marriages, which are available to same-sex couples in only a few U.S. states. Were the commencement speaker simply to encourage graduates to thank their "families" instead of their "spouses and families," that statement would include both legally recognized marriages and other committed romantic relationships.

Culture The United States is among the most culturally diverse countries in the world.[3] As you may recall from Chapter 2, cultural groups can vary significantly in their perceptions of communication behaviors. Consequently, effective speakers must take into account the cultural makeup of their audiences and speak in culturally sensitive ways.

Culturally sensitive speakers recognize that many cultural minorities have histories of social, economic, or political oppression. To avoid perpetuating such oppression, they are careful to avoid using words or phrases that insult, mock, or belittle cultural groups. Importantly, speakers who aren't culturally sensitive can cause offense even if they don't intend to do so. In October 2006, for instance, the Fox Sports Network fired baseball announcer Steve Lyons for making a culturally insensitive remark on the air about his colleague Lou Piniella's Hispanic heritage. While announcing Game 3 of the American League Championship Series, Piniella used some Spanish phrases and then made an analogy about unexpectedly finding a wallet. In response, Lyons said Piniella was "hablaing Español" (a mutilation of the Spanish verb "to speak") and then implied that Piniella had stolen his wallet. Network executives considered Lyons's remarks insulting to Piniella and to the Hispanic community, and they terminated his employment at the end of that game.

In an interview after the incident, Lyons said that his remarks were a joke and that he did not intend to insult Piniella. Often, however, what matters is how one's comments are *interpreted* rather than how they are *intended*. Speakers who are insensitive to how listeners might interpret their remarks risk offending or alienating cultural groups in their

A Joke Gone South: Offending Your Listeners

Even if they aren't speaking to entertain, good speakers often interject humor into their remarks. When used appropriately, humor can help speakers to connect emotionally with their listeners. Unfortunately, some jokes can backfire, causing the audience to take offense at the speaker's remarks. A notable example occurred on August 15, 2006. Virginia senator George Allen, speaking at a campaign stop, spotted in the audience a young man of Indian descent named S. R. Sidarth. Because he knew Sidarth worked for his challenger, Jim Webb, Allen decided to poke some fun at him:

> This fellow here, over here with the yellow shirt, Macaca, or whatever his name is. He's with my opponent. . . . Let's give a welcome to Macaca, here. Welcome to America and the real world of Virginia.

In some European cultures, *macaca* is considered a racial slur against people of African descent. Allen claimed he used the term jokingly and didn't intend to degrade Sidarth. Many in the audience—and many more who watched media broadcasts of his speech—were nonetheless offended by Allen's remarks, especially because Sidarth was a U.S. citizen, born in Fairfax, Virginia. Allen was forced to apologize publicly, and he went on to lose the senatorial race.

To avoid similar fates, competent speakers must exercise caution when using humor—particularly humor directed at a specific group of people—to ensure that it won't seem offensive or derogatory.

audiences, even if their intentions are honorable. The risk of causing unintended offense is often heightened when speakers use humor inappropriately, as The Dark Side of Communication box details.

Economic Status The United States is diverse not only culturally but also economically. According to the U.S. Census Bureau, approximately the same percentage of U.S. American households earn below $10,000 per year as earn more than $150,000 per year.[4] Considering the economic status of your listeners can help you tailor your message to their priorities and experiences. For instance, wealthy listeners are often older, more educated, and more widely traveled than are less wealthy listeners. As a result, they may be more likely than less wealthy listeners to take for granted certain expectations, such as home ownership and health insurance coverage. Wealthy audiences are often conservative as well, so they may be more resistant to change. In contrast, less wealthy audiences are often more liberal and more open to new ways of thinking.

Physical and Mental Capabilities Many audiences include people with differing physical and mental capabilities. Some may have a sensory impairment, such as being deaf or blind. Some may need a walker or a wheelchair to get around, and others may cope with physical disfigurements or deformities. Still others may face cognitive limitations, such as those associated with autism, a psychological disorder characterized by impaired communication and social skills, and dyslexia, a learning disability that affects reading and writing.

Although many people function well despite physical or mental challenges, a speaker still must sensitively accommodate listeners' needs. If you're speaking at a senior center, for instance, many of your listeners are likely to have impaired hearing and vision. To accommodate them, you need to speak clearly and at an appropriate volume, and your visual aids must be large enough to be easily seen. You may even need to describe your visual aids verbally for the benefit of those who cannot see them. In addition, if several of your listeners are in wheelchairs or have limited mobility, you should avoid asking them to take part in activities that require standing or moving about. You can appear insensitive if you don't consider your listeners' particular needs.

Political Orientation During the 2000 U.S. presidential election, journalist Tim Russert devised the method of dividing the country into "red states" and "blue states." Red states—such as Kansas, Texas, Utah, and Georgia—tend to support political candidates from the Republican Party because their populations are politically more conservative. Blue states—such as California, Illinois, Pennsylvania, and New York—usually support political candidates from the Democratic Party because their populations tend to be more liberal. Knowing whether your audience is primarily conservative, primarily liberal, or a mix of the two can help you tailor your message accordingly.

Being aware of listeners' political orientation is particularly important if you are speaking on a politically contentious topic such as gay marriage, gun rights, abortion, or universal health care. Conservative audiences will feel quite differently about those issues than will liberal ones. Your listeners' political leanings will also affect what evidence they will find persuasive. Liberal listeners are more persuaded by arguments from liberal sources than conservative ones, whereas conservative listeners follow the opposite pattern.[5] If you know something about your listeners' political orientation, you can consider which types of statements and which forms of evidence they are most likely to accept.

The politics of an audience is one of the many characteristics to which a political communication professional must be sensitive. For a look at an individual who's engaged in that career, see the Putting Communication to Work box.

Depending on who your listeners are, you may not know much about their age, experience with computer-mediated communication, sex and sexual orientation, culture, socioeconomic status, physical and mental capabilities, and political orientation prior to your speech. If, however, you are able to gather at least some of that information beforehand, you can use it to make your presentation more appropriate and more effective. Figure 11.2 provides guidance for learning about your listeners in advance of your speech.

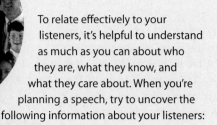

To relate effectively to your listeners, it's helpful to understand as much as you can about who they are, what they know, and what they care about. When you're planning a speech, try to uncover the following information about your listeners:

- How old are they? How much variation in age do they have?
- How familiar are they with computer-mediated communication and popular culture?
- What percentage is male and what percentage is female?
- What are their cultural backgrounds?
- What is their economic status?
- What mental or physical impairments do they have, if any?
- How do they feel about politics?

FIGURE 11.2 Who's Listening? Learning About Your Audience

CONSIDER THE SITUATION OF YOUR LISTENERS

As useful as it is to know the composition of your audience, it's equally helpful to consider the context of your speaking engagement. To do so, you need to think about several issues: the purpose of your audience, its size, the time available for your speech, the demands competing for your listeners' attention, and your audience's existing knowledge about your topic.

Purpose To maximize your effectiveness as a speaker, consider *why* your audience will come together to hear you. Will your listeners be required to attend, or will they assemble by choice? Will they anticipate being taught? Persuaded? Entertained? Is the context formal or informal? Is it joyous or somber? Those issues matter because they influence the behaviors your audience will expect from you.

Suppose you're leading a fire safety course that all new employees at your company are required to complete. In that situation, your listeners are probably

Putting Communication to Work

Name: Isaac "Zac" Wright

College(s): BA, University of Tennessee, 2003

Major(s): Journalism and public relations communication

Job Title: Political Communication and Public Policy Consultant (self-employed)

Salary: Varies

Time in Job: 1 year in present position

Work Responsibilities: I've been employed in political communication for almost a decade, working on everything from crafting broad messages of why to vote for a candidate or why to support or oppose an issue to the tactical execution of communication strategy, including writing news releases and being a pundit on the local morning news. My career has included serving as a communication operative or strategist in three U.S. Senate races, two gubernatorial efforts, and two presidential campaigns. In 2007, I was the youngest communication director to any sitting governor in the country. Recently, I began my own business offering communication consulting for candidates for public office and focusing on public policy issues.

Why Communication? I always wanted to work in a field that offered me the opportunity to help people and to make a difference in the broader world and that would be exciting and offer a creative outlet. The world of political campaigns and communication seemed like a perfect fit. I have had the opportunity to do the work I love, engaging in the democratic process and contributing to the greater good. I'm honored to have stood next to a president, would-be presidents, governors, and members of Congress and to have helped communicate their messages. I've briefed the national press corps and argued policy and politics on television and in newspapers. It's been a fun way to spend my 20s.

My Advice to Students Think in terms of building a career. Sometimes, it's about making the less attractive choice in jobs in order to open the door for what's next. Always take opportunities that are bigger than you are. It's the fastest way to grow. And make yourself indispensable. Become the person that everyone wants in the room when decisions are made.

---

expecting you to teach them what they need to know as efficiently as possible. Because they are not attending the workshop by choice, their motivation to pay attention is likely to be low. You can speak effectively to them by being clear, concise, and informative and by incorporating humor to lighten their experience. The most effective speakers think carefully about what their audience expects and requires of them in each specific situation, and they adapt their presentations accordingly.

Size A second factor to consider is the size of your audience. In general, the larger the group, the more formally structured you should make your presentation.

If you're speaking to a youth group with only a dozen members, for instance, you might be most effective by behaving somewhat informally. You might choose to sit instead of stand, ask your listeners to introduce themselves, request audience participation in an activity, speak in an informal, conversational tone, and encourage your listeners to interrupt you with questions. None of those behaviors would be effective with an

SHARPEN Your Skills

Students taking a class certainly represent one type of audience. The next time you're in a class and the opportunity arises, do an audience analysis as if you were preparing to speak to the students. Consider what you know about the students' characteristics. Then write down three ways you could adapt your speech to that audience.

audience of 300, however. With that many listeners, activities and audience participation could easily become unmanageable, and an informal style of speaking would be inappropriate. Consider how you would feel, for example, if you were one of 300 people in the audience and the speaker asked each of you to introduce yourself. You would probably find such a request unreasonable (if not bizarre) for an audience of that size, and you would likely lose respect for the speaker as a result. To be effective, the speaker should adapt his or her presentation style to fit the size of the audience.

Available Time Have you had the frustrating experience of taking a course in which the time allotted for class runs out but the speaker continues speaking anyway? If so, you can appreciate that listeners have only a finite amount of time to spend listening to a speaker. To be effective, speakers must be aware of how long their presentations are supposed to last, and they must be realistic about how much material they can cover.

Suppose you're preparing a speech about gun safety. If you have 45 minutes to speak, you might choose to discuss the 10 most dangerous mistakes gun owners make. If you have only 15 minutes to speak, however, then trying to cover the 10 most dangerous mistakes is probably a mistake itself. In that context, you'll give a more effective speech by covering, say, the *three* most dangerous mistakes. Whatever the situation, your listeners are likely aware of how long your speech is supposed to last, and they may get restless and lose interest if you speak longer than you should. In contrast, if you speak for slightly less than your allotted time, your audience is likely to be appreciative.

Competing Demands You probably know from your own experience that it's difficult to give your undivided attention to anyone for very long. No matter who's listening to your speech, other factors are almost always competing for their attention. Perhaps your speech is right before lunch, and your listeners are distracted by hunger. Perhaps it's on a Friday afternoon, and they're eager to leave for the weekend. Maybe your microphone is faltering, and your listeners can't hear you clearly. Those and many other issues can make it challenging for your listeners to pay close attention to your words.

You can address many of the factors that might be competing for your audience's attention if you're aware of what they are. If your speech is right before lunch, for instance, you can try to reschedule it for a time when your audience will be less distracted. If resched-

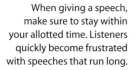
When giving a speech, make sure to stay within your allotted time. Listeners quickly become frustrated with speeches that run long.

uling isn't an option, then you can say to your listeners, "I know we're all eager to get to lunch, so if you'll give me your attention, I'll make my remarks as briefly as I can." Audiences will understand that certain factors, such as the time of your speech, may be beyond your control. They often will appreciate it, however, if you acknowledge their situation ("I know we're all eager to get to lunch") and pledge to do what you can to minimize it ("I'll make my remarks as briefly as I can").

Prior Knowledge of Your Topic Finally, it's important to consider what your audience already knows about the topic of your speech. Armed with this information, you can avoid two mistakes: talking down to your listeners and talking over their heads. *Talking down* means telling people what they already know as if they didn't already know it. *Talking over people's heads* means assuming they have information or an understanding that they don't actually have.

Let's say you're leading a workshop to teach adolescents about personal finance. If your listeners are members of their school's accounting club, they probably know the basics of how credit works, what a profit margin is, and how to reconcile a checking account statement. They would likely feel annoyed if you stopped to define a term such as *annual interest rate,* because they probably already know what that term means. You can cover more advanced topics with such an audience than you could with a group of students who lack training in the basics of finance. Many students without such training would feel frustrated if you used a term such as *annual interest rate* without defining it, because unlike the accounting club members, they may not know what it means.

Public speakers are most effective when they tailor their presentations to meet their listeners' needs and expectations. Doing so requires considering not just who their listeners are but also their listeners' situation. Analyzing the audience and adapting one's presentation to it can help anyone speak effectively and memorably.

How do you feel when a speaker talks down to you or talks over your head?

Test Yourself

- In what ways might your listeners' ages or cultural backgrounds influence your speech?
- What can you do if several demands are competing for your audience's attention?

>> Know Where to Find Information

When planning a speech, you'll often find it helpful to consult various sources for information or guidance. You may already have used some or all of these sources to prepare papers or other class assignments, and they can be just as valuable when you are developing a speech. In this section, we'll look at Internet research, library research, personal observations, and interviews and questionnaires as potential sources of good supporting material.

INTERNET RESEARCH

The Internet puts a wealth of information at your fingertips, and it can be an invaluable source of supporting material if you use it responsibly. One of the Internet's greatest assets as a source of supporting material is also its greatest liability, and that is the sheer volume of information it can provide. Having an enormous amount of information at your disposal can be a great advantage when you're searching for supporting material. Indeed, you can use the Internet to find material on almost any topic imaginable, so it's unlikely you would fail to discover something useful for your speech. The disadvantage is that the breadth of information available on the Internet can seem overwhelming. Particularly if you are searching for material on a popular topic, such as the policy goals of President Barack Obama, you could easily identify hundreds or even thousands of sources after just a few moments of searching. Because it would be nearly impossible to read and evaluate all of those sources, you might find Internet searches to be more trouble than they're worth. As we'll see, however, it's easy to narrow the parameters of an Internet search so that only specific types of information are identified.

Many public speakers use one or more of three resources when searching online for supporting material: general search engines, research search engines, and website-specific searches. The broadest of these, the **general search engine,** is a website that allows you to search for other websites containing information on a topic that you specify. General search engines include, for example, yahoo.com, google.com, altavista.com, lycos.com, and ask.com. On those sites, you can enter words or phrases and the search engine will produce a list of other websites on which those words or phrases appear. For instance, if you type "Yellowstone National Park" into google.com, that search engine will produce a list of over 3 million other websites offering information about the park. You can then scroll through the list to identify those sites you want to read.

In most cases, using a general search engine will identify a wide range of sources. Some may be helpful to you, and others may not. Among the 3 million websites about Yellowstone National Park, for instance, are bound to be thousands that advertise the park's services or describe family vacations taken there. Those may not be particularly useful sources of supporting material for the claims you want to make in your speech. You can reduce the number of websites identified in a search by submitting more terms to the search engine. For instance, if you type "Yellowstone National Park future volcanic eruptions" into google.com, the search will identify approximately 15,000 websites. Although that's still a large number, it is considerably less than 3 million.

Because of the overwhelming amount of information a general search engine can produce, it's essential to evaluate the usefulness of what you find, as Fact or Fiction? explains. If you know ahead of time that you want to look specifically for published research on your topic, you may prefer to use a research search engine such as scholar.google.com.

Typing "Yellowstone National Park" into google.com will identify over 3 million websites offering information about the park and its residents.

A **research search engine** doesn't scan the Internet as broadly as general search engines do but rather looks only for research that has been published in books, academic journals, and other periodicals. If you type "Yellowstone National Park" into scholar.google.com, the search will identify approximately 48,000 sources reporting published research on the park. In many instances, the publications are available to read online.

Finally, you can do a website-specific search, which means confining your search to specific websites that you know will contain the information you're seeking. To find information about Yellowstone National Park, for instance, you could consult the website for the U.S. National Park service, www.nps.gov. That page provides information about Yellowstone's history, location, geographic characteristics, climate, and visitor hours. Similarly, you could use websites for various organizations to search for information relevant to those groups. For example, you might consult the site for the American Medical Association if you were interested in health or the site for the United Nations if you were interested in international politics.

Table 11.2 gives examples of general search engines, research search engines, and specific websites. You may find these handy when doing research for a speech.

The Internet is an extraordinary research tool, but it isn't your only option. Your local library may also provide many useful resources that can help you prepare a speech.

LIBRARY RESEARCH

As a student, you likely have access to one or more libraries at your college or university. The town or city in which you attend school may also have its own public library system. Libraries vary in the resources they provide, so it is often worth investigating what your local or school library can offer you.

One valuable resource of most libraries is the assistance of trained professionals who can help you navigate the library's research assets. If you are uncertain where to begin to search for supporting material, ask a library staff member for help. Many large libraries

general search engine A website on which one can search for other websites containing information on a specified topic.

research search engine A website on which one can search for research published in books, academic journals, and other periodicals.

Fact or Fiction?

All Information Found Online Is Equally Valuable

When people do online research for a speech, they sometimes believe that any information they find will be valuable. As you prepare your own speeches, be careful not to fall victim to that false idea. There's no question that the web provides access to a wide range of information, but not all of the information is equally trustworthy.

Suppose you were researching the effectiveness of acupuncture for treating migraine headaches. You would undoubtedly come across hundreds of websites offering people's personal testimonies of how effective—or ineffective—acupuncture was for them. Some of their comments might be on blogs, others on bulletin boards, and others on their Facebook pages. To find out if acupuncture has genuine value for treating migraines, however, you need to look at reports of research, not personal accounts.

Indeed, although they may be convincing, personal reports can be invalid for at least two reasons. First, the people making them might be exceptional. For example, the fact that acupuncture works for some people doesn't necessarily mean it works for most people. Second, people don't always know what affects their health. Continuing with our migraine example, even if individuals' migraines improved, that doesn't necessarily mean that acupuncture treatments caused the improvement. Researchers design studies to overcome both of those types of problems, so the findings from research studies are more valid than people's reports of their personal experiences. That point is essential to keep in mind when you search online for information.

ASK YOURSELF

- How do you know if someone's personal testimony is valid for other people besides that individual?
- Are you generally more persuaded by research findings or reports of personal experiences? Why?

Table 11.2   Find It Online: Examples of Internet Search Tools

The following examples of general search engines, research search engines, and specific websites might be useful when you conduct research on a particular speech topic, such as medicine, psychology, art, or the environment.

General Search Engines	Research Search Engines	Website Searches organization in parentheses
google.com	scholar.google.com	ama-assn.org (American Medical Association)
yahoo.com	scirus.com	apa.org (American Psychological Association)
about.com	highbeam.com	arts.gov (National Endowment for the Arts)
bing.com	doaj.org	doi.gov (U.S. Department of the Interior)
altavista.com	pubmed.gov	epa.gov (U.S. Environmental Protection Agency)

One of the most valuable library resources are the trained professionals who can help you navigate the library's research assets.

even have offices or divisions dedicated to helping people locate the information they're seeking. Staff members are trained to help you search the library's resources, and their help can be invaluable.

Libraries often divide their collections into books, periodicals, nonprint materials, and electronic print materials. Books include both fictional and nonfictional works, as well as reference volumes such as dictionaries and encyclopedias. You are likely to find books containing information on almost any speech topic you could choose. Typically, each book has a unique catalog number—its "call number"—that helps you locate the book on the library shelf. Most libraries allow you to search for books by author, subject, title, and/or publisher so that you can easily find what you want. Figure 11.3 gives an example of how a book would be listed in a library's online catalog.

Periodicals are materials that are published on a regular basis, such as magazines, newspapers, and scientific journals. Newspapers are often published daily, whereas magazines might be published weekly or monthly and journals are typically published quarterly. Because they are produced on a recurring basis, periodicals generally provide more current information than books do. Thus, if you're preparing a speech about the economy, you will find more recent information in the *Wall Street Journal,* a daily financial newspaper, than in a book that was published several months ago.

Nonprint materials are audiovisual resources such as sound recordings, movies, and photographs. Many libraries have extensive collections of records, videotapes, CDs, DVDs, and photographs that patrons can check out. You can use nonprint materials both as sources of research and as audiovisual aids to enhance your presentation.

Finally, for their older resources, most libraries also have collections of electronic print materials, such as microfilm, a medium that stores reproductions of books and periodicals on film at a greatly reduced font size. Libraries often transfer printed materials to microfilm both to preserve the materials and to conserve space. With a special device, you can read materials on microfilm and even print them in their original font size.

By the Numbers

4.6

Percentage of articles in scientific journals that are available online immediately upon publication.[6]

Author	Chinn, Sarah E.
Title	Inventing modern adolescence: The children of immigrants in turn-of-the-century America
Publisher	New Brunswick, N.J.: Rutgers University Press
Series	The Rutgers series in childhood studies
Copyright year	2009
Call number	HQ792.U5 C45 2009
Description	xi, 199 p. : ill. ; 23 cm.
ISBN	9780813543093
Subject	Children of immigrants – United States – History – 20th century
Contents	"Youth must have its fling": the beginnings of modern adolescence – Picturing labor : Lewis W. Hine, the child labor movement, and the meanings of adolescent work – "Irreverence and the American spirit": immigrant parents, American adolescents, and the invention of the generation gap – "Youth demands amusement": dancing, dance halls, and the exercise of adolescent freedom – "Youth is always turbulent": reinterpretations of adolescence from Bohemia to Samoa.

FIGURE 11.3 Example of a Catalog Entry for a Book

In addition to their collections of physical resources, most libraries offer access to online research databases. A **database** is an electronic storehouse of specific information that people can search. Using a research database is much like using a research search engine. The major difference is that databases tend to be narrower and more specialized in the sources they include. Most research databases, that is, are focused on specific academic disciplines. Such databases include ComIndex for communication studies, PsycInfo for psychology, Sociological Abstracts for sociology, ERIC for education, and Criminal Justice Abstracts for criminal justice. If you want to search for research published within a particular field, using one of a library's online research databases is a good option.

PERSONAL OBSERVATIONS

When you think of doing research, you may—if you are like many students—think only about locating information that already exists in books or on websites. However, an additional option is to do original research by gathering information yourself. One way is by observing a phenomenon yourself and taking notes about what you see and hear.

Let's say you were preparing a speech about nonverbal greeting behaviors, and you wondered how they differed in same-sex and other-sex pairs. To learn about the topic, you might spend a few hours watching people at the airport. You could sit close to the area where arriving passengers meet their friends and relatives, and you could observe and take note of their greeting behaviors. Specifically, you could note similarities and differences in how people greet women and men, and see if any patterns emerge.

As part of your speech, you might describe how you conducted your observations and what you found:

> *To observe greeting behaviors in same-sex and other-sex pairs, I spent two hours on the visitors' side of the main security screening gate at the airport and watched how people greeted arriving passengers. Within two hours, I observed almost 100 greetings. In that time, I noted some stark differences in greeting behavior. Specifically, arriving male passengers were much more likely to kiss and hug women than they were to display that behavior with other men. When greeting another man, male passengers were more likely only to shake hands. Arriving female passengers, however, were equally likely to kiss and hug men and other women.*

What are some issues or phenomena on which you could gather information through personal observations?

When using personal observations as supporting material, it's vital to remember that your observations may not accurately reflect the behaviors of the population at large. After observing people for two hours at one security gate at one airport, you could not say with certainty that *all* women and men differ in their greeting behaviors. You could, however, use this personal observation in conjunction with other forms of data, such as findings from behavioral research, to illustrate how patterns of behavior are enacted in a local environment.

SURVEYS

Personal observation is a good way to collect original data, but it is only effective if the topic is directly observable, such as public behavior. What if you want to learn about something that you cannot directly observe, such as people's attitudes, beliefs, or histories? To learn about those topics, you can conduct a **survey,** which means collecting data by asking people directly about their experiences.

One method of surveying people is by interviewing them. An **interview** is a structured conversation in which one person poses questions to which another person responds. Some interviews are brief, making use of a few questions that probe the person's experiences. Others are in-depth conversations in which the respondent speaks in great detail about his or her experiences. Many interviews take place in a face-to-face setting, but interviews can also be conducted over the telephone, via text messaging or e-mail, or in an online chat room.

A second method of surveying people is by distributing a **questionnaire,** a written instrument containing questions for people to answer. Like interviews, questionnaires

database An electronic storehouse of specific information that people can search.

survey A method of collecting data by asking people directly about their experiences.

interview A structured conversation in which one person poses questions to which another person responds.

questionnaire A written instrument containing questions for people to answer.

Select a current issue on which people's opinions vary, such as what the government's position on immigration reform should be. Conduct informal interviews with eight or so family members, co-workers, and classmates in which you ask what people's opinions are on the issue and why they hold those opinions. As you conduct each interview, try to keep your own opinions private so you don't influence what others say. Write a paragraph describing the results of your interviews, which could be one form of evidence you use in a speech.

help you learn about people's attitudes, preferences, values, and experiences. Using a questionnaire, you might survey students at your school about their use of the campus health service or their preferences for community arts and entertainment. Compiling people's responses to your questionnaire allows you to find out which preferences or experiences are the most common among your respondents. Let's say that you discovered that 87 percent of students had used your campus health service within the previous six months. You could use that information to argue for expanding health services for students.

Compared to interviews, questionnaires have the advantage of allowing you to collect data from a large number of people efficiently. Using a questionnaire, for instance, you could collect data from every student in your communication course in the same amount of time it might take you to interview one person. The disadvantage of questionnaires is that you usually cannot get the detailed answers that are possible in an interview. For those reasons, surveys that include data from both in-depth interviews and questionnaires are often more informative than those that rely on only one method.

Internet research, library research, personal observations, and surveys can all yield quality supporting material for your presentation. Because these sources differ in the information they provide, however, it's often to your advantage to use more than one when you're preparing a speech.

- How are general search engines different from research search engines?
- What types of resources do libraries offer for research?
- Why is personal observation valuable?
- What is the difference between an interview and a questionnaire?

Test Yourself

For
REVIEW >>

- For what reasons might you plan a speech?

  People plan speeches to inform their listeners of information, persuade their listeners to think or act in a particular way, entertain their listeners, introduce someone to their audience, and give honor to a person, place, or event.

- How can you select a topic that is right for you and your audience?

  You can brainstorm to identify a list of potential topics. Choose one by considering what you know and care about, what your listeners will know and care about, and what would work well for the occasion.

- Where can you find supporting information?

  The Internet, the library, personal observations, interviews, and questionnaires can all give you access to supporting material that will assist you with planning your speech.

Pop Quiz

Multiple Choice

1. A type of speech that amuses or inspires listeners is a(n)

   a. persuasive speech
   b. introductory speech
   c. informative speech
   d. entertainment speech

2. While brainstorming potential speech topics, you should avoid

   a. considering what you care about
   b. identifying unusual ideas
   c. evaluating ideas as you generate them
   d. thinking about topics in the news

3. In general, the larger the audience, the greater the need for a speaker's presentation to be

   a. short and to the point
   b. formal in structure
   c. positive in tone
   d. politically neutral

4. The website scholar.google.com is an example of a

   a. general search engine
   b. research search engine
   c. library database
   d. microfilm

5. A form of research that involves collecting data by asking people directly about their experiences is

   a. personal observation
   b. a research database search
   c. a web search
   d. a survey

Fill in the Blank

6. When we speak to _____ , our goal is to teach listeners something they don't already know.

7. The process of thinking carefully about the characteristics of one's listeners is called _____ .

8. A library's _____ is an electronic storehouse of specific information that people can search.

9. Audiences in _____ states tend to be politically conservative.

10. A _____ is a written instrument containing questions for people to answer.

Answers: 1. d; 2. c; 3. b; 4. b; 5. d; 6. inform; 7. audience analysis; 8. database; 9. red; 10. questionnaire

KEY TERMS

audience analysis 268	database 279
general search engine 276	survey 279
	interview 279
research search engine 276	questionnaire 279

ORGANIZING SUPPORT

PREPARATION MEANS SUCCESS

In the movie *A Time to Kill* (1996), Matthew McConaughey stars as Jake Brigance, a lawyer defending Carl Lee Hailey, played by Samuel L. Jackson. Hailey is on trial for killing two young men who had brutally assaulted his 10-year-old daughter. Because Hailey is an African American and his jury is entirely white, Brigance is challenged by how to help the jury members identify with his client. He knows that his best opportunity to appeal to the jury will be during his closing statement, his last speech before the end of the trial. To prepare, Brigance determines what points he must prove during that speech. He then interviews witnesses, examines documents, and gathers the information he'll need to make his points persuasively. Eventually, Brigance realizes that he must appeal to the jury emotionally as well as intellectually, so he crafts a memorable story with which to conclude his speech. His preparations pay off in the end, as the jury finds Hailey not guilty and sets him free.

AND FINDING FOR YOUR SPEECH

- What are the important elements of any speech?
- Why are formal outlines and speaking notes useful?
- What evidence should you use to support your claims?

A Time to Kill is a work of fiction, but the methods Jake Brigance uses to prepare his speech are not. You don't have to be organizing the closing statement in a murder trial to appreciate the benefits of solid preparation. As you'll see in this chapter, a little effort can go a long way toward making your speech a success. Preparing a good speech requires an appropriate topic and an understanding of the audience, as you learned in Chapter 11, but it also requires a detailed speaking plan.

>> State Your Purpose and Thesis

Benjamin Franklin once said, "By failing to prepare, you are preparing to fail." As his words convey, success in many endeavors relies on solid planning, and public speaking is no exception. One of the first steps in planning a successful speech is to decide on the message of your speech. That is, once you've chosen your topic, you must consider what you want to say about it.

Suppose you've identified Australia as your topic. You could use your presentation to teach your audience about the nation's cultural history or political climate. You could try to persuade your listeners to visit the country's famous Great Barrier Reef. You could amuse your audience with bits of Australian humor. The point is that Australia is a broad topic that you could address in many possible ways. To be effective, you'll need to narrow the scope of your speech by choosing what, in particular, you want to address. In this section, you'll learn how to focus your topic by taking two important steps: crafting a purpose statement and crafting a thesis statement.

CRAFT A PURPOSE STATEMENT

We saw in Chapter 11 that a speech can have several *general* goals, such as to inform, to persuade, to entertain, to introduce, and to give honor. To create a speech that meets one of those general goals, it is useful to craft a purpose statement. A **purpose statement** is a declaration of your *specific* goal for your speech. It expresses precisely what you want to accomplish during your presentation.

Let's say that the topic of your speech is Italian cuisine. With that topic in mind, consider the range of specific goals you might have. You could choose to describe the varieties of Italian wines. You could demonstrate pasta making. You could explain the similarities and differences between Italian and French cuisine and argue for the superiority of one.

purpose statement A declaration of the specific goal for a speech.

Most likely, you would not attempt to meet all of those goals in the same speech. Rather, you would select one purpose on which to focus. You can articulate that specific goal in the form of a purpose statement.

To craft a purpose statement, first identify your topic and your general goal. Sticking with your topic of Italian cuisine, let's say your general goal is to inform. Next, consider exactly what you want to inform your listeners *about*. In other words, make your general goal—to inform—specific. Perhaps you decide to teach your audience how to make ravioli. In that scenario, you might articulate your purpose statement in this way:

> **Purpose statement:** *Demonstrate the process of making ravioli.*

Suppose instead that you want to inform your audience about Italian wines. You might express your purpose statement in this way:

> **Purpose statement:** *Teach listeners the differences among five Italian red wines.*

Notice that each of these purpose statements reflects the general goal of your speech, which is to inform. Importantly, however, each purpose statement makes your general goal focused and specific.

What if your goal is to persuade rather than to inform? In that case, you will need to consider exactly what you want to persuade your listeners to think or do. Once again, you can use your purpose statement to make your general goal more specific. For example, you may want to persuade your listeners that Italian cuisine is better than French cuisine. In that case, you might articulate your purpose statement in this way:

> **Purpose statement:** *Persuade listeners that Italian cuisine is superior to French cuisine.*

Suppose instead that you want to encourage consumption of Italian olive oil because of its benefits for heart health. You might articulate your purpose statement in this way:

> **Purpose statement:** *Persuade listeners to consume more Italian olive oil.*

Notice again that each purpose statement reflects the general goal—to persuade—but it makes the goal specific.

A focused purpose statement can launch the creation of a great speech. Constructing a workable outline for your presentation becomes much easier after you have articulated a specific goal. Indeed, your purpose statement will help you determine the content of your speech, in ways we will explore below.

To craft a strong purpose statement, follow these guidelines:

- *Be specific.* A purpose statement such as "Teach my audience about the weather" is vague because the weather has so many facets. Thus, that statement won't help you to determine the content of your speech as effectively as a sharper, more specific purpose statement, such as "Teach my audience how tornadoes form."
- *Be declarative.* Write your purpose statement as a directive such as "Explain the process of creating a MySpace page." Simply posing a question, such as "How does one create a MySpace page?" doesn't indicate as clearly what you plan to accomplish in your speech.
- *Be concise.* Focus your purpose statement on one specific goal for your speech. A statement such as "Persuade my listeners that government should provide universal health care and that the free market economy hurts working families" is too broad because it expresses more than one distinct purpose. Limiting your purpose statement to one goal will help you organize your speech effectively.

Why do you think it is useful to have a sharply defined purpose statement?

Once you have selected your topic and crafted your purpose statement, you're almost ready to begin constructing your speech. One task remains, however—to articulate the message you want to get across. You can express that message in the form of a thesis statement, as we'll see next.

CRAFT A THESIS STATEMENT

During the 2009 Super Bowl, a 30-second television commercial cost a staggering $3 million.[1] That high price prompted the Miller Brewing Company to run an advertisement for only 1 second, just long enough for the announcer to mention the name of the product. Under such circumstances, the message has to be concise. Suppose *you* had only one sentence in which to deliver an entire speech. What would your sentence be? What single specific message would you want your listeners to remember? You can formulate an answer to that question by crafting a **thesis statement,** a one-sentence version of the message in your speech.

Let's say your speech topic is alternative medicine and your purpose statement is "Teach about the effectiveness of herbal supplements." Before you develop your speech, consider what you want your take-home message to be. You might articulate your message in this way:

Thesis statement: *Although sales of herbal supplements are growing, medical research shows most of their effects to be nothing more than placebos.*

As another example, suppose your topic is personal finance, and your purpose statement is "Persuade my listeners to invest in gold." You could convey your message in this way:

Thesis statement: *Because gold prices rise even in a weak economy, investing in gold is a sound financial decision.*

Notice how each of these thesis statements expresses the *message* of the speech. That is, it identifies what you would want your listeners to take away from your presentation. With a strong thesis statement, you'll find it much easier to construct the rest of your speech because you'll know exactly what you want to say to your audience.

To craft a strong thesis statement, follow these guidelines:

- *Be concrete.* Good thesis statements should be concrete, not vague or abstract. For an informative speech about the 2010 volcanic eruptions in Iceland, a concrete thesis statement would be, "Volcanic eruptions in Eyjafjallajökull, Iceland, caused widespread air travel restrictions in western Europe in the spring of 2010." In contrast, the thesis statement "A volcano influenced travel" is vague because it doesn't specify which volcano was involved, what type of travel it affected, or how or when that travel was impacted.

- *Make a statement.* Frame your thesis statement as a sentence rather than a question. In a persuasive speech calling for more attention to the food crisis in Kenya, the thesis statement "Four million Kenyans in urban areas are in immediate danger of starvation" works well because it declares the point of your speech. In comparison, a question—such as "What is the food crisis in Kenya?"—doesn't indicate the point you plan to make, only the topic you intend to discuss.

- *Tell the truth.* Good speakers communicate ethically with their listeners. To speak ethically, you must be sure that you believe in the truth of your thesis statement, so that you don't knowingly mislead your audience. Crafting an ethical thesis statement doesn't just mean avoiding claims that you know to be false. It also means ensuring that you don't exaggerate your claims beyond what your supporting evidence warrants. To do so risks deceiving your listeners, a topic explored in The Dark Side of Communication.

Table 12.1 presents examples of good thesis statements for three different speech topics. Armed with a topic, a purpose statement, and a thesis statement, you are ready to build your presentation. In the next sections, we'll explore the organization of a speech and see how to create a useful outline.

By the Numbers

1

Number of sentences composing a thesis statement.

SHARPEN Your Skills

Select a topic you find interesting. Write a purpose statement and thesis statement for an informative speech about that topic. Then write a purpose statement and thesis statement for a persuasive speech about the same topic. Notice how your purpose and thesis statements differ for the two speeches.

thesis statement A one-sentence version of the message in a speech.

THE DARK SIDE of Communication

Stretching the Truth: Exaggeration or Deception?

Most people would consider it lying if you were to use a thesis statement in your speech that is blatantly false. What if you were just exaggerating beyond what the evidence shows, however? While preparing a persuasive speech about antibacterial soap, for example, suppose you were to discover research indicating that the product provides minimal health benefits. Would you therefore be lying if you claimed in your thesis statement, "Washing with antibacterial soap is a good way to stay healthy"? Or would you simply be exaggerating—stretching the truth?

According to communication researchers, exaggeration is a form of deception. If your thesis statement makes claims that you know your evidence doesn't fully support, then you are lying to your audience just as surely as if your thesis statement were a complete fabrication. The reason is that by stretching the truth, you are knowingly giving your audience a false impression. If your listeners discover that you have been less than forthright with them, that knowledge is likely to damage your credibility as a speaker. Once your credibility with an audience has been damaged, it can be difficult—if not impossible—to regain. Even if your audience never discovers your exaggeration, however, stretching the truth beyond what your evidence supports is always an unethical communication act.

Table 12.1 Writing an Effective Thesis Statement

Topic	Goal	Purpose Statement	Thesis Statement
Human rights for sexual minorities	To persuade	Persuade listeners that the United States should take a more proactive role to ensure human rights for sexual minorities.	The United States should issue severe economic sanctions to countries that impose capital punishment or life imprisonment for homosexual or bisexual behavior.
Boston Marathon	To inform	Teach listeners about the qualifications for entering the Boston Marathon.	Prospective competitors in the Boston Marathon must have achieved a minimum time on an approved marathon within 18 months of the event.
New high school library	To dedicate	Mark the opening of the new high school library and acknowledge those who made it possible.	Due to the selfless contributions of multiple individuals, a new high school library is now available to meet the needs of students and community members.

Test Yourself

- What are the characteristics of a strong purpose statement?
- What is the primary goal of a thesis statement?

>> Organize Your Speech

On occasion, you've probably had the frustrating experience of listening to a disorganized speech. Maybe the speaker jumped from point to point with little apparent direction. You might have wondered if anyone—including the speaker—was following along. Chances are, you didn't learn much about the topic of the speech, and you left with a poor impression of the speaker's competence. If you've had such an experience, then you already understand the benefits of a clearly organized speech.

As an expert public speaker in the making, you can use that negative experience to your advantage by learning how to organize your speech for maximum effectiveness. Even if you have a fascinating topic and a compelling thesis statement, your audience will quickly lose interest if your presentation lacks coherence and order. Several studies conducted in educational settings have formally demonstrated that effect. Research shows that when teachers present material in an organized, coherent manner, their students are more motivated to learn,[2] take more detailed course notes,[3] and recall more of the material than when teachers' presentations are disorganized.[4]

As you'll see in this section, an organized presentation has several features:

- An *introduction* that previews the information to be presented
- A *body* composed of specific main points
- A *conclusion* that summarizes the main points
- *Transitions* that connect the main points to one another

Figure 12.1 summarizes how those elements come together to form an effective speech.

Introduction
1. Generate interest in topic
2. Preview main points

Transition

Body
1. First main point

Transition

2. Second main point

Transition

3. Third main point

Conclusion
1. Reinforce central point
2. Create memorable moment

FIGURE 12.1 Putting It All Together: The Parts of an Organized Presentation An organized presentation features an introduction, a body, a conclusion, and transitions to link the main points.

THE INTRODUCTION TELLS THE STORY OF YOUR SPEECH

As the saying goes, you get only one chance to make a good first impression. The same is true when you're preparing a speech. A good presentation starts with an introduction that

If you've ever listened to someone give a disorganized speech, you know how frustrating that experience can be.

accomplishes two goals: It captures your listeners' interest in your topic, and it previews the points you plan to make.

The Introduction Generates Interest in Your Topic First, your introduction should grab your listeners' attention and arouse their interest in your topic. One way to accomplish that goal is to open with a story that will spark your audience's curiosity. Imagine a speech that begins with the following:

> *I was running late that morning, so I threw my belongings in my backpack and rushed out of my house. I set my coffee on the roof of my car while I opened the driver's side door and tossed my bag in the back seat. No sooner had I gotten behind the wheel than I heard car alarms all around the neighborhood going off. I saw my coffee cup fall to the ground and shatter. It felt like someone was jumping up and down on the back bumper. Then, as quickly as it started, it was over. It took me a few moments to realize I had just experienced my first earthquake.*

That story would be an effective start to a speech about earthquakes because it begins with an easily relatable experience ("I was running late that morning"), describes unusual events (coffee cup shattering, car shaking), and reveals the explanation for those events (an earthquake) only at the end.

Another way to spark your listeners' interest in your topic is to use statistics that illustrate its importance. For example:

> *Children in the United States are dealing with a growing problem, literally speaking. Over 9 million of them are overweight or obese. That's more than the populations of Los Angeles, Chicago, San Antonio, and Detroit* put together. *Unfortunately, the problem is getting worse. In the past three decades, the childhood obesity rate has more than tripled for children aged 6 to 11. Obesity raises the risks of a range of health problems, including diabetes, hypertension, and heart disease. Every year, Americans collectively spend nearly $150 million treating obesity-related disorders for children.*

That introduction uses a few well-chosen statistics to illustrate the gravity of the problem of childhood obesity. It also provides an example to help the audience interpret the number of obese children. Simply saying that obesity affects 9 million children may be ineffective if listeners aren't sure whether that's a large or small number of American children. Explaining that the number exceeds the combined population of four major U.S. cities gives listeners a context for understanding its importance.

In addition to using a story or a statistic to generate interest in your topic, you can use any of the following techniques:

- *Present a quotation.* Many speakers capture attention with a well-crafted quote that is relevant to their topic. For instance, "As former U.S. senator Elizabeth Dole once said, 'Power is a positive force if it is used for positive purposes.' Today, I'd like to discuss some of the many ways we can use power to improve the lives of others."
- *Tell a joke.* Opening your speech with a joke can be a particularly effective way to capture your listeners' attention, put them at ease, and generate positive feelings toward yourself. Always make certain that your humor is appropriate for your audience and for the occasion and that it won't be interpreted as offensive.
- *Pose a question.* Beginning your speech with a question is a great way to get your audience thinking about your topic. You could ask question that you want listeners to answer, such as "By show of hands, how many of you have ever been called for jury duty?" You can also pose a *rhetorical question*, one that you want your listeners to think about but not respond to. For instance, "Why do you suppose you can't tickle yourself?"
- *Cite an opinion.* Provocative opinions from well-known people can also get your listeners' attention. For example, "World-renowned physicist Stephen Hawking recently

warned scientists that making contact with aliens would be disastrous for the human race. In this speech, I'll be exploring some of the reasons why he may be exactly right."

- *Note the occasion.* Particularly if you are speaking to give honor to a person, place, or event, you can generate attention by noting the importance of the occasion. For instance, "We have come together in this beautiful place on this most joyous of days to honor the 50th wedding anniversary of two very special people."
- *Identify something familiar.* An excellent way to establish rapport with your listeners is to refer to something with which they are familiar. If you're speaking in a very small community, for example, you might start by saying, "As I was driving in this morning, I was a little unsure of my directions, which simply said to 'turn left after the big red house.' Once I got to town, though, it made perfect sense!" By noting something with which your audience is familiar—in this case, the smallness of the town—you make a personal connection with your listeners.

The Introduction Previews Your Main Points Once you have aroused your listeners' interest in your topic, your second goal is to preview the points you plan to make in your speech. A preview will help your listeners pay attention to the body of your speech by identifying ahead of time what they should listen for. Previews can be simple and straightforward, as in the following example from a speech about music education:

Today I'd like to talk about the importance of funding music education in our public schools. First, I'll explain how learning about music helps children both intellectually and socially. Then I'll discuss the challenges to music education funding that our public schools have faced in recent years. Finally, I'll offer some ideas for ensuring that music education is supported for generations to come.

Notice that this preview clearly identifies the major ideas that the speaker plans to address. It isn't necessary to explain or justify the ideas during the preview; that's the purpose of the body of the speech. Rather, it's only necessary to identify the points you intend to make. If you put your preview at the end of your introduction, it will also serve as a lead-in to the body of your speech.

THE BODY EXPRESSES YOUR MAIN POINTS

If the introduction is the warm-up for your presentation, the body is the main act. The body will be the longest part of your speech because it's where you will deliver the message you previewed in the introduction.

To organize the body of your speech, identify the main points you want to address. A **main point** is a statement expressing a specific idea or theme related to the speech topic. Most speeches have between two and five main points; if you have more than five, your audience may have difficulty remembering them. As you'll see in this section, you want to ensure that your main points are related, distinct, and equally important. You'll also want to consider your best option for arranging your main points.

Main Points Should Be Related Suppose you wanted to craft an informative speech about hormones, using the following purpose and thesis statements:

Purpose statement: *Explain the structure and function of the human hormone system.*

Thesis statement: *The human hormone system releases chemical messengers to affect the activity of organs and tissues in the body.*

For that speech, you might propose the following main points:

Main point 1: *Hormones are chemicals that affect the cell metabolism of organs and tissues.*

main point A statement expressing a specific idea or theme related to the speech topic.

Main point 2: *Hormones are produced and released into the bloodstream by a system of glands.*

Main point 3: *Hormones produce different effects on the body, depending on their chemical compositions.*

Notice that the main points relate to one another. Those relationships are key because the main points all address the speech topic, the hormone system. The first main point defines what hormones are, the second indicates where hormones come from, and the third states what different effects hormones can have. You don't want any of your points to seem out of place or unrelated to the topic of the presentation. For example, suppose you had proposed the following main points:

Main point 1: *Hormones are chemicals that affect the cell metabolism of organs and tissues.*

Main point 2: *Hormones are produced and released into the bloodstream by a system of glands.*

Main point 3: *The immune system also releases chemicals into the bloodstream that affect the body.*

The third main point may interest you, but it does not relate to the purpose statement and thesis statement of your speech. If you wanted to keep the third main point in your outline, you would need to expand your purpose and thesis statements to include information about the immune system. Otherwise, you are better off replacing the third main point with one that better relates to your topic.

Main Points Should Be Distinct Main points must also be distinct from one another. Although they all address the same topic, each main point in the above example expresses a different idea: what hormones are, where they come from, and what they do. If two points express the same idea, they do not constitute distinct points. Let's say, for instance, that you proposed the following main points:

Main point 1: *Hormones are chemicals that affect the cell metabolism of organs.*

Main point 2: *Hormones are chemicals that affect the cell metabolism of tissues.*

Those two statements are probably not different enough to justify being separated into two main points. Rather, you should combine those messages into one main point:

Hormones are chemicals that affect the cell metabolism of organs and tissues.

Main Points Should Be Equally Important A third consideration about your main points is their relative importance. The importance of each main point will dictate how much time you spend discussing it in your speech. Ideally, you want to give approximately the same amount of time to each of your main points.

Let's say you have three main points but plan to spend 95 percent of your time discussing the first two. That leaves only 5 percent of your time for your third point. In this situation, you would need to reconsider the relative importance of your three points. Perhaps you actually have only two main points, in which case you might delete the third. Alternatively, perhaps you aren't devoting sufficient time to the third point, in which case you should spend less time discussing the first two and more time discussing the third. If all the main points in the body of your speech are relatively equal in importance, you should give them roughly equal time.

Main Points Can Be Organized in Various Patterns In addition to being related, distinct, and equally important, your main points should be organized in a manner that makes sense for your topic. You can organize the main points in several different patterns, depending on what those points are and how they are related to one another. Consider which of the following options might work best for your speech:

- *Arranging points by topic:* When you adopt a **topic pattern,** you organize your main points to represent different categories. Let's say you are preparing an informative

topic pattern A pattern of organizing the main points of a speech to represent different categories.

speech about aquatic life. You might include separate main points about different categories of aquatic life, with an outline that looks like this:

    A. Fish
    B. Amphibians
    C. Reptiles
    D. Mammals

If your points don't lend themselves to already-established categories, you can create categories of your own. In a speech about friendships, for instance, you might distinguish various types of friends along the lines of this outline:

    A. Good-time friends: those you always have fun with
    B. Counselor friends: those with whom you share your problems
    C. Downer friends: those who frequently put you in a bad mood
    D. Connected friends: those who seem to know everything about everyone

- *Arranging points by time:* A second option for organizing your main point is to use a **time pattern,** which means arranging your points in chronological order. This option is particularly useful when you are describing the steps of a process, such as the designing a scientific study:

    A. Pose a testable question
    B. Construct a hypothesis
    C. Collect data
    D. Analyze data and draw a conclusion

A time pattern is also useful when your main points describe a historical sequence of events, such as in this outline of a speech about the events leading to the decline of the Roman Empire:

    A. Reign of Theodosius I
    B. Crossing of the Rhine
    C. Rise of the Hunnic Empire
    D. Deposition of Julius Nepos and Romulus Augustus

- *Arranging points by space:* A **space pattern** organizes your main points according to areas. In a speech about the earth's atmosphere, you might arrange the various atmospheric layers as they exist from the ground up:

    A. Troposphere
    B. Stratosphere
    C. Mesosphere
    D. Thermosphere
    E. Magnetosphere

- *Arranging points by cause and effect:* In a **cause-and-effect pattern,** you organize your points so that they describe the causes of an event or a phenomenon and then identify its consequences. If you wanted to discuss the effects of acid rain, you could arrange your main points in this way:

    A. Causes of acid rain
      1) Natural causes, such as volcanic eruptions
      2) Human-made causes, such as industrial pollution
    B. Effects of acid rain
      1) Effects on plants and wildlife
      2) Effects on surface waters and aquatic animals
      3) Effects on human health

- *Arranging points by problem and solution:* A **problem-solution pattern** is similar to a cause-and-effect pattern, except that you are organizing your points so that they describe a problem and then offer one or more solutions for it. Notice that pattern in this example of a speech about victims of identity theft:

    A. The problem of identity theft
      1) Using your name, Social Security number, or bank accounts without permission
      2) Increases in incidence of identity theft
    B. What you should do if you're a victim
      1) Inform credit bureaus
      2) Notify the police
      3) Check your banking statements for any discrepancies

time pattern A pattern of organizing the main points of a speech in chronological order.

space pattern A pattern of organizing the main points of a speech according to areas.

cause-and-effect pattern A pattern of organizing the main points of a speech so that they describe the causes of an event and then identify its consequences.

problem-solution pattern A pattern of organizing the main points of a speech so that they describe a problem and then offer solutions for it.

Some ways of organizing your main points are likely to work better than others, depending on what those main points are. If they describe a series of events, then a time pattern will work better than a space pattern. If they identify types or categories of something, then a topic pattern is probably best. Consider what your main points are and how they are related to one another to select the organizational method that will work best for your speech.

THE CONCLUSION SUMMARIZES YOUR MESSAGE

If your introduction is the warm-up for your speech and the body is the main act, then your conclusion is the grand finale. Your conclusion should accomplish two main tasks: reinforce your central message and create a memorable moment for your listeners.

The Conclusion Reinforces Your Central Message First, you want your conclusion to reinforce your thesis statement, which is your speech's central message. Good speakers often accomplish this goal by repeating the thesis statement and then summarizing the main points they have made in support of it.

Suppose you're concluding an informative speech about the recent increase in Americans' adoptions of children from foreign countries. Here's an example of how you might reinforce your message:

> As I've explained, foreign adoptions are on the rise in the United States for three primary reasons. First, the number of children in foreign orphanages is growing. Second, increasing numbers of American adults are choosing to adopt instead of having biological children of their own. Finally, changes in foreign adoption laws have streamlined the process of adopting children from overseas. Although foreign adoptions still have their challenges, more and more American families are deciding to pursue them.

Notice that the conclusion begins with the central idea of the speech (foreign adoptions are increasing in the United States), repeats the three main points of the speech (number of children in foreign orphanages, numbers of Americans choosing to adopt, changes in adoption laws), and then restates the central idea even more strongly (more and more American families are pursuing foreign adoptions). By accomplishing these three tasks, the conclusion clearly reinforces the speech's thesis statement.

The Conclusion Creates a Memorable Moment The second goal for your conclusion is to create a *memorable moment* for your audience. A memorable moment is something your listeners will remember about the speech even if they no longer recall all of your specific points. You can probably think of movies, for instance, that had memorable endings—although you may not remember every detail of the plot, you remember how they ended. Creating a memorable moment in your conclusion will similarly help your listeners to recall your presentation.

One strategy for making your speech memorable is to end it with humor. If the concluding lines of your presentation make the audience laugh, your listeners are likely to remember your speech—and remember it positively. Another option for creating a memorable conclusion is to surprise your audience. You might begin your speech by telling part of a story, for instance, and then give the story an unexpected ending in your conclusion.

Finally, many great speeches end on an emotionally dramatic note. In his 1963 speech on the steps of the Lincoln Memorial in Washington, DC, Martin Luther King Jr. concluded his stirring call for racial equality with this dramatic appeal:

What do you tend to remember about good speeches you've heard?

> Let freedom ring from the snowcapped Rockies of Colorado! Let freedom ring from the curvaceous slopes of California! But not only that; let freedom ring from Stone Mountain of Georgia! Let freedom ring from Lookout Mountain of Tennessee! Let freedom ring from every hill and molehill of Mississippi. From every mountainside, let freedom ring. And when this happens, when we allow freedom to ring, when we let it ring from every village and every hamlet, from every state and every city, we

will be able to speed up that day when all of God's children, black men and white men, Jews and Gentiles, Protestants and Catholics, will be able to join hands and sing in the words of the old Negro spiritual, "Free at last! Free at last! Thank God Almighty, we are free at last!"

Whether you use humor, surprise, or drama, creating a memorable moment in your conclusion will help ensure that your audience remembers your presentation.

Together, the introduction, body, and conclusion compose the essential elements of your speech. Connecting these elements with one another is the job of transitions.

TRANSITIONS HELP YOUR SPEECH FLOW SMOOTHLY

A **transition** is a statement that logically connects one point in a speech to the next. Good public speakers use transitions to link the introduction to the body of the speech, and the body to the conclusion. They also use transitions to connect the main points in the body of the speech to one another. Effective transitions give a speech "flow" by bridging each part of the presentation to the next. Some transitions are full statements that provide previews and internal summaries of the material. Other transitions are single words or phrases, called "signposts," that help distinguish one point from another. Finally, many nonverbal behaviors can signal transitions.

Many great speeches end on an emotionally dramatic note that captivates the audience. Martin Luther King Jr. used that technique to conclude his famous "I have a dream" speech.

Some Transitions Preview and Internally Summarize One type of transition is a **preview,** a statement alerting listeners that you are about to shift to a new topic. Notice how each of the following examples preview a change of topic:

- *Next, I'd like to discuss recent innovations in standardized testing.*
- *Let's now turn our attention to the health implications of a vegetarian diet.*

As you can see, previews need only to be short statements. By signaling a change of topic, they help your listeners to track where you are in your speech.

A second type of transition is the **summary,** a statement that briefly reminds listeners of points you have already made. For example:

- *As we've seen, some military personnel lack adequate training and resources to accomplish their missions.*
- *So far, we have discussed two of the three forms that water can take: gas and liquid.*

transition A statement that connects one point in a speech to the next.

preview A statement alerting listeners that a speaker is about to shift to a new topic.

summary A statement that briefly reminds listeners of points a speaker has already made.

signposts Single words and phrases that distinguish one point in a presentation from another and help listeners follow the speaker's "path."

Notice that each statement simply identifies the points already covered. Each reminds listeners about what they have learned so far, and signals that those points are complete.

It is possible to combine summaries and previews. Many speakers will use a summary when they are finishing a point and then use a preview to start the next point. For instance:

- *At this point, we have covered the early life and reign of Mary, Queen of Scots. Next, let's examine her imprisonment and trial.*

Some Transitions Are Signposts Previews and summaries typically comprise full sentences, but you can also use single words or phrases to distinguish one point in your presentation from another. Such words and phrases are known as **signposts** because they serve as signs to help listeners follow the "path" or outline of your speech.

As you'll see in Table 12.2, signposts can serve several specific functions, including comparing or contrasting points, indicating a sequence of events, providing an explanation, and emphasizing the importance of a point. The signposts that will work best for your presentation will depend on the particular points you intend to make.

Some Transitions Are Nonverbal In addition to using verbal transitions, you can also help listeners follow your speech by incorporating specific nonverbal behaviors, including

- *Body movement:* Unless you are standing behind a podium during your speech, use the available space to move around during your presentation. You can highlight transitions from one point to the next nonverbally by changing where you are standing as you discuss each point.
- *Vocal inflection: Inflection* refers to variation in the pitch and volume of your voice. You can increase your volume and pitch to emphasize that a specific point is very important. As you prepare to transition between points, let your volume and pitch drop as you conclude one point and then rise again as you begin the next point.
- *Pauses:* Pauses—silences you interject into your speech— are an effective way to signal that you have finished your current point and are about to start your next point. You can also pause for effect, such as after you've made a very important statement that you want your listeners to think about before you move on.
- *Gestures:* You can use hand movements to punctuate your speech. If you intend to present three main points in the body of your presentation, you might signal the start of your first, second, and third points by holding up one, two, or three fingers, respectively. If you're comparing two arguments to each other, you might hold out your right hand and say, "on one hand . . ." and then hold out your left as you say, "on the other hand . . ."

Nonverbal transition behaviors are generally effective only to the extent that they seem natural rather than staged. As you rehearse your speech, practice using movement, inflection, pauses, and gestures until they feel natural. When you can incorporate those behaviors without consciously thinking about them, they are likely to look and seem natural to your audience.

Using effective transitions ensures that the shifts from one part of your speech to the next don't seem abrupt. You want all parts of your speech to fit together seamlessly so that your listeners can easily follow your presentation from start to finish.

Now that you know how to construct an introduction, a body, a conclusion, and transitions, it's time to create an outline for your speech. Preparing a good outline requires effort, but it is a useful step in the development of an effective speech.

Table 12.2	Follow Along: Some Effective Signposts
Specific Purpose	**Examples**
Compare or contrast points	On the other hand In contrast Similarly
Indicate a sequence of events	First, Second, Third Primarily Now, Then Finally
Provide explanation	For instance To illustrate In other words
Emphasize importance	Most importantly Remember that Above all
Show cause and effect	If, Then Consequently Therefore
Give additional examples	Likewise In a similar way As a second example
Summarize	Finally As I've explained In summary

Good speakers use gestures and movement to signal transitions between topics.

Test Yourself

- Why are stories often useful in speech introductions?
- What are three properties of effective main points?
- What is a memorable moment, and why is this device important in a speech?
- How are preview transitions different from review transitions?

>> Create an Effective Outline

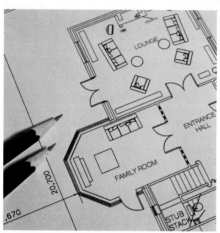

In architecture, a blueprint is a technical drawing that reflects the design of a structure, such as a house, ship, or bridge. Engineers use the blueprint as a guide for determining the types of materials required to build the structure effectively. When you're building a speech, a good outline serves the same purpose: It reflects your speech's design and helps you decide what materials you'll need.

We'll begin this section by examining three rules of outlining. Next, we'll walk through the process of creating a formal speech outline. Finally, we'll see how to convert your formal outline into useful speaking notes.

KNOW THE THREE RULES OF OUTLINING

Following three basic rules will help you create an efficient outline for your speech. Those rules involve subordination, division, and parallel wording.

The Rule of Subordination First, the **rule of subordination** specifies that some concepts in your speech are more important than others. As a result, you want to make the most important concepts your main points and the less important concepts your subordinate points, or *subpoints.*

Let's say you're preparing an informative speech about how to become a U.S. Secret Service agent. When considering what you want to say, you compile the following list of points:

1. Prospective agents must meet specific criteria.
2. Prospective agents must be U.S. citizens.
3. Prospective agents must be between 21 and 37 years of age.
4. Prospective agents must have 20/20 eyesight.
5. Prospective agents must pass an extensive training program.

If the purpose of your speech is to explain how one becomes a Secret Service agent, then all of these points are important, but they are not *equally* important. Specifically, the first and fifth points are broad statements about the requirements for agents. The second, third, and fourth points, however, are specific examples of the criteria referred to in the first point. Thus, it would make more sense to organize your points in this way:

1. Prospective agents must meet specific criteria.
   a. Prospective agents must be U.S. citizens.
   b. Prospective agents must be between 21 and 37 years of age.
   c. Prospective agents must have 20/20 eyesight.
2. Prospective agents must pass an extensive training program.

Notice that this outline includes all five of your original concepts. It is now organized according to the rule of subordination, however. The most important concepts are the main points, and the less important concepts are now subpoints.

The Rule of Division The second rule of outlining is the **rule of division,** which specifies that if you divide a point into subpoints, you must create at least two subpoints. Suppose the only criterion for becoming a Secret Service agent were U.S. citizenship. In that case, your outline would look like this:

1. Prospective agents must meet specific criteria.
   a. Prospective agents must be U.S. citizens.
2. Prospective agents must pass an extensive training program.

According to the rule of division, however, if a point has one subpoint, it must have at least one more. The reason is that if there is only one subpoint, it communicates the same

rule of subordination A rule of speech organization specifying that some concepts in the speech are more important than others.

rule of division A rule of speech organization specifying that if a point is divided into subpoints, it must have at least two subpoints.

amount of information as the main point. In that instance, it would be better to replace the main point with the subpoint, so that your outline looked like this:

1. Prospective agents must be U.S. citizens.
2. Prospective agents must pass an extensive training program.

Notice that this outline gives the same amount of information as the one before it.

The Rule of Parallel Wording The third requirement of outlining is to follow the **rule of parallel wording,** which states that all points and subpoints in your outline should have the same grammatical structure. If you write some points as complete sentences, you should write them all that way. Avoid writing some points as complete sentences, others as incomplete sentences, and others as single words. Following the rule of parallel wording ensures that all the points on your outline have a uniform structure, which will help those points fit together to form your speech.

Notice that our three subpoints from the previous example are all worded in the form of complete sentences and are therefore parallel:

1. Prospective agents must be U.S. citizens.
2. Prospective agents must be between 21 and 37 years of age.
3. Prospective agents must have 20/20 eyesight.

Suppose instead that we had worded our three subpoints as follows:

1. Prospective agents must be U.S. citizens.
2. How old do prospective agents have to be?
3. 20/20 eyesight

Those subpoints would violate the rule of parallel wording, because the first subpoint is a complete sentence, the second subpoint is a question, and the third subpoint is a sentence fragment.

Once you've mastered the rules of subordination, division, and parallel wording, you're ready to develop a formal outline for your presentation.

CREATE A FORMAL OUTLINE

A **formal outline** is a structured set of all the points and subpoints in your speech. Creating a formal outline helps ensure that you're covering all the points you wish to make. It also assists you with identifying the places in your speech where you will need to include supporting material. Compiling a formal outline takes some time and effort, but it will pay off by helping you develop a high-quality speech.

Most formal outlines for a speech include the following elements:

- Title
- Purpose statement
- Thesis statement
- Main points and subpoints composing the body of the speech
- Conclusion
- Bibliography of sources

We have already covered the process of creating a purpose statement, a thesis statement, main points, and subpoints. When compiling a formal outline, you'll want to start with those elements and add the title, conclusion, and bibliography. Importantly, you'll want to array this information in outline form.

Let's say you're preparing a persuasive speech about the dangers of buying prescription medications online. Figure 12.2 provides an example of what your formal outline might look like.

Several characteristics of this formal outline warrant attention. The title expresses what you intend to say in your speech. The purpose and thesis statements are clear and easy to understand. The body is composed of three main points, each of which is supported

By the Numbers

2

Smallest number of subpoints that a main point can have, if it has any.

rule of parallel wording A rule of speech organization specifying that all points and subpoints in an outline should have the same grammatical structure.

formal outline A structured set of all the points and subpoints in a speech.

TITLE: Buying Prescription Drugs Online Is Risky

Purpose statement: *Persuade my audience that buying prescription medications online involves some risks.*

Thesis statement: *Buying prescription medications online is too risky to do.*

INTRODUCTION

I. Buying prescription medications online entails many risks.
   A. According to the National Institute of Drug Abuse, online sales of prescription medications have nearly quadrupled in the past five years.
   B. My friend Terrie bought an antidepressant from an online pharmacy and ended up seriously ill and in legal trouble.
   C. **Thesis:** Buying prescription medications online is too risky to do.

Transition: We will now look at three of the biggest risks of buying prescription medications online: financial risks, medical risks, and legal risks.

BODY

I. **Main Point 1:** Buying prescription medications online poses financial risks.
   A. Purchases made from online pharmacies may not be covered by insurance, leaving consumers to bear the cost.
      1. Many insurance plans identify specific pharmacies from which patients can order medications.
      2. Out-of-pocket payments for medications can pose a large financial burden for a middle-class family.
   B. Some pharmacies may not ship products that online customers order, causing consumers to lose money for purchases they never receive.
      1. Consumer research indicates that unfilled online orders are increasing in frequency.
      2. Patients who do not receive their products have few options for legal recourse against an online pharmacy.

Transition: Many people have lost significant amounts of money buying prescriptions online. Others have encountered medical risks.

II. **Main Point 2:** Buying prescription medications online poses medical risks.
   A. Online pharmacies may not be subject to government safety standards.
      1. Pharmacies registered outside of the United States are not subject to oversight by the U.S.

Food and Drug Administration the way that U.S. pharmacies are.
      2. Some online pharmacies are registered in countries with few, if any, government standards for pharmaceutical safety.
   B. Consumers may receive medications containing unsafe ingredients.
      1. Medications sold online may contain inconsistent quantities of active ingredients.
      2. A study by the World Health Organization found that more than half of the medications sold online contained dangerous levels of potentially toxic substances.

Transition: Using medications bought online can put people's health at risk. It can also pose legal risks.

III. **Main Point 3:** Buying prescription medications online poses legal risks.
   A. Some online pharmacies may not be properly licensed to dispense medications.
      1. In the United States, a pharmacy must be staffed by a registered pharmacist who has a license to dispense medication.
      2. Online pharmacies registered outside the United States may employ few people, if any, with the credentials to practice pharmacy.
   B. Consumers may be violating the law by purchasing prescription medications from unlicensed vendors.
      1. Purchasing controlled pharmaceutical products without a prescription is illegal in the United States, even if the products were purchased outside the country.
      2. U.S. customs officials have recently announced that locating and confiscating illegally purchased medications is an agency priority.

Transition: Many people find themselves in trouble with the law after buying prescription medications from online pharmacies.

CONCLUSION

I. Review of main points
   A. Ordering medications over the Internet may be convenient.
   B. The financial, medical, and legal risks it entails make it irresponsible and unwise.

II. Final remarks
   A. It is crucial to exercise extreme caution when buying medications online.
   B. People are much safer purchasing their prescription medications from reputable, licensed pharmacies in their own communities.

FIGURE 12.2 Formal Speech Outline: Buying Prescription Drugs Online Is Risky

	APA Format	MLA Format
Book	Gottman, J., & Silver, N. (2004). *The seven principles for making marriage work*. New York: Three Rivers Press.	Gottman, John, and Nan Silver. <u>The Seven Principles for Making Marriage Work</u>. New York: Three Rivers Press, 2004.
Journal Article	Chesebro, J. L. (2003). Effects of teacher clarity and nonverbal immediacy on student learning, receiver apprehension, and affect. *Communication Education, 52*, 135–147	Chesebro, Joseph L. "Effects of Teacher Clarity and Nonverbal Immediacy on Student Learning, Receiver Apprehension, and Affect." <u>Communication Education</u> 52 (2003): 135–147.
Magazine article	Gandel, S. (2010, May 3). The case against Goldman Sachs. *Time, 175*, 30–37.	Gandel, Stephen. "The Case Against Goldman Sachs." <u>Time</u> 3 May 2010: 30–37.
Website	http://owl.english.purdue.edu	*The Purdue OWL Family of Sites*. The Writing Lab and OWL at Purdue and Purdue U, 2008. Web. 23 April 2010.

FIGURE 12.3 APA and MLA Citation Formats The figure compares the APA and MLA formats, both of which are popular in the communication field.
For more on APA format, go to owl.english.purdue.edu/owl/resource/560/01/
For more on MLA format, visit owl.english.purdue.edu/owl/resource/557/01/

by two subpoints. The conclusion indicates the exact message you want your listeners to remember.

Your formal outline will often conclude with a **bibliography,** a list of the sources you used in preparing your speech. To develop a speech about buying prescription drugs online, you would likely consult books, journal articles, websites, and/or other sources to learn more about Internet drug sales and people who have been hurt by such transactions. You would probably cite some of those sources directly when delivering your speech. Others you would use only as a source of background information. Usually you would include all your sources in your bibliography.

To list your sources in a bibliography, you'll need to follow a particular format. Of the several available citation formats, most people in the communication field use either the American Psychological Association (APA) format or the Modern Language Association (MLA) format. Both formats specify how to cite a source properly. Figure 12.3 provides examples of APA and MLA formats for citing books, journal articles, magazine articles, and websites. You can learn more about both formats by visiting the websites listed in Figure 12.3.

When you prepare speeches for class, your instructor may assign you a minimum number of citations to include in your bibliography and may indicate which citation format to use. You will learn more about finding appropriate sources for your speech—and evaluating whether they are credible—in the final section of this chapter.

SHARPEN Your Skills

Construct a formal outline for a speech on a topic of your choosing. Make sure it contains all of the required elements. Also take care to follow the rules of subordination, division, and parallel wording.

CONVERT YOUR FORMAL OUTLINE INTO SPEAKING NOTES

As we've seen, a formal outline helps you organize the structure and content of your speech. When you're delivering your speech, however, you may find your formal outline too long and detailed to help you. For that reason, many speakers convert their formal outlines into a set of speaking notes. **Speaking notes** (also called a *speaking outline*) are an abbreviated version of your formal outline. Their purpose is to aid your delivery by reminding you of each of your points and subpoints.

bibliography A list of the sources used in preparing a speech.

speaking notes An abbreviated version of a formal speech outline.

Suppose you're preparing to deliver the speech about buying prescription drugs online that we outlined previously, and you want to convert your formal outline into speaking notes. First, delete the title, purpose statement, and thesis statement. Replace those elements with a brief reminder about your speech's introduction. Let's say you want to begin your presentation with an anecdote about a friend whose health was compromised by medications purchased online. To remind yourself of that introduction, you might use the phrase "Story about my friend" in your speaking notes.

How much detail do you think you personally would want in a set of speaking notes? Why?

Next, abbreviate each of your main points and subpoints into a *keyword*—a word or short phrase that will help you remember it. For instance, you could abbreviate the first main point, "Buying prescription medications online poses financial risks," with the phrase "Financial risks." Your purpose is to use as few words as possible to remind yourself about each point and subpoint. Finally, abbreviate your conclusion in the same way. Use the keyword approach to cue yourself to your ending. When you've finished your speaking notes, you should have a brief outline that will be quick to read and easy to follow as you present.

Figure 12.4 provides an example of how you could convert your formal outline about buying medications online into useful speaking notes.

Notice that each note contains only a few words—just enough detail to jog your memory about the purpose of each point. A brief outline such as this will help you stay on track as you deliver your speech, without forcing you to ignore your listeners by reading long strings of text.

The Competent Communicator provides a handy checklist for preparing a speech. Consulting it will help ensure that you have completed all the steps necessary to develop a successful speech.

TITLE: Buying Prescription Drugs Online Is Risky

INTRODUCTION
I. National Institute of Drug Abuse: Near-quadrupling of online sales of prescription medications in past five years
II. Friend Terrie's problems with antidepressants bought online
III. **Thesis:** Buying prescription medications online = too risky

　Transition: Review financial, medical, legal risks

BODY
I. **Main Point 1:** Financial risks of buying prescription medications online
　A. Insurance coverage
　　1. Insurance plan restrictions
　　2. Out-of-pocket costs
　B. Orders not shipped
　　1. Increasingly frequent problem
　　2. Few options for recourse

　Transition: Significant money lost buying prescriptions online; medical risks

II. **Main Point 2:** Medical risks
　A. Safety standards lacking
　　1. No FDA oversight for foreign pharmacies

　　2. Some countries with few pharmaceutical safety standards
　B. Unreliable, unsafe ingredients
　　1. Inconsistent quantities of active ingredients
　　2. WHO study: potentially toxic ingredients

　Transition: Health risks of medications; legal risks, too

III. **Main Point 3:** Legal risks
　A. Unlicensed pharmacies
　　1. U.S. requires licensed pharmacies
　　2. Online pharmacies—possibly lacking credentials
　B. Violating prescription laws
　　1. Purchasing controlled medications without prescription illegal
　　2. U.S. customs increasing surveillance

　Transition: Legal problems after buying prescription medications from online pharmacies

CONCLUSION
I. Review of main points
　A. Convenience of online ordering
　B. Magnitude of financial, medical, legal risks
II. Final remarks
　A. Extreme caution needed when buying medications online
　B. Safer to purchase from reputable, licensed pharmacies in community

FIGURE 12.4 Speaking Notes: Buying Prescription Drugs Online Is Risky

Speech Preparation Checklist—Dot Your i's and Cross Your t's

You have learned about several tasks that are essential to preparing a good speech. You will soon put your new knowledge and skills into practice by preparing a speech of your own. How will you know you have prepared adequately? Use the checklist below to ensure that you have completed each required step.

Speech Preparation Tasks

_____ I have crafted a purpose statement reflecting the specific goal of my speech.

_____ I have written a thesis statement summarizing the principal message of my speech.

_____ I have created an introduction that generates interest and previews my main points.

_____ I have organized my speech around related, distinct, and equally important main points.

_____ I have crafted a conclusion that summarizes my message and creates a memorable moment.

_____ I have used transitions throughout my speech to preview and review.

_____ I have created an outline that follows the rules of subordination, division, and parallel wording.

_____ I have converted my outline to a set of speaking notes.

_____ I have included a bibliography of all of the sources I used when preparing my speech.

Now that you have created a formal outline and speaking notes, you need to identify appropriate supporting material to help you make your points convincingly. Let's turn to that essential task.

Test Yourself

- **What do the rules of subordination, division, and parallel wording specify?**
- **What elements should a complete formal outline contain?**
- **How detailed should speaking notes be?**

>> Find Support

Especially when your goal is to inform or to persuade, you will require supporting material to back up the claims you make in your speech. Finding supporting material is not difficult. However, as you will see in this section, to use it effectively you will need to

- Identify places in your speech where you need support.
- Determine the type of support you require.
- Evaluate the quality of supporting material.
- Avoid plagiarism.

IDENTIFY PLACES WHERE YOU NEED SUPPORT

Before locating supporting material for your speech, you must determine where you need it. Essentially, you need to provide support whenever you make a factual claim. Recall from Chapter 4 that a factual claim is a statement asserting that something is objectively

true. Each of the following statements is a factual claim because it argues that something is true in an objective sense:

- The Ebola virus causes high fever, abdominal pain, dizziness, and exhaustion.
- Chinese is the most commonly spoken language in the world.
- Syrah is a dark-skinned type of grape used for making red wine.
- Islam is the world's largest religion.

We can distinguish factual claims from opinions, which are statements of belief about what *ought to be* true, not about what *is* true. The statement "Every person should learn to speak Chinese" is an opinion because it conveys what the speaker believes *should be*. The speaker might argue persuasively for that opinion and even cite opinions of political scientists or expert linguists as support. He or she cannot cite evidence showing that the statement is true, however, because opinions are never true or false in an objective sense.

In contrast, the statement "Chinese is the most commonly spoken language in the world" is a factual claim because it is either true or false no matter how the speaker thinks or feels about it. When you make such a factual claim in a speech, you need to provide evidence that the claim is true. To locate effective supporting material, therefore, start by identifying the factual claims you intend to make, and then search for appropriate material to support each one.

DETERMINE THE TYPE OF SUPPORT YOU REQUIRE

Your options for supporting your speech claims include definitions, examples, statistics, quotations, and narratives. Each type of support is most appropriate under certain circumstances, as follows:

- *Definitions:* When your speech focuses on a concept that may be unfamiliar to your audience—or one that can have multiple meanings—you can support your use of that concept by defining it explicitly. In a presentation about conjunctivitis, you might say, "According to Stedman's medical dictionary, conjunctivitis is an inflammation of the mucous membrane that lines the inner surface of the eye." By identifying the source of your definition, you give that definition credibility.
- *Examples:* Another way to help your audience understand a concept is to give examples of it. Suppose you're giving an informative speech about conspiracy theories. Even if your listeners understand in principle what a conspiracy theory is, they may benefit from hearing specific examples, which might include the conspiracy theories surrounding the assassination of President John F. Kennedy in 1963 and the attacks on the World Trade Center and Pentagon in 2001.
- *Statistics:* Statistics are numbers—usually identified through research—that you can use to support your claims. If your focus is on teen pregnancy, for instance, you might support the importance of that topic in this way: "According to the Centers for Disease Control, the United States has the highest rate of teen pregnancy among all industrialized nations. Nearly 500,000 babies are born each year to mothers aged 15 to 19, and almost two-thirds of those pregnancies are unintended." By providing such statistics, you support your claim that teen pregnancy is a significant issue. Because some statistics are more reliable than others, however, it is always important to identify their source. The next section will give you some hints for determining the merit of your statistics.
- *Quotations:* Quotations from people who are recognized experts on your topic can serve as valuable supporting material. Suppose your presentation is about the future of the British monarchy. To address the question of whether the monarchy is stable, you might say, "As British historian Dr. David Starkey has noted, 'Will there still be a king to be crowned, or will the monarchy follow so many other English institutions into oblivion? History suggests that monarchies rarely disappear, save as a result of defeat in war or revolution, and neither seems in prospect in Britain.'" As with defini-

tions and statistics, it is critical to identify the source of the quotation and his or her qualifications for speaking on that topic.

- *Narratives:* Many speakers use narratives—such as personal stories or testimonies—to support their claims. If you're speaking about the benefits of laser eye surgery, you might relate stories of individuals who have had the procedure and experienced improvements in their life. When speaking about something that is personally relevant to you, you may also elect to share a story or testimony of your own. Narratives can be especially compelling for listeners because they often make a topic feel personal in a way that examples or statistics do not.

KNOW HOW TO EVALUATE SUPPORTING MATERIAL

Not all supporting material is equally valuable. You'll want to find the best possible supporting material, and that means checking carefully for three particular characteristics: credibility, objectivity, and currency.

Credibility As you learned in Chapter 4, information has credibility if it is believable and trustworthy. Using credible supporting material helps you make the points in your speech convincingly. To be credible, supporting material must come from a trustworthy source. A source is convincing if its experience, training, and expertise give its claims more authority than the claims of others.

Suppose your speech focuses on adolescent health. Which of the following statements do you think has more credibility?

- *According to Wikipedia.com, most adolescents have dietary habits that elevate their risk of cardiovascular disease.*
- *According to a report from the U.S. Surgeon General, most adolescents have dietary habits that elevate their risk of cardiovascular disease.*

Both statements make exactly the same claim. The first statement attributes the claim to Wikipedia.com, a website that anyone—regardless of his or her credentials—can edit. The second statement attributes the claim to the U.S. Surgeon General, a recognized national authority on public health. As such an authority, the Surgeon General is a more credible source to cite on matters of public health than Wikipedia. Note, however, that the health information on Wikipedia isn't necessarily inaccurate. Rather, the issue is that the Surgeon General—because of his or her professional training and medical expertise—is a more trustworthy source of medical information.

Besides coming from an appropriate source, credible supporting material often also includes statistics that enumerate an effect. Statistics are simply numbers that you can use to help make a point more informatively. Imagine that you're speaking about safe driving, and you want to argue that talking on a cell phone while driving is dangerous. Which of the following statements makes that point more credibly?

- *According to the National Safety Council, talking on a cell phone while driving increases the chances of a collision.*
- *According to the National Safety Council, talking on a cell phone while driving increases the chances of a collision by 400 percent.*

You'll notice that the second statement specifies *how much* the risk of collision increases when the driver uses a cell phone. Saying that cell phone use increases the chance of a collision may be interesting, but it doesn't help your audience understand the magnitude of the issue. That is, your listeners won't know whether cell phone use poses a significant risk—which may cause them to

By far the most terrifying film you will ever see.

aninconvenient**truth**

A GLOBAL WARNING

Hollywood movies may be entertaining or provocative, but they are not necessarily good sources of credible, objective information.

pay close attention to your point—or a relatively minor risk—which may cause them to ignore your point. In contrast, explaining that cell phone use raises the chance of a collision *by 400 percent* is more provocative, because it gives listeners a specific criterion for judging the importance of the issue.

Objectivity When evaluating the potential usefulness of supporting material, consider how objective the source is. A source is *objective* to the extent that it presents information in an unbiased fashion. In contrast, sources are *subjective* when they offer information in a manner that supports only their favored position on an issue. That distinction matters because many people will consider data from subjective sources to be untrustworthy.

Let's say that you're preparing a speech about the effects of global warming on arctic animal life. Which is a more objective source to cite—a university study of climate change funded by the National Science Foundation or the movie *An Inconvenient Truth,* based on a book of the same title written by former U.S. vice president Al Gore? To what extent is each source objective? Most people would consider the scientific study to be more objective, because the scientific method requires conclusions to be dictated by data. That is, regardless of what scientists *want* to be true, they can claim only what their data tell them. Moreover, a scientist's work is heavily reviewed and scrutinized by other scientists before it can be published. The scientific process therefore demands objectivity. Hollywood movies, in contrast, do not require objectivity. The purpose of most movies is to entertain, not to inform the audience of objective facts. That doesn't necessarily mean that statements made in a movie aren't true, but it does mean that movies are more subjective than scientific studies.

When you are evaluating a source's objectivity, consider the extent to which that source has a political or financial interest in the content of the message. A report on the effectiveness of childproof locks is likely to be more objective if issued by a consumer interest group than by a manufacturer of childproof locks. The reason is that the latter group has a financial interest in reporting that the locks are effective, whereas the former group may not lean toward any particular outcome. Likewise, the report would be less objective if it were funded, or otherwise facilitated, by someone with a political or financial interest in the outcome.

Currency A final consideration when selecting supporting material is the currency of the information. Information that was produced or published recently is likely to be more up-to-date than older information. Using recent supporting material is particularly important when you're speaking about issues that change continually, such as technology and world politics.

Suppose you're developing a speech about how people communicate online. Which of the following sources would provide better supporting material?

Lea, M., & Spears, R. (1992). Paralanguage and social perception in computer-mediated communication. *Journal of Organizational Computing, 2,* 321–341.

Lewis, K., Kaufman, J., & Christakis, N. (2008). The taste for privacy: An analysis of college student privacy settings in an online social network. *Journal of Computer-Mediated Communication, 41,* 79–100.

Because of its more recent publication date, the second article would clearly provide more up-to-date information than the first. Given how rapidly computer-mediated communication technology develops, having the most recent information to support the points in your speech would be very advantageous.

plagiarism Knowingly using information from another source without giving proper credit to that source.

verbal footnote A statement giving credit for the words to their original source.

As you search for appropriate supporting material, remember that credibility, objectivity, and currency are all important, but they are not necessarily equally important. When preparing a speech on British history, for instance, you may find the credibility of your sources to be more important than their currency, because the facts about British history don't change as rapidly as the facts about computer-mediated communication. If you're speaking about the safety of a new treatment for muscle pain, then the objectivity of your supporting material may be paramount, to ensure that the facts you present are as unbiased as possible. You should always consider the credibility, objectivity, and currency of potential supporting material, but you'll want to think about which of those properties are most important for your particular topic.

Finding appropriate supporting material is essential. So, too, is our next topic: using that material appropriately and responsibly, to ensure that you aren't passing off someone else's work as your own.

SHARPEN
Your Skills

Consider the factual claim "Smoking causes high blood pressure." Make a list of three websites that would give you credible and objective evidence relevant to that claim. Then list three websites whose information on the topic would not be credible or objective. What differences do you notice about the sites on your two lists?

DON'T PLAGIARIZE

To support our claims or arguments in a speech or paper, many of us routinely use someone else's words, ideas, or data. Although incorporating material from other sources is perfectly acceptable, you must take care to avoid plagiarism when you do so. Committing **plagiarism** means knowingly using information from another source without giving proper credit to that source. You plagiarize, that is, when you misrepresent someone else's words or ideas as your own. As an act of academic and professional dishonesty, plagiarism is subject to serious punishment and should always be avoided.

Plagiarism Can Take Several Forms When people prepare speeches, it is possible for them to commit plagiarism in at least three different ways. Understanding each will help you avoid plagiarism when you put together a public presentation.

- *Global plagiarism* means stealing your entire speech from another source and presenting it as if it were your own. You would commit global plagiarism if you downloaded a persuasive speech from the Internet and passed it off as your own, for instance. Similarly, if a friend allowed you to use an informative speech he wrote for another class as your own, that would also constitute global plagiarism because you are representing the words as yours rather than his.
- *Patchwork plagiarism* occurs when you copy words from multiple sources and put them together to compose your speech. Suppose you took large sections of your introduction from a magazine article, portions of your main points from a website, and the bulk of your conclusion from a television show. Even though you compiled those sources and wrote portions of your speech to tie them together, you would still be committing plagiarism because you are passing off someone else's words as your own.
- *Incremental plagiarism* means failing to give credit for small portions of your speech—such as a phrase or paragraph—that you did not write. It is entirely acceptable to quote other people's words in your speech, particularly if those words generate audience interest or support a claim. Whenever you do so, however, it is essential that you use a **verbal footnote,** a statement giving credit for the words to their original source. For example, you might say, "According to the April 2010

As renowned opera singer José Carreras once noted . . .

Fact or Fiction?

Using Information from the Internet Constitutes Plagiarism

Plagiarism involves presenting someone else's words as your own. If you use a passage from a magazine article or dialogue from a television show in your speech without properly acknowledging the source, you are committing plagiarism because the words belong to someone else.

Some people believe that words posted online are an exception to that rule, because the Internet doesn't technically *belong* to anyone in the way a magazine or television show does. According to that perspective, using words from the Internet in your speech would not constitute plagiarism, even if you represented those words as your own. However, that way of thinking is incorrect. If you did not write the words in your speech but you represent them as though you did, you are committing plagiarism, regardless of where those words came from. The rules are no different for the Internet than for any other source. You can use words in your speech from any source—including books, movies, and even websites—but you must indicate clearly that you are quoting someone else's words, and you must identify who wrote them.

ASK YOURSELF

- How is plagiarism a form of intellectual dishonesty?
- What can you do to ensure you aren't plagiarizing your speech?

---

edition of *Psychology Today*, . . ." or "As renowned opera singer José Carreras once noted, . . ." If you are using the person's words exactly as he or she wrote them, say "quote" when you begin reciting the quoted passage and "end quote" when you have finished.

Plagiarism Is a Serious Offense Those who commit plagiarism are stealing someone else's work and committing academic dishonesty by passing that work off as theirs. Colleges and universities enforce codes of student conduct that prohibit plagiarism and identify punishments for offenders. At many schools, students convicted of plagiarism can be given failing grades for a course, suspended from school, or even permanently expelled. Being found guilty of plagiarism can also cast doubt over your credibility in the future. Professional associations in the communication discipline, including the National Communication Association and the International Communication Association, condemn plagiarism as a serious professional offense.

How would you feel if someone used your ideas without giving you credit?

Given the amount of information readily available online, some students are tempted to commit plagiarism in their speeches and papers because they believe the likelihood of getting caught is small. To combat plagiarism, however, instructors at many colleges and universities now employ plagiarism-prevention software, such as SafeAssignment, iThenticate, or Turnitin. Those software programs check the text of speeches and papers against a wide variety of sources online, and they clearly identify passages of text that are copied verbatim from another source. With those programs as a resource, many instructors are finding it increasingly easy to spot plagiarism. For that rea-

Table 12.3 Avoiding Plagiarism: Some Helpful Websites

Website	Materials
plagiarism.org	Types of plagiarism; instructions for citing sources; frequently asked questions about plagiarism
owl.english.purdue.edu/owl/resource/589/1	Specific tips for avoiding plagiarism; an exercise to identify properly cited sources
collegeboard.com/student/plan/college-success/10314.html	Instructions for citing sources; instructions for paraphrasing; discussion of when citing sources is unnecessary

son alone, it is worth ensuring that you properly cite your sources and clearly identify any verbatim quotes in the speeches you prepare. You can learn more about plagiarism and the Internet by reading the Fact or Fiction? box.

The Internet also provides resources to help students avoid plagiarism. Table 12.3 describes three such websites that you might find useful when you prepare a speech.

Test Yourself

- **What is a factual claim?**
- **What makes a source current?**
- **Why is it important to avoid plagiarism?**

For REVIEW >>

- ### What are the important elements of any speech?
  When preparing a speech, it is important to craft purpose and thesis statements to guide your speech, as well as the introduction, body, conclusion, and transitions that will compose your speech.

- ### Why are formal outlines and speaking notes useful?
  Creating a formal outline helps ensure that you have made all the points you wish to make in a logical manner. Speaking notes help you remember each of your points while you are delivering your speech.

- ### What evidence should you use to support your claims?
  To support claims you have made in your speech, you need evidence that is credible, objective, and current. When using evidence in your speech, you must take care not to plagiarize someone else's work.

Pop Quiz

Multiple Choice

1. A good purpose statement has all of the following properties *except*

   a. it is concise
   b. it poses a question
   c. it is specific
   d. it makes a declarative statement

2. A one-sentence version of the message of your speech is known as a

   a. purpose statement
   b. main point
   c. conclusion
   d. thesis statement

3. Of the forms of transitions, _____ alert listeners that you are about to shift to a new topic, and _____ remind listeners of points you have already made.

   a. previews; reviews
   b. reviews; main points
   c. conclusions; previews
   d. reviews; previews

4. When preparing her speech, Alana makes certain that if a main point has one subpoint, then it has at least one more. She is following the rule of

   a. parallel wording
   b. subtraction
   c. subordination
   d. division

5. Colin makes sure that he only uses supporting material from sources that present information in an unbiased way. By doing so, he ensures that his supporting material has

   a. credibility
   b. currency
   c. objectivity
   d. subjectivity

Fill in the Blank

6. A statement that connects one part of your speech to another is called a(n) _____ .

7. When you create a structured set of all the points and subpoints in your speech, you are creating a(n) _____ .

8. A(n) _____ is a statement expressing a specific idea or theme related to your topic.

9. The rule of _____ states that all points and subpoints should have the same grammatical structure.

10. A list of the sources you used when preparing your speech is called a(n) _____ .

Answers: 1. b; 2. d; 3. a; 4. d; 5. c; 6. transition; 7. formal outline; 8. main point; 9. parallel wording; 10. bibliography

KEY TERMS

13

PRESENTING
CONFIDENTLY AND

THE MISTAKE HEARD 'ROUND THE WORLD

One traditional responsibility of the chief justice of the United States is to administer the oath of office to newly elected presidents. Presidential inaugurations are grand events that are watched by hundreds of millions of people around the world on television and online. With such an important task to undertake before such a large audience, many chief justices choose to read the oath from a printed card, even though it is only 35 words long and is familiar to anyone with a background in constitutional law. During the inauguration of Barack Obama on January 20, 2009, however, Chief Justice John Roberts chose to "wing it" by administering the oath from memory. That proved to be a questionable decision, as Roberts mixed up the order of some of the words. His mistake created an awkward moment as the new president tried to repeat the incorrect phrase Roberts had delivered. Although the error was minor, it raised enough concern that the president had been properly sworn in that Roberts readministered the oath to Obama the following evening. That time, in front of only nine observers, it came out perfectly.

A SPEECH
COMPETENTLY

- What are the most common forms of speech delivery?
- How can you manage stage fright?
- How can you deliver a speech effectively?

Few of us will ever have occasion to speak before an audience of millions. For many people, however, giving a speech—even in front of a small group of peers—can be a challenge. In the previous two chapters, you saw how to plan and prepare a successful speech. In this chapter, you'll learn what it takes to deliver your speech confidently and competently. You'll discover the various delivery options, examine ways to deal effectively with stage fright, see how to practice delivering a speech, and learn to use presentation aids to maximize the impact of your presentation.

>> Styles of Delivering a Speech

As you learned in Chapter 11, people prepare speeches for many different reasons, such as to inform, to persuade, and to entertain. No matter *why* you're speaking, however, you have various options for *how* to deliver your speech. In this section, we'll examine four basic styles of delivery: impromptu, extemporaneous, scripted, and memorized. Because each style has specific benefits and drawbacks, it's important to consider which would work best in the contexts in which you might be speaking.

SOME SPEECHES ARE IMPROMPTU

An **impromptu speech** is a speech that you deliver on the spot, with little or no preparation. Suppose you're meeting with your project team at work and your manager asks you

to share your marketing ideas with the group. If she had mentioned a week ago that she wanted you to speak at the meeting, you might have used that time to consider your message and prepare your remarks. Instead, she expects you to speak without the benefit of planning. Making an impromptu speech requires you not only to think spontaneously about what you want to say but also to organize your thoughts quickly into a set of speaking points. Being asked to speak impromptu can be nerve-wracking, particularly for individuals who are already afraid of public speaking.

If you're called upon to deliver an impromptu speech, these hints can help you succeed:

- *Don't panic.* Many people feel pangs of fear when asked to speak impromptu. That's a normal response, and it needn't prevent you from speaking well. If you react that way, take a deep breath and tell yourself "I can do this." Remember that you wouldn't be asked to speak if you didn't have something worthwhile to say.

- *Think in threes.* Whatever the topic of your impromptu speech, identify three points you want to make about it. Ask yourself, "What three things do I want my audience to know?" Make those messages the three main points of your speech. If you include more than three points, it will be harder for your listeners—and you—to remember them all.

- *Draw from what's happened.* Consider what else has been said or done in the context you're in and make reference to it. For example, you might begin your speech by responding to someone's previous observations. Likewise, you might end your remarks by commenting on the occasion or on the audience.

- *Be brief.* Because impromptu speeches are spontaneous, people usually expect them to be short. Giving a long, detailed description of each point in your speech is usually unnecessary and will reduce your listeners' ability to remember what you've said. Instead, make your points concisely, provide a brief conclusion, and then thank your audience for listening.

SHARPEN Your Skills

Suppose you were asked to deliver an impromptu speech addressing the question, "What do you want your life's legacy to be?" Identify three points you would make in such a speech.

Although impromptu speaking can be stressful, it is certainly possible to do it well. As with many communication skills, you'll get more comfortable with it the more you practice.

SOME SPEECHES ARE EXTEMPORANEOUS

One benefit of giving an impromptu speech is that listeners may believe your words are genuine or from the heart because you didn't have time to prepare them in advance. Another style of delivery that gives you that advantage—but also allows you some planning time—is the extemporaneous style. An **extemporaneous speech** is one that is carefully prepared to *sound* as though it is being delivered spontaneously.

Preparing to speak extemporaneously involves steps we examined in Chapter 12: constructing purpose and thesis statements, identifying main points and subpoints, choosing how to introduce and conclude your speech, creating a formal outline, and crafting a set of informal speaking notes. Using your informal speaking notes, you can practice making your speech sound off the cuff or not heavily prepared. As an extemporaneous speaker, your goal is to communicate in a natural, conversational manner—to give the impression that you are simply *talking with* your listeners instead of *formally addressing* them. Analyzing and understanding your audience (see Chapter 11) will help you to relate to your speakers as effectively as possible.

Extemporaneous speaking offers some advantages over other styles of delivery. Because extemporaneous speakers use minimal notes, they can maintain audience eye contact, which helps their listeners be attentive and engaged. They can also speak with a more relaxed tone of voice than if they were reading a script. Yet using speaking notes helps to ensure that extemporaneous speakers won't forget their main points or lose their place.

Despite those important advantages, the extemporaneous style of delivery is not the best option in every situation. For instance, many speakers would find it difficult to deliver an extemporaneous speech within a narrow time frame, such as might be required if they were speaking on television or on the radio. If a speech *must* last a specified period of time, then it is safer to read the speech from a script that has been timed to fit that period. The extemporaneous style can also be challenging if the speech must have perfect grammar or if large sections of the speech must be exactly worded. Such instances call for the use of a script.

SOME SPEECHES ARE SCRIPTED

Unlike an extemporaneous speech, a **scripted speech** is composed word for word on a manuscript and then read aloud exactly as it is written. Scripted speeches are particularly

impromptu speech A speech delivered with little or no preparation.

extemporaneous speech A speech that is carefully prepared to sound as though it is being delivered spontaneously.

scripted speech A speech composed word for word on a manuscript and then read aloud exactly as it is written.

News anchors frequently read the day's stories word for word from a teleprompter.

common in situations when the exact wording of the speech is crucial or when the speech must fit within a predetermined time frame. For instance, politicians often use teleprompters when delivering important speeches before large audiences. In such cases, the manuscript is projected onto the teleprompter in such a way that only the speaker can see it. Similarly, television news anchors read the day's stories word for word from a manuscript that is projected next to the cameras they are facing. A scripted speech allows the speakers to deliver grammatically accurate, well-planned messages within a specified time frame.

Many people opt for scripted speeches when they are nervous about speaking. Perhaps you've noticed that it is easy to become distracted when you're nervous. Distraction can cause you to stumble over your words or forget parts of what you want to say. Chief Justice John Roberts may have been particularly nervous administering the presidential oath of office to Barack Obama in January 2009, given the momentous occasion and the enormity of the audience. His nervousness could have been to blame for the problems he encountered with the oath. You might have experienced some of the same nervousness while giving a speech in class or before a student organization. On such occasions, having a manuscript with all your words can be comforting because it ensures that you will always know exactly what you want to say.

Scripted delivery is probably the easiest form of speaking, because it requires speakers simply to recite the words of the speech from a manuscript. Delivering a scripted speech has some clear disadvantages, however. First, compared to impromptu and extemporaneous speeches, scripted speeches often take much more time and energy to prepare. Not only must you create a detailed outline for a scripted speech—as you would for an extemporaneous speech—but you also must then compose every part of the speech word for word. That process can be time-consuming, particularly when you generate several drafts.

Second, unless you are using a teleprompter, delivering a scripted speech requires you to manipulate a manuscript—a potentially tricky chore, especially when you're nervous. If you were to drop your manuscript or shuffle the pages in the wrong order, you could lose your place. Even if you handle your manuscript without incident, turning the pages can distract your listeners from paying attention to your words. Finally, consider that it is often challenging to sound energetic and sincere when reading a speech verbatim. Because you use your voice differently when you read something aloud than when you engage in conversation, reading a speech can make you sound stiff or uninteresting.[1] The best way to deal with that challenge is to practice reading your speech while varying your tone, volume, and speaking rate, as you would during a conversation. In that way you can help ensure that your speech won't *sound* read even if you are reading it.[2]

SOME SPEECHES ARE MEMORIZED

Perhaps you like the control over your words that a scripted speech gives you, but you can't use or don't want to use a manuscript. In that case, you probably want to give a **memorized speech,** a speech that you compose word for word and then deliver from memory. Memorizing their words allows people to speak without having to handle a script or set of notes. Because they have no papers to hold or look at, speakers can gesture naturally and maintain an effective level of eye contact with their listeners. As we'll see later in this chapter, both of those behaviors can enhance the credibility of a speech. Going "noteless" also frees a speaker to move around during a speech.

Like scripted speeches, memorized speeches are useful when individuals must speak within a specified time frame. In political debates, for instance, candidates are often al-

memorized speech A speech composed word for word and then delivered from memory.

lowed only a certain number of minutes for their opening and closing statements. They can therefore prepare and rehearse memorized speeches that conform to those time limits.

As with all forms of delivery, memorized speeches have some drawbacks. One disadvantage is that like scripted speeches, memorized speeches take a good deal of time and energy to prepare. Not only must you write the speech itself, you must also commit it to memory—a possibly burdensome task, especially if your speech is relatively long. Another drawback of memorized speeches is that they can come across as excessively prepared and overly formal. As a result, they may not sound as sincere as impromptu or extemporaneous speeches often do. You can overcome that disadvantage by rehearsing to make your speech *seem* as though you are presenting it for the first time.

Memorizing their words allows speakers to gesture naturally and to maintain effective eye contact with their listeners.

A third disadvantage of giving a memorized speech is that a speaker's memory can fail. Many people have had the experience of practicing a speech so many times that they can practically recite it in their sleep, only to forget the words in the middle of their delivery. If you ever encounter that problem, the best way to recover is to improvise. Consider what you were saying right before your memory failed, and then speak extemporaneously about it. Improvising for even a few moments may jog your memory, allowing you to resume your memorized speech without anyone's noticing that you temporarily forgot your words.

Have you ever tried to give a memorized speech but forgotten the words? What did you do to recover during your presentation?

Impromptu, extemporaneous, scripted, and memorized speeches offer a range of options for delivery. As summarized in Table 13.1, each style of delivery provides specific benefits but entails certain drawbacks. To succeed at any of these forms of delivery, however, you must first learn how to manage stage fright, our next topic.

Table 13.1 Benefits and Drawbacks of Four Styles of Delivery

Style	Benefits	Drawbacks
Impromptu	Requires little preparation. Often makes the speaker sound genuine.	Lack of opportunity to prepare can be stressful. Thinking on the spot can be difficult.
Extemporaneous	Provides the speaker with notes while making the speech sound spontaneous.	Takes time to prepare. Difficult to do well under strict time constraints or if perfect grammar is required.
Scripted	Provides maximum control over the verbal content. Ensures the speaker always knows what to say.	Takes much time to prepare. Use of a manuscript can be distracting for speaker and audience.
Memorized	Allows high control over verbal content. Requires no notes, so speaker can use natural gestures and maintain eye contact.	Requires considerable effort to write and memorize. Can sound insincere. Speaker's memory can fail during delivery.

- Why is impromptu speaking often difficult to do well?
- What tasks are involved in preparing an extemporaneous speech?
- When is using a scripted speech the best option?
- What are the primary drawbacks of a memorized speech?

Test Yourself

>> Managing Stage Fright

Every few years, the Gallup organization polls U.S. American adults about what they most fear. In a 2001 survey of over a thousand people, the most commonly mentioned fear was snakes—and the second most commonly cited fear was public speaking.[3] Incidentally, the fear of death didn't make the top 10 list, a finding suggesting that some respondents were more afraid of giving a speech than they were of dying. That reality once prompted comedian Jerry Seinfeld to joke that at a funeral, most people would rather be in the casket than giving the eulogy.

All joking aside, public speaking can be a terrifying prospect for people who suffer from **stage fright:** anxiety or fear that is brought on by performing in front of an audience. As you'll learn in this section, stage fright is a type of stress that affects individuals psychologically, physically, and behaviorally.[4] It can be debilitating, causing people to deliver poor performances. Fortunately, you can learn to use stage fright to your advantage by overcoming some of its problematic effects.

STAGE FRIGHT IS A COMMON FORM OF STRESS

Actress Kim Basinger is one of the most recognizable performers in Hollywood. She has appeared in nearly three dozen motion pictures in the last 30 years and had major roles in such movies as *Batman* (1989) and *8 Mile* (2002). Her 10-year marriage to actor Alec Baldwin also contributed to her high public profile. Given the extent of her acting experience and media attention, you might expect Basinger to be the last person who would be nervous giving a speech. Yet Basinger has suffered from debilitating stage fright for much of her life.[5] When she stepped to the podium in 1998 to accept the Academy Award for best supporting actress for her role in the movie *L.A. Confidential* (1997), she was too overcome with stage fright to deliver her prepared acceptance speech, even though she had practiced it multiple times.

As Basinger's example illustrates, even seasoned performers can experience stage fright. The anxiety or fear that many people feel before giving a speech or performing in front of a crowd is a form of stress. **Stress** is the body's reaction to any type of perceived threat. You may feel stress, for instance, when you see a growling dog running toward you, when you sit down to take a final exam, or when you are laid off from a job. Although those are different situations, each poses some type of threat, whether it's to your physical health, academic record, or financial well-being. Scientists use the term *stressor* to refer to events that cause the body to experience stress.

As communication scholar James McCroskey has documented, public speaking is a common stressor.[6] Research indicates that the stage fright associated with public speaking—which some scholars call *speech anxiety*—affects more than one in five adults,[7] a figure that has remained stable for the last four decades.[8] Public speaking stress is so common, in fact, that many scientific experiments about stress use a public speaking activity purposely to elevate participants' stress levels.[9]

Although public speaking may not threaten a person's physical, academic, or financial well-being as do other stressors, many people feel that public speaking threatens their emotional well-being. For instance, they might worry about experiencing embarrassment, disapproval, or ridicule if their speech doesn't go well. Those may seem like mild threats, particularly when compared to being physically harmed, failing a class, or losing a job. As

stage fright Anxiety or fear brought on by performing in front of an audience.

stress The body's reaction to any type of perceived threat.

anxiety A psychological state of worry and unease.

anticipatory anxiety The worry people feel when looking ahead to a speech.

fight-or-flight response A reaction that helps prepare the body either to confront or to avoid a stressor.

anyone who has experienced stage fright can attest, however, public speaking can be just as stressful as—if not more stressful than—many more serious threats.

When we feel stress, our body reacts in ways that affect us psychologically, physically, and behaviorally. Let's examine how those components of the stress response are related to the stage fright associated with public speaking.

Psychological Effects of Stage Fright Stage fright routinely causes people to experience **anxiety,** a psychological state of worry and unease. Communication scholars Ralph Behnke and Chris Sawyer have devoted much of their careers to studying the anxiety associated with public speaking. One of their most important findings is that anxiety often begins long before speakers stand in front of an audience. According to Behnke and Sawyer, many people experience **anticipatory anxiety,** which is the worry they feel when looking ahead to a speech.[10] Research shows that anticipatory anxiety often starts when the speech is assigned. Perhaps you can recall feeling worried or stressed when you learned that you would have to make a speech in class or at work. Anticipatory anxiety usually decreases as individuals begin preparing their speeches, probably because preparation gives them a sense that they can control their performance.[11] Then, just before delivering the speech, people's anxiety peaks as they feel the pressure to perform.

Not every speech will evoke the same level of anxiety. For instance, you've probably found that you're less anxious when speaking about a topic you understand well than one that is less familiar. The reason is that having a command of your topic gives you confidence in what you're saying. Delivery style also appears to affect how much anxiety people experience about public speaking. One study found that speakers had the most anxiety when anticipating an impromptu speech, less anxiety when anticipating an extemporaneous speech, and the least anxiety when anticipating a scripted speech.[12]

People vary with respect to how much speaking anxiety they experience. Research shows that public speaking anxiety is lowest among people who are outgoing,[13] uninhibited,[14] intellectually sophisticated,[15] and not prone to worry.[16] Another study found that women had higher levels of anticipatory anxiety than did men[17]—perhaps a reflection of differences in how women and men react physically to stress.[18]

When do you feel anxiety? What do you do to deal with it?

Physical Effects of Stage Fright Beyond their psychological impact, stressful situations such as public speaking affect the body. Try to recall a time when you experienced stress. Perhaps you can remember that your heart beat faster, you breathed more heavily, and you perspired more than normal. Other physical changes were occurring outside your conscious awareness. Your body was producing more stress hormones, for instance, and the pupils of your eyes were dilating. Those physical effects of stress are part of the body's **fight-or-flight response,** a reaction that helps prepare the body either to confront the stressor (through a fight) or to avoid it (through flight).[19] Your heart and breathing rates increase to get more oxygen to your muscles so that you have more energy for fighting or fleeing from the stressor. You perspire more to keep from overheating. Your stress hormones temporarily increase your strength, and your pupils dilate so that you can take in as much visual information about the situation as possible.[20] In those ways, the physical effects of stress enable you to deal as effectively as possible with the stressor.

Stage fright produces many of the same physical stress reactions from person to person, including increased heart rate and blood pressure and elevated stress hormones.[21] You will find more detail about one study on stage fright in the The Dark Side of Communication box.

Stress related to public speaking produces effects similar to those of other forms of stage fright, such as the physical reactions people might experience before acting in a play or dancing in a recital. One study found that people training to be professional musicians experienced increases in heart rate and stress hormones when they performed in front

SHARPEN
Your Skills

When you feel your body getting worked up over the stress of public speaking, close your eyes and pay attention to your breathing. Focus on the sensation of each breath entering and leaving your body. Research shows that focusing on breathing for 15 minutes helps people deal more effectively with stressful situations.[22]

THE DARK SIDE of Communication

Stressing Out: Public Speaking Elevates Stress Hormone Levels

The ability to speak in public is critical for success in a range of careers. For many individuals, however, public speaking has a dark side: It causes them to experience physical stress. Some of the effects of stress are relatively noticeable, such as increases in heart rate and perspiration. The experience of stress also causes rises in stress hormones, which, although they may not be immediately obvious, have multiple effects on the body.

Research by communication scientists James Roberts, Chris Sawyer, and Ralph Behnke indicates that when college students deliver a speech in front of a group of their peers, their level of the stress hormone cortisol rises. Specifically, students showed a dramatic increase in cortisol from before the speech to 8 minutes after they began speaking. Cortisol level continually decreased from that point on, as students recovered from their stress.

Stress hormones such as cortisol prepare the body in multiple ways to deal effectively with a stressor. For instance, they reduce blood flow to the extremities—the reason why our hands and feet may feel cold when we're nervous—so that more blood is available to our internal organs. They also increase the level of sugar in our blood so that the muscles have more fuel than normal, and they activate the immune system in case it needs to respond to an injury. Such reactions can be helpful in the short term by giving us more physical resources to manage a stressor. However, repeated exposure to stress has many negative effects on the body, including reduced muscle mass and decreased immune system strength.

ASK YOURSELF

- What physical reactions do you notice in your body when you're under stress?
- Instead of studying students, what if the researchers had studied teachers, television reporters, or others who do public speaking for a living? How do you think their results would have been different, if at all?

Source: Roberts, J. B., Sawyer, C. R., & Behnke, R. R. (2004). A neurological representation of speech state anxiety: Mapping salivary cortisol levels of public speakers. *Western Journal of Communication, 68,* 219–231.

of an audience as opposed to practicing on their own.[23] Even college instructors are sometime prone to experience stage fright before they teach.[24] Fears of making a mistake and being embarrassed can invoke physical stress for anyone performing in front of a crowd, including public speakers.

As with psychological anxiety, there is a good deal of diversity from person to person in the level of physical stress experienced when speaking in public. Some studies have demonstrated, for example, that individuals with a strong tendency to worry experience more physical stress when anticipating, preparing, and delivering a speech than do non-worriers.[25] Moreover, those who react strongly to other stressful situations tend to experience highly elevated stress during a speech.[26] There are also some sex differences in public speaking stress. Although women report more psychological anxiety than men about public speaking, research shows that men experience more physical stress overall while delivering a speech. In particular, men demonstrate greater elevations in stress hormones[27] and blood pressure,[28] although women appear to experience greater elevations than men in heart rate.[29]

Behavioral Effects of Stage Fright In addition to its psychological and physical effects, stage fright also influences how people behave.[30] You can probably recall from your own experience how you act when you're nervous. Perhaps you fidget or pace. Maybe you find it difficult to speak. Researchers have been examining those and other behavioral effects of stage fright for several decades.[31] Their work indicates that stage fright—including that evoked by public speaking—affects behavior in at least five separate domains:

- *Voice:* Stage fright often causes the voice to quiver or sound tense. It can also cause the voice to sound monotonous or lifeless.
- *Mouth and throat:* People experiencing stage fright often swallow and clear their throat more frequently than normal.
- *Facial expression:* Muscle tension in the face causes a general lack of expression and eye contact. It can also make the face twitch slightly.
- *General movement:* Stage fright frequently causes people to fidget or engage in random movement. It can also cause them to pace, sway, or shuffle their feet.
- *Verbal behavior:* People experiencing stage fright often stammer or stutter more than usual. They also increase their use of filler words, such as "um" or "uh," and they are more likely to forget what they want to say.[32]

Each of those behaviors is an effect of feeling nervous, stressed, and distracted, the way people feel when they experience stage fright. As we'll discover in the next sections, the psychological, physical, and behavioral effects of stage fright can inhibit your ability to speak effectively, but stage fright can also improve your performance if you know how to manage it successfully.

STAGE FRIGHT CAN BE DEBILITATING

When stage fright is particularly intense, it can become debilitating—that is, it can overwhelm people and prevent them from speaking or performing effectively. Kim Basinger's stage fright incapacitated her and prevented her from giving the acceptance speech she had prepared for the Academy Awards ceremony. Like a deer caught in the headlights, people with debilitating stage fright can become immobilized and unable to deliver their speech, even if they have rehearsed extensively.

The stress of stage fright can cause the face to appear expressionless, much like the look of a deer caught in a car's headlights.

Putting Communication to Work

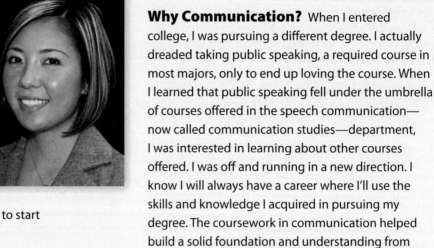

Name: Cristina Lane

College(s): BA, Colorado State University, 2004

Major(s): Communication

Job Title: Donor Relations Coordinator

Salary: $30,000 to $45,000 to start

Time in Job: 2 years

Work Responsibilities: My current position is in development for the College of Liberal Arts at Colorado State University. As Donor Relations Coordinator, I plan all of our events, including fundraisers. A typical workweek is never typical. Each day brings new challenges and new opportunities.

Why Communication? When I entered college, I was pursuing a different degree. I actually dreaded taking public speaking, a required course in most majors, only to end up loving the course. When I learned that public speaking fell under the umbrella of courses offered in the speech communication—now called communication studies—department, I was interested in learning about other courses offered. I was off and running in a new direction. I know I will always have a career where I'll use the skills and knowledge I acquired in pursuing my degree. The coursework in communication helped build a solid foundation and understanding from which to grow personally and professionally.

My Advice to Students: Doing what you love will make you feel fulfilled. If you find particular passion in a course, figure out where that passion is rooted and pursue a career where you can access that passion—not necessarily on a daily basis but enough that you feel satisfaction and contentment.

Debilitating stage fright often causes two distinct sensations. The first is that your mind seems to go blank. In the grip of intense stage fright, you can easily forget words or information that you would readily remember under normal circumstances. The reason you forget when you experience an intense negative emotion—fear in the case of stage fright—is that you become distracted by your body's efforts to manage that emotion. As a result, your ability to think and remember temporarily suffers, causing your mind to draw a blank when you attempt to recall what you had planned to say.[33]

The second sensation that occurs during an episode of intense stage fright is an urge to escape the situation. As we've seen, stressful events often trigger a fight-or-flight response, motivating you either to confront the stressor or to flee from it. When the stressful event causes fear, you're more likely to want to flee than fight.[34] Because the stress and fear of the situation make you perceive that your well-being is threatened, you want to get away to protect yourself from harm.[35] If you feel intensely nervous about giving a speech, for example, you may find yourself wishing you could postpone the speech or trying to get it over with as quickly as possible. You may also avoid eye contact with your listeners as a subconscious way to escape acknowledging their attention.

It's difficult to speak effectively when your mind goes blank and you feel the urge to escape. Just because stage fright *can* have those debilitating effects, however, doesn't mean that it *must*.

visualization Developing a mental image, such as an image of oneself giving a successful performance.

desensitization The process of confronting frightening situations directly, to reduce the stress they cause.

avatars Graphic representations of people.

MAKING STAGE FRIGHT AN ADVANTAGE

Although stage fright is common, you can learn to turn it to your advantage. This section offers five pieces of advice for making stage fright your friend—as the individual who's profiled in "Putting Communication to Work" did with great success.

Accept Stage Fright as a Normal Response When you are working to become a better speaker or performer, you might be inclined to focus on trying to eliminate your stage fright. You may reason that if stage fright inhibits your ability to perform well, it makes sense to get rid of it. Such efforts would be largely wasted, however. All forms of fear, including stage fright, are deeply rooted in humans' ancestral experiences. The fear response is largely innate, and although people who perform frequently in front of audiences usually become less nervous over time, stage fright rarely goes away entirely. Thus, rather than trying to eliminate stage fright, accept it as a normal part of the performance experience. In fact, stage fright can even help you to perform better than you would if you didn't feel nervous.

Focus the Nervous Energy Recall that the stress of public speaking causes bodily changes—including elevated heart rate, breathing rate, and stress hormone levels—that increase your energy stores. That energy boost is meant to help you deal effectively with a threatening situation. You can train yourself to focus the nervous energy on the goal of giving the best speech possible rather than letting it distract you. Just as many athletes try to get psyched up before a game so that they have more energy to channel toward their performance, so too can you use your nervousness to energize your speech.

Visualize a Successful Performance A technique that often helps individuals perform well, even if they are experiencing stage fright, is **visualization:** developing a particular mental image—in this case, an image of oneself giving a successful performance.[36] Practice visualization by closing your eyes and imagining yourself delivering an expert speech. As you visualize, see yourself giving your entire speech in a confident and relaxed manner. Research shows that people who visualize a successful speech performance experience less stage fright and fewer negative thoughts when they actually deliver their speeches, compared to people who don't use visualization.[37]

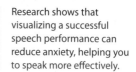

Research shows that visualizing a successful speech performance can reduce anxiety, helping you to speak more effectively.

Desensitize As we've seen, people generally avoid what they fear. For instance, if you're afraid of flying, you will tend not to fly. The more you avoid flying (or something else you're afraid of), however, the scarier it often seems. In contrast, when people face their fears and encounter the situations that frighten them, they often realize that those situations aren't as scary as they once seemed; your fear of flying may lessen after you have taken a flight and experienced a safe take-off and landing. You will gradually feel less and less afraid of flying each time you take a flight.

The process of confronting frightening situations head-on is called **desensitization,** and research shows that it can significantly reduce the anxiety individuals experience about all sorts of fears, including public speaking.[38] That research suggests that the more you practice speaking in front of people, the less frightening public speaking will become, because over time you will be desensitized to it.

One way to desensitize yourself to public speaking anxiety is to take every opportunity you have to speak in public, even if the prospect scares you. Remind yourself that you're facing your fears so that you can overcome them, and you will be stronger and more confident after each speech. Another way to desensitize yourself is to practice speaking in front of a computer-generated audience. Using a virtual world such as Second Life, find an area with several **avatars,** which are graphic representations of other people. Then deliver speeches to that virtual audience before you deliver them to real-life listeners. In the safety of a computer-mediated environment, you will gain practice in the public speaking context—practice that can help to desensitize you to public speaking anxiety.[39]

Practicing your speech in the safety of the virtual world can help you desensitize yourself to public speaking anxiety.

Stay Positive Finally, approach the delivery of your speech with a positive, optimistic attitude. Tell yourself that you can—and will—succeed. This positive self-talk can be difficult, particularly if you're very nervous or if you have had negative experiences with prior performances. Staying as positive as you can is important for two reasons, however. First, research shows that positive thoughts and emotions help to relieve the body of the negative effects of stress.[41] Therefore, you'll approach your speech in a more relaxed manner than you otherwise would. Second, recall from Chapter 3 that negative thoughts can turn into a self-fulfilling prophecy, causing you to have a poor performance simply because you expect that you will. Approaching your speech with an optimistic attitude, in contrast, can encourage the behaviors that will help you succeed.

In summary, stage fright is a common experience and one that can either inhibit or enhance your ability to give an effective speech. The key is knowing how to manage stage fright and how to make it work to your advantage. Yet even if you feel nervous about delivering a speech, you don't have to look or sound nervous. In the next section, you'll discover how to deliver a speech so that you come across as calm and confident in the eyes of your audience.

- **How does the stress of stage fright affect individuals psychologically, physically, and behaviorally?**
- **In what ways can stage fright be debilitating?**
- **Why should you practice visualization before giving a speech?**

Test Yourself

>> Practicing Effective Delivery

Think about the most memorable speech you can recall hearing. What makes it stick in your mind? Perhaps it's partly what the speaker said, but what you probably remember most is the speaker's delivery. After all, we don't usually read others' speeches—instead, we watch and listen to them. As we considered in Chapter 5, most of us pay more attention to how people look and sound than to what they say. An effective speech therefore requires an effective delivery. We can categorize the behaviors of effective delivery according to visual elements and vocal elements.

VISUAL ELEMENTS AFFECT DELIVERY

Humans have a strong tendency to evaluate a situation—including a speech—according to what they see. Visual cues are thus important elements of effective speech delivery. This section describes how you can use facial expression, eye contact, posture and body position, gestures, and personal appearance to your advantage.

Facial Expression Recall from Chapter 5 that the face communicates more information than any other nonverbal channel. For that reason, you can use your facial expressions during a speech to add impact to your words and credibility to your message.

Research indicates that two aspects of your facial expression are particularly important for an effective speech. The first is that your facial expressions should match the tone of your words. When your words are serious, your facial expression should be serious as well. You should smile when telling positive stories and express concern when telling troubling stories. Doing so creates congruence between your facial expressions and your verbal message that makes your audience more inclined to believe what you're saying.[42]

The second aspect of using facial expressions effectively is that your expressions should vary over the course of your speech. Presenting the same expression throughout your speech may cause listeners to tune you out. Researchers have found that speakers who vary their facial expressions—as long as they do so in ways that are appropriate to their words—are seen as competent and credible.[43]

Eye Contact A second element of effective delivery is eye contact. Inexperienced presenters often stare at the floor or the ceiling while speaking. If they look at their audience at all, it is only with short glances, often over the top of their listeners' heads.

Avoiding eye contact with your audience is a response to fear that makes you feel hidden and protected. When you avert your eyes, your subconscious is saying, "If I can't see my listeners, then they can't see me." In contrast, looking your audience in the eye can make you feel vulnerable because it acknowledges that your listeners are evaluating you.

Effective speakers know that maintaining eye contact with their listeners is extremely important.[44] Imagine carrying on a face-to-face conversation with someone who never looks you in the eye. You would likely get the impression that the person isn't interested in you or perhaps that he or she isn't being honest with you. Research shows that your listeners will probably form the same impressions of you if you don't look them in the eye while speaking.[45]

Of course, it's not necessary to stare at your listeners. Rather, you should make eye contact with one person in your audience, hold it for a moment, and then make eye contact with another audience member. Focus on one section of the audience at a time. Look at people in the front row for a minute or two and then direct your eye contact to those in the back corner or in the middle of the group. Try to make eye contact with each person at least once during your speech. When you look your listeners in the eye, you come across as confident and believable even if you feel nervous.[46]

Posture and Body Position Whether you're sitting or standing during your speech, it's important to adopt a posture that is relaxed but confident. Slouching or hanging your head will make you appear uninterested in what you're saying. Instead, keep your back straight, your shoulders square, and your head up. That posture makes you appear strong, composed, and in control.[47]

You should also be aware of your body movement and position, particularly if you're standing. First, make sure that you stand facing your listeners. That advice may seem obvious, but it is particularly easy to forget if your speech incorporates visual aids, such as a PowerPoint presentation. When showing PowerPoint slides, for instance, some speakers turn away from the audience and speak in the direction of the screen on which the slides appear. Doing so makes it seem as though they are ignoring their audience and can also make it difficult for listeners to hear them. A better approach is to stand alongside the screen so that you are still facing your audience, and to turn your head—instead of your whole body—when you need to see the next slide.

Depending on the size and layout of the room in which you're speaking, you may also have the option of walking around during your speech. Moving around while you speak can make your presentation more visually interesting to your audience than standing in one spot. That visual variety encourages the audience to pay attention to your speech. Research shows that a speaker's engaging in natural body movement can also help the audience understand what the speaker is saying.[48]

If you choose to move around during your speech, it's important that your movements appear casual but deliberate. Move slowly to one position, stay there for a few minutes, and then move slowly to another spot. A particularly good time to move from one place to another is during a transition in your speech, because your change in position will correspond to a change in your remarks. You want to avoid random movement, as that will suggest you are moving simply to expend nervous energy. Similarly, avoid movement that looks overly contrived and thus unnatural, such as circulating continuously around three specific spots. If you can move in a natural and relaxed manner, you will hold your listeners' attention and enhance your credibility.

Gestures As we saw in Chapter 5, gestures are movements of the hands, arms, or head that express meaning. Most of us gesture naturally as we converse with other people. Studies indicate that the use of gestures also enhances the effectiveness of a speech.[49]

Three factors are particularly important when gesturing during a speech. First, gestures should look spontaneous rather than planned. Spontaneous gestures naturally follow what people are saying and thus appear well connected to the verbal message. Planned gestures, in contrast, appear contrived and insincere. Perhaps the best way to keep your gestures from looking planned is not to plan them. Rather, let them arise naturally from the words you're speaking.

A second key factor is that gestures should be appropriate in number. Some speakers, especially when they're anxious, gesture almost constantly because the motion helps them get rid of excess nervous energy. If you've ever listened to such a speaker, however, you know that using too many gestures can distract an audience and make it difficult for listeners to concentrate on the speaker's words. While some speakers show nervousness by overdoing gestures, other speakers become physically tense and barely gesture at all. As a result, they appear stiff and rigid. Effective speakers, then, use a *moderate* number of gestures—not too many or too few.

Finally, gestures should be appropriate in size for your proximity to the audience. If your listeners are relatively close to you,

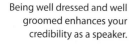

Effective gestures look spontaneous, are appropriate in number, and are appropriate in size for your proximity to the audience.

as in a conference room or a small classroom, you should use gestures similar to those you would use in face-to-face conversations. If you are farther away from your listeners, as in an auditorium, it's important to use larger, more dramatic gestures so that your audience can see them.

Personal Appearance A final visual element of an effective delivery is personal appearance—clothing, accessories, and grooming. As a general rule, your appearance should be appropriate for your audience and for the occasion on which you're speaking. Select clothing that will match the formality of—or will be slightly more formal than—the clothes your listeners will be wearing. The more your personal appearance reflects theirs, the more your listeners will perceive you as similar to them, and that perception enhances your credibility.[50] In contrast, dressing far more formally or far less formally than your listeners will lead your audience to see you as more of an outsider.

Jewelry and accessories should complement your clothing but should not attract attention. Long, flashy earrings or multiple bracelets that clang together whenever you move your arm will distract your audience. Effective speakers also know that it's important to be well groomed when giving a speech. You can use the checklist in The Competent Communicator to ensure you've attended adequately to your personal appearance before presenting a speech.

Being well dressed and well groomed enhances your credibility as a speaker.

An exception to this advice arises if you are using your personal appearance as a presentation aid. If you are speaking about stereotypes, for example, you might deliberately dress or project yourself to evoke certain judgments from your listeners, which you can then discuss in your speech. Likewise, if your speech is about military uniforms, you might choose to wear one. Unless your appearance is a presentation aid, however, it's best to dress similarly to your audience, to wear conservative jewelry and accessories, and to be well groomed.

Your facial expressions, eye contact, posture and body position, gestures, and personal appearance all influence the effectiveness of your speech by affecting what your audience *sees*. However, effective delivery also relies on what your audience *hears*.

VOCAL ELEMENTS AFFECT DELIVERY

Several elements of the voice influence how people understand and evaluate what the speaker says. Here we'll examine the importance of rate, volume, pitch, articulation, and fluency as vocal elements of effective speech delivery.

Personal Appearance Checklist

When you're getting ready to present a speech, use this checklist to make sure you have given adequate attention to your personal appearance. Check either "True" or "False" following each item.

		True	False
1.	My clothing is far more formal than that of my audience.	_____	_____
2.	I am wearing jewelry that makes noise when I move.	_____	_____
3.	I am dressed far more casually than my listeners are.	_____	_____
4.	My appearance is unkempt.	_____	_____
5.	I am wearing accessories that will attract attention.	_____	_____
6.	My clothing is similar to what my listeners will be wearing.	_____	_____
7.	I look well groomed.	_____	_____
8.	Everything I am wearing is clean.	_____	_____
9.	I'm not wearing any flashy jewelry.	_____	_____
10.	I believe my appearance will make the impression I want to make.	_____	_____

As you might guess, you should answer "False" in response to the first five items and "True" in response to the second five items. If any of your answers are otherwise, recheck your personal appearance before your speech to ensure that you are making the visual impression on your listeners that you intend to make.

Rate One vocal factor in effective delivery is your speech rate, or the speed at which you speak. In normal conversation, most U.S. American adults speak approximately 150 words per minute.[51] Studies find, though, that speaking at a faster rate makes a speaker more persuasive[52] and more credible[53] than speaking at an average or a slower rate. The explanation may be that speakers who talk at a fast rate appear to be in command of what they're saying, whereas slower speakers sound less sure of themselves.

There are two important caveats about speaking rate, however. The first is that it is possible to speak *too* fast. If you speak unusually fast, your listeners will begin paying attention to your speaking rate and will tune out your message. The second caution is that you should adapt your speaking rate to your audience. Speaking at a brisk rate may work well with most audiences, but you'll likely need to speak more slowly if your audience is composed of young children, the elderly, people with developmental disabilities, or people who don't speak your language fluently, so that those listeners can understand you.

Volume Vocal volume is the loudness or softness of the voice. The appropriate volume for your speech depends on several factors, such as the size of your audience, the size of the room in which you're speaking, and whether you're using a microphone. Just as you would in a face-to-face conversation, you want to ensure that you are speaking loudly enough that your listeners can hear you but not so loudly as to make them uncomfortable. In general, you will speak more loudly if you have a large audience than a small one, but only if you aren't using a microphone. Because a microphone amplifies the volume of your voice, you need only speak at a normal conversational volume to be heard.

Effective speakers also vary their volume during their speech to create certain effects. They may speak more loudly when making particular points to express

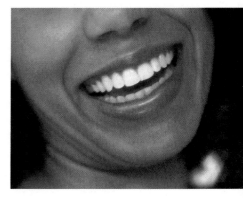

enthusiasm or conviction about those points. At other times, they may speak softly to create a serious tone or to encourage the audience to pay close attention. Varying your vocal volume will add variety to your speech and help to keep your listeners engaged in it.

What perceptions do you have of adults with high-pitched voices? How about adults with low-pitched voices?

Pitch Vocal pitch is a measure of how high or how low the voice is. Every voice has a range of pitches that it typically produces. Some voices have a naturally high pitch, others have a medium pitch, and still others have a deep, low pitch. When speakers are nervous, however, their vocal pitch becomes higher than normal. As a result, high-pitched speech often makes the speaker sound nervous and unsure, whereas a deeper pitch may convey greater confidence. If you focus on relaxing while you speak, your voice may also relax, allowing you to speak at a deeper pitch.

Perhaps more important than pitch itself is the variation in pitch used while speaking. Speakers who vary their pitch sound energetic and dynamic and are judged by others as friendly[54] and caring.[55] In contrast, those who speak in a monotone voice, with little or no variety in pitch, often come across as tired or annoying.[56] Just as effective speakers vary their volume to create certain effects, so too do they vary their pitch to hold their listeners' attention.

Articulation **Articulation** is the extent to which the speaker pronounces words clearly. A speaker who mumbles has poor articulation, which makes it difficult for listeners to understand what he or she is saying. In contrast, a speaker with good articulation enunciates each word clearly and correctly.

You can improve your articulation by avoiding five common articulation problems:

- *Addition* is caused by adding unnecessary sounds to words. For example, a person might say "real-ah-tor" instead of "realtor" or "bolth" instead of "both."
- *Deletion* occurs when a speaker omits part of a word sound, usually at the beginning or end of a word. Someone may say "frigerator" instead of "refrigerator," or "goin" instead of "going."
- *Transposition* means reversing two sounds within a word. Examples include saying "hunderd" instead of "hundred" and "perfessor" instead of "professor."
- *Substitution* is caused by replacing one part of a word with an incorrect sound. A person might say "Sundee" instead of "Sunday" or "wit" instead of "with."
- *Slurring* occurs when a speaker combines two or more words into one. "Going to" becomes "gonna" and "sort of" becomes "sorta."

Articulation errors like those aren't necessarily problematic when they occur in face-to-face conversations. Many of us are so used to committing such errors in our everyday communication that we don't even notice them. In a speech, however, poor articulation can damage the speaker's credibility.

SHARPEN
Your Skills

Record yourself practicing the delivery of a speech. Afterward, ask someone who has not heard your speech to listen carefully to the recording and to point out any words and phrases that you did not articulate clearly. Re-record your speech, taking care to correct any articulation errors.

articulation The extent to which a speaker pronounces words clearly.

fluency The smoothness of a speaker's delivery.

stuttering A speech disorder that disrupts the flow of words with repeated or prolonged sounds and involuntary pauses.

presentation aids Anything used in conjunction with a speech or presentation to stimulate listeners' senses.

Fluency Whereas articulation refers to the speaker's clarity, **fluency** refers to the smoothness of the speaker's delivery. Speeches that are fluent have an uninterrupted flow of words and phrases. There is a smooth rhythm to the delivery, without awkward pauses or false starts. In contrast, disfluent speeches are characterized by the use of filler words, such as "um" and "uh," and by the unnecessary repetition of words. Researchers have known for some time that people who speak with fluency are perceived as more effective communicators than people who do not.[57]

Speaking with fluency is a particular challenge for individuals who stutter. **Stuttering** is a speech disorder that disrupts the flow of words with repeated or prolonged sounds and involuntary pauses.[58] Stuttering usually strikes individuals early in life and can significantly impair their ability to communicate.[59] With treatment, many can overcome their stuttering before reaching adulthood. For those who do not, ongoing speech therapy can often help to improve the fluency of speech, even if it doesn't eliminate the person's stuttering entirely.[60] Vice President Joseph Biden, actors Julia Roberts and James Earl Jones, journalist John Stossel, and baseball star Johnny Damon are among many famous people who have dealt with stuttering and gone on to lead successful lives in the public sphere.

Rate, volume, pitch, articulation, and fluency aren't the only vocal elements of an effective speech delivery, but they are among the most noticeable to listeners. Paying attention to those vocal aspects as you speak will help you sound confident and credible.

Test Yourself

- What are the characteristics of effective facial expressions and eye contact?
- Why is vocal articulation important?

>> Using Presentation Aids

The Home Shopping Network (HSN) airs infomercials for everything from jewelry and handbags to steam cleaners and computers. The speakers in infomercials don't simply *tell* you about their products—they also *show* you what the products are and how they work. They may demonstrate the products in use, show photographs of the sizes and colors in which they are available, or present video-recorded testimonials from satisfied customers. Their sales strategies center on **presentation aids,** which comprise anything used in conjunction with a speech or presentation to stimulate listeners' senses. Presentation aids help the viewing audience understand the products those HSN presenters are pitching.

You can similarly incorporate presentation aids into your speech to make it memorable and engaging for your listeners. In this section, we'll look first at the benefits of using presentation aids and then at the electronic and non-electronic forms available. Finally, we'll focus on some tips for choosing and using presentation aids effectively.

Speakers in infomercials don't simply *tell* you about their products—they also *show* you what the products are and how they work.

PRESENTATION AIDS CAN ENHANCE YOUR SPEECH

Although presentation aids take time and energy to prepare, research shows that using them properly can dramatically enhance a presentation. They work by improving at least three audience responses—attention, learning, and recall.

Presentation Aids Improve Attention One benefit of using presentation aids is that the audience will pay more attention.[61] Most listeners can think much faster than you can talk, so if all they have to attend to are your words, their minds will likely wander. Incorporating one or more presentation aids will better hold your listeners' attention.

Presentation Aids Improve Learning A second benefit of using presentation aids is that the audience will learn more from the speech. One reason is that the listeners are paying closer attention, as we just considered. Another is that most people learn better when more than one of their senses is engaged. Research shows that if the speaker incorporates materials that involve the listeners' sense of sight, hearing, touch, or smell, they will learn more from the presentation than if they are only listening to the speaker's words.[62]

Presentation Aids Improve Recall Listeners will also remember more of what is said if the speaker incorporate presentation aids. One study compared listeners' recall of material from a speech that included visual aids to one that did not. Three hours after the

By the Numbers

600

Words per minute the average listener can understand.[63]

speech, audience members recalled 85 percent of the content if visual aids were used but only 70 percent if no visual aids were used. The difference was even more striking three days later, when listeners exposed to visual aids still remembered 65 percent of the content, compared to only 10 percent for listeners who did not have the benefit of visual aids.[64]

Improving attention, learning, and recall are three ways that presentation aids can benefit your listeners, thereby enhancing the effectiveness of your speech. You have several options to choose from when selecting presentation aids, including a variety of electronic and non-electronic forms.

ELECTRONIC PRESENTATION AIDS

Technology provides a wealth of opportunities for creating interesting and memorable computer-mediated presentation aids. Software programs such as PowerPoint allow speakers to integrate many of these forms into a unified presentation. In this section, we'll look at the use of text slides, graphic slides, video, and audio.

Text Slides One form of electronic presentation aid is a **text slide,** an electronic display of text used to accompany a speech. Perhaps some of your instructors use text slides created in PowerPoint to convey course material in the classroom. Text slides often take the form of bulleted lists of words or phrases that are relevant to the presenter's topic. Figure 13.1 illustrates an example of a text slide that might be used in a speech about healthy living.

Effective text slides are clear and brief. Notice, for instance, that the slide in Figure 13.1 doesn't go into detail about how much sleep a person should get or what a healthy diet should include. That detail is for the speaker to present. The slide itself should give only enough information to introduce each new point. We'll continue the discussion about maximizing the effectiveness of presentation aids later in this chapter.

Tips for Staying Healthy

- Get enough sleep
- Eat a healthy diet
- Take a multivitamin
- Avoid smoking
- Exercise daily

FIGURE 13.1 Example of a Text Slide

Graphic Slides Text slides work particularly well for presenting a bulleted list of items, such as tips for staying healthy. Another practical electronic presentation aid is a **graphic slide,** the electronic display of information in a visually compelling format that can enhance listeners' attention. Graphic slides include

- *Tables:* A **table** is the display of words or numbers in a format of columns and rows. It is a particularly effective option when you want to compare the same information for two or more groups. For instance, Figure 13.2 compares starting salaries for high school and college graduates in various fields. This simple illustration makes it easy to spot large and small differences.
- *Charts:* A **chart** is a graphic display of numeric information. Like a table, it is also useful for comparing data between two or more groups. Whereas a table presents the actual text or numbers being compared, a chart converts numbers into a *visual* display. Three types of charts are commonly used. A **pie chart,** as seen in Figure 13.3, is a graphic display of numbers in the form of a circle that is divided into segments, each of which represents a percentage of the whole; for example, a pie chart could illustrate the percentages of people around the world who practice various religions. A **line chart,** as shown in Figure 13.4, is a graphic display of numbers in the form of a line or lines that connect various data points; for example, a line chart could illustrate the percentage of U.S. American children living in poverty in various years. Finally, a **bar chart,** as seen in Figure 13.5, depicts numbers as bars on a graph, such as the percentages of people in various parts of the world who regularly use the Internet.
- *Pictures:* Visual images can be very provocative, so many speakers use pictures as presentation aids. You can embed drawings or photographs into an electronic presen-

text slide An electronic display of text used to accompany a speech.

graphic slide An electronic display of information in a visually compelling format.

table The display of words or numbers in a format of columns and rows.

chart A graphic display of numeric information.

pie chart A graphic display of numbers in the form of a circle that is divided into segments, each of which represents a percentage of the whole.

line chart A graphic display of numbers in the form of a line or lines that connect various data points.

bar chart A graphic display of numbers as bars on a graph.

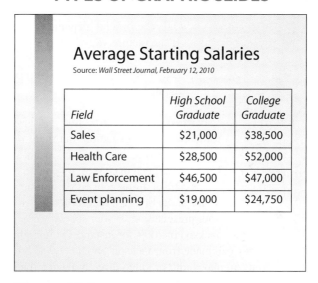

Figure 13.2 Example of a Table Slide

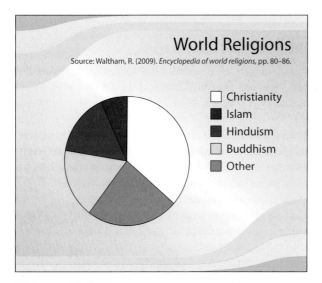

Figure 13.3 Example of a Pie Chart Slide

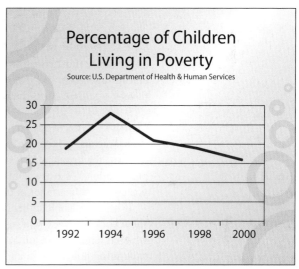

Figure 13.4 Example of a Line Chart Slide

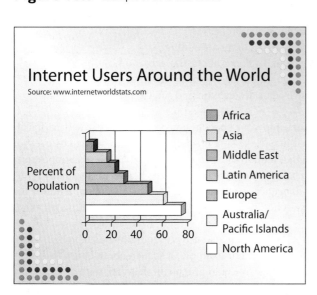

Figure 13.5 Example of a Bar Chart Slide

Figure 13.6 Example of a Photographic Slide

SHARPEN
Your Skills

Use your college website to determine the 10 most popular majors at your school. Represent your findings in a pie chart, a line chart, and a bar chart. Which one of those formats do you think an audience would find the most visually appealing? Why?

tation such as a PowerPoint document. For instance, Figure 13.6 illustrates the use of a photograph in a presentation about Air Force One, the official airplane of the president of the United States. If the picture you want to use is already in electronic form, you can easily add it to a PowerPoint slide. If you have only a hard copy of the picture, you will need to scan it first and save it in a digital format.

Video and Audio Text and graphic slides are excellent options for displaying information, but there may be occasions when you want your audience to listen to or see an audio or a video recording. Perhaps you've been in classes, for example, in which the instructor had you watch part of a movie or listen to a musical recording. You may choose to use audio or video recordings in a speech as well, when they will aid your presentation. If your speech were about the death of singer Michael Jackson in 2009, for instance, you might have your audience listen to the 911 emergency call made from Jackson's home or watch footage from his public memorial service. You can play audio or video directly from a media player, such as a CD or DVD player, or you can embed it in a PowerPoint presentation.

Electronic presentation aids are popular and can be highly effective, but they are not your only options. Non-electronic presentation aids can also enhance your speech.

NON-ELECTRONIC PRESENTATION AIDS

Some of the most engaging presentation aids are decidedly low tech. Besides using PowerPoint and other electronic media, you can also make presentation aids out of objects, flavors, textures, odors, handouts, and even people.

Objects Almost any physical object can be an effective presentation aid if it is relevant to your topic and if it can be incorporated easily and safely. If your speech is about the culture of Peru, for instance, you might bring examples of Peruvian currency or artwork to your presentation to use as visual aids. If you're speaking about French fashion, you could bring articles of clothing to show your audience.

If it isn't feasible to bring the actual object you want to show your listeners, you may be able to bring a **model,** which is a representation of the object. Suppose you're explaining how the human brain is divided into four different lobes. Chances are you won't have an actual brain to use as a visual aid, so you can bring a plastic model that will be just as effective.

You can also use objects to demonstrate processes. Let's say your goal is to explain how to decorate a wedding cake. Rather than simply telling your listeners about the process, you could bring a cake and decorate it as you describe what you're doing. That way, your listeners hear your description and see the process at the same time.

Before incorporating any object into your speech, consider whether it will be feasible for the space in which you're speaking. Make sure it is large enough to be seen by everyone in your audience but not so large that it dominates your presentation. It is also important to check with your instructor or the person in charge of the venue before bringing any type of object that might be considered dangerous or unsanitary, such as a weapon, a power tool, a hot plate, or a live animal. Some school policies prohibit having such objects on campus.

Flavors, Textures, and Odors You can also use presentation aids to appeal to your listeners' senses of taste, touch, and smell. For example, a speech about citrus fruit might incorporate slices of orange, lemon, tangerine, and grapefruit that your audience can taste. A presentation about interior design might use swatches of different types of carpeting that

model A representation of an object.

your listeners can feel. If you're speaking about men's cologne, you might bring fragrance samples for your audience to smell. When your topic relates to something that is tasted, touched, or smelled, using those types of presentation aids can be a particularly effective way of demonstrating your speech points.

Handouts Another type of non-electronic presentation aid is a handout. Most handouts are copies of written material that listeners keep after the speech is over. Using a handout can be especially effective when you want your listeners to have more information than you can reasonably address during your presentation. When incorporating a handout, make certain to bring enough copies for everyone in the audience. If you need your listeners to see your handout while you're speaking, distribute it at the beginning of your speech. If not, distribute it at the end so that it doesn't distract your listeners' attention while you're speaking.

People Finally, you can use people—including yourself—as presentation aids. Suppose your speech is about the Chinese martial art of tai chi. You might choose to show your audience some of the fundamental movements of tai chi by either performing them yourself or having someone else perform them. Similarly, if you are speaking about the procedure for measuring blood pressure, you might perform a blood pressure test on someone to demonstrate the technique. In both cases, using a person as a presentation aid is more engaging than showing your audience photographs or video recordings, because your demonstration is live.

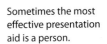

Sometimes the most effective presentation aid is a person.

CHOOSING AND USING PRESENTATION AIDS

If they are used well, presentation aids can greatly enhance a speech. However, if they are not incorporated correctly, presentation aids can be distracting or even dangerous, greatly diminishing the effectiveness of a speech. This section gives tips for choosing and using presentation aids for maximum effectiveness.

Remember the Goal No matter what type of presentation aids you choose, remember that they are meant to *aid* your speech. Your presentation aids should never themselves become your focus. Instead, they should be like accessories, embellishing your delivery but not overpowering it. Remember that your listeners' primary focus should be on you and what you have to say.

Consider the Context Think about which presentation aids will work best for your audience, the layout of the room, and the resources available to you. Pay particular attention to

- *The size and arrangement of the room:* Make sure that everyone will be able to see, hear, touch, taste, or smell the presentation aids you plan to use. If you're creating a PowerPoint presentation, use a font that is large enough for everyone to read comfortably. Before your speech, try out your presentation aids in the space where you'll be speaking; check that every listener will be able to take advantage of them.
- *The time available for the speech:* Be certain that you'll have adequate time to set up and use your presentation aids effectively. If you can, load your PowerPoint onto the computer in the presentation room before your speech so that you need only to open the document when you are ready to speak. Also be sure that you don't have too many slides to get through in the time allotted for your speech. You don't want to have to rush through or skip slides to stay within your time limit.
- *The resources available:* Determine beforehand whether you will have everything you need to make your presentation aids work. If you're bringing an object that requires electric power, make certain that there is an accessible outlet and that you have a long enough power cord to reach it. If you plan to use PowerPoint, ensure ahead of time that a computer, projector, and screen are all available. Particularly when you're

My PowerPoint Slides Need Bells and Whistles—Right?

PowerPoint gives speakers the ability to create colorful, eye-catching audiovisual aids for their presentations. Even if their primary purpose in using PowerPoint is to communicate text, many speakers enhance their PowerPoint slides with features such as pictures and sound effects. They often do so out of the belief that such embellishments will grab their listeners' attention and thus cause them to remember more of the speech. Is it fact—or fiction—that these special effects work?

Research has found that they usually do *not* serve that intended purpose. Although pictures and sound effects might successfully capture your listeners' attention, they will draw that attention away from the content of your speech. As a result, your audience will learn and remember less from your presentation than if you use simple, straightforward PowerPoint slides with text only. A study by behavioral scientists Robert Bartsch and Kristi Cobern found that pictures in PowerPoint slides were particularly distracting if they were not directly relevant to the content of the text. To use PowerPoint effectively, it's therefore best to forgo unnecessary sights and sounds, making sure that pictures and sound effects you do include are directly related to your various points.

Source: Bartsch, R. A., & Cobern, K. M. (2003). Effectiveness of PowerPoint presentations in lectures. *Computers & Education, 41*, 77–86.

speaking in an unfamiliar room, don't take anything for granted. Rather, double-check to be sure you will have everything you need.

Strive for Simplicity Choose or create presentation aids that are as simple and straightforward as possible so that your listeners will pay attention to their content instead of their form. For example, develop PowerPoint slides that are clean and uncluttered. Stay away from sound effects, fancy slide transitions, and pictures or photographs that are irrelevant to the content of the slide. As you'll discover in Fact or Fiction? distracting features can reduce your listeners' ability to learn.

Strive for simplicity with the timing of your presentation aids as well. Make a presentation aid visible to your audience only when you are ready to use it. Then turn it off or put it away when you no longer need it. In this way, you will encourage your audience to pay attention to your aids only when you are using them.

Is it ethical to include racially offensive language in a speech if you are simply quoting someone else? Why or why not?

Be Ethical Stay away from any presentation aid that might harm your audience physically or emotionally. In that category are horrifying or disgusting photographs, audio or video recordings with profane or offensive language, and objects that produce dangerously loud sounds or noxious fumes. Using those sorts of presentation aids is unethical because it places your listeners in danger of being hurt, either physically or emotionally. If you must use a potentially harmful aid in your speech, explicitly warn your audience about it at the beginning of your presentation and again right before you introduce it. For instance, if you're speaking about open-heart surgery and feel you should include a photograph of the surgical procedure, tell your listeners beforehand that you will be showing a picture that they may find distasteful, so that they have the option to look away.

If you plan to incorporate presentation aids into your speech, be sure to use them when you rehearse.

In addition, give credit to the source of any information you present. When you prepare a PowerPoint slide with data that you did not generate yourself, include the source of the data on the slide. Doing so is an important way to avoid plagiarism (see Chapter 12).

Practice with Your Presentation Aids If you will be incorporating presentation aids when you deliver your speech, be sure to use them when you rehearse. Practice advancing from slide to slide in your PowerPoint document—manually or with a remote control—so that you can do so effortlessly during your presentation. Perhaps you must set up or uncover your presentation aid *during* your speech instead of beforehand. If so, rehearse those moves so that you can continue speaking while doing the necessary tasks. That way, you will avoid disrupting the flow of your speech with long, awkward pauses.

Have a Backup Plan Regardless of the type of presentation aid you plan to use, something can always go wrong that will prevent you from using it. You might forget the USB drive containing your PowerPoint document, or the computer on which you planned to run it might fail. The light bulb in your projector could burn out, or the room could lose power. The photocopier on which you planned to duplicate your handouts might be jammed, or the person who was to demonstrate tai chi moves might get sick and cancel.

Before using any presentation aid, it's thus crucial to think through everything that might go wrong and to have a backup plan. Bring a laptop computer containing your PowerPoint document to use in case you forget your USB drive or in the event that the computer in the room fails. Copy your handouts a day or two before your speech. Learn the tai chi moves well enough to demonstrate them yourself if you have to. Being prepared to respond to such contingencies will help your speech succeed under any circumstances.

Test Yourself

- Why is it beneficial to use presentation aids?
- What options are available for creating graphic slides?
- How can you engage your listeners' senses of touch, taste, and smell?
- What must you do to use presentation aids effectively?

For REVIEW >>

- **What are the most common forms of speech delivery?**

  Most speakers deliver their speeches in one of four formats: impromptu, extemporaneous, scripted, or memorized.

- **How can you manage stage fright?**

  Remember that stage fright is normal, and try to channel your excess energy toward a good performance. Practice visualizing a successful speech, and maintain a positive attitude.

- **How can you deliver a speech effectively?**

  Pay attention to what you look like (including your facial expressions, eye contact, posture, gestures, and personal appearance) and what you sound like (including your vocal rate, volume, pitch, articulation, and fluency). Select presentation aids that will enhance your speech, and incorporate them appropriately.

Pop Quiz

Multiple Choice

1. Ping is called upon to give a speech with almost no preparation. Her style of delivery will be
   a. impromptu
   b. extemporaneous
   c. scripted
   d. memorized

2. Research shows that anticipatory public speaking anxiety usually peaks
   a. when the speech is first assigned
   b. during preparation of the speech
   c. immediately before delivery of the speech
   d. two minutes after delivery is complete

3. Effective speakers ensure that their gestures
   a. appear planned rather than spontaneous
   b. are appropriate in size
   c. are excessive in number
   d. all of the above

4. Alan has a habit of pronouncing the word *both* as "bolth." The articulation error he is making is
   a. addition
   b. transposition
   c. substitution
   d. slurring

5. The type of chart that displays percentages of a whole, such as the percentage of people who practice each major world religion, is a

   a. table
   b. pie chart
   c. line chart
   d. bar chart

Fill in the Blank

6. A _____ speech is written word for word and then read aloud exactly as written.

7. _____ is your body's reaction to any type of perceived threat.

8. _____ is a technique whereby you develop a mental image of yourself giving a successful speech.

9. The smoothness of your vocal delivery is known as your _____.

10. A representation of an object that you might use as a presentation aid is called a _____.

Answers: 1. a; 2. c; 3. b; 4. a; 5. b; 6. scripted; 7. stress; 8. visualization; 9. fluency; 10. model

KEY TERMS

impromptu speech   312
extemporaneous speech   313
scripted speech   313
memorized speech   314
stage fright   316
stress   316
anxiety   317
anticipatory anxiety   317
fight-or-flight response   317
visualization   321

desensitization   321
avatars   321
articulation   326
fluency   326
stuttering   326
presentation aids   327
text slide   328
graphic slide   328
table   328
chart   328
pie chart   328
line chart   328
bar chart   328
model   330

14

SPEAKING IN

DANGERS OF MISINFORMATION ONLINE

Sexually active adolescents often seek information about sexual health online, especially if they feel uncomfortable talking to a parent or doctor. The Internet can be a rich source of medical information, but it can also foster misinformation. Do most websites offer teenagers accurate data about sexual health? To find out, Dr. Sophia Yen, a professor of medicine at Stanford University, surveyed 35 of the most popular websites that adolescents consult for sexual health information. She looked specifically at what each site said about issues such as birth control, emergency contraception, and sexually transmitted diseases. Her analysis uncovered incorrect or incomplete information on 41 percent of the sites. In particular, she found that many sites perpetuate myths about sexual health, such as that emergency contraception triggers spontaneous abortion, that hormonal contraceptives cause weight gain, and that herpes cannot be transmitted through kissing. Dr. Yen warns that such misinformation can hurt adolescents by encouraging them to adopt unsafe sexual practices. She recommends that anyone seeking medical information online steer toward websites associated with university medical centers, as experts will have reviewed the information on those sites to ensure its accuracy.[1]

FORMATIVELY

- What methods can we use to inform?
- In what ways should we frame an informative speech?
- Through what strategies can we hone our informative-speaking skills?

We rely on accurate information from websites, newspapers, interpersonal encounters, and many other sources to make decisions in our personal and professional lives. Having good information can empower us to make wise choices. Often, however, the manner in which information is presented matters as much as the information itself. If the information we receive from others isn't accurate, complete, or understandable, or if it doesn't grab our attention, it may lead us to make poor decisions. The same is true when we have occasion to speak informatively to others. Unless we convey our message clearly and completely and in a way that engages our listeners' attention, their decision making might be compromised.

In this chapter, we'll explore the various methods for informing an audience and ways to frame the speech topic for maximum effectiveness. We'll also examine several techniques for presenting successfully and peruse an award-winning informative speech.

>> Choosing a Method of Informing

In the past two decades, more than 24,000 college graduates have participated in Teach for America, a nonprofit organization that recruits individuals to teach for two years in low-income communities throughout the United States.[2] Unlike traditional teachers who have earned undergraduate degrees in education, most Teach for America instructors have no training in teaching practices when they apply for the program. However, many recruits quickly learn that there are several ways to impart knowledge to their students and that although one method may be ineffective, another often works well. The same can be said for any type of informative speaking.

We can approach **informative speaking**—publicly addressing others to increase their knowledge, understanding, or skills—in several different ways. The techniques available to us include defining, describing, explaining, and demonstrating. Which method or methods we choose depends on our speech topic and audience.

INFORMATIVE SPEECHES CAN DEFINE

One method of informing an audience is **defining:** providing the meaning of a word or concept. Let's say you want to educate your listeners about the credit industry. You might focus part of your speech on defining the term *FICO score,* a widely used personal credit score calculated by the Fair Isaac Corporation. An individual's FICO score strongly influ-

informative speaking Publicly addressing others to increase their knowledge, understanding, or skills.

defining Providing the meaning of a word or concept.

etymology The origin or history of a word.

synonyms Words that have the same meaning.

antonyms Words that have opposite meanings.

ences his or her ability to obtain credit, so knowing what a FICO score is can help your audience to understand how the credit industry works.

Defining a term may sound straightforward because it only requires that you connect the term to its meaning. Meanings can be highly contested, however. How a society defines the word *marriage,* for instance, differentiates those who can enjoy the benefits of such a relationship from those who cannot. Likewise, how a government defines the word *torture* dictates what methods its military personnel can use in combat and interrogations. Individuals often have dramatically different perspectives on how words such as *marriage* and *torture* ought to be defined, largely because the definitions of such terms have consequences for so many people.

If defining a word or concept will help you inform your listeners, you can choose from several methods:

- *Identify the denotative meaning.* You may recall from Chapter 4 that a term's denotative meaning is its dictionary definition. In a speech about global warming, for instance, you could define *greenhouse gases* as "atmospheric gases that absorb and emit radiation."
- *Explain the connotative meaning.* A term's connotative meaning is its socially or culturally implied meaning. One connotative meaning of the word *home,* for example, is "a place where you feel safe and secure."
- *Provide the etymology.* The **etymology** of a term is its origin or history. In a speech about affectionate communication, you could explain that the word *affection* derives from the Latin word *affectio,* meaning "an emotion of the mind."
- *Give synonyms or antonyms.* You can define a word by identifying **synonyms,** words that have the same meaning, or **antonyms,** words that have the opposite meaning. Synonyms for the term *normal* include *usual, ordinary,* and *typical,* whereas antonyms include *abnormal, irregular,* and *odd.*
- *Define by example.* You may help your audience understand a concept by providing examples that illustrate its meaning. In a speech about the immune system, you might define the term *pathogen* by giving examples of types of pathogens, such as viruses, bacteria, fungi, and parasites.
- *Compare-and-contrast definitions.* You can discuss similarities and differences between two or more definitions of a term. To some

SHARPEN Your Skills

Select one word or concept and define it according to its denotative and connotative meanings, etymology, synonyms, antonyms, and examples.

people, the definition of *family* is limited to legal and biological relationships, whereas to others, it includes anyone to whom they feel emotionally close. If you were speaking about the concept of family, you could compare and contrast those two definitions of the term.

INFORMATIVE SPEECHES CAN DESCRIBE

A second way to inform your audience about something is to describe it. **Describing** means using words to depict or portray a person, a place, an object, or an experience. You might describe the arrangement of rooms in the campus student center or the experience of having your eyes dilated by an optometrist using language that creates a mental image for your listeners.

Two forms of description are common in informative speeches. The first form, **representation,** means describing something in terms of its physical or psychological attributes. You could represent the Great Wall of China by telling your audience what it looks like or what kind of awe it inspires when people see it. When you describe by representation, you are helping your listeners imagine their physical or emotional experiences if they were to encounter what you are describing.

The second form of description common in informative speeches is **narration,** which means describing a series of events in sequence. You can think of narra-

An informative speech about the Great Wall of China could describe its physical dimensions or detail the awe it inspires in visitors.

tion as storytelling. In an informative speech about the field of veterinary medicine, for instance, you could describe what your aunt went through to become a veterinarian or tell a story about your first visit to an animal hospital.

Many speakers combine representation and narration. Let's say you wanted to teach your audience about the work of film director James Cameron. You could use representation to describe some of the memorable characters he has featured in his movies, such as *Avatar* and *Titanic.* You could use narration to describe how Cameron and his former wife, Kathryn Bigelow, were both nominated for the Academy Award for best director in 2010 and how Bigelow edged out Cameron for her work on the film *The Hurt Locker.* Incorporating both forms of description can produce a richer mental image for your listeners than either form can evoke on its own.

INFORMATIVE SPEECHES CAN EXPLAIN

In many informative presentations, the speaker explains something to the audience. **Explaining** means revealing why something occurred or how something works. For example, you might explain how Larry Page and Sergey Brin, two PhD students at Stanford University, developed the search engine Google. You could also explain how cancer cells spread through the body or why people in Great Britain drive on the left side of the road.

When offering an explanation, speakers must use clear, concrete language and avoid jargon that will be unfamiliar to listeners. Suppose that in an informative speech about statistics, you hear a speaker explain, "Mean scores are considered significantly different only if the p-value is smaller than the critical alpha." Although that explanation would make perfect sense to a statistician, it won't make sense to you unless you already understand what mean scores, p-values, and critical alphas are and why they matter. It is always useful to assess how much your listeners already know about your speech topic. That consideration is particularly crucial when you are explaining something, to ensure that your audience will understand all of the elements of your explanation.

describing Using words to depict or portray a person, a place, an object, or an experience.

representation Describing something in terms of its physical or psychological attributes.

narration Describing a series of events in sequence.

explaining Revealing why something occurred or how something works.

In Chapter 11 we examined the various goals a speaker might have in planning a public presentation, and we differentiated between speaking to inform and speaking to persuade. Of all the techniques speakers can use to inform an audience, explaining often comes closest to crossing the line from informing to persuading. The reason is that people's opinions and perspectives frequently influence their explanations of events or processes. In July 2009, for instance, Henry Louis Gates, a renowned African American scholar at Harvard University, was arrested while entering his own home after a neighbor allegedly mistook him for a burglar. The Cambridge, Massachusetts, police department explained the arrest as stemming from a simple misunderstanding. Gates explained it as the result of overt racism. Either explanation may have merit, but the explanation you believe may be influenced by your own attitudes about race or your own experiences with law enforcement. Therefore, by explaining Gates's arrest as the product of either an innocent mistake or a racist act, an informative speaker would implicitly be persuading the audience to believe the explanation being offered.

You can avoid crossing the line from informative to persuasive speaking by keeping your remarks **objective**—that is, based on facts rather than opinions. When you speak objectively, you avoid trying to convince listeners of a particular point of view. In comparison, remarks in a persuasive speech are **subjective**—that is, biased toward a specific conclusion. Consult Table 14.1 for some key differences between informative and persuasive speaking.

Henry Louis Gates

INFORMATIVE SPEECHES CAN DEMONSTRATE

Many people learn better by *seeing* how to do something rather than by simply hearing how to do it. Therefore, one way to maximize the effectiveness of an explanation is to incorporate a demonstration. **Demonstrating** means showing how to do something by doing it as it is explained. For instance, you could teach listeners how to do a Sudoku puzzle, clean a camera lens, or stretch properly before exercise by demonstrating those activities during your speech.

When you're demonstrating a process, it's important to describe each step as you do it. Let's say your informative speech is about how to prepare a Caprese salad. You might start by identifying each of the ingredients you'll be using: tomato, mozzarella cheese, basil, black pepper, and balsamic vinegar. Then, as you slice the tomatoes and mozzarella, tell your audience what you're doing ("I am slicing the tomato and cheese into equal-size pieces so they'll be easier to eat"). When you chop the basil, describe how you're doing it ("First I'm going to cut the stem off each basil leaf; then I'll roll the leaves together and give them a rough chop"). Explain how you are arranging the tomatoes, cheese, and basil on a plate ("I'm interspersing slices of tomato and cheese on the

How could you explain the Gates story in a way that simply informs but does not persuade your audience?

Table 14.1   To Inform or To Persuade?

Avoid turning an informative speech into a persuasive speech by keeping in mind these fundamental differences.

	Persuasive Speech	Informative Speech
Focus	What should be	What is
Evidence	Facts and opinions that support the predetermined conclusion	Facts and information relevant to the topic
Goal	To convince listeners to adopt a particular belief or action	To educate listeners about the speech topic

objective Based on facts rather than opinions.

subjective Biased toward a specific conclusion.

demonstrating Showing how to do something by doing it as it is explained.

Show and Tell: People Learn Best by Seeing *and* Hearing

Speech instructors often encourage students to use demonstrations on the assumption that listeners learn best by seeing *and* hearing rather than by just seeing *or* just hearing. Is that assumption fact or fiction?

Research suggests that it is a fact. Let's say that in addition to describing how to download applications on the iPad, you also *demonstrate* that task by downloading applications during your speech. Studies show that students who encounter both visual and auditory stimuli accurately recall 11 percent more of what they learn than do students exposed only to visual stimuli, and 8 percent more than students exposed only to auditory stimuli. The explanation may be that we process verbal and visual information separately, so that when we are presented with both types of information, they reinforce each other. Some of us seem to be primarily *visual learners,* who learn best by seeing. Others seem to be primarily *auditory learners,* who learn best by hearing. Studies have found, however, that most of us learn well from both what we see *and* what we hear. So, for most listeners, a presenter who both shows and tells in a demonstration enhances the listeners' ability to learn.

ASK YOURSELF

- How do you learn best? In what ways do you notice that your own learning is influenced by verbal and visual stimuli?
- Based on the research described here, how do you think listeners' learning would be affected if a speaker engaged an additional sense—such as their sense of touch or smell—in addition to using visual and auditory stimuli?

Sources: See Paivio, A. (1990). *Mental representations: A dual-coding approach.* Oxford, England: Oxford University Press; Plass, J. L., Chun, D. M., Mayer, R. E., & Leutner, D. (1998). Supporting visual and verbal learning preferences in a second-language multimedia learning environment. *Journal of Educational Psychology, 90,* 25–36.

plate in a vertical pattern and then sprinkling the chopped basil over the top"). Describe seasoning the salad with black pepper and balsamic vinegar as you do so. In this way, your audience will both *see* and *hear* every step of the process.

Does demonstrating while giving a speech enhance listeners' ability to learn? Check out the Fact or Fiction? box to find out.

If you want to include a demonstration in your informative speech, take note of the advice offered in Chapter 13 about using presentation aids. In particular, make sure you will have everything you need to run your demonstration, such as adequate space, the right equipment, and access to a power supply if you require one. Ensure that you can conduct the demonstration safely and that it won't pose a threat to anyone in your audience. Be certain that you can complete the demonstration within the time allocated for your speech, and have a backup plan in case any elements of your demonstration fail.

- What options do you have for defining a term or concept?
- How are representation and narration different?
- What does it mean to explain?
- Why are demonstrations effective?

Test Yourself

>> Selecting and Framing the Topic

Students who compete in speech and debate understand the importance of choosing a compelling topic and framing it appropriately for their listeners. They put their speaking skills on the line in tournament after tournament, so they can't afford to bore their audiences.

Imagine that *you* are taking part in an informative-speaking competition with undergraduates from around the country. How will you choose an intriguing topic? How can you frame your presentation in such a way that your listeners will care about and pay attention to the content? In this section, we'll explore eight categories of topics for informative speeches, and we'll see that effective informative speakers frame their presentations in two connected ways: first by relating themselves to their topic and then by relating the topic to their audience.

SELECT A CAPTIVATING TOPIC

When planning an informative speech, many people have difficulty selecting a topic that will capture and hold their listeners' attention. That decision needn't be a challenge, however, because the list of potential topics for an informative speech is virtually unlimited. Communication scholars Ron Allen and Ray McKerrow have identified eight categories of topics that work particularly well for informative speeches:[3]

- *Issues:* According to Allen and McKerrow, *issues* are problems or points of controversy concerning which people desire resolution. You could choose to speak on a contemporary issue facing the United States, such as the economic recession, unemployment, or the wars in Afghanistan and Iraq. You might also select an issue that has been controversial for some time, such as affirmative action or sex education in public schools. When you focus your informative speech on an issue, your purpose isn't to persuade your listeners to adopt any particular point of view but rather to give them the facts necessary to form their own opinions.

- *Events:* *Events* are occurrences that are noteworthy for the meanings they represent. You may choose to speak about an event that was publicly experienced, such as the swine flu or the death of Senator Edward Kennedy. You might also elect to speak about a significant event in your personal life, such as spending time in a foreign culture or going through a religious conversion. In each instance, you can educate your audience about the event and communicate the significant meaning it has, either for your listeners or for you.

- *People:* Many informative speakers focus their presentations on other people. You might choose to discuss an individual who made history, such as Keith Ellison, the first Muslim elected to the U.S. Congress. You could talk about someone who is noteworthy for acts of charity, such as the late Mother Teresa of Calcutta. You might talk about the life of a person in the public spotlight, such as golfer Tiger Woods or pop singer Lady Gaga. You could also focus your remarks on a group, such as the Amish or the Apollo 11 astronauts.

- *Places:* Cable television's Travel Channel is popular because it informs viewers about interesting and exotic places. You can do the same by focusing your speech on a place you find significant or intriguing. It might be a place you have personally visited, or it could be a locale where daily life is substantially different than it is for your listeners, such as Cuba, Iceland, or Yemen. You can even focus on a place in a specific historical period, such as China during the Shang Dynasty or Moscow before the breakup of the former Soviet Union.

- *Objects:* Allen and McKerrow have categorized as *objects* any entities that are nonhuman. Those can include living or animate objects, such as the California giant redwoods and Comet Hale-Bopp. They can also include inanimate objects, such as the guillotine and the Empire State Building. Effective speeches about an object often

Who are three people you think your peers would find fascinating to learn more about?

By the Numbers

195

Number of countries in the world on which you could focus your informative speech.[4]

educate listeners about the object's evolution and development or its significance in history, culture, politics, or ecology.

- *Concepts:* Whereas objects are tangible items, *concepts* are abstract ideas. Oppression, compassion, integrity, bias, and forgiveness are all examples of concepts because each is a notion or an idea rather than a concrete object. Some powerful speeches have focused on concepts that were significant to their audiences. In March 2008, for instance, then–presidential hopeful Barack Obama delivered what has become a landmark speech about the politics of race in the United States. Race isn't an object that can be seen or felt; it's a complex idea and one that affects millions of lives as a social concept.

- *Processes:* As we saw earlier in the chapter, many informative speeches describe or demonstrate a *process,* which is a series of actions that culminates in a specific result. For instance, you might focus on a natural process, such as how coal becomes diamond or how a canyon forms from water erosion. You might instead focus on a human-created process, such as the design of currency or the line of succession to the British throne. You can also use your informative speech to teach your listeners a process, such as how to tie a bowline knot or crop a digital photo.

- *Policies:* Finally, informative speeches can focus on *policies,* that is, programs that aim to guide future decision making or to achieve some goal. For instance, you might inform your listeners about policies that existed in the past but were overturned, such as school segregation in the United States and apartheid in South Africa. You might also speak on current policies, such as those affecting gays and lesbians in the military. Some humorous informative speeches focus on bizarre policies and laws, such as the New Jersey prohibition against frowning at police officers and the Nevada law against riding a camel on public highways.

SHARPEN
Your Skills

Generate a list of eight topics—one representing each of Allen and McKerrow's categories—about which you could speak informatively.

As we've seen, a wide range of topics is available for an informative speech, so be creative! Consider issues, events, people, places, objects, concepts, processes, or policies that you feel are well suited to yourself and your audience. As you do so, however, remember that your listeners' cultural background can influence what topics are appropriate. Although to U.S. audiences few topics are considered *taboo*—or impolite to discuss publicly—listeners from other cultures may be surprised or even offended by certain topics. Table 14.2 presents some examples of culturally taboo topics.

Once you have selected your topic, you will want to frame it for your listeners in a compelling way, as we'll see in the next two sections.

Children of deaf adults, or CODAs, often learn to communicate through sign language even before they can speak.

RELATE YOURSELF TO YOUR TOPIC

Recall the discussion in Chapter 11 of the advantages of choosing a speech topic that you know and care about. By doing so, you ensure that you'll have both the knowledge and the enthusiasm to speak in a way that engages and informs. In some instances, your personal connection to the topic may be evident to your audience when you begin speaking. For example, if everyone in your public speaking class knows that you come from abroad, your listeners will understand why you have chosen to speak informatively about international students' experiences. On some occasions, however, your personal connection to your topic may not be immediately evident. In such cases, it is important to explain why your topic is meaningful to you.

For example, one student expressed her personal connection to the topic of the children of deaf adults in this way:

Unlike most of you, I didn't speak my first word. Rather, I communicated my first word—mother—in American Sign Language. You see, I'm what is commonly referred to as a "CODA," a child of deaf adults. As the only person in my immediate family who can hear, I learned to sign before

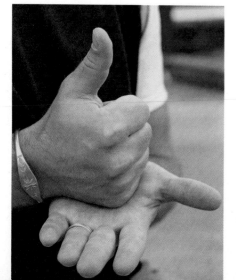

Table 14.2 Cultural Do's and Don'ts: Managing Taboo Topics

Teachers of English as a second language (ESL) are taught to avoid particular topics when speaking to certain groups around the world. If your audience consists largely of listeners from one of these societies, you, too, may find it prudent to avoid certain speech topics—or at least to exercise sensitivity when discussing them. What topics, if any, would you consider taboo in *your own* culture?

Country	Topics to Avoid
China	Tibet and the Dalai Lama; the Falun-Gong movement
France	Jobs, financial success, and wealth; immigration
India	Poverty; religious beliefs; India's relationship with Pakistan
Muslim countries	Sex and sexual practices
Japan	World War II
Korea	Politics; personal family matters; the relationship between North and South Korea
Mexico	Pollution; illegal immigration; sexuality
Taiwan	Politics; Taiwan's relationship with mainland China
Thailand	National security; criticisms of the monarchy

I learned to speak. I'd like to tell you today about what it's like to grow up as a CODA, straddling the fence between the deaf and hearing worlds.

To make her connection to the topic of CODAs more evident to her audience, this student augmented parts of her speech with sign language. By explaining her background and demonstrating her fluency in signing, she made clear to her listeners why the topic of CODAs and their experiences was relevant to her.

Relating yourself to your topic is advantageous for two reasons. First, it establishes for your audience that you have the credibility to speak with authority about the topic. If you have training, personal experience, or a vested interest in what you're discussing, you are

Listeners will be more interested and invested in your topic if they believe it matters personally to you.

likely to be knowledgeable about it. Explaining your connection to the topic establishes you as a qualified speaker whose words can be trusted. The second advantage is that your listeners will care more about the topic if they believe it matters personally to you than if they do not. You may know from your own experience that it is difficult to get excited about a speech when not even the speaker seems to care about the topic. In contrast, when you make clear to your audience that you are enthusiastic about or deeply invested in the topic of the speech, the audience is more likely to care about what you have to say.

RELATE YOUR TOPIC TO YOUR AUDIENCE

Seeing that *you* know and care about your topic will matter to your listeners. What will matter to them even more, however, is seeing why *they* should know and care about your topic. To frame an informative speech effectively, you must therefore make clear how the topic is relevant to your audience.

Establish Listeners' Vested Interest in Your Topic Some topics will be easy to relate to your listeners' current experiences. Suppose you are speaking to a group of college-bound high school students about strategies for getting financial aid. That topic will matter to your listeners because many of them will require financial assistance to get a college education. Those listeners therefore have a **vested interest**—an inherent motivation to pay attention—in your topic, and you need only point that out to relate your topic to your audience successfully.

Establish Your Topic's Relevance to Listeners In other instances, it's necessary to tell your listeners why they should care about your topic. Even if your audience doesn't have direct experience with the topic of your speech, you can often make it relevant by asking your listeners to imagine themselves in a hypothetical situation. Notice how the following introduction accomplishes that goal:

> *Imagine this: You're spending the holidays with family and you've just gotten up from a delicious dinner when you see your dad stumble and fall to the floor. At first, you think he just tripped, but his eyes are closed and he isn't moving. Your mom runs to call 911, but it could be several minutes before anyone arrives. Would you know what to do to keep your father alive until help gets there? You would if you'd been trained in cardiopulmonary resuscitation, or CPR. Today, I'm going to tell you what CPR is, how it works, and where you can learn to perform it. If you know how to administer CPR properly, you may be able to save the life of someone near and dear to you.*

In that introduction, the speaker makes clear why the topic of CPR is relevant to the listeners. The speaker relates the topic to listeners, even if they have no direct experience with it.

Check out The Competent Communicator to practice framing topics for an informative speech.

- **What are Allen and McKerrow's categories of informative speech topics?**
- **Why is it advantageous to relate yourself to your speech topic?**
- **What is a vested interest?**

Test Yourself

>> Honing Your Informative-Speaking Skills

Even if you have chosen a compelling topic and successfully framed it for your audience, you must still deliver your speech in a way that will draw—and hold—your listeners' attention. In this section, we'll explore several strategies for delivering an informative

vested interest An inherent motivation to pay attention.

It's All Relative: Framing Your Informative Topic

When selecting the topic of your informative speech, consider how you can relate yourself to your topic and how you can relate your topic to your audience. Doing so with a few different topics can help you decide which topic is best for your presentation. In this exercise, select three potential informative-speaking topics, each of which represents a different category in Allen and McKerrow's list. For each topic, list two ways you could relate yourself to the topic and two ways you could relate the topic to your audience.

	Topic	How the Topic Relates to Me	How the Topic Relates to My Listeners
1.	_____	_____	_____
		_____	_____
2.	_____	_____	_____
		_____	_____
3.	_____	_____	_____
		_____	_____

Based on your responses, which of the three topics you chose do you think you could frame most effectively? Why?

speech effectively, including creating information hunger, being organized, making learning easy, involving your audience, and being ethical.

CREATE INFORMATION HUNGER

Perhaps you've had the experience of taking a high school or college course that you thought would be boring, only to be surprised by how interesting the instructor made the material. The instructor inspired your interest by creating **information hunger,** the desire to learn. As an informative speaker, you can do the same with your listeners by sparking their curiosity and giving them reason to want the information you have. In short, you can show your listeners "what's in it for them" if they pay attention to your speech.

Recall from Chapter 1 the five types of needs—physical, relational, identity, spiritual, and instrumental—that communication helps us meet. An excellent way to generate information hunger is to connect your topic to one or more of those needs. By doing so, you imply the benefits of listening to the information you have to share, creating a desire for that information among your listeners.

Imagine that you're preparing a speech about food. Let's look at some examples of how you might connect that topic to each of those five needs:

- *Physical needs:* Teach listeners to prepare a meal that is both healthy and flavorful.
- *Relational needs:* Discuss the importance of cooking rituals—such as preparing a Thanksgiving dinner—in maintaining family relationships.
- *Identity needs:* Explain how individuals with an eating disorder view their consumption of food as a central component of their identity.
- *Spiritual needs:* Explore various uses and meanings of food and drink in religious ceremonies, such as communion, with your audience.
- *Instrumental needs:* Teach your listeners how to find the best deals on food staples, such as meat, bread, and milk.

information hunger The desire to learn.

An informative speech about food presents many opportunities to connect to your listeners' needs, including their relational needs.

By connecting the information in your speech to one or more of your listeners' needs, you make that information relevant to *them* and thereby motivate the audience to pay attention to your words and message.

What particular aspects of a presentation motivate you to learn?

BE ORGANIZED

Studies confirm what you probably already know: We learn better from presentations that are well organized.[5] That may be so because most of us process information best in a limited number of segments at a time; thus, a speech that presents easily identified "chunks" of information in a coherent order is easiest for listeners to follow.[6] Just *appearing* organized, in fact, is enough to boost your listeners' retention of what you say—that's how powerful organization is.[7]

Creating a well-organized informative speech is easy. Recall the different components of a speech—introduction, body, conclusion, and transitions—and the role each component plays in making your presentation coherent. As you prepare your informative speech, work on each component individually to ensure that it is serving its necessary functions. If each component does its job, your speech will have a logical, organized structure, and you will be poised for success.

Use the checklist in Table 14.3 to make certain that your informative speech includes all the elements necessary for an organized presentation.

MAKE IT EASY TO LISTEN

We've all encountered speakers who seem oblivious to their listeners' needs and desires—for example, presenters who talk too long or use unfamiliar technical jargon. It is difficult to pay attention to such speakers or to care about what they're saying. To avoid that reaction from your own audience, make it easy for them to listen to you by keeping your message short, using clear language, starting with familiar concepts, repeating your key points, and sprinkling in humor when it's appropriate.

Keep It Short In most instances, you will have a specific time slot for your informative speech. Your time frame will limit the amount of material you can effectively discuss in your presentation, so make sure you include only as much information as you can reasonably cover.

Table 14.3   Pull It Together: Organize Your Informative Speech

As you prepare an informative speech, remember your priorities for each component of your presentation.

Section	Priorities
Introduction	1. Generate interest in your topic. 2. Present your thesis statement. 3. Relate your topic to yourself and to your listeners. 4. Preview your main points.
Body	1. Present each of your main points, with appropriate transitions between them. 2. Make sure you have at least three main points and that they are sufficiently related to each other.
Conclusion	1. Reinforce your central idea by reviewing your main points. 2. Create a memorable moment for your audience.
Transitions	1. Use transitions to review the material you've presented already. 2. Use transitions to preview material yet to be presented.

By the Numbers

14

Percentage more material that college students recalled after listening to a presentation with humor versus one without humor.[8]

Keep It Simple It might seem self-evident to say that your listeners must understand what you're saying before they can learn from it, but many speakers forget that crucial consideration. A common mistake for informative speakers is to use technical language or jargon that they erroneously assume their audience understands. A better approach—particularly if you're unsure whether certain words will be familiar to your listeners—is to use plain, simple language that everyone will understand.

Start with What's Familiar Many of us feel uneasy when we're asked to learn a new skill or understand new information. To reduce that anxiety among your listeners, begin your informative speech by describing something that is familiar to them. Then discuss how that familiar concept is related to the new information or skill you intend to describe. For instance, being "psychologically flooded" means experiencing thoughts and feelings so intense that you become unable to continue interacting with others. To describe that phenomenon, you might begin by reminding your listeners what happens to a car engine when it gets flooded. As most drivers know, a flooded engine won't start. You can then make comparisons between that familiar concept and the new knowledge you wish to impart.

Repeat Key Points Audiences pay more attention to information that is repeated. Take advantage of that fact by repeating your most important points during your speech. Research shows that repetition of critical points will help your listeners remember more of what you say.[9] To use repetition effectively, however, repeat only the important points, not trivial ones, and do not to repeat them so many times that your audience tunes out.[10]

Make It Fun Like repetition, humor can also enhance your presentation and increase your listeners' retention if you use it appropriately. Research suggests that humor in informative presentations promotes relaxation that allows listeners to understand and assimilate the information.[11] When using humor, remember to consider who your listeners are and what they are likely to find funny. Humor that is distasteful, obscene, or disrespectful of others is never appropriate in an informative speech *unless* the humor itself is the topic.

Effective speakers make it easy for the audience to listen to their presentations.

INVOLVE THE AUDIENCE

Many of us learn better when we're somehow involved in the lesson than when we're passively receiving it. Skillful informative speakers use several techniques to involve listeners in their presentations.

Invite Direct Participation In this method, you ask your listeners to perform some action that helps them understand your topic. In an informative speech about relaxation techniques, for instance, you might instruct your listeners to close their eyes, let their facial muscles go slack, and breathe slowly and deeply, to help them grasp how the techniques work.

Ask for Volunteers If you're teaching something too complex to involve everyone in the audience, ask for one or more volunteers with whom you can demonstrate your lesson for the rest of the listeners. In a speech about self-defense, you could ask for a volunteer on whom to demonstrate ways of fending off an attacker.

Poll the Audience A good way to gauge your listeners' opinions or experiences is to take an informal poll related to your topic. You might say "Raise your hand if you've ever known anyone who has suffered from asthma." If you're speaking in a room with a classroom response system—commonly known as *clicker technology*—your audience can respond to your questions anonymously.

Pose a Hypothetical Situation A technique similar to polling your audience is to ask your listeners to consider a hypothetical situation in which the information you have to share would be useful. For example: "Imagine you're driving late at night along a back road, hit a patch of ice, and end up in a ditch with no way to get out. You're alone, the temperature is below freezing, and there's no cell phone coverage where you are. What would you do?" Asking listeners to picture themselves in such a situation can spark their interest in your speech. The difference between that technique and polling your audience is that you are not asking your listeners to respond.

Refer to Individual Listeners Particularly if your audience is small, an excellent way to connect to your listeners is to refer to them individually during your speech when appropriate. For instance, "Last week we heard Tariq describe his life-changing experience of visiting Mecca. Today, I'd like to tell you about the two major denominations of Islam: the Sunni and the Shi'a." Even though you're referring only to one specific listener, the technique connects all of your listeners to you and to your presentation.

Invite Questions At the end of some informative speeches, presenters involve listeners by inviting and responding to their questions. If you have the time and wish to use that technique, it's often helpful to tell your audience early in your speech that you'll be taking questions at the end. That way, you will encourage listeners to think of questions as you speak. During a question-and-answer period, be mindful of the time allotted so that you don't run over.

BE ETHICAL

Finally, treat your listeners ethically. In the context of an informative speech, one of the most important requirements of ethical behavior is truthfulness. Because your purpose is to impart information to your audience, you have a responsibility as an ethical speaker to ensure that your information is true and accurate. Specifically, you should

- *Use information only from reputable sources.* Scientific journals and major newspapers are more reputable sources than tabloids and Wikipedia pages, for instance, because information in journals and large mainstream newspapers is checked for accuracy before being published.

- *Understand the information you're reporting.* If you're unsure how to interpret the meaning of a report or a statistic, ask an instructor for help. If you don't, you risk drawing conclusions from your information that are unwarranted.

- *Incorporate verbal footnotes.* When you use information in your speech from another source, identify that source while you're speaking. For example, you might say, "According to the U.S. Bureau of Labor Statistics, occupational therapy is one of the fastest-growing professions."

- *Be clear about when you're speculating.* Many sources of information allow us to infer ideas or speculate about possibilities, and it is fine to include those inferences or speculations in an informative speech as long as you make it clear that they aren't facts.

Inviting and responding to questions can be an excellent way to draw listeners into your presentation.

Ethical speakers also avoid using offensive language, exposing their audience to sensitive sights and sounds, and engaging in behaviors that would make their listeners uncomfortable—*unless* they have specifically warned their listeners in advance.

One highly unethical use of informative speaking is to coerce your audience into believing or doing something. If your purpose is to persuade individuals to adopt a particular belief, opinion, or behavior—a topic we'll examine in Chapter 15—you owe it to your listeners to be upfront about that objective. Speakers who hide their persuasive intentions in seemingly objective informative speeches often cross an ethical boundary by engaging in propaganda. Read more about propaganda—and learn how to identify it—in The Dark Side of Communication.

Test Yourself

- **What is information hunger?**
- **How can you ensure that your speech is well organized?**
- **When are repetition and humor useful?**
- **In what ways can you involve your audience in your informative speech?**
- **What should you do to ensure that your information is true and accurate?**

>> A Sample Informative Speech

When we're learning or polishing a skill such as informative speaking, it's often helpful to study excellent examples provided by others. Beginning on page 353 is the text of an informative speech by Eric Dern, an economics major at Arizona State University and a member of the school's speech and debate team. The speech describes the Golden Shield surveillance project in China. In April 2009, Eric tied for first place in informative speaking with this speech at the national tournament of the American Forensics Association, a teachers' association dedicated to cultivating excellence in public speaking and debate. Alongside the text are comments about what makes each section of his speech—the introduction, body, and conclusion—so effective. Figure 14.1, which follows the speech, provides the formal outline for Eric's speech and helps you to appreciate its organizational structure.

THE DARK SIDE of Communication

Listener Beware: When "Information" Becomes Propaganda

It's easy to think of informative speeches as offering only objective details and facts. Some speakers, however, use "informative" speeches to disguise their attempts to persuade or coerce their listeners. When they do, they are no longer simply informing but engaging in propaganda.

Informative speeches whose true purpose is coercive often contain one or more of the following elements. How many political speeches that you've recently heard have included these elements?

- *Moral labeling:* Using terms with negative connotations to refer to one's opponent. Politicians denounce "special-interest groups," for instance, to put down groups whose priorities contradict their own. They may use words such as *radical* and *extremist* to describe people with whom they disagree. In recent years, it has become fashionable to call one's opponents "Nazis," drawing comparisons to the fascist German group responsible for killing millions of Jews, Gypsies, homosexuals, and others in the twentieth century. The problem with such labeling is that calling someone a "radical," an "extremist," or a "Nazi" doesn't mean the person actually has any of the characteristics of such groups. Therefore, the labels are meaningless, although highly provocative.

- *Glowing generalizations:* Using positive terms to refer to oneself or one's allies. While applying negative terms to their opponents, lawmakers might refer to people and policies in their own parties as "patriotic," "loyal," "democratic," and "fair to working families." Likewise, food and drug companies might describe their products as "100 percent natural" to highlight their quality, even though many 100 percent natural substances are poisonous! Just as denouncing an opponent with negative terms doesn't mean those terms are accurate, referring to oneself or one's products with positive terms doesn't necessarily make those any more positive.

- *False dichotomy:* Conveying the idea that "if you aren't *for* us, you're *against* us" to cast anyone with a different opinion as an opponent. Such a ploy categorizes everyone into one of two groups: us or them. It separates people and discourages attempts at reaching compromise or finding common ground in their opinions.

- *Ordinary folk:* Describing oneself as "of the people" while depicting one's opponent as "out of touch with the average citizen." A particularly common tactic among U.S. American politicians is to campaign on the premise that the federal government is "broken" and "out of touch with" the realities of American life and that the candidate is a "Washington outsider" who will "fix" the system once he or she is elected. That approach garners support because it casts the speaker as "one of us."

Keep in mind that propaganda does not mean everything you disagree with when you're listening to a speech. Rather, propaganda is a speaker's deliberate attempts to make coercive messages sound like objective information. Knowing the common techniques of propaganda can help you resist its influence when you encounter it.

Sources: Caplan, A. L. (2005). Misusing the Nazi analogy. *Science, 309,* 535; for further information see Jowett, G. S., & O'Donnell, V. (2006). *Propaganda and persuasion.* Thousand Oaks, CA: Sage.

China's Golden Shield Surveillance Project

COMMENTARY >>	SPEECH

This introduction opens with a short story introducing listeners to the topic of the speech, the Golden Shield.

Southeastern China's Shenzhen was once a simple fishing community, only truly notable for its proximity to the border of Hong Kong. In 1979, the Chinese Communist Party stepped in and chose Shenzhen as the first of four Special Economic Zones, areas where capitalism would be allowed on a trial basis. Today, this Gotham-like metropolis, widely known as China's organized crime capital, is home to 12.4 million people—twice the size of Los Angeles—and is a city of pure commerce.

Notice here how the speaker relates his topic to his audience.

But this rags-to-riches story has its own interesting twist. *Rolling Stone,* on May 29, 2008, reports that it's only fitting that this concoction of crime and capitalism should once again serve as a laboratory, this time for the largest surveillance project in history. Golden Shield, a system of over 2 million cameras, not only watches every move of the city's population, but also detects emotion and predicts thoughts. And surprisingly, the communist country's best imitation of George Orwell is far more American that some would like to admit. *Rolling Stone* reports $30 billion of the $33-billion Golden Shield system consists of American investments, so just like everything else made in China with American parts, "Police State 2.0" is ready for export to a neighborhood near you.

Here, the speaker previews the topics to be covered in the body of the speech.

Golden Shield not only is significant for its giant leaps in human tracking technology, but also has implications for how our democratic society functions as a whole. To understand the impact Golden Shield will have on the world, we will first examine the technology of Shenzhen's Golden Shield, next understand its applications, and finally draw some implications from China's massive social experiment.

In the body of the speech, the speaker uses transitions to indicate when he is beginning a new topic.

What separates Golden Shield from London's famous security set-up or the surveillance of the Patriot Act is the system's sheer size and sophistication. To get a full picture of Golden Shield, let's first examine the technology that makes up the system, which is intended to be able to "see" and "hear."

First, if I were to stand at the corner at Shenzhen's Civic Centre, the area of the city where most security and government buildings are located, I would be watched by 38 different cameras. The *Brunei Times* of August 30, 2008, details the cameras' technology that allows subjects' eyes, facial features, and walking mannerisms to be checked against a database containing names, photos, and even reproductive information. Additionally, Malcolm Gladwell's 2002 book *Blink* chronicles the exploration of involuntary facial "microexpressions," explaining "When we experience a basic emotion, a corresponding message is sent to the muscles in our face." Golden Shield's software is so advanced that it is capable of reading these involuntary microexpressions within a millisecond, giving authorities the ability to instantly read motives and predict behavior. "The smallest thing could give you away. A nervous tic, a look of anxiety, a habit of muttering to yourself—anything that carries with it the suggestion of having something to hide is itself a punishable offense." This may sound familiar. George Orwell wrote this prediction of a dystopian future in his novel *1984.* Orwell's fantasy may certainly become a reality.

The speaker is careful throughout the speech to cite his sources properly.

By saying "second," the speaker signals that he is shifting to a new dimension of his topic.

Second, Golden Shield has been equipped to "hear" the sounds of the city. According to the 2006 essay *China's Golden Shield,* the system is capable of listening in on every cell phone signal in the city and saving these voice recordings in a huge database. So, if I were standing on that same corner in the Civic Centre, my cell phone would be constantly tracked and recorded, and my voice could be immediately recognized if I uttered a single word on the street. By utilizing the

Here, the speaker uses a quote from an expert as supporting material for the point he is making.

system's ability to both see and hear, China has reached a state of constant surveillance that few countries can rival.

Now that we know how Golden Shield works, we can see its applications in the world. Golden Shield has applications on crime and security not only in China, but also right here in the United States. But first, let's admit it, 2 million cameras spying on every move you make sounds pretty wrong. And creepy. But in a post-9/11 era, when terrorism and mass attacks are very real possibilities, China doesn't necessarily seem so out of line in installing Golden Shield. In fact, Golden Shield is devastatingly effective at preventing crime in Shenzhen. According to the January 24, 2007, *Shenzhen Daily,* in the very first week of Golden Shield's installation, robberies in the city dropped by 15 percent. Since then, the city's crime rate, once 9 times higher than Shanghai and 3 times higher than New York City, has fallen by nearly 14 percent. Golden Shield has time and time again proved its ability to make Shenzhen a much safer and more secure city.

But Golden Shield is not simply a Chinese security system. It is a cooperative effort between Chinese communism and American investment. The *International Herald Tribune* of September 10, 2008, reveals that 91 percent of Golden Shield's face- and behavior-recognition software was paid for by American hedge fund money in the last year. Robin Huang, chief operating officer of China Public Security, stated that Golden Shield has "a very good relationship with U.S. companies like Google, Honeywell, IBM, Cisco, HP, and Dell." *Rolling Stone* speculates that "these global corporations currently earning profits from Golden Shield are unlikely to be content if the lucrative new market remains confined to Shenzhen." And, accordingly, this technology is already being applied by these companies in the United States. The *Huffington Post* of August 7, 2008, reports that the same Golden Shield backers are also the companies invested in a Defense Department project auspiciously named "Operation Noble Shield." This virtual database can create constantly updated dossiers and surveillance footage for every U.S. citizen. The July 9, 2008, *New York Times* reports that the first 3,000 of these high-tech cameras were installed in New York, while another 2,200 were installed in Chicago in the past year.

There is a good chance that half of everything you own was made in Shenzhen: iPods, sneakers, maybe your car, and almost certainly your cell phone. And now population surveillance devices. There are three far-reaching implications for Golden Shield, related to American involvement in foreign policy, the meaning of privacy rights, and the intrusion of government into individual affairs.

First, Western powers claim that by doing business in China, they are spreading democracy. But the September 20, 2007, *American Prospect* points out, "We are now seeing the reverse: investment is helping China . . . actively repress a new generation of activists." This means America must disenthrall itself from one of its most cherished cornerstones in foreign policy: the idea that capitalism and democracy go hand in hand. As Naomi Klein states, "Remember how we've

COMMENTARY >>   **SPEECH**

always been told that free markets and free people go hand in hand? That was a lie. It turns out that the most efficient delivery system for capitalism is actually a communist-style police state, fortressed with American 'homeland security' technologies, pumped up with 'war on terror' rhetoric." By changing the foundation on which the United States spreads democracy, the existence of Golden Shield may very well alter the course of American foreign policy.

Next, privacy rights. Mike Sullivan, a police technology consultant, states in a November 24, 2008, MSNBC interview that "the difference between the Noble Shield and Golden Shield is the Supreme Court. We have the ability as U.S. citizens to cry foul. In China, citizens do not." However, in the 1973 decision *United States v. Dionisio,* the Supreme Court found a person's physical characteristics, like the eyes or face, are not protected by constitutional privacy rights. This means that while the Fourth Amendment protects us from searches and seizures without probable cause, it does not protect us against Golden Shield's ability to read one's emotions and motives. Golden Shield is redefining the term "probable cause" and may even redefine what we all consider to be privacy.

Finally, in his book *Discipline and Punish,* philosopher Michel Foucault examines Jeremy Bentham's panopticon, a prison layout where prisoners are allowed to roam freely under the permanent visibility of guards in a central tower. Foucault further explains that these guards do not even have to be in the tower for the panopticon to work; the very potential of visibility traps prisoners into disciplining themselves. Golden Shield works in the same way, using cameras instead of towers to ensure the automatic functioning of power.

However, *Rolling Stone* details the repression of Tibetan protestors by everyday Chinese citizens who aided authorities in the capture of political activists. This self-enforcement among Chinese citizens implies that Golden Shield could be turned off completely and citizens would police themselves. Traditionally, governments have always been responsible for the security of their citizens. But when citizens begin to check themselves, instead of the government, that frees the state to carry out oppressive agendas. For China, a country that has multiple regional conflicts, this could provide the final silencing of opposition to the cultural extermination of Tibet and Taiwan.

In his conclusion, the speaker reiterates the main points he has made in the speech.

When Beijing was awarded the Olympics seven years ago, the theory was that international scrutiny would force China's government to grant more rights to its people. Instead, the Olympics opened up a back door for the regime to massively upgrade its systems of population control. After examining how Golden Shield works, its applications, and finally its implications, we better understand how the system affects China and the world. No longer is Golden Shield confined to distant and unfamiliar worlds where most of us have probably never been. With the Olympics potentially coming to Chicago in 2016, it seems like only a matter of time before Operation Noble Shield brings this reality closer to home. Maybe George Orwell was right when he wrote, "Big Brother is watching."

He ends with a quote that will make his conclusion memorable.

TITLE: China's Golden Shield Surveillance Project

General purpose: To inform

Purpose statement: Inform audience about the Golden Shield surveillance project in China.

INTRODUCTION

I. The Chinese fishing community of Shenzen has been transformed into a metropolis and a unique lab for Golden Shield, history's largest surveillance project.

II. Golden Shield's more than 2 million cameras watch the population's every move.

Thesis: The Golden Shield surveillance project has far-reaching implications regarding U.S. foreign policy, privacy rights, and the role of government in individual lives.

Transition: To understand Golden Shield's impact, we first examine its technology, then its applications, and finally its implications.

BODY

I. Golden Shield stands out due to its technological sophistication.

   A. *Brunei Times:* Golden Shield has advanced camera technology.
      1. Subjects' facial features and walking mannerisms can be tracked.
      2. *Blink:* Detection of involuntary facial microexpressions allows authorities to read motives and predict behavior.

   B. Golden Shield can listen in on every cell phone signal in the city.
      1. *China's Golden Shield:* Voice recordings are saved in a huge database.
      2. Surveillance is constant and exceeds the level of most countries.

   Transition: Now that we know how Golden Shield works, we can see its applications in the world.

II. Golden Shield has applications related to crime prevention and security in China and the United States.

   A. *Shenzen Daily:* Golden Shield is extremely effective in preventing crime.
      1. Shenzhen's crime rate has fallen by nearly 14 percent
      2. The city is much safer and more secure.

   B. Several U.S. companies are investors in Golden Shield.
      1. *International Herald Tribune:* American hedge funds paid for 91 percent of Golden Shield's face- and behavior-recognition software in the last year.
      2. Golden Shield has an excellent relationship with major U.S. firms.

   C. *New York Times:* Thousands of the same high-tech cameras used by Golden Shield have been installed in New York and Chicago.

   Transition: There are three far-reaching implications for Golden Shield.

III. Golden Shield has three far-reaching implications.

   A. By affecting the foundation on which the United States advances democracy, Golden Shield may alter U.S. foreign policy.
      1. *American Prospect:* American investment is helping China suppress internal political activism.
      2. U.S. policymakers must rethink the long-held notion that capitalism and democracy go hand in hand.

   B. MSNBC: Golden Shield may redefine privacy as Americans understand it.
      1. *United States v. Dionisio:* The Fourth Amendment does not protect Americans against Golden Shield's ability to read emotions and motives.
      2. Golden Shield has prompted a redefinition of "probable cause."

   C. *Discipline and Punish:* Promotion of citizen self-policing could free governments to suppress political opponents.
      1. A precedent for self-enforcement among Chinese citizens implies that Golden Shield could be turned off and citizens would police themselves.
      2. The state would thus be freed to carry out repressive agendas.

   Transition: After examining Golden Shield's technology, applications, and implications, we better understand the system's worldwide effects.

CONCLUSION

I. Review of main points
   A. Golden Shield is unique in its size and technological sophistication.
   B. Golden Shield has applications related to crime prevention and security.
   C. Golden Shield has implications for U.S. foreign policy, the meaning of privacy rights, and the intrusion of government into individual affairs.

II. Final remarks
   A. Golden Shield has profound implications for how U.S. democratic society functions.
   B. It seems inevitable that a population control system such as Golden Shield will become a larger reality in the United States.

FIGURE 14.1 Formal Speech Outline: China's Golden Shield Surveillance Project

For REVIEW >>

- **What methods can we use to inform?**

  In an informative speech, we can define, describe, explain, and demonstrate.

- **In what ways should we frame an informative speech?**

  We should begin by relating ourselves to the topic of the speech. We should then relate the speech topic to our listeners.

- **Through what strategies can we hone our informative-speaking skills?**

  We can create information hunger, present a speech that is well organized, make it easy for our audience to listen, involve our listeners in our presentation, and communicate in an ethical manner.

Pop Quiz

Multiple Choice

1. Caroline's informative speech reveals how the Federal Reserve System works. Her speech is an example of one that
   a. defines
   b. describes
   c. explains
   d. demonstrates

2. In his informative speech, Jake defines the word *romance* by detailing the word's origin and history. Jake's method of definition is
   a. providing etymology
   b. identifying denotative definition
   c. defining by example
   d. explaining connotative definition

3. Tara wants to focus her speech on a problem or a point of controversy. In Allen and McKerrow's list of categories, that focus exemplifies a(n)
   a. event
   b. concept
   c. process
   d. issue

4. Compared to those who listen to lectures that are not humorous, people who listen to lectures that include humor do all of the following *except*
   a. evaluate the lecture more positively
   b. more accurately recall the material
   c. perceive the lecture to be shorter
   d. make more positive assessments of the lecturer

5. When speaking to a group of Japanese businesspeople, Lance would do well to remember that a taboo topic for this audience is
   a. immigration
   b. World War II
   c. pollution
   d. criticisms of the monarchy

Fill in the Blank

6. Describing a series of events in sequence, as you would when telling a story, is called _____ .

7. _____ are words that have opposite meanings.

8. A person's _____ is his or her inherent motivation to pay attention to something.

9. A series of actions that culminates in a specific result is called a _____ .

10. When you create _____ , you spark your listeners' desire to learn.

Answers: 1. c; 2. a; 3. d; 4. c; 5. b; 6. narration; 7. antonyms; 8. vested interest; 9. process; 10. information hunger

KEY TERMS

informative speaking 338	narration 340
defining 338	explaining 340
etymology 339	objective 341
synonyms 339	subjective 341
antonyms 339	demonstrating 341
describing 340	vested interest 346
representation 340	information hunger 347

15

SPEAKING

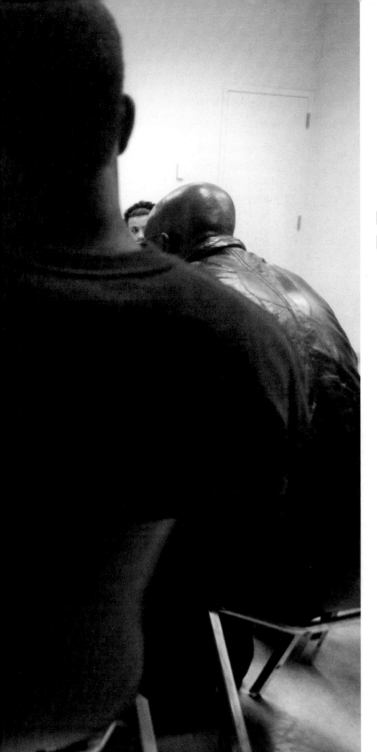

PERSUASION CAN PRESERVE A LIFE

The A&E television series *Intervention* chronicles stories of young adults with dependencies on alcohol or drugs, or other destructively compulsive behaviors, who have put themselves at serious physical, emotional, and social risk. Each episode includes a real-life intervention—a structured conversation in which the young person's family and friends try to persuade the individual to get professional help. Such was the experience of Brooks, a 21-year-old man who became addicted to drugs after an automobile accident had left him paralyzed from the waist down. When his family intervened, his younger brother Chace pleaded with Brooks to enter a treatment facility: "Brooks, I have seen your drug addiction affect your life negatively in the following ways. By destroying the close relationships that you and I once had. You sleep all day and party all night. It is not all right for me to keep enabling you to live like this. I can only support your life if you are willing to help yourself. Will you go to treatment today?" As a result of his family's persuasive efforts, Brooks agreed to begin rehabilitation. Although his recovery was long and painful, he finally became sober.

PERSUASIVELY

- What does it mean to persuade?
- In what ways can we craft a persuasive message?
- Through what strategies can we hone our persuasive-speaking skills?

Actor Sean Penn used the occasion of winning the Academy Award for best actor in 2009 to make a persuasive statement about same-sex marriage.

We have many occasions to persuade others for our own personal gain. Perhaps we're trying to convince someone to buy the car we wish to sell or to support a political cause we care about. In some situations, however, our attempts at persuasion are for the benefit of others. Had his relatives not succeeded in persuading Brooks to treat his drug addiction, his story may have ended tragically instead of triumphantly. Our ability to persuade can therefore have significant effects on other people's lives. In this chapter, you'll discover what it means to persuade others and how you can craft a successful persuasive message. You'll also learn several techniques for presenting effectively, and you'll see an example of an award-winning persuasive speech.

>> The Meaning and Art of Persuasion

Performers who win major awards frequently use their acceptance speeches as an opportunity to persuade their audiences to adopt their views on politically controversial issues. Upon winning the 2009 Academy Award for best actor for his role in *Milk,* Sean Penn sharply attacked California's Proposition 8, outlawing same-sex marriage in that state. In his speech, Penn remarked, "For those who saw the signs of hatred as our cars drove in tonight, I think that it is a good time for those who voted for the ban against gay marriage to sit and reflect, and anticipate their great shame, and the shame in their grandchildren's eyes if they continue that way of support. We've got to have equal rights for everyone." By expressing those sentiments, Penn wasn't merely conveying his own viewpoint—he was trying to persuade others to share that viewpoint and to act accordingly. Although the occasion may not have called for it, Penn was using **persuasive speaking**—public speech that aims to influence listeners' beliefs, attitudes, and actions.

We can think of **persuasion** as an attempt to motivate others, through communication, to adopt or to maintain a specific manner of thinking or doing. Some persuasion—including national advertising campaigns and Sean Penn's speech in front of a television audience of millions—occurs on a broad scale and seeks to motivate large numbers of people at once. Other persuasion—including the types most of us undertake in our daily interactions—occurs one-on-one or with small groups, such as a family and a work staff. In this section, we'll see that persuasion can influence beliefs, opinions, and/or actions. We'll also discover that good persuasive speakers support their arguments with appeals to integrity, emotion, and/or reason.

WHAT IT MEANS TO PERSUADE

When we try to motivate people to adopt a specific manner of thinking or doing, we usually have one of three concrete goals in mind:

• To persuade them to believe that a claim we're making is true
• To convince them to share our opinion on a particular issue
• To get them to do something

We may also be working toward more than one of those goals at a time. Let's take a close look at how we can use persuasion to influence others' beliefs, opinions, and actions.

Some Persuasion Affects Beliefs Our **beliefs** are perceptions about what is true or false, accurate or inaccurate. When others attempt to persuade us to believe something, they are trying to convince us that their words are a valid reflection of reality.

Suppose that several weeks after having a traffic accident, you and the other driver appear before a judge. Each of you tells the judge, in your own words, what led to your collision. You indicate that the other driver made an illegal turn, hitting your car. The other driver claims that the collision occurred because you failed to stop completely at a stop sign. Each of you is trying to convince the judge that your description of the events is true in an objective sense—that is, an accurate depiction of what *really* happened. In that instance, you are attempting to persuade the judge's beliefs by causing her to accept your description as true.[1] To help your case, you might offer evidence that supports your description, such as photos from the collision scene or statements from witnesses.

Some Persuasion Affects Opinions Whereas our beliefs are our perceptions of what's true and false, our **opinions** are our evaluations about what's good and bad. Opinions reflect what we think *should be*, not necessarily what *is*. When people attempt to persuade our opinions, they want us to evaluate something in the same way they do.

Perhaps you've attended rallies at your school where the speakers are voicing an opinion on a specific issue, such as the war in Afghanistan or abortion rights. Although they may present facts in support of their position, their goal is not simply for you to accept the facts as true. Rather, it's to cause you to agree with their position on the issue—that is, to ar-

SHARPEN
Your Skills

Find and examine five examples of attempts to persuade an opinion. They could be from a political speech, a television advertisement, a magazine column, a website, or from many other sources. For each, identify the opinion that is being advocated, and list the arguments offered in support of that opinion.

People attending rallies on controversial issues often try to persuade others to accept their position.

persuasive speaking Public speech that aims to influence listeners' beliefs, attitudes, and actions.

persuasion An attempt to motivate others, through communication, to adopt or to maintain a specific manner of thinking or doing.

belief Perception about what is true or false, accurate or inaccurate.

opinion Evaluation about what is good and bad.

Advertisements try to persuade us to buy a product or a service.

rive at the same evaluation of the issue that they hold. To help their case, the speakers might appeal to your morals or your sense of fairness.

Some Persuasion Affects Actions Our beliefs and opinions are what we think, but our actions are what we do. **Actions** are the behaviors we undertake, and many persuasive messages attempt to influence them.

Suppose that you see a television commercial advertising a product that makes hands-free cell phone use seem easy to manage while one is driving. The commercial first shows drivers who are frustrated and distracted when using their cell phone; then they appear happy and unencumbered while using the advertised product. The advertisement claims that similar devices are more expensive or poorly manufactured, implying that the featured product is a good value. By suggesting that the device is both convenient to use and reasonably priced, the commercial's producers are attempting to motivate you to take a specific action—to buy the product.[2]

Today, many companies use the Internet as a major channel for advertising their products or services. What characteristics make Internet advertisements persuasive? Check out Figure 15.1 to find out.

THREE FORMS OF RHETORICAL PROOF

In one of his major writings, *Treatise on Rhetoric,* the Greek philosopher Aristotle (384–322 B.C.) described three **forms of rhetorical proof,** which are ways to support a persuasive argument. He explained that persuasive messages could be supported by appeals to ethos, pathos, and logos.

Ethos Imagine listening to a speaker about whom you know nothing as he makes a persuasive appeal for money to help the victims of the devastating Haitian earthquake of 2010. He claims that if you donate your funds to him, he will use them directly for the benefit of the Haitian people instead of deducting a large proportion of the money to fund his operating costs. Moreover, he claims to know where the needs in Haiti are most dire, and he assures you that he will fund those needs first. Do you donate?

Many people, although inclined to help the victims of natural disasters, would want to know more about the speaker before they decided whether to give him their money. The reason is that a speaker who's respectable and trustworthy is generally more persuasive than one who isn't.[3] Aristotle recognized that, to be persuaded, people needed to have positive regard for the person whose message they were considering. He used the term **ethos** to refer to a speaker's respectability, trustworthiness, and moral character.[4]

Speakers can establish ethos with listeners by displaying these specific qualities:

- *Knowledge, experience, and wisdom with respect to the topic:* Does the speaker have adequate expertise with the issue to be persuasive? The individual appealing for your donations to Haiti could establish knowledge, experience, and wisdom by describing his extensive experience working in Haiti and his many professional connections in Port-au-Prince, its capital.

Internet advertisements—such as the boxes and banners that pop up on websites—persuade people to spend billions of dollars annually on the products or services they tout. The ads are usually effective, however, only if people click on them to get the details of the advertised product or service. What persuades us to click through? According to research, three features of an Internet advertisement draw us:

- *Size matters.* We are more likely to click on large ads than small ones.
- *Specificity matters.* Online ads that describe their products or services specifically, rather than vaguely, are more effective.
- *Amount of text matters.* We favor online ads with lots of text over ads with little text.

FIGURE 15.1 Cyberpersuasion: What Makes Us Click Through?

Source: Robinson, H., Wysocka, A., & Hand, C. (2007). The effect of design on click-through rates for banner ads. *International Journal of Advertising, 26,* 527–541.

Fact or Fiction?

Hooked on a Feeling: Emotion Persuades

From advertisers to political candidates to addiction counselors, many people appeal to emotion based on Aristotle's idea that feeling can affect beliefs, opinions, and behaviors. Is it fact or fiction that emotion has this effect?

A wide variety of experiments indicates that it's a fact. When researchers examine the findings of multiple studies, they conclude that appeals to positive emotion are often most effective at persuading people to change their attitudes or opinions, whereas appeals to negative emotion (particularly fear) are frequently most effective at inducing behavioral change. Some persuasion scientists believe that we are most likely to change our mind about something when we feel good, because we don't scrutinize the arguments very closely, but are most likely to change our behavior when we feel bad, because we want to end the bad feelings. You can use the findings from that research to craft your own persuasive messages, depending on whether you are trying to change someone's beliefs, opinions, or actions.

ASK YOURSELF

- Besides happiness or joy, to what other positive emotions could you appeal?
- Which emotions most strongly affect your own behaviors?

Sources: Dillard, J. P., & Meijnders, A. (2002). Persuasion and the structure of affect. In J. P. Dillard & M. W. Pfau (Eds.), *The persuasion handbook: Developments in theory and practice* (pp. 309–328). Thousand Oaks, CA: Sage; Witte, K., & Allen, M. (2000). A meta-analysis of fear appeals: Implications for effective public health campaigns. *Health Education & Behavior, 27,* 591–615.

- *Integrity and virtue:* Is the speaker honest and trustworthy, or do you have reason to doubt his integrity? The fundraiser for Haiti could establish integrity and virtue by mentioning his moral standards and his intolerance for individuals who cheat or steal.[5]
- *Goodwill toward the audience:* Does the speaker care about the welfare of his listeners, or is he only trying to use them? The speaker asking for donations could establish goodwill by acknowledging his audience's concerns about giving money and by addressing them to his listeners' satisfaction.

Note that judgments about ethos belong to the audience. Listeners decide for themselves how much experience, integrity, and goodwill a speaker has. Good persuasive speakers therefore establish and reinforce their ethos with every audience, knowing that it will enhance their persuasive abilities.

What makes a speaker seem knowledgeable and trustworthy to you? How can you display those qualities when you speak?

Pathos Many compelling persuasive appeals are memorable and effective because they stir people's emotions. Although it's helpful for a speaker to convince listeners of his or her integrity, it's often much more powerful if the speaker can generate a strong emotional reaction from the audience. The reason is that when people are emotionally aroused, their receptivity to new ideas is enhanced. Aristotle used the term **pathos** to refer to listeners' emotions, and he understood that emotion can be a significant persuasive tool. Was he right? Check out Fact or Fiction? to find out.

Consider the experience of Brooks in the vignette at the start of the chapter. Many people had tried to persuade him over the years to seek treatment, but he never did. Reasoning with drug or alcohol addicts that they should end their harmful behaviors is often ineffective because that approach underestimates the powerful force of addictions.[6] Even

action A behavior someone undertakes.

forms of rhetorical proof Ways to support a persuasive argument, including ethos, pathos, and logos.

ethos A speaker's respectability, trustworthiness, and moral character.

pathos Listeners' emotions.

By the Numbers

48

Percentage more likely women were to perform self-examinations for breast cancer after being exposed to a fear appeal versus no emotional appeal.[7]

if addicts rationally understand *why* they need help, they may not be sufficiently persuaded to seek it until they have had a significant emotional experience. In a typical intervention such as the one Brooks received, the letters of friends and relatives describe how the addict's behaviors have negatively affected them. They also explain the potential consequences if the person does not accept help, including ending contact with the addict and cutting off offers of money or shelter.

When friends and family members read their letters aloud during the intervention, their intent is to elicit emotional reactions in the addict that are strong enough to persuade the individual to get medical help. To generate sorrow and guilt, they describe the negative effects of the addict's behavior on their own lives. To generate fear, they spell out the consequences of continued drug or alcohol use. And to generate hope, someone at the intervention, usually a professional counselor, describes the treatments available to the addict. Those emotions—sorrow, guilt, and fear about one's current behavior, and hope for changing it—can persuade the individual to modify his or her behavior significantly, where reasoning alone did not work.

Although stirring virtually any emotion can be persuasive, emotional appeals often focus on generating negative emotions such as fear, guilt, disgust, anger, and sadness.[8] The reason is that we generally dislike experiencing such emotions, so we are motivated to respond to the persuasive appeal as a way of reducing those feelings. Table 15.1 presents examples of emotional appeals that might be used in a campaign to encourage people to quit smoking.

Logos A third way to persuade people is to appeal to their sense of reason. If a particular belief, opinion, or behavior makes good sense, then people will be inclined to adopt it if they have the capacity to do so. As we saw in the previous example, appealing to reason doesn't always work, particularly if some other force—such as an addiction—influences a person's behavior. When people are free to choose their beliefs, opinions, and behaviors, however, they are frequently persuaded by a solidly logical argument. Aristotle used the term **logos** to refer to listeners' ability to reason.

To **reason** means to make judgments about the world based on evidence rather than emotion or intuition. When we appeal to logos, we provide our listeners with certain evidence, hoping they will arrive at the same conclusion we have reached. People can engage in the reasoning process in two ways: inductively and deductively.

Table 15.1 Some Examples of Emotional Appeals	
Suppose you were designing a message to persuade people to stop smoking. Here are examples of appeals to pathos that you might use.	
Type of Appeal	**Example Statement**
Appeal to fear	Thousands of people die from lung cancer every year; you could be next.
Appeal to guilt	Think about how many children you're hurting with second-hand smoke.
Appeal to joy	Imagine how happy you'd be if you were free of your nicotine addiction.
Appeal to disgust	See this charred skin tissue? That's what your lungs look like right now.
Appeal to shame	You're an embarrassment to your family when you smoke.
Appeal to anger	If you're sick and tired of nicotine controlling your life, then kick the habit.
Appeal to sadness	Imagine saying goodbye to your kids because smoking claimed your life.

logos Listeners' ability to reason.

reason To make judgments about the world based on evidence rather than emotion or intuition.

Inductive Reasoning In **inductive reasoning,** we first consider the specific evidence and then draw general conclusions from it. As the evidence changes or as new evidence becomes available, we modify our conclusions accordingly.

For example, when you get sick and visit the doctor, she asks you about your symptoms, runs diagnostic tests, and examines your medical record. Each of those sources provides evidence. Let's say your symptoms are a rash, fever, and persistent headache. After considering those symptoms, ordering blood tests, and noticing from your records that you haven't had chicken pox, the doctor diagnoses your condition as chicken pox.

To apply inductive reasoning, that is, the doctor started with the specific evidence and drew her general conclusion from it. It is possible, of course, that her conclusion is incorrect. Even though your symptoms are consistent with a diagnosis of chicken pox, they may also be consistent with another diagnosis, such as meningitis or Rocky Mountain spotted fever. When making an inductive claim, your doctor considers the evidence available to her and draws the conclusion she believes that evidence best supports. If you later developed symptoms that are inconsistent with a diagnosis of chicken pox, she would have to reconsider her conclusion based on the new evidence.

Deductive Reasoning In **deductive reasoning,** we start with a general conclusion and then use it to explain specific individual cases. Deductive claims often make use of a **syllogism,** a three-line argument consisting of a major premise, a minor premise, and a conclusion. In a valid syllogism, if both the major and minor premises are true, then the conclusion logically *must* be true. Consider the following example:

Major premise: All fruits contain seeds.
Minor premise: Tomatoes are fruits.
Conclusion: Therefore, tomatoes contain seeds.

Let's consider the logic of that argument. If it is true that all fruits contain seeds, and if it is true that tomatoes are fruits, then logically it must be the case that tomatoes contain seeds. There is no logical way that the major and minor premises could be true and the conclusion false. We would therefore say that the conclusion *follows* from the premises, producing a valid syllogism.

When using a syllogism to persuade, it is important to establish the accuracy of the premises. Listeners may not be convinced by the logic of your argument if they don't believe that both premises are true. Suppose everyone in your audience accepts that all fruits contain seeds, but some listeners believe that tomatoes are vegetables, not fruits. They may not find your argument persuasive unless you first convince them that the tomato is a fruit. To do so, you might quote an authority on botany or plant biology to support that claim.

Establishing the truth of the premises is necessary, but it isn't sufficient for producing a valid argument. Consider the following syllogism:

Major premise: All mothers are women.
Minor premise: Lucy is a woman.
Conclusion: Therefore, Lucy is a mother.

That syllogism is not valid. The reason is that, even if both premises are true, the conclusion could still be false. Just because Lucy is a woman and all mothers are women, it doesn't follow that Lucy is a mother, because even though all mothers are women, not all women are mothers.

A second way we can reason deductively is with an enthymeme. An **enthymeme** is a syllogism in which one of the premises is already so widely known and accepted that it isn't mentioned.[9] Consider the now-famous statement made by seventeenth-century French philosopher René Descartes: *I think, therefore I am.* If we were to state his argument in the form of a syllogism, it would look like this:

Major premise: Anyone who thinks must exist.
Minor premise: I think.
Conclusion: Therefore, I exist.

inductive reasoning A form of reasoning in which one considers evidence and then draws general conclusions from it.

deductive reasoning A form of reasoning in which one starts with a general conclusion and then uses it to explain specific individual cases.

syllogism A three-line argument consisting of a major premise, a minor premise, and a conclusion.

enthymeme A syllogism in which one of the premises is already so widely known and accepted that it is omitted.

Descartes may have believed that the major premise ("Anyone who thinks must exist") was so obviously true that it didn't require articulating. If so, then he could safely construct his argument based only on the minor premise and the conclusion, which results in an enthymeme. Enthymemes can be just as persuasive as full syllogisms, but only if listeners accept the validity of both the omitted premise and the premise that is included.

Whether we do it inductively or deductively, appealing to reason means providing our audience with the evidence and explaining how it led us to our conclusions. Our goal in doing so is to persuade our listeners to adopt the same conclusions we have.

- **How are beliefs, opinions, and actions different?**
- **What does it mean to appeal to ethos, pathos, and logos?**

Test Yourself

>> Creating a Persuasive Message

In 1997, Oregon became the first U.S. state permitting physicians to help terminally ill patients end their own lives. Such doctor-assisted suicide is highly controversial. Supporters argue that people with terminal illnesses deserve to die with dignity and that a doctor's primary role should be to relieve suffering. Opponents say that the practice undermines society's respect for human life and transforms doctors from healers into killers.

Suppose you had the opportunity to persuade lawmakers to vote one way or the other on the issue of doctor-assisted suicide. Your success would rely not only on the strength of your convictions but also on your ability to communicate them in a compelling way. In this section, we'll consider the types of persuasive propositions you can employ, the options you have for organizing your persuasive message, and the logical fallacies you should avoid.

TYPES OF PERSUASIVE PROPOSITIONS

As we saw in Chapter 12, preparing a speech includes crafting a thesis statement, a one-sentence version of your message. In persuasive speaking, we sometimes call the thesis statement a **proposition,** because in a persuasive speech we are proposing something that we want our audience to accept. Recall that some persuasive messages influence beliefs, others influence attitudes, and others influence actions. As we'll see next, we use different types of propositions to achieve those various persuasive goals.

We Influence Beliefs with Propositions of Fact When we ask people to believe some statement, we are asserting that the statement is true. To achieve that persuasive goal, we use a **proposition of fact,** a claim that a particular argument is supported by the best available evidence and should therefore be taken as factual. Some examples of propositions of fact are

- Barack Obama was born in Hawaii.
- Flying is the safest mode of transportation.
- Solar power is not capable of meeting the energy demand in the United States.

Notice that the first and second examples make a claim about *what is,* whereas the third example makes a claim about *what is not.* All three are propositions of fact, however, because in each case we are asking our listeners to accept what we say as true. If it's true that flying is the safest mode of transportation, then that's our proposition, and our speech would need to provide the evidence to support that claim. Similarly, if it's true that solar power cannot meet U.S. energy demand, we would give the evidence necessary to support that argument.

proposition That which a persuasive speech attempts to convince an audience to accept.

proposition of fact A claim that a particular argument is supported by the best available evidence and should therefore be taken as factual.

proposition of value A claim that evaluates the worth of a person, an object, or an idea.

proposition of policy A claim about what should be done.

Propositions of fact are claims about reality. It isn't a matter of opinion whether Barack Obama was born in Hawaii—either he was or he was not. When we assert propositions of fact, our persuasive goal is to make our listeners believe in the objective truth of what we're saying. That goal requires us to support propositions of fact with credible—that is, believable—evidence. We'll examine what makes evidence credible and strong later in this chapter.

We Influence Opinions with Propositions of Value Whereas propositions of fact are statements about what is objectively true, **propositions of value** are claims that evaluate the worth of a person, an object, or an idea. When we assert propositions of value, our persuasive goal isn't to make someone *believe* us—it's to make someone *agree with* us. Some examples of propositions of value are

- Fathers are just as important as mothers.
- Animal cloning is immoral.
- Our country is right to do anything it can to protect its citizens.

Notice that all three statements make claims, but they are not claims about facts. Rather, they are judgments that reflect the speaker's opinions about what is important, moral, and right. Unlike facts, opinions are never true or false in an absolute sense—they are only correct or incorrect in the minds of the people who discuss them. Therefore, we can't *prove* an opinion in the way we prove a factual claim. We might use facts to establish a basis for advocating a specific opinion—for instance, we may quote evidence about threats of terrorism and the safety of Americans—but the facts themselves will never settle the issue. One person might interpret that evidence as justifying our nation's right to defend itself against its enemies. Another person might interpret the same evidence as proof of our failed foreign policy and the need for greater diplomacy.

Note that the people in that example interpreted the same piece of evidence differently, based on their different ideas about what *should be.* Who is right? That's a matter of opinion.

We Influence Actions with Propositions of Policy Closely tied to propositions of value are **propositions of policy,** claims about *what we should do.* Speakers offer propositions of policy to suggest a specific course of action for listeners to follow or to support. Some examples of propositions of policy are

- The federal government should ban the use of human stem cells in medical research.
- Hate crimes against ethnic, religious, and sexual minorities should be capital offenses.
- Everyone should eat only locally grown, organic foods whenever possible.

Notice that each statement contains the word *should,* a characteristic that makes it closer to a proposition of value than a proposition of fact. Whereas propositions of value suggest what we should *think,* however, propositions of policy suggest what we should *do.* Each of the examples, that is, suggests a specific course of action, either for individuals ("eat only locally grown, organic foods") or for the government ("ban the use of human stem cells"). When advocating for individual action, speakers attempt to persuade listeners to adopt the action themselves. When advocating for government action, speakers are usually trying to persuade listeners to support the action, such as by voting for it or encouraging their elected officials to do the same.

Some persuasive speakers include propositions of fact, value, and policy in their presentations.

Some Persuasive Speeches Include More Than One Type of Proposition Although each type of proposition can be persuasive on its own, many persuasive speeches integrate two or even all three types to support their message. Let's say, for instance, that you wanted to advocate expanding affirmative action laws that help members of minority groups to get jobs. You might begin your speech with a proposition of value, such as

SHARPEN
Your Skills

Write a proposition of value, a proposition of fact, and a proposition of policy that you would use if you were persuading lawmakers how to vote with respect to doctor-assisted suicide.

"Diversity in the workplace is important," and persuade your listeners to adopt that opinion. Next, you might introduce a proposition of fact, such as "Affirmative action laws have increased workplace diversity by 27 percent in the past three decades," and provide the evidence for your listeners to believe that factual claim. Finally, you might assert a proposition of policy, such as "The U.S. government should expand affirmative action laws to increase workplace diversity even further," and use your earlier claims about values and facts to persuade listeners to support that action. In that speech, each new proposition you introduce is supported by the propositions that preceded it, and that model can add up to a powerfully persuasive argument.

FOUR WAYS TO ORGANIZE A PERSUASIVE MESSAGE

How you organize a persuasive message often matters as much as the message itself. Even good arguments can lose their persuasive appeal if they aren't presented in a meaningful sequence. In this section, we'll look at four options for organizing a persuasive message.

Problem-Solving Pattern One way to organize a persuasive speech is to use a **problem-solving pattern,** in which you establish the existence of a problem and then propose a solution to it. The problem-solving approach requires you persuade your listeners on two separate points. First, you must show that the problem exists and is serious enough to warrant intervention. Second, you must establish that your proposed solution is possible and practical and will be effective at reducing or eliminating the problem.

Suppose your persuasive speech is about family farms. You might begin by pointing out how many family farms in the United States have gone out of business in the last 50 years due to competition from corporate mega-farms. Because the loss of family farms is the problem you're aiming to address, you would need to explain why it's a problem worth solving. For instance, you could show that the demise of family farms eliminates thousands of jobs and requires stores to buy food that is grown hundreds of miles away and thus has decreased nutritional value.

Perhaps your proposed solution is that the government increase its subsidies to family farms to help keep them in business. You would then need to provide evidence that such a solution is *possible* (the government has the money to fund the subsidies), *practical* (an infrastructure exists to dispense the subsidies to family farmers), and *effective* (providing the subsidies will keep more family farms in business).

Refutational Approach A problem-solving pattern can work well when your audience is open-minded about the problem and solution you describe. Sometimes, however, your audience may be predisposed toward a certain position that you plan to refute. Let's say, for instance, that you're speaking in favor of capital punishment, and you already know that some of your listeners oppose it. In that instance, you might use a **refutational approach,** a method whereby you begin by presenting the main arguments against your position, and you then immediately refute them.

One common argument against capital punishment is that it won't bring the victims back. That statement is often persuasive because it's true: Putting a criminal to death won't bring that individual's victims back to life. Many people use that point to argue that capital punishment is therefore futile. If you plan to advocate the death penalty in your speech, you might begin by acknowledging that statement and admitting that it is true. You could then point out, however, that *no* form of punishment will bring the victims back. The fact that the victims won't come back is therefore not a valid argument against capital punishment.

In the refutational method, after you've acknowledged and responded to the main arguments against your position, you would then state your own position and argue for it.

problem-solving pattern A way of organizing a persuasive speech in which the speaker establishes the existence of a problem and then proposes a solution to it.

refutational approach A way of organizing a persuasive speech in which the speaker begins by presenting the main arguments against his or her position and then immediately refutes those arguments.

comparative advantage method A way of organizing a persuasive speech in which the speaker explains why his or her point of view is superior to others on the same topic.

Monroe's motivated sequence A way of organizing a persuasive speech consisting of appeals to attention, need, satisfaction, visualization, and then action.

The refutational approach is designed to dispense with the arguments against your position first—or at least to weaken them—so that your own position looks stronger by comparison.[10]

Comparative Advantage Method On occasion, you may find yourself speaking to people who already agree that a problem exists—they just can't agree on the best way to solve it. In that situation, it's often best to use the **comparative advantage method,** in which you explain why your point of view is superior to others on the same topic.

Imagine that you're speaking to a group of schoolteachers on the topic of teacher evaluations. Your listeners all agree that evaluations are important, but they have little consensus on how evaluations should be done. To persuade the audience to adopt *your* suggestion, you begin by reminding everyone of the importance of the problem: "Although teacher evaluations are critical to school success, there's no fair way of conducting them."

Next, you identify the various alternative viewpoints and explain why each one is deficient:

> *Evaluating teachers on the basis of student test scores is unfair because that rewards the teachers who "teach to the test." Having principals evaluate teachers is unfair because principals can play favorites. Evaluating teachers based on student feedback is unfair because only popular teachers receive good evaluations.*

After identifying the shortcomings of the alternatives, you propose your own solution to the problem:

> *The only fair way to evaluate teachers is by using expert evaluators from other school districts. Because they won't know the content of student exams, they cannot reward teachers for "teaching to the test." Because they don't know the teachers they're evaluating personally, they won't be inclined to play favorites. Finally, because they are experts, their evaluations won't be swayed by teacher popularity.*

By using the comparative advantage method, you acknowledge that other viewpoints exist, but you give your listeners reason to discount them in favor of the viewpoint you are advocating.

Monroe's Motivated Sequence A final way of organizing a persuasive speech is with **Monroe's motivated sequence,** a problem-oriented structure for persuasive arguments. The sequence, developed by former Purdue University professor Alan Monroe, has proved to be particularly effective at motivating listeners to adopt a specific *action,* such as buying a product or giving money to a charity.

Let's say that you must give a speech persuading people to donate blood. Monroe's motivated sequence includes five stages that you would address in order:

- *Attention:* The attention stage arouses people's interest and sparks their desire to listen, often by making the topic personally relevant to them. Your message at the attention stage is: *Please listen!*

  Example
  Imagine you're badly injured in a head-on car crash, and you're quickly losing blood. After you arrive by ambulance to the emergency room, the doctor says you need an immediate blood transfusion to save your life. The only problem is that they don't have enough blood to give you.

- *Need:* Once you've aroused your listeners' attention, your next priority is to identify the need or problem that requires their action. Your message at the need stage is: *Something must be done.*

  Example
  In the past few years, community blood drives have been less and less successful at collecting enough blood to meet our area's medical needs. Our supply of healthy, usable blood is drying up fast.

- *Satisfaction:* After you've established the problem at the need stage, you use the satisfaction stage to propose your solution. Your message at the satisfaction stage is: *This is what should be done.*

  Example
  We need an association of healthy, committed volunteers who will donate blood on a regular basis and will encourage their friends, relatives, co-workers, and acquaintances to do the same. That will ensure an ongoing supply of blood to meet our needs.

- *Visualization:* At the visualization stage, you ask your audience to imagine how much better their situation will be if they do what you're proposing. Your message at the visualization stage is: *Consider the benefits.*

  Example
  With a continuous supply of blood on hand, our area hospitals will be well equipped to respond to a wide range of medical situations, ensuring the health and welfare of the people in our community.

- *Action:* Finally, at the action stage, you tell your listeners what you want them to do. Your request could be that they change their opinions or their beliefs, but often it's that they change their actions. Your message at the action stage is: *Act now!*

  Example
  You can make a difference by filling out the blood donor cards I'm passing around and dropping them in the cardboard box at the back of the room as you leave.

Each of the four options for organizing a persuasive speech that we've reviewed in this section has its strengths. Every situation is different, and you will need to choose the best option for the specific circumstances. As you consider ways to organize your presentation, think about what you are trying to accomplish and how sympathetic you expect your audience to be. You can use that information to select the organizational approach that will work best for you.

No matter how you organize your persuasive appeal, it's critical that you use valid arguments. Many arguments might seem valid when you first hear them, but they may actually be problematic on closer inspection, as we consider next.

> *Suppose you were trying to persuade a group of college students to vote in favor of a proposed tuition surcharge. Which organizational pattern do you think would work best for that speech? Why?*

AVOIDING LOGICAL FALLACIES

A **logical fallacy** is a line of reasoning that, even if it makes sense, doesn't genuinely support a speaker's point. Some logical fallacies are easy to spot; others are subtle and more difficult to identify. Competent speakers avoid logical fallacies and instead focus on providing real support for their points.

The most common logical fallacies in persuasive speaking include

- Ad hominem *fallacy:* A common but illogical way to counter arguments is to criticize the person who makes them—for instance, "I wouldn't believe anything Senator Rodgers says about fiscal responsibility; the man's an idiot." That line of reasoning, called an ***ad hominem* fallacy,** implies that if a person has shortcomings, his or her arguments are therefore deficient. That implication is a fallacy, however; consider that, in our example, even if the speaker doesn't respect Senator Rodgers, the lawmaker's arguments about fiscal responsibility aren't necessarily wrong. To show that they are, the speaker would need to attack the arguments themselves.

- *Slippery slope:* A **slippery slope fallacy**—also called a *reduction to the absurd*—unfairly tries to shoot down an argument by taking it to such an extreme that it appears ludicrous. An activist advocating a ban on same-sex marriage might state, "If we allow gay marriage, pretty soon we'll be legalizing polygamy and allowing people to marry animals." Such a method tries to persuade people not to adopt an argument by extending the argument to a ridiculous and undesirable extreme.

- *Either/or fallacy:* An **either/or fallacy** identifies two alternatives and falsely suggests that if one is rejected, the other must be accepted. Take the statement, "Either we

logical fallacy A line of reasoning that, even if it makes sense, does not genuinely support a speaker's point.

***ad hominem* fallacy** A statement that attempts to counter an argument by criticizing the person who made it.

slippery slope fallacy A statement that attacks an argument by taking it to such an extreme that it appears ludicrous.

either/or fallacy A statement that identifies two alternatives and falsely suggests that if one is rejected, the other must be accepted.

make condoms available in public schools or we prepare for an epidemic of sexually transmitted infections among our teenagers." That statement argues for providing condoms by identifying an epidemic of infections as the only possible alternative. The reasoning is invalid—a fallacy—because it ignores the possibility that there may be other ways to keep sexually active adolescents infection-free.

- *False-cause fallacy:* A **false-cause fallacy**—also known as the *post hoc ergo prompter hoc* fallacy—asserts that if an event occurs before some outcome, the event therefore caused that outcome. Consider the claim, "I started taking ginseng and fish oil supplements three years ago, and I haven't gotten sick once during that time." That claim implies that because the speaker's streak of wellness *followed* her use of supplements, it was therefore *caused by* her use of supplements. Her reasoning is a fallacy, however, because she has no way of knowing whether she would have been free of illness even if she hadn't taken the supplements. The fact that one occurrence preceded the other doesn't mean it caused the other.

- *Bandwagon appeal:* **Bandwagon appeal** suggests that a listener should accept an argument because of how many other people have already accepted it. Think about the assertion "Over 15 million people buy Vetris motor oil each month, and you should too—15 million satisfied customers can't be wrong!" The implication is that if an argument (such as to use a particular brand) is popular, it therefore has merit. That may well be true—good products are often popular *because* they are good—but it isn't necessarily true. Can 15 million people be wrong? Absolutely—so the popularity of an argument is no guarantee of its merit.

- *Hasty generalization:* A **hasty generalization** is a broad claim that is based on insufficient evidence. Usually, the "evidence" for the generalization comprises one or two isolated examples. Suppose you were to claim in your speech that it is unsafe to travel in Turkey. To support your claim, you tell the story of having had your passport stolen out of your hotel room during your study abroad experience in Turkey the previous year. Your argument would be a hasty generalization because your evidence is limited to one incident in one hotel.

- *Red herring fallacy:* When people are unable to respond legitimately to an argument, they sometimes introduce an irrelevant detail—thus committing what is known as the **red herring fallacy**—to divert attention from the point of the argument. Suppose you hear someone say, "We shouldn't prosecute people for smoking marijuana when there are so many more dangerous drugs out there." Smoking marijuana is still illegal even if other drugs are more dangerous, so the danger of other drugs is irrelevant to the claim that marijuana users shouldn't be prosecuted.

- *Straw man fallacy:* A speaker uses a **straw man fallacy** when he or she refutes a claim that was never made. Let's say the governor of your state proposes to reduce the drinking age in your state to 19 for beer and wine. A legislator responds in a televised interview by saying, "Our governor thinks kids should be able to sit in bars drinking martinis! I doubt most parents in this state want to see children getting hammered with hard liquor after school." In that instance, the legislator is trying to refute an argument that the governor hasn't made. After all, the governor's proposal is about 19-year-olds, not children, and about beer and wine, not hard liquor.

- *Begging the question:* **Begging the question** means supporting an argument with claims whose truth is taken for granted but never verified. Suppose a speaker says, "Banning the use of cell phones while driving would save thousands of lives every year." Perhaps that claim sounds reasonable—and perhaps it is even true—but where is the evidence? No data are presented to verify the claim, so listeners shouldn't assume it's true.

false-cause fallacy A statement asserting that if an event occurs before some outcome, the event therefore caused that outcome.

bandwagon appeal A claim that a listener should accept an argument because of how many other people have already accepted it.

hasty generalization A broad claim that is based on insufficient evidence.

red herring fallacy A statement that responds to an argument by introducing an irrelevant detail to divert attention from the point of the argument.

straw man fallacy A statement that refutes a claim that was never made.

begging the question Supporting an argument with claims whose truth is taken for granted but never verified.

- *Appeal to false authority:* An **appeal to false authority** uses as evidence the testimony of someone who is not an expert on a given topic. In a persuasive speech about the benefits of a vegan diet, for instance, a student might say, "According to an interview with Ellen DeGeneres, a vegan diet is the healthiest way to eat." The problem is that although DeGeneres is a vegan, she is not a physician, nutritionist, or medical scientist. Therefore, despite her high public profile, she is unqualified to comment with authority on the health benefits of veganism or any other diet.

Although comedian Ellen DeGeneres is a vegan, she is not a physician, nutritionist, or medical scientist. Therefore, despite her high public profile, she is unqualified to comment with authority on the health benefits of veganism.

The lines of reasoning described above are fallacies because they each represent an illogical way of supporting an argument. Two important caveats are worth noting, however. First, *arguments supported by logical fallacies may still be true.* Although Ellen DeGeneres is not a medical authority, that fact does not mean, by itself, that she's inaccurate in saying that a vegan diet is healthful. It simply means that DeGeneres does not have the credibility (about which we will read below) to make that claim. Knowing whether the claim is true or false would require more believable evidence.

Second, *even though they are illogical, fallacies may still be persuasive.* Consider that politicians frequently use *ad hominem* attacks during campaigns, pointing out, say, that an opponent has failed in her business or in his marriage. Although such a statement doesn't logically mean that the individual is unfit for public office, people aren't persuaded only by logic, as you'll recall from the earlier discussion of rhetorical proof. People are also persuaded by emotion. If politicians can arouse negative emotion about their opponents, even with illogical arguments, they can be—and often are—persuasive in discrediting their rivals. That practice, known as *negative campaigning* or *mudslinging,* is highly controversial and often considered unethical, particularly when politicians make misleading statements about each other. Although the practice is an example of the dark side of communication, research indicates that negative campaign ads can be just as persuasive as positive ads.[12]

Those caveats aside, however, good persuasive speakers know how to avoid committing logical fallacies. To do so, they first have to be able to spot them accurately. Check out "The Competent Communicator" to see how well *you* can identify some of the most common fallacies.

By the Numbers

62

Percentage of high school students who were able to identify logical fallacies in written arguments, according to one study.[11]

- What do propositions of fact, value, and policy each propose?
- When is it advantageous to use Monroe's motivated sequence?
- What makes a statement a logical fallacy?

Test Yourself

>> Honing Your Persuasive-Speaking Skills

Much of our ability to persuade others comes not from the words we use but from the style in which we deliver them. Just as an exceptional salesperson can sell almost anything to almost anyone, an outstanding persuasive speaker has the skills to persuade even the most resistant audiences. In this section, we'll explore several strategies for delivering a persuasive speech effectively, including adapting to your audience, building rapport, and establishing your credibility.

appeal to false authority A claim that uses as evidence the testimony of someone who is not an expert on the topic.

Name That Fallacy!

It's time to put your understanding of logical fallacies to the test. Match each of the fallacies listed below with the statement that exemplifies it.

Fallacy	**Statement**
_____ 1. Bandwagon appeal	A. If we restrict oil drilling in Alaska, then eventually we won't be able to drill for oil anywhere and we'll be back in the Stone Age.
_____ 2. Either/or argument	B. You should get an LCD television because that's the type that 9 out of 10 consumers prefer.
_____ 3. *Ad hominem* attack	C. Joining a fraternity made my son an alcoholic. He never drank before he moved into that frat house.
_____ 4. Red herring	D. My pediatrician overcharged me for some tests last year. Doctors are crooks!
_____ 5. Slippery slope	E. Richard Jones would make a terrible mayor; his daughter's in rehab, for goodness' sake!
_____ 6. Hasty generalization	F. You should try acupuncture; Michael Phelps swears by it, and he's won 14 Olympic gold medals.
_____ 7. Appeal to false authority	G. Grading on a curve is unfair because teaching shouldn't be a popularity contest; it's about educating our students.
_____ 8. False cause	H. If you're not pro-life, then you're in favor of killing millions of innocent babies.

Spotting logical fallacies can be tricky, but it's a skill you can improve with practice. Answers for this exercise appear at the end of the chapter on page 383. Not all fallacies addressed in the chapter are included here because some are impossible to identify without knowing the arguments that preceded them.

ADAPT TO YOUR AUDIENCE

As we've discussed in earlier chapters, it's always important to know who your listeners are and to adapt to their needs. Accommodating listeners' needs is useful when you give an informative speech, because it helps to ensure that you present information that your listeners can understand and don't already know. It is equally important when you are speaking persuasively, because it gives your message the best chance for acceptance. Adapting to your audience requires identifying its general disposition and neutralizing hostility when you encounter it.

Identify Your Audience's Disposition Before presenting a persuasive speech, it is advantageous to know how your audience is likely to react. Some audiences will be receptive to your message, others will be neutral, and still others will be hostile. Connecting with each type of audience requires a different presentational style:

- A **receptive audience** is composed of people who already accept and agree with all or most of what you plan to say. We sometimes use the phrase "preaching to the choir" to describe speaking to a receptive audience. When you have such an audience, your persuasive task is relatively easy because your listeners are likely to respond favorably to whatever you say.

receptive audience An audience composed of people who already accept and agree with all or most of what a speaker plans to say.

Table 15.2 Culture Matters: Cultural Differences in Persuasion

Cultural background can influence the persuasive strategies to which listeners respond. In one study, researchers from Stanford University observed employees of the same international corporation in four different countries. Each employee was asked to comply with a request from another employee. The researchers found noteworthy cultural differences in what persuaded the employees. How might you use this information to understand your audience better?

Culture	Most Effective Persuasive Strategy
Chinese	Authority: Chinese employees complied with requests made by higher-status individuals.
Spanish	Liking: Spanish employees complied with requests made by people they liked.
German	Consistency: German employees complied with requests if such requests were consistent with the organization's rules.
U.S. American	Reciprocity: U.S. American employees complied with requests made by people who had recently done something for them

Source: Morris, M. W., Podolny, J. M., & Ariel, S. (2000). *Innovations in international and cross-cultural management.* Thousand Oaks, CA: Sage.

- A **neutral audience** doesn't have strong feelings for or against the topic of your speech. Perhaps such listeners don't know enough about your topic to have formed a strong opinion on it, or maybe they don't care enough about your topic—or see enough of a personal connection to them—to bother forming a strong opinion. When speaking to a neutral audience, it's therefore helpful to inform listeners about what your topic is and why it should matter to them. Once you make the issue relevant to your listeners, you'll find it easier to persuade them to adopt your viewpoint on the topic.

- The most difficult audience to persuade is a **hostile audience,** one in which listeners are predisposed to disagree with you. Their hostile disposition may reflect that they already have a viewpoint on the issue that conflicts with yours, or it may be that they dislike you personally. Whatever the reason, hostile audiences are challenging because they are against you even before you start speaking. Good persuasive speakers can neutralize hostility, however, as we will see later.

Your audience's disposition—and the kinds of persuasive appeals to which it will respond—can also depend on your listeners' cultural background. Research shows that people from different cultures are persuaded by different types of messages. See Table 15.2 for specific examples.

Neutralize Hostility Many people find it difficult to listen to—let alone to be persuaded by—someone toward whom they feel hostility. If a portion of an audience already is disapproving of a speaker, his or her ideas, or the occasion on which the person is speaking, it is difficult to convey the message effectively. Many speakers are so uncomfortable with such situations that they ignore the hostility, hoping that their message will be enough to persuade their listeners. Skilled persuasive speakers, however, acknowledge the listeners' negative feelings and then identify points on which they and the listeners agree.

When President Barack Obama delivered the commencement speech at the University of Notre Dame in May 2009, he faced just such a situation. As a Catholic institution, Notre Dame and many of its students oppose abortion, so they protested the selection of the pro-choice Obama. Instead of shying away from their concerns, the president acknowledged them respectfully and focused on points on which he and his audience could agree:

When we open up our hearts and our minds to those who may not think precisely like we do or believe precisely what we believe, that's when we discover at least the possibility of common ground. That's when we begin to say, "Maybe we won't agree

neutral audience An audience lacking strong feelings for or against the topic of a speech.

hostile audience An audience in which listeners are predisposed to disagree with the speaker.

on abortion, but we can still agree that this heart-wrenching decision for any woman is not made casually, it has both moral and spiritual dimensions. So let us work together to reduce the number of women seeking abortions, let's reduce unintended pregnancies. Let's make adoption more available. Let's provide care and support for women who do carry their children to term. Let's honor the conscience of those who disagree with abortion, and draft a sensible conscience clause, and make sure that all of our health care policies are grounded not only in sound science, but also in clear ethics, as well as respect for the equality of women." Those are things we can do.

During his commencement speech at the University of Notre Dame in May 2009, President Barack Obama respectfully acknowledged differences of opinion regarding the controversial issue of abortion.

By giving voice to his opponents' views on abortion, Obama made his critics feel respected instead of maligned. Further, by identifying points on which he and his critics agreed, he provided a way for people on all sides of this divisive issue to communicate with one another, neutralizing much of the opposition that surrounded his selection as commencement speaker.

To read about how one former communication major uses his understanding of his audiences to make his presentations persuasive, check out the Putting Communication to Work box on the following page.

BUILD RAPPORT WITH YOUR LISTENERS

Knowing your audience will also help you build rapport with your listeners. To **build rapport** is to create the perception that your listeners and you see things similarly. Having rapport establishes trust and encourages audience members to listen to you even if they disagree with you.

Several behaviors can help you build rapport with your audience:

- *Interact with listeners before your speech.* Particularly when you're speaking to people you don't know well, spend time talking to them—and listening to them—before your speech. Not only will you get information about who your listeners are and what they're thinking, but you will signal to your audience that you care about them.
- *Maintain eye contact while you speak.* According to research, most people believe that a lack of eye contact indicates that the speaker is being deceptive.[13] If you don't look at your audience while you speak, you're likely to come across as untrustworthy—an undesirable effect when you're trying to persuade. Practice establishing and maintaining eye contact with each person in your audience for three to four seconds at a time.
- *Open with a story.* Because everyone loves a good story, an excellent way to build rapport with your audience is to open with one. Stories are especially effective when they include information to which your audience can relate. If you live in a cold climate but are speaking in a hot one, for instance, you could describe your experience of dealing with the heat, because your listeners will be able to relate to it themselves.
- *Use humor when appropriate.* It's difficult not to like people who make us laugh. Therefore, a particularly effective way to establish rapport is to use humor in your presentation. Humor can consist of short jokes or one-liners and can also be reflected in the stories you tell. Incorporating humor can help your listeners relax and enjoy your presentation—and be receptive to your message. When considering the use of humor, however, think carefully about what your audience is likely to find funny and in good

SHARPEN Your Skills

Suppose you were speaking on a controversial topic to a hostile audience. Select a topic on which you and your audience would disagree, and then outline at least three ways you could establish common ground with your listeners on the topic.

When is humor an effective way to establish rapport with an audience? When can it backfire?

build rapport Create the perception that listeners and the speaker see things similarly.

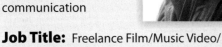

Name: Chris Folkens

College(s):
Bachelor's degree, University of Illinois at Urbana/Champaign, spring 2005

Major(s): Speech communication

Job Title: Freelance Film/Music Video/Commercial Director

Salary: There is really no "salary" per se, but rather day rates for directing and hourly rates for editing.

Time in Job: 1 year full-time (since February 2009)

Work Responsibilities: I've been directing and editing projects ranging from music videos for major-label rock groups to corporate videos, viral videos for ad agencies, and short films. I've also written two feature film screenplays that I'm currently pitching to producers.

This year I directed and edited a high-end rock music video for The Red Jumpsuit Apparatus (Virgin Records / EMI), as well as a slick and stylized movie-trailer-esque advertisement for the Facebook game Mob Wars. I also directed and edited a visually compelling cinema advertisement for the American Red Cross of Greater Chicago that depicts a family who lose their house to a tragic fire, for which we staged real fire sequences.

Why Communication? I originally intended to go to law school and become an entertainment attorney or trial lawyer. I ended up discovering the merit communication had in media studies. The principles of communication, persuasion, argumentation theory, organizational communication, and leadership studies have been a huge asset.

Every time I pitch a project to a rock band, record label, or an ad agency, I am making a persuasive speech or written presentation. I have to understand my audience and fit my presentation to the group's core intentions. Some groups value the art more; some value the budget more. Either way, I have to show a total commitment to the idea I'm presenting, and that confidence comes from my studies in communication.

My Advice to Students: Focus on the field you want to pursue, and pick classes that support that area of work. Diversity of studies is good, but you also want your choices to make sense long-term, based on the field you want to end up in. I would suggest following your passions and dreams as well. My passion was (and is) film, and in studying communication, I've been able to pursue my lifelong dream of becoming a film director.

taste. It is best to stay away from jokes that risk offending listeners and jokes that your audience may not understand or appreciate.

ESTABLISH YOUR CREDIBILITY

Earlier in this chapter, we considered the value of appealing to ethos, which is the integrity, trustworthiness, and goodness of the speaker. Knowing that ethos is important, good persuasive speakers work to establish credibility with their audiences. **Credibility** means believability—if you're credible, people will believe what you have to say. If you have a good deal of credibility, audiences will take your words seriously and be open to new ideas. If your credibility is low, however, you will find it hard to persuade, even if your evidence is strong. Establishing credibility is thus vital for persuasive speakers. Researchers believe that credibility has three different components: competence, character, and charisma.[14]

credibility A speaker's believability.

Demonstrate Your Competence People have *competence* when they have the required skills, knowledge, and organization to perform a task well. Think back to the first day of this class. What impressions did you have of your instructor? Did he or she seem knowledgeable, organized, well prepared, and professional? If so, those characteristics probably gave you confidence in what your instructor had to say. By comparison, when you've had instructors who appeared ignorant, disorganized, unprepared, and unprofessional, you probably lacked confidence in their abilities.

Just as you have more confidence in a competent instructor, listeners will have more confidence in you if you come across as a competent speaker. Describing the experience and knowledge you have of your topic, and speaking in a polished, well-organized manner, will demonstrate your competence.

Accent Your Character A person's *character* is his or her honesty. People who appear honest are more credible than those who appear dishonest, because we can have greater confidence that what honest individuals say is accurate and true. In jury trials, for example, lawyers frequently cast doubt on the testimony of their opponents' witnesses by questioning their character. If an attorney can establish that an opposing witness has been caught lying in the past, that history makes the witness appear to be of questionable character and can lead the jury to doubt his or her testimony in the current trial. By comparison, witnesses who appear honest are more likely to be believed.

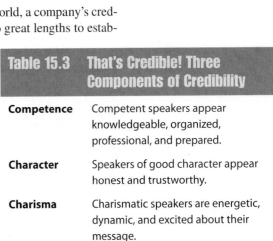

Charismatic speakers are often more persuasive than speakers who lack energy and excitement.

Good persuasive speakers establish their character by incorporating stories and anecdotes about themselves that demonstrate their honesty. In addition, speakers who enact *high-immediacy behaviors*—such as standing close to others, leaning forward, using eye contact, and maintaining an open posture—are judged to be of more positive character than speakers who do not enact those behaviors.[15]

Communicate with Charisma A final component of credibility is *charisma,* which is a speaker's enthusiasm. As you know, it's much easier to listen to—and to be persuaded by—someone who speaks dynamically and energetically than by someone who seems bored by his or her own words. So, when you're giving a persuasive speech, approach your topic and your audience with enthusiasm. Smile! Use gestures and vary your tone of voice to keep your presentation interesting. Look at your audience and use facial expressions that reflect the mood of your message. Bringing energy and excitement to your presentation will encourage your listeners to pay attention and make them receptive to your words.

A quick summary of the three components of credibility appears in Table 15.3.

The Bottom Line: Credibility Matters In the business world, a company's credibility often directly affects its profits. Corporations therefore go to great lengths to establish and maintain their credibility.

In late 2009 and early 2010, for instance, Toyota voluntarily recalled thousands of its cars because of problems with the accelerator and brakes. In an attempt to protect its credibility as a manufacturer of quality automobiles, Toyota placed advertisements on U.S. television and in major publications reinforcing its commitment to stand by its products and fix the problems.[16] By taking that action, the company tried to assure consumers that it was assuming responsibility and was committed to fixing the problems. That strategy was intended to minimize damage to Toyota's credibility that could result in lost sales and reduced profits.

In contrast, companies that are found to use false or misleading statements to persuade customers often lose credibility and

Table 15.3	That's Credible! Three Components of Credibility
Competence	Competent speakers appear knowledgeable, organized, professional, and prepared.
Character	Speakers of good character appear honest and trustworthy.
Charisma	Charismatic speakers are energetic, dynamic, and excited about their message.

THE DARK SIDE of Communication

Misleading to Persuade: A Threat to Credibility

Perhaps the most annoying aspect of renting a DVD is having to return it before it is overdue and subject to late fees. In January 2005, video rental giant Blockbuster attempted to persuade customers to patronize its stores by announcing—through a multimillion-dollar advertising campaign—that it was eliminating late fees. Large posters in the front windows of thousands of Blockbuster stores announced the new "No Late Fees" policy. Only one month later, however, the attorney general of New Jersey sued Blockbuster, claiming that the company's persuasive tactic amounted to false advertising.

The lawsuit, which was prompted by multiple consumer complaints, disclosed that instead of assessing a late fee to videos that were not returned on time, Blockbuster was charging the renters' credit cards for the purchase price of the products. That detail, the lawsuit alleged, was not properly disclosed to consumers, creating a false belief that the "No Late Fees" policy meant that customers could keep their rentals as long as they wanted.

In March 2005, Blockbuster agreed to make refunds to thousands of consumers and to reimburse 47 states for the cost of their investigations into customer complaints. The settlement, and the media coverage of the controversy, probably cast doubt on Blockbuster's credibility in the minds of its customers and perhaps served as an example for other companies wishing to protect their own credibility.

suffer decreased profits as a result. The reason is that consumers find deceptive practices in advertising to be unethical. To read about the problems one company encountered after losing credibility due to misleading statements, see "The Dark Side of Communication."

- As a speaker, in what different ways should you approach receptive, neutral, and hostile audiences?
- How can you establish rapport with your listeners?
- What are the components of credibility?

Test Yourself

>> A Sample Persuasive Speech

A good way to develop persuasive-speaking skills is to study excellent examples. Below is the text of a persuasive speech by Jennifer Wells, a communication studies major at the University of Alabama and a member of the school's speech and debate team. Jennifer's speech advocates expanding laws that protect people from sexual harassment in the workplace. Jennifer was a quarter-finalist in persuasive speaking with this speech at the American Forensics Association National Tournament in April 2009. Alongside the text are comments about what makes each section of her speech so effective. The formal outline for Jennifer's speech appears in Figure 15.2 on page 382.

Closing the Loophole on Sexual Harassment

COMMENTARY >>

SPEECH

This introduction opens with a compelling story introducing listeners to the problem described in the speech, same-sex sexual harassment in the workplace.

Joseph Oncale is not a household name . . . at least, not yet. After taking a job as a roughneck on an oil rig with Sundowner Offshore Services, Oncale's outgoing personality was incorrectly perceived as stereotypically homosexual behavior by his co-workers. They verbally and physically abused Oncale, culminating in an episode in which Oncale's arms were pinned behind his back in the shower while cheering co-workers looked on as a Sundowner supervisor simulated raping Oncale with a bar of soap.

Certain that he would be protected against such unrestrained subjugation and cruelty, Oncale sued Sundowner for sexual harassment. According to the *Labor Law Journal* of April 1, 2005, the Louisiana Supreme Court found that the atrocities committed against the heterosexual Oncale by Sundowner Services were perfectly excusable under the law. After all, boys will be boys. A loophole in Title 7—the federal safeguard protecting against sexual harassment and discrimination—permits heinous same-sex sexual harassment.

The starkest ramifications of this loophole can be seen in discriminatory practices between men. According to a report from the Equal Employment Opportunity Commission, or EEOC, between 1997 and 2007, 1 out of every 6 reports of sexual harassment was filed by a man. While significant, the scope of the issue is blurred by the fact that, according to the *Mondaq Legal News Network* on July 31, 2008, of those incidents, only a few make it to the verdict stage of a trial, and even fewer survive the appellate proceedings.

Here, the speaker makes her persuasive appeal. Notice that she offers a proposition of value: *we should protect people from same-sex sexual harassment.* Later, she will advocate changing the law, which is a proposition of policy.

Notice how the speaker effectively previews the topics she plans to address.

Regardless of one's moral, ethical, or religious views on sexuality, everyone deserves the protection of a safe workplace. Therefore, it is our duty as a vigilant society to ensure that we recognize the extent of this social injustice, identify the sources allowing this backwater practice to persist, and unite to protect those whose fundamental human rights have been ignored.

To understand this problem better, let's first examine the ramifications of a hostile work environment, and second, the loophole in the law. First, men deciding to report harassment risk escalating a hostile work environment into an openly discriminatory work environment. Servers who filed suit against the Cheesecake Factory stated in the July 11, 2008, *Los Angeles Times,* "It's just different when it happens to a guy; there's always the fear that they're going to question your manhood." The fact that the servers reported anything is unusual, because on top of the vulnerability involved in reporting harassment, co-workers and companies often make it even harder. *PR Week* of May 2, 2008, reports a case in which a finance director assaulted his male assistant during a trip. When the assistant reported it, he was forced to leave his job, but the finance director remains unpunished.

The speaker is careful throughout the speech to cite her sources. These citations help to give her words credibility.

Second, those brave enough to report sexual harassment often do so without the support of the law. The protection of Title 7 of the Civil Rights Act of 1964 extends only to individuals who are discriminated against on the basis of race, color, religion, sex, or national origin. This wording means that the law provides no protection from harassment based on sexual orientation or assumed sexual orientation, or from a member of one's own sex. Therefore, if you are a man and another man sexually harasses you in some way, you have no federally secured recourse. Contending that it is impossible for a man to sexually harass another man, the courts and Congress have repeatedly refused to acknowledge same-sex sexual harassment as an actionable discrimination, especially harassment based on sexual orientation. The December 2006 *Journal of Individual Employment Rights* succinctly explains that, as a federally unprotected class, homosexuals remain extremely exposed to discrimination in the form of sexual harassment.

COMMENTARY >>

SPEECH

Here, the speaker offers another brief preview of points she plans to make. By doing so, she helps her listeners follow the organization of her speech.

The same misconceptions that permitted the Title 7 loophole in 1964 perpetuate today. To better understand why, we must first understand the motivations behind sexual harassment and then examine the short-sighted view many take of it. First, although most people blame sexual desire for demeaning behavior, more often than not desire has nothing to do with motivating perpetrators. The *Journal of Individual Employment Rights* asserts that same-sex sexual harassment usually cannot be attributed to the sexual orientation of the victim or the perpetrator. Instead, it is a "power issue." A 2004 *Journal of Sex Roles* study clarifies that hostile sexism results from the belief that heterosexual men are superior to women and effeminate or homosexual men. That motivation means that the loophole in Title 7 not only permits heinous discrimination, but also perpetuates behaviors that invoke heterosexual as the "normal" or "superior" lifestyle. This desire to maintain the status quo propels perpetrators to exploit positions of power, resulting in increasingly hostile work environments.

Here, the speaker uses a quote from an attorney involved in the lawsuit as a way of supporting her point.

The second reason why same-sex sexual harassment is so often overlooked is because of general attitudes toward interpersonal relationships between men. When the law was written over 40 years ago, the sexual harassment tenet was included solely to safeguard women from men. That concentrated focus kept lawmakers from realizing that sexual harassment may occur in ways outside of their hetero-normative viewpoint. As the attorney in the lawsuit against the Cheesecake Factory stated in the *Los Angeles Times*, "There's this expectation that this doesn't happen to men. It's almost this boys-will-be-boys attitude of 'Oh, it's just hazing, it's just teasing, you can't take it seriously.'" The servers of the Cheesecake Factory restaurant in the lawsuit reported harassment that included simulated gang rape. The managers—who were fully aware of the problem—seemed amused and took no action to prohibit the offensive behavior. Their attitude of amusement carried into the court proceedings where, according to the previously cited article from *Mondaq Legal News Network*, in the appeal of *EEOC v. Harbert-Yeargin, Inc.*, the court furthered the "horseplay" excuse and overturned the original guilty verdict by asking, "What's next? Towel slapping in the locker room?"

COMMENTARY >>

SPEECH

The speaker introduces her proposition of policy, which is a change in Title 7.

This shamefully outdated view of sexual harassment provides a breeding ground for hostility and degradation. However, solutions exist on the government and personal levels. We as citizens must petition our government officials, letting them know that we do not agree with the loophole in Title 7 but we do agree that action must be taken. I have with me a petition. At the end of this speech round, please add your name to the list alongside those who disagree with allowing a law that permits discrimination to stand. At the end of the year I will send this petition to the EEOC, the organization spearheading the movement to close the loophole in Title 7. This petition will show our support of their activism and our willingness to add our names to the cause. In an open letter released on February 28, 2008, President Obama told the LGBT [lesbian, gay, bisexual, and transgender] community that he would end workplace discrimination based on sexual orientation or gender identity. Hopefully, our outpouring of support will further encourage the president to make good on his promise and move toward equality for all by closing the loophole.

A mandate on the national level would force corporations to update and streamline their policies in accordance with federal law. On a personal level, we can all take a stand against sexual harassment in any form. Most importantly, we must reshape our paradigms regarding what constitutes harassment. If you see something that would be considered harassment were it to take place between a man and a woman, it is harassment. Teasing is never an excuse. After all, as a community that generally prides itself in promoting acceptance, if change does not begin with us, where will it begin?

In her conclusion, the speaker reminds her listeners of her opening story, a technique that personalizes the issue.

Anytime sexual harassment occurs it is disgraceful, yet when sexual harassment is all but sanctioned under the law it is despicable. Fortunately, Joseph Oncale took his case before the U.S. Supreme Court, who decided that what happened to Oncale was indeed sexual harassment. The decision read by Justice Antonin Scalia laid the foundation to eventually protect the rights of all workers. Hopefully, the name Joseph Oncale will eventually be remembered as a pioneer in defending those whom the government had left to defend themselves.

TITLE: Closing the Loophole on Sexual Harassment

General purpose: To persuade

Purpose statement: Persuade my audience that it is the duty of a vigilant society to protect individuals from same-sex sexual harassment in the workplace.

INTRODUCTION

I. Joseph Oncale was subjected to simulated rape by his fellow male oil rig workers.

II. Despite his protests, no punishment ensued because same-sex sexual harassment is not recognized under the law.

III. **Thesis:** Regardless of one's moral, ethical, or religious views on sexuality, everyone deserves the protection of a safe workplace.

Transition: Describe ramifications of hostile work environment; identify loophole in sexual harassment law; offer solutions.

BODY

I. What is same-sex sexual harassment?
   A. Reporting same-sex harassment risks escalating hostility.
      1. Reporting harassment can turn a hostile work environment into an openly discriminatory one.
      2. *PR Week:* Financial director accused of assault of a male subordinate was allowed to keep his job.
   B. Those brave enough to report sexual harassment often do so without the support of the law.
      1. Title 7 of the Civil Rights Act of 1964 provides no protection from same-sex sexual harassment.
      2. *Journal of Individual Employment Rights:* As a federally unprotected class, homosexuals remain exposed to discrimination.

Transition: To understand why same-sex harassment is permitted by the loophole, we must understand the nature of sexual harassment.

II. The law overlooks same-sex sexual harassment.
   A. Power is a motivator of demeaning behavior.
      1. *Journal of Sex Roles:* Hostile sexism results from the belief that heterosexual men are superior to women and homosexual men.

2. The loophole therefore perpetuates the stereotype of heterosexuality as "normal."
   B. Outdated attitudes and beliefs persist about interpersonal relationships between men.
      1. Sexual harassment laws were originally intended to protect women from men.
      2. *Mondaq Legal News Network:* Courts accept the "boys will be boys" explanation for same-sex harassment.

Transition: Obsolete views of sexual harassment encourage hostility and degradation. Solutions exist, however.

III. Solutions exist at government and personal levels.
   A. The Title 7 loophole needs to be closed.
      1. Sign petition to the Equal Employment Opportunity Commission.
      2. Obama: I will end workplace discrimination based on sexual orientation or gender identity.
   B. People should take individual stands against sexual harassment.
      1. We must reshape our ideas about what constitutes sexual harassment.
      2. Any sexual harassment should be reported to authorities.

Transition: Any sexual harassment is disgraceful, but when sexual harassment is all but sanctioned under the law, it is despicable and must be legally prohibited.

CONCLUSION

I. Review of main points
   A. People deserve protection from sexual harassment, whether same-sex or opposite-sex.
   B. Sexual harassment that is sanctioned by law is despicable.

II. Final remarks
   A. Joseph Oncale's case has been heard by the U.S. Supreme Court.
   B. His case hopefully will prompt changes to federal sexual harassment laws in the United States.

FIGURE 15.2 Formal Speech Outline: Closing the Loophole on Sexual Harassment

For REVIEW >>

- **What does it mean to persuade?**

  Persuasion is an attempt to motivate others to adopt a specific belief, opinion, or behavior. We persuade others by appealing to ethos, pathos, and/or logos.

- **In what ways can we craft a persuasive message?**

  Persuasive messages can propose facts, values, or policies. They are organized in a compelling manner and avoid the use of logical fallacies.

- **Through what strategies can we hone our persuasive-speaking skills?**

  We can adapt to our audience, build rapport with our listeners, and establish our credibility.

Pop Quiz

Multiple Choice

1. Kellie tries to convince her instructor that she did her homework but left it in her car. Kellie is trying to influence her instructor's
   a. belief
   b. opinion
   c. evaluation
   d. action

2. The statement below that constitutes a proposition of fact is
   a. English should be the official language of the United States.
   b. College tuition should be made fully tax-deductible.
   c. National security is more important than individual rights.
   d. Platinum is three times as heavy as gold.

3. In Monroe's motivated sequence, the message "consider the benefits" would occur at the stage called
   a. need
   b. satisfaction
   c. visualization
   d. action

4. Mac suggests that you should accept his argument because of how many other people have already accepted it. Mac is using the logical fallacy known as
   a. false cause
   b. straw man
   c. red herring
   d. bandwagon appeal

5. The aspect of credibility that reflects a speaker's honesty is
   a. competence
   b. character
   c. charisma
   d. enthusiasm

Fill in the Blank

6. Aristotle used the term _____ to refer to listeners' emotions.

7. _____ reasoning starts with a general conclusion and then applies it to individual cases.

8. A _____ approach to persuasion begins by presenting, and then arguing against, the main objections to your position.

9. A "reduction to the absurd" is also called a _____.

10. When you build _____, you create the perception that you and your listeners see things similarly.

Answers for **The Competent Communicator** *exercise:*
5-A; 1-B; 8-C; 6-D; 3-E; 7-F; 4-G; 2-H

KEY TERMS

Appendix

WORKPLACE COMMUNICATION AND INTERVIEWING

- What communication processes are important in the workplace?
- What communication challenges do workplaces face today?
- In what ways can we improve our interviewing skills?

Nearly all of us will be employed at some point in our lives. Whether we work for a large multinational corporation or a small business with only a few employees, our ability to communicate effectively in the workplace can matter greatly to those whose lives are affected by our work. In this appendix, we'll explore **workplace communication,** the interactions people have as part of their employment.

>> Communicating in the Workplace

Many popular television shows—from dramas such as *NCIS* and *Grey's Anatomy* to comedies such as *30 Rock* and *The Office*—focus their storylines on how the characters communicate in the workplace. Most viewers can relate to the communication behaviors and challenges depicted in such shows. Building and maintaining workplace relationships is often difficult, although it can be highly rewarding. In this section, we'll survey the challenges and benefits of communicating within the workplace, look at employees' communications with people outside the workplace, and examine some key dimensions of creating a positive workplace culture.

COMMUNICATING WITHIN THE WORKPLACE

Much of workplace communication is **internal communication,** that is, the messages people within the workplace convey to one another. A meeting of managers, a company-wide e-mail message, and an employee suggestion box are all examples of internal communication. Internal workplace communication can be either formal or informal.

Formal Workplace Communication **Formal communication** comprises messages that come from the work organization and relate to its operations. Memos, official announcements, company newsletters, mission statements, and employee evaluations are all types of formal communication that members of many organizations regularly encounter.

Formal communication in the workplace varies according to the relative status of the sender and the audience. For instance, few of us would speak in the same way to our boss as to our peers. We can understand the effects of relative status on formal workplace communication by differentiating among communication that is upward, downward, and lateral.

- **Upward communication** consists of messages we send to people at higher levels of the organizational hierarchy than ours. Those include communications to immediate

---

workplace communication The interactions people have as part of their employment.

internal communication The messages people within the workplace convey to one another.

formal communication Messages that come from the work organization and relate to its operations.

upward communication Messages people send to those at higher levels of the organizational hierarchy than themselves.

supervisors as well as to higher-level personnel, such as an e-mail message we might send to the company president. When communicating upwardly, we're most likely to be taken seriously if our statements are clear, concise, and respectful.

- **Downward communication** comprises messages we send to people at lower levels of the organizational hierarchy, such as subordinates, interns, and staff members who report to us. Although such messages are often instructions regarding work assignments, they may also be general announcements, explanations of policy, or notes of encouragement. When communicating downwardly, it's best to avoid specialized jargon and to use language that anyone—regardless of his or her job—can understand. If our message contains criticism, we should choose our words tactfully and avoid embarrassing people by singling them out.

- **Lateral communication** involves the messages we share with peers or anyone who occupies the same position as we do in the workplace hierarchy. It includes communication with co-workers and anyone else whose level of power is similar to ours. Recall from Chapter 7 that effective communication with peers contributes to a positive work environment and makes the work experience more satisfying. Good lateral communication treats people as equals and helps them accomplish their mutual goals.

Informal Workplace Communication Formal communication—whether upward, downward, or lateral—is critical to any organization's ability to manage its image and conduct its operations. However, much of the communication in workplaces is informal. Unlike formal communication, **informal communication** is not sanctioned by the employer itself but arises from the social interactions of its members.

Many people say that informal communication travels along a **grapevine,** a metaphor indicating that informal messages are often conveyed in upward, downward, and lateral directions simultaneously. Just as a grapevine twists and turns in seemingly unpredictable ways as it grows, in many workplaces informal messages take a similarly unpredictable path.

Regarding communication grapevines, research tells us that

- *Grapevines use multiple communication channels.* Much communication along the grapevine is accomplished face-to-face, as people visit informally (and perhaps even secretly) to share information and gossip. Workplace grapevines also make use of telephone, e-mail, text messaging, instant messaging, and other forms of electronically mediated communication, allowing for the participation of people who aren't physically present.[1]

- *People rely heavily on the grapevine during a crisis.* When employees feel threatened by a situation, such as the announcement of upcoming layoffs, they can spend as much as 70 percent of their workplace communication time on the grapevine, listening to what others know and speculating about what they've heard. Particularly when a situation is ambiguous, we seem to crave the comfort of our informal communication networks.[2]

- *Communication along the grapevine can be remarkably accurate.* The informality of grapevine communication doesn't mean that it's inaccurate. Studies show that grapevine messages are substantially accurate from 75 percent to 95 percent of the time. Importantly, employees tend to *believe* that grapevine messages are accurate, maybe even more so than the employer's formal communication.[3]

COMMUNICATING TO EXTERNAL AUDIENCES

Nearly all organizations also communicate regularly with external audiences. When conducted effectively, **external communication**—that is, the messages people within the workplace convey to people outside the organization—can significantly enhance reputation, productivity, community support, and economic success. In contrast, poorly managed external communication can cause a workplace irreparable harm.

Among the multiple potential external audiences with whom companies must communicate are

- *Consumers,* who include anyone who buys or might buy a company's products or services. For many organizations, a primary vehicle for communicating with consumers

downward communication Messages people send to those at lower levels of the organizational hierarchy than themselves.

lateral communication Messages people share with peers in an organization.

informal communication Messages that are not sanctioned by an organization but arise from the social interactions of its members.

grapevine A metaphor indicating that informal messages are often conveyed in upward, downward, and lateral directions simultaneously.

external communication The messages people within the workplace convey to people outside the organization.

Putting Communication to Work

Name: Sunmit Singh

College(s):
Bachelor's degree,
University of Maryland
University College,
December 2009

Major(s): Business
administration, with a
concentration in communication, marketing,
and finance

Job Title: Owner of two small businesses,
including Rootsgear, a manufacturer and seller of
screen-printed apparel

Salary: Variable, as the business is young and still
growing

Time in Job: 4 years

Work Responsibilities: I have a wide range
of responsibilities, from bringing in clients, to
processing orders, to graphic design. The work starts
at 9 A.M. with sending out proofs for design jobs, and
then I meet with clients or vendors during the rest of
the day.

One of the exciting things that happened this
past year was the launch of our new website for
Rootsgear. After we worked on the site for two to
three months, international orders tripled, local
orders became steadier, and reviews from local
customers have been very positive.

Why Communication? Growing up, I always
wanted to be a business owner, but I never had
any plans to start out in college—it sort of just
happened. After taking a course in business speech,
I realized the importance of communication in the
business world.

A communication course that I learned a
tremendous amount from, and applied directly to my
daily work, was business communication. The course
focused on everyday business communication, with
a concentration on e-mails. As a business owner
today, writing e-mails is a daily task. Knowing how to
compose these in a conscientious and professional
manner makes all the difference.

My Advice to Students: Apply what you
have learned in college to the real world. For a
communication major, your skills could move you up
the ladder in a company very quickly. For example,
while applying for most jobs, understand that salaries
are negotiable. Most first-time employees tend to take
what they get, not realizing that all they had to do was
initiate a conversation about salary requirements.

---

is advertising. Companies advertise their goods or services in multiple ways, including television and radio commercials; print advertisements in newspapers and magazines; electronic ads posted on the Internet or sent to e-mail distribution lists; signs and billboards visible to drivers; unsolicited sales calls made in person or by telephone; and booths at fairs, trade shows, and sporting events. To see how one former communication major uses his communication skills to interact with consumers, check out Putting Communication to Work.

- *Potential personnel,* who include anyone who might come to work for a workplace as either a paid employee or a volunteer. Corporations, nonprofit groups, and the military are among the organizations that frequently recruit employees or volunteers through television, radio, and Internet ads.
- *Stockholders,* or people who own shares of a publicly traded company. Companies communicate with their stockholders primarily through their annual reports, which detail the financial gains and losses of a company's endeavors over the course of a year.
- *The media,* which include both broadcast and print forms of mass communication. Many large corporations have spokespersons or media relations divisions that accom-

workplace culture The values, customs, and communication behaviors that workplace members share and that reflect their organization's distinct identity.

rites Ceremonial acts and practices that convey one or more characteristics of a workplace's culture.

rituals Repeated behaviors that provide a familiar routine to a workplace's experiences.

modate reporters' requests for informational interviews or statements to include in news features.

- *Lawmakers,* including local elected officials, state legislators, and members of Congress. In November 2008, for instance, the chief executive officers of the largest three American automobile manufacturers testified before a committee of the U.S. House of Representatives to ask for several billion dollars in loans to keep their companies operational.
- *The general public,* which includes current or potential customers and employees and anyone else to whom an employer's reputation matters. Many large companies employ public relations experts who use communication to shape their public image.

WORKPLACE CULTURE

Pixar Animation Studios in Emeryville, California, is an unconventional place to work. To stimulate innovative, outside-the-box thinking, company president Ed Catmull instituted Pixar University. This professional-development program encourages risk taking and invites irrational thought as avenues to creativity. To minimize stress, Catmull makes a physician and a massage therapist available to Pixar employees several times a month, and he requires animators to get special permission to work more than 50 hours in a single week. The animation studio boasts a café, break rooms with pool and foosball tables, and an open area for concerts and lectures. At the urging of former Pixar CEO Steve Jobs, Catmull even created one giant bathroom for the company's 700 employees so that people across the organization would regularly interact and talk. Its innovations have put Pixar on the map as a company with a remarkable workplace culture.

Throughout this book, we have talked about culture as the collective values, customs, and communication behaviors shared among people in a particular country or social group. Communication researchers believe that workplaces have their own cultures. We can think of **workplace culture** as the values, customs, and communication behaviors that workplace members share and that reflect their organization's distinct identity. We can understand workplace culture by examining its rites, rituals, and roles.

Workplaces Have Rites **Rites** are ceremonial acts and practices that convey one or more characteristics of a workplace's culture. Organizational behavior scholars Harrison Trice and Janice Beyer identified six types of workplace rites:[4]

- *Rites of passage* signify people's advancement to a higher status or level in a workplace. Ceremonies to celebrate an employee's promotion are examples of rites of passage.
- *Rites of integration* enhance feelings of inclusion and community in the workplace. Participation in a company's annual picnic, for instance, can reinforce employees' sense of belonging to the group.
- *Blaming rites* are concerned with consequences for poor or unethical performance. For example, attorneys who violate client confidentiality might be reprimanded, demoted, or fired and may lose their license to practice law.
- *Enhancement rites* relate to consequences for superior performance. Excellent salespeople might receive plaques, cash bonuses, trips, or recognition as Salesperson of the Year in acknowledgment of outstanding achievement.
- *Renewal rites* update and revitalize a workplace. After a particularly disappointing year of collecting donations, a nonprofit group, for example, might organize a retreat to boost morale and refresh its employees' solicitation skills.
- *Conflict resolution rites* aim to manage disagreements and discord. To resolve conflicts between management and employees, a large corporation might use a mediator to help representatives from each group reach consensus on their disagreements.

Workplaces Have Rituals Whereas rites occur when circumstances call for them, **rituals** are repeated behaviors that provide a

SHARPEN
Your Skills

Identify a rite that is common in your workplace. In a short paragraph, indicate whose communication behaviors that rite affects, and in what ways.

familiar routine to a workplace's experiences.[5] We examined family rituals in Chapter 8. In workplaces, three types of rituals are especially common:

- *Personal rituals* are routine behaviors through which individuals convey their workplace identity.[6] On the first day of each fiscal year, a manager might personally greet each arriving employee as a way of communicating her interest in their well-being.
- *Social rituals* are recurring events that reinforce personal relationships among workplace members.[7] The custodial staff at a government agency might meet every other Thursday for happy hour, for example, in a ritual that allows them to socialize, share information, and affirm their personal bonds.
- *Task rituals* are repeated activities that enhance people's abilities to do their jobs. For example, when greeting a patient at a clinic, a medical assistant typically performs a series of ritualized tasks, such as asking about symptoms, current medications, and drug allergies and then taking the patient's vital signs.

Many rites and rituals reinforce a workplace's current cultural practices. As a workplace culture evolves, however, its rites and rituals often follow suit. In response to various threats to traveler safety, for instance, the U.S. Transportation Security Administration has changed its task rituals for screening airline passengers. Recent changes include requiring passengers to remove their shoes for X-ray and limiting the types and amounts of liquid that passengers can bring aboard an airplane.

Workplaces Have Roles As we saw in Chapter 8, people in families enact different *roles,* which embody their functions within the family system. The same can be said of people in workplaces. Each employee has certain responsibilities to the group that reflect his or her role.

Some workplace roles are **formal roles,** functions that are prescribed by the employer itself. The formal role of a receptionist, for instance, may be to greet visitors, provide directions to specific company facilities, issue visitor passes, and answer incoming telephone calls. Formal roles are interconnected in a system that fulfills all necessary functions of the workplace. Organizational charts, such as the one in Figure A.1, specify the connections among various roles in a fictitious manufacturing company.

Formal roles are tied to *positions* within the workplace rather than to particular individuals. The formal role of a receptionist is the same no matter who has that job. In contrast, **informal roles** are functions adopted by specific people rather than being dictated by the workplace. Whereas formal roles serve the organization's professional needs, informal roles often evolve to serve social and interpersonal needs. At his advertising agency, for instance, Jay is known as someone with an exceptional sense of humor who can always be counted on to bring comic relief to stressful situations. We might say that Jay has assumed the informal role of company comedian. No one formally assigned Jay that responsibility; it wasn't included in his job description or detailed in his contract. Moreover, that role is tied specifically to Jay because of his personality and sense of humor; it would not necessarily be expected of the next person to occupy Jay's position. For those reasons, company comedian is an informal role.

An informal role isn't necessarily any less important than a formal role. Indeed, research shows that sharing humor in the workplace—as Jay does informally—can reinforce company culture,[8] alleviate tension,[9] foster creativity,[10] and enhance interpersonal relationships.[11] Many informal roles that employees might play—including conflict mediator, confidante, or social event organizer—are seen by others as indispensable to the group's success.

- How do upward communication, downward communication, and lateral communication differ?
- What are workplace rites?
- How do rituals function in the workplace?
- In what ways are formal workplace roles different from informal roles?

Test Yourself

Organizational Chart
South Bend Industrial, Inc.

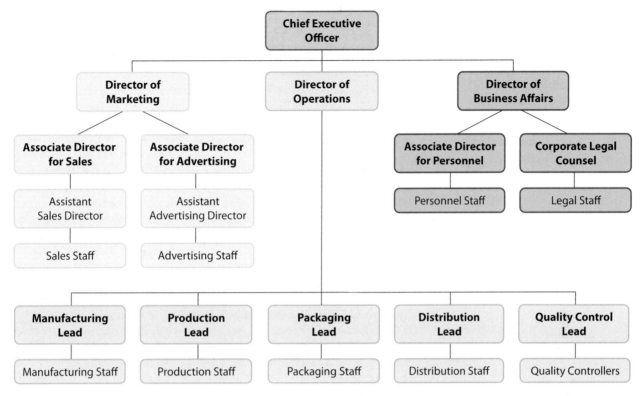

FIGURE A.1 Organizational Chart

>> Managing Workplace Communication Challenges

Everyone in workplace organizations—large and small—encounters communication challenges from time to time. Although no list can enumerate every possible challenge, we can appreciate the communication trials that employees face by examining four issues: globalization, communication technology, work/life conflict, and diversity.

GLOBALIZATION AND CROSS-CULTURAL CHALLENGES

The world has shrunk considerably—figuratively speaking, at least—in the past hundred years. Almost unbelievably, travel time between continents used to be measured in weeks rather than hours. Only a few decades ago, telephone calls to other countries were extremely expensive, and mail service was unreliable and slow. Consequently, only very large organizations had the means to communicate and do business with overseas organizations. Today, we can chat online in real time with anyone in the world who has a computer and an Internet connection. We can fax documents to any corner of the globe in minutes, and we can send a package by overnight delivery to virtually any country. Advances in transportation and communication technology have significantly expanded the audience with which we can interact and have made it possible for companies to do business around the world. The term **globalization** describes the increasing interconnectedness of societies and their economies as a result of developments in transportation and communication.

Millions of items—from cars and computers to clothes, food products, and DVDs—are either manufactured or assembled in other countries and then imported into the United States for sale. When we buy those products, we are affecting, and being affected by, globalization. When we call to receive technical support for a new purchase, we are as

formal roles Responsibilities and functions that are prescribed by the employer.

informal roles Responsibilities and functions adopted by specific people rather than being dictated by the workplace.

globalization The increasing interconnectedness of societies and their economies as a result of developments in transportation and communication.

likely to speak with someone in New Delhi as in New York City. As companies have expanded to include employees, suppliers, customers, and members around the world, they have had to adapt to a diversity of languages, customs, and ways of doing business.

COMMUNICATION TECHNOLOGY CHALLENGES

Few organizations today could operate as they do without communication technology. E-mail, videoconferencing, text messaging, telephone and fax machines, and workplace websites allow individuals to work together without *being* together and to communicate with unprecedented efficiency. Nearly two-thirds of U.S. American workers use electronically mediated forms of communication, such as e-mail and the Internet, on a daily basis at their jobs.[12] Such technologies have significantly expanded the audience a workplace can reach, while simultaneously making communication faster and more cost-effective. As with many innovations, however, communication technology has also presented new challenges.

Choosing a Communication Channel One challenge for using communication technology in the workplace is deciding which technology to employ in a given situation. Recall from Chapter 1 that some communication contexts are *channel-rich,* meaning they allow people to perceive several communication behaviors at once. The most channel-rich context is the face-to-face conversation, because it provides communicators access to each other's words, gestures, facial expressions, vocalic behaviors, touch, and scent. When face-to-face meetings are not feasible, however, a videoconference provides the next most channel-rich context. In a videoconference, participants can see and hear each other in **real time,** meaning as they are communicating.

Other communication technologies provide *channel-lean* contexts, meaning they restrict the number of communication channels people can perceive. Conversing by text messaging or instant messaging, for instance, allows people to communicate in real time but only with words and emoticons that approximate facial expressions. The communicators cannot feel each other's touch, smell each other's scent, or see each other's gestures and facial expressions as they can in contexts that offer more communication channels. Sending e-mail messages and posting notes to an electronic bulletin board, blog, or Facebook wall are even more channel-lean than text and instant messages because they normally do not constitute real-time communication. Rather, an e-mail message or a blog posting you generate today may not be read for hours or even days.

Ensuring Security A second challenge for workplaces—and for many individuals—is ensuring the security of information they communicate, particularly online. Because companies rely so heavily on e-mail to communicate with their internal and external audiences, concerns over the security of e-mail messages have become paramount. In 1986, the U.S. Congress enacted the Electronic Communications Privacy Act (ECPA) to protect the privacy of electronic communication. The ECPA prohibits intercepting a person's private e-mail messages without consent and prevents the government from requiring electronic communication providers (such as Yahoo, Google, and AOL) to disclose their subscribers' identity except in a narrow range of circumstances. Although the ECPA safeguards electronic communication even when this protection isn't explicitly mentioned, some workplaces have required their e-mail messages to include an addendum notifying the recipient that the messages are protected. Such an addendum usually appears below the user's signature file on every e-mail message he or she generates. Figure A.2 provides an example of one such addendum.

Reducing Distraction A third challenge posed by communication technology is the time it takes to keep up with it. According to one survey, the average person received 13,505 e-mail messages in 2009 alone, an average of 37 messages every day.[13] Although some of those messages are related to work, others are personal messages or unsolicited

real time At the actual time when a communication or an event takes place.

```
CONFIDENTIAL COMMUNICATION
This Email is covered by the Electronic Communications Privacy Act, 18 U.S.C.
2510-2521 and is legally privileged. The information contained in this Email
is intended only for use of the individual or entity named above. If the
reader of this message is not the intended recipient, or the employee or agent
responsible to deliver it to the intended recipient, you are hereby notified
that any dissemination, distribution or copying of this communication is
strictly prohibited.
```

FIGURE A.2 E-Mail Message Addendum Regarding Privacy

advertisements. Attending to all that e-mail during work hours can be distracting and can reduce productivity.

Distraction is an even bigger danger when employees use the Internet during work hours for personal activities such as shopping, banking, blogging, and social networking. One survey found that 69 percent of office workers—and 77 percent of those aged 18 to 24—conduct personal business online during work hours.[14] According to another study, 1.5 percent of total office productivity is lost every year to U.S. businesses just because of employees' personal use of Facebook during work hours.[15] Know your employer's policy on using the Internet for personal business, and be mindful of the ways it can reduce your own productivity.

WORK/LIFE CONFLICT

The typical U.S. American family of the 1950s was supported financially by only one parent (usually the father) working full-time. In the twenty-first century, however, *dual-career families*—in which both adults work full-time—are the norm.[16] The pressure of balancing the demands of work with the rest of one's activities creates a **work/life conflict** for many people. Such a conflict can be highly problematic for employers and their employees if not managed constructively.

Two types of work/life conflict occur. The first type is *life interference with work,* which happens when people's life responsibilities impede their job performance. If Ramon's elderly mother falls ill and requires his help, for instance, he may miss work or important deadlines. The second type is *work interference with life,* which happens when people's job responsibilities hinder their ability to fulfill personal obligations. If Simone's position requires her to travel frequently, for example, her repeated absences may make it difficult to maintain close friendships.

Studies have shown that individuals with significant work/life conflict are at elevated risk of health problems such as clinical depression[17] and sleep disorders.[18] They also experience increased job stress and reduced satisfaction with life,[19] their marriage,[20] and their family relationships.[21] Finally, individuals with substantial work/life conflict aren't very happy.[22] One of the most harmful effects of work/life conflict is **burnout,** a chronic sense of exhaustion or apathy that can come from long-term frustration and stress. Burnout isn't a component of work/life conflict; it's a result of it. When their employees experience burnout, workplaces suffer in the form of increased absenteeism,[23] lost productivity,[24] and decreased communicative effectiveness.[25]

Individuals can also feel conflicted about their work lives when they experience sexual harassment in the workplace. See The Dark Side of Communication to explore this problem.

work/life conflict Conflict created by the pressure of balancing the demands of work with the rest of one's activities.

burnout A chronic sense of exhaustion or apathy that can come from long-term frustration and stress.

WORKPLACE DIVERSITY

In many workplaces, employees represent a mix of different cultures, religious beliefs, mental and physical abilities, educational achievements, ages, genders, and political orientations.[26] It's therefore likely that workplace experiences will expose us to people with

THE DARK SIDE of Communication

Sexual Harassment in the Workplace

A serious problem arises in the workplace when employees feel they have been sexually harassed by their superiors. In the United States, the federal Equal Employment Opportunity Commission (EEOC) defines **sexual harassment** as unsolicited, unwelcome behavior of a sexual nature in the workplace.[27] You might intend to be friendly or supportive by putting your arm around a subordinate, for instance, but if the subordinate feels uncomfortable by your behavior, it may constitute harassment.

According to the EEOC, sexual harassment can occur in two forms. The first, *quid pro quo* (Latin for "this for that") *harassment,* happens when a supervisor offers an employee rewards in exchange for sexual favors. A statement such as "I'll give you tomorrow off if you have a drink with me tonight" can qualify as quid pro quo harassment if it is directed at a subordinate. The second form, *hostile work environment harassment,* occurs when work conditions are sexually offensive or intimidating. Telling sexually suggestive jokes when both men and women are present, or making derogatory comments about a person's sexual orientation, can qualify as hostile work environment harassment. Sexual harassment is a serious and pervasive problem in some workplaces, and its victims often suffer long-term emotional and psychological harm. If you ever feel you are being sexually harassed, it can be hard to speak up, but ignoring the situation won't make it go away. Remember that sexual harassment is illegal and that you have a right not to be victimized. Sometimes, all it takes to stop harassment is for you to speak up and tell another person that his or her behavior offends you. If you're uncomfortable doing so, or if the offensive behavior continues afterward, report the situation to your organization's human resources department or affirmative action office.

backgrounds, customs, and ways of thinking that are quite different from our own.[28] Many organizations regard such diversity as an essential asset on the reasoning that a diverse work force may produce more innovative ideas than a homogeneous staff.

Yet diversity can pose challenges for communication and interpersonal interaction. Working with people whose capabilities, beliefs, and life experiences differ dramatically from our own can be frustrating. Our personal background leads each of us to take certain ideas and experiences for granted that others may not. For instance, when scheduling a meeting of a work team, it may not occur to you that the date you set is an important religious holiday for some in the group. Recognizing and adapting to people's differences can improve our ability to work harmoniously and productively with others.

You can improve your adaptability to workplace diversity if you

- *Check your assumptions.* When you send an e-mail message to co-workers, for instance, do you tend to assume everyone will understand your terminology? Do you assume the recipients will all share the priorities your message conveys? If there's a chance your assumptions may not be valid, adjust your message before sending it.
- *Remember that being different doesn't mean being wrong.* If, say, your religious beliefs are very important to you, you might tend to see alternative ideas as wrong. That

sexual harassment Unsolicited, unwelcome behavior of a sexual nature in the workplace.

tendency can make it difficult to communicate openly and respectfully with people whose beliefs differ from yours. There are many ways to think about religion, and your beliefs are only "right" because *you* believe them. Others see their beliefs as right because *they* believe them. Having a different orientation from you doesn't make someone else wrong, only different. Just as you would want others to treat your beliefs respectfully, it's important to extend that courtesy to them.

- *Help others adapt.* Being adaptable to diversity doesn't mean only respecting and accommodating others—it also means informing others when they're ignoring your needs or beliefs. Through your honest input, they can learn to be more adaptable as well. So, when someone doesn't acknowledge your uniqueness, point out—tactfully and respectfully—that your background gives you experiences, beliefs, priorities, and needs that he or she may not be recognizing.

Test Yourself

- In what ways can globalization affect how people in organizations communicate?
- Why is security such a large concern in the context of communication technology?
- What types of problems result from work/life conflict?
- How can we adapt successfully to workplace diversity?

>> Interviewing Successfully

People conduct interviews for various reasons, many of which are related to the workplace. Your ability to participate successfully in interviews can therefore be an asset when communicating in the workplace. We'll begin this section by exploring the diverse purposes of interviewing. We'll then consider how you can land, and subsequently prepare for, a successful job interview and how you should respond to discriminatory questions if you encounter them.

WHAT IS AN INTERVIEW?

A useful and versatile component of workplace communication is the **interview,** a structured conversation that focuses on questions and answers.[29] When we hear the word *interview,* many of us think immediately of a job interview. The job interview—which we will examine below as an example of a *selection interview*—is critical in the workplace; after all, most of us won't be hired in the first place unless we succeed at the job interview. There are, however, *many* forms of interviewing, some of which occur commonly in the workplace.

TYPES OF INTERVIEWS

Interviews are of different types and have varying purposes, including

- *The appraisal interview:* Whenever you sit down with someone to discuss your performance and your goals for the future, you're taking part in an **appraisal interview.** In many lines of work, managers and supervisors conduct appraisals of all their employees on a yearly basis. The appraisal interview can encourage you to continue what you're doing well and guide you in ways to improve.[30]
- *The problem-solving interview:* A **problem-solving interview** occurs to identify solutions to a problem or conflict. The primary goals are to understand the nature of the problem and to identify potential solutions. You take part in problem-solving interviews, for instance, when you discuss treatment options for an illness with your physician and financial options for a mortgage with your banker.[31]

interview A structured conversation that focuses on questions and answers.

appraisal interview A discussion focused on an employee's performance and goals for the future.

problem-solving interview A discussion conducted to identify solutions to a problem or conflict.

- *The exit interview:* If you've resigned from an organization to take a job elsewhere, you typically are asked to complete an **exit interview,** a conversation about your experiences with the organization you're leaving. During an exit interview, you usually would describe both positive and negative aspects of your job, your supervisors, and the organization.
- *The counseling interview:* When you go through a difficult time, you might reach out to close friends, relatives, or a professional therapist. With those people, you can express your feelings, receive empathy, and gain an outside perspective on your situation. That type of conversation—whether conducted with a therapist or a loved one—constitutes a **counseling interview,** an interaction aimed at supporting an individual through a personal problem.
- *The service-oriented interview:* A **service-oriented interview** is a conversation oriented toward helping you with a product or service you have purchased. When you tell the customer service representative at the clothing store that you've discovered a torn lining in a jacket you just bought, he may examine the jacket and offer either to refund your money or to exchange your damaged jacket.
- *The persuasive interview:* If you've ever received a telephone call asking you to support a political candidate or vote a certain way on a proposition, you've participated in a **persuasive interview,** a conversation intended to affect your belief, opinion, or behavior. During elections, it's common for campaign workers to call or visit registered voters to encourage them to vote in a particular way. You also take part in persuasive interviews when people try to convince you to donate money or volunteer your time.
- *The survey interview:* Each decade, the federal government conducts a *census,* a survey to count and gather information about the U.S. population. To collect census data, government workers visit or call households and businesses. If you were to be visited by a census surveyor, you would likely be asked a variety of questions, including "How many people live in your household?" and "How many of you are employed full-time?" Your conversation with the census worker would constitute a **survey interview,** an interaction aimed at gathering information.
- *The selection interview:* A **selection interview** is a conversation intended to help the interviewer choose the most appropriate person for a position, an assignment, a promotion, or an award. When you interview for a job, you are taking part in a selection interview. The ability to succeed in selection interviews is critical to your chances for employment.

LANDING A JOB INTERVIEW

Your first conversation with a potential employer is likely to be during a selection interview in which you're competing for a specific job. Only rarely do jobs come looking for you. Landing a job interview typically requires identifying employment opportunities in your field of interest and preparing a professional resume and cover letter to submit for those vacancies. This section contains tips for accomplishing those tasks and also for ensuring that your hard work is not undermined by your online persona.

Conduct a Job Search The first step in landing a job interview is to identify positions for which to apply. An excellent place to start is with your friends, family members, instructors, and anyone you know who works in your field of interest. Tell those people the kind of work you want to do, and ask for ideas about where to look. They may be able to put you in touch with employers in your field who are looking for people to hire. They may also give you pointers for how to connect with potential employers.

Most colleges and universities also have job placement centers where employers can post announcements of vacancies. Because those centers exist specifically to help students find jobs, they can be a valuable resource for identifying opportunities. Get to know the staff at your placement office and find out about the resources available to you there.

You can also search for job openings on your own. Websites such as CareerBuilder.com and Monster.com allow you to search for jobs by location, field, or company. Those

exit interview A conversation about an employee's experiences with an organization that he or she is leaving.

counseling interview An interaction aimed at supporting an individual through a personal problem.

service-oriented interview A conversation oriented toward helping people with a product or service they have purchased.

persuasive interview A conversation intended to affect beliefs, opinions, or behaviors.

survey interview An interaction aimed at gathering information.

selection interview A conversation intended to help the interviewer choose the most appropriate person for a position, an assignment, a promotion, or an award.

sites will describe available openings and allow you to apply for the jobs online. Some websites specialize in advertising positions with a specific field. For instance, TeacherJobs.com posts vacancies for educators, and Firefighter-Jobs.com lists openings for positions in the fire service. You can also identify vacancies at specific companies by looking at their individual websites.

Prepare a Cover Letter and Resume When you find job postings that catch your interest, the next step is to communicate that interest to the employers. In many cases, your first contact with an employer will be made in writing, in the form of a cover letter and resume. Because many employers receive dozens or even hundreds of applications for each available position, you need to ensure that your cover letter and resume make a positive first impression.

The Cover Letter A **cover letter** is a one-page letter in which you formally apply for a specific position. In your cover letter, you have the opportunity to express your interest in the job and to describe how your education, skills, and experience would benefit the employer.

Some applicants write long, detailed cover letters describing their every qualification for the position. That approach is almost never a good strategy. The reason is that your potential employer may have stacks of cover letters to read and may not have the time to read yours in depth. Remember that the goal of your cover letter isn't to land you the job—it's to land you the job interview. Cover letters shouldn't contain your life story; they should hit the highlights and make the employer want to know more about you.

Figure A.3 contains a sample cover letter. Notice how the writer expresses his interest in the job, mentions his qualifications, and then says he looks forward to discussing the position further. For most positions, a brief and direct letter such as the sample is best.

The Resume A **resume** is a short document listing your employment qualifications. When you're applying for an entry-level position, it is usually best to keep your resume to one page. As you progress in your career, your resume may grow in length, but you should always strive to keep it straightforward and clear.

There are several ways to compile a resume. You'll generally want to include the following details:

- *Name and contact information:* Be certain that your name appears at the top of your resume and is followed by your mailing address, telephone number, and e-mail address. Ensure that the telephone number you provide has an answering machine or voice mail that contains a clear, professional message.
- *Employment objective:* Briefly describe the type of position you are seeking and the kind of employer for whom you wish to work. If you will be applying for several different types of jobs, create different versions of your resume so that you can keep your employment objectives as specific as possible.
- *Education:* Identify the schools you have attended and the degrees or certificates you have earned (or are expecting to earn) at each. Note your academic major and areas of concentration, and list your grade point average if you think it will help make your application competitive.
- *Employment experience:* Starting with your current or most recent job, list the jobs you have had that are relevant to the type of employment you are seeking. For each job, identify your job title, employer, dates of employment, and primary responsibilities. Even if you worked on a volunteer basis in some cases, include the positions that are most relevant to the work you are seeking now.
- *Skills and interests:* In this section, tell your potential employer about any special skills you have and about your major interests. If you're fluent in sign language, certified in CPR, or proficient at computer programming, say so. Potential employers may find your skills and interests to be particularly attractive.
- *References:* Your employment references should be individuals who can attest to your skills, work ethic, and character. They typically include current or former employers,

cover letter A one-page letter in which a person formally applies for a specific position.

resume A short document listing a person's employment qualifications.

1001 Main Street
Seattle, WA 98195

May 2, 2010

Dr. Ellen Hurston, Sales Manager
Chrysalis Publishing
342 Eighth Avenue, Suite 11
Chicago, IL 60603

Dear Dr. Hurston:

In response to your advertisement in the April 28, 2010 issue of *The Chicago Sun-Times,* enclosed is my resume for the position of sales associate with Chrysalis Publishing. I am currently a senior majoring in communication at the University of Washington and have a strong interest in using my sales experience and interpersonal skills in the field of academic publishing.

Currently I am the Sales Manager for *The Daily,* the student newspaper at the University of Washington, which has a daily circulation of nearly 30,000. In my position, I coordinate the sale of classified advertising for both campus and corporate clients, and I oversee a staff of 12 part-time student salespeople. This position has given me valuable experience with building and maintaining professional relationships and ensuring high-quality customer service for the newspaper's clients. I would love the opportunity to put those skills to use for Chrysalis Publishing.

My publishing experience also includes work as a copyeditor for Grand Systems Publishing, a producer of technical writing textbooks, and as a sales associate for Borders Books. Both of those positions have helped me to hone my communication, sales, and customer service skills, which I believe would be advantageous in the academic publishing industry.

I am fluent in both English and Spanish and have experience working with people from diverse ethnic and cultural backgrounds. I am also proficient in Microsoft computer programs, including Word, Excel, PowerPoint, and Pages. If you would like a list of personal and professional references, I would be glad to furnish it.

Thank you for the opportunity to apply for the position of sales associate with Chrysalis Publishing. I will look forward to discussing my skills and experience with you in person.

Sincerely yours,

David Shaffer

David Shaffer

FIGURE A.3 Sample Cover Letter

college instructors, coaches, and others who can verify that you are responsible and proficient. It is usually best not to include relatives, romantic partners, and others whose assessments of you would seem biased by their personal feelings. You can either list your references and their contact information on your resume or indicate that you will provide those details upon request.

Figure A.4 illustrates a sample resume. You might consult with the placement office at your college or university for additional examples.

Check Your Online Persona In your job search, you have carefully crafted your resume and cover letter to portray yourself as competent, professional, and responsible. However, don't make the mistake of believing that those documents constitute all the information that a potential employer could find about you. What would a human resources director learn about you if she Googled your name? Would she find your Facebook page containing unflattering photos and information? Would she read on MySpace that your interests include "getting smashed every weekend"?

There's a simple way to find out. Google your own name, and see what comes up. Whatever information you can find about yourself online will be easily accessible to any potential employer. You may consider it an invasion of your privacy for employers to consult the Internet for information about you. Once you post something online, however, it becomes accessible not only to your friends but also to anyone seeking information about you, including a prospective employer.

Before you send out a resume, Google your name. If your search returns anything that you wouldn't want a potential employer to see, take down that information or make it accessible only to authorized viewers (such as your Facebook friends). The last thing you want is to lose a job opportunity because a personnel manager sees your spring break pictures online and concludes that you don't have the character or the maturity to perform competently in the job.

SUCCEEDING IN A JOB INTERVIEW

Now that you've landed a job interview, how can you ensure that you're ready to negotiate the interview successfully? Job selection interviews can be stressful and even daunting, but you can manage those challenges if you're prepared. In this section, we'll survey some crucial strategies for winning the job.

Research Your Potential Employer One of the best ways to prepare for a successful job selection interview is to learn as much as you can about your potential employer. Let's say you are interviewing for a marketing position at a major sportswear retailer. Before your interview, you will want to find out about the company's size, the location of its headquarters and major divisions, its top officers, and its history. Explore the company's website (or other sites that discuss the firm) for that information, or look for it in the company's annual report, which you may be able to download.

In addition, learn as much as you can about the specific position for which you're applying, such as the facility where you would be working, the size of the marketing division, and the manager to whom you'd be reporting. Carefully reading the job description and searching the website for information on the marketing division—if there is one—should give you some clues.

Anticipate Likely Questions A major reason why job selection interviews are stressful is that you don't usually know beforehand what questions the interviewer will ask. However, you can anticipate many of the questions you are likely to encounter. Let's first briefly examine the most common types of questions and identify successful responses to each.

- *Open-ended questions* are questions that invite a broad range of answers. Examples include "Tell me about yourself," and "What are your goals for the future?" An

David Shaffer

1001 Main Street, Seattle WA 98195
206.965.2482 • dshaffer@gmail.com

Employment Objective
To obtain an entry-level sales position for an academic publishing company.

Education
Bachelor of Arts, Communication, University of Washington   May 2010
  Cumulative GPA: 3.69/4.00
  Dean's List five out of six quarters

Associate of Arts, Liberal Studies, Seattle Community College   May 2008
  Cumulative GPA: 3.80/4.00
  Graduated *magna cum laude*

Employment Experience
Sales Manager, *The Daily,* University of Washington   April 2009–present
  Coordinate sales of advertising for major university student newspaper. Maintain business
  relationships with nearly 100 corporate accounts. Provide customer service and editorial support.
  Responsible for increasing advertising revenue by 15%.

Copyeditor, Grand Systems Publishing, Seattle WA   February 2006–April 2009
  Edited technical writing book produced for undergraduate and graduate students in engineering,
  city planning, and design. Developed software to reduce copyediting errors.

Sales Associate, Borders Books, Seattle WA   September 2003–January 2006
  Assisted customers with locating books. Conducted sales transactions. Stocked book shelves.
  Provided assistance for publication deliveries. Responsible for closing store at night.

Skills and Interests
Computer skills: Word, Excel, PowerPoint, Pages.

Language skills: Fluent in English and Spanish.

Other interests: Writing, software design, cross-country skiing.

References
Gladly furnished upon request.

FIGURE A.4 Sample Resume

open-ended question gives you the opportunity to reply in such a way that reflects positively on you. In response to a question about your goals, for instance, you can focus on goals that are relevant for the job and explain how you are already working toward attaining them.

- *Closed-ended questions* are questions that prompt brief, specific answers. Some call for a simple yes or no, such as "Can you work weekends?" Others elicit particular pieces of information, such as "What was your college major?" When you're asked closed-ended questions, it is best to provide short, direct answers. If the interviewer wants you to elaborate on your answer, he or she will ask you to do so.

- *Hypothetical questions* describe a situation and ask you to speculate about how you would react if you encountered it. An interviewer might ask, "Suppose you were su-pervising an employee whom you suspected was having an affair with your boss. How would you handle that?" By posing such a question, the inter-viewer assesses how you would analyze and ap-proach the situation.

- *Probing questions* are questions that request more detail on answers you have already provided. Let's say you are asked why you left your previ-ous job, and you cite the lack of opportunities for advancement as the reason. A probing question would be, "What opportunities for advancement would make a job more appealing to you?" Use probing questions as your chance to elaborate on what you've said.

Most job selection interviews include a mix of gen-eral questions and position-specific questions. Interview-ers commonly begin with broad, open-ended questions, such as "Tell me a little about yourself." From there, they typically move to more specific, closed-ended, hypothet-ical, and probing questions about the candidate's educa-tion, work history, skills and talents, and qualifications for the job. Many interviews end with the interviewer's asking whether the applicant has any questions. Al-though it is impossible to anticipate every question, you can prepare for your interview by formulating answers to commonly asked questions such as those in Table A.1.

Table A.1 Questions Commonly Asked During Selection Interviews
Tell me about yourself.
What are your primary strengths?
What do you consider your most serious weaknesses?
Why are you interested in this particular job/company?
Describe a difficult situation you've been in and how you handled it. How would you handle it differently today?
Who have been the biggest influences in your life? Why?
What can you do for this company? Why should we hire you instead of someone else?
What are your professional goals for the next five years? Ten years?
What do you value in a co-worker?
Are you willing to relocate if necessary?
How is your academic background/work experience relevant for this job?
Do you have any questions for me?

Generate Questions of Your Own Always prepare at least three or four ques-tions to ask if given the opportunity. Some strategies for formulating good questions are to

- *Ask questions that allow the interviewer to reflect on his or her own experiences.* An excellent question to ask the interviewer is, "What have you most enjoyed about working here?" That type of question allows the interviewer to tell you about himself or herself and also to identify the aspects of the employer that he or she most appreciates.

- *Ask questions that indicate your long-term interest in the job.* A question such as, "What opportunities would this position offer for someone who is interested in growing with this company?" suggests that you are thinking about your career in the long term and that you would be serious about your commitment to your employer.

- *Don't ask for details about the company that you should already know.* Recall that part of preparing for a job selection interview is researching your potential employer. Therefore, you don't want

SHARPEN
Your Skills

Think of a job you would like to have when you graduate. Review the questions in Table A.1, and write out a short answer for each. Afterward, ask a trusted relative or instructor to go through your answers and offer you feedback about how you might improve them.

your questions to reveal ignorance about the company, such as "Where is this company's headquarters located?"

- *Never ask about salary or benefits unless the interviewer has brought up those subjects.* Some interviewers may ask you about your salary requirements. However, unless the interviewer introduces the topic, don't inquire about the salary, vacation time, or medical benefits. Those are questions to be posed after you have a job offer.

May 30, 2010

Dear Dr. Hurston,

Thank you for taking the time to meet with me last week about the sales associate position at Chrysalis Publishing. It was a pleasure to visit with you and learn more about the company. I left our meeting feeling very excited about the possibility of working with your sales team.

Sincerely,

David Shaffer

FIGURE A.5 Sample Thank-You Note

Follow Up After the Interview Finally, send your interviewer a thank-you note shortly after your interview. As illustrated in Figure A.5, indicate that you appreciate the interviewer's having taken time to speak with you, how you benefited from the interview experience, and that you are excited about the position. You might want to close with the statement that you look forward to hearing back. Sending a thank-you note requires only a few moments but may be the one gesture that sets you apart from equally qualified competitors. After you send your note, however, resist the urge to call or e-mail the interviewer with a question such as, "When do you expect to make a hiring decision?" Although the temptation to do so can be great, you run the risk of annoying the interviewer and thereby potentially reducing—or eliminating—whatever goodwill you created during your interview.

Table A.2 provides quick tips on some interviewing do's and don'ts.

IDENTIFYING AND RESPONDING TO ILLEGAL QUESTIONS

In the United States, the Equal Employment Opportunity Commission (EEOC) is the federal agency that monitors unfair discrimination in hiring and firing decisions. For the last four decades, the EEOC has enforced guidelines that specify what an employer may and may not ask prospective job candidates during employment interviews and on application

Table A.2 Prepare to Succeed: Interview Do's and Don't's	
Do	**Don't**
Find out as much about the company as you can.	Ask questions about the company to which you should already know the answer
Anticipate likely questions and practice your answers to them.	Go into a job interview intending to "wing it."
Keep your answers short and to-the-point.	Monopolize the conversation by giving long, rambling answers.
Dress professionally.	Look as if you gave no thought to your appearance.
Arrive on time or a few minutes early.	Arrive late.
Prepare thoughtful questions to ask of your interviewer.	Indicate a lack of interest in the position by asking no questions about it.
Follow up with a thank-you note.	Think that a thank-you note won't make any difference.

forms. The guidelines are intended to ensure that employers ask only for information that is relevant to the position being sought.

During a job selection interview, you may be asked a question that violates federal employment discrimination laws. If such a question should arise, it is often an honest mistake reflecting the interviewer's lack of awareness of the EEOC guidelines. On occasion, however, it represents an intentional attempt to gain information about you that the prospective employer doesn't need. When faced with an illegal question, many job candidates feel caught in an impossible position. They may recognize the question as discriminatory but feel compelled to answer anyway. If you find yourself in such a situation, you can respond effectively by knowing the law and dealing tactfully with the question.

Be Aware of Employment Law Companies can only make employment decisions based on information that is relevant to job performance. In most cases, the law prohibits employers from considering factors such as a person's sex, age, ethnicity, sexual orientation, religion, marital status, political orientation, or disability status in decisions to hire, promote, or fire someone. Exceptions are allowed only when there is a *bona fide,* or legally legitimate, reason to allow them. For instance, if the position legitimately requires someone of a certain sex (such as a men's locker room attendant), a certain ethnicity (such as an actress playing a ethnic-specific movie role), or a certain physical ability (such as a firefighter, who must be able to walk and carry loads of a certain weight), those factors may be considered in employment decisions.

Most jobs, however, require only the skills and training necessary to perform the assigned tasks. If there is no bona fide reason to require applicants to fit a specific demographic profile (such as being of a particular age, marital status or political orientation, or practicing a particular religion), employers cannot legally ask about those characteristics during a job selection interview. Even if one characteristic (such as ethnicity or physical ability) is a bona fide job requirement, the employer can ask only about *that* attribute, not the others.

As a job applicant, you benefit by knowing the laws regarding employment and illegal discrimination. Table A.3 offers a list of questions that are generally illegal for employers to ask in an interview, alongside similar, job-related questions that *are* legal to ask.

Respond Tactfully to Illegal Questions If you are asked illegal questions during a job interview, there are ways you can respond that will provide the necessary

Table A.3 What Can and Can't Be Asked During a Job Interview

Legal to Ask	Illegal to Ask
Are you authorized to work in the United States?	Are you a citizen of the United States?
What languages do you speak, read, or write fluently?	What is your native language?
Are you available to work on the days this job requires?	What religious holidays or days of worship do you observe?
Are you 18 years of age or older?	How old are you?
Have you worked or earned a degree under another name?	Is this your maiden name?
What is your experience with such-and-such an age group?	Do you have children?
Are you able to perform the specific duties of this position?	Do you have any disabilities?
Do you have upcoming events that would require extensive time away from work?	Are you a member of the National Guard or military reserves?
Are you willing to relocate if necessary?	Do you live nearby?
Tell me about your experience managing others.	How do you feel about supervising men or women?

Source: hrworld.com/features/30-interview-questions-111507

information without embarrassing the interviewer and causing everyone's discomfort to escalate. Communication professors Charles Stewart and William Cash suggest five potential ways of responding effectively to illegal questions:[32]

- *Answer directly but briefly.* "Do you go to church?" "Yes, I do."
- *Pose a tactful inquiry.* "What is your political orientation?" "Why do you ask?"
- *Tactfully refuse to answer.* "Do you plan to have children?" "My family plans won't interfere with my ability to do this job."
- *Neutralize the question.* "What happens if your spouse gets called for military duty?" "My spouse and I would discuss the logistical requirements of any change in our circumstances."
- *Take advantage of the question.* "Do you have any disabilities?" "As someone with mild dyslexia, I've learned to treat people with a wide range of abilities empathically and respectfully."

Although you may feel uncomfortable or even offended when asked an illegal question, it is seldom best to respond defensively ("You can't ask me that; that's none of your business"). Instead, use one of Stewart and Cash's strategies to defuse the tension and show that you can react tactfully and professionally in an uncomfortable situation.

For REVIEW >>

- **What communication processes are important in the workplace?**

  In the workplace, people must communicate in upward, downward, and lateral ways to those within the organization, and to multiple constituencies outside of the organization. Organizational culture is reflected in an organization's rites, rituals, rules, and roles.

- **What common communication challenges do workplaces face today?**

  Many workplaces struggle with the communication challenges of globalization, communication technology, sexual harassment, work/life conflict, and diversity.

- **In what ways can we improve our interviewing skills?**

  We can succeed at job selection interviews by researching our potential employer, anticipating likely questions, formulating questions of our own, and engaging in appropriate follow-up communication after an interview.

Pop Quiz

Multiple Choice

1. Tara sends a memo to her interns at the accounting firm where she works. Her memo is an example of

   a. informal communication
   b. lateral communication
   c. upward communication
   d. downward communication

2. Research tells us that grapevine communication
   a. usually uses only one communication channel
   b. is typically ignored by those who receive it
   c. can be remarkably accurate
   d. is an example of formal workplace communication

3. Peter is leaving his current position to take a job at another company. To learn more about his experiences in the job he is leaving, his supervisors might conduct
   a. an exit interview
   b. a counseling interview
   c. a problem-solving interview
   d. a service-oriented interview

4. An example of quid pro quo sexual harassment is
   a. work conditions that are sexually offensive or intimidating
   b. an employee's confiding in her peer about her sexual attraction to her boss
   c. a supervisor's offer of rewards to an employee in exchange for sexual favors
   d. an employee telling a sexually obscene joke in mixed company

5. The question "What was your college major?" is an example of a(n)
   a. open-ended question
   b. closed-ended question
   c. hypothetical question
   d. probing question

Fill in the Blank

6. People who own shares of a publicly traded company are called _____.

7. Rites of _____ enhance feelings of inclusion and communication in the workplace.

8. _____ is the increasing connectedness of societies and their economies as a result of developments in transportation and communication.

9. Sending e-mail messages and posting notes to an electronic bulletin board, blog, or Facebook wall are considered channel- _____ contexts.

10. A _____ job requirement is one that is legally legitimate.

Answers: 1. d; 2. c; 3. a; 4. c; 5. b; 6. stockholders; 7. integration; 8. globalization; 9. lean; 10. bona fide

KEY TERMS

workplace communication 386	informal roles 390
internal communication 386	globalization 391
formal communication 386	real time 392
upward communication 386	work/life conflict 393
downward communication 387	burnout 393
lateral communication 387	sexual harassment 394
informal communication 387	interview 395
grapevine 387	appraisal interview 395
external communication 387	problem-solving interview 395
workplace culture 389	exit interview 396
rites 389	counseling interview 396
rituals 389	service-oriented interview 396
formal roles 390	persuasive interview 396
	survey interview 396
	selection interview 396
	cover letter 397
	resume 397

A

action   A behavior someone undertakes.

action model   A model describing communication as a one-way process.

ad hominem **fallacy**   A statement that attempts to counter an argument by criticizing the person who made it.

adapt   To change one's behavior to accommodate what others are doing.

adaptors   Gestures used to satisfy a personal need.

affect displays   Gestures that communicate emotion.

ambiguous language   Words that can have more than one meaning.

anchor-and-contrast approach   A persuasion technique by which one precedes a desired request with a request that is outrageously large.

anticipatory anxiety   The worry people feel when looking ahead to a speech.

antonyms   Words that have opposite meanings.

anxiety   A psychological state of worry and unease.

appeal to false authority   A claim that uses as evidence the testimony of someone who is not an expert on the topic.

appraisal interview   A discussion focused on an employee's performance and goals for the future.

articulation   The extent to which a speaker pronounces words clearly.

artifacts   Objects and visual features that reflect a person's identity and preferences.

attending   Paying attention to someone's words well enough to understand what that person is trying to communicate.

attraction theory   A theory that explains why individuals are drawn to others.

attribution   An explanation for an observed behavior.

audience analysis   Carefully considering the characteristics of one's listeners when preparing a speech.

authority rule   A decision-making process in which the leader of the group makes the decisions.

autocratic style   A leadership style in which leaders see themselves as having both the authority and the responsibility to take action on a group's behalf.

autonomy face   The need to avoid being imposed upon by others.

avatars   Graphic representations of people.

avoiding stage   The stage of relationship dissolution at which partners create physical and emotional distance from each other.

B

bandwagon appeal   A claim that a listener should accept an argument because of how many other people have already accepted it.

bar chart   A graphic display of numbers as bars on a graph.

begging the question   Supporting an argument with claims whose truth is taken for granted but never verified.

belief   Perception about what is true or false, accurate or inaccurate.

bibliography   A list of the sources used in preparing a speech.

bonding stage   The stage of relationship development at which partners make a public announcement of their commitment to each other.

brainstorming   An idea-generating process in which group members offer whatever ideas they wish before any are debated.

breadth   The range of topics one discusses with various people.

build rapport   Create the perception that listeners and the speaker see things similarly.

burnout   A chronic sense of exhaustion or apathy that can come from long-term frustration and stress.

C

cause-and-effect pattern   A pattern of organizing the main points of a speech so that they describe the causes of an event and then identify its consequences.

channel   A pathway through which messages are conveyed.

channel-lean contexts   Communication contexts involving few channels at once.

channel-rich contexts   Communication contexts involving many channels at once.

chart   A graphic display of numeric information.

chronemics   The use of time.

circumscribing stage   The stage of relationship dissolution at which partners begin to decrease the quality and quantity of their communication with each other.

closed-mindedness   The tendency not to listen to anything with which one disagrees.

co-cultures   Groups of people who share values, customs, and norms related to mutual interests or characteristics besides their national citizenship.

coercive power   A form of power that comes from the ability to punish.

cognitive complexity   The ability to understand a given situation in multiple ways.

cohesion The force by which the members of a group work together in the service of a common goal.

collectivistic culture A culture in which people believe that their primary responsibility is to their families, their communities, and their employers.

commitment The desire to stay in a relationship no matter what happens.

communication The process by which people use signs, symbols, and behaviors to exchange information and create meaning.

communication apprehension Anxiety or fear about communicating with others.

communication codes Verbal and nonverbal behaviors whose meanings are often understood only by people from the same culture.

communication competence Communication that is effective and appropriate for a given situation.

communication privacy management (CPM) theory A theory explaining how people in relationships negotiate the tension between disclosing information and keeping it private.

comparative advantage method A way of organizing a persuasive speech in which the speaker explains why his or her point of view is superior to others on the same topic.

comparison level A realistic expectation of what one wants and thinks one deserves from a relationship.

comparison level for alternatives An assessment of how much better or worse one's current relationship is than one's other options.

competence face The need to be respected and viewed as competent and intelligent.

competitive interrupting The practice of using interruptions to take control of the conversation.

complementarity The beneficial provision by another person of a quality that one lacks.

confirmation bias The tendency to pay attention only to information that supports one's values and beliefs, while discounting or ignoring information that does not.

confirming messages Behaviors that convey how much another person is valued.

conflict An expressed struggle between at least two interdependent parties who perceive incompatible goals, scarce resources, and interference from the other party in achieving their goals.

connotative meaning The ideas or concepts a word suggests in addition to its literal definition.

contempt Hostile behavior in which people insult each other and attack the other's self-worth.

content dimension Literal information that is communicated by a message.

context The physical or psychological environment in which communication occurs.

counseling interview An interaction aimed at supporting an individual through a personal problem.

cover letter A one-page letter in which a person formally applies for a specific position.

credibility A speaker's believability.

credibility The extent to which others perceive us to be competent and trustworthy.

critical listening Listening to evaluate or analyze.

criticism The act of passing judgment on someone or something.

criticisms Complaints about another person or the person's behaviors.

culture The totality of learned, shared symbols, language, values, and norms that distinguish one group of people from another.

cyberbullying Using the Internet to inflict emotional or psychological harm.

D

database An electronic storehouse of specific information that people can search.

deception The act of leading others to believe something the speaker knows to be untrue.

decode To interpret or give meaning to a message.

deductive reasoning A form of reasoning in which one starts with a general conclusion and then uses it to explain specific individual cases.

defamation Language that harms a person's reputation or image.

defensiveness Seeing oneself as a victim and denying responsibility for one's behaviors.

defining Providing the meaning of a word or concept.

democratic style A leadership style in which every member of a group has the right to participate in decision making.

demonstrating Showing how to do something by doing it as it is explained.

denotative meaning The literal meaning of a word.

depth The intimacy of one's self-disclosures.

describing Using words to depict or portray a person, a place, an object, or an experience.

desensitization The process of confronting frightening situations directly, to reduce the stress they cause.

dialectical tensions Conflicts between two important but opposing relational needs or desires.

differentiating stage The stage of relationship dissolution at which partners begin to view their differences as undesirable or annoying.

disconfirming messages Behaviors that imply a lack of respect or value for others.

divorce The legal discontinuation of a marriage.

downward communication Messages people send to those at lower levels of the organizational hierarchy than themselves.

E

either/or fallacy A statement that identifies two alternatives and falsely suggests that if one is rejected, the other must be accepted.

emblems Gestures that have a direct verbal translation.

emoticons Textual representations of facial expressions.

empathic listening Listening to experience what the speaker thinks or feels.

empathy The ability to think and feel as others do.

encode To put an idea into language or gesture.

enculturation The process of acquiring a culture.

enthymeme A syllogism in which one of the premises is already so widely known and accepted that it is omitted.

equity theory Theory that a good relationship is one in which a person's ratio of costs and benefits is equal to his or her partner's.

ethics Principles that guide judgments about whether something is morally right or wrong.

ethnicity People's perceptions of ancestry or heritage.

ethnocentrism The tendency to judge other cultures' practices as inferior to one's own.

ethos A speaker's respectability, trustworthiness, and moral character.

etymology The origin or history of a word.

euphemism A vague, mild expression that symbolizes and substitutes for something blunter or harsher.

exit interview A conversation about an employee's experiences with an organization that he or she is leaving.

experimenting stage The stage of relationship development at which people converse to learn more about each other.

expert opinion Recommendations of individuals who have expertise in a particular area that are sometimes the basis of a group's decision-making process.

expert power A form of power that stems from having expertise in a particular area.

explaining Revealing why something occurred or how something works.

explicit rules Rules that have been clearly articulated.

extemporaneous speech A speech that is carefully prepared to sound as though it is being delivered spontaneously.

external communication The messages people within the workplace convey to people outside the organization.

extroversion A personality trait shared by people who are friendly, assertive, and outgoing with others.

F

face A person's desired public image.

face needs Important components of one's desired public image.

face-threatening act Any behavior that threatens one or more face needs.

facework The behaviors people use to establish and maintain their desired public image with others.

facial displays Facial expressions that are an important source of information in nonverbal communication.

false-cause fallacy A statement asserting that if an event occurs before some outcome, the event therefore caused that outcome.

false consensus An outcome where some members of a group say they support the unanimous decision even though they do not.

family of origin The family in which one grows up, usually consisting of parents and siblings.

family of procreation The family one starts as an adult, usually consisting of a spouse or romantic partner and children.

family rituals Repetitive activities that have special meaning for a family.

feedback Verbal and nonverbal responses to a message.

fellowship face The need to be liked and accepted by others.

feminine culture A culture in which people cherish traditionally feminine qualities and prefer little differentiation in the roles of women and men.

fight-or-flight response A reaction that helps prepare the body either to confront or to avoid a stressor.

fluency The smoothness of a speaker's delivery.

formal communication Messages that come from the work organization and relate to its operations.

formal outline A structured set of all the points and subpoints in a speech.

formal roles Responsibilities and functions that are prescribed by the employer.

forms of rhetorical proof Ways to support a persuasive argument, including ethos, pathos, and logos.

fundamental attribution error The tendency to attribute others' behaviors to internal rather than external causes.

G

general search engine A website on which one can search for other websites containing information on a specified topic.

gesticulation The use of arm and hand movements to communicate.

glazing over Daydreaming or allowing the mind to wander while another person is speaking.

globalization The increasing interconnectedness of societies and their economies as a result of developments in transportation and communication.

gossip Informal, and frequently judgmental, talk about people who are not present.

grapevine A metaphor indicating that informal messages are often conveyed in upward, downward, and lateral directions simultaneously.

graphic slide An electronic display of information in a visually compelling format.

groupthink A situation in which group members seek unanimous agreement despite their individual doubts.

H

halo effect A predisposition to attribute positive qualities to physically attractive people.

haptics The study of the sense of touch.

hasty generalization A broad claim that is based on insufficient evidence.

hate speech Language used to degrade, intimidate, or dehumanize specific groups of people.

hearing The sensory process of receiving and perceiving sounds.

high-context culture A culture in which people are taught to speak in an indirect, inexplicit way.

high-power-distance culture A culture in which certain groups, such as the royal family or the members of the ruling political party, have much greater power than the average citizen.

hostile audience An audience in which listeners are predisposed to disagree with the speaker.

HURIER model A model describing the stages of effective listening as hearing, understanding, remembering, interpreting, evaluating, and responding.

I

ideawriting An idea-generating process in which each member adds three or four ideas to a pile and then offers comments on others' ideas. Afterward, members respond to comments made about their ideas and generate a master list of ideas worthy of consideration.

identity The set of perceptions a person has about who he or she is; also known as *self-concept*.

illustrators Gestures that go along with a verbal message to clarify it.

image The way one wishes to be seen or perceived by others.

image management The process of projecting one's desired public image.

immediacy behaviors Nonverbal signals of affection and affiliation.

implicit rules Rules that have not been clearly articulated but are nonetheless understood.

impromptu speech A speech delivered with little or no preparation.

individualistic culture A culture in which people believe that their primary responsibility is to themselves.

inductive reasoning A form of reasoning in which one considers evidence and then draws general conclusions from it.

infidelity Romantic or sexual interaction with someone outside one's romantic relationship.

informal communication Messages that are not sanctioned by an organization but arise from the social interactions of its members.

informal roles Responsibilities and functions adopted by specific people rather than being dictated by the workplace.

information hunger The desire to learn.

information overload The state of being overwhelmed by the enormous amount of information encountered each day.

informational listening Listening to learn.

informational power A form of power that stems from the ability to control access to information.

informative speaking Publicly addressing others to increase their knowledge, understanding, or skills.

in-groups Groups of people with which a person identifies.

initiating stage The stage of relationship development at which people meet and interact for the first time.

instrumental needs Practical, everyday needs.

integrating stage The stage of relationship development at which a deep commitment has formed, and the partners share a strong sense that the relationship has its own identity.

intensifying stage The stage of relationship development at which people move from being acquaintances to being close friends.

interaction model A model describing communication as a process shaped by feedback and context.

interdependence The state in which what happens to one person affects everyone else in the relationship.

interdependence (groups) With respect to groups, a state in which each member of a group affects, and is affected by, every other member.

internal communication The messages people within the workplace convey to one another.

interpersonal attraction The force that draws people together.

interpersonal communication Communication that occurs between two people in the context of their relationship.

interpretation The process of assigning meaning to information that has been selected for attention and organized.

interview A structured conversation in which one person poses questions to which another person responds.

intimacy Significant emotional closeness experienced in a relationship, whether romantic or not.

intimate distance The zone of space willingly occupied only with intimate friends, family members, and romantic partners.

intrapersonal communication Communication with oneself.

introversion A personality trait shared by people who are shy, reserved, and aloof.

investment The commitment of one's energies and resources to a relationship.

I-statement A statement that claims ownership of the communicator's feelings or thoughts.

J

jargon Technical vocabulary of a certain occupation or profession.

Johari Window A visual representation of components of the self that are known or unknown to the self and to others.

K

kinesics The study of movement.

L

laissez-faire style A leadership style in which leaders offer minimal supervision.

language A structured system of symbols used for communicating meaning.

lateral communication Messages people share with peers in an organization.

legitimate power A form of power in which leaders' status or position gives them the right to make requests with which others must comply.

life story A way of presenting oneself to others that is based on one's self-concept but is also influenced by other people.

line chart A graphic display of numbers in the form of a line or lines that connect various data points.

listening The active process of making meaning out of another person's spoken message.

loaded language Words with strongly positive or negative connotations.

logical fallacy A line of reasoning that, even if it makes sense, does not genuinely support a speaker's point.

logos Listeners' ability to reason.

low-context culture A culture in which people are expected to be direct and to say what they mean.

low-power-distance culture A culture in which people believe that no one person or group should have excessive power.

M

main point A statement expressing a specific idea or theme related to the speech topic.

majority rule A decision-making process that follows the will of the majority.

masculine culture A culture in which people cherish traditionally masculine values and prefer sex-specific roles for women and men.

mass communication Communication to a large audience that is transmitted by media.

memorized speech A speech composed word for word and then delivered from memory.

message Verbal and nonverbal elements of communication to which people give meaning.

metacommunication Communication about communication.

mindful Aware—as in being aware of how other cultures' behaviors and ways of thinking are likely to differ from one's own.

minority rule A decision-making process in which a small number of members makes a decision on behalf of the group.

mnemonics Devices that can aid short- and long-term memory.

model A formal description of a process.

model (speech) A representation of an object.

monochronic culture A culture that views time as a finite and tangible commodity.

monogamy The state of being in only one romantic relationship at a time and avoiding romantic or sexual involvement with others outside that relationship.

Monroe's motivated sequence A way of organizing a persuasive speech consisting of appeals to attention, need, satisfaction, visualization, and then action.

N

narration Describing a series of events in sequence.

nationality One's status as a citizen of a particular country.

need to belong theory   A psychological theory proposing a fundamental human inclination to bond with others.

neutral audience   An audience lacking strong feelings for or against the topic of a speech.

noise   Anything that interferes with the encoding or decoding of a message (distracts people from listening to what they wish to listen to).

nominal group technique (NGT)   An idea-generating process in which group members generate their initial ideas silently and independently and then combine them and consider them as a group.

nonverbal channels   The various behavioral forms that nonverbal communication takes.

nonverbal communication   Behaviors and characteristics that convey meaning without the use of words.

norm of reciprocity   The social expectation that favors should be reciprocated.

O

objective   Based on facts rather than opinions.

oculesics   The study of eye behavior.

olfactics   The study of the sense of smell.

opinion   Evaluation about what is good and bad.

organization   The process of categorizing information that has been selected for attention.

out-groups   Groups of people with which a person does not identify.

over-benefited   A state in which one's relational benefits outweigh one's costs.

P

paralanguage   Vocalic behaviors that communicate meaning along with verbal behavior.

pathos   Listeners' emotions.

peer   A person similar to oneself in status or power.

perception   The process of making meaning from environmental experiences.

perceptual schema   A mental framework for organizing information.

perceptual set   A person's predisposition to perceive only what he or she wants or expects to perceive.

personal distance   The zone of space occupied with close friends and relatives.

persuasion   An attempt to motivate others, through communication, to adopt or to maintain a specific manner of thinking or doing.

persuasion   The process of convincing people to think or act in a certain way.

persuasive interview   A conversation intended to affect beliefs, opinions, or behaviors.

persuasive speaking   Public speech that aims to influence listeners' beliefs, attitudes, and actions.

physical attraction   Attraction to someone's appearance.

physical traits   The body's physical attributes.

pie chart   A graphic display of numbers in the form of a circle that is divided into segments, each of which represents a percentage of the whole.

plagiarism   Knowingly using information from another source without giving proper credit to that source.

polychronic culture   A culture that views time as holistic, fluid, and infinite.

polygamy   The state of having two or more romantic partners at once.

power   The ability to influence or control people or events.

presentation aids   Anything used in conjunction with a speech or presentation to stimulate listeners' senses.

preview   A statement alerting listeners that a speaker is about to shift to a new topic.

primacy effect   The tendency to emphasize the first impression over later impressions when forming a perception.

problem-solving interview   A discussion conducted to identify solutions to a problem or conflict.

problem-solving pattern   A way of organizing a persuasive speech in which the speaker establishes the existence of a problem and then proposes a solution to it.

profanity   Language considered to be vulgar, rude, or obscene.

proportionality   The relative sizes of facial or body features.

proposition   That which a persuasive speech attempts to convince an audience to accept.

proposition of fact   A claim that a particular argument is supported by the best available evidence and should therefore be taken as factual.

proposition of policy   A claim about what should be done.

proposition of value   A claim that evaluates the worth of a person, an object, or an idea.

proxemics   The study of the use of space.

proximity   Closeness, as in how closely together people live or work.

pseudolistening   Pretending to listen.

psychosocial traits   Characteristics of one's personality and ways of relating to others.

public communication   Communication directed at an audience that is larger than a small group.

public distance   The zone of space maintained during a public presentation.

purpose statement A declaration of the specific goal for a speech.

Q

questionnaire A written instrument containing questions for people to answer.

R

real time At the actual time when a communication or an event takes place.

reason To make judgments about the world based on evidence rather than emotion or intuition.

rebuttal tendency The propensity to debate a speaker's point and formulate a reply while that person is still speaking.

receiver The party who interprets a message.

recency effect The tendency to emphasize the most recent impression over earlier impressions when forming a perception.

receptive audience An audience composed of people who already accept and agree with all or most of what a speaker plans to say.

red herring fallacy A statement that responds to an argument by introducing an irrelevant detail to divert attention from the point of the argument.

referent power A form of power that derives from attraction to the leader.

refutational approach A way of organizing a persuasive speech in which the speaker begins by presenting the main arguments against his or her position and then immediately refutes those arguments.

regulators Gestures that control the flow of conversation.

relational dimension Signals about the relationship in which a message is being communicated.

relational maintenance behaviors theory Theory specifying the primary behaviors people use to maintain their relationships.

relational needs The essential elements people seek in their relationships with others.

representation Describing something in terms of its physical or psychological attributes.

research search engine A website on which one can search for research published in books, academic journals, and other periodicals.

resources Entities that enable a group to be productive.

resume A short document listing a person's employment qualifications.

reward power A form of power based on the leader's ability to reward another for doing what the leader says.

rites Ceremonial acts and practices that convey one or more characteristics of a workplace's culture.

rituals Repeated behaviors that provide a familiar routine to a workplace's experiences.

role A pattern of behavior that defines a person's function within a group or larger organization.

rule of division A rule of speech organization specifying that if a point is divided into subpoints, it must have at least two subpoints.

rule of parallel wording A rule of speech organization specifying that all points and subpoints in an outline should have the same grammatical structure.

rule of subordination A rule of speech organization specifying that some concepts in the speech are more important than others.

S

Sapir-Whorf hypothesis A theory that language shapes a person's views of reality.

scripted speech A speech composed word for word on a manuscript and then read aloud exactly as it is written.

selection The process of paying attention to a certain stimulus.

selection interview A conversation intended to help the interviewer choose the most appropriate person for a position, an assignment, a promotion, or an award.

selective attention Listening only to what one wants to hear and ignoring the rest.

self-concept The set of perceptions a person has about who he or she is; also known as *identity*.

self-disclosure Act of intentionally giving others information about oneself that one believes is true but thinks others don't already have.

self-esteem One's subjective evaluation of one's value and worth as a person.

self-fulfilling prophecy An expectation that gives rise to behaviors that cause the expectation to come true.

self-monitoring Awareness of one's behavior and how it affects others.

self-serving bias The tendency to attribute one's successes to stable internal causes and one's failures to unstable external causes.

service-oriented interview A conversation oriented toward helping people with a product or service they have purchased.

signposts Single words and phrases that distinguish one point in a presentation from another and help listeners follow the speaker's "path."

skepticism An attitude that involves raising questions or having doubts.

slang Informal and unconventional words often understood only within a particular group.

slippery slope fallacy   A statement that attacks an argument by taking it to such an extreme that it appears ludicrous.

small group   A collection of people working interdependently to accomplish a task; small groups typically include 3 to 20 members.

small group communication   Communication occurring within small groups of three or more people.

social attraction   Attraction to someone's personality.

social distance   The zone of space occupied with casual acquaintances.

social exchange theory   Theory suggesting that people seek to maintain relationships in which their benefits outweigh their costs.

social loafing   The tendency of some members of a group to contribute less to the group than the average member does, particularly as the group grows in size.

social penetration theory   Theory indicating that the depth and breadth of self-disclosure help us learn about a person we're getting to know.

social validation principle   The idea that people will comply with requests if they believe that others are also complying.

societies   Groups of people who share common symbols, language, values, and norms.

source   The originator of a thought or an idea.

space pattern   A pattern of organizing the main points of a speech according to areas.

speaking notes   An abbreviated version of a formal speech outline.

stage fright   Anxiety or fear brought on by performing in front of an audience.

stagnating stage   The stage of relationship dissolution at which the relationship stops growing and the partners feel as if they are just "going through the motions."

stalemate   An outcome where members' opinions are so sharply divided that consensus is impossible to achieve.

stereotype   A generalization about a group or category of people that is applied to individual members of that group.

stonewalling   Withdrawing from a conversation.

straw man fallacy   A statement that refutes a claim that was never made.

stress   The body's reaction to any type of perceived threat.

stuttering   A speech disorder that disrupts the flow of words with repeated or prolonged sounds and involuntary pauses.

subjective   Biased toward a specific conclusion.

summary   A statement that briefly reminds listeners of points a speaker has already made.

survey   A method of collecting data by asking people directly about their experiences.

survey interview   An interaction aimed at gathering information.

syllogism   A three-line argument consisting of a major premise, a minor premise, and a conclusion.

symbol   A representation of an idea.

symmetry   The similarity between the left and right sides of a face or body.

synergy   A collaboration that produces more than the sum of its parts.

synonyms   Words that have the same meaning.

T

table   The display of words or numbers in a format of columns and rows.

task attraction   Attraction to someone's abilities or dependability.

terminating stage   The stage of relationship dissolution at which the relationship is officially deemed to be over.

text slide   An electronic display of text used to accompany a speech.

thesis statement   A one-sentence version of the message in a speech.

threat   A declaration of the intention to harm someone.

time pattern   A pattern of organizing the main points of a speech in chronological order.

topic pattern   A pattern of organizing the main points of a speech to represent different categories.

traits   Defining characteristics of a person that are often relatively enduring and not easily changeable.

transaction model   A model describing communication as a process in which everyone is simultaneously a sender and a receiver.

transition   A statement that connects one point in a speech to the next.

U

unanimous consensus   Uncontested support for a decision—sometimes the only option in a group's decision-making process.

uncertainty avoidance   The extent to which people try to avoid situations that are unstructured, unclear, or unpredictable.

uncertainty reduction theory   Theory suggesting that people find uncertainty to be unpleasant, so they are motivated to reduce their uncertainty by getting to know others.

under-benefited   A state in which one's relational costs outweigh one's benefits.

upward communication   Messages people send to those at higher levels of the organizational hierarchy than themselves.

V

verbal footnote   A statement giving credit for quoted words in a speech to their original source.

vested interest   An inherent motivation to pay attention.

visualization   Developing a mental image, such as an image of oneself giving a successful performance.

vividness effect   The tendency of dramatic, shocking events to distort one's perceptions of reality.

vocalics   Characteristics of the voice that communicate meaning.

W

work/life conflict   Conflict created by the pressure of balancing the demands of work with the rest of one's activities.

workplace communication   The interactions people have as part of their employment.

workplace culture   The values, customs, and communication behaviors that workplace members share and that reflect their organization's distinct identity.

Y

you-statement   A statement that shifts responsibility for the communicator's feelings or thoughts to the other party in the communication.

Chapter 1

1. http://blog.compete.com/2009/02/09/facebook-myspace-twitter-social-network/

2. See Rubin, B. D. (2005). Linking communication scholarship and professional practice in colleges and universities. *Journal of Applied Communication Research, 33,* 294–304.

3. Bonta, J., & Gendreau, P. (1995). Re-examining the cruel and unusual punishment of prison life. In T. J. Flanagan (Ed.), *Long-term imprisonment: Policy, science, and correctional practice* (pp. 75–84). Thousand Oaks, CA: Sage.

4. See, e.g., Ray, E. B. (Ed.). (1996). *Communication and disenfranchisement: Social health issues and implications.* Mahwah, NJ: Lawrence Erlbaum Associates; Takahashi, L. M. (1998). *Homelessness, AIDS, and stigmatization: The NIMBY syndrome in the United States at the end of the twentieth century.* New York: Oxford University Press.

5. Perry, B. D. (2002). Childhood experience and the expression of genetic potential: What childhood neglect tells us about nature and nurture. *Brain and Mind, 3,* 79–100.

6. Field, T. (2001). *Touch.* Cambridge, MA: MIT Press.

7. Cacioppo, J. T., Ernst, J. M., Burleson, M. H., McClintock, M. K., Malarkey, W. B., Hawkley, L. C., Kowalewski, R. B., Paulsen, A., Hobson, J. A., Hugdahl, K., Spiegel, D., & Berntson, G. G. (2000). Lonely traits and concomitant physiological processes: The MacArthur Social Neuroscience Studies. *International Journal of Psychophysiology, 35,* 143–154; Narem, R. (1980). Try a little TLC. *Science, 80,* 15; Ruberman, R. (1992). Psychosocial influences on mortality of patients with coronary heart disease. *Journal of the American Medical Association, 267,* 559–560.

8. Cohen, S., Doyle, W. J., Skoner, D. P., Rabin, B. S., & Gwaltney, J. M. (1997). Social ties and susceptibility to the common cold. *Journal of the American Medical Association, 277,* 1940–1944; Kiecolt-Glaser, J. K., Loving, T. J., Stowell, J. R., Malarkey, W. B., Lemeshow, S., Dickinson, S. L., & Glaser, R. (2005). Hostile marital interactions, proinflammatory cytokine production, & wound healing. *Archives of General Psychiatry, 62,* 1377–1384.

9. Rubin, R. B., Perse, E. M., & Barbato, C. A. (1988). Conceptualization and measurement of interpersonal communication motives. *Human Communication Research, 14,* 602–628.

10. Yingling, J. (1994). Constituting friendships in talk and metatalk. *Journal of Social and Personal Relationships, 11,* 411–426.

11. Figure is from statistics compiled by the Nielsen Company during the second quarter of 2008 for U.S. subscribers only. Source: http://blog.nielsen.com/nielsenwire/online_mobile/in-us-text-messaging-tops-mobile-phone-calling/

12. Parks, M. R., & Floyd, K. (1996). Making friends in cyberspace. *Journal of Communication, 46,* 80–97.

13. See, e.g., Usita, P. M., & Blieszner, R. (2002). Immigrant family strengths: Meeting communication challenges. *Journal of Family Issues, 23,* 266–286.

14. Baumeister, R. F., & Leary, M. R. (1995). The need to belong: Desire for interpersonal attachments as a fundamental human motivation. *Psychological Bulletin, 117,* 497–529.

15. Diener, E., & Seligman, M. E. P. (2002). Very happy people. *Psychological Science, 13,* 81–84.

16. Popenoe, D. (2007). *The state of our unions: The social health of marriage in America.* Piscataway, NJ: The National Marriage Project.

17. Weissman, M. M. (1987). Advances in psychiatric epidemiology: Rates and risks for major depression. *American Journal of Public Health, 77,* 445–451.

18. Cooley, C. H. (1983). *Human nature and the social order.* Edison, NJ: Transaction.

19. Higher Education Research Institute, University of California, Los Angeles. (2005). *The spiritual life of college students: A national study of college students' search for meaning and purpose.* Los Angeles: Author. Retrieved April 20, 2006, from: www.spirituality.ucla.edu

20. Maslow, A. H. (1970). *Motivation and personality* (2nd ed.). New York: Harper & Row.

21. Shannon, C. E., & Weaver, W. (1949). *The mathematical theory of communication.* Urbana: University of Illinois Press.

22. Laswell, H. (1948). The structure and function of communication in society. In L. Bryson (Ed.), *The communication of ideas.* New York: Harper.

23. See, e.g., Schramm, W. (1954). How communication works. In W. Schramm (Ed.), *The process and effects of mass communication.* Urbana: University of Illinois Press.

24. Barnlund, D. C. (1970). A transactional model of communication. In K. K. Sereno & C. D. Mortensen (Eds.), *Foundations of communication theory* (pp. 83–102). New York: Harper & Row.

25. Trevino, L. K., Draft, R. L., & Lengel, R. H. (1990). Understanding managers' media choices: A symbolic interactionist perspective. In J. Fulk & C. Steinfield (Eds.), *Organizations and communication technology* (pp. 71–94). Newbury Park, CA: Sage.

26. Watzlawick, T., Beavin, J., & Jackson, D. (1967). *The pragmatics of human communication.* New York: Norton.

27. Motley, M. T. (1990). On whether one can(not) communicate: An examination via traditional communication postulates. *Western Journal of Speech Communication, 54,* 1–20.

28. This position is usually attributed to Watzlawick, Beavin, & Jackson, 1967.

29. Shimanoff, S. B. (1980). *Communication rules: Theory and research.* Beverly Hills, CA: Sage.

30. Wheeler, L., & Nelek, J. (1977). Sex differences in social participation. *Journal of Personality and Social Psychology, 35,* 742–754.

31. National Communication Association. (1999). *How Americans communicate* [online]. Retrieved April 16, 2006, from http://www.natcom.org/research/Roper/how_americans_communicate.htm

32. Gottman, J. M., & Silver, N. (1999). *The seven principles for making marriage work.* New York: Crown.

33. National Communication Association. (1999). *How Americans communicate.* Washington, DC: Author.

34. For a classic text, see Katriel, T., & Philipsen, G. (1981). "What we need is communication": "Communication" as a cultural category in some American speech. *Communication Monographs, 48,* 300–317.

35. McDaniel, S. H., Beckman, H. B., Morse, D. S., Silberman, J., Seaburn, D. B., & Epstein, R. M. (2007). Physician self-disclosure in primary care visits: Enough about you, what about me? *Archives of Internal Medicine, 167,* 1321–1326.

36. Chesley, N. (2005). Blurring boundaries? Linking technology use, spillover, individual distress, and family satisfaction. *Journal of Marriage and the Family, 67,* 1237–1248.

37. National Association of Colleges and Employers. (2009). *Job outlook 2009: Spring update.* Bethlehem, PA: Author.

38. Graduates are not prepared to work in business. (1997, June). *Association Trends, 4;* Windsor, J. L., Curtis, D. B., & Stephens, R. D. (1997). National preferences in business and communication education: A survey update. *Journal of the Association for Communication Administration, 3,* 170–179; Work Week. (1998, December 29). *Wall Street Journal,* A1.

39. Beatty, M. J., Marshall, L. A., & Rudd, J. E. (2001). A twins study of communicative adaptability: Heritability of individual differences. *Quarterly Journal of Speech, 87,* 366–377; Beatty, M. J., McCroskey, J. C., & Heisel, A. D. (1998). Communication apprehension as temperamental expression: A communibiological paradigm. *Communication Monographs, 65,* 197–219.

40. Spitzberg, B. H. (2000). What is good communication? *Journal of the Association for Communication Administration, 29,* 103–119.

41. Spitzberg, B. H., & Cupach, W. (1989). *Handbook of interpersonal competence research*. New York: Springer-Verlag.

42. Chen, G. M., & Starosta, W. J. (1996). Intercultural communication competence: A synthesis. In B. R. Burleson & A. W. Kunkel (Eds.), *Communication yearbook 19* (pp. 353–383). Thousand Oaks, CA: Sage.

43. Schraw, G. (1998). Promoting general metacognitive awareness. *Instructional Science, 26,* 113–125; Sypher, B. D., & Sypher, H. E. (1983). Perceptions of communication ability: Self-monitoring in an organizational setting. *Personality and Social Psychology Bulletin, 9,* 297–304.

44. Goleman, D. (2006). *Social intelligence: The new science of human relationships*. New York: Bantam; Goleman, D. (1996). *Emotional intelligence: Why it can matter more than IQ*. New York: Bantam.

45. Stamp, G. H. (1999). A qualitatively constructed interpersonal communication model: A grounded theory analysis. *Human Communication Research, 25,* 531–547.

46. Ifert, D. E., & Roloff, M. E. (1997). Overcoming expressed obstacles to compliance: The role of sensitivity to the expressions of others and ability to modify self-presentation. *Communication Quarterly, 45,* 55–67.

47. Burleson, B. R., & Caplan, S. E. (1998). Cognitive complexity. In J. C. McCroskey, J. A. Daly, M. M. Martin, & M. J. Beatty (Eds.), *Communication and personality: Trait perspectives* (pp. 233–286). Cresskill, NJ: Hampton.

Chapter 2

1. Tajfel, H., & Turner, J. C. (1986). The social identity theory of intergroup behavior. In S. Worchel & W. G. Austin (Eds.), *The psychology of intergroup relations* (pp. 7–24). Chicago: Nelson-Hall.

2. Levitt, M. J., Lane, J. D., & Leavitt, J. (2005). Immigration stress, social support, and adjustment in the first postmigration year: An intergenerational analysis. *Research in Human Development, 2,* 159–177.

3. Öhman, L., Bergdahl, J., Nyberg, L., & Nilsson, L.-G. (2007). Longitudinal analysis of the relation between moderate long-term stress and health. *Stress and Health, 23,* 131–138.

4. Rushton, J. P. (2005). Ethnic nationalism, evolutionary psychology and Genetic Similarity Theory. *Nations and Nationalism, 11,* 489–507.

5. McConnell, A. R., & Leibold, J. M. (2001). Relations among the Implicit Association Test, discriminatory behavior, and explicit measures of racial attitudes. *Journal of Experimental Social Psychology, 37,* 435–442.

6. Suransky-Polakov, S. (2002). Denmark: Rebuffing immigrants. Retrieved July 27, 2007, from http://www.worldpress.org/Europe/642.cfm

7. Padden, C., & Humphries, T. (1988). *Deaf in America: Voices from a culture*. Cambridge, MA: Harvard University Press.

8. Holcomb, R. K., Holcomb, S. K., & Holcomb, T. K. (1995). *Deaf culture our way* (3rd ed.). San Diego: DawnSign.

9. See Lane, H., Hoffmeister, R., & Bahan, B. (1996). *A journey into the deaf world*. San Diego: DawnSign.

10. See groups.google.com; groups.yahoo.com.

11. Gordon, R. G. (Ed.). (2005). *Ethnologue: Languages of the world* (15th ed.). Dallas: SIL International.

12. Office of the New York State Comptroller: http://www.osc.state.ny.us/

13. Foundation for Endangered Languages: http://www.ogmios.org/home.htm

14. See Williams, R. M. (1970). *American society: A sociological interpretation* (3rd ed.). New York: Knopf.

15. Yin, L. (2009). Cultural difference of politeness in English and Chinese. *Asian Social Science, 5*(6), retrieved February 5, 2010, from: www.ccsenet.org/journal/index.php/ass/article/view/2492/2338

16. Triandis, H. C. (1990). Cross-cultural studies of individualism and collectivism. In J. Berman (Ed.), *Nebraska symposium on motivation* (pp. 41–133). Lincoln: University of Nebraska Press.

17. Hofstede, G. (2003). *Culture's consequences: Comparing values, behaviors, institutions, and organizations across nations* (2nd ed.). Thousand Oaks, CA: Sage.

18. Piot, C. (1999). *Remotely global: Village modernity in West Africa*. Chicago: University of Chicago Press.

19. Hofstede, 2003.

20. Cai, D. A., & Fink, E. L. (2002). Conflict style differences between individualists and collectivists. *Communication Monographs, 69,* 67–87.

21. Burgoon, J. K., Guerrero, L. K., & Floyd, K. (2010). *Nonverbal communication*. Boston: Allyn & Bacon.

22. Hall, E. T. (1959). *Beyond culture*. New York: Doubleday.

23. Ambady, N., Koo, J., Lee, F., & Rosenthal, R. (1996). More than words: Linguistic and nonlinguistic politeness in two cultures. *Journal of Personality and Social Psychology, 70,* 996–1011.

24. Hofstede, 2003.

25. Hofstede, D., & Hofstede, G. J. (2004). *Cultures and organizations: Software of the mind* (2nd ed.). Boston: McGraw-Hill.

26. Andersen, P. (1991). Explaining intercultural differences in nonverbal communication. In L. A. Samovar & R. E. Porter (Eds.), *Intercultural communication: A reader* (6th ed., pp. 289–296). Belmont, CA: Wadsworth.

27. Yook, E. L., & Albert, R. D. (1998). Perceptions of the appropriateness of negotiation in educational settings: A cross-cultural comparison among Koreans and Americans. *Communication Education, 47,* 18–29.

28. Hofstede & Hofstede, 2004.

29. Hofstede & Hofstede, 2004.

30. Hall, E. T., & Hall, M. R. (1990). *Understanding cultural differences: Germans, French, and Americans*. Boston: Intercultural.

31. Hall, E. T. (1990). *The silent language*. New York: Anchor.

32. Hilton, B. A. (1994). The Uncertainty Stress Scale: Its development and psychometric properties. *Canadian Journal of Nursing Research, 26,* 15–30.

33. Hofstede, G. (1986). Cultural differences in teaching and learning. *International Journal of Intercultural Relations, 10,* 301–320.

34. Lee, W. S. (1994). On not missing the boat: A processual method for intercultural understanding of idioms and lifeworld. *Journal of Applied Communication Research, 22,* 141–161.

35. Pease, A., & Pease, B. (2004). *The definitive book of body language: The secret meaning behind people's gestures*. London: Orion.

36. Berger, C. R. (1988). Uncertainty and information exchange in developing relationships. In S. Duck & D. F. Hay (Eds.), *Handbook of personal relationships: Theory, research and intervention* (pp. 239–255). New York: Wiley.

37. Rainie, L., Madden, M., Boyce, A., Lenhart, A., Horrigan, J., Allen, K., & O'Grady, E. (2003, April 16). *The ever-shifting Internet population: A new look at Internet access and the digital divide*. Pew Internet & American Life Project. Retrieved February 17, 2010, from http://www.pewinternet.org/Reports/2003/The-EverShifting-Internet-Population-A-new-look-at-Internet-access-and-the-digital-divide.aspx

38. See Giles, H., Mulack, A., Bradac, J. J., & Johnson, P. (1987). Speech accommodation theory: The first decade and beyond. In M. L. McLaughlin (Ed.), *Communication yearbook, 10* (pp. 13–48). Newbury Park, CA: Sage.

39. Natalie, M. (1975). Convergence of mean vocal intensity in dyadic communication as a function of social desirability. *Journal of Personality and Social Psychology, 32,* 790–804.

Chapter 3

1. Ambady, N., Bernieri, F. J., & Richeson, J. A. (2000). Toward a histology of social behavior: Judgmental accuracy from thin slices of the behavioral stream. *Advances in Experimental Social Psychology, 32,* 201–271; Borkenau, P., Mauer, N., Riemann, R., Spinath, F. M., & An-

gleitner, A. (2004). Thin slices of behavior as cues of personality and intelligence. *Journal of Personality and Social Psychology, 86,* 599–614.

2. Kenny, D. A. (1994). *Interpersonal perception: A social relations analysis.* New York: Guilford.

3. Schermerhorn, J. R., Hunt, J. H., & Osborn, R. N. (2003). *Organizational behavior* (8th ed.). New York: Wiley.

4. Goldstein, E. B. (2007). *Sensation and perception* (7th ed.). Pacific Grove, CA: Wadsworth.

5. Floyd, K., Ramirez, A., & Burgoon, J. K. (2008). Expectancy violations theory. In L. K. Guerrero, J. A. DeVito, & M. L. Hecht (Eds.), *The nonverbal communication reader: Classic and contemporary readings* (3rd ed., pp. 503–510). Prospect Heights, IL: Waveland.

6. Zajonc, R. B. (2001). Mere exposure: A gateway to the subliminal. *Current Directions in Psychological Science, 10,* 224–228.

7. Goldstein, 2007.

8. Floyd, K., Mikkelson, A. C., & Hesse, C. (2007). *The biology of human communication* (2nd ed.). Florence, KY: Thomson/Cengage.

9. Andersen, P. A. (1998). *Nonverbal communication: Forms and functions.* New York: McGraw-Hill.

10. Sowa, J. F. (2000). *Knowledge representation: Logical, philosophical, and computational foundations.* Pacific Grove, CA: Brooks/Cole.

11. Funder, D. C. (1999). *Personality judgment: A realistic approach to person perception.* San Diego: Academic.

12. Kelley, H. H. (1967). Attribution theory in social psychology. In D. Levine (Ed.), *Nebraska Symposium on Motivation* (vol. 15, pp. 192–238). Lincoln: University of Nebraska Press.

13. Jones, E. E., & Davis, K. E. (1965). From acts to dispositions: The attribution process in person perception. In L. Berkowitz (Ed.), *Advances in experimental social psychology* (vol. 2, pp. 219–266). New York: Academic.

14. See, e.g., Manusov, V. (1993). It depends on your perspective: Effects of stance and beliefs about intent on person perception. *Western Journal of Communication, 57,* 27–41.

15. Andersen, 1998.

16. Ji, L. K., Peng, K., & Nisbett, R. E. (2000). Culture, control, and perception of relationships in the environment. *Journal of Personality and Social Psychology, 78,* 943–955; Knowles, E. D., Morris, M. W., Chiu, C. -Y., & Hong, Y. -Y. (2001). Culture and the process of person perception: Evidence for automaticity among East Asians in correcting for situational influences on behavior. *Personality and Social Psychology Bulletin, 27,* 1344–1356.

17. Luszcz, M. A., & Fitzgerald, K. M. (1986). Understanding cohort differences in cross-generational, self, and peer perceptions. *Journal of Gerontology, 41,* 234–240.

18. Farwell, L., & Weiner, B. (2000). Bleeding hearts and the heartless: Popular perceptions of liberal and conservative ideologies. *Personality and Social Psychology Bulletin, 26,* 845–852.

19. Lepore, L., & Brown, R. (1997). Category and stereotype activation: Is prejudice inevitable? *Journal of Personality and Social Psychology, 72,* 275–287.

20. Buttney, R. (1997). Reported speech in talking race on campus. *Human Communication Research, 23,* 477–506; Nelson, T. D. (2005). Ageism: Prejudice against our feared future self. *Journal of Social Issues, 61,* 207–221.

21. See, e.g., Hendrix, K. G. (2002). "Did being Black introduce bias into your study?" Attempting to mute the race-related research of black scholars. *Howard Journal of Communication, 13,* 153–171; Hughes, P. C., & Baldwin, J. R. (2002). Communication and stereotypical impressions. *Howard Journal of Communication, 13,* 113–128.

22. Aronson, J., Lustina, M. J., Good, C., & Keough, K. (1999). When white men can't do math: Necessary and sufficient factors in stereotype threat. *Journal of Experimental Social Psychology, 35,* 29–46.

23. Snyder, M., & Uranowitz, S. (1978). Reconstructing the past: Some cognitive consequences of person perception. *Journal of Personality and Social Psychology, 36,* 941–950.

24. Allen, M. (1998). Methodological considerations when examining a gendered world. In D. J. Canary & K. Dindia (Eds.), *Handbook of sex differences and similarities in communication* (pp. 427–444). Mahwah, NJ: Lawrence Erlbaum Associates.

25. Lee, Y. -T., Jussim, L. J., & McCauley, C. R. (1996). *Stereotype accuracy: Toward appreciating group differences.* Washington, DC: American Psychological Association.

26. Tetlock, P. E. (1983). Accountability and the perseverance of first impressions. *Social Psychology Quarterly, 46,* 285–292.

27. Lindgaard, G., Fernandes, G., Dudek, C., & Brown, J. (2006). Attention web designers: You have 50 milliseconds to make a good first impression! *Behaviour and Information Technology, 25,* 115–126.

28. Asch, S. (1946). Forming impressions of personality. *Journal of Abnormal and Social Psychology, 41,* 258–290.

29. Parsons, C. K., Liden, R. C., & Bauer, T. N. (2001). Personal perception in employment interviews. In M. London (Ed.), *How people evaluate others in organizations* (pp. 67-90). Mahwah, NJ: Lawrence Erlbaum Associates.

30. Luchins, A. (1957). Primacy-recency in impression formation. In C. Hovland (Ed.), *The order of presentation in persuasion.* New Haven, CT: Yale University Press.

31. Baddeley, A. D., & Hitch, G. (1993). The recency effect: Implicit learning with explicit retrieval? *Memory and Cognition, 21,* 146–155.

32. McCann, C. D., Higgins, E. T., & Fondacaro, R. A. (1991). Primacy and recency in communication and self-persuasion: How successive audiences and multiple encodings influence subsequent evaluative judgments. *Social Cognition, 9,* 47–66.

33. Schyns, P. G., & Oliva, A. (1999). Dr. Angry and Mr. Smile: When categorization flexibly modifies the perception of faces in rapid visual presentations. *Cognition, 69,* 243–265.

34. Stern, M., & Karraker, K. H. (1989). Sex stereotyping of infants: A review of gender labeling studies. *Sex Roles, 20,* 501–522.

35. King, D. E., & Bushwick, B. (1994). Beliefs and attitudes of hospital inpatients about faith healing and prayer. *Journal of Family Practice, 39,* 349–352.

36. Floyd, K. (2000). Affectionate same-sex touch: Understanding the influence of homophobia on observers' perceptions. *Journal of Social Psychology, 140,* 774–788.

37. Floyd, K., & Yoshimura, C. G. (2002). The extended self-serving bias in attribution making about communication behavior. In A. V. Stavros (Ed.), *Advances in communications and media research* (vol. 1, pp. 129–138). Hauppauge, NY: Nova Science.

38. Manusov, V., & Harvey, H. J. (Eds.). (2001). *Attribution, communication behavior, and close relationships.* Cambridge, England: Cambridge University Press.

39. Weiner, B. (2000). Intrapersonal and interpersonal theories of motivation from the attributional perspective. *Educational Psychology Review, 12,* 1–14.

40. Pascarella, E. T., Edison, M., Hagedorn, L. S., Nora, A., & Terenzini, P. T. (1996). Influences on students' internal locus of attribution for academic success in the first year of college. *Research in Higher Education, 37,* 731–756.

41. Weiner, B. (1985). An attributional theory of achievement motivation and emotion. *Psychological Review, 92,* 548–573.

42. Hooley, J. M., & Campbell, C. (2002). Control and controllability: Beliefs and behaviour in high and low expressed emotion relatives. *Psychological Medicine, 32,* 1091–1099.

43. Block, J., & Funder, D. C. (1986). Social roles and social perception: Individual differences in attribution and error. *Journal of Personality and Social Psychology, 51,* 1200–1207.

44. Sedikides, C., Campbell, W. K., Reeder, G. D., & Elliott, A. J. (1998). The self-serving bias in relational context. *Journal of Personality and Social Psychology, 74,* 378–386.

45. Sillars, A., Roberts, L. J., Dun, T., & Leonard, K. (2001). Stepping into the stream of thought: Cognition during marital conflict. In

V. Manusov & J. H. Harvey (Eds.), *Attribution, communication behavior, and close relationships* (pp. 193-201). Cambridge, England: Cambridge University Press.

46. Ross, L. (1977). The intuitive psychologist and his shortcomings: Distortions in the attribution process. In L. Berkowitz (Ed.), *Advances in experimental social psychology* (vol. 10, pp. 173–220). New York: Academic; Tetlock, P. E. (1985). Accountability: A social check on the fundamental attribution error. *Social Psychology Quarterly, 48,* 227–236.

47. Luft, J., & Ingham, H. (1955). The Johari window: A graphic model of interpersonal awareness. *Proceedings of the Western Training Laboratory in Group Development.* Los Angeles: UCLA.

48. Reported in Myers, D. G. (1980). *The inflated self.* New York: Seabury.

49. Brown, J. D., & Mankowski, T. A. (1993). Self-esteem, mood, and self-evaluation: Changes in mood and the way you see you. *Journal of Personality and Social Psychology, 64,* 421–430; Campbell, J. D. (1990). Self-esteem and clarity of the self-concept. *Journal of Personality and Social Psychology, 59,* 538–549.

50. Tarlow, E. M., & Haaga, D. A. F. (1996). Negative self-concept: Specificity to depressive symptoms and relation to positive and negative affectivity. *Journal of Research in Personality, 30,* 120–127.

51. Kolligan, J. (1990). Perceived fraudulence as a dimension of perceived incompetence. In R. J. Sternberg & J. Kolligan (Eds.), *Competence considered* (pp. 261–285). New Haven, CT: Yale University Press; Downey, G., & Feldman, S. I. (1996). Implications of rejection sensitivity for intimate relationships. *Journal of Personality and Social Psychology, 70,* 1327–1343.

52. Shaw, L. H., & Gant, L. M. (2002). In defense of the Internet: The relationship between Internet communication and depression, loneliness, self-esteem, and perceived social support. *CyberPsychology & Behavior, 5,* 157–171.

53. Campbell, J. D., & Lavallee, L. F. (1993). Who am I? The role of self-concept confusion in understanding the behavior of people with low self-esteem. In R. F. Baumeister (Ed.), *Self-esteem: The puzzle of low self-regard* (pp. 3–20). New York: Plenum.

54. Buhrmester, D., Furman, W., Wittenberg, M. T., & Reis, H. T. (1988). Five domains of interpersonal competence in peer relations. *Journal of Personality and Social Psychology, 55,* 991–1008; Murray, S. L., Rose, P., Bellavia, G., Holmes, J. G., & Kusche, A. (2002). When rejection stings: How self-esteem constrains relationship-enhancement processes. *Journal of Personality and Social Psychology, 83,* 556–573.

55. Baumeister, R. F. (2001). Violent pride: Do people turn violent because of self-hate, or self-love? *Scientific American, 284*(4), 96–101; Olweus, D. (1994). *Bullying at school: What we know and what we can do.* Malden, MA: Blackwell.

56. Baumeister, R. F., Campbell, J. D., Krueger, J. I., & Vohs, K. D. (2003). Does high self-esteem cause better performance, interpersonal success, happiness, or healthier lifestyles? *Psychological Science in the Public Interest, 4,* 1–44.

57. Bishop, J., & Inderbitzen-Nolan, H. M. (1995). Peer acceptance and friendship: An investigation of their relation to self-esteem. *Journal of Early Adolescence, 15,* 476–489; Rusbult, C. E., Morrow, G. D., & Johnson, D. J. (1987). Self-esteem and problem solving behavior in close relationships. *British Journal of Social Psychology, 26,* 293–303.

58. McAdams, D. P. (1996). Personality, modernity, and the storied self: A contemporary framework for studying persons. *Psychological Inquiry, 7,* 295–321.

59. Donath, J. S. (1999). Identity and deception in the virtual community. In P. Kollock & A. S. Smith (Eds.), *Communities in Cyberspace* (pp. 29–59). London: Routledge.

60. Kendall, L. (1998). Meaning and identity in "Cyberspace": The performance of gender, class, and race online. *Symbolic Interaction, 21,* 129–153.

61. Herring, S. C., Scheidt, L. A., Bonus, S., & Wright, E. (2004). Bridging the gap: A genre analysis of weblogs. *Proceedings of the 37th Hawaii International Conference on System Sciences (HICSS-37).* Los Alamitos, CA: IEEE. Retrieved October 15, 2009, from http://csdl.computer.org/comp/proceedings/hicss/2004/2056/04/205640101b.pdf

62. Huffaker, D. A., & Calvert, S. L. (2005). Gender, identity, and language use in teenage blogs. *Journal of Computer-Mediated Communication, 10*(2), article 1. http://jcmc.indiana.edu/vol10/issue2/huffaker.html

63. Goldschmidt, M. M. (2004). Good person stories: The favor narrative as a self-presentation strategy. *Qualitative Research Reports in Communication, 5,* 28–33.

64. See Ting-Toomey, S., Oetzel, J. G., & Yee-Jung, K. (2001). Self-construal types and conflict management styles. *Communication Reports, 14,* 87–104; Ting-Toomey, S., & Oetzel, J. G. (2001). *Managing intercultural conflict effectively.* Thousand Oaks, CA: Sage.

65. Goffman, E. (1959). *The presentation of the self in everyday life.* New York: Doubleday; see also Brown, P., & Levinson, S. C. (1987). *Politeness: Some universals in language usage.* Cambridge, England: Cambridge University Press.

66. Lim, T. S., & Bowers, J. W. (1991). Facework: Solidarity, approbation, and tact. *Human Communication Research, 17,* 415–449.

67. Cupach, W. R., & Metts, S. (1994). *Facework.* Thousand Oaks, CA: Sage.

68. Brocklehurst, J., & Dickinson, E. (1996). Autonomy for elderly people in long-term care. *Age and Aging, 25,* 329–332.

69. See, e.g., Takahashi, L. M. (1998). *Homelessness, AIDS, and stigmatization: The NIMBY syndrome in the United States at the end of the twentieth century.* New York: Oxford University Press.

Chapter 4

1. Baker, M. C. (2002). *The atoms of language: The mind's hidden rules of grammar.* New York: Basic.

2. Pinker, S. (2007). *The stuff of thought: Language as a window into human nature.* New York: Viking.

3. Ogden, C. K., & Richards, I. A. (1927). *The meaning of meaning: A study of the influence of language upon thought and of the science of symbolism* (2nd ed.). Orlando: Harcourt Brace.

4. British Council. (2004). Mum's the word: British Council announces results of 70 most beautiful words survey. Retrieved online September 23, 2006, from: http://www.britishcouncil.de/e/about/70words.htm

5. Bryson, B. (1990). *The mother tongue: English and how it got that way.* New York: William Morrow.

6. Hayakawa, S. I., & Hayakawa, A. R. (1991). *Language in thought and action.* San Diego: Harcourt.

7. Gudykunst, W., & Lee, C. (2002). Cross-cultural communication theories. In W. Gudykunst & B. Mody (Eds.), *The handbook of international and intercultural communication* (2nd ed., pp. 25–50). Thousand Oaks, CA: Sage.

8. Schultz, E. A. (1990). *Dialogue at the margins: Whorf, Bakhtin, and linguistic relativity.* Madison: University of Wisconsin Press.

9. Gumperz, J. J., & Levinson, S. C. (Eds.). (1996). *Rethinking linguistic relativity.* New York: Cambridge University Press.

10. For more detail on the Sapir-Whorf hypothesis, see Pütz, M., & Verspoor, M. (Eds.). (2000). *Explorations in linguistic relativity.* Amsterdam: John Benjamins Publishing Company.

11. Marcus, M. G. (1976, October). The power of a name. *Psychology Today, 9,* 75–77, 106.

12. Steele, K. M., & Smithwick, L. E. (1989). First names and first impressions: A fragile relationship. *Sex Roles, 21,* 517–523.

13. See Bertrand, M., & Mullainathan, S. (2004). Are Emily and Greg more employable than Lakisha and Jamal? A field experiment on labor market discrimination. *American Economic Review, 94,* 991–1013; but see Fryer, R. G., & Levitt, S. D. (2004). The causes and consequences of distinctively black names. *Quarterly Journal of Economics, 119,* 767–805.

14. Giles, H., & Wiemann, J. M. (1987). Language, social comparison and power. In C. R. Berger & S. H. Chaffee (Eds.), *The handbook of communication science* (pp. 350–384). Newbury Park, CA: Sage.

15. Bavelas, J. B., Black, A., Bryson, L., & Mullett, J. (1988). Political equivocation: A situational explanation: *Journal of Language and Social Psychology, 7,* 137–145; Bavelas, J. B., Black, A., Chovil, N., & Mullett, J. (1990). *Equivocal communication.* Newbury Park, CA: Sage.

16. Hamilton, M. A., & Mineo, P. J. (1998). A framework for understanding equivocation. *Journal of Language and Social Psychology, 17,* 3–35.

17. Daly, J. A., Diesel, C. A., & Weber, D. (1994). Conversational dilemmas. In W. R. Cupach & B. H. Spitzberg (Eds.), *The dark side of interpersonal communication* (pp. 127–156). Mahwah, NJ: Lawrence Erlbaum Associates.

18. Huston, T. L., Caughlin, J. P., Houts, R. M., Smith, S. E., & George, L. J. (2001). The connubial crucible: Newlywed years as predictors of marital delight, distress, and divorce. *Journal of Personality and Social Psychology, 80,* 237–252.

19. Floyd, K., & Riforgiate, S. (2008). Affectionate communication received from spouses predicts stress hormone levels in healthy adults. *Communication Monographs, 75,* 351–368.

20. Floyd, K., Mikkelson, A. C., Tafoya, M. A., Farinelli, L., La Valley, A. G., Judd, J., Davis, K. L., Haynes, M. T., & Wilson, J. (2007). Human affection exchange: XIV. Relational affection predicts resting heart rate and free cortisol secretion during acute stress. *Behavioral Medicine, 32,* 151–156.

21. Floyd, K., Boren, J. P., Hannawa, A. F., Hesse, C., McEwan, B., & Veksler, A. E. (2009). Kissing in marital and cohabiting relationships: Effects on blood lipids, stress, and relationship satisfaction. *Western Journal of Communication, 73,* 113–133; Floyd, K., Mikkelson, A. C., Hesse, C., & Pauley, P. M. (2007). Affectionate writing reduces total cholesterol: Two randomized, controlled trials. *Human Communication Research, 33,* 119–142.

22. Floyd, K., Mikkelson, A. C., Tafoya, M. A., Farinelli, L., La Valley, A. G., Judd, J., Haynes, M. T., Davis, K. L., & Wilson, J. (2007). Human affection exchange: XIII. Affectionate communication accelerates neuroendocrine stress recovery. *Health Communication, 22,* 123–132.

23. Floyd, K., Hesse, C., & Haynes, M. T. (2007). Human affection exchange: XV. Metabolic and cardiovascular correlates of trait expressed affection. *Communication Quarterly, 55,* 79–94.

24. Floyd, K. (2002). Human affection exchange: V. Attributes of the highly affectionate. *Communication Quarterly, 50,* 135–154; Floyd, K., Hess, J. A., Miczo, L. A., Halone, K. K., Mikkelson, A. C., & Tusing, K. J. (2005). Human affection exchange: VIII. Further evidence of the benefits of expressed affection. *Communication Quarterly, 53,* 285–303; Hesse, C., & Floyd, K. (2008). Affectionate experience partially mediates the effects of alexithymia on mental health and interpersonal relationships. *Journal of Social and Personal Relationships, 25,* 793–810.

25. Jorm, A. F., Dear, K. B. G., Rodgers, B., & Christensen, H. (2003). Interaction between mother's and father's affection as a risk factor for anxiety and depression symptoms. *Social Psychiatry and Psychiatric Epidemiology, 38,* 173–179; Schwartz, G. E., & Russek, L. G. (1998). Family love and lifelong health? A challenge for clinical psychology. In D. K. Routh & R. J. DeRubeis (Eds.), *The science of clinical psychology: Accomplishments and future directions* (pp. 121–146). Washington, DC: American Psychological Association.

26. ASD/AMD Merchandise Group. (2006). Greeting card marketers and retailers struggle. Retrieved September 18, 2006, from: http://www.merchandisegroup.com/merchandise/newsletter/newsletter_display.jsp?vnu_content_id=1001306530

27. www.bluemountain.com

28. Dunbar, R. (1996). *Grooming, gossip, and the evolution of language.* Cambridge, MA: Harvard University Press.

29. McAndrew, F. T., Bell, E. K., & Garcia. C. M. (2007). Who do we tell and whom do we tell on? Gossip as a strategy for status enhancement. *Journal of Applied Social Psychology, 37,* 1562–1577.

30. See De Backer, C. J. S., Nelissen, M., Vyncke, P., Braeckman, J., & McAndrew, F. T. (2007). Celebrities: From teachers to friends. A test of two hypotheses on the adaptiveness of celebrity gossip. *Human Nature, 18,* 334–354.

31. Wert, S. R., & Salovey, P. (2004). A social comparison account of gossip. *Review of General Psychology, 8,* 122–137; see also McAndrew, F. T., & Milenkovic, M. A. (2002). Of tabloids and family secrets: The evolutionary psychology of gossip. *Journal of Applied Social Psychology, 32,* 1064–1082.

32. Figure is current as of July 2009 according to "Top 20 Most Popular Gossip Websites July 2009," available online at: http://www.ebizmba.com/articles/gossip

33. Martin, P. S. (2004). Inside the black box of negative campaign effects: Three reasons why negative campaigns mobilize. *Political Psychology, 25,* 545–562.

34. Freedman, P., & Goldstein, K. (1999). Measuring media exposure and the effects of negative campaign ads. *American Journal of Political Science, 43,* 1189–1208.

35. Burger, J. M. (1986). Increasing compliance by improving the deal: The that's-not-all technique. *Journal of Personality and Social Psychology, 31,* 277–283.

36. Gouldner, A. W. (1960). The norm of reciprocity: A preliminary statement. *American Sociological Review, 25,* 161–178.

37. Cialdini, R. B. (1994). Interpersonal influence. In S. Shavitt & T. C. Brock (Eds.), *Persuasion: Psychological insights and perspectives* (pp. 195–218). Boston: Allyn & Bacon.

38. Cody, M. J., Seiter, J., & Montagne-Miller, Y. (1995). Women and men in the marketplace. In P. Kalbfleisch & M. J. Cody (Eds.), *Gender, power, and communication in human relationships* (pp. 305–328). Hillsdale, NJ: Lawrence Erlbaum Associates.

39. Wiseman, R. (2002). *Laughlab: The scientific search for the world's funniest joke.* London: Random House.

40. Goel, V., & Dola, R. J. (2001). The functional anatomy of humor: Segregating cognitive and affective components. *Nature Neuroscience, 4,* 237–238.

41. Mobbs, D., Greicius, M. D., Abdel-Azim, E., Menon, V., & Reiss, A. L. (2003). Humor modulates the mesolimbic reward centers. *Neuron, 40,* 1041–1048.

42. Norrick, N. R. (1993). *Conversational joking: Humor in everyday talk.* Indianapolis: Indiana University Press.

43. Keller, K. (1984). *Humor as therapy.* Wauwatosa, WI: Med-Psych.

44. Feingold, A. (1992). Gender differences in mate selection preferences: A test of the parental investment model. *Psychological Bulletin, 112,* 125–139.

45. Alberts, J. K. (1992). Teasing and sexual harassment: Double bind communication in the workplace. In L. A. Perry, H. Sterk, & L. Turner (Eds.), *Constructing and reconstructing gender* (pp. 150–120). Albany: SUNY Press.

46. Makin, V. S. (2004). Face management and the role of interpersonal politeness variables in euphemism production and comprehension. *Dissertation Abstracts International, 64,* 4077; McGlone, M. S., & Batchelor, J. A. (2003). Looking out for number one: Euphemism and face. *Journal of Communication, 53,* 251–264.

47. Butler, J. (1997). *Excitable speech: A politics of the performative.* New York: Routledge.

48. Waltman, M. S., & Haas, J. W. (2007). Advertising hate on the Internet. In D. W. Schumann & E. Thorson (Eds.), *Internet advertising: Theory and practice* (pp. 397–426). Mahwah, NJ: Lawrence Erlbaum Associates.

49. Bryant, S. (2006). Feds retrieve Google records after Gmail used for hate speech. Retrieved September 6, 2006, from: http://googlewatch.eweek.com/blogs/google_watch/archive/2006/07/27/11852.aspx

1. Nierenberg, G. (1990). *How to read a person like a book.* New York: Pocket; Calero, H. H. (2005). *The power of non-verbal communication: What you do is more important than what you say.* Lansdowne, PA: Silver Lake.

2. Mehrabian, A. (1968). Communication without words. *Psychology Today, 2,* 51–52.

3. Birdwhistell, R. L. (1970). *Kinesics and context.* Philadelphia: University of Pennsylvania Press; see also Philpott, J. S. (1983). *The relative contribution to meaning of verbal and nonverbal channels of communication: A meta-analysis.* Unpublished master's thesis, University of Nebraska, Lincoln; Burgoon, J. K., & Hoobler, G. (2002). Nonverbal signals. In M. L. Knapp & J. A. Daly (Eds.), *Handbook of interpersonal communication* (3rd ed., pp. 240–299). Thousand Oaks, CA: Sage.

4. Burgoon, J. K. (1985). Nonverbal signals. In M. L. Knapp & G. R. Miller (Eds.), *Handbook of interpersonal communication* (pp. 344–390). Beverly Hills, CA: Sage.

5. See Guerrero, L. K., & Floyd, K. (2006). *Nonverbal communication in close relationships.* Mahwah, NJ: Lawrence Erlbaum Associates.

6. See Hall, J. A. (2006). How big are nonverbal sex differences? The case of smiling and nonverbal sensitivity. In K. Dindia & D. J. Canary (Eds.), *Sex differences and similarities in communication* (2nd ed., pp. 59–81). Mahwah, NJ: Lawrence Erlbaum Associates.

7. Ekman, P., & Friesen, W. V. (1975). *Unmasking the face: A field guide to recognizing emotions from facial clues.* Englewood Cliffs, NJ: Prentice-Hall.

8. Ekman, P. (1972). Universals and cultural differences in facial expressions of emotion. In J. Cole (Ed.), *Nebraska symposium on motivation, 1971* (vol. 19, pp. 207–282). Lincoln: University of Nebraska Press.

9. Boucher, J. D., & Carlson, G. E. (1980). Recognition of facial expression in three cultures. *Journal of Cross-Cultural Psychology, 11,* 263–280; Cüceloglu, D. M. (1970). Perception of facial expressions in three cultures. *Ergonomics, 13,* 93–100; Ekman, P., Friesen, W. V., O'Sullivan, M., Chan, A., Diacoyanni-Tarlatzis, I., Heider, K., Krause, R., LeCompte, W. A., Pitcairn, T., Ricci-Bitti, P. E., Scherer, K., Tomita, M., & Tzavaras, A. (1987). Universals and cultural differences in the judgments of facial expressions of emotion. *Journal of Personality and Social Psychology, 53,* 712–717; Izard, C. E. (1971). *The face of emotion.* New York: Appleton-Century-Crofts; McAndrew, F. T. (1986). A cross-cultural study of recognition thresholds for facial expression of emotion. *Journal of Cross-Cultural Psychology, 17,* 211–224; Niit, T., & Valsiner, J. (1977). Recognition of facial expressions: An experimental investigation of Ekman's model. *Acta et Commentationes Universitatis Tarvensis, 429,* 85–107.

10. Elfenbein, H. A., & Ambady, N. (2002). On the universality and cultural specificity of emotion recognition: A meta-analysis. *Psychological Bulletin, 128,* 203–235.

11. Kappas, A., Hess, U., & Scherer, K. R. (1991). Voice and emotion. In R. S. Feldman & B. Rimé (Eds.), *Fundamentals of nonverbal communication* (pp. 200–237). Cambridge, England: Cambridge University Press.

12. Bavelas, J. B., Coates, L., & Johnson, T. (2002). Listener responses as a collaborative process: The role of gaze. *Journal of Communication, 52,* 566–580.

13. Guerrero, L. K., & Floyd, K. (2006). *Nonverbal communication in close relationships.* Mahwah, NJ: Lawrence Erlbaum Associates.

14. See, e.g., Carroll, L., & Gilroy, P. J. (2002). Role of appearance and nonverbal behavior in the perception of sexual orientation among lesbians and gay men. *Psychological Reports, 91,* 155–122; Douglas Creed, W. E., Scully, M. A., & Austin, J. R. (2002). Clothes make the person? The tailoring of legitimating accounts and the social construction of identity. *Organization Science, 13,* 475–496; Schötz, S. (2003). Towards synthesis of speaker age: A perceptual study with natural, synthesized, and resynthesized stimuli. *PHONUM, 9,* I–X.

15. Cha, A., Hecht, B. R., Nelson, K., & Hopkins, M. P. (2004). Resident physician attire: Does it make a difference to our patients? *American Journal of Obstetrics and Gynecology, 190,* 1484–1488.

16. See Morry, M. M. (2007). The attraction-similarity hypothesis among cross-sex friends: Relationship satisfaction, perceived similarities, and self-serving perceptions. *Journal of Social and Personal Relationships, 24,* 117–138; Watkins, L. M., & Johnston, L. (2000). Screening job applicants: The impact of physical attractiveness and application quality. *International Journal of Selection and Assessment, 8,* 76–84.

17. Ekman, P., Friesen, W. V., & Scherer, K. R. (1976). Body movement and voice pitch in deceptive interaction. *Semiotica, 16,* 23–27.

18. Ekman, P., Friesen, W. V., & O'Sullivan, M. (1997). Smiles when lying. In P. Ekman & E. L. Rosenberg (Eds.), *What the face reveals: Basic and applied studies of spontaneous expression using the facial affect coding system (FACS)* (pp. 201–214). New York: Oxford University Press.

19. Vrij, A., Semin, G. R., & Bull, R. (1996). Insight into behavior displayed during deception. *Human Communication Research, 22,* 544–562.

20. Knapp, M. L. (1978). *Nonverbal communication in human interaction* (2nd ed.). New York: Holt.

21. Ellis, H. D., & Young, A. W. (1989). Are faces special? In A. W. Young & H. D. Ellis (Eds.), *Handbook of research on face processing* (pp. 1–26). Amsterdam: North-Holland.

22. Smith, C., Lentz, E. M., & Mikos, K. (1988). *Signing naturally.* San Diego: DawnSign.

23. Iverson, J. M., Tencer, H. L., Lany, J., & Goldin-Meadow, S. (2000). The relation between gesture and speech in congenitally blind and sighted language-learners. *Journal of Nonverbal Behavior, 24,* 105–130.

24. Floyd, K. (2006). *Communicating affection: Interpersonal behavior and social context.* Cambridge, England: Cambridge University Press.

25. Field, T. M. (Ed.). (1995). *Touch in early development.* Mahwah, NJ: Lawrence Erlbaum Associates.

26. Zuckerman, M., & Miyake, K. (1993). The attractive voice: What makes it so? *Journal of Nonverbal Behavior, 17,* 119–135.

27. Wolvin, A., & Coakley, C. (1996). *Listening.* Dubuque, IA: Brown & Benchmark.

28. Burgoon, J. K., Guerrero, L. K., & Floyd, K. (2010). *Nonverbal communication.* Boston: Allyn & Bacon.

29. Hall, E. T. (1959). *The silent language.* Garden City, NY: Doubleday; Hall, E. T. (1963). System for the notation of proxemic behavior. *American Anthropologist, 65,* 1003–1026.

30. Dion, K. K., Berscheid, E., & Walster, E. (1972). What is beautiful is good. *Journal of Personality and Social Psychology, 24,* 285–290; Eagley, A. E., Ashmore, R. D., Makhijani, M. G., & Longo, L. C. (1991). What is beautiful is good, but . . . : A meta-analytic review of research on the physical attractiveness stereotype. *Psychological Bulletin, 110,* 109–139; Kuhlenschmidt, S., & Conger, J. C. (1988). Behavioral components of social competence in females. *Sex Roles, 18,* 107–112.

31. O'Grady, K. E. (1989). Physical attractiveness, need for approval, social self-esteem, and maladjustment. *Journal of Social and Clinical Psychology, 8,* 62–69; Curran, J. P., & Lippold, S. (1975). The effects of physical attraction and attitude similarity on attraction in dating dyads. *Journal of Personality, 43,* 528–539.

32. Efran, M. G. (1974). The effect of physical appearance on the judgment of guilt, interpersonal attraction, and severity of recommended punishment in a simulated jury task. *Journal of Experimental Research in Personality, 8,* 45–54; Efran, M. G., & Patterson, E. (1974). Voters vote beautiful: The effect of physical appearance on a national debate. *Canadian Journal of Behavioral Science, 6,* 352–356; West, S. G., & Brown, T. J. (1975). Physical attractiveness, the severity of the emer-

gency and helping: A field experiment and interpersonal simulation. *Journal of Experimental Social Psychology, 11,* 531–538.

33. Jandt, F. E. (1995). *Intercultural communication: An introduction.* Thousand Oaks, CA: Sage.

34. Burgoon et al., 2010.

35. Feghali, E. K. (1997). Arab cultural communication patterns. *International Journal of Intercultural Relations, 21,* 345–378.

36. Watson, O. M. (1970). *Proxemic behavior: A cross-cultural study.* The Hague: Mouton.

37. Iizuka, Y. (1994). Gaze during speaking as related to shyness. *Perceptual and Motor Skills, 78,* 1259–1264; Larsen, R. J., & Shackelford, T. K. (1996). Gaze avoidance: Personality and social judgments of people who avoid direct face-to-face contact. *Personality and Individual Differences, 21,* 907–917.

38. Matsumoto, D. (2006). Culture and nonverbal behavior. In V. Manusov & M. L. Patterson (Eds.), *The Sage handbook of nonverbal communication* (pp. 219–236). Thousand Oaks, CA: Sage.

39. Ekman, P. (1993). Facial expression and emotion. *American Psychologist, 48,* 384–392; Ekman, P., & Friesen, W. V. (1986). A new pan-cultural facial expression of emotion. *Motivation and Emotion, 10,* 159–168; Scherer, K. R., & Wallbott, H. G. (1994). Evidence for universality and cultural variation of differential emotion response patterning. *Journal of Personality and Social Psychology, 66,* 310–328.

40. Matsumoto, D. (1991). Cultural influences on facial expressions of emotion. *Southern Communication Journal, 56,* 128–137; Matsumoto, 2006.

41. Burgoon et al., 2010.

42. Hall, E. T., & Hall, M. R. (1990). *Understanding cultural differences: Germans, French, and Americans.* Yarmouth, ME: Intercultural.

43. Levine, R., & Wolff, E. (1985, March). Social time: The heartbeat of culture. *Psychology Today,* 28–35.

44. McDaniel, E. R., & Andersen, P. A. (1998). Intercultural variations in tactile communication: A field study. *Journal of Nonverbal Behavior, 22,* 59–75; see also Field, T. (1999). American adolescents touch each other less and are more aggressive toward their peers as compared with French adolescents. *Adolescence, 34,* 753–758.

45. Andersen, P. A. (2008). *Nonverbal communication: Forms and functions* (2nd ed.). Long Grove, IL: Waveland; Andersen, P. A., & Wang, H. (2006). Unraveling cultural cues: Dimensions of nonverbal communication across cultures. In L. A. Samovar, R. E. Porter, & E. R. McDaniel (Eds.), *Intercultural communication: A reader* (pp. 250–266). Belmont, CA: Wadsworth.

46. Kramsch, C. (1998). *Language and culture.* New York: Oxford University Press.

47. Field, T. (1999). American adolescents touch each other less and are more aggressive toward their peers as compared with French adolescents. *Adolescence, 34,* 753–758.

48. Fridlund, A. J. (1994). *Human facial expression: An evolutionary view.* San Diego: Academic.

49. Grieser, D. L., & Kuhl, P. K. (1988). Maternal speech to infants in a tonal language: Support for universal prosodic features in motherese. *Developmental Psychology, 24,* 14–20.

50. Wood, J. T. (2009). *Gendered lives: Communication, culture, and gender* (8th ed.). Belmont, CA: Cengage/Wadsworth.

51. Floyd, K., Mikkelson, A. C., & Hesse, C. (2007). *The biology of human communication* (2nd ed.). Florence, KY: Thomson.

52. Burgoon, J. K., & Bacue, A. (2003). Nonverbal communication skills. In B. R. Burleson & J. O. Greene (Eds.), *Handbook of communication and social interaction skills* (pp. 179–219). Mahwah, NJ: Lawrence Erlbaum Associates.

53. Floyd, 2006. (See note 24.)

54. Blier, M. J., & Blier-Wilson, L. A. (1989). Gender differences in sex-rated emotional expressiveness. *Sex Roles, 21,* 287–295.

55. Nolen-Hoeksema, S. (1987). Sex differences in unipolar depression: Evidence and theory. *Psychological Bulletin, 101,* 259–282.

56. Coats, E. J., & Feldman, R. S. (1996). Gender differences in nonverbal correlates of social status. *Personality and Social Psychology Bulletin, 22,* 1014–1022.

57. Burrowes, B. D., & Halberstadt, A. G. (1987). Self- and family-expressiveness styles in the experience and expression of anger. *Journal of Nonverbal Behavior, 11,* 254–268.

58. Mulac, A., Studley, L. B., Wiemann, J. W., & Bradac, J. J. (1987). Male/female gaze in same-sex and mixed-sex dyads: Gender-linked differences and mutual influence. *Human Communication Research, 13,* 323–344.

59. Wada, M. (1990). The effects of interpersonal distance change on nonverbal behaviors: Mediating effects of sex and intimacy levels in a dyad. *Japanese Psychological Research, 32,* 86–96.

60. Exline, R. V. (1963). Explorations in the process of person perception: Visual interaction in relation to competition, sex, and the need for affiliation. *Journal of Personality, 31,* 1–20.

61. Mulac et al., 1987.

62. Patterson, M. L., & Schaeffer, R. E. (1977). Effects of size and sex composition on interaction distance, participation, and satisfaction in small groups. *Small Group Behavior, 8,* 433–442.

63. Shaffer, D. R., & Sadowski, C. (1975). This table is mine: Respect for marked barroom tables as a function of gender of spatial marker and desirability of locale. *Sociometry, 38,* 408–419.

64. Marieb, E. N. (2003). *Essentials of human anatomy and physiology* (7th ed.). San Francisco: Benjamin Cummings.

65. Fitzpatrick, M. A., Mulac, A., & Dindia, K. (1994, July). *Convergence and reciprocity in male and female communication patterns in spouse and stranger interaction.* Paper presented at the Fifth International Conference on Language and Social Psychology, Brisbane, Australia.

66. Major, B., Schmidlin, A. M., & Williams, L. (1990). Gesture patterns in social touch: The impact of setting and age. *Journal of Personality and Social Psychology, 58,* 634–643.

67. Major et al., 1990.

68. See Dortch, S. (1997). Women at the cosmetics counter. *American Demographics, 19,* 4.

69. Gray, J. (1992). *Men are from Mars, women are from Venus: A practical guide to improving communication and getting what you want in your relationships.* New York: HarperCollins.

70. Dindia, K. (2006). Men are from North Dakota, women are from South Dakota. In K. Dindia & D. J. Canary (Eds.), *Sex differences and similarities in communication* (2nd ed., pp. 3–20). Mahwah, NJ: Lawrence Erlbaum Associates.

71. See, e.g., Hall, J. A. (2006). How big are nonverbal sex differences? The case of smiling and nonverbal sensitivity. In K. Dindia & D. J. Canary (Eds.), *Sex differences and similarities in communication* (2nd ed., pp. 59–81). Mahwah, NJ: Lawrence Erlbaum Associates.

72. Ekman, P., & Friesen, W. V. (1982). Felt, false, and miserable smiles. *Journal of Nonverbal Behavior, 6,* 238–252.

73. Riggio, R. E. (2005). The Social Skills Inventory (SSI): Measuring nonverbal and social skills. In V. Manusov (Ed.), *The sourcebook of nonverbal measures: Going beyond words* (pp. 25–34). Mahwah, NJ: Lawrence Erlbaum Associates.

74. Riggio, R. E. (2006). Nonverbal skills and abilities. In V. Manusov & M. L. Patterson (Eds.), *The Sage handbook of nonverbal communication* (pp. 79–96). Thousand Oaks, CA: Sage.

75. Riggio, R. E. (1986). Assessment of basic social skills. *Journal of Personality and Social Psychology, 51,* 649–660.

76. See Friedman, H. S., & Riggio, R. E. (1981). Effects of individual differences in nonverbal expressiveness on transmission of emotion. *Journal of Nonverbal Behavior, 6,* 96–102.

77. Friedman, H. S., Prince, L. M., Riggio, R. E., & DiMatteo, M. R. (1980). Understanding and assessing nonverbal expressiveness: The Affective Communication Test. *Journal of Personality and Social Psychology, 39,* 333–351.

Chapter 6

1. See Spitzberg, B. H. (1994). The dark side of (in)competence. In W. R. Cupach & B. H. Spitzberg (Eds.), *The dark side of interpersonal communication* (pp. 25–50). Hillsdale, NJ: Lawrence Erlbaum Associates.

2. Emmert, P. (1996). President's perspective. *ILA Listening Post, 56,* 2–3.

3. Dindia, K., & Kennedy, B. L. (2004, November). *Communication in everyday life: A descriptive study using mobile electronic data collection.* Paper presented at the annual conference of the National Communication Association, Chicago, IL.

4. Barker, L., Edwards, R., Gaines, C., Gladney, K., & Holley, F. (1980). An investigation of proportional time spent in various communicating activities by college students. *Journal of Applied Communication Research, 8,* 101–109; Hargie, O., Saunders, C., & Dickson, D. (1994). *Social skills in interpersonal communication* (3rd ed.). New York: Routledge.

5. Windsor, J. L., Curtis, D. B., & Stephens, R. D. (1997). National preferences in business and communication education: An update. *Journal of the Association for Communication Administration, 3,* 170–179.

6. Wolvin, A. D. (1984). Meeting the communication needs of the adult learner. *Communication Education, 33,* 267–271.

7. See, e.g., Prager, K. J., & Buhrmester, D. (1998). Intimacy and need fulfillment in couple relationships. *Journal of Social and Personal Relationships, 15,* 435–469.

8. Brownell, J. (1990). Perceptions of effective listeners: A management study. *Journal of Business Communication, 27,* 401–415.

9. Carrell, L. J., & Willmington, S. C. (1996). A comparison of self-report and performance data in assessing speaking and listening competence. *Communication Reports, 9,* 185–191.

10. See Lane, K., Balleweg, B. J., Suler, J. R., Fernald, P. S., & Goldstein, G. S. (2000). Acquiring skills—Undergraduate students. In M. E. Ware & D. E. Johnson (Eds.), *Handbook of demonstrations and activities in the teaching of psychology: Vol. 3. Personality, abnormal, clinical-counseling, and social* (2nd ed., pp. 109–124). Mahwah, NJ: Lawrence Erlbaum Associates.

11. Spinks, N., & Wells, B. (1991). Improving listening power: The payoff. *Bulletin of the Association for Business Communication, 54,* 75–77.

12. Wolvin, A. D. (1987, June). *Culture as a listening variable.* Paper presented at the summer conference of the International Listening Association, Toronto, Ontario, Canada.

13. Chen, G.-M., & Chung, J. (1997). The "Five Asian Dragons": Management behaviors and organization communication. In L. A. Samovar & R. E. Porter (Eds.), *Intercultural communication: A reader* (pp. 317–328). Belmont, CA: Wadsworth.

14. Egan, G. (1998). *The skilled helper* (6th ed.). Pacific Grove, CA: Brooks/Cole.

15. Brownell, J. (2002). *Listening attitudes, principles, and skills* (2nd ed.). Boston: Allyn & Bacon.

16. Macrae, C. N., & Bodenhausen, G. V. (2001). Social cognition: Categorical person perception. *British Journal of Psychology, 92,* 239–255.

17. Thomas, L. T., & Levine, T. R. (1994). Disentangling listening and verbal recall: Separate but related constructs? *Human Communication Research, 21,* 103–127.

18. Benoit, S. S., & Lee, J. W. (1986). Listening: It can be taught. *Journal of Education for Business, 63,* 229–232.

19. Bellezza, F. S., & Buck, D. K. (1988). Expert knowledge as mnemonic cues. *Applied Cognitive Psychology, 2,* 147–162.

20. Verhaeghen, P., Marcoen, A., & Goossens, L. (1992). Improving memory performance in the aged through mnemonic training: A meta-analytic study. *Psychology and Aging, 7,* 242–251.

21. Duncan, S., & Fiske, D. W. (1977). *Face-to-face interaction: Research, methods, and theory.* New York: Wiley.

22. Kuhn, J. L. (2001). Toward an ecological humanistic psychology. *Journal of Humanistic Psychology, 41,* 9–24.

23. Duan, C., & Hill, C. E. (1996). The current state of empathy research. *Journal of Counseling Psychology, 43,* 261–274.

24. Stiff, J. B., Dillard, J. P., Somera, L., Kim, H., & Sleight, C. (1988). Empathy, communication, and prosocial behavior. *Communication Monographs, 55,* 198–213.

25. See Armstrong, B. G., Boiarsky, G. A., & Mares, M. L. (1991). Background television and reading performance. *Communication Monographs, 58,* 235–253.

26. Haider, M. (1970). Neuropsychology of attention, expectation, and vigilance. In D. I. Mostofsky (Ed.), *Attention: Contemporary theory and analysis* (pp. 419–432). New York: Appleton-Century-Crofts.

27. Ball, S. A., & Zuckerman, M. (1992). Sensation seeking and selective attention: Focused and divided attention on a dichotic listening task. *Journal of Personality and Social Psychology, 63,* 825–831.

28. Media Dynamics, Inc. (2007, February 15). Our rising ad dosage: It's not as oppressive as some think. *Media Matters, XXI*(3), 1–2.

29. Toffler, A. (1970). *Future shock.* New York: Random House.

30. Keller, E. (2007, July 19). Why you can't get any work done: Workplace distractions cost U.S. business some $650 billion a year. Retrieved online November 23, 2007, from: http://www.businessweek.com/careers/content/jul2007/ca20070719_880333.htm

31. American Psychiatric Association. *Diagnostic and statistical manual of mental disorders* (4th ed.). Washington, DC: Author.

32. Attention-deficit hyperactivity disorder: ADHD in adults. Retrieved online March 8, 2008, from: http://www.webmd.com/add-adhd/guide/adhd-adults

33. Versfeld, N. J., & Dreschler, W. A. (2002). The relationship between the intelligibility of time-compressed speech and speech-in-noise in young and elderly listeners. *Journal of the Acoustical Society of America, 111,* 401–408; Wolvin, A., & Coakley, C. (1996). *Listening.* Dubuque, IA: Brown & Benchmark.

34. Golen, S. (1990). A factor analysis of barriers to effective listening. *Journal of Business Communication, 27,* 25–36.

35. Golen, 1990.

36. Watson, K. W., & Smeltzer, L. R. (1984). Barriers to listening: Comparisons between students and practitioners. *Communication Research Reports, 1,* 82–87.

37. Golen, 1990.

38. James, D., & Clarke, S. (1993). Women, men, and interruptions: A critical review. In D. Tannen (Ed.), *Gender and conversational interaction* (pp. 231–267). New York: Oxford University Press.

39. Redeker, G., & Maes, A. (1996). Gender differences in interruptions. In D. Slobin, J. Gerhardt, A. Kyratzis, & J. Guo (Eds.), *Social interaction, social context, and language* (pp. 579–612). Mahwah, NJ: Lawrence Erlbaum Associates.

40. Gilovich, T. (1997, March/April). Some systematic biases of everyday judgment. *Skeptical Inquirer,* 31–35.

41. Taylor, S. E., & Thomson, S. C. (1982). Stalking the elusive "vividness" effect. *Psychological Review, 89,* 155–181.

42. http://www.planecrashinfo.com/rates.htm

43. Glassman, J. K. (1998, May 29). Put shootings in proper perspective. *San Jose Mercury News,* B7.

44. Ruggeiro, V. (1988). *Teaching thinking across the curriculum.* New York: Harper & Row.

45. Tannen, D. (1990). *You just don't understand: Women and men in conversation.* New York: Ballantine.

46. Pollak, K. I., Arnold, R. M., Jeffreys, A. S., Alexander, S. C., Olsen, M. K., Abernethy, A. P., Skinner, C. S., Rodriguez, L. K., & Tulsky, J. A. (2007). Oncologist communication about emotion during visits with patients with advanced cancer. *Journal of Clinical Oncology, 25,* 5748–5752.

47. Floyd, K. (2006). *Communicating affection: Interpersonal behavior and social context*. Cambridge, England: Cambridge University Press.

Chapter 7

1. Parks, M. R. (2007). *Personal relationships and personal networks*. Mahwah, NJ: Lawrence Erlbaum Associates; quote is from page 1.

2. See Fiske, A. P. (1992). The four elementary forms of sociality: Framework for a unified theory of social relations. *Psychological Review, 99*, 689–723.

3. Baumeister, R. F., & Leary, M. R. (1995). The need to belong: Desire for interpersonal attachments as a fundamental human motivation. *Psychological Bulletin, 117*, 497–529.

4. See Bonta, J., & Gendreau, P. (1995). Re-examining the cruel and unusual punishment of prison life. In T. J. Flanagan (Ed.), *Long-term imprisonment: Policy, science, and correctional practice* (pp. 75–84). Thousand Oaks, CA: Sage.

5. Schumm, W. R., Bell, D. B., Knott, B., & Rice, R. E. (1996). The perceived effect of stressors on marital satisfaction among civilian wives of enlisted soldiers deployed to Somalia for Operation Restore Hope. *Military Medicine, 161*, 601–606.

6. Dykstra, P. A., van Tilburg, T. G., & De Jong-Gierveld, J. (2005). Changes in older adult loneliness: Results from a seven-year longitudinal study. *Research on Aging, 27*, 725–747; Sorkin, D., Rook, K. S., & Lu, J. L. (2002). Loneliness, lack of emotional support, lack of companionship, and the likelihood of having a heart condition in an elderly sample. *Annals of Behavioral Medicine, 24*, 290–298; Tijhuis, M. A., De Jong-Gierveld, J., Feskins, E. J., & Kromhout, D. (1999). Changes in and factors related to loneliness in older men: The Zutphen Elderly Study. *Age and Ageing, 28*, 491–495.

7. Haney, C. (1993). Mental health issues in long-term solitary and "supermax" confinement. *Crime & Delinquency, 49*, 124–156.

8. Parks, M. R., & Floyd, K. (1996). Making friends in cyberspace. *Journal of Communication, 46*, 80–97.

9. Bryant, J. A., Sanders-Jackson, A., & Smallwood, A. M. K. (2006). IMing, text messaging, and adolescent social networks. *Journal of Computer-Mediated Communication, 11*, article 10. Available online: http://jcmc.indiana.edu/vol11/issue2/bryant.html

10. Whitty, M. (2001). Age/sex/location: Uncovering the social cues in the development of online relationships. *CyberPsychology & Behavior, 4*, 623–630.

11. Bonebrake, K. (2002). College students' Internet use, relationship formation, and personality correlates. *CyberPsychology & Behavior, 5*, 551–557.

12. See, e.g., Halsen, M., Wolleberg, W., & Meeus, W. (2000). Social support from parents and friends and emotional problems in adolescence. *Journal of Youth and Adolescence, 29*, 319–335.

13. Rawlins, W. K. (1992). *Friendship matters: Communication, dialectics, and the life course*. New York: Aldine de Gruyter.

14. Cohen, S., Doyle, W. J., Turner, R., Alper, C. M., & Skoner, D. P. (2003). Sociability and susceptibility to the common cold. *Psychological Science, 14*, 389–395.

15. Ruberman, W., Weinblatt, E., Goldberg, J. D., & Chaudhary, B. S. (1984). Psychosocial influences on mortality after myocardial infarction. *New England Journal of Medicine, 311*, 552–559.

16. House, J. S., Landis, K. R., & Umberson, D. (1988). Social relationships and health. *Science, 241*, 540–545.

17. See, e.g., Schnurr, P. P., & Green, B. L. (Eds.). (2004). *Trauma and health: Physical health consequences of exposure to extreme stress*. Washington, DC: American Psychological Association.

18. Gallant, M. P. (2003). The influence of social support on chronic illness self-management: A review and directions for research. *Health Education & Behavior, 30*, 170–195.

19. McCroskey, J. C., & McCain, T. A. (1974). The measurement of interpersonal attraction. *Speech Monographs, 41*, 261–266.

20. Adams, G. R., & Roopnarine, J. L. (1994). Physical attractiveness, social skills, and same-sex peer popularity. *Journal of Group Psychotherapy, Psychodrama and Sociometry, 47*, 15–35; Speed, A., & Gangestad, S. W. (1997). Romantic popularity and mate preferences: A peer-nomination study. *Personality and Social Psychology Bulletin, 23*, 928–936.

21. Mehrabian, A., & Blum, J. S. (2003). Physical appearance, attractiveness, and the mediating role of emotions. In N. J. Pallone (Ed.), *Love, romance, sexual interaction: Research perspectives from current psychology* (pp. 1–29). New Brunswick, NJ: Transaction.

22. Barber, N. (1995). The evolutionary psychology of physical attractiveness: Sexual selection and human morphology. *Ethology and Sociobiology, 16*, 395–424; Hume, D. K., & Montgomerie, R. (2001). Facial attractiveness signals different aspects of "quality" in women and men. *Evolution and Human Behavior, 22*, 93–112.

23. Festinger, L., Schachter, S., & Back, K. W. (1963). *Social pressures in informal groups: A study of human factors in housing*. Stanford, CA: Stanford University Press.

24. Urberg, K. A., Degirmencioglu, S. M., & Tolson, J. M. (1998). Adolescent friendship selection and termination: The role of similarity. *Journal of Social and Personal Relationships, 15*, 703–710.

25. See Byrne, D. (1997). An overview (and underview) of research and theory within the attraction paradigm. *Journal of Social and Personal Relationships, 14*, 417–431.

26. For an extended discussion, see Guerrero, L. K., & Floyd, K. (2006). *Nonverbal communication in close relationships*. Mahwah, NJ: Lawrence Erlbaum Associates.

27. Dutilleux, J. P. (1994). *L'indien blanc: Vingt ans de sortilege amazonien* [The white Indian: Twenty years of the Amazonian curse]. Paris: R. Laffont.

28. Thesander, M. (1997). *The feminine ideal*. London: Reaktion.

29. Singh, D., & Luis, S. (1995). Ethnic and gender consensus for the effect of waist-to-hip ratio on judgments of women's attractiveness. *Human Nature, 6*, 51–65; Singh, D., & Young, R. K. (1995). Body weight, waist-to-hip ratio, breasts, and hips: Role in judgments of female attractiveness and desirability for relationships. *Ethology and Sociobiology, 16*, 483–507.

30. Singh, D. (1995). Female judgment of male attractiveness and desirability for relationships: Role of waist-to-hip ratio and financial status. *Journal of Personality and Social Psychology, 69*, 1089–1101.

31. Workman, L., & Reader, W. (2004). *Evolutionary psychology: An introduction*. Cambridge, England: Cambridge University Press.

32. Berger, C. R., & Calabrese, R. J. (1975). Some explorations in initial interaction and beyond: Toward a developmental theory of interpersonal communication. *Human Communication Research, 1*, 99–112.

33. Sunnafrank, M. (1986). Predicted outcome values: Just now and then? *Human Communication Research, 13*, 39–40.

34. Sunnafrank, M. (1990). Predicted outcome value and uncertainty reduction theories: A test of competing perspectives. *Human Communication Research, 17*, 76–103.

35. Vishwanath, A. (2003). Comparing online information effects. *Communication Research, 30*, 579–598.

36. Gudykunst, W. G., & Nishida, T. (1984). Individual and cultural influences on uncertainty reduction. *Communication Monographs, 51*, 23–36.

37. Gergen, K. J., Greenbert, M. S., & Willis, R. H. (1980). *Social exchange: Advances in theory and research*. New York: Plenum; Thibaut, J. W., & Kelley, H. H. (1959). *The social psychology of groups*. New York: Wiley.

38. See, e.g., Lloyd, S. A., Cate, R. M., & Henton, J. M. (1984). Predicting premarital relationship stability: A methodological refinement. *Journal of Marriage and the Family, 46*, 71–76.

39. Messick, R. M., & Cook, K. S. (Eds.). (1983). *Equity theory: Psychological and sociological perspectives*. New York: Praeger.

40. Stafford, L., & Canary, D. J. (1991). Maintenance strategies and romantic relationship type, gender, and relational characteristics. *Journal of Social and Personal Relationships, 8,* 217–242.

41. Canary, D. J., & Stafford, L. (1992). Relational maintenance strategies and equity in marriage. *Communication Monographs, 59,* 243–268.

42. See Hecht, M. L., Shepard, T., & Hall, T. J. (1979). Multivariate indices of the effects of self-disclosure. *Western Journal of Speech Communication, 43,* 235–245.

43. Argyle, M., & Henderson, M. (1984). The rules of friendship. *Journal of Social and Personal Relationships, 1,* 211–237.

44. Milardo, R. M. (1986). Personal choice and social constraint in close relationships: Application of network analysis. In V. J. Derlega & B. A. Winstead (Eds.), *Friendship and social interaction* (pp. 145–166). New York: Springer-Verlag.

45. Coltrane, S. (1996). *Family man.* New York: Oxford University Press.

46. Floyd, K., & Morman, M. T. (1997). Affectionate communication in nonromantic relationships: Influences of communicator, relational, and contextual factors. *Western Journal of Communication, 61,* 279–298.

47. Altman, I., & Taylor, D. (1973). *Social penetration: The development of interpersonal relationships.* New York: Holt.

48. Gouldner, A. W. (1960). The norm of reciprocity: A preliminary statement. *American Sociological Review, 25,* 161–178.

49. Miller, L. C., & Kenny, D. A. (1986). Reciprocity of self-disclosure at the individual and dyadic levels: A social relations analysis. *Journal of Personality and Social Psychology, 50,* 713–719.

50. Derlega, V. J., Metts, S., Petronio, S., & Margulis, S. T. (1993). *Self-disclosure.* Newbury Park, CA: Sage.

51. See Wood, J. T. (2007). *Gendered lives: Communication, gender, and culture* (7th ed.). Belmont, CA: Wadsworth.

52. Dindia, K., & Allen, M. (1992). Sex differences in self-disclosure: A meta-analysis. *Psychological Bulletin, 112,* 106–124.

53. See, e.g., Triandis, H. C. (1989). The self and social behavior in differing cultural contexts. *Psychological Review, 96,* 506–520.

54. Dindia, K. (2000). Sex differences in self-disclosure, reciprocity of self-disclosure, and self-disclosure and liking: Three meta-analyses reviewed. In S. Petronio (Ed.), *Balancing the secrets of private disclosures* (pp. 21–35). Mahwah, NJ: Lawrence Erlbaum Associates.

55. Lippert, T., & Prager, K. J. (2001). Daily experiences of intimacy: A study of couples. *Personal Relationships, 8,* 283–298.

56. Dindia, K. (2002). Self-disclosure research: Knowledge through meta-analysis. In M. Allen & R. W. Preiss (Eds.), *Interpersonal communication research: Advances through meta-analysis* (pp. 169–185). Mahwah, NJ: Lawrence Erlbaum Associates.

57. Kelly, A. E., Klusas, J. A., von-Weiss, R. T., & Kenny, C. (2001). What is it about revealing secrets that is beneficial? *Personality and Social Psychology Bulletin, 27,* 651–665.

58. See Kacewicz, E., Slatcher, R. B., & Pennebaker, J. W. (2007). Expressive writing: An alternative to traditional methods. In L. L'Abate (Ed.), *Low-cost approaches to promote physical and mental health: Theory, research, and practice* (pp. 271–284). New York: Springer.

59. Helgeson, V. S., & Gottlieb, B. H. (2000). Support groups. In S. Cohen, L. G. Underwood, & B. H. Gottlieb (Eds.), *Social support measurement and intervention* (pp. 221–245). New York: Oxford University Press.

60. Wright, P. H. (1984). Self-referent motivation and the intrinsic quality of friendship. *Journal of Social and Personal Relationships, 1,* 115–130.

61. See Shimanoff, S. B. (1980). *Communication rules: Theory and research.* Beverly Hills, CA: Sage.

62. Argyle & Henderson, 1984. (See note 43.)

63. Parks, M. R., & Floyd, K. (1996). Meanings for closeness and intimacy in friendship. *Journal of Social and Personal Relationships, 15,* 517–537.

64. Wood, J. T., & Inman, C. C. (1993). In a different mode: Masculine styles of communicating closeness. *Journal of Applied Communication Research, 21,* 279–295.

65. Floyd, K. (1995). Gender and closeness among friends and siblings. *Journal of Psychology, 129,* 193–202; see also Morman, M. T., & Floyd, K. (1998). "I love you, man": Overt expressions of affection in male-male interaction. *Sex Roles, 38,* 871–881.

66. Sapadin, L. A. (1988). Friendship and gender: Perspectives of professional men and women. *Journal of Social and Personal Relationships, 5,* 387–403.

67. Rawlins, 1992. (See note 13.)

68. Kaplan, D. L., & Keys, C. B. (1997). Sex and relationship variables as predictors of sexual attraction in cross-sex platonic friendships between young heterosexual adults. *Journal of Social and Personal Relationships, 14,* 191–206; Sapadin, 1988.

69. Egland, K. I., Spitzberg, B. G., & Zormeier, M. M. (1996). Flirtation and conversational competence in cross-sex platonic and romantic relationships. *Communication Reports, 9,* 105–118.

70. Fuiman, M., Yarab, P., & Sensibaugh, C. (1997, July). *Just friends? An examination of the sexual, physical, and romantic aspects of cross-gender friendships.* Paper presented at the biennial meeting of the International Network on Personal Relationships, Oxford, OH.

71. Afifi, W. A., & Faulkner, S. L. (2000). On being "just friends": The frequency and impact of sexual activity in cross-sex friendships. *Journal of Social and Personal Relationships, 17,* 205–222.

72. Werking, K. J. (1997). *We're just good friends: Women and men in nonromantic relationships.* New York: Guilford.

73. Hughes, M., Morrison, K., & Asada, K. J. K. (2005). What's love got to do with it? Exploring the impact of maintenance rules, love attitudes, and network support on friends with benefits relationships. *Western Journal of Communication, 69,* 49–66.

74. Messman, S. J., Canary, D. J., & Hause, K. S. (2000). Motives to remain platonic, equity, and the use of maintenance strategies in opposite-sex friendships. *Journal of Social and Personal Relationships, 17,* 67–94.

75. Rose, S. M. (1985). Same- and cross-sex friendships and the psychology of homosociality. *Sex Roles, 12,* 63–74.

76. Sias, P. M., Krone, K. J., & Jablin, F. M. (2002). An ecological systems perspective on workplace relationships. In M. L. Knapp & J. A. Daly (Eds.), *Handbook of interpersonal communication* (3rd ed., pp. 615–642). Thousand Oaks, CA: Sage.

77. Sias, P. M., & Cahill, D. J. (1998). From co-workers to friends: The development of peer friendships in the workplace. *Western Journal of Communication, 62,* 273–300.

78. Marks, S. R. (1994). Intimacy in the public realm: The case of co-workers. *Social Forces, 72,* 843–858.

79. Winstead, B. A., Derlega, V. J., Montgomery, M. J., & Pilkington, C. (1995). The quality of friendships at work and job satisfaction. *Journal of Social and Personal Relationships, 12,* 199–215.

80. Straits, B. C. (1996). Ego-net diversity: Same- and cross-sex co-worker ties. *Social Networks, 18,* 29–45.

81. Zorn, T. E. (1995). Bosses and buddies: Constructing and performing simultaneously hierarchical and close friendship relationships. In J. T. Wood & S. Duck (Eds.), *Under-studied relationships: Off the beaten track* (pp. 122–147). Thousand Oaks, CA: Sage.

82. Largent, R. N. (1987). *The relationship of friendship with a supervisor to job satisfaction and satisfaction with the supervisor.* Unpublished master's thesis, University of North Dakota, Grand Forks, ND.

83. See Fiedler, F. E. (1957). A note on leadership theory: The effect of social barriers between leaders and followers. *Sociometry, 20,* 87–94.

84. Zorn, 1995.

85. Adelman, M. B., Ahuvia, A., & Goodwin, C. (1994). Beyond smiling. In R. T. Rust & R. L. Oliver (Eds.), *Service quality: New directions in theory and practice* (pp. 139–171). Thousand Oaks, CA:

Sage; Locke, K. (1996). A funny thing happened! The management of consumer emotions in service encounters. *Organizational Science, 7,* 40–59.

86. Gwinner, K. P., Gremler, D. D., & Bitner, M. J. (1998). Relational benefits in service industries: The customer's perspective. *Journal of the Academy of Marketing Science, 26,* 101–114.

87. American College of Physicians. *Ethics manual.* Retrieved February 9, 2008, from: http://www.acponline.org/running_practice/ethics/

Chapter 8

1. Hecht, M. L., Marston, P. J., & Larkey, L. K. (1994). Love ways and relationship quality in heterosexual relationships. *Journal of Social and Personal Relationships, 11,* 25–44.

2. Baxter, L. A., & Montgomery, B. M. (1996). *Relating: Dialogues and dialectics.* New York: Guilford.

3. Peterson, G. W., & Bush, K. R. (1999). Predicting adolescent autonomy from parents: Relationship connectedness and restrictiveness. *Sociological Inquiry, 69,* 431–457.

4. U.S. Census Bureau. (2007). Marriage and divorce. Downloaded January 19, 2007, from: http://www.census.gov/population/www/socdemo/marr-div.html

5. Kaplan, R. M., & Kronick, R. G. (2006). Marital status and longevity in the United States population. *Journal of Epidemiology and Community Health, 60,* 760–765; Manzoli, M., Villarti, P., Pirone, G. M., & Boccia, A. (2007). Marital status and mortality in the elderly: A systematic review and meta-analysis. *Social Science & Medicine, 64,* 77–94.

6. Macintyre, S. (1992). The effects of family position and status on health. *Social Science & Medicine, 35,* 453–464.

7. Duncan, G., Wilkerson, B., & England, P. (2006). Cleaning up their act: The effects of marriage and cohabitation in licit and illicit drug use. *Demography, 43,* 691–710.

8. Bachman, J. G., Wadsworth, K. N., O'Malley, P. M., Johnston, L. D., & Schulenberg, J. E. (1997). *Smoking, drinking, and drug use in young adulthood: The impacts of new freedoms and new responsibilities.* Mahwah, NJ: Lawrence Erlbaum Associates.

9. Kim, H. K., & McKenry, P. (2002). The relationship between marriage and psychological well-being. *Journal of Family Issues, 23,* 885–911; Lamb, K. A., Lee, G. R., & DeMaris, A. (2003). Union formation and depression: Selection and relationship effects. *Journal of Marriage and Family, 65,* 953–962.

10. Ross, C. E., Mirowsky, J., & Goldsteen, K. (1990). The impact of the family on health: The decade in review. *Journal of Marriage and the Family, 52,* 1059–1078.

11. See Kiecolt-Glaser, J. K., & Newton, T. L. (2001). Marriage and health: His and hers. *Psychological Bulletin, 127,* 472–503.

12. Waldron, I., Hughes, M. E., & Brooks, T. L. (1996). Marriage protection and marriage selection—Prospective evidence for reciprocal effects of marital status and health. *Social Science & Medicine, 43,* 113–123.

13. Bringle, R. G., & Buunk, B. P. (1991). Extradyadic relationships and sexual jealousy. In K. McKinney & S. Sprecher (Eds.), *Sexuality in close relationships* (pp. 135–153). Mahwah, NJ: Lawrence Erlbaum Associates.

14. Mazur, R. M. (2000). *The new intimacy: Open-ended marriage and alternative lifestyles.* Boston: iUniverse.com Inc.

15. Rust, P. C. (2003). Monogamy and polyamory: Relationship issues for bisexuals. In L. Garnets & D. Kimmel (Eds.), *Psychological perspectives on lesbian, gay, and bisexual experiences* (pp. 475–495). New York: Columbia University Press.

16. Bettinger, M. (2004). Polyamory and gay men: A family systems approach. *Journal of GLBT Family Studies, 1,* 97–116; Blasband, D., & Peplau, L. A. (1985). Sexual exclusivity versus openness in gay male couples. *Archives of Sexual Behavior, 14,* 395–412.

17. Munson, M., & Stelbourn, J. P. (Eds.). (1999). *The lesbian polyamory reader: Open relationships, non-monogamy, and casual sex.* Binghamton, NY: Haworth.

18. Priambodo, N. (2006, April 17). Dating trends jump on the technological train. *University of La Verne Campus Times,* available online at: http://www.ulv.edu/ctimes/web_exclusives_stories/datingtrends.htm

19. See Uebelacker, L. A., Courtnage, E. S., & Whisman, M. A. (2003). Correlates of depression and marital dissatisfaction: Perceptions of marital communication style. *Journal of Social and Personal Relationships, 20,* 757–769.

20. Previti, D., & Amato, P. R. (2003). Why stay married? Rewards, barriers, and marital stability. *Journal of Marriage and Family 65,* 561–573.

21. Dion, K. K., & Dion, K. L. (1996). Cultural perspectives on romantic love. *Personal Relationships, 3,* 5–17.

22. Amato, P. R., & Previti, D. (2003). People's reasons for divorcing. *Journal of Family Issues 24,* 602–626.

23. Smock, P. J., Manning, W. D., & Porter, M. (2005). "Everything's there except money": How money shapes decisions to marry among cohabitors. *Journal of Marriage and Family, 67,* 680–696.

24. Compton, J., & Pollak, R. A. (2007). Why are power couples increasingly concentrated in large metropolitan areas? *Journal of Labor Economics, 25,* 475–512.

25. Kurdek, L. A. (2004). Are gay and lesbian cohabiting couples *really* different from heterosexual married couples? *Journal of Marriage and Family, 66,* 880–900.

26. Kurdek, L. A. (1998). Relationship outcomes and their predictors: Longitudinal evidence from heterosexual married, gay cohabiting, and lesbian cohabiting couples. *Journal of Marriage and the Family, 60,* 553–568.

27. Kurdek, L. A. (1994). Conflict resolution styles in gay, lesbian, heterosexual nonparent, and heterosexual parent couples. *Journal of Marriage and the Family, 56,* 705–722.

28. Kurdek, L. A. (1994). Areas of conflict for gay, lesbian, and heterosexual couples: What couples argue about influences relationship satisfaction. *Journal of Marriage and the Family, 56,* 923–934.

29. Kurdek, L. A., & Schmitt, J. P. (1987). Perceived emotional support from family and friends in members of homosexual, married, and heterosexual cohabiting couples. *Journal of Homosexuality, 14,* 57–68.

30. Kurdek, L. A. (1993). The allocation of household labor in gay, lesbian, and heterosexual married couples. *Journal of Social Issues, 49,* 127–139.

31. Balsam, K. F., Beauchaine, T. P., Rothblum, E. D., & Solomon, S. E. (2008). Three-year follow-up of same-sex couples who had civil unions in Vermont, same-sex couples not in civil unions, and heterosexual married couples. *Developmental Psychology, 44,* 102–116; Roisman, G. I., Clausell, E., Holland, A., Fortuna, K., & Elieff, C. (2008). Adult romantic relationships as contexts of human development: A multimethod comparison of same-sex couples with opposite-sex dating, engaged, and married dyads. *Developmental Psychology, 44,* 91–101.

32. Bringle & Buunk, 1991. (See note 23.)

33. Levine, R. B. (1993). Is love a luxury? *American Demographics, 15,* 27–28.

34. Hsu, F. L. K. (1981). The self in cross-cultural perspective. In A. J. Marsella, B. De Vos, & F. L. K. Hsu (Eds.), *Culture and self* (pp. 24–55). London: Tavistock; quote is from p. 50.

35. Knapp, M. L. (1978). *Social intercourse: From greeting to goodbye.* Boston: Allyn & Bacon; see also Knapp, M. L., & Vangelisti, A. L. (2000). *Interpersonal communication and human relationships* (4th ed.). Boston: Allyn & Bacon.

36. Peplau, L. A. (2003). Lesbian and gay relationships. In L. Garnets & D. Kimmel (Eds.), *Psychological perspectives on lesbian, gay, and bisexual experiences* (pp. 395–419). New York: Columbia University Press.

37. See, e.g., Donn, J. A., & Sherman, R. C. (2002). Attitudes and practices regarding the formation of romantic relationships on the Internet.

CyberPsychology & Behavior, 5, 107–123; Parks, M. R., & Roberts, L. D. (1988). "Making MOOsic": The development of personal relationships online and a comparison to their off-line counterparts. *Journal of Social and Personal Relationships, 15,* 517–537.

38. See Walther, J. B. (2010). Computer-mediated communication. In C. R. Berger, M. E. Roloff, & D. R. Roskos-Ewoldsen (Eds.), *Handbook of communication science* (2nd ed., pp. 489–505). Los Angeles: Sage.

39. Wilmot, W. W., & Hocker, J. L. (2001). *Interpersonal conflict.* New York: McGraw-Hill.

40. Gottman, J. M., & Levenson, R. W. (1992). Marital processes predictive of later dissolution: Behavior, physiology, and health. *Journal of Personality and Social Psychology, 63,* 221–233.

41. Gottman, J. M. (1994). *What predicts divorce?* Hillsdale, NJ: Lawrence Erlbaum Associates.

42. Holman, T. B., & Jarvis, M. O. (2003). Hostile, volatile, avoiding, and validating couple-conflict types: An investigation of Gottman's couple-conflict types. *Personal Relationships, 10,* 267–282.

43. Petronio, S. (2002). *Boundaries of privacy.* Albany: SUNY Press.

44. See Dindia, K., Fitzpatrick, M. A., & Kenny, D. A. (1997). Self-disclosure in spouse and stranger interaction: A social relations analysis. *Human Communication Research, 23,* 388–412.

45. Cordova, J. V., Gee, C. B., & Warren, L. Z. (2005). Emotional skillfulness in marriage: Intimacy as a mediator of the relationship between emotional skillfulness and marital satisfaction. *Journal of Social and Clinical Psychology, 24,* 218–235.

46. Mirgain, S. A., & Cordova, J. V. (2007). Emotion skills and marital health: The association between observed and self-reported emotion skills, intimacy, and marital satisfaction. *Journal of Social and Clinical Psychology, 26,* 983–1009.

47. Gottman, J. M., & Levenson, R. W. (1986). Assessing the role of emotion in marriage. *Behavioral Assessment, 8,* 31–48.

48. Carstensen, L. L., Gottman, J. M., & Levenson, R. W. (1995). Emotional behavior in long-term marriage. *Psychology and Aging, 10,* 140–149.

49. Gottman, 1994. (See note 41.)

50. Gottman & Levenson, 1986; Gottman, 1994.

51. Kluwer, E. S., Heesink, J. A. M., & Van de Vliert, E. (1997). The marital dynamics of conflict over the division of labor. *Journal of Marriage and the Family, 59,* 635–653; Perry-Jenkins, M., & Folk, K. (1994). Class, couples, and conflict: Effects of the division of labor on assessments of marriage in dual-earner families. *Journal of Marriage and the Family, 56,* 165–180.

52. Alberts, J. K., Yoshimura, C. G., Rabby, M., & Loschiavo, R. (2005). Mapping the topography of couples' daily conversation. *Journal of Social and Personal Relationships, 22,* 299–322.

53. Kluwer, E. S., Heesink, J. A. M., & Van de Vliert, E. (1996). Marital conflict about the division of household labor and paid work. *Journal of Marriage and the Family, 58,* 958–969.

54. Coltrane, S. (2000). Research on household labor: Modeling and measuring the social embeddedness of routine family work. *Journal of Marriage and the Family, 62,* 1208–1233; Coltrane, S., & Adams, M. (2001). Men's family work: Child-centered fathering and the sharing of domestic labor. In R. Hertz & N. L. Marshall (Eds.), *Working families: The transformation of the American home* (pp. 72–99). Berkeley: University of California Press.

55. Zvonkovic, A. M., Schmiege, C. J., & Hall, L. D. (1994). Influence strategies used when couples make work-family decisions and their importance for marital satisfaction. *Family Relations, 43,* 182–188.

56. Zvonkovic et al., 1994.

57. Mannino, C. A., & Deutch, F. M. (2007). Changing the division of household labor: A negotiated process between partners. *Sex Roles, 56,* 309–324.

58. Johnson, E. M., & Huston, T. L. (1998). The perils of love, or why wives adapt to husbands during the transition to parenthood. *Journal*

of Marriage and the Family, 60, 195–204; Kluwer, E. S., Heesink, J. A. M., & Van de Vliert, E. (2000). The division of labor in close relationships: An asymmetrical conflict issue. *Personal Relationships, 7,* 263–282.

59. Kluwer, E. S. (1998). Responses to gender inequality in the division of family work: The status quo effect. *Social Justice Research, 11,* 337–357.

60. Boren, J. P. (2007, November). *Negotiating the division of household labor in same-sex romantic partnerships.* Paper presented at the annual meeting of the National Communication Association, Chicago.

61. Knapp, 1978; Knapp & Vangelisti, 2000.

62. Duck, S. (1987). How to lose friends without influencing people. In M. E. Roloff & G. R. Miller (Eds.), *Interpersonal processes: New directions in communication research* (pp. 278–298). Beverly Hills, CA: Sage.

63. Kellerman, K., Reynolds, R., & Chen, J. B. (1991). Strategies of conversational retreat: When parting is not sweet sorrow. *Communication Monographs, 58,* 362–383.

64. Kreider, R. M. (2005). *Number, timing, and duration of marriages and divorces, 2001.* Washington, DC: U.S. Census Bureau; Munson, M. L., & Sutton, P. D. (2004, June 10). Births, marriages, divorces, and deaths: Provisional data for 2003. *National Vital Statistics Report, 52*(22). Hyattsville, MD: National Center for Health Statistics.

65. Amato, P. R. (2000). The consequences of divorce for adults and children. *Journal of Marriage and the Family, 62,* 1269–1287.

66. Hetherington, E. M., & Stanley-Hagen, M. (1999). The adjustment of children with divorced parents: A risk and resiliency perspective. *Journal of Child Psychology and Psychiatry, 40,* 129–140.

67. American Bar Association. (1996). *Guide to family law.* New York: Times Books.

68. General Accounting Office. (1997). Memo B-275860. Retrieved online at: http://www.gao.gov/archiva/1997/og97016.pdf

69. Satir, V. (1972). *Peoplemaking.* Palo Alto, CA: Science and Behavior Books.

70. U.S. Census Bureau. (2005). *Living arrangements of children: 2001* (Current Population Reports, P70–104). Washington, DC: Author.

71. Satir, 1972.

72. Braithwaite, D. O., Baxter, L. A., & Harper, A. M. (1998). The role of rituals in the management of dialectical tensions of "old" and "new" in blended families. *Communication Studies, 49,* 105–120.

73. Braithwaite et al., 1998; quote is from page 113.

74. Stone, E. (1989). *Black sheep and kissing cousins: How our family stories shape us.* New York: Penguin.

75. Vangelisti, A. L., & Caughlin, J. P. (1997). Revealing family secrets: The influence of topic, function, and relationships. *Journal of Social and Personal Relationships, 14,* 679–705.

76. Aron, A., Norman, C. C., Aron, E. N., McKenna, C., & Heyman, R. E. (2000). Couples' shared participation in novel and arousing activities and experienced relationship quality. *Journal of Personality and Social Psychology, 78,* 273–284.

77. Gottman, J. M. (1993). A theory of marital dissolution and stability. *Journal of Family Psychology, 7,* 57–75.

78. Ellis, K. (2002). Perceived parental confirmation: Development and validation of an instrument. *Southern Communication Journal, 67,* 319–334.

79. Gibb, J. R. (1961). Defensive communications. *Journal of Communication, 3,* 141–148.

80. Gottman, J. (2003). Why marriages fail. In K. M. Galvin & P. J. Cooper (Eds.), *Making connections: Readings in relational communication* (pp. 258–266). Los Angeles: Roxbury.

81. Gottman, 1993. (See note 41.)

82. Gottman, 1994.

83. Kiecolt-Glaser, J. K., Glaser, R., Cacioppo, J. T., & Malarkey, W. B. (1998). Marital stress: Immunologic, neuroendocrine, and auto-

nomic correlates. *Annals of the New York Academy of Sciences, 840,* 656–663.

84. Kiecolt-Glaser, J. K., Loving, T. J., Stowell, J. R., Malarkey, W. B., Lemeshow, S., Dickinson, S. L., & Glaser, R. (2005). Hostile marital interactions, proinflammatory cytokine production, and wound healing. *Archives of General Psychiatry, 62,* 1377–1384; Kiecolt-Glaser, J. K., Newton, T., Cacioppo, J. T., MacCallum, R. C., Glaser, R., & Malarkey, W. B. (1996). Marital conflict and endocrine function: Are men really more physiologically affected than women? *Journal of Consulting and Clinical Psychology, 64,* 324–332.

85. Baxter, L. A., & Montgomery, B. M. (1996). *Relating: Dialogues and dialectics.* New York: Guilford.

Chapter 9

1. Relethford, J. (2003). *Reflections of our past: How human history is revealed in our genes.* New York: Basic.

2. www.habitat.org

3. Myers, S. A., & Anderson, C. M. (2008). *The fundamentals of small group communication.* Thousand Oaks, CA: Sage.

4. Socha, T. J. (1997). Group communication across the life span. In L. R. Frey & J. K. Barge (Eds.), *Managing group life: Communicating in decision-making groups* (pp. 3–28). Boston: Houghton Mifflin.

5. Cragan, J. F., & Wright, D. W. (1999). *Communication in small groups: Theory, process, skills* (5th ed.). Belmont, CA: Wadsworth.

6. Rothwell, J. D. (2004). *In mixed company: Small group communication* (5th ed.). Belmont, CA: Wadsworth.

7. Henman, L. D. (2003). Groups as systems. In R. Y. Hirokawa, R. S. Cathcart, L. A. Samovar, & L. D. Henman (Eds.), *Small group communication theory & practice: An anthology* (8th ed., pp. 3–7). Los Angeles: Roxbury.

8. Carron, A. V., & Brawley, L. R. (2000). Cohesion: Conceptual and measurement issues. *Small Group Research, 31,* 89–106.

9. See Rovio, E., Esokla, J., Kozub, S. A., Duda, J. L., & Lintunen, T. (2009). Can high group cohesion be harmful? A case study of a junior ice-hockey team. *Small Group Research, 40,* 421–435.

10. Kjormo, O., & Halvari, H. (2002). Two ways related to performance in elite sport: The path of self-confidence and competitive anxiety and the path of group cohesion and group goal-clarity. *Perceptual and Motor Skills, 94,* 950–966.

11. Craig, T. Y., & Kelly, J. R. (1999). Group cohesiveness and creative performance. *Group Dynamics: Theory, Research, and Practice, 3,* 243–256.

12. Fujishin, R. (2007). *Creating effective groups: The art of small group communication* (2nd ed.). Lanham, MD: Rowman & Littlefield.

13. Riddle, B. L., Anderson, C. M., & Martin, M. M. (2000). Small group socialization scale: Development and validity. *Small Group Research, 31,* 554–572.

14. Wittenbaum, G. M., Hollingshead, A. B., Paulus, P. B., Hirokawa, R. Y., Ancona, D. G., Peterson, R. S., Jehn, K. A., & Yoon, K. (2004). The functional perspective as a lens for understanding groups. *Small Group Research, 35,* 17–43.

15. Mayer, M. E. (1998). Behaviors leading to more effective decisions in small groups embedded in organizations. *Communication Reports, 11,* 123–132.

16. Southwell, D., & Twist, S. (2007). *Secret societies.* New York: Rosen; see also Bond, M. (2007). The dining Freemasons: Security protocols for secret societies. *Lecture Notes in Computer Science, 4631,* 266–275.

17. See, e.g., Newer, H. (1999). *From wrongs of passage: Fraternities, sororities, hazing, and binge drinking.* Bloomington: Indiana University Press.

18. Decker, S. H., & Van Winkle, B. (1996). *Life in the gang: Family, friends, and violence.* Cambridge, England: Cambridge University Press.

19. www.redhatsociety.com

20. Frey, L. R., & Sunwolf. (2005). The communication perspective on group life. In S. A. Whelan (Ed.), *The handbook of group research and practice* (pp. 158–186). Thousand Oaks, CA: Sage.

21. Cragan & Wright, 1999. (See note 5.)

22. Staples, D. S., & Webster, J. (2007). Exploring traditional and virtual team members' "best practices." *Small Group Research, 38,* 60–97.

23. Schiller, S. Z., & Mandviwalla, M. (2007). Virtual team research: An analysis of theory use and a framework for theory appropriation. *Small Group Research, 38,* 12–59.

24. Johnson, S. K., Bettenhausen, K., & Gibbons, E. (2009). Realities of working in virtual teams: Affective and attitudinal outcomes of using computer-mediated communication. *Small Group Research, 40,* 623–649.

25. Hardin, A. M., Fuller, M. A., & Davison, R. M. (2007). I know I can, but can we? Culture and efficiency beliefs in global virtual teams. *Small Group Research, 38,* 130–155.

26. Majchrzak, A., Malhotra, A., Stamps, J., & Lipnack, J. (2004). Can absence make a team grow stronger? *Harvard Business Review, May 2004,* 1–8.

27. http://www.9-11commission.gov/

28. National Commission on Terrorist Attacks Upon the United States. (2004). *The 9/11 Commission report: Final report of the National Commission on Terrorist Attacks Upon the United States.* New York: Norton.

29. Grossman, M. (2000). *Encyclopedia of the United States cabinet.* Santa Barbara, CA: ABC-Clio.

30. Langford, J., & McDonagh, D. (Eds.). (2002). *Focus groups: Supporting effective product development.* London: Taylor & Francis.

31. www.riaa.com/goldandplatinumdata.php?resultpage=1&table= tblTopArt&action=

32. www.kiwanis.org

33. www.lionsclubs.org

34. Davison, K. P., Pennebaker, J. W., & Dickerson, S. S. (2000). Who talks? The social psychology of illness support groups. *American Psychologist, 55,* 205–217.

35. Goodwin, P. J., Leszcz, M., Ennis, M., Koopmans, J., Vincent, L., Guther, H., Drysdale, E., Hundleby, M., Chochinov, J. M., Navarro, M., Speca, M., Masterson, J., Dohan, L., Sela, R., Warren, B., Patterson, A., Pritchard, K. I., Arnold, A., Doll, R., O'Reilley, S. E., Quirt, G., Hood, N., & Hunter, J. (2001). The effect of group psychosocial support on survival in metastatic breast cancer. *New England Journal of Medicine, 345,* 1719–1726; see also Gilden, J. C., Hendryx, M. S., Clar, S., & Singh, S. P. (1992). Diabetes support groups improve health care of older diabetic patients. *Journal of the American Geriatrics Society, 40,* 147–150.

36. Wright, K. B., & Bell, S. B. (2003). Health-related support groups on the Internet: Linking empirical findings to social support and computer-mediated communication theory. *Journal of Health Psychology, 8,* 39–54.

37. Based on the number of hits from a Google search conducted in November 2008 using the phrase "online support group."

38. McPherson, M., Smith-Lovin, L., & Cook, J. M. (2001). Birds of a feather: Homophily in social networks. *Annual Review of Sociology, 27,* 415–444.

39. Peris, R., Gimeno, M. A., Pinazo, D., Ortet, G., Carrero, V., Sanchiz, M., & Ibáñez, I. (2002). Online chat rooms: Virtual spaces of interaction for socially oriented people. *CyberPsychology & Behavior, 5,* 43–51.

40. For discussion, see Ellison, N. B., Steinfield, C., & Lampe, C. (2007). The benefits of Facebook "friends": Social capital and college students' use of online social network sites. *Journal of Computer-Mediated Communication, 12,* 1143–1168.

41. www.collegequizbowl.org

42. Gokhale, A. A. (1995). Collaborative learning enhances critical thinking. *Journal of Technology Education, 7,* 22–30.

43. See Young, C. B., & Henquinet, J. A. (2000). A conceptual framework for designing group projects. *Journal of Education for Business, 76,* 56–60.

44. Keyton, J., Harmon, N., & Frey, L. R. (1996, November). *Grouphate: Implications for teaching small group communication.* Paper presented at the annual meeting of the Speech Communication Association, San Diego.

45. Louis, M. R. (1980). Surprise and sense making: What newcomers experience in entering unfamiliar organizational settings. *Administrative Science Quarterly, 25,* 226–251.

46. Moreland, R. L. (1985). Social categorization and the assimilation of "new" group members. *Journal of Personality and Social Psychology, 48,* 1173–1190.

47. Sinclair-James, L., & Stohl, C. (1997). Group endings and new beginnings. In L. R. Frey & J. K. Barge (Eds.), *Managing group life: Communicating in decision-making groups* (pp. 308–334). Boston: Houghton Mifflin.

48. Keyton, J. (1993). Group termination: Completing the study of group development. *Small Group Research, 24,* 84–100.

49. Baker, D. F., & Campbell, C. M. (2004). When is there strength in numbers? A study of undergraduate task groups. *College Teaching, 53,* 14–18.

50. Sunwolf. (2002). Getting to "groupaha!": Provoking creating processes in task groups. In L. R. Frey (Ed.), *New directions in group communication* (pp. 203–217). Thousand Oaks, CA: Sage.

51. Williams, K., Harkins, S., & Latané, B. (1981). Identifiability as a deterrent to social loafing: Two cheering experiments. *Journal of Personality and Social Psychology, 40,* 303–311.

52. Hung, T.-K., Chi, N.-W., & Lu, W.-L. (2009). Exploring the relationships between perceived coworker loafing and counterproductive work behaviors: The mediating role of a revenge motive. *Journal of Business and Psychology, 24,* 257–270.

53. Høigaard, R., Säfvenbom, R., & Tønnessen, F. E. (2006). The relationship between group cohesion, group norms, and perceived social loafing in soccer teams. *Small Group Research, 37,* 217–232.

54. Wheelan, S. A., & McKeage, R. L. (1993). Developmental patterns in small and large groups. *Small Group Research, 24,* 60–83.

55. Bertcher, H. J., & Maple, F. F. (1996). *Creating groups* (2nd ed.). Thousand Oaks, CA: Sage.

56. Myers & Anderson, 2008. (See note 3.)

57. Hess, J. A. (1993). Assimilating newcomers into an organization: A cultural perspective. *Journal of Applied Communication Research, 21,* 189–210.

58. See Moreland, R. L., & Levine, J. M. (2002). Socialization and trust in work groups. *Group Processes & Intergroup Relations, 5,* 185–201.

59. Keyton, J. (2000). Introduction: The relational side of groups. *Small Group Research, 31,* 387–396.

60. Mullen, B., & Cooper, C. (1994). The relation between group cohesiveness and performance: An integration. *Psychological Bulletin, 115,* 210–227; Welch, B. A., Mossholder, K. W., Stell, R. P., & Bennett, N. (1998). Does work group cohesiveness affect individuals' performance and organizational commitment? *Small Group Research, 29,* 472–494.

Chapter 10

1. Fok, S. (2009, February 17). Group of downtown retailers brainstorm ideas to battle recession. *Hanford Sentinel.* Available online: http://www.hanfordsentinel.com/articles/2009/02/17/news/doc499b090a5e4eb299711745.prt

2. Osborn, A. F. (1953). *Applied imagination: Principles and procedures of creative problem solving.* New York: Scribner.

3. Anderson, J., Foster-Kuehn, M., & McKinney, B. C. (1996). *Communication skills for surviving conflicts at work.* Cresskill, NJ: Hampton.

4. Osborn, A. F. (1963). *Applied imagination: Principles and procedures of creative problem solving* (3rd ed.). New York: Scribner.

5. Gautschi, T. F. (1990). How to improve group decisions. *Design News, 47*(17), 188.

6. MacPhail, A. (2001). Nominal group technique: A useful method for working with young people. *British Educational Research Journal, 27,* 161–170.

7. Gautschi, T. F. (1990). Group decision-making—Part III. *Design News, 46*(19), 336; Offner, A. K., Kramer, T. J., & Winter, J. P. (1996). The effects of facilitation, recording, and pauses on group brainstorming. *Small Group Research, 27,* 283–298.

8. Seibold, D. R., & Krikorian, D. H. (1997). Planning and facilitating group meetings. In L. R. Frey & K. J. Barge (Eds.), *Managing group life: Communicating in decision-making groups* (pp. 270–305). Boston: Houghton Mifflin.

9. Eitington, J. E. (2002). *The winning trainer: Winning ways to involve people in learning* (4th ed.). Woburn, MA: Butterworth-Heinemann/Elsevier.

10. Moore, C. M. (1987). *Group techniques for idea building.* Newbury Park, CA: Sage.

11. See Adler, R. B., & Elmhorst, J. M. (2005). *Communicating at work: Principles and practices for business and the professions* (8th ed.). New York: McGraw-Hill.

12. Eagly, A. H., & Karau, S. J. (2002). Role congruity theory of prejudice toward female leaders. *Psychological Review, 109,* 573–598.

13. Koch, S. C. (2005). Evaluative affect display toward male and female leaders of task-oriented groups. *Small Group Research, 36,* 678–703.

14. Eagly, A. H., Makhijani, M. G., & Klonsky, B. G. (1992). Gender and the evaluation of leaders: A meta-analysis. *Psychological Bulletin, 111,* 3–22.

15. Koch, S. C. (2005). Evaluative affect display toward male and female leaders II: Transmission among group members and leader reactions. *Journal of Articles in Support of the Null Hypothesis, 3,* 51–72.

16. Koch, 2005.

17. Cohen, A. (2009). *The tall book.* New York: Bloomsbury.

18. See Burgoon, J. K., & Dunbar, N. E. (2006). Nonverbal expressions of dominance and power in human relationships. In V. L. Manusov & M. L. Patterson (Eds.), *The Sage handbook of nonverbal communication* (pp. 279–297). Thousand Oaks, CA: Sage; see also Frieze, I. H., Olson, J. E., & Good, D. C. (1990). Perceived and actual discrimination in the salaries of male and female managers. *Journal of Applied Social Psychology, 20,* 46–67; Montepare, J. M. (1995). The impact of variations in height on young children's impressions of men and women. *Journal of Nonverbal Behavior, 19,* 31–47.

19. Judge, T. A., & Cable, D. M. (2004). The effect of physical height on workplace success and income: Preliminary test of a theoretical model. *Journal of Applied Psychology, 89,* 428–441.

20. See Kane, J. N., Anzovin, S., & Podell, J. (2001). *Facts about the presidents: A compilation of biographical and historical information.* Bronx, NY: Wilson.

21. Judge & Cable, 2004.

22. Statistics are from the National Health and Nutrition Examination Survey. The figure is the mean of the average height for women (63.8 inches) and the average height for men (69.2 inches).

23. Sczesny, S., & Kühnen, U. (2004). Meta-cognition about biological sex and gender-stereotypic physical appearance: Consequences for the assessment of leadership competence. *Personality and Social Psychology Bulletin, 30,* 13–21.

24. Sczesny, S., Spreeman, S., & Stahlberg, D. (2006). Masculine = competent? Physical appearance and sex as sources of gender-stereotypic attributions. *Swiss Journal of Psychology, 65,* 15–23.

25. Cherulnik, P. D., Turns, L. C., & Wilderman, S. K. (2006). Physical appearance and leadership: Exploring the role of appearance-based attribution in leader emergence. *Journal of Applied Social Psychology, 20,* 1530–1539.

26. Paglis, L. L., & Green, S. G. (2002). Leadership self-efficacy and managers' motivation for leading change. *Journal of Organizational Behavior, 23,* 215–235; see also House, R. J., & Aditya, R. N. (1997). The social scientific study of leadership: Quo vadis? *Journal of Management, 23,* 409–473.

27. Chemers, M. M., Watson, C. B., & May, S. T. (2000). Dispositional affect and leadership effectiveness: A comparison of self-esteem, optimism, and efficacy. *Personality and Social Psychology Bulletin, 26,* 267–277.

28. Özalp Türetgen, I., Unsal, P., & Erdem, I. (2008). The effects of sex, gender role, and personality traits on leader emergence: Does culture make a difference? *Small Group Research, 39,* 588–615; see also Ellis, R. J., Adamson, R. S., Deszca, G., & Cawsey, T. F. (1988). Self-monitoring and leadership emergence. *Small Group Research, 19,* 312–324; Miller, J. S., & Cardy, R. L. (2000). Self-monitoring and performance appraisal: Rating outcomes in project teams. *Journal of Organizational Behavior, 21,* 609–626.

29. Ellis, R. J. (1988). Self-monitoring and leadership emergence in groups. *Personality and Social Psychology Bulletin, 14,* 681–693.

30. Judge, T. A., Bono, J. E., Ilies, R., & Gerhardt, M. W. (2002). Personality and leadership: A qualitative and quantitative review. *Journal of Applied Psychology, 87,* 765–780.

31. Hawkins, K., & Stewart, R. A. (1991). Effects of communication apprehension on perceptions of leadership and intragroup attraction in small task-oriented groups. *Southern Communication Journal, 57,* 1–10.

32. O'Hair, D., & Wiemann, M. O. (2004). *The essential guide to group communication.* Boston: Bedford/St. Martin's.

33. Van Vugt, M., Jepson, S. F., Hart, C. M., & De Cremer, D. (2004). Autocratic leadership in social dilemmas: A threat to group stability. *Journal of Experimental Social Psychology, 40,* 1–13.

34. Hackman, M. Z., & Johnson, C. E. (2004). *Leadership: A communication perspective* (4th ed.). Long Grove, IL: Waveland.

35. Foels, R., Driskell, J. E., Mullen, B., & Salas, E. (2000). The effects of democratic leadership on group member satisfaction: An integration. *Small Group Research, 31,* 676–701.

36. Dunbar, N. E., & Burgoon, J. K. (2005). Perceptions of power and interactional dominance in interpersonal relationships. *Journal of Social and Personal Relationships, 22,* 207–233.

37. French, J. P. R., & Raven, B. H. (1959). The bases of social power. In D. Cartwright & A. Zander (Eds.), *Group dynamics* (pp. 607–623). New York: Harper & Row; Raven, B. H. (1965). Social influences and power. In I. D. Steiner & M. Fishbein (Eds.), *Current studies in social psychology* (pp. 371–381). New York: Holt, Rinehart & Winston.

38. Baron, J. N., & Pfeffer, J. (1994). The social psychology of organizations and inequality. *Social Psychology Quarterly, 57,* 190–209.

39. Gaski, J. F. (1986). Intercorrelations among a channel entity's power sources: Impact of the exercise of reward and coercion on expert, referent, and legitimate power sources. *Journal of Marketing Research, 23,* 62–77.

40. Till, B. D., & Busler, M. (2000). The match-up hypothesis: Physical attractiveness, expertise, and the role of fit on brand attitude, purchase intent and brand beliefs. *Journal of Advertising, 29,* 1–13.

41. Andreoni, J., & Petrie, R. (2008). Beauty, gender and stereotypes: Evidence from laboratory experiments. *Journal of Economic Psychology, 29,* 73–93.

42. See Clegg, S. R. (1989). Radical revisions: Power, discipline, and organizations. *Organization Studies, 10,* 97–115.

43. Blake, R. R., & Mouton, J. S. (1984). *The managerial grid III* (3rd ed.). Houston: Gulf.

44. Messman, S. J., & Mikesell, R. L. (2000). Competition and interpersonal conflict in dating relationships. *Communication Reports, 13,* 21–34.

45. Olson, L. N., & Braithwaite, D. O. (2004). "If you hit me again, I'll hit you back": Conflict management strategies of individuals experiencing aggression during conflicts. *Communication Studies, 55,* 271–285.

46. Cahn, D. D. (1992). *Conflict in intimate relationships.* New York: Guilford.

47. Wilmot, W. W., & Hocker, J. L. (2007). *Interpersonal conflict* (7th ed.). New York: McGraw-Hill.

48. Oetzel, J. G., & Ting-Toomey, S. (2003). Face concerns in interpersonal conflict: A cross-cultural empirical test of the face negotiation theory. *Communication Research, 30,* 599–625.

49. Solomin, M. (2006). Groupthink versus The Wisdom of Crowds: The social epistemology of deliberation and dissent. *Southern Journal of Philosophy, 44,* 28–42.

50. Janis, I. L. (1972). *Victims of groupthink.* Boston: Houghton Mifflin.

51. See McCauley, C. (1998). Group dynamics in Janis's theory of groupthink: Backward and forward. *Organizational Behavior and Human Decision Processes, 73,* 142–162.

52. Schafer, M., & Crichlow, S. (1996). Antecedents of groupthink: A quantitative study. *Journal of Conflict Resolution, 40,* 415–435; Vaughan, D. (1996). *The Challenger launch decision: Risky technology, culture, and deviance at NASA.* Chicago: University of Chicago Press.

53. Courtright, J. A. (1978). A laboratory investigation of groupthink. *Communication Monographs, 45,* 229–246.

54. Ginnett, R. (2005, May/June). What can leaders do to avoid groupthink? *Leadership in Action, 25*(2), 14.

Chapter 11

1. www.wired.com/wired/archive/13.09/stewart.html

2. www.marketingcharts.com/television/academy-awards-fewest-viewers-in-39-years-3612/

3. factfinder.census.gov

4. DeNavas-Walt, C., Proctor, B. D., & Smith, J. C. (2008). *U.S. Census Bureau current population reports, P60–235: Income, poverty, and health insurance coverage in the United States: 2007.* Washington, DC: U.S. Government Printing Office.

5. Lupia, A. (2002). Who can persuade whom? Implications from the nexus of psychology and rational choice theory. In J. H. Kuklinski (Ed.), *Thinking about political psychology* (pp. 51–88). New York: Cambridge University Press.

6. Björk, B. C., Roos, A., & Lauri, M. (2009). Scientific journal publishing: Yearly volume and open access availability. *Information Research, 14*(1), paper 391. Available online at http://InformationR .net/ir/14-1/paper391.html

Chapter 12

1. http://www.sportsbusinessjournal.com/index.cfm?fuseaction=article .preview&articleid=61260

2. Comadena, M. E., Hunt, S. K., & Simonds, C. J. (2007). The effects of teacher clarity, nonverbal immediacy, and caring on student motivation, affective, and cognitive learning. *Communication Research Reports, 24,* 241–248.

3. Titsworth, B. S. (2004). Students' notetaking: The effects of teacher immediacy and clarity. *Communication Education, 53,* 305–320.

4. Houser, M. L. (2006). Expectancy violations of instructor communication as predictors of motivation and learning: A comparison of traditional and nontraditional students. *Communication Quarterly, 54,* 331–349; see also Chesebro, J. L. (2003). Effects of teacher clarity and

nonverbal immediacy on student learning, receiver apprehension, and affect. *Communication Education, 52,* 135–147.

Chapter 13

1. Rubin, D. L., Hafer, T., & Arata, K. (2000). Reading and listening to oral-based versus literate-based discourse. *Communication Education, 49,* 121–133.

2. See Hayes, D. P. (1988). Speaking and writing: Distinct patterns of word choice. *Journal of Memory and Language, 27,* 572–585.

3. Gallup, G. (Ed.). (2001). *The 2001 Gallup poll: Public opinion.* Lanham, MD: Rowman & Littlefield.

4. Marshall, J. R. (1996). *Social phobia: From shyness to stage fright.* New York: Basic.

5. Actress Archives. (2006, May 6). Basinger battles stage fright as she considers Broadway dream. Retrieved July 9, 2009, from http://www.actressarchives.com/news.php?id=1092

6. McCroskey, J. C. (2006). Oral communication apprehension: A summary of recent theory and research. *Human Communication Research, 4,* 78–96.

7. Pollard, C. A., & Henderson, J. G. (1988). Four types of social phobia in a community sample. *Journal of Nervous and Mental Disease, 176,* 440–445.

8. Heimberg, R. G., Stein, M. B., Hiripi, E., & Kessler, R. C. (2000). Trends in the prevalence of social phobia in the United States: A synthetic cohort analysis of changes over four decades. *European Psychiatry, 15,* 29–37.

9. Kirschbaum, C., Pirke, K.-M., & Hellhammer, D. H. (1993). The "Trier Social Stress Test"—A tool for investigating psychobiological stress responses in a laboratory setting. *Neuropsychobiology, 28,* 76–81.

10. Behnke, R. R., & Sawyer, C. R. (1998). Conceptualizing speech anxiety as a dynamic trait. *Southern Communication Journal, 63,* 160–168.

11. Behnke, R. R., & Sawyer, C. R. (1999). Milestones of anticipatory public speaking anxiety. *Communication Education, 48,* 165–172.

12. Witt, P. L., & Behnke, R. R. (2006). Anticipatory speech anxiety as a function of public speaking assignment type. *Communication Education, 55,* 167–177.

13. MacIntyre, P. D., & Thivierge, K. A. (1995). The effects of speaker personality on anticipated reactions to public speaking. *Communication Research Reports, 12,* 125–133.

14. Freeman, T., Sawyer, C. R., & Behnke, R. R. (1997). Behavioral inhibition and the attribution of public speaking state anxiety. *Communication Education, 46,* 175–187.

15. MacIntyre & Thivierge, 1995.

16. Mladenka, J. D., Sawyer, C. R., & Behnke, R. R. (1998). Anxiety sensitivity and speech trait anxiety as predictors of state anxiety during public speaking. *Communication Quarterly, 46,* 417–429.

17. Behnke, R. R., & Sawyer, C. R. (2000). Anticipatory anxiety patterns for male and female public speakers. *Communication Education, 49,* 187–195.

18. Hollander, E., Liebowitz, M. R., Cohen, B., & Gorman, J. M. (1989). Prolactin and sodium lactate-induced panic. *Psychiatry Research, 28,* 181–191.

19. Jansen, A. S., Nguyen, X. V., Karpitsky, V., Mettenleiter, T. C., & Loewy, A. D. (1995). Central command neurons of the sympathetic nervous system: Basis of the fight-or-flight response. *Science, 270,* 644–646.

20. Floyd, K., Mikkelson, A. C., & Hesse, C. (2007). *The biology of human communication* (2nd ed.). Florence, KY: Thomson.

21. Roberts, J. B., Sawyer, C. R., & Behnke, R. R. (2004). A neurological representation of speech state anxiety: Mapping salivary cortisol levels of public speakers. *Western Journal of Communication, 68,* 219–231.

22. Arch, J. J., & Craske, M. G. (2006). Mechanisms of mindfulness: Emotion regulation following a focused breathing induction. *Behaviour Research and Therapy, 44,* 1849–1858.

23. Fredrikson, M., & Gunnarsson, R. (1992). Psychobiology of stage fright: The effect of public performance on neuroendocrine, cardiovascular, and subjective reactions. *Biological Psychology, 33,* 51–61.

24. Scott, S. (2007). College hats or lecture trousers? Stage fright and performance anxiety in university teachers. *Ethnography and Education, 2,* 191–207.

25. Witt, P. L., Brown, K. C., Roberts, J. B., Weisel, J., Sawyer, C. R., & Behnke, R. R. (2006). Somatic anxiety patterns before, during, and after giving a public speech. *Southern Communication Journal, 71,* 87–100; see also Roberts, Sawyer, & Behnke, 2004.

26. Finn, A. N., Sawyer, C. R., & Behnke, R. R. (2009). A model of anxious arousal for public speaking. *Communication Education, 58,* 417–432.

27. Kirschbaum, C., Wust, S., & Hellhammer, D. H. (1992). Consistent sex differences in cortisol responses to psychological stress. *Psychosomatic Medicine, 54,* 648–657; Kudielka, B. M., Hellhammer, J., Hellhammer, D. H., Wolf, O. T., Pirke, K.-M., Varadi, E., Pilz, J., & Kirschbaum, C. (1998). Sex differences in endocrine and psychological responses to psychosocial stress in healthy elderly subjects and the impact of a 2-week dehydroepiandrosterone treatment. *Journal of Clinical Endocrinology & Metabolism, 83,* 1756–1761.

28. Traustadóttir, T., Bosch, P. R., & Matt, K. S. (2003). Gender differences in cardiovascular and hypothalamic-pituitary-adrenal axis responses to psychological stress in healthy older adult men and women. *Stress, 6,* 133–140.

29. Heponiemi, T., Keltikangas-Järvinen, K., Kettunen, J., Puttonen, S., & Ravaja, N. (2004). BIS-BAS sensitivity and cardiac autonomic stress profiles. *Psychophysiology, 41,* 37–45.

30. Paul, G. L. (1966). *Insight vs. desensitization in psychotherapy: An experiment in anxiety reduction.* Palo Alto, CA: Stanford University Press.

31. Clevinger, T., & King, T. R. (1961). A factor analysis of the visible symptoms of stage fright. *Speech Monographs, 28,* 296–298.

32. Bulleted list was adapted from Table 1 of Mulac, A., & Sherman, A. R. (1974). Behavioral assessment of speech anxiety. *Quarterly Journal of Speech, 60,* 134–143.

33. Borhis, J., & Allen, M. (1992). Meta-analysis of the relationship between communication apprehension and cognitive performance. *Communication Education, 41,* 68–76.

34. Frijda, N. H. (1993). Moods, emotion episodes, and emotions. In M. Lewis & J. M. Haviland (Eds.), *Handbook of emotions* (2nd ed., pp. 381–403). New York: Guilford.

35. Lazarus, R. S. (1991). *Emotion and adaptation.* New York: Oxford University Press.

36. Ayres, J., & Hopf, T. (1992). Visualization: Reducing speech anxiety and enhancing performance. *Communication Reports, 5,* 1–10.

37. Ayres, J., Hopf, T., & Ayres, D. M. (1994). An examination of whether imaging ability enhances the effectiveness of an intervention designed to reduce speech anxiety. *Communication Education, 43,* 252–258.

38. Ayres, Hopf, & Ayres, 1994. Figure represents the average reduction in negative thoughts attributed to the "vivid imaginers" and "less vivid imaginers" in the performance visualization condition.

39. Hopf, T., & Ayres, J. (1992). Coping with public speaking anxiety: An examination of various combinations of systematic desensitization, skills training, and visualization. *Journal of Applied Communication Research, 20,* 183–198.

40. See Pertaub, D.-P., Slater, M., & Barker, C. (2002). An experiment on public speaking anxiety in response to three different types of virtual audience. *Presence: Teleoperators and Virtual Environments, 11,* 68–78.

41. Tugage, M. M., Fredrickson, B. L., & Barrett, L. F. (2004). Psychological resilience and positive emotional granularity: Examining the benefits of positive emotions on coping and health. *Journal of Personality, 72,* 1161–1190.

42. Hale, J. L., & Stiff, J. B. (1990). Nonverbal primacy in veracity judgments. *Communication Reports, 3,* 75–83.

43. Burgoon, J. K., Birk, T., & Pfau, M. (1990). Nonverbal behaviors, persuasion, and credibility. *Human Communication Research, 17,* 140–170.

44. Beebe, S. A. (1974). Eye contact: A nonverbal determinant of speaker credibility. *Speech Teacher, 23,* 21–25.

45. Burgoon, J. K., Manusov, V., Mineo, P., & Hale, J. L. (1985). Effects of gaze on hiring, credibility, attraction and relational message interpretation. *Journal of Nonverbal Behavior, 9,* 133–146.

46. Napieralski, L. P., Brooks, C. I., & Droney, J. M. (1995). The effect of duration of eye contact on American college students' attributions of state, trait, and test anxiety. *Journal of Social Psychology, 135,* 273–280.

47. Burgoon, J. K. (1991). Relational message interpretations of touch, conversational distance, and posture. *Journal of Nonverbal Behavior, 15,* 233–259.

48. Munhall, K. G., Jones, J. A., Callan, D. E., Kuratate, T., & Vatikiotis-Bateson, E. (2004). Visual prosody and speech intelligibility: Head movement improves auditory speech perception. *Psychological Science, 15,* 133–137; see also McClave, E. V. (2000). Linguistic functions of head movements in the context of speech. *Journal of Pragmatics, 32,* 855–878.

49. Gundersen, D. F., & Hopper, R. (1976). Relationships between speech delivery and speech effectiveness. *Communication Monographs, 43,* 158–165.

50. Elsbach, K. D. (2004). Managing images of trustworthiness in organizations. In K. M. Roderick & K. S. Cook (Eds.), *Trust and distrust in organizations* (pp. 275–292). New York: Russell Sage Foundation.

51. Wolvin, A., & Coakley, C. (1996). *Listening.* Dubuque, IA: Brown & Benchmark.

52. Miller, N. (1976). Speed of speech and persuasion. *Journal of Personality and Social Psychology, 34,* 15–24.

53. Street, R. L., & Brady, R. M. (1982). Speech rate acceptance ranges as a function of evaluative domain, listener speech rate, and communication context. *Speech Monographs, 49,* 290–308.

54. Rockwell, P., & Hubbard, A. E. (1999). The effect of attorneys' nonverbal communication on perceived credibility. *Journal of Credibility Assessment and Witness Psychology, 2,* 1–13.

55. Ray, G. B. (1986). Vocally cued personality prototypes: An implicit personality theory approach. *Communication Monographs, 53,* 266–276.

56. Miley, W. M., & Gonsalves, S. (2003). What you don't know can hurt you: Students' perceptions of professors' annoying teaching habits. *College Student Journal, 37,* 447–455.

57. Miller, G. R., & Hewgill, M. A. (1964). The effect of variations in nonfluency on audience ratings of source credibility. *Quarterly Journal of Speech, 50,* 36–44.

58. Kalinowski, J. S., & Saltuklaroglu, T. (2006). *Stuttering.* San Diego: Plural.

59. Yairi, E., & Ambrose, N. (1992). Onset of stuttering in preschool children: Selected factors. *Journal of Speech and Hearing Research, 35,* 782–788.

60. Guitar, B. (2005). *Stuttering: An integrated approach to its nature and treatment.* San Diego: Lippincott, Williams & Wilkins.

61. Alley, M. (2003). *The craft of scientific presentations: Critical steps to succeed and critical errors to avoid.* New York: Springer.

62. Versfeld, N. J., & Dreschler, W. A. (2002). The relationship between the intelligibility of time-compressed speech and speech-in-noise in young and elderly listeners. *Journal of the Acoustical Society of America, 111,* 401–408.

63. Gellevij, M., van der Meij, H., de Jong, T., & Pieters, J. (2002). Multimodal versus unimodal instruction in a complex learning context. *Journal of Experimental Education, 70,* 215–239.

64. Zayas-Baya, E. P. (1997). Instructional media in the total language picture. *International Journal of Instructional Media, 5,* 145–150.

Chapter 14

1. Tolani, A. T., & Yen, S. (2009, March). *Many websites fail to dispel myths about IUDs, emergency contraception, birth control, and proper timing of pap smears.* Paper presented at the annual meeting of the Society for Adolescent Medicine, Los Angeles.

2. http://www.teachforamerica.org

3. Allen, R. R., & McKerrow, R. E. (1985). *The pragmatics of public communication* (3rd ed.). Dubuque, IA: Kendall/Hunt.

4. For a list of the countries, their capitals, and information about their geographies, see http://geography.about.com/library/maps/blindex.htm

5. Garner, R. (1992). Learning from school texts. *Educational Psychologist, 27,* 53–63; see also Miller, R. B., & McCown, R. R. (1986). Effects of text coherence and elaboration on recall of sentences within paragraphs. *Contemporary Educational Psychology, 11,* 127–138.

6. Fransden, K. D., & Clement, D. A. (1984). The functions of human communication in informing: Communicating and processing information. In C. C. Arnold & J. W. Bowers (Eds.), *Handbook of rhetorical and communication theory* (pp. 338–399). Boston: Allyn & Bacon.

7. Pascarella, E., Edison, M., Nora, A., Hagedorn, L. S., & Braxton, J. (1996). Effects of teacher organization/preparation and teacher skill/clarity on general cognitive skills in college. *Journal of College Student Development, 37,* 7–19.

8. Garner, 2006.

9. Thompson, F., & Grundgenett, D. (1999). Helping disadvantaged learners build effective learning skills. *Education, 120,* 130–135.

10. See Cacioppo, J. T., & Petty, R. E. (1979). Effects of message repetition and position on cognitive response, recall, and persuasion. *Journal of Personality and Social Psychology, 37,* 97–109.

11. Garner, R. L. (2006). Humor in pedagogy: How ha-ha can lead to aha! *College Teaching, 54,* 177–180.

Chapter 15

1. Stiff, J. B., & Mongeau, P. (2003). *Persuasive communication.* New York: Guilford.

2. Homer, P. M. (2006). Relationships among ad-induced affect, beliefs, and attitudes: Another look. *Journal of Advertising, 35,* 35–51.

3. Priester, J. R., & Petty, R. E. (1995). Source attributions and persuasion: Perceived honesty as a determinant of message scrutiny. *Personality and Social Psychology Bulletin, 21,* 637–654.

4. Reynolds, N. (1993). Ethos as location: New sites for discursive authority. *Rhetoric Review, 11,* 325–338.

5. Stewart, R. A. (1994). Perceptions of a speaker's initial credibility as a function of religious involvement and religious disclosiveness. *Communication Research Reports, 11,* 169–176.

6. Gardner, M. P. (1994). Responses to emotional and informational appeals: The moderating role of context-induced mood states. In E. Clark, T. Brock, & D. Stewart (Eds.), *Attention, attitude, and affect in response to advertising* (pp. 207–223). Mahwah, NJ: Lawrence Erlbaum Associates.

7. Meyerowitz, B. E., & Chaiken, S. (1987). The effect of message framing on breast self-examination attitudes, intentions, and behavior. *Journal of Personality and Social Psychology, 52,* 500–510.

8. See, e.g., Rothman, A. J., Salovey, P., Turvey, C., & Fishkin, S. A. (1993). Attributions of responsibility and persuasion: Increasing mammography utilization among women over 40 with an internally oriented message. *Health Psychology, 12,* 39–47.

9. Crick, N. (2004). Conquering our imagination: Thought experiments and enthymemes in scientific argument. *Philosophy and Rhetoric, 37,* 21–41.

10. DiSanza, J. R., & Legge, N. J. (2002). *Business and professional communication: Plans, processes, and performance* (2nd ed.). Boston: Allyn & Bacon.

11. Weinstock, M., Neuman, Y., & Tabak, I. (2004). Missing the point or missing the norms? Epistemological norms as predictors of students' ability to identify fallacious arguments. *Contemporary Educational Psychology, 29,* 77–94.

12. Lau, R. L., Sigelman, L., Heldman, C., & Babbit, P. (1999). The effects of negative political advertisements: A meta-analytic assessment. *American Political Science Review, 93,* 851–875.

13. Burgoon, J. K., Guerrero, L. K., & Floyd, K. (2010). *Nonverbal communication.* Boston: Allyn & Bacon.

14. See DeVito, J. A. (1986). *The communication handbook: A dictionary.* New York: Harper & Row.

15. Burgoon, J. K., & Hale, J. L. (1988). Nonverbal expectancy violations: Model elaboration and application to immediacy behaviors. *Communication Monographs, 55,* 58–79.

16. http://pressroom.toyota.com/pr/tms/default.aspx

Appendix

1. See Crampton, S. M., Hodge, J. M., & Mishra, J. M. (1998). The informal communication network: Factors influencing grapevine activity. *Public Personnel Management, 27,* 569–584.

2. Crampton et al., 1998; Smith, B. (1996). Care and feeding of the office grapevine. *Management Review, 85,* 6.

3. Hellweg, S. A. (1992). Organizational grapevines. In K. L. Hutchinson (Ed.), *Readings in organizational communication* (pp. 159–172). Dubuque, IA: Brown; see also Davis, K. (1980). Management communication and the grapevine. In S. Ferguson & S. D. Ferguson (Eds.), *Intercom: Readings in organizational communication* (pp. 55–66). Rochelle Park, NJ: Hayden.

4. Trice, H., & Beyer, J. (1984). Studying organizational cultures through rites and ceremonials. *Academy of Management Review, 9,* 653–669.

5. Mokros, H. (2006). Composing relationships at work. In J. T. Wood & S. W. Duck (Eds.), *Composing relationships: Communication in everyday life* (pp. 175–185). Belmont, CA: Thomson Wadsworth.

6. Pacanowsky, M., & O'Donnell-Trujillo, N. (1983). Organizational communication as cultural performance. *Communication Monographs, 30,* 126–147.

7. Mumby, D. K. (2006). Constructing working-class masculinity in the workplace. In J. T. Wood & S. W. Duck (Eds.), *Composing relationships: Communication in everyday life* (pp. 89–95). Belmont, CA: Thomson Wadsworth.

8. Holmes, J., & Marra, M. (2002). Having a laugh at work: How humour contributes to workplace culture. *Journal of Pragmatics, 34,* 1683–1710.

9. Vinton, K. L. (1989). Humor in the workplace: It is more than telling jokes? *Small Group Behavior, 20,* 151–166.

10. Romero, E. J., & Cruthirds, K. W. (2006). The use of humor in the workplace. *Engineering Management Review, IEEE, 34*(3), 58–69.

11. Morreall, J. (1991). Humor and work. *Humor—International Journal of Humor Research, 4,* 359–374.

12. Pew Internet & American Life Project. (2009). *Networked workers.* Retrieved December 24, 2009, from http://www.pewinternet.org/Reports/2008/Networked-Workers.aspx?r=1

13. *Time.* (2009, December 28). p. 35.

14. Schweitzer, T. (2007). Seven out of 10 employees admit to abusing office computers, phones. *Inc.* Retrieved December 24, 2009, from: http://www.inc.com/news/articles/200701/workers.html

15. Figure is according to Nucleus Research.

16. See Orrange, R. (2002). Aspiring law and business professionals' orientations to work and family life. *Journal of Family Issues, 23,* 287–317.

17. Frone, M. R., Russell, M., & Cooper, M. L. (1992). Prevalence of work-family conflict: Are work and family boundaries asymmetrically permeable? *Journal of Organizational Behaviour, 13,* 723–729.

18. Geurts, S., Rutte, C., & Peeters, M. (1999). Antecedents and consequences of work-home interference among medical students. *Social Scientific Medicine, 48,* 1135–1148.

19. Burke, R. J. (1989). Some antecedents and consequences of work-family conflict. In E. B. Goldsmith (Ed.), *Work and family: Theory, research, and applications* (pp. 287–302). Newbury Park, CA: Sage.

20. Adams, G. A., King, L. A., & King, D. W. (1996). Relationships of job and family involvement, family social support, and work-family conflict with job and life satisfaction. *Journal of Applied Psychology, 81,* 411–420.

21. Perrewe, P. L., & Hochwarter, W. A. (1999). Value attainment: An explanation for the negative effects of work-family conflict on job and life satisfaction. *Journal of Occupational Health, 4,* 318–326.

22. Adams et al., 1996; see also Maslach, C., Schaufeli, W. B., & Leiter, M. P. (2001). Job burnout. *Annual Review of Psychology, 52,* 387–422.

23. Eisenberg, E. M., Monge, P. R., & Miller, K. I. (1983). Involvement in communication networks as a predictor of organizational commitment. *Human Communication Research, 10,* 179–201.

24. Neuman, J. H. (2004). Injustice, stress, and aggression in organizations. In R. W. Griffin & A. M. O'Leary-Kelly (Eds.), *The dark side of organizational behavior* (pp. 62–102). San Francisco: Jossey-Bass.

25. Pincus, J. D., & Acharya, L. (1988). Employee communication strategies for organizational crises. *Employee Responsibilities and Rights Journal, 1,* 181–199.

26. http://www.eeoc.gov/types/sexual_harassment.html

27. Earley, P., & Gibson, C. (2002). *Multinational work teams.* Mahwah, NJ: Lawrence Erlbaum Associates; Padavic, I., & Reskin, B. (2002). *Women and men at work.* Thousand Oaks, CA: Sage.

28. Farr, J. (Ed.). (2003). Stereotype threat effects in employment settings. [Special issue.] *Human Performance, 16.*

29. Lumsden, G., & Lumsden, D. (2004). *Communicating in groups and teams* (4th ed.). Belmont, CA: Wadsworth.

30. Arvey, R. D., & Murphy, K. R. (1998). Performance evaluation in work settings. *Annual Review of Psychology, 49,* 141–168.

31. Coulehan, J. L., & Block, M. L. (2006). *The medical interview: Mastering skills for clinical practice.* Philadelphia: Davis.

32. Stewart, C. J., & Cash, W. B. (2007). *Interviewing: Principles and practices* (12th ed.). New York: McGraw-Hill.

Photos

Chapter 1

p. 1, © Jose Luis Pelaez Inc/Blend Images/Corbis; p. 2TL, OJO Images/Getty Images; p. 2TM, © PhotoAlto/PunchStock; p. 2TR, © Royalty-Free/Corbis; p. 2B, © Thor Swift/The New York Times/Redux; p. 3, Photodisc Collection/Getty Images; p. 4, © Purestock/Alamy; p. 6, © moodboard/Corbis; p. 7, Glow Images/Superstock; p. 8, © Eileen Bach/Lifesize/Getty Images; p. 9, © Thinkstock/Getty Images; p. 11, © Warner Bros./Courtesy Everett Collection; p. 12, © George Doyle/Stockbyte/Getty Images; p. 14, © Thinkstock; p. 16, Courtesy Everett Collection; p. 17T, © Lane Oatey/Getty Images; p. 17B, © Jupiterimages/Brand X Pictures/Getty Images; p. 19, © Fancy/Veer; p. 20, Courtesy of Erika Lake; p. 21, © Ghislain and Marie David de Lossy/Cultura/Getty Images; p. 22, © Ozier Muhammad/The New York Times/Redux.

Chapter 2

p. 26, © AP Photo/The Canadian Press, Darryl Dyck; p. 28TL, James Darell/Getty Images; p. 28TM, © Huntstock/Getty Images; p. 28TR, © Royalty-Free/Corbis; p. 29, © AP Photo/Lynne Sladky; p. 30, Dimitri Vervitsiotis/Getty Images; p. 31T, © David McNew/Getty Images; p. 31B, © Steve Skjold/Alamy; p. 32T, James Woodson/Getty Images; p. 32B, © Michael Newman/PhotoEdit; p. 34TL, © Adam Woolfitt/Corbis; p. 34TR, © AP Photo/Brainerd Dispatch, Steve Kohls; p. 34B, © Eyewire/PhotoDisc/PunchStock; p. 36, © Patrick Sheandell/Photo Alto; p. 37B, Photo: Michael Becker/TM and Copyright © 20th Century Fox Film Corp. All rights reserved, Courtesy Everett Collection; p. 39, © Tim Graham/Getty Images; p. 40, © Brand X Pictures/PunchStock; p. 41, Courtesy of Deborah Therrien; p. 42T, © AP Photo/CP, Winnipeg Free Press - Ken Gigliotti; p. 43, © Markus Kirchgessner/laif/Redux; p. 44, © Jupiter Images/Workbook Stock/Getty Images; p. 46, moodboard/Corbis.

Chapter 3

p. 50, Courtesy Everett Collection; p. 52TL, Comstock Images/Alamy; p. 52TM, BananaStock/JupiterImages; p. 52TR, © Glowimages/Getty Images; p. 52B, © AP Photo/Chris Gardner; p. 54, © Comstock Images/Getty Images; p. 55T, Photomondo/Getty Images; p. 55B, © Glow Images/Alamy; p. 56, © Joe Raedle/Getty Images; p. 57, © Spencer Grant/PhotoEdit; p. 58L, © Ethan Miller/Getty Images; p. 58M, Jules Frazier/Getty Images; p. 58R, © Ron Chapple/Taxi/Getty Images; p. 59, © Comedy Central/Courtesy Everett Collection; p. 60B, © Jeff Kravitz/FilmMagic/Getty Images; p. 61T, © MIXA/PunchStock; p. 61B, © Jose Luis Pelaez, Inc./Blend Images/Corbis; p. 64, © Image Source/Getty Images. p. 67, Courtesy Everett Collection; p. 70, © Robert Warren/Taxi/Getty Images; p. 71, © Larry Hirshowitz/Corbis.

Chapter 4

p. 74, © Bloomberg/Getty Images; p. 76L, © Bettmann/Corbis; p. 76M, © Darren McCollester/Getty Images; p. 76R, © Alex Wong/Getty Images; p. 77T, © Darrell Gulin/Stone/Getty Images; p. 77M, © AFP/Getty Images; p. 77B, © Tim O'Hara/Corbis; p. 78, © Ariel Skelley/Blend Images/Getty Images; p. 79T, Courtesy of Jennifer Hesse; p. 82, © Flying Colours/Iconica/Getty Images; p. 83, Brand X/Getty Images; p. 85, © Luedke and Sparrow/Digital Vision/Getty Images; p. 86, © AP Photo/Lawrence Jackson; p. 87, © Dave & Les Jacobs/Superstock; p. 89, © Felipe Trueba/epa/Corbis; p. 90, © Robert Glenn/Getty Images; p. 91, © John Medina/WireImage/Getty Images; p. 93, © Jim West/The Image Works; p. 94, © Radius Images/Corbis; p. 96, Comstock Images/JupiterImages; p. 97, © Brand X Pictures/PunchStock.

Chapter 5

p. 100, © Reuters/Landov; p. 102TL, © AP Photo/Jay LaPrete; p. 102TM, © John Rensten/Taxi/Getty Images; p. 102TR, D.Falconer/PhotoLink/PhotoDisc/Getty Images; p. 102B, © Fox. Courtesy Photofest; p. 103, © Stephen Mallon/Photonica/Getty Images; p. 105, Martial Colomb/Getty Images; p. 106, Greg Gayne / TM and Copyright © 20th Century Fox Film Corp. All rights reserved, Courtesy: Everett Collection; p. 107, Creatas Images/JupiterImages; p. 109T, Courtesy Martin Gruendl; p. 109B, Courtesy of the author; p. 111L, © Erik Isakson/Blend Images/Getty Images; p. 111R, © Bob Thomas/Photodisc/Getty Images; p. 112T, Dougal Waters/Getty Images; p. 112B, © Tetra Images/Getty Images; p. 114T, © Dorling Kindersley/Getty Images; p. 114B, Keith Brofsky/Getty Images; p. 115, © Image Club; p. 116, © BBS United/Photodisc/Getty Images; p. 117T, © Andy Clark/Reuters/Corbis; p. 117B, © Martin Hunter/Getty Images; p. 118, Courtesy of Robert Schlehuber; p. 119, © Jon Feingersh/The Image Bank/Getty Images; p. 121, Justin Lubin/© NBC/Courtesy Everett Collection; p. 122, U.S. Air Force photo by Staff Sgt. Marcus McDonald.

Chapter 6

p. 126, Joseph Sohm/Visions of America/Corbis; p. 128L, Asia Images Group/Getty Images; p. 128M, © Royalty-Free/Corbis; p. 128R, © Dynamic Graphics Group/PunchStock; p.

p. 130, © Royalty-Free/Corbis; p. 131L, © JupiterImages/Workbook Stock/Getty Images; p. 131R, © Lane Oatey/Getty Images; p. 133, © Comstock/PunchStock; p. 134, © Solid Porcupine/Photographer's Choice/Getty Images; p. 135T, © Digital Vision/Getty Images; p. 135B, © Digital Vision; p. 137, © Universal/courtesy Everett Collection; p. 138, © William Andrew/Photographer's Choice/Getty Images; p. 139, © Katrina Wittkamp/Digital Vision/Getty Images; p. 140, © INSADCO Photography/Alamy; p. 141, © Jeffrey Coolidge/Riser/Getty Images; p. 145, © Derek Berwin/The Image Bank/Getty Images; p. 148, © Thinkstock/Masterfile.

Chapter 7

p. 150, © Steve Lipofsky/Corbis; p. 152TL, © Frank and Helena/Cultura/Getty Images; p. 152TM, © Andreas Kindler/Getty Images; p. 152TR, © Brian Erier/Taxi/Getty Images; p. 152B, © Johnny Franzen/Johner Images/Getty Images; p. 153T, Getty Images/Image Source; p. 153B, © Joe Raedle/Getty Images; p. 155, © AP Photo/Tom Gannam; p. 156, © Tony Garcia/Taxi/Getty Images; p. 157, © Masterfile; p. 158, © Yellow Dog Productions/The Image Bank/Getty Images; p. 160T, © The McGraw-Hill Companies, Inc./Barry Barker, photographer;

p. 161, © Design Pics Inc./Alamy; p. 163, © Image Source/Getty Images; p. 164, © Vstock LLC/Vladimir Godnik/Getty Images; p. 167, © Allan Baxter/Photodisc/Getty Images; p. 168, © Juli Balla/Stockbyte/Getty Images; p. 169, © Barbara Peacock/Taxi/Getty Images; p. 170, © Yellow Dog Productions/The Image Bank/Getty Images; p. 171, © BananaStock Ltd.; p. 172, © AP Photo/M. Spencer Green; p. 173, Courtesy of Mary Dawson; p. 174, Ingram Publishing/SuperStock; p. 175, Dynamic Graphics Group/PunchStock.

Chapter 8

p. 178, © Brand X Pictures/PunchStock; p. 180TL, © Lars A. Niki; p. 180TM, © Chris Whitehead/Cultura/Getty Images; p. 180TR, © ImageMore Co, Ltd./Getty Images; p. 180B, © AP Photo/Kirkland; p. 181, © Paul Barton/Corbis; p. 182T, © Image Source/Getty Images; p. 182B, © Jihn Lund/Sam Diephuis/Blend Images/Getty Images; p. 183, © Image Source/Getty Images; p. 184T, © Chris Noble/Stone/Getty Images; p. 184B, © Ingram Publishing/Alamy; p. 185, © Jim

Wilson/The New York Times/Redux; p. 186, © Photo Japan/Alamy; p. 188, © Jack Hollingsworth/Photodisc/Getty Images; p. 190, © Stock4B-RF/Getty Images; p. 191T, © Tom Stewart/Corbis; p. 191B, © Andy Reynolds/Stone/Getty Images; p. 192T, © Brandon Harman/Taxi/Getty Images; p. 192B, © Buena Vista Images/Stockbyte/Getty Images; p. 193, © Roy Botterell/Corbis; p. 194T, © Blend Images/Alamy; p. 194B, © Sean Justice/Corbis; p. 195, © 2009 Jupiterimages Corporation; p. 197L, Getty Images/Foodcollection; p. 197R, © Lars A. Niki; p. 198, © Digital Vision; p. 200, Getty Images.

Chapter 9

p. 206, © Mark Wilson/Getty Images; p. 208TL, Jon Feingersh/Getty Images; p. 208TM, © Martin Roe/Retna Ltd./Corbis; p. 208TR, © Tim Pannell/Corbis; p. 208B, © Mark Wilson/Getty Images; p. 210T, © Joe Raedle/Getty Images; p. 210B, © Patrick Andrade/The New York Times/Redux; p. 211, © Don Smith/Getty Images; p. 212, © Paramount/Courtesy Everett Collection; p. 213T, © John G. Mabanglo/AFP/Getty Images; p. 213B, © AP Photo/Sentinel-Tribune, Michael Lehmkuhle; p. 215, © Ross Anania/Photographer's Choice/Getty Images; p. 216, © Samuel Zuder/laif/Redux; p. 217TL, Brand X Pictures; p. 217TM, © Getty Images; p. 217TR, © AP Photo/The Ames Tribune, Jon Britton; p. 217BL, © Blend Images/PunchStock; p. 217BR, © AP Photo/Matt Sayles; p. 217ML, © Shaun Botterill/Getty Images; p. 217MR, Michel Touraine/pixland/Corbis; p. 220L, © S. Meltzer/PhotoLink/Getty Images; p. 220R, © Stockdisc/PunchStock; p. 222, Getty Images/Blend Images; p. 223, Danny Feld/© ABC/Courtesy Everett Collection; p. 225, © Blend Images/ColorBlind Images/Getty Images; p. 229T, Courtesy of Erika Lake; p. 229B, © Dann Coffey/Riser/Getty Images.

Chapter 10

p. 232, © Jupiterimages/Botanica/Getty Images; p. 234L, Will Hart/© NBC/Courtesy Everett Collection; p. 234M, Joshua Scott, Courtesy Department of Defense; p. 234R, © Royalty-Free/Corbis; p. 235T, © Bob Sacha/Corbis; p. 235B, © Photodisc/PunchStock; p. 237, Ryan McVay/Getty Images; p. 239, © AP Photo/Karim Kadim; p. 241, © Spathis and Miller/FoodPix/Getty Images; p. 242, © Thony Belizaire/AFP/Getty Images; p. 245, Manchan/Getty Images; p. 246, © Scott Olson/Getty Images; p. 247T, © Michael Caulfield/WireImage/Getty Images; p. 247B, © Creatas/PunchStock; p. 249, © Adrian Weinbrecht/Stone/Getty Images; p. 250, © AP Photos/Ben Liebenberg; p. 251T, © Ko Sasaki/The New York Times/Redux; p. 251B, © Diana Koenigsberg/Stone/Getty Images; p. 253T, © The McGraw-Hill Companies Inc./Ken Cavanagh Photographer; p. 253B, © AP Photo/Bruce Weaver; p. 254, © Royalty-Free/Corbis.

Chapter 11

p. 258, © Joe Bavier/Reuters/Landov; p. 260TL, James Woodson/Getty Images; p. 260TM, © Veer; p. 260TR, © Kayte M. Deioma/PhotoEdit Inc.; p. 260B, © Kevin Winter/Getty Images; p. 261, © Mike Cardew/MCT/Landov; p. 262, © C. Flanigan/FilmMagic/Getty Images; p. 263, Maria Teijeiro/Getty Images; p. 264B, © Dimitri Vervitsiotis/Digital Vision/Getty Images; p. 266, © Jeff Greenberg/Alamy; p. 267, © Hill Street Studios/Blend Images/Getty Images; p. 269, © Ethan Miller/Getty Images; p. 270, © AP Photo/Darryl Bush; p. 271T, © Win McNamee/Getty Images; p. 271B, Photodisc Collection/Getty Images; p. 272T, JupiterImages/Comstock Images/Alamy; p. 272B, © Dirk Anschutz/Stone/Getty Images; p. 273, Courtesy of Erika Lake; p. 274, © Dirk Anschutz/Stone/Getty Images; p. 276, © W. Wayne Lockwood, M.D./Corbis; p. 278L, © SuperStock/Alamy; p. 278R, © Walt Disney/Courtesy Everett Collection; p. 279, © Burke/Triolo Productions/Brand X/Corbis.

Chapter 12

p. 282, Courtesy Everett Collection; p. 284L, © Inti St. Clair/Digital Vision/Getty Images; p. 284M, © Stockbyte/PunchStock; p. 284R, © David Young-Wolff/PhotoEdit; p. 285, Spike Mafford/Getty Images; p. 286, © AP Photo/Paul Spinelli; p. 287T, © liquidlibrary/PictureQuest; p. 288, © Tim Sloan/AFP/Getty Images; p. 289, © David Muir/PhotoDisc/Getty Images; p. 292, © Hulton Archive/Getty Images; p. 294, © Flip Schulke/Corbis; p. 295T, © The McGraw-Hill Companies, Inc./Jill Braaten, Photographer; p. 296, mage Source/SuperStock; p. 302, Gallo Images-Lanz von Horsten/Getty Images; p. 303, © Nicole Hill/Rubberball/Corbis; p. 304, Lawrence Bender Prods./The Kobal Collection; p. 305, © Corbis.

Chapter 13

p. 310, © Alex Wong/Getty Images; p. 312TL, © Image Source/Getty Images; p. 312TM, © Tony Freeman/PhotoEdit; p. 312TR, © Bonnie Kamin/PhotoEdit; p. 312B, Digital Vision Ltd./SuperStock; p. 314, ©Bob Daemmrich/The Image Works; p. 315, © Kevin Winter/Getty Images; p. 318, © Brand X Pictures/PunchStock; p. 319L, © Jonathan Kirn/Photographer's Choice/Getty Images; p. 319R, © Bryan Allen/Corbis; p. 320, Courtesy of Erika Lake; p. 321T, © Shelby Ross/Riser/Getty Images; p. 321B, © Tina Stallard/Getty Images; p. 323, © Gen Nishino/Riser/Getty Images; p. 324T, © Spencer Grant/PhotoEdit; p. 324B, © PhotoAlto/Alamy; p. 325, © Royalty-Free/Corbis; p. 327, © AP Photo/Chris O'Meara; p. 330, © Royalty-Free/Corbis; p. 331, © Bellurget Jean Louis/Stock Image/Getty Images; p. 333, © Jeff Jacobson/Redux.

Chapter 14

p. 336, © Anthony Ong/Digital Vision/Getty Images; p. 338TL, Pierre Vauthey/Corbis Sygma; p. 338TM, © Royalty-Free/Corbis; p. 338TR, © Nik Wheeler/Corbis; p. 338B, © Najlah Feanny/Corbis; p. 340, Glen Allison/Getty Images; p. 341T, © Leo Sorel/Retna Ltd./Corbis; p. 341B, © Tom Grill/Iconica/Getty Images; p. 343, © Steve Granitz/WireImage/Getty Images; p. 344T, © Royalty-Free/Corbis; p. 344B, © Lisa Petkau/First Light/Getty Images; p. 345, © Jeff Greenberg/Alamy; p. 348, Ryan McVay/Getty Images; p. 349, © wonderlandstock/Alamy; pp. 351, 352, © AP Photo/Eric Risberg.

Chapter 15

p. 358, © AP Photo/Bebeto Matthews; p. 360TL, © AP Photo/Ross D. Franklin; p. 360TM, © AP Photo/Jason DeCrow; p. 360TR, © John Neubauer/PhotoEdit; p. 360B, © Gabriel Bouys/AFP/Getty Images; p. 361, © Alex Wong/Getty Images; p. 362T, © Susan Van Etten/PhotoEdit; p. 362B, © Imagno/Hulton Archive/Getty Images; p. 365T, Image Source/Getty Images; p. 365B, Ingram Publishing/SuperStock; p. 367, © Jon Feingersh/Blend Images/Corbis; p. 369, © Linda Ketelhut/Illustration Works/Corbis; p. 371, © TS Photography/Photographer's Choice/Getty Images; p. 372, © Kevin Winter/Getty Images; p. 375, © AP Photo/Gerald Herbert; p. 377, © Najlah Feanny/Corbis SABA; p. 378, © Justin Sullivan/Getty Images.

Appendix

p. 386L, Barbara Nitke/© NBC/Courtesy Everett Collection; p. 386M, John Lund/Nevada Wier/Blend Images/Getty Images; p. 386R, Blend Images/Getty Images; p. 394, Photodisc/Getty Images; p. 388, Courtesy of Sunmit Singh.

Text and Figures

Chapter 1

p. 17, Hall, J.A., Park, N., Song, H., & Cody, M.J. (2010). Strategic misrepresentation in online dating: the Effects of gender, self-monitoring, and personality traits. *Journal of Social and Personal Relationships, 27*, 117–135.

p. 19,National Association of Colleges and Employers (2009). *Job Outlook 2009: Spring update.* Bethlehem, PA. Reprinted from Job Outlook 2009, with permission of the National Association of Colleges and Employers, copyright holders.

p. 23, Items adapted from Mehrabian, A., & Epstein, N. (1972). A measure of emotional empathy. *Journal of Personality, 40*(4), pp. 525–543. Used by permission of John Wiley & Sons.

Chapter 2

p. 31, Kerr, M. (2009, May 17). Muslims face discrimination and intolerance. The Statesman. Retrieved February 17, 2010. Used by permission of The Statesman.

p. 45, "Assessing the reliability and validity of the generalized ethnocentrism scale" by J.W. Neuliep from JOURNAL OF INTERCULTURAL COMMUNICATION RESEARCH, 31, 201–215.

p. 47, http://www.itu.int/ITU-D/ict/statistics/ict/graphs/internet.jpg. Reprinted by permission of International Telecommunication Union.

Chapter 3

p. 53, Gosling, S.D., Ko, S.J., Mannarelli, T., & Morris, M.E. (2002). A room with a cue: Personality judgments based on offices and bedrooms. *Journal of Personality and Social Psychology, 82*, 379–398. Used by permission of American Psychological Association.

p. 66, Rosenberg, M. (1965). *Society and the adolescent self-image.* Princeton, NJ: Princeton University Press. Used by permission.

p. 69, Derlega, V.J., & Winstead, B.A. (2001). HIV-infected persons' attributions for the disclosure and nondisclosure of the seropositive diagnosis to significant others. In V. Manusov & J.H. Harvey (Eds.), *Attribution, communication behavior,a dn close relationships* (pp 266–284). New York: Cambridge University Press.

Chapter 4

p. 82, Pinker, S. (1994). *The language instinct.* New York: HarperCollins.

Chapter 5

p. 110, Langlois, J.H., Kalakanis, L.E., Rubenstein, A.J., Larson, A.D., Hallam, M.J., & Smoot, M.T. (2002). Maxims or myths of beauty: A meta-analytic and theoretical review. *Psychological Bulletin, 126*, 380–423. Reprinted by permission of American Psychological Association.

p. 123, Riggio, R.E. (1986). Assessment of basic social skills. *Journal of Personality and Social Psychology, 51*, 649–660. Reprinted by permission of American Psychological Association.

Chapter 6

p. 136, Watson, D.W., Barker, L.L., & Weaver, J.B. (2005). The listening styles profile (LSP-16): Development and validation of an instrument to assess four listening styles. *International Journal of Listening, 9*, 1–13. Reprinted by permission of Taylor & Francis.

p. 142, Sargent, S.L., & Weaver, J.B. 92003). Listening styles: Sex differences in perceptions of self and others. *International Journal of Listening, 17*, 5–18. Reprinted by permission of Taylor & Francis.

p. 148, Adapted from St. Mary's College Counseling Center Grief and Loss Guidelines: www.stmarys-ca.edu/prospective/undergraduate_admissions/

Chapter 7

p. 154, mlyn959. Used by permission of CartoonStock. www.CartsoonStock.com.

p. 155, Hinduja, S., & Patchin, W.J. (2009). *Bullying beyond the schoolyard: Preventing and responding to cyberbullying.* Thousand Oaks, CA: Sage. Reprinted by permission.

p. 158, Items adapted from McCroskey, J.C., & McCain, T.A. (1974). The measurement of interpersonal attraction. *Speech Monographs, 41*, 261–266. Reprinted by permission of Speech Communication Association.

p. 159, Neimeyer, R.A., & Mitchell, K.A. (1988). Similarity and attraction: A Longitudinal study. *Journal of Social and Personal Relationships, 5*, 131–148. Reprinted by permission of Sage Publications.

p. 169, Argyle, M., & Henderson, M. (1984). The rules of friendship. *Journal of Social and Personal Relationships, 1*, 211–237. Reprinted by permission of Sage Publications.

Chapter 8

p. 189, cwln162. Used by permission of CartoonStock. www.CartoonStock.com.

Chapter 9

p. 209, jfa2788. Used by permission of CartoonStock. www.CartoonStock.com.

p. 211, Aube, C., Rousseau, V., Mama, C., & Morin, E.M. (2009). Counterproductive behaviors and psychological wel-being: The moderating effect of task interdependence. Journal of Business and Psychology, 24, 351–361.

Chapter 10

p. 243, Items adapted from Snyder, M. (1974). Self-monitoring of expressive behavior. Journal of Personality and Social Psychology, 30, 526–537. Used by permission of American Psychological Association.

p. 246, National Clearinghouse on Family Violence Information.

Chapter 13

p. 318, Roberts, J. B., Sawyer, C. R., & Behnke, R. R. (2004). A neurological representation of speech state anxiety: Mapping salivary cortisol levels of public speakers. *Western Journal of Communication, 68*, 219–231.

p. 332, Bartsch, R. A., & Cobern, K. M. (2003). Effectiveness of PowerPoint presentations in lectures. *Computers & Education, 41*, 77–86. Used by permission of Elsevier.

uncertainty reduction theory, 160–161
under-benefited, 162–163
verbal abuse, 87–88
relationships, intimate, 52, *178–179.*
See also families; marriage; physical attraction
autonomy *vs.* connection, 183
avoiding stage of, 193
bonding stage of, 188–189
characteristics of, 184–188
circumscribing stage of, 192–193
commitment, 180–181
communicating in, 189–192
confirming messages in, 199–200
conflict in, 189–190, 200–201
conflict-avoiding couples, 190
CPM, 190–191
culture and, 186–187, 189
developmental stages of, 188–189
dialectical tensions of, 183–184, 202–203
differentiating stage of, 192
disconfirming messages in, 199–200
divorce, 193, 199
emotional communication in, 191
ending, 192–193
exclusivity in, 184–185, 186
expectations of, 187, 201
experimenting stage, 188
fairy tales and, 179
forming, 188–189
friendships and, 170–171
fun in, 198–200
HIV/AIDS and, 69
hostile couples, 190
improving communication in, 198–203
initiating stage, 188
instrumental communication in, 191–192
integrating stage of, 188
intensifying stage, 188
interdependence, 181–183
intimacy, 180–181
investment in, 183
kissing, *36, 44*
love, 185
nature of, 180–184
online dating, 17, 185, 189
open, 184–185
openness *vs.* closedness, 183
ORI, 182
predictability *vs.* novelty, 183–184
privacy, 190–191
sexuality, 185–186, 187
smell and sexual attraction, 114
speed dating, 52
stagnation stage of, 192, 193
terminating stage, 193
validating couples, 190

volatile couples, 190
relative power, 248
remembering, 132
representation, 340
research. *See* speaking/speech, research
resentment, 251
resources, small group, 223–224
respect, 46–48
within small groups, 229
responding, 133–134
resume, 397, 399, *400*
reticular formation, 54
reward power, 244, 245–246, 248
rhetorical proof
deductive reasoning, 365–366
enthymeme, 365–366
ethos, 362–363
inductive reasoning, 365
logos, 364–366
pathos, 363–364
syllogisms, 365–366
Richards, Michael, 93
rites, 388, 389
rituals, 388, 389–390
Roberts, James, 318
Roberts, John, 311, 314
Roberts, Julia, 326–327
Rock, Chris, 262
role(s)
communication, 214
constructs, 54
family, 195, 196–197
small group, 212–213
in workplace, 390, *391*
romance. *See* relationships, intimate
rule of division, 296–297
rule of parallel wording, 297
rule of subordination, 296
rules, 12–13
brainstorming, 235
culture and, 19
by small groups, enforcement of, 211–212
Russert, Tim, 272

S

sacrifices, small group, 224–225
SafeAssignment, 306
same-sex friendships, 170
same-sex marriage, 185–186, 360
Sanders-Jackson, Ashley, 154
Sapir, Edward, 81
Sapir-Whorf hypothesis, 81, 82
Sargent, Stephanie, 142
Satir, Virginia, 197
Saudi Arabia, *39*
Sawyer, Chris, 317, 318
Schlehuber, Robert, 118
scripted speech, 313–314, 315
search engines, 276–277
secrets, 198

security, 392
segmentation, 202
Seinfeld, 103
Seinfeld, Jerry, 316
selection, 54
selection interview, 396
selective attention, 138, 139, 141
selective memory bias, 58
self. *See also* image
assessment, 64
concept, 62–65, 67
disclosure, 164, *165,* 166–168
esteem, 64, 65–66, 115, 242
expression, 38, 122–123
fulfilling prophecy, 65
identity, 62–63
Johari Window, 62, *63*
judgment, 64
monitoring, 20, 21, 64–65, 242–243
perception of, 62–66
serving bias, 61
semantic rules, 78
semantic triangle, 78, *79*
senses, 104
smell, 113–114
touch, 3, *100–101,* 112, 119, 120
separation, language and, 87–88
service-oriented interview, 396
sex. *See* gender
sexual attraction, 114
sexual harassment, 394
sexual health, 337
sexuality, 185–186, 187
sharing tasks, 164
Sidarth, S. R., 271
sign language, 108–109, *109, 344*
signposts, of speech, 294, *295*
Silva, Danny, 27
similarity
assumption, 43
attraction to, 158–159
The Simpsons, 102
Singh, Sunmit, 388
single-parent family, 196
Sistine Chapel, 233
skepticism, 144–145
skills, 20–21
Skype, 269
slander, 92
slang, 90–91. *See also* jargon
slippery slope fallacy, 370, 373
Slow Food movement, 215
small groups. *See* groups, small
Smallwood, Amber, 154
smell, 113–114
social attraction, 157, 158
social behavior, 60
social cohesion, 211
social commitment, 181
social distance, 114, 115
social exchange theory, 161–162